*The Goodheart-Willcox home economics series*

# Working with Young Children

*Dr. Judy Herr, C.H.E.*
*Director, Child and Family Studies Center*
*and*
*Graduate Home Economics Program Director*
*University of Wisconsin—Stout*
*Menomonie, Wisconsin*

**The Goodheart-Willcox Company, Inc.**
*South Holland, Illinois*

Library of Congress Catalog Card Number 89-33752
International Standard Book Number 0-87006-732-X

1234567890-90-9876543210

*Cover photos:*

*by John Shaw*
*taken in cooperation*
*with the Child Development*
*Center at Northwestern*
*State University of Louisiana*

**Library of Congress Cataloging in Publication Data**

Herr, Judith
  Working with young children / by Judy Herr.
    p.    cm.
  Includes index.
  ISBN 0-87006-732-X
  1. Child care services--United States. 2. Child care workers-
-United States  I.  Title.
HQ778.7.U6H47   1990                                        89-33752
362.7--dc20                                                        CIP

# Introduction

*Working with Young Children* is designed to help you prepare for a career in child care. It teaches practical ways to guide children through a variety of daily experiences in safe, educational ways.

Success in working with children begins by understanding children. This book starts with an overview of the physical, intellectual, social, and emotional characteristics of young children. Using this information will help you plan for and react to children with confidence that your actions are developmentally appropriate.

Once you understand children, you are ready to develop and build your guidance skills. This text teaches you practical techniques for guiding children as you establish rules and handle daily routines. It also gives helpful suggestions for dealing with guidance problems.

An important part of child care involves creating a safe, healthy learning environment. As you read this text, you will learn techniques for keeping children safe, healthy, and nourished. In addition, you will learn to provide experiences that build children's enthusiasm for learning.

*Working with Young Children* prepares you for other important aspects of child care. These include planning classroom curriculum and developing strategies for involving parents in child care programs. The book also prepares you to handle special care concerns related to infants, toddlers, and special needs children. Finally, the book prepares you to launch a career in child care, helping you explore the types of programs and refine your job hunting skills.

# About the Author

The quality of this textbook reflects Judy Herr's intense dedication to early childhood education. With over 20 years of experience in the field, Judy currently supervises and administers seven children's programs at the University of Wisconsin-Stout. She also supervises preschool teachers on campus and kindergarten teachers in the public schools.

Judy has published several books, manuals, and articles on early childhood education. Her articles have been printed in such noted journals as *Child Care Professional, Journal of Home Economics,* and *Texas Child Care Quarterly.* She has been a guest speaker at local, regional, national, and international conferences.

Judy is active in several professional associations including the National Association for the Education of Young Children, National Association of Early Childhood Teacher Educators, and American Home Economics Association. Her many contributions and accomplishments in these and other organizations have resulted in much recognition. Recently, Judy was given the Shirley Dean Award for Distinguished Service from the Midwestern Association for the Education of Young Children.

# Contents

**part six**
# Other Children You will Meet

**part seven**
# Exploring Careers with Young Children

# part 1

# The Children and You

Who you are and what you know affects your ability to work with young children. In this part, you will explore current career opportunities in early childhood. You will also examine the responsibilities and characteristics of successful early childhood teachers.

This part will help you understand the characteristics of children at different ages. It will give you an overview of their physical, intellectual, social, and emotional development. You will learn how to change your teaching and care techniques to fit the developmental needs of children at different ages.

Working with young children is challenging,
but rewarding. Do you have the characteristics
needed to have a successful career in child care?

# Chapter 1

# *You: Working with Young Children*

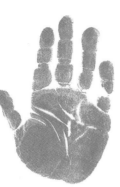

After studying this chapter, you will be able to:
- ☐ Explain how social changes will increase the need for child care services.
- ☐ Describe job opportunities in early childhood.
- ☐ List responsibilities of the early childhood teacher.
- ☐ Explain how certain characteristics can help early childhood teachers be successful.

Mary takes care of infants, 1-1. Suzie, who has been a preschool teacher for two years, just took a job as a center director. Her friend Toby is the parent coordinator in a local Head Start center, while Tom, who was another classmate, is a parent educator. Two other classmates, Pat and Sally, recently opened a children's clothing store. Each of these individuals studied early childhood.

Already you may be asking yourself, "What is early childhood?" *Early childhood* covers the period from birth up to nine years of age. During this period of time, growth is very rapid. The child develops a sense of self as well as language, social, problem solving, and motor skills. These accomplishments are an important foundation for later learning and life.

People who explore careers in early childhood often have at least two main questions. First, they want to know whether there will be a need for people trained in early childhood. They also want to know about the responsibilities of early childhood educators and the characteristics they need to succeed.

This chapter reviews social changes that will create a need for more child care services. It also gives an overview of teachers' responsibilities and characteristics of successful teachers.

1-1 Taking care of infants is one of many job opportunities for people who study early childhood.

## SOCIAL CHANGES AND CHILD CARE

Social changes will create a need for more child care services. These changes occur in the family, employers' attitudes, educators' attitudes, and in job opportunities.

### Changes in families

Families no longer fit the traditional model—a mother as homemaker and a father as breadwinner. The traditional family only accounts for a small percentage of the population. An even smaller percentage is expected in the future. Several trends support this prediction:
- Women are becoming more highly educated.
- Families are smaller.
- Women with preschool children are returning to the labor force rather than remaining out for several years.
- Women are working for economic reasons.
- Many working women are widowed, divorced, single, separated, or married to men earning a salary that is too low to support the family.

Other significant changes will influence the need for child care services. The number of dual-worker families is increasing. Likewise, the number of single parents is continuing to rise. In the last decade alone, they have doubled in number.

The need for early childhood teachers is expected to grow. In the next decade, the under-five population is expected to increase in numbers parallel to the "baby boom" of the 1950s. It is also projected that the number of children under six years of age will increase. More children will need child care. Consequently, there will be an increasing need for early childhood teachers.

### Changes in employers' attitudes

Corporate or employer-sponsored child care will grow in the future. This growth will present many opportunities for early childhood professionals. The United States Chamber of Commerce has reported that child care will be one of the fastest growing benefits provided by companies in future years.

Companies have reported tangible payoffs. Included are positive effects on recruitment, morale, productivity, and absenteeism. Other positive influences are related to turnover, public relations, taxes, scheduling, and the quality of the work force.

In addition to the on-site model of care, other models will be provided. Included may be a referral matching type of assistance. Lists of day care providers, maps, and brochures will be provided to parents. This type of service respects the employee's right to choose a suitable arrangement.

Some corporations may even hire early childhood specialists to provide sick child care. This model provides short-term home health care for sick children. The average child experiences ten days of illness each year. As a result, many parents are forced to stay home from work. This model has been designed to help reduce the parents' stress, guilt, and worry that occur when inappropriate child care is provided. See 1-2.

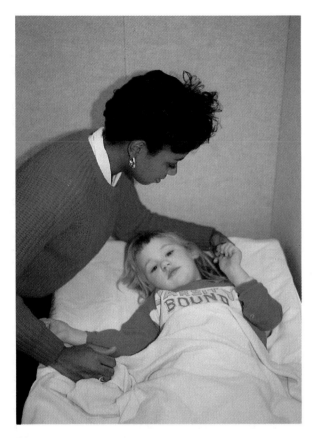

1-2 Parents can concentrate on their work when they feel sure that their sick children are getting proper care.

## Changes in education attitudes

Full-day kindergartens are increasing in numbers. There is a movement toward full-day kindergartens throughout the nation. This, in turn, will create a need for more certified teachers and aides. Some school districts are even discussing the concept of kindergarten programs for four-year-old children.

Professionals are working toward greater allocation of public educational resources for early childhood. Their purpose is to remedy some current problems in education for young chidren. Many four-year-olds already attend a preschool program. They may be enrolled in a government subsidized program, such as Head Start, for low income famlies. They may also be enrolled in programs supported by middle and upper-class families.

## Changes in job opportunities

Never have there been more job opportunities in early childhood. As a result, you as an early childhood specialist may find yourself choosing from among a number of job alternatives. Nannies, kindergarten teachers, day care teachers and directors, and licensing specialists all will be needed. In addition, you may find other possibilities in business settings. See 1-3.

| JOB POSSIBILITIES | |
|---|---|
| • Aide in the public school system<br>• Beautician for children<br>• Children's art instructor<br>• Children's book salesperson<br>• Children's clothing designer<br>• Children's clothing salesperson<br>• Children's furniture salesperson<br>• Children's librarian<br>• Children's photographer<br>• Children's shoe salesperson<br>• Children's ski instructor<br>• Children's swimming instructor<br>• Children's toy designer<br>• Director of preschool or Head Start center | • Entertainer for parties<br>• Foster parent<br>• Head Start teacher<br>• Licensing specialist<br>• Nanny<br>• Parent educator<br>• Preschool teacher<br>• Recreation director<br>• Religious education director<br>• Referral specialist for corporate day care<br>• School supply salesperson<br>• Sick-child-care specialist for corporate day care<br>• Toy salesperson |

1-3 A variety of job opportunities exist in eary childhood.

**Nannies.** There is currently a great demand for the nanny. A *nanny* provides care in a child's home. Some nannies live in the child's home. Other nannies have their own homes or apartments, depending on the parents' needs.

The dual-career family has contributed to the increasing demand for nannies. One employment service reported that it received over 50 requests for nannies per day. Due to a lack of personnel, the placement officers were able to place only 50 nannies in an entire year. Since many nannies have come from other countries, tighter immigration controls have decreased the supply of nannies in the United States. This has created new opportunities for nannies who are trained in the United States.

**Kindergarten teachers.** Although kindergarten attendance is not required in all states, the opportunity is provided. Thus kindergarten teachers are needed in public as well as private schools. Even many day care centers hire kindergarten teachers. These centers provide all day kindergarten to children of working parents.

**Day care teachers and directors.** Because of the rapid increase in day care services, teachers and directors are needed. Usually the teacher is responsible for planning curriculum and teaching children. The director's responsibilities are broader. Recruiting children, hiring and supervising staff, and managing the budget are all included. Building maintenance is also the responsibility of the director in some centers.

**Licensing specialists.** Due to the rapid increase in day care centers, the number of licensing positions are expanding. The *licensing specialist* is usually employed by the state. The role of this person is to ensure that the state's rules and regulations are followed. These regulations vary somewhat from state to state.

Specialists make on-site visits to assigned centers. During each visit, the licensing specialist observes to see that the center is following state guidelines. Included are the number of children in the center, adult-child ratio, facility size, food served, and curriculum provided.

**Other opportunities.** Many other opportunities exist for you as an early childhood specialist. With this background, you are prepared to hold a variety of positions. You may open a children's toy or clothing store. Perhaps you may even be interested in opening a shoe or book store. Because they understand curriculum needs, some early childhood teachers sell school supplies for book and stationery companies. Others work as authors of children's books or as aides in the public school system.

You may start a company related to child care. For example, in a larger city you could start a company that specialized in providing substitute teachers for day care centers. When a center needed personnel to cover for a teacher who was on vacation, at a conference, or ill, the administrator could call you. Your responsibility would be to furnish a substitute teacher.

The job responsibilities of a parent educator may also appeal to you. In this position, you would work with parents to help them learn child care skills, 1-4. You might work days, evenings, or weekends. You could design written materials or produce visuals to help parents better understand their roles and the nature of young children.

There are many, many job opportunities for people studying early childhood. Knowledge of child growth and development is necessary for the community recreation leader. Children's furniture salespersons will also find a background in this field valuable. They can share children's growth rates and safety needs with parents while selecting furniture. Indeed, the demand for workers educated in early childhood exceeds the supply.

## THE TEACHER'S RESPONSIBILITIES

Many employment opportunities exist in early childhood. The majority, however, will be as a teacher or teacher's aid. These professionals are needed for day care centers and preschools. Because of this need, the contents of this book will focus on skills for teaching young children.

Your responsibilities as an early childhood teacher will be complex. You will have direct and indirect influences on children. Directly, you will interact with children. Indirectly, you will influence children through the arrangement of space and activities. Basically, you as an early childhood teacher will serve a dual role. Often you will play both the teacher and parent educator role. Usually, the younger the child, the more support you need to provide to the parent in the transition from home to school. The parent may also seek advice on such aspects of child development as toilet training and thumbsucking.

You will also need to be a friend, colleague, janitor, nurse, and even a cook on some days. Not all of your tasks will be pleasant. Sometimes your work may be dirty, including changing messy diapers and cleaning up after a sick child. Noses have to be wiped and messes — such as spilled milk, dumped paint, or a leaky sensory table — must be cleaned.

Challenging and rewarding are two words that can best describe the responsibilities of an early childhood teacher. You will be challenged planning appropriate, interesting curriculum, designing class materials, and coping with behavior problems in the classroom. At times you may become discouraged, particularly when behavioral changes are slow. But once the changes occur, the rewards are well worth the time and effort. Early childhood teachers usually feel useful, needed, and important, 1-5. Equally important, they usually feel loved by the children. For these reasons, most early childhood teachers thoroughly enjoy their profession.

**To know the principles of child development**

Regardless of your position, you will need a thorough understanding of child growth and development. This understanding will help you prepare an appropriate environment for young children. Likewise, it will help you design appropriate educational experiences for the children.

Understanding children's behavior will help you work well with individuals and groups of children. You will learn that children behave the way they do because their behavior brings them pleasure. That is, what happens to the child after he acts determines whether this

1-4 Parent educators present information that will help parents improve their child care skills.

1-5 Love from children helps make teaching in early childhood a rewarding career.

behavior will be continued. A child who throws a temper tantrum to get a second turn on a bike (and gets a second turn) will usually repeat this behavior. Thus, you will teach children to behave the way they do. Most of what they learn, they will learn from other people and you.

Working with young children, you will notice differences in behavior. Children can learn to be friendly, and they can learn to be aggressive. As a teacher, you will be responsible for teaching children to interact positively. Thus, you will teach them to be cooperative and skillful in getting along with others. To do this, you will need to learn and model guidance principles.

### To develop the curriculum

Teachers are responsible for developing an appropriate developmental curriculum. The focus of such a curriculum is on the total development of the child. Physical, social, intellectual, and emotional development are all emphasized in this type of program. All of these areas must be considered when planning curriculum.

**Physical development.** Physical development is stressed in a quality early childhood curriculum. Young children develop a variety of skills through physical experiences which are a foundation for later learning. Coordination, stamina, flexibility, strength, and sensory awareness are all included. See 1-6.

**Social development.** Social development is another important aspect of a quality curriculum. Young children must learn to interact with other children and adults. Likewise, they need to learn to adapt to the expectations that are established in the center.

**Intellectual development.** Young children need to acquire information to be able to understand and function in the world. As a result, intellectual development is an important area of the child's development. Thus, problem solving through hands-on activities will be an important part of the children's learning.

**Emotional development.** Emotional development is the fourth area included in a developmental curriculum. Young children need to

understand themselves. Sensitivity is needed toward others as is self-knowledge. Feelings need to be understood in order to develop self-awareness and self-knowledge.

Your curriculum will need to be designed for the children. A broad knowledge of all the curriculum areas outlined in this book is important. You will find that an understanding of science, math, music, art, dramatic play, and storytelling will influence what you do with children.

### To prepare the environment

A large part of the teaching process involves preparing the environment. Learning is an active process whereby children gain knowledge. The environment that you provide must encourage children to experiment, explore, and manipulate, 1-7.

As a teacher, you will need to provide a variety of materials. These materials will en-

1-6 Curriculum should include activities that help improve muscle strength and coordination.

courage children to engage in positive social activities. They also will promote physical, intellectual, and emotional development. Lack of variety or quantity can lead to lags in development. For instance, if there are not enough interesting materials, children may fight over the few that they like. Chapters have been included in this book to teach you how to arrange space and select toys, equipment, and supplies.

### To communicate effectively

To be an effective teacher, you need to have good communication skills. This involves easily expressing ideas and gaining trust with children, their families, and your peers. Not only will you need to relate to the child, but you will also need to relate to his or her parents. Most preschool teachers have daily contact with a child's parent or parents. Thus, information is usually exchanged on a continuous basis. Early childhood teachers must also be able to form meaningful relationships with their colleagues. To provide a quality educational program for young children, all staff must work cooperatively. This requires open communication with others.

### To get along with co-workers

An important part of any job is getting along with your co-workers. Staff in a child care center need to work as a team, 1-8. To be a team member, you will need to help make your co-workers feel important. Everyone enjoys feeling important and wanted.

To work well with a staff, you need to provide support to your co-workers through actions and words. Share ideas with them. Tell them when they have planned an interesting activity. Praise them for meaningful interactions with the children. Furthermore, accept their style of caregiving.

### To manage time wisely

Rarely does an early childhood teacher have time to do everything he or she wants to do. Thus, time management skills are important. Time management skills help teachers work smarter, not harder. They help you organize

1-7 It is up to you as a teacher to make learning an active process.

1-8 When staff members take and give suggestions on curriculum, they are able to give children the best care possible.

your time, set priorities, and distinguish between important and urgent.

No matter what you accomplish, there is always more that could be done. You might want to make one more bulletin board, write a letter to a parent, or develop new teacher-made materials. Time management skills will help you make choices and use your time wisely.

### To continue education

A teacher never finishes learning. In order to keep up with happenings in the field, you need to be a continuous learner. Conferences, in-service training, course work, journals, and books all help teachers learn more about their field. See 1-9. In addition, participating in one or more professional organizations is essential to learning new developments in the field.

The National Association for the Education of Young Children, with over 65,000 members, is the primary organization for teachers of young children. This organization has state and local affiliates. Membership services include an annual conference, a journal, and other professional publications. Reading the journal will provide you with recent teaching trends, research, legislation, schedule of conferences, and current publications including children's books.

Career advancement often requires experience and more education. After completing an associate degree in early childhood, many students enroll in bachelors degree programs. After this, they may even continue in a graduate degree program.

## CHARACTERISTICS OF SUCCESSFUL TEACHERS

As an early childhood teacher, you will need to build on your own strengths and develop your own style. Each teacher is different. Some teachers are outgoing and lively. Other teachers may be reserved and naturally quiet. Both styles can be effective.

Simply copying the style of another teacher will not necessarily make you a successful teacher. You must develop a style that best suits

1-9 Reading is an important part of continuing education for early childhood teachers.

your temperament. When your style suits your personality, you will feel more comfortable working with children and adults. You will find more enjoyment and success in your profession.

Although teachers may use very different styles, successful teachers tend to have some common characteristics. See 1-10. These traits help teachers deal effectively with the day-to-day situations that are naturally part of their work.

### Fondness of children

The most important trait of an early childhood teacher is fondness of children. The rapport established with each child will reflect the program's success. Every child needs to be understood and accepted. Each child's family background, interests, and desires also need to be respected.

As an early childhood teacher, you will need to notice and show love for each child that you work with. You need to be kind, firm, and understanding with each child. These actions do not just affect how children feel about themselves. They show children how they should treat each other. As part of their social development, young children need to be taught that people and feelings are important.

Feeling loved also helps children develop intellectually and emotionally, 1-11. As you show children that they are important, children have confidence in themselves. They are more willing to try new activities.

## Patience

Effective teachers are also patient. Young children often need extra time to complete tasks. Children also need the opportunity to repeat tasks. Much of a child's learning occurs as the result of repetition.

Children are naturally curious and may constantly repeat simple questions. Children do not always remember everything they have been told. Repeating information and reminding children of rules may seem tedious at times. But

1-11 Children who feel loved are more receptive to learning.

## CHARACTERISTICS OF A SUCCESSFUL TEACHER

- Is fond of children.
- Relates easily and spontaneously to others.
- Is a patient, confident, and caring individual.
- Is a positive, happy individual.
- Is dependable and reliable.
- Makes friends easily.
- Possesses a sense of humor.
- Is flexible and adapts well to the requirements of others.
- Is compassionate, accepting children's strong emotions such as anger, love, and wonder.
- Takes initiative in the classroom.
- Has knowledge in curriculum, child growth and development, and child guidance.
- Keeps abreast of changes in the field by reading, attending conferences, seminars, and courses.
- Desires continuous learning.
- Enjoys challenge and problem solving.
- Can juggle several activities at one time.
- Feels rewarded by progress even if it is minimal.

1-10 Teachers who have these characteristics tend to have high success in teaching and caring for young children.

when these situations are handled patiently, teachers will help children grow and learn while building their self-esteem.

## Compassion

Compassionate teachers are able to accept others without prejudice. Being compassionate requires self-knowledge and self-acceptance. It involves accepting any emotion from others such as grief, joy, fear, love, or even hate.

A compassionate teacher does not simply observe a child's feelings. He or she takes part in the feelings of a child and reacts accordingly. The teacher is sensitive to both positive and negative feelings.

Teachers show compassion by praising and complimenting children for their successes. They also avoid actions that make children feel worthless, such as punishment and shaming. Compassionate teachers work to help children understand the feelings of other children and motivate children to respect each other.

## Confidence

Having confidence in your abilities helps you relax in the classroom. Teachers who are re-laxed and natural tend to be more successful with children. Children, especially the younger ones, can become easily excited. By remaining calm and self-assured, you will have a calming effect on the children.

Your confidence is affected by your ability to make sensible decisions. You need to feel sure that the choices you make are in the best interest of the children. For instance, when it is raining, children should not be taken outside. Children may not always understand such decisions. But if you stand by them with confidence, children will accept them.

## Sense of humor

A sense of humor is helpful when working with children. Children enjoy adults who can laugh. Laughter helps children relax and feel content. And when children see a teacher with a positive, cheerful attitude, they are more likely to be positive and cheerful. See 1-12.

Keeping a sense of humor also can make your work more enjoyable. Seeing the funny side of children can be a rewarding experience. Seeing the humor in situations can also help you cope with some of the daily stresses of

1-12 A teacher who smiles and laughs encourages children to smile and laugh.

teaching. Of course, you must be careful to laugh with, not at, children.

## Commitment

In many ways, the job of an early childhood teacher is anything but easy. Demands on your energy will be high. You will be expected to be an expert in child development, child guidance, and curriculum. Parents will ask your advice on child rearing. Questions such as, "When should I begin toilet training?" or, "What kinds of toys should two-year-olds have?" are common.

You will find that meeting the demands of this field requires a serious commitment. To keep up with current developments in the field, you must constantly study. This can be accomplished through reading books and attending seminars, classes, and conferences. Discussions with other teachers are also helpful.

Preparing for daily teaching is also time consuming. To be a successful teacher, you must be prepared. You, as a teacher, must fully understand the purpose of each activity. You also need to be sure that the activities planned for the day address all areas of a child's development. You must also balance activities so that children are not constantly active or still. Providing a curriculum that best meets children's needs takes much time and careful thought, 1-13.

## Personal desire

Knowing that you really want to teach young children is important to your success. Although you may have doubts, you need to feel that working with young children is rewarding for you. Hearing children make comments such as, "I love you," or "You're pretty," should boost your self-esteem. Otherwise, you will not feel enthusiastic enough about your work to do a good job.

It is not unusual for you to question your career choice. Even experienced teachers will have days when they wonder why they chose this career. These questions are healthy. If they help you determine that you do belong in early childhood teaching, you will feel more confident and committed to your career choice.

1-13 Spending the time needed to plan an effective curriculum takes a strong commitment from a teacher.

Only you can answer the question, "Is teaching really for me?" You will need to examine carefully your own interests, feelings, and satisfactions. See 1-14. Studying the chapters in this book can help you. Each chapter contains important concepts. Explore possibilities for applying these concepts to a group of young children.

Working with children will increase your insights. Until you understand the program and children, you might not find much self-satisfaction. Given time, however, you are bound to discover the real joys and rewards of working with young children.

## SUMMARY

Many changes in society are creating new opportunities in child care. With fewer traditional families, the demand for quality child care services is growing. Employers are becoming more willing to sponsor child care programs for their employees. Educators are working to expand the availability of kindergarten programs. New job opportunities are being created and expanded.

Most employment opportunities in early childhood are as teachers or teachers' aides. The main focus of this book is to prepare you for

## A LETTER TO A NEW TEACHER

Dear Teacher:

As you begin your work, you will meet new challenges and find new answers. This process will continue throughout your teaching career.

There will be exciting days that will be fulfilling. The children will experience many new discoveries. Many times over they may also tell you that "you're beautiful" or "you have a pretty voice."

You will also have discouraging days. Teaching is not an easy job. It is physically and mentally exhausting. At times, the costs seem to exceed the rewards. Luckily, the majority of the time, teaching is most rewarding and satisfying.

Remember that you will only get out of a career what you invest in it. You must always be willing to work overtime and to seek new answers.

When you leave the center at night, you may reflect on the daily happenings. Replaying something a child said or did is not uncommon. You may also want to think about your responses. This will prepare you for the next time.

Try to learn as much as you can about child development, child guidance, and curriculum. Talk to your colleagues, read professional journals, and attend conferences. Additional course work and degrees will help strengthen your understanding of young children. Chances are, if you are actively involved, you will never lose your enchantment of teaching.

1-14 Deciding whether you want to be an early childhood teacher is an important step in having a successful career.

a career as an early childhood teacher.

Teachers have many important responsibilities. They must understand the principles of child growth and development. Teachers develop curriculum and create a classroom environment that meets children's developmental needs. They need to communicate effectively and get along with their coworkers. Teachers must manage their time wisely. They need to constantly update and expand their knowledge in early childhood.

A successful teacher develops a style that works well for him or her. However, most successful teachers have many traits in common. These teachers are fond of children, patient, and compassionate. They have confidence in their abilities and know how to keep a sense of humor. Successful teachers are committed to teaching young children. They have a strong desire to be with and guide children. They find their work a rewarding and joyous experience.

If you have the commitment and desire, you can develop skills as an early childhood teacher by studying and by spending time with children.

## to Know

early childhood
nanny
licensing specialist

## to Review

1. _____ _____ covers the period from birth up to nine years of age.

2. True or false. Social changes have created a need for more day care services.

3. Why do companies provide child care?

4. _____ provide care for children in the parents' homes.

5. A _____ _____ is responsible for enforcing state day care rules and regulations.

6. Give two job opportunities in which education in early childhood is helpful. Explain how a background in early childhood is helpful in those jobs.

7. True or false. Curriculum that enhances a developmental program focuses almost completely on intellectual development.

8. How does the environment affect a child's development?

9. In teaching, _____ _____ skills are needed to work smarter, not harder.

10. The primary organization for teachers of young children is called:
   a. Children's Rights.
   b. Early Childhood Teachers' Group.
   c. The National Association for the Education of Young Children.
   d. The Teaching Association for the Advancement of Young Children.

11. True or false. People who are naturally quiet and reserved cannot be effective early childhood teachers.

12. Give two common characteristics of successful early childhood teachers and explain why these characteristics are helpful.

## to Do

1. Look through the want-ad section of a newspaper. Write down jobs listed in which early childhood training would be helpful.

2. Take a survey of early childhood teachers. Ask them to share the advantages and disadvantages of teaching. Share your findings with the class.

3. Review the qualities of a successful teacher given in chart 1-10. Make a list of qualities from the chart that you possess.

4. Design a bulletin board displaying characteristics of successful teachers.

5. Survey parents of young children to find out what qualities they value in teachers.

6. Write a one-page paper on why you want to teach children.

# Chapter 2

# *Understanding Children from Birth to Age Two*

After studying this chapter, you will be able to:
- ☐ Describe the areas and characteristics of development.
- ☐ Explain how developmental scales are used.
- ☐ Chart the physical development of children in the first two years after birth.
- ☐ Describe how children develop intellectually in the first two years after birth.
- ☐ Explain how children in the first two years after birth develop socially and emotionally.

Studying and understanding child development is an important part of teaching young children. No two children are alike. Children differ in physical, intellectual, social, and emotional growth patterns. They also differ in the ways they respond to play, affection, and other factors in their environment.

Think of the children that you know. Each is different, 2-1. Some may always appear to be happy. Other children's personalities may not seem as pleasant. Some children are active. Still others are typically quiet. You may even find that some children are easier to like. To help all of these children, you need to understand the sequence of their development. Knowledge of child development is essential to guiding young children and to planning curriculum.

## CHILD DEVELOPMENT

*Development* refers to change or growth in a child. Understanding growth and development will help you plan appropriate programs for children. For instance, you will learn that two-year-old children like to run. This means that you should provide space for them to move freely. Likewise, you will learn that infants explore through their senses, often mouthing ob-

2-1 Knowledge of child development can help you understand how to work with children who have very different personalities.

*Physical development* refers to physical body changes. Changes in bone thickness, vision, hearing, and muscles are all included. Changes in size and weight are also part of physical development. See 2-2.

Changes in physical skills, such as crawling, walking, hopping, and writing, are another part of physical development. These skills fall into two main areas of development. *Gross motor development* involves improvement of skills using the large muscles. Such activities as running, skipping, and lifting weights fall into this category. *Fine motor development* involves the small muscles. Grasping, holding, cutting, and drawing are some activities requiring fine motor development.

jects. Knowing this, you will need to make sure that all toys for infants are clean.

Different names are often used to describe young children at different ages. For the first year after birth, a child is called an *infant*. From the first year until the third birthday, children are often called *toddlers*. (The name toddlers was given to this age group because of their awkward style of walking.) The name *preschooler* is often used to describe children ages three to six.

Child development is a relatively new area of study. Researchers are continually discovering new information on how children grow and develop. So studying the basics of child development should just be the beginning for you. Throughout your career, you will need to update your knowledge through seminars, courses, professional articles, and conferences.

### Areas of development

The study of child development is often divided into three main areas. These include physical, intellectual, and social-emotional development. Dividing development into these areas makes it easier to study.

2-2 Changes in height and weight are two of the most obvious signs of physical development.

*Intellectual development* refers to mental processes used to gain knowledge. Thought, language, reasoning, and imagination are all included. Identifying colors such as red and blue would be an intellectual task. So would knowing the difference between one and many.

The third area of development is called *social-emotional development*. These two areas are grouped together because they are so interrelated. Learning to relate to others is social development. Emotional development involves refining feelings and expressions of feelings. Trust, fear, confidence, pride, friendship, and humor are all part of social-emotional development. See 2-3. A person's self-concept and self-esteem are also part of this area.

These areas of development are interrelated. Development in one area can have a strong effect on development in another area. For instance, both fine motor development and intellectual development are needed to write words. Language, a part of intellectual development, is needed to communicate with others and develop socially and emotionally.

## Characteristics of development

Although each child is different, the basic pattern of development is predictable. Development tends to proceed from the head downward. This is called the *cephalocaudal principle*. According to this principle, the child first gains control of the head, then the arms, then the legs. Therefore, infants gain control of head and face movements within the first two months after birth. In the next few months, they are able to lift themselves up using their arms. By 6 to 12 months of age, children start to gain leg control and may be able to crawl, stand, or walk.

Development also proceeds from the center of the body outward according to the *principle of proximodistal development*. This means that the spinal cord develops before outer parts of the body. The child's arms develop before the hands, and the hands develop before the fingers. Finger and toe muscles are the last to develop.

Development depends on maturation. *Maturation* refers to a sequence of biological changes in a child. These changes give children new abilities. Much of maturation depends on changes in the brain and the nervous system. These changes allow children to have improved thinking abilities and motor skills.

Children must mature to a certain point before they can gain some skills, 2-4. For instance, the brain of a four-month-old has not matured enough to allow the child to use language. But by two years of age, with help from others, the child will be able to say and understand many words.

The characteristics of development help you understand the order of development in children. But each child develops at his or her own rate. You may find children the same age who have developed to different levels in different areas. But knowing the patterns of development will help you understand what abilities each child already has. And it will help you plan activities that will help the children develop new skills successfully.

## Using developmental scales

As you teach children, you may use developmental scales. *Developmental scales* (sometimes

2-3 Learning to trust and show affection for others is a part of social-emotional development.

referred to as *normative scales*) are lists of characteristics that are considered normal for children in certain age groups. They are designed by researchers who observe large numbers of children. The researchers then analyze the information gathered and determine normal developmental characteristics for each age group. (Many characteristics of children from birth to age six are charted in the appendix.)

You can use developmental scales to help you plan curriculum that is appropriate for the children you teach. You can also use them as a yardstick to assess each child's developmental level.

Developmental scales can be used to assess development formally or informally. Using formal methods, you would observe one child at a time. To do this, you may have to remove the child from the group. You could use another room in the center that is quiet and convenient. This reduces the number of disruptions from other children. It may also increase the validity of the assessment since the child will not be prompted by others.

Assessing children individually is time-consuming. Most centers do not use this type of assessment very often. Instead, they are more likely to use informal assessments. Teachers can make these assessments throughout the day in a normal setting.

To make informal assessments, observe children in their regular routine. Record your observations on plain paper, note cards, or on a developmental scale. Then when you have more time, you can compare your observations to the norms on the developmental scale.

**Applying assessment information.** Growth is an individual process. Depending on maturation and environment, each child develops at his or her own rate. For instance, not every two-year-old will have all of the skills identified on the scales for two-year-olds. It is not uncommon for a child's growth to be uneven in different areas. According to the scales, the child could be advanced in language development and behind in motor development.

When results do not match norms, avoid panicking. Rather, try to find out why. A child may not follow the norm for several reasons.

2-4 Improved muscle strength and coordination are needed before a child can climb.

These may result from lack of opportunity. For instance, if a child's family does not speak or allow the child to speak often, the child may not have normal language skills. Self-help skills may not be mastered if someone always dresses the child. See 2-5. Other problems may be the result of a handicap. For instance, you may find through assessment that a child does not have normal language skills. Further observation may uncover a hearing problem that has resulted in language problems.

## PHYSICAL DEVELOPMENT IN THE FIRST TWO YEARS

Growth is rapid during the first two years of life. The child's size, shape, senses, and organs change. Some changes are rapid; others are more gradual. With each change, children gain new abilities.

As a caregiver, you need to be aware of physical changes in the first two years. Activities, diets, sleep schedules, and safety policies need to be adjusted as children grow. For instance, infants less than four months old do not have enough muscle strength to move around much. These children can be kept in cribs or playpens or held for most of the day. But by twelve months, the children's large muscles have developed much. These children need time and space for crawling and walking.

### Size and shape

An infant's weight may change almost daily. The average weight at birth is 7 1/2 pounds. Four months later, the infant will have doubled in weight. By one year, the typical child weighs about 22 pounds—about three times birth weight. By two years of age, most children weigh almost four times their birth weight.

The infant's length also changes rapidly. The average newborn measures 20 inches. Twelve months later, the infant has usually grown 10 inches. During the second year of life, most children grow 2 to 6 inches. So by 24 months, most children measure 32 to 36 inches in height.

There are weight and height differences between boys and girls by two years of age. At this age, most boys are slightly heavier and

2-5 Children who are always dressed by others may be behind the norms in self-help skills.

taller than girls. Most boys reach about half of their adult height by two years of age. At the same age, girls will have passed their halfway mark by one or two inches.

### Reflexes

At birth, the infant's physical abilities are limited to reflexes. A *reflex* is an automatic body response to a stimulus. The person does not control this response. Blinking when something is coming toward your face is an example of a reflex. Some reflexes are part of a person for life. Others appear in young infants and disappear after several months.

Some of the infant's reflexes are needed for survival. See 2-6. These include the rooting and sucking reflexes. The rooting reflex causes infants to turn their heads toward anything that brushes their faces. This action helps them find a food source such as a nipple. Once an object is near a healthy infant's lips, the child will immediately start to suck. This reflex helps the child get food.

2-6 The rooting and sucking reflexes help an infant get food.

Doctors and others who work with children check reflexes to assess brain and nerve development. If reflexes that are normal in infants are not present, this may be a sign of brain or nerve damage. Professionals often test infants for the Moro, grasping, Babinski, swimming, and stepping reflexes.

**Moro reflex.** The Moro reflex occurs when a baby is startled by a noise or a sudden movement. When this happens, the infant will fling the arms outward. Then the infant will quickly draw the arms into the chest. This reflex lasts from birth to about three months of age.

**Grasping reflex.** The grasping reflex is easy to observe. When you touch the infant's palms, the hands will grip tightly. The grip is tight enough that you can lift the infant into a sitting position. This reflex can also be seen if a rattle or another object is placed across the palm. This reflex disappears after the first three or four months after birth.

**Babinski reflex.** The Babinski reflex is present at birth in normal babies who were born at full term. To test for this reflex, stroke the sole of the foot on the outside from the heel to the toe. When you do this, the infant will fan the toes upward. This reflex usually lasts for the first year after birth.

**Swimming reflex.** If you hold an infant horizontally, face down, you will observe the swimming reflex. The child will stretch out the arms and legs in a swimming motion. This reflex usually lasts for the first six months after birth.

**Stepping reflex.** A stepping reflex can be observed in normal, full-term babies. It occurs if you hold an infant so that the feet are flat on a surface. The infant will move the legs in a walking motion. This reflex usually disappears a few months after birth.

### Motor sequence

*Motor sequence* refers to the order in which a child is able to perform new movements. Each new movement builds upon the previous abilities. Motor sequence depends on the development of the brain and nerves. For this reason, movements tend to develop in areas closest to the brain and spinal cord first.

In the first months after birth, head and trunk control develops. When this occurs, the infant can lift the head from a surface. The infant also can watch a moving object by moving the head from side to side.

By four or five months of age an infant can roll over. Most infants are first able to turn from the stomach to the back. Soon after, the child will be able to roll from back to stomach.

Most infants are able to sit upright in a high chair from four to six months of age. To accomplish this, the infant first needs to gain strength in the neck and back.

Gradually, infants are able to pull themselves into sitting positions. After this, *crawling* is the next skill in the motor sequence. This skill occurs shortly after the child learns to roll onto the stomach. To crawl, the child pulls with the arms and wiggles the stomach. Some infants may even push with their legs.

*Hitching* is another movement used by infants. Before they can hitch, infants must be able to sit without support. From this position, they move their arms and legs, sliding their buttocks across the floor.

As the arms and legs strengthen, infants are able to creep. *Creeping* is a movement in which infants support their weight on their hands and knees. See 2-7. They then move their arms and legs to go forward. As arms and legs become stronger, infants are able to stand with help from an adult. Soon after, they are able to stand while supporting themselves with furniture.

With better leg strength and coordination, infants are able to walk when led by an adult. Soon after, they are able to pull themselves up into a standing position. Next, infants are able to stand without any support. Finally, they become true toddlers—able to walk without support or help.

2-7 Creeping requires stronger leg muscles and better leg control than crawling.

Many other motor skills are gained in the first two years. These skills are listed in the appendix. The skills listed are norms for each age group. They are considered norms because about half of infants at that age can do the skills. For this reason, you should not worry if a child cannot do every skill listed for his or her age. However, you should seek help for a child who is way behind the norms. For instance, if a 17-month-old cannot roll over, help should be sought.

## INTELLECTUAL DEVELOPMENT IN THE FIRST TWO YEARS

At birth, most of an infant's movements are the result of reflexes. But as infants grow, they begin to learn how to make things happen for themselves. Soon they are able to coordinate the movements needed to grab a bottle and suck milk from it. They also begin to react differently depending on their needs. A baby may spit out a pacifier if he or she is not hungry. But a hungry baby may be content to suck on the pacifier.

Two main forces—heredity and environment—influence a child's intellectual development. Heredity determines when a child's brain and senses will be mature enough to learn certain skills. Environmental factors also affect learning. Children need opportunities to use their senses and try new things, 2-8. As a caregiver, you need to provide an environment that allows children to develop to their full potential intellectually.

Being able to see, hear, feel, taste, and smell are important to learning. Through these senses, children learn about many objects and concepts. All of the senses develop during the first two years of life. Sight and hearing develop especially quickly.

### Birth to three months
A newborn's vision is blurry. During the first few weeks after birth, infants appear to focus on objects 7 to 10 inches from them. Their near vision is better developed than their far vision.

As their vision improves, infants show preferences for certain objects. Studies show that infants will gaze longer at patterned disks than at disks of one solid color. Infants also pay more attention to faces than to other objects, 2-9. By two months of age, an infant will gaze longer at a smiling face than at a face with no expression.

As infants grow older, they tend to shift their attention on the face. At one month of age, infants appear to focus on the hairline. By two months, infants show more interest in the eyes. The adult's facial expression is most interesting to a three-month-old child. These changes show that children are giving thought to areas of the face that interest them.

Hearing also develops early in life. Newborns are startled by loud noises. They often react to these noises by crying. These same newborns are lulled to sleep by rhythmic sounds such as a lullaby or a heartbeat. They also react to human voices while ignoring other sounds. By three weeks, a newborn can distinguish between the voice of the mother or father and that of a stranger.

During the first three months after birth, infants do not distinguish between themselves and the objects around them. If infants see their hands moving, they do not think of themselves

2-9 Infants prefer faces to most other objects.

2-8 The activities that you provide infants and young toddlers help them develop intellectually.

as making this movement. In their thinking, it could easily be someone else's hand.

Children this age start to experiment with reflex actions. Newborns suck everything that touches their lips. They even make sucking motions in their sleep. Gradually, these children adapt such reflexes to the environment. They learn to suck on bottles, pacifiers, and fingers in different ways.

### Three to six months

During this time, children start to focus on their surroundings. Before this time, a child would just gaze at objects. But infants now begin to examine objects more closely. By six months of age, the child can distinguish between familiar and unfamiliar faces.

Infants also start to learn that they can touch, shake, and hit objects that they see. Memory, foresight, and self-awareness are all developing. The child learns that hitting the crib gym makes a noise. The infant also learns that his or her own movement caused the noise.

Infants from three to six months of age also start to show judgment. For instance, they prefer the smell and voice of a parent to that of a stranger. Infants in this stage also try to locate noises by turning toward them. Many times, though, they will turn in the wrong direction.

From birth an infant makes noises. During this stage, vocalizations begin to increase. You will find that children this age make many noises when you hold and play with them.

Infants in this stage also respond in new ways to touch. If you blow on or kiss the baby's stomach, the child may smile or coo in response. Children this age also respond happily to light touches and tickling.

Infants in this stage think with their senses and movements. By four months, an infant will start using a predictable pattern to learn about objects. If you give a child at this stage an object, you will see this pattern. The child will first look at the object. Then he or she will mouth it and try shaking it, 2-10. The child may also try banging the object on the floor. This is the infant's way of learning what the object can do or be used for.

Toward the end of this period, body awareness begins to develop. The infant may bite his or her toe while playing. If the child has a tooth, he or she may be surprised by the hurt this causes. This does not stop the child, however, from making the same mistake with other toes or fingers.

### Six to nine months

The concept of *object permanence* begins to develop at this stage. This concept is the understanding that objects continue to exist even if you cannot see them. Before this time, anything out of sight was out of mind for the infant. For instance, if a rattle was placed under a blanket, the young infant would not search for it. Now, the child begins to understand that the rattle is still there even though it is covered.

Beginning to understand object permanence shows that these infants are developing memory and goal-oriented thinking. The child will search under a blanket for a rattle that has been covered. This means that the child remembers that the rattle was there. It also means that the child takes actions with the goal of finding the rattle. At this time though, infants give up within a few seconds if they do not find the rattle.

2-10 Mouthing is a major way that infants learn about objects.

You can test for object permanence by showing the infant an interesting toy. Then cover the toy with a towel or blanket while the child is looking. If the child attempts to uncover the toy, the child shows an understanding of object permanence. This child also shows goal-oriented behavior.

Part of object permanence involves understanding that other people exist all the time. Before this stage, children would simply cry if uncomfortable and stop crying when needs were met. Now, children begin to understand that they can cry as a call to parents or other caregivers. They know that even if a person is not within sight, the person still exists. Their cry will call the person to them.

Crying to call a person is also a sign that infants are learning to communicate. The child learns that making noises can get an adult to understand the child's needs. At this point, the child starts communicating in other ways. When the infant makes a noise, he or she will often listen for a response. If you make a noise in return, the infant will answer back.

### Nine to twelve months

At this point, infants become more intentional about their goals. The child has definite ideas about what he or she wants. If confined to a playpen, the child may cry to be taken out. Once out, the child may crawl across the room to get a forbidden object. At the same time, the child may ignore many interesting objects along the way.

These infants also begin to anticipate certain events. A child at this stage may cry when a parent puts on a coat. The infant has learned that when this happens, the parent will leave. When the child sees the parent enter the day care center, he or she may become excited and happy.

### Twelve to eighteen months

Children at this stage enjoy trial-and-error problem solving. They experiment with objects to find new ways to use them, 2-11. These might include rolling, tossing, or bouncing. These children express joy when they find that toys can make noise. They start to understand that the force they use affects the loudness or softness of noise in a toy.

Relationships between cause and effect fascinate these young toddlers. For instance, the child loves to hit water and watch it splash. Children also learn ways to use cause and effect to reach goals at this age. For instance, the child may learn that by pulling on a tablecloth, he or she can reach a plate of cookies.

Language becomes a bigger part of communication at this stage. Before this time, some children may say a few words, such as daddy or mommy. Now, children learn to say many new words. Most children at this age can understand even more words than they can say. Mostly, children use one or two words to communicate in this stage. They do not yet understand how to put words together to form sentences.

Books become more important to children at this time. A child in this age group will love to sit on your lap and have you read a story. The child may be able to identify many pictures in simple books. As you point to the pictures, the child may give the names of the objects.

2-11 Young toddlers often look for new ways to use objects.

## Eighteen to twenty-four months

At this stage, children start to think before they do things. They are able to apply what they know about objects to solve problems without as much trial-and-error. For instance, the child may know that standing on a stool in the bathroom helps the child reach the sink. This same child may apply this knowledge to get a cookie on the kitchen counter. Instead of a stool, the child may use a chair or even an open drawer. Children in this stage still tend to think in terms of actions.

Improved thinking skills and motor skills can make toddlers in this stage exhausting to care for. These children want to actively explore everything. They want to find out as much as they can about new places and objects. But these children are not old enough to understand the dangers that may be involved in exploring. For instance, they may step in an open drawer to reach something without realizing that the drawer may fall. Therefore, you must carefully watch these children and try to make sure their environment is as safe as possible.

Pretending starts to be part of a child's world at this stage. A young toddler's pretending is often a form of deferred imitation. *Deferred imitation* is watching another person's behavior and then acting out that behavior later, 2-12. For instance, a father may tuck his child into bed each night and give him or her a kiss on the forehead. At the center the next day, the child may tuck in a doll and give it a kiss on the forehead. Children may also pretend to be animals they have seen, such as dogs.

Children in this stage understand that symbols may represent other real objects. For instance, a younger child might play with a doll by swinging it around and hitting things with it. But now the child will hold the doll like a baby and cover it with a blanket.

Children are learning more and more words. By this age, they may even combine two words into little sentences. For instance, the child might say, "doggie bark," to let you know that he or she hears a dog barking.

Children like to share what they know with you. As you read to them, they may point to objects to tell you what they are. And they enjoy pointing to things that you name. For instance, you may say to the child, "Touch your toes." Children at this age are quick to point to such parts of their bodies. A little later, you may get them to point to other objects in the room.

## SOCIAL-EMOTIONAL DEVELOPMENT IN THE FIRST TWO YEARS

When children are first born, they do not show a wide range of emotions. They seem to be basically comfortable or uncomfortable. With time, they begin to show such emotions as happiness, fear, and love. By the end of the second year, children are expressing their emotions in many ways.

Socially, young children tend to focus on a few adults who are close to them. This is

2-12 This child is imitating behavior that she has seen at home.

2-13 One-year-olds start to take more interest in their peers.

especially true of infants. After the first birthday, children may take more interest in other toddlers, 2-13. But adults are still most important to children in this age group. As a caregiver, you need to realize that your actions will have a strong effect on children's social-emotional development.

## Temperament

Even from birth, children differ in *temperament* or the ways that they react to their environment. Such factors as passivity, irritability, and activity patterns are part of a child's temperament.

*Passivity* relates to how actively involved a child is with his or her surroundings. A passive infant withdraws from a new person or event. An active infant does something in response to a new person or event.

Children also differ in their level of *irritability* or tendency to feel distressed. Some infants cry easily. They may be difficult to comfort, even if you hold them and try to soothe them. There are other infants who rarely cry. These infants do not let changes bother them as much. Caring for these infants is usually easier for adults.

*Activity patterns* or levels of movement also vary in infants. Some infants can be described as quiet, making few movements. When asleep, these infants may hardly move. Others are constantly moving their arms and legs. These infants may even sleep restlessly.

If you care for infants, you need to work with the temperaments of different children. All infants need loving attention. If given patient, tender care, most children will grow to be happy and well-adjusted. This is even true of very irritable infants.

## Attachment

Most infants become attached to a small group of people early in life. They mainly become attached to the people who care for them. Included may be mothers, fathers, caregivers, or older siblings. Young infants learn that when they are hungry, wet, or frightened, they can depend on these people to make them feel better.

Several early *attachment behaviors* are shown by infants. These behaviors show that infants care for and respond to certain people who are important to them. Smiling, crying, looking, and making vocal sounds are examples of attachment behaviors. These behaviors show that the child is signaling to others.

Attachment begins early in life. Studies show that one-month-old babies show signs of distress if they are cared for by an unfamiliar person. These distress signs appear as irregular sleeping or eating patterns.

*Separation distress* is another attachment behavior shown by infants. This happens when a child is unhappy because a familiar caregiver is leaving. The child often cries as a sign of distress. The first signs of separation distress appear at about six months of age. The reaction becomes clearer by nine months of age. By 15 months of age, separation distress is very strong. After this point, this distress gradually weakens.

As a caregiver, you need to be prepared for the attachment behaviors of children in this age group. Children between 9 and 18 months of age will usually have the most difficulty beginning a day care program. To make the transition easier, you should encourage parents to bring the child's favorite toy and/or blanket.

As children show separation distress, you need to remind yourself not to take the reaction personally. These children are simply fearful because their familiar caregivers are leaving them. They do not know what to expect next. And they are in an unfamiliar surrounding with unfamiliar people. As children become more familiar with the center, its people, and its routine, they will show less distress.

## Changes over time

In the first two years after birth, you will see many changes in children socially and emotionally. As a caregiver, your actions will affect how these children change. If you meet children's needs and encourage them to interact with others, children will learn to trust and care for others. They will feel safe and happy.

**Birth to three months.** At birth, newborns do not have very refined emotions. General excitement and general distress are the only emotions shown. The child may show excitement by looking alert, smiling, or wiggling. Distress is shown by crying. Observing a child in this stage, you may notice that there are no tears when the child cries.

**Three to six months.** By three months, children respond to people with smiles and laughter. They may make happy sounds as adults play with, hold, or feed them. During this stage, infants start to notice and smile at other babies. Crying is still used to show distress. Early in this stage, tears begin to appear. Later, children start to use different cries to signal different types of distress.

**Six to twelve months.** Infants in this stage become actively involved with their caregivers. As adults play with and care for them, these children express happiness, joy, and surprise. They also make sounds in response to the speech of others. Infants in this stage also begin to develop fear. You should not be surprised if a child this age cries at the sight of a stranger. By this age, children have also developed attachment to their caregivers. They may cry and even show anger when their caregivers leave them.

This stage may be the most difficult for the child's parents and for you. Separation distress starts to show at this stage. As a result, a child may start crying upon entering the center. When you try to take the child from the parent, the child may try to push you away. After the parent leaves, the child may continue to cry.

**Twelve to twenty-four months.** Early in this stage, children still show separation distress. Children in this age group also show anxiety. In other words, they become upset because of something they think will happen in the future. For instance, this child may cling to a parent who will be leaving soon.

These children become more interested in exploring. Although they still fear the unfamiliar, they are curious about new places and objects, 2-14. Children who feel secure are more likely to explore than those who feel unsure of their surroundings. By this age, children start to take more interest in other children. They like to play next to other children, but they do not interact much with other children.

Children start to become more aware of their own abilities at this point. This self-awareness

2-14 Curiosity helps toddlers explore new places and objects.

is a source of joy and anger for children. Toddlers are proud and happy when they can do things for themselves. But sometimes they insist on doing things for themselves that they can't do yet. This can cause frustration and anger for the child.

Children who are becoming self-aware also like to say "no." These children like to know that they can make things happen, and they do not always want to do what adults want. Sometimes they may say no to you just to see what will happen. You will need to be kind but firm with these children. You must help them understand that there are rules that must be followed. But at the same time, you need to reassure these children that their wants and needs are important.

## SUMMARY

Understanding child development will help make you a successful caregiver or child care teacher. The study of child development is broken into three main areas—physical, intellectual, and social-emotional development. Certain characteristics of development make the sequence of development predictable. Because the sequence is fairly predictable, developmental scales can be used to predict and assess growth in children. Of course, teachers must allow for individual difference when using these scales.

Growth in the first two years of life is rapid. Physically, children start with many reflexes that are eventually replaced with voluntary movements. As they become bigger and stronger, infants are able to roll over, crawl, creep, and eventually walk.

Intellectual growth shows in children's reactions to the environment. As infants, children will mouth and hit with objects to learn how they work. With growth, children begin to understand how different objects work. They also begin to understand that objects exist even if they are not seen. Children begin to think about how they can reach goals. They also learn to communicate, first by crying, and later by using words.

Each child is born with a temperament that sets the stage for social-emotional development. Young infants tend to show two main emotions—distress and excitement. As infants grow, they become attached to caregivers. They express joy, happiness, surprise, and fear. These children may experience separation distress when loved ones leave them. As children grow older, they show interest in other children. They also become interested in their own abilities. These children may often test adults by saying no to rules and suggestions. But they also take pride in their own achievements. These children still look to adults for love and attention.

# to Know

# to Review

1. Changes in bone thickness, vision, and hearing are part of _____ _____.
2. True or false. Trust, fear, and pride are part of intellectual development.
3. List and explain three characteristics of development.
4. What does it mean if a child does not follow the norms in one or two areas on a developmental scale?
5. True or false. Reflex testing can be used to detect whether an infant has brain or nerve damage.
6. Why are infants able to crawl before they are able to creep?
7. If you place a toy car near an infant who is three to six months old, what is the child most likely to do?
  a. Ignore the toy.
  b. Cry.
  c. Put the toy in his or her mouth.
  d. Slide the toy along the floor making car noises.
8. Describe how to test a child for an understanding of object permanence.
9. If a toddler sees his or her mother mowing the lawn one day and then pretends to mow the lawn at the day care center, the toddler is practicing _____ _____.
10. Describe three factors that affect a child's temperament.
11. True or false. Children do not start to show attachment behaviors until after their first birthday.
12. How would the social-emotional development of a three-month-old differ from that of a one-year-old?

# to Do

1. Visit a day care center serving infants. Observe differences among them.
2. Invite a pediatrician to class to describe the sequences in infant development.
3. Observe a parent playing with or caring for an infant. Record the child's age in months and observations on how the child interacts with the parent. Share your observations with the class.
4. Use pictures from magazines or catalogs to make a bulletin board on infant development.

# Chapter 3

## Understanding Two- and Three-Year-Olds

After studying this chapter, you will be able to:
- ☐ Describe the physical, intellectual, and social-emotional development of two-year-olds.
- ☐ Explain how three-year-olds develop physically, intellectually, socially, and emotionally.
- ☐ Relate how the development of two- and three-year-olds will affect your role as a teacher.

To better understand two- and three-year-olds, you need to develop a mental picture. You need to understand how children in these age groups behave. There are differences between two-year-olds and three-year-olds. Generally, two-year-olds are active and demanding. Three-year-old children tend to be more calm. Understanding differences will help you plan programs that best meet the needs of each child.

### PHYSICAL DEVELOPMENT OF TWO-YEAR-OLDS

Children continue to grow physically in many ways. They become stronger. Their organs, such as the eyes, stomach, heart, and lungs, become stronger. But these children still have a long way to grow to be as developed as adults.

The digestive system matures slowly in children. The appetites of two-year-olds vary from day to day. Some days they may be excited about eating at snack time; other days they may reject their snacks. Likewise, what they eat at lunch time may vary.

The coordination of the two-year-old's body is improving. Provided equipment, space, and support, these children can master a variety of gross motor skills, 3-1. They can usually run and jump without falling. The fine motor skills of these children are improving.

## Gross motor development

Improved coordination and body control makes playing with balls great fun for two-year-olds. They are able to pick up a ball by bending at the waist. Likewise, they can kick a large ball. These children are usually able to throw a ball without falling.

Two-year-olds have more control in leg and foot muscles than before. They can walk up and down stairs placing both feet on each stair. (Most children this age need to hold on to a rail as they step.) They also are able to stand with both feet on a balance beam. These children have the skill to walk on their toes. From a standing position, balancing on one foot is also possible. So is jumping. Most children this age can do a standing broad jump of about eight and one-half inches.

## Fine motor development

Two-year-old children are rapidly developing finger dexterity and control. They are able to insert keys into a lock and turn pages in a book one at a time. Most children this age also can string large beads or spools and lace cards, 3-2. They also can hold scissors properly. By two years of age, they can open and close scissors.

Hand preference is fairly developed by this age. Children will use the same hand for many fine motor activities. However, these children still switch hands.

You will see children using writing tools at this age. At about 24 months of age, children can scribble. By about 30 months, children can draw horizontal lines, vertical lines, and circles. Most children draw by holding the crayon or pencil in their fist.

Two-year-olds become skilled at building with blocks. They can build towers of six to seven blocks. They can also use two or more blocks to make a train and push the blocks along.

## Self-help skills

With a little help, two-year-olds can accomplish many self-help skills. At this age, they begin to cooperate in dressing. First, they can undress themselves. They are able to remove socks, shoes, and pants. Next, they begin to dress themselves. At first, this involves pulling on simple garments. Zippers and snaps can be opened successfully. By thirty months, most children can unbutton large buttons, close snaps, and put on their socks. However, you will need to help children as they try these skills.

3-1 Two-year-olds have improved muscle strength and coordination.

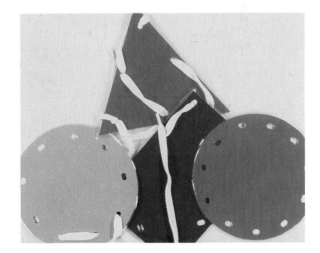

3-2 Having lacing cards like these for two-year-olds helps them improve their fine motor skills.

By this age, children can drink from a cup or glass without help. These children do spill fairly often. But their drinking skills improve with practice. Children this age are also able to drink using a straw.

Strides are normally made in toilet training during this time. At two years of age, most children learn to use the toilet or potty chair with reminders. However, accidents are common. Between 24 and 35 months, children seldom have bowel accidents. But they may still have problems with wetting for several months. By 33 months, many children can use the toilet without help.

## INTELLECTUAL DEVELOPMENT OF TWO-YEAR-OLDS

The two-year-old's intellectual development focuses on three main areas. These include language comprehension skills, expressive language skills, and math readiness skills. All of these areas reflect the child's intelligence.

### Language comprehension skills

A person's understanding of language is called *language comprehension.* Some experts refer to this as receptive or inner language. This form of language is more advanced than expressive language skills in children. For instance, a 20-month-old child may be able to follow directions. But this child may not be able to say more than a few words.

Language comprehension grows quickly in two-year-olds. These children can understand and answer routine questions. While reading a story, you may point to a picture and ask, "What is that?" the child may respond by saying, "Baby." See 3-3.

By 24 months of age, most children can identify at least six body parts. Children can point to these parts on themselves, others, or dolls. They enjoy playing games in which you state, "Find your toes," or "Where are your eyes?"

Many other new skills develop around 24 months. Children can comprehend the pronouns I, my, mine, and me. They also can

3-3 Two-year-olds will answer questions about pictures in the stories you read them.

provide appropriate answers to yes and no questions.

By 30 months of age, other milestones are reached. When asked, children can give you one cookie. They also can follow two-step directions. For instance, you can tell a child, "Take off your coat and put it in your locker."

These children can also give answers to "where" questions. For instance, you may ask a child, "Where do you sleep?" or "Where do you eat?"

Understanding of meanings of words continues through the second year. When picking up objects, two-year-olds can tell the difference between soft and heavy. Size concepts are also developing. Children understand such words as big and tall. Children also start to understand words related to space. These include such words as on, under, out of, together, and away from.

### Expressive language skills

*Expressive language* is the ability to produce language forms. It is a tool that can be used to express a person's thoughts to others.

For most two-year-olds, expressive language quickly develops. Like other aspects of development, if follows a sequence. The child's experiences affect the rate and content of expressive language development.

Speech usually involves simple sentences by two years of age. At the beginning only two words may be used. "Johnny hurt" or "Tom dog" are examples. After this, the child will begin to put three words together. Examples include "Tom go home," "I eat corn," or "See my truck."

The vocabulary of the average two-year-old is 50 to 200 words. You will notice that these children often use words without fully understanding them.

Two-year-olds do not understand how to use grammar to make questions. Instead, they use the tone of their voice. They may ask in a questioning tone, "Grandma go?" or "Milk all gone?"

Two-year-olds often make negative sentences. They do this by adding no to positive sentences. For instance, a child may say, "No milk," meaning that he or she does not want any milk. Or the child may say, "Teacher no here," meaning that he or she cannot find the teacher.

Between 27 and 30 months children may begin to use prepositions. For instance, children may say, "Cookies in jar." Around this age, children also begin using plurals. They may request "cookies" or "candies."

Modifiers are also added to the vocabulary. Some, a lot, all, and one are used as quantifiers. Mine, his, and hers are used as possessives. Pretty, new, and blue are some adjectives that might be used as modifiers.

Between 31 and 34 months of age, children may begin adding "ed" to verbs to show past tense. At about the same time, present tense verb helpers appear. These include such terms as can, are, will, and am.

### Math readiness skills

Math skills are developed as children interact with others and with objects. When you ask, a child can give you "just one" of something. Children also understand size concepts such as big and small. Awareness of shapes, forms, and colors is also developing during this stage.

## SOCIAL-EMOTIONAL DEVELOPMENT OF TWO-YEAR-OLDS

Two-year-olds continue to grow socially and emotionally. At this age, children tend to show many negative attitudes. Children like instant gratification and find it difficult to wait. These qualities make patience an important quality as you work with two-year-olds.

### Social development

At the beginning of this developmental stage, children play next to each other. But they do not play cooperatively with each other, 3-4. Children at this stage still tend to be more interested in adults. Therefore, they tend to act out adult experiences as they play. These might include driving a car, making a bed, and talking on the phone.

The average two-year-old tends to be possessive. Usually these children do not want to

3-4 Two-year-olds do not interact much as they play.

screaming, crying, stamping, and kicking. Their anger is not usually at any one person or object; they are simply frustrated. Children this age still have not learned more appropriate ways of expressing anger.

Fears are more common at this age. Two-year-olds are often afraid of being hurt or harmed. Many of their fears have to do with the imagination. Two-year-olds don't always separate pretend from reality. So they may be afraid of a monster from a story. Or a dream may frighten them because they think the characters from it are real. As a teacher, you need to comfort children when they are afraid. Even if fears are imagined, they are real to toddlers.

Love and caring are shown often by these children. They need to receive love and caring in return. Two-year-olds need to know that people still care for them even if they get angry. They also need to know that they can depend

share. They tend to use body language to let people know how they feel about their possessions. Two-year-old children may push, hit, or shove another child who approaches their toys. Although they have difficulty understanding the concept of sharing, two-year-olds may return a toy that belongs to someone else.

In spite of their negativism and possessiveness, two-year-olds are usually affectionate. They may hug you and hold your hand. Two-year-olds depend on love and caring from adults.

**Emotional development**

These children like to be able to control their surroundings. But because they can't always do that, they tend to get frustrated and angry. Trying to do a task that is too hard for them may cause anger, 3-5. Not being allowed to do or have something may stir angry feelings as well. Two-year-olds may have temper tantrums if they do not get their way. These may include

3-5 Being able to meet goals quickly is important to two-year-olds. If they do not get instant results, they often become angry.

on others. To build trust and security, these children need regular routines. For instance, they may need to sit next to the same person or group of people at every meal or snack time.

## TEACHING TWO-YEAR-OLDS

The development of two-year-olds has a strong effect on the way you teach and work with them. You need to be prepared to handle those situations that are typical with these children.

If you were to observe a group of two-year-olds, your first observation might be that they are negative. Two-year-olds often use the word "no." At times, they may even mean "yes" when they say "no." For instance, you may ask, "Do you want more milk?" The child may say "no" while extending his or her glass toward you for more milk.

You may find yourself becoming impatient with two-year-old children at times. They always seem to want their own way. Whether you want to read a story or take the children on a field trip, you are bound to find a two-year-old who refuses. The child may refuse to leave his or her present activity. Or the child may refuse to put on his or her coat.

Prepare yourself for the dawdling behavior of the typical two-year-old. These children insist on doing things at their own pace. Because of this, routines take longer. When planning a schedule, be aware of this type of behavior. These young children need plenty of time to move from one activity to the next.

Noise is common in a room full of two-year-olds. When they discover a drum, they will hit it over and over again. Likewise they may repeat a new vocal sound many times. If one child starts clapping and stamping his or her feet, the other children may join in. You will need to be prepared for high noise levels and for controlling that noise from time to time.

Children this age are curious. They want to explore. When new materials are brought into the classroom, the children will carefully inspect them. If you ask them what toy you want, they may have difficulty choosing. Therefore, you should add only a few new items at a time.

Gross motor activity is a favorite of two-year-old children. They delight in movement and are not afraid to try out new equipment. They love to run and chase others. Therefore, adequate supervision is crucial. On field trips, these children like to run ahead. For this reason, you may want to have extra adults on the trips to help supervise.

Two-year-olds like to act out life experiences. They especially like to imitate the activities of adults, 3-6. Therefore, they need a dramatic play corner. Housekeeping equipment, mirrors, dolls, dress-up clothes, toy telephones, trucks, and cars should all be included.

Two-year-olds need some rituals in their day. They like to have things done the same way. And these children look forward to certain parts of the day, such as story time. Therefore, you need to be careful to follow a similar

3-6 Teachers should provide many dramatic play materials so two-year-olds can act out such everyday experiences as shaving.

routine from day to day. A few changes add interest. But children need to rely on a regular schedule.

## PHYSICAL DEVELOPMENT OF THREE-YEAR-OLDS

Three-year-olds explore by doing. They are constantly moving, tasting, smelling, and touching. As a result, their body coordination shows great improvement. You will notice that the arms, hands, legs, and feet are all becoming more coordinated.

### Gross motor development

The improvement of body coordination is reflected in the climbing skills of three-year-olds. Now these children can climb and descend stairs easily. In fact, these children can walk up stairs with alternating feet.

By 36 months of age, children can catch balls with their arms. Their catching skill gradually becomes more refined. Eventually, they can catch bouncing balls with their hands. This skill usually emerges toward the end of the third year.

Leg coordination and balancing skills improve. Three-year-olds can ride tricycles. They can walk heel-to-toe for four steps. They can balance on one foot for up to eight seconds. And they can hop on one foot up to three times.

### Fine motor development

The fine motor skills of three-year-olds continue to develop. Cutting skills become more refined. The two-year-old could only hold and work scissors. But a three-year-old can use the scissors to cut paper, 3-7. They can cut five-inch squares of paper into two. Young three-year-olds can cut across the paper. But they cannot cut along a line. By 42 to 48 months, children can cut along a line staying no more than one-half of an inch away from it.

Three-year-olds have improved drawing skills. They often make simple shapes as they

3-7 This three-year-old can use scissors to cut paper.

draw. If you show these children the shape of a cross, they can copy the shape. They also can trace the shape of a diamond. These children draw faces. The faces usually include the mouth, eyes, nose, and/or ears. They are not drawn in proportion, but these features usually are placed in the correct position on the face.

Three-year-olds also enjoy manipulating blocks and puzzles. They can build towers with 9 to 10 cubes. They also can put together simple puzzles.

### Self-help skills

Three-year-olds become increasingly more self-sufficient, needing less help from you with daily care routines. These children can turn the water faucet on and off as long as they can reach it, 3-8. As a result, they can attend to routines such as washing and drying their hands and face. They also can brush their own teeth.

Three-year-olds become better at dressing themselves. They can now open buckles and put on shoes that do not tie. These children do best with clothing that has elastic waists or large button openings. They still are not able to work small buttons and hooks. Three-year-olds have trouble telling the front from the back on clothing, too. They do better with clothing that has a design on the front or a label in the back.

At snack and meal time, these children are now able to use knives. They can spread butter, jelly, and soft peanut butter on bread. They also can pour liquid from a small pitcher. As a result, these children may enjoy assisting at snack time.

Another step toward independence is mastered at this age. Three-year-olds have almost full control over toilet routines. They are even able to get through a night without wetting. This accomplishment is made possible through improved motor control.

## INTELLECTUAL DEVELOPMENT OF THREE-YEAR-OLDS

By the third birthday, the ability to think matures. Children move away from thinking only in terms of actions. They are able to solve simple problems. For instance, if you place an

3-8 Being able to turn water on and off increases this three-year-old's ability to help himself.

object under a cup and place nothing under another cup, the child knows which cup the object is under. If you switch the cups while the child is watching, the child still knows where the object is.

Children at this age still do not think logically. They have not yet learned to see things from more than one perspective. For instance, they do not realize that something that seems tall to them might actually seem short to an adult. They also get confused about time concepts. And these children may become confused about cause and effect. For instance, if a bell rings before each snack is served, children may think the bell causes the snack to appear.

Even though thinking is still flawed, these children learn quickly. Their language comprehension skills, expressive language skills, and math readiness skills continue to improve.

## Language comprehension skills

Understanding of language continues to grow in three-year-olds. On request, the child can now give you two objects. These children can also remember and follow three-part instructions. For example, you might say, "Go to the sink, wash your hands, and dry them with a towel." See 3-9.

Three-year-olds begin to understand the pronouns you and they. They also understand such words as who, whose, why, and how. They are able to provide answers to questions based on these words. For instance, you may ask the child, "Who lives at the North Pole?" Another question might be, "Whose teddy bear is this?" Or you may ask while reading a story, "Why is the girl crying?" And children will be able to answer such questions as, "How will your mother bake the pie?"

Space concepts become clearer. While moving objects, children will understand your instructions that include such words as toward, up, top, and apart. Toward the end of the third year, children master more space concepts. They understand such ideas as around, in front of, in back of, and next to.

## Expressive language skills

Children's ability to produce language continues to increase. By now, children may use more than 900 words. These children also have improved grammar. They may make sentences of four or five words. They may even join sentences together with a conjunction. For instance, the child may say, "The bunny died and we don't have it."

Three-year-olds begin to understand the difference between past and present tense. They like to make verbs past tense by adding "ed" to them. These children make statements such as, "I talked," or "Daddy walked." However, they do not yet understand that there are exceptions to this rule. They may use such past tense verbs as "runned" and "goed." They may even use the correct form, but still add "ed." For instance, they may say "ranned" or "wented."

Children start to understand possessive nouns. Three-year-olds may refer to Mommy's

3-9 Three-year-olds can follow your three-part instructions.

car, Daddy's hammer, and Teacher's coat.

Negatives are not fully understood by three-year-olds. They understand that such words as no, not, can't, don't, nothing, and never are negative. But they use all negative terms when they form negative statements. For instance, a three-year-old may say, "Kelsie can't do nothing," or "Jackson can't never go nowhere."

During this stage, children start to use question words, especially why and when. These children tend to just add on the question word to a regular sentence. For instance, they may ask, "When Daddy is coming?" or "Why the cloud is moving?"

## Math readiness skills

Three-year-olds continue to learn concepts basic to math. They start to understand the concepts full, more, less, smaller, and empty. By 42 months of age, most children understand the concept of largest. These children like to constantly compare objects, saying one object is bigger or another is smaller.

Counting skills also begin at this stage. If you

ask, a three-year-old can give you two objects. These children can also count to three while pointing to corresponding objects. They may be able to recite numbers in order higher than three, but they are not able to count that number of objects.

Children in this age group can distinguish between one and many. To check for this skill, place one chip on the table. Nearby, place a pile of chips. Ask the child to point to one chip. Repeat the question asking the child to point to many chips. Children who respond correctly have learned the difference between one and many.

## SOCIAL-EMOTIONAL DEVELOPMENT OF THREE-YEAR-OLDS

After the third birthday, children start to grow out of the temper tantrums and contrariness of the two-year-old stage. They become cooperative, happy, and agreeable, 3-10. By this time, children start to learn socially acceptable ways of expressing their feelings. They can use more language to communicate with others. And they start to form friendships with their peers.

### Social development

Three-year-olds are eager to help others, especially adults. They like to help with such tasks as passing out crayons and pouring juice. They are learning new ways of showing concern for others. And they are learning positive ways to get attention from others. These children are more willing to accept attention from adults and children who are not well-known. They adjust to new people more easily than two-year-olds do.

By the third birthday, children begin to play with, rather than next to, other children. See 3-11. Although these children interact with each other, their play is not truly organized. For instance, they may play house and each child playing may be the daddy.

Children this age are not as possessive as two-year-olds. They will share with others, but they do not like to share too much. For this reason, three-year-olds usually play with only one or

3-10 Three-year-olds tend to be more content and agreeable than two-year-olds.

3-11 Although their play is not organized, three-year-olds will play with each other.

**Understanding Two- and Three-Year-Olds  51**

two main friends. These children use language more to communicate with friends and other children. For instance, they may say to a friend, "You play with the baby." But to another child, they may say, "You can't play with us."

Children this age also begin to learn **gender roles.** These are behaviors that are expected of girls or boys. Gender roles are not as clearly defined as they once were, but they are still an important part of learning. Children this age realize that there are physical differences between boys and girls. With the proper role models, they begin to learn how to treat members of the opposite sex with respect.

### Emotional development

Three-year-olds have strong visible emotions. They get excited. They get angry. They get discouraged. But they are beginning to understand that there are appropriate ways to express these emotions. They realize that adults do not approve of such actions as temper tantrums. And they are eager to act in ways that please others. Therefore, these children have some control over their strong feelings. Instead of striking another child, they may scream, "Stop it!"

Many situations do not cause as much anger as two-year-olds feel. Three-year-olds have improved coordination. Therefore, they are less likely to get frustrated because they cannot do something. They also have improved language skills. When children can understand why something is happening, they are less likely to get angry. For instance, a child may want a drink. You can explain, "It's only a few minutes until lunch. You can have a drink then." When the child understands that he or she will have a drink soon, he or she is less likely to get angry.

Three-year-olds are likely to become angry when things do not go their way. But they begin to direct their anger at objects. For instance, they may be angry at a pitcher if they spill their milk. Children this age are more likely to express their anger in words. They do not hit, stamp, or cry as much as two-year-olds do.

By this stage, children are not as likely to be frightened by objects that they know. For instance, they are not frightened by the noise

from a car. But these children are quite fearful of imagined dangers. They may be especially afraid of the dark. These children also become more fearful of pain. They may be scared that a dog will bite them or that they will be hurt during a doctor's visit.

Three-year-olds are affectionate. But they tend to seek affection in return. They may follow, cling to, or help an adult in an effort to get attention, approval, or comfort. Three-year-olds still do not think in terms of the feelings of others.

## TEACHING THREE-YEAR-OLDS

Three-year-olds are typically happy, sociable, and agreeable. Furthermore, they are very eager to please. As a result, they are likely to accept your suggestions, 3-12. They also adjust easily to new adults, classmates, and situations. For these reasons, you will find that most adults enjoy working with these children.

Three-year-olds enjoy playing. They still like to play alone. But they also like to play in groups of two or three. You can work with them to introduce themes to their play. Some themes include treating and healing others. One child will help another who is injured. Another theme is avoiding danger. For instance, children may pretend to save themselves from a fire and put the fire out.

The objects that you supply in the classroom will influence a three-year-old's dramatic play. Cooking supplies, tools, phones, and suitcases are popular. These children enjoy pretending to cook, make repairs, call others, and take trips.

Three-year-old children are becoming increasingly independent. They feel a need to do things for themselves. Signs of independence include such statements as, "I can do it," or "Let me do it." These statements are healthy signs that children are gaining confidence in their abilities.

Some three-year-olds need encouragement to become more independent. They may make such statements as, "You do it," or "I can't." When these words are spoken, you need to provide encouragement. These children need to know that you value their independence. They need to develop a feeling that they can do things.

## SUMMARY

Two-year-olds grow and change in many ways. Their motor skills improve so that they can run, jump, and balance. They also can scribble, drink, and undress. These children are learning to control their elimination.

Two-year-olds are able to understand and say many words. They can answer simple questions and follow simple directions. And they are beginning to learn basic math concepts related to size, number, shape, and color.

Socially and emotionally, these children are striving to be independent. They want to do things their own way, and when they can't, they may have temper tantrums. These children still need love and affection, especially from adults.

Three-year-olds grow out of many of the problems of two-year-olds. They have better muscle control and coordination. These children can draw, cut with scissors, and work simple puzzles. They can dress themselves without much help from adults.

The thinking abilities of three-year-olds improve. Their thought is no longer entirely in terms of actions. These children have growing understanding and use of language. They have a better understanding of questions and instructions. They use more complex sentences to communicate. And they are beginning to learn grammar rules for past tense. These children are also developing more refined concepts of number and size.

Socially, three-year-olds are beginning to reach out. They seek the favor of adults. And they start to make friends with other children. These children have strong emotions. But they are learning appropriate ways to express these emotions to others.

3-12 By the third year, children are more willing to accept and try suggestions from teachers.

## to Know

expressive language
gender roles
language comprehension

## to Review

1. List three motor skills of two-year-olds.
2. True or false. Most two-year-olds can dress themselves without help from adults.
3. Language comprehension is _____ advanced than expressive language in two-year-olds.
4. Which sentence is typical of a two-year-old?
   a. "Mommy."
   b. "Mommy go."
   c. "Mommy go and I go too."
   d. "Is Mommy going?"
5. How do most two-year-olds express their anger?
6. When working with two-year-olds, why do you need to allow plenty of time for transitions between activities?
7. True or false. Three-year-olds can climb and descend stairs easily.
8. Describe two self-help skills of three-year-olds.
9. Most three-year-old children can count to _____ while pointing to corresponding objects.
10. Why are three-year-olds less likely to become angry than two-year-olds?

## to Do

1. Visit a local day care center and observe the motor skills of two- and three-year-olds. Use notes from your observations to write a report comparing the motor skills of the two age groups.
2. Design a toy, activity, or teaching aid to help improve the self-help skills of a two- or three-year-old.
3. Invite a day care teacher to discuss the differences in expression of emotions between two-year-olds and three-year-olds.
4. Visit a children's library and find books designed to help young children express their feelings in positive ways. Write a report on one of these books.

# Chapter 4

# *Understanding Four- and Five-Year-Olds*

After studying this chapter, you will be able to:
- ☐ Describe the physical, intellectual, and social-emotional development of four- and five-year-olds.
- ☐ Explain how you as a teacher can plan programs and relate to four- and five-year-olds in developmentally appropriate ways.

Your days with four- and five-year-olds (preschoolers) will be filled with fun and challenges. These children are developed enough to handle many basic self-help skills. But they need new experiences and challenges to keep them growing and learning. These children have many questions about the world around them. Helping them answer these questions can be a rewarding part of teaching.

## PHYSICAL DEVELOPMENT

Increased body strength and coordination makes movement great fun for preschoolers, 4-1. Physical skills become easier partly because body proportions are changing. Compared to their total height, toddlers have fairly short legs. But by five and one-half years, most children's legs are about half the length of the body. Their proportions are more similar to adult proportions. This makes running, jumping, and balancing easier for children.

Preschool children are growing in more than just size. Their bones are becoming harder and stronger. And beneath the gums, their permanent teeth are forming. Many children in this age group begin losing their baby teeth. These children need good nutrition to assure that their

4-1 Preschoolers enjoy such large motor activities as climbing.

bones and permanent teeth form properly. This should include sources of calcium and vitamin D, such as milk and other dairy products.

### Gross motor development

As coordination improves, preschoolers gain many new skills. At four years, these children can hop on one foot. They also can walk down stairs with alternating feet. Four-year-olds can balance on one foot for about 10 seconds. And they can walk backwards, toe-to-heel, for four consecutive steps.

Late in the fourth year, many children may begin to learn how to skip. Most five-year-olds have developed this skill. Older four-year-olds may also ride a bike with training wheels. If they have the opportunity, most children have developed this skill by five years. Five-year-olds also can walk forward and backward on a balance beam. See 4-2. They can climb fences and march to music. They also can jump from table height and land on both feet.

Throwing and catching skills improve in these years also. Most four- and five-year-olds can throw overhand. As they grow, they become better at using their bodies to direct a ball as they throw. They rotate their bodies and shift their weight from the back foot to the front foot as they throw. These children are able to catch a ball with both hands. A five-year-old is able to keep the hands close to the body until just before they catch the ball. Four- and five-year-olds have an easier time catching balls that bounce first than catching fly balls.

Children this age enjoy working to improve their physical skills. They try to use their skills to the fullest. Sometimes, they may even become reckless. For instance, they may try to ride scooters as fast as they can.

### Fine motor development

Children's fine motor skills improve rapidly in the preschool years. These children find it easier to string beads and work with small game or puzzle pieces. See 4-3. When they build

4-2 Improved balance allows this five-year-old to walk forward and backward on a balance beam.

4-3 Four-year-olds have an easier time working game pieces than younger children do.

towers from blocks, the towers are straight and tall. By four years, most children can complete a five-piece puzzle. By five years, children can put together puzzles with eight or more pieces. Five-year-olds are also becoming skilled at working clay. They may sculpt simple forms and figures.

Writing and drawing skills also improve quickly. By four years of age, children's drawing forms are more refined. As a result, you will have an easier time recognizing their drawings. These children can also copy a square and print a few letters. Often the letters are printed improperly, though. For instance, the child may print "b" for "d" or even for "p." Or the child may place five or six horizontal lines on an E.

Five-year-olds show marked improvement in controlling a writing tool. They can copy triangles and trace diamond shapes. They are also fairly skilled at staying within the lines when they color. Most five-year-olds can print their first names. These children can copy most letters and print some simple words. (Children may still have problems printing some letters properly.)

**Self-help skills**

Preschoolers become more and more self-sufficient. They can dress and undress themselves with very little help. These children have learned how to tell the front from the back of clothing. But you may need to give them reminders from time to time. By four years of age, most children can buckle belts and close zippers. By five years, many children can even button and unbutton fasteners on the backs of garments. They also can put shoes on the correct feet. Some five-year-olds can even tie their own shoe laces.

Self-feeding is easier for preschoolers, too. These children like to help with serving. They can use spoons and forks with ease. By four years of age, children can use their forks to cut some large pieces of food. They may even try cutting foods with a knife. Most five-year-olds are able to cut fairly soft foods with knives. Preschoolers are also able to clean up their places after they finish eating.

Preschoolers are also better able to take care of their own hygiene. They become more skilled at handling a toothbrush and brushing their teeth. They also can use a wash cloth to wipe their hands and faces. These children become more skilled at brushing and combing their hair, too.

## INTELLECTUAL DEVELOPMENT

Children in this age group make many gains in understanding the world around them. They become more skilled in thinking without having to act things out. As a result, they have a better understanding of symbols than younger children. These children also have increased language comprehension and expressive language skills. Language is a tool that can help children solve problems mentally.

Children start to create their own symbols in this stage, 4-4. This is reflected in play. Instead of just imitating the actions of adults, these children add their own ideas. Instead of using a bowl for mixing, they may pretend the bowl is a hat.

New symbols also appear in art. Before the fourth year, children tend to scribble or just draw simple shapes. Now, children make drawings that represent real objects. These drawings are simple and do not always look like what the child really sees. For instance, a hand may have six or even ten fingers. Four-year-olds often make drawings and then decide what they are. By five years, children decide what they want to draw and then draw it.

Understanding symbols is important to developing more advanced intellectual skills. Symbols are a part of learning in language, math, science, social science, and many other areas of education. Therefore, intellectual development during these years helps prepare children for learning to come in the school years.

These children are eager to learn about why things happen around them. They may ask, "Why do dogs bark?" or, "Why do boats float?" With their endless string of questions, they are trying to make sense of their world. These children still have flaws in their thinking, as three-year-old preschoolers do. But through asking questions again and again, thinking becomes more and more logical.

Your curriculum will help children grow intellectually. As you provide new experiences, children's vocabularies will grow. And they will learn about new concepts. For instance, you may show the children a live bunny. These children will explore concepts about the bunny, such as size, color, and method of eating. Children may learn new vocabulary words as you show the animal. For instance, you might explain that the bunny is "timid." Each new experience helps the children grow intellectually, 4-5.

**Language comprehension skills**

The language comprehension skills of four- and five-year-olds are constantly growing. New

4-4 Four- and five-year-olds may make paper cones to symbolize hats.

4-5 A visit from a resource person can help children's intellectual growth in many ways.

58

words related to space concepts are added to their understanding. These include such words as beside, bottom, backward, and forward. They also understand such words as down, low, different, and thin. By the fifth year, the words behind, ahead of, first, and last are added to children's understanding. As you instruct children using these words, children will be able to understand and follow directions. For instance, you may tell a child, "Place the green block *behind* the blue block."

Children this age become even better at following three-step commands. These children will be able to follow the directions in the order that they are given. For instance, you may tell a child, "Pick up the puzzle, put it on the table, and wash your hands."

Children have a better understanding of the difference between plural and singular nouns at this age. For instance, you may tell a child to take a sandwich at lunch time. The child understands that he or she is to take only one sandwich. If you tell the child to take cookies, the child knows that he or she can have more than one.

Children start to understand the passive voice at this time. In a *passive voice* sentence, the object of the sentence is placed before the subject. An example of a passive voice sentence would be, "The orange was eaten by Brock." Three-year-olds do not usually understand this word order. They think the sentence means that the orange ate Brock. Four- and five-year-olds understand that Brock ate the orange.

Because many words and phrases have more than one meaning, these children may become confused about some statements. They tend to take literally such comments as, "Wanda just flew out the door." See 4-6. You need to be careful about the phrases that you use around these children. For instance, a phrase such as, "I'm dying of hunger," may scare children.

4-6 Preschoolers may have trouble understanding figurative speech.

Anne just flew out the door . . .

**Reading.** Most four- and five-year-olds cannot really read. But they are developing abilities that lead to reading skills. These abilities are made possible as children begin to understand symbolism. Before children learn to read, they need to understand that a group of letters on paper can symbolize any object, from a ball to an airplane.

Four- and five-year-olds can recognize and name many letters of the alphabet. They also can recognize their own names. Children in this age group enjoy having stories read to them over and over again. As you reread stories, these children may be able to pick out and say words that they recognize. The children will also try to guess words that they do not recognize. They tend to look at the first letter of a word and then name any word that begins with that letter. For instance, they may point to the word "ball" and say "baby."

### Expressive language skills

Preschoolers in this age group become quite talkative. As their vocabularies and grammar skills grow, they enjoy talking to others. See 4-7. At this age, children tend to talk to you rather than have a conversation with you. When you talk about one subject, a child may interrupt to tell you about something entirely unrelated. The child may even make two or three unrelated comments to you in the same conversation. These children can answer your questions. They also listen to answers to their own questions. In later years, these children become better at true two-way communication.

**Articulation.** *Articulation* is the ability to speak in clearly pronounced sounds. Articulation of these children improves in many ways. They can make most of the sounds needed to form words. Many children still have trouble making the "ch" sound and the "th" sound in words. Others may have trouble with the "s" sound, causing a lisp.

Some preschoolers also have *stuttering* problems. These include repeating sounds or words and pausing for unusually long times while speaking. For most preschoolers, stuttering is a result of thinking faster than they can talk. As children's speech ability catches up to think-

4-7 Four- and five-year-olds like to talk to you about their projects.

ing ability, the stuttering problem tends to disappear.

**Vocabulary.** Vocabulary grows quickly over these two years. Most four-year-olds have about 1500 words in their vocabularies. Five-year-olds have about 2000. Children do not always have clear ideas of the meanings of all the words they use. And they may make up their own meanings to some words. For instance, they may use up to mean up or down.

These children have mainly concrete nouns and action verbs in their vocabularies. They are beginning to add some modifiers and adjectives. But words related to ideas or thought are still not a big part of vocabulary. For instance, children this age would be unlikely to use the words freedom or unfair, unless they were simply imitating the words of adults.

Children this age do imitate phrases that they hear from adults or television. See 4-8. After

4-8 Children may imitate a phrase from television such as, "My teeth feel minty fresh and tingly." These children do not always understand the meaning of the phrase.

a meal, a child may say, "That was simply delectable!" This child is most likely imitating a statement heard at home or on television. If you ask, the child could not tell you what delectable means. Children might also use such words as bionic, biodegradable, and computer chip.

**Grammar.** Children's grammar improves during these years. Children start to learn that there are exceptions to rules for past tense. They use such irregular verbs as ate, ran, and went properly. These children still put "ed" at the end of these words occasionally.

Children also learn how to properly form questions. The three-year-old would say, "Why the sky is blue?" But four- and five-year-olds know to say, "Why is the sky blue?"

Some grammar rules still give these children problems. They especially have trouble using the proper forms of pronouns in sentences. For

instance, a child may say, "Him and me are going to the zoo." They also have trouble with noun/verb agreement. For instance, a child may say, "Tommy don't have a crayon."

**Math skills**

Number concepts become easier for children in this age group. Rote counting skills increase quickly. *Rote counting* is reciting numbers in their proper order. This skill is gained by most children before they fully understand that each number represents a certain amount. At four years of age, most children can rote count from one to nine. By the end of the fifth year, most children can rote count to 20. Rote counting skills develop at different rates for children in this age group. Therefore, you need to observe these children to make sure your curriculum fits their skill levels.

True counting, in which an object is counted for each number named, develops more slowly. For instance, a child may try to count ten objects. The child may touch one object and say "one," another and say "two," and another saying "three." But the child may then point to another object three times in a row, saying "four, five, six." Children in this age group may be able to count three or four objects. But they have trouble counting more objects.

Children start to recognize numerals in this stage. A four-year-old usually recognizes the numerals 1, 2, 3, 4, and 5. Five-year-olds learn to recognize 6, 7, 8, 9, and 10 as well. By five years of age, many children can dial their own telephone numbers.

Other math skills grow at this age. Children become better at recognizing shapes. About 80 percent of five-year-olds can recognize the square and rectangle shapes. Four- and five-year-olds also understand more terms related to size and number. These include short, fat, tallest, same size, first, and last.

Children start to understand money concepts in this stage. Most of these children can identify a penny, a nickel, and a dime. These children do not yet understand the true value of money, though. If you ask a child this age whether a nickel or a dime is worth more, the child is likely to choose the nickel. Since it is bigger, children think that it is worth more. They do not yet realize that a nickel is worth five pennies and a dime is worth ten.

Time concepts become more clear at this age. They start to understand the difference between today, tomorrow, and yesterday. But many time concepts are still confusing for these children. These children don't really understand how long an hour or a minute takes. They also get confused because time is described in so many ways. An adult may tell a child that puppet time is at 3:30, at half past three, this afternoon, or in a few hours.

## SOCIAL-EMOTIONAL DEVELOPMENT

Preschoolers continue to be helpful and cooperative, 4-9. With improved language skills, children become more involved with each other. Friendships become more important. Emotions are changing in these children. As they learn and grow, the causes of happiness, fear, anger, and sadness change. And the ways children react to these emotions change.

### Social development

Companionship is important to preschoolers. Friendships, attention, and approval are important to these children. But these children are also becoming more independent of adults. They like to play on their own or with other children. They may not always want you or other adults to participate in play. They may still need your help to get materials or settle disputes.

Children this age start to value their friendships with others. They tend to have only a few friends. They also prefer friends of the same sex. Children in this age group become more willing to cooperate as they play with others. They are more likely than younger children to offer a liked toy to a friend. Many children in this age group choose best friends. They tend to change best friends fairly often, though.

Play involves more and more interaction. Play groups are still small—only two or three children. But children talk to each other more and do more as a group, 4-10. Play still is not very organized. Children do not usually set

4-9 Four- and five-year-olds are usually cheerful and cooperative.

4-10 Play becomes more cooperative for four- and five-year-olds.

goals or stick with themes as they play on their own. But they will play more organized games with adult supervision.

Children this age accept supervision. They know their own abilities, and they realize that adults have reasons for rules. These children will accept your instructions. And they will ask your permission before doing certain activities.

### Emotional development

Causes and expressions of emotions change during these years. Children start to realize new ways of showing love and caring. They still understand hugs and other physical signs of affection. But they start to realize that helping others is a way of showing love. These children may show love for others by sharing something or helping with a task. They may also seek this sign of love from others. At times, children may ask for help with a task even if they don't need it. These children are looking for assurance that you care.

Children in this age group start to develop a sense of humor. See 4-11. Laughter becomes a fun way of expressing their happiness. These children do not yet understand most verbal jokes. But they laugh at funny faces or actions. They also laugh at things that they know are unusual. For instance, they may laugh at a dog that says "meow." These children also need good role models to learn that harm done to others is not funny.

**Fear.** Causes of fears change at this stage. These children are still afraid of imagined creatures. They may be especially fearful of dreams, because they seem so real. But they also start to realize that there is a difference between the real and the imagined. This helps children deal with some of these fears. For this reason, you may hear these children state firmly, "There's no such thing as dragons." Or they may ask you repeatedly, "The story was just pretend, right?"

Other fears may be created by the new knowledge of preschoolers. They are aware of more dangers. But they do not know enough to fully understand what is and is not dangerous. For instance, a child may learn that sharks live in the ocean. This may cause fear of being hurt in the ocean. But the child may also become afraid of sharks in rivers, pools, and even bathtubs.

Preschoolers are also more afraid of being hurt than younger children are. And they know of more things that can hurt them. They may be afraid of dogs, high places, doctors, and dentists. This is because they are aware of pain or injuries associated with these things.

These children sometimes work through fears in play. For instance, a child who is afraid of dogs may pretend to be a fierce dog. A child who is afraid of heights may pretend to be a bird. This play helps children let out some of their feelings and deal with their fears.

**Anger.** Like three-year-olds, children in this age group do not have as many causes for anger as toddlers do. But they can become angry if they are not able to reach their goals. These children are more likely to use words and yelling rather than hitting or kicking to express anger. If they do express anger physically, they are more likely to take out their anger on objects or other children. They do not usually

4-11 Children this age enjoy humor.

respond to adults physically because they know this action is not accepted.

Some preschoolers respond more physically to anger than others. These children may become angry more easily than others also. They may use pushing, hitting, or kicking to show anger. These children may not have learned better ways of expressing anger from adult role models. Or they may want attention.

**Jealousy.** Jealousy may be a problem for some children in this age group. These children are most likely to become jealous of a new brother or sister. They may resent the fact that their parents are spending so much time with a new child. And they may fear that their parents do not love them as much.

Jealousy may surface in children in many ways, 4-12. The child may regress to earlier behaviors, such as crying, following adults, and having toileting accidents. Or the child may develop physical problems such as stomach aches or nightmares.

4-12 Children who are jealous of a new sibling may become withdrawn or show regressive behaviors at the center.

These children need to be reassured that they are still loved and cared for. Sometimes, they may need a little extra attention away from home to make them feel special. Showing these children that their sibling needs help from a good "big sister" or "big brother" can make them feel better, too.

**Sadness.** Four- and five-year-olds start to learn that some situations are sad. They become aware of the concept of death. Their first experiences with death may be the loss of a pet. It may take children a while to realize that the pet will not come back to life. But once they understand this, they often become sad.

Children are not always sure how to express sadness. They need help from adults to learn that it is okay to cry and talk about their feelings. They also need adults to model appropriate responses to sadness. Children may deal with sadness in play. They may pretend to be the lost pet or to talk to the lost pet.

Some children must also deal with the death of a close family member. These children need to have as much explained about the situation as they can understand. They also need help from adults in dealing with the loss and sadness.

## TEACHING FOUR- AND FIVE-YEAR-OLDS

Like three-year-olds, four- and five-year-olds tend to be cooperative and helpful. These children are eager to please you, 4-13. If you ask a child to help you, the child feels complimented. These children enjoy feeling needed and important. These children may even ask you if there is any way they can help you.

Because these children like to help, you need to carefully select helpers. Choosing the same few helpers time after time can make others feel unimportant. Even children who do not volunteer need to be asked from time to time. These children may be too shy to ask. Or they may not feel confident in their abilities to help. Your choosing these children can help build their self-esteem.

By this age, children become quite talkative. They still enjoy physical play. But they like to spend more time talking. You can spend time carrying on conversations with these children. These conversations may become a part of learning activities or story time. After you read a story, these children may wish to retell the story. They can usually retell the story in detail and in the proper sequence.

Children in this age group will imitate your speech also. You may hear one child tell another, "Christopher, we walk, we don't run, when we are in the hallway." For this reason, you need to be careful of your statements around these children. You should never use words or statements that you would not want children to repeat.

Children are more content to play with each other. You do not need to function as a playmate as much. But you will need to handle more disputes among children. These children may have conflicts over group rules. They will look to you for advice on settling these problems. You may also want to add new ideas to play. These children enjoy playing some simple, organized games that you may lead.

Some children may have imaginary playmates. A child may come to school explaining that Ralph, his playmate, asked to come with him. He may provide space for Ralph on his cot at nap time. He may have conversations with Ralph throughout the day. This kind of

4-13 Preschoolers are eager to help you in such ways as caring for plants.

play does not necessarily indicate problems. It is simply a way of using the imagination and having fun.

Children in this age group are often proud of their possessions and family members, 4-14. They may like to bring favorite toys to the center. They may also call attention to new shoes or a new jacket. And they may beam with pride when their parents visit the center. Children enjoy talking to you and others about their belongings. Asking children questions about something of theirs can help them build their self-esteem.

Children in this age group enjoy working on projects. Their attention span and their ability to set goals are improving. Children's ideas for projects may come from play with peers or from adult activities. Such projects as woodworking, cooking, and sculpting clay may be fun for these children. See 4-15.

## SUMMARY

The growth of four- and five-year-olds helps them become more and more independent. These preschoolers become stronger and more coordinated. Their changing body proportions help them improve their balance and skills. These children become more skilled at running, jumping, throwing, and catching. They also become better at printing, drawing, working clay, and putting together puzzles. These children also have improved dressing, eating, and hygiene skills.

Children's thought becomes more and more adult-like. These children begin to understand and use symbols in play, drawing, and learning. Language skills improve quickly. These children understand and use more words. Their grammar improves also. Much new knowledge helps prepare children for later math learning.

4-14 Preschoolers are proud to have their parents visit the center.

These include rote counting and understanding of size and number concepts.

Children become more social with their peers at this age. Their play becomes more cooperative. Children still seek favor and approval from adults. They like to help and talk to adults. Children are learning acceptable ways of expressing their feelings. They are also experiencing feelings for different reasons.

As a teacher, you will enjoy working with four- and five-year-olds. These children can be independent in terms of self-care. They are eager and able to help you. And they enjoy talking with you and learning about new ideas.

4-15 Woodworking projects are popular with four- and five-year-olds.

## to Know

articulation
rote counting
stuttering

## to Review

1. Why is it important to include sources of calcium and vitamin D in the diets of four- and five-year-olds?

2. True or false. Four- and five-year-olds stand perfectly still when they throw a ball.

3. Describe the writing skills of four- and five-year-olds.

4. Which of the following dressing skills do most five-year-olds have?
   a. Knowing the front from the back of a garment.
   b. Buckling belts.
   c. Putting shoes on the right feet.
   d. All of the above.

5. Children age _____ tend to make drawings and then decide what they are.

6. Describe the reading abilities of four- and five-year-olds.

7. True or false. A four-year-old who uses the word "imitation" probably does not know what the word means.

8. Why are time concepts confusing for four- and five-year-olds?

9. True or false. Five-year-olds prefer friends of the opposite sex.

10. Describe a situation that is likely to cause fear in a five-year-old. Explain why this situation would cause fear.

11. Typically, what is the teacher's role in the play of four- and five-year-olds?

## to Do

1. Play catch with a four- or five-year-old. Make sketches or written descriptions of the movements used by the child to catch and to throw. Report on your findings to the class.

2. Invite a preschool teacher to show the class samples of artwork from four- and five-year-olds. Discuss the types of symbolism used in the artwork.

3. Make a bulletin board based on phrases that might be misinterpreted by four- and five-year-olds. The bulletin board could contain drawings of the preschooler's interpretation of the phrase.

4. Write a research report on recommended ways of helping four- and five-year-olds deal with death.

# part 2

# Guiding Children

As you work in child care, guidance will be a routine part of your experiences with children. Children need proper guidance to learn how to get along with others and to stay safe.

In this part, you will learn guidelines for establishing and enforcing rules throughout the classroom. You will study and practice techniques for guiding children throughout the day.

This part will also teach you ways to guide children through such daily routines as dressing, eating, and napping. And you will gain insight into methods for handling such guidance problems as negativism and fear.

# Chapter 5

# *Establishing Classroom Rules*

After studying this chapter, you will be able to:
- [ ] Explain the importance of rules.
- [ ] Discuss reasons rules are needed in all areas of the classroom.
- [ ] Describe methods for enforcing rules.
- [ ] List useful rules for a variety of situations.

Effective rules serve as a kind of shorthand that state the goals of the center. As such, *rules* should focus on actions and behaviors that reflect these goals. As a teacher, you are responsible for suggesting new rules to the director and staff. Likewise, you will help determine what will happen when rules are broken.

Every area of the classroom needs to have rules. As the classroom teacher, it is your responsibility to maintain rules. In addition, you should make sure that each adult working in the classroom is given a copy of the rules. A copy of the rules should be posted on a bulletin board in the teachers' lounge and/or in the classroom. You should also provide all new employees with a list of classroom and/or center rules.

## ESTABLISHING RULES

There are three reasons for establishing classroom rules. First, according to the law, children's health and safety must be protected. Second, children feel freer to explore when they know their teacher will stop them if they go too far, 5-1. Thus, they feel protected from mistakes. In this instance, rules are also known as *limits.* Finally, rules also help children develop self-control. As children learn to accept and obey rules, they gradually come to learn that rules are part of life. One of the center's goals should be to develop socially responsible behavior in young children. Establishing rules will help the center reach this goal.

When setting rules for children, make the rules short. Write them in language that the children can understand. State the rules in terms of the positive behavior that you expect.

Set rules that are reasonable and serve a useful purpose. Unreasonable rules can cause young children to feel angry.

Define both acceptable and unacceptable behavior. Decide how to deal with unacceptable behavior. Normally, the best approach is to stop such action firmly and quickly. You may find, however, that the child will become angry, 5-2. This anger may show in several ways. The child may resist set limits, cry, yell, or simply stare at you.

5-2 Undesirable behavior should be stopped, even if the child becomes upset.

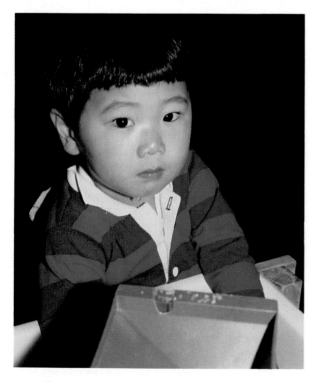

5-1 Setting rules helps children feel freer to explore.

On a regular basis, rules need to be re-examined by the entire staff. Children's behavior will change as they grow and develop. Therefore, rules should change as the children change. Any rule changes must be discussed with the staff. At that time, you should discuss what changes need to be made and why. If you determine that a rule no longer fits the group's needs, discard it.

## ENFORCING RULES

Children follow rules best when the rules are enforced in a regular, unchanging manner. This is known as *consistency.* Children then know what is expected of them. However, children will often test these well-established rules. You should feel comfortable with this testing process. At the same time you should also maintain your position. Do not be afraid or back down. For example, if you said that each child may do only one painting, make sure that no child paints two.

Enforcing rules also requires that rules be flexible at times. *Flexible rules* allow you to adapt to the needs of an individual or situation. For instance, your rule states that children are allowed thirty minutes to eat lunch. A sick child may need extra time to finish. Or perhaps the children are required to eat at a table. On a field trip, however, tables may not be available. The children will have to sit on the ground in this instance. Your rules must be flexible enough to handle such situations, 5-3.

The way you react to children who break rules affects children's feelings of security. Children feel secure knowing that the rules protect them. But when one child breaks a rule, another child's security may be threatened. For instance, a child may express his or her anger in a violent way, such as hitting. That child is breaking a rule. You must tell the child that hitting is wrong. But the child who was hit is also affected. He or she has lost some security. You need to reassure and pay attention to

this child. In fact, giving attention to the injured child shows the child who hit that hitting is not a good way to gain attention.

## SETTING RULES

The rules you set may be very different from the rules set at a center in the next town. This is because no two centers are alike. Equipment, facilities, and staff vary among centers. However, similar activities take place at many centers, regardless of location. For instance, cooking, blockbuilding, and reading occur at most centers. General rules for some of these areas and activities can be used as guidelines for all centers.

### Sensory play

In some classrooms, sensory activity is provided each day. A water table is often used for this activity. During a typical week, shaving cream, ice cubes, dried beans, seed corn,

5-3 Rules may need to be adapted to the needs of an individual child or situation.

colored water, and soapy water may all be used at the table.

Depending on the material being used, the rules may change somewhat. For instance, a child would not need to wear a smock for protection when playing with dried seed corn. When using shaving cream, however, the smock may be required.

Rules for the children should include:
- Wear smocks for all wet and/or messy activities, 5-4.
- Wipe up splashes and spills immediately.
- Keep sand and water in the sandbox. Throwing sand and water is not allowed. If a child does not follow the rule, direct the child from the area.

## Dramatic play

The dramatic play area might be called the home living or housekeeping area in some centers. Materials should be provided to help the children gain a better understanding of themselves and others around them. Dramatic play also allows children to work out their own feelings. Thus, to provide the children with the least restrictive environment, limit rules to the following:
- Wipe up all spilled water.
- Replace materials after they have been used.
- Respect the participation of other children.

## Small manipulative activities

This area of the classroom contains games and small objects. With these materials, children learn to build, compare, sort, arrange, and match. Also, color, number, size, and shape concepts can be mastered. As children use these materials, they also develop small muscle coordination and hand-eye coordination.

Usually, rules in this area are limited to include:
- Return toys to the shelf after use.
- Keep games and puzzle pieces in this area of the classroom.

## Cooking

Children learn about food by participating in cooking activities. Cooking allows the

5-4 Wearing smocks during messy activities will keep children clean and dry.

children to feel a sense of accomplishment. Tasting, smelling, touching, listening, and seeing help build language, number, sequence, and physics concepts.

Arrangements for health and safety must be included in the rules. Therefore, the following rules should be included:
- Wash hands before cooking.
- Wear aprons during messy activities.
- Wipe up spills immediately.
- Only teachers pick up hot kettles.
- Everyone assists with clean-up, 5-5.
- Children may taste their products during lunch or snack time. There is no eating or tasting during the activity.

Supervision is required during all cooking activities. Whenever appliances are being used, never leave the activity area! If more supplies are needed, signal for another teacher to get them for you. Always use pot holders and hot pads with cooking appliances.

Use recipe cards for all cooking activities. By following directions, children will learn sequencing. Recipes will also call attention to the importance of good reading skills. Chapter 21 contains many ideas for cooking activities.

5-5 After cooking activities, children must help with clean-up.

5-6 Blocks are to be used for building only.

## Blockbuilding

Blockbuilding encourages children to be productive and creative. Blockbuilding also provides children with a way to release energy. The children's safety is important in this area. Rules must stress safety.

Close supervision is always required in this area. Because of this need, building activities should be allowed only during a set time period.

Rules for blockbuilding activities include the following:

- Use blocks for building only, 5-6. Blocks are not to be used to threaten or hit other children.
- Keep blocks in the block building area.
- Return blocks to the storage shelves after use. Adults may have to assist.
- Do not touch another child's building.

## Music

Children from all cultures enjoy music, 5-7. It is a universal language. By participating in

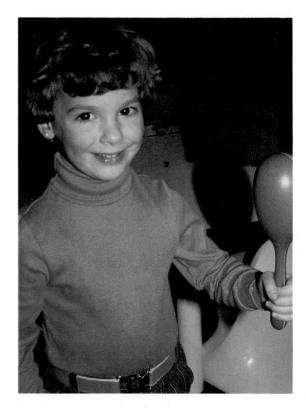

5-7 Children enjoy listening to and creating music.

music activities, children can develop self-expression, listening, language, and coordination skills. Music, like other activities, needs to have specific rules:

- Children select the instruments they want to use.
- Return instruments to their assigned places on the shelves after use.
- Use musical instruments only for creating sounds. (Hitting others is not allowed.)

## Art

For children, art is usually a pleasing activity. Therefore, they may want to spend a lot of time playing in this area. Art is available in most centers every day, most often during the self-selected activity period.

Children in this area should be encouraged to explore materials. They should not be told what to make. As a result, the rules in this area are minimal. Most centers use only the following rules:

- Cover tables.
- Wear smocks for messy activities.
- Children's names should be written across the top left hand corner of their projects. This is helpful to children in this culture because people read from left to right. If a child is not able to write his or her name, the teacher should write it.
- Wipe up spills immediately.
- Do not compare artwork. (Teachers also need to follow this rule.)

## Book corner

In the book corner, children can develop language and pre-reading skills. Children should be encouraged to explore the books in this area, 5-8. In doing so, they will learn about their own family and community. They also will learn about other cultures.

Rules for the book corner are:
- Turn one page at a time.
- After use, return books to the shelf.
- Give torn books to the teacher.

In order to encourage the children to explore, you also need to follow some rules. Change books on a regular basis. Some teachers change books on a weekly basis, leaving several

favorites to carry over. Control the number of books available at any given time. When too many books are in the area, it can become cluttered. Likewise, a child may have difficulty locating a favorite storybook.

## Science

All children need science activities. These activities encourage them to discover their own environment. As they observe and question, they will see relationships and draw conclusions.

Teachers need to follow several rules when planning science activities. Include a variety of classroom and outdoor activities. Emphasize hands-on activities that allow children time to explore their surroundings, 5-9. During these activities, encourage the children to participate by studying, questioning, touching, and holding.

5-8 Children can learn valuable pre-reading and language skills in the book corner.

As a teacher, you will also need to demonstrate some of the rules in this area. For example, you will need to show the children how to hold a bunny, water a plant, or feed classroom pets. Using equipment and handling living things will also need to be demonstrated for the children. You may even choose to have some children assist with cleaning the animal cages.

The science rules should include the following:

- Feed pets and water plants only under teacher supervision.
- Keep science equipment in the area.
- Handle pets with care.

## Playground activity

On the playground, children can express themselves in creative ways. They can build ships, houses, forts, and other objects with wooden crates and other materials. Through play, children develop motor coordination skills, social play skills, and a sense of cooperation.

The primary concern of the teacher is the children's safety. You will be responsible for helping the children develop safe play habits. Rules must be set and enforced if children are to play happily and safely on the playground. These rules will vary, depending upon the specific piece of equipment being used.

**Swings.** Swings are not found on all playgrounds. One reason is that they require a great deal of teacher supervision. If swings are available, specific rules must be followed. Included should be the following:

- Sit on the center of the swing.
- Use both hands for holding on.
- Stay on the swing until it has stopped.
- Only teachers push children on swings.
- Only one child may sit on a swing at a time.

**Slides.** Slides are also a source of hazard for young children. Accidents happen when children bump into each other. Some children are

5-9 Hands-on activities encourage children to become involved in the world around them.

injured when they stand up as they go down the slide or when they slide head first. As a result, follow these rules:

- Use both hands when climbing up the stairs.
- Stay one arm's length behind the child in front of you.
- Wait until the person in front of you has gotten off the slide before you slide down.
- Slide down feet first and sitting up.
- Get off the slide as soon as you get to the bottom.

**Jungle gyms.** Jungle gyms are very appealing to young children. Their natural curiosity leads them to explore each inch of the jungle gym. Since children are adventurous, any activity on this piece of equipment has to be carefully supervised. Children must also be taught the correct and safe way to use the jungle gym. Include the following rules for jungle gym use:

- Use both hands to hold on, 5-10.
- Look down to see that you do not step on another child's hand when climbing.
- Only four or five children may use the jungle gym at one time.

**Seesaws.** Seesaws are another piece of equipment that require constant supervision when being used. Therefore, the rules you establish should stress safety. Include the following:

- Hang on to the handle with both hands.
- Keep feet out from under the board as it goes down.
- Stop before the board hits the ground.
- Tell your partner when you are getting off.

## SUMMARY

Rules focus on actions and behaviors that reflect the goals of the center. Rules must be made for all areas of the classroom and for all activities.

Rules that are consistently enforced and fair help create a relaxed atmosphere at the center. Children know what is expected of them. Adults know what to expect. Both groups find the center a pleasant place to be.

5-10 Children need to hold on with both hands when they play on the jungle gym.

## to Know

consistency                    limits
flexible rules                 rules

## to Review

Write your answers on a separate sheet of paper.

1. Explain the importance of effective rules.

2. List three reasons for establishing classroom rules.

3. True or false. When defining acceptable and unacceptable behavior, teachers must also decide how to deal with unacceptable behavior.

4. _____ rules allow you to adapt to the needs of an individual or situation.

5. Does your reaction to a child who breaks a rule affect other children's feeling of security? Explain your answer using an example.

6. Which of the following rules for sensory play is not flexible?

   a. Wipe up splashes and spills immediately.

   b. Always wear a smock.

   c. Keep sand and water in the sandbox.

7. By following directions on a recipe card, children may learn _____.

8. List two rules teachers should obey in the book corner.

9. True or false. Teacher supervision is always required on the playground.

## to Do

1. Discuss ways in which rules may change as children grow. Give some specific examples.

2. Collect classroom rules from two centers. Discuss the similarities and differences between the two sets of rules.

3. Role play the following scenes:

   a. Toby is in the book corner. While looking at a book, she accidentally tears a page.

   b. Tommy goes down the slide. When he reaches the bottom, he continues to sit there.

   c. Sarah and Frank are on the seesaw. Suddenly, Sarah jumps off.

   d. During a cooking activity, Mark accidentally spills his milk.

4. Cut pictures of two pieces of outdoor play equipment from a catalog. Write rules for each piece.

# Chapter 6

# *Building Guidance Skills*

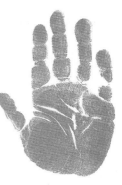

After studying this chapter, you will be able to:
- ☐ Outline the goals of effective guidance.
- ☐ Explain how a useful observation is made.
- ☐ Describe various direct guidance and indirect guidance principles.
- ☐ List techniques for effective guidance.

Kris sat in the corner looking at a library book. Slowly he ripped a page from the book. On the other side of the room, Kelsie knocked Wendy's block tower over. Then she sped to the art table and grabbed John's play dough. At the same time, Paula entered the room, greeted another child, and threw her coat on the floor.

How will you, as a teacher, guide each of these children? Guiding children is a complex process. *Guidance* consists of direct and indirect actions used by an adult to help children develop socially acceptable behavior, 6-1. Effective guidance should maintain children's self-esteem and produce a growth or desired change in children. Self-control is the long-term goal of guidance. That is, the children should learn to direct their own behavior without outside control.

Understanding and guiding children's behavior requires knowledge of child growth and development. It also requires the ability to understand each child's behavior. This is a constant process that never ends. As a teacher, you will constantly learn more about your role in guiding young children as you study each situation.

6-1 Younger children often require more guidance than older children.

## GUIDANCE AND YOU

As a teacher, your personality will affect the behavior of your children. Many studies have been conducted to determine the effect that specific personality traits have on children's behavior. You should be aware of the results of some of these studies.

Studies show that effective early childhood teachers encourage and show interest in children. These teachers use more suggestions than commands. Children respond faster to suggestions than commands.

According to research, teachers should interact often with their children and ask *open-ended questions*. These questions require more than one-word answers. Children in this type of environment will show certain positive characteristics. These include independence, verbalization, cooperation, task persistence, and high self-esteem. See 6-2.

Studies also note that uncooperative teachers have more hyperactive, disruptive, and bored students. On the other hand, talkative teachers have children who are more shy. Nurturing teachers have children who get along with others easily.

Aggressive and attention-seeking behavior is also influenced by the teacher. This behavior occurs most often with permissive teachers. Such teachers often fail to get involved with or stop aggressive and attention-seeking behavior. The children who behave this way may see the teacher's lack of involvement as permission to engage in such behavior.

Studies also show that a teacher's behavior is affected by available space. When the ratio of space to children is low, teachers are more demanding. They tend to restrict play. For example, self-selected play may be limited to playing with toys at a table. Likewise, a greater ratio of space to children results in a more relaxed teacher.

6-2 This child will learn a great deal through interaction with the teacher.

## PREPARING FOR GUIDANCE

There are some general guidelines for developing effective guidance skills. Study these guidelines. They will help you become an effective teacher.

One of the first steps toward effective guidance is *observation* of the children. Watch and note how individual children behave in certain situations. This will help you understand the children in your class.

To make observations that will be useful to you, you will need to do the following:
- Put a group of blank index cards in a card box or gather paper in a three-ring binder.
- On a card or piece of paper, record the child's name, observation date, activity area, and time of day.
- Record the actual event. Include full details.
- Record the time you finish the observation.

For instance, note how long a crying child cries. Note who reinforces the child's behavior. Was it the teacher, an aide, or another child? If possible, include any conversation that occurred. For instance, Johnny's mother brought him to the center. Johnny began to cry. Describe this scene in full detail. Describe actions. Instead of saying "Johnny is crying because he does not want to leave his mother," say, "Johnny continued clinging to his mother as she walked toward the door. She bent down and put her arms around Johnny, yet he continued to cry. Finally, Johnny's mother gave Johnny a package of gum. He stopped crying."

Another important guideline is to plan with other teachers. Sharing observations, feelings, and suggestions will help you fully understand the children. One teacher may be able to add to your observations, 6-3. As a result, you will better understand why a child refuses to take part in art activities.

Next, do not talk to other adults when you are teaching, unless it is important. The children's needs should always come first. Being alert to these needs requires your full attention. Make a practice of talking with other teachers only if necessary. Save other comments for after program hours.

Finally, sit with the children whenever possible. You will be closer to the children's level. As a result, they will find it easier to approach you and gain your attention. Stay in the background in this situation. Do not interrupt an activity unless you can add to knowledge or safety. Let the children begin interaction with you. Remember that to develop independence and self-confidence, never do for the children what they can do for themselves.

## DIRECT GUIDANCE

Child guidance may be direct or indirect. *Indirect guidance* involves outside factors that influence behavior. The layout of the center is a form of indirect guidance. Indirect guidance will be discussed later in the chapter.

*Direct guidance* involves physical and verbal actions. Included may be facial gestures such as eye contact, a smile, or even a surprised look. Body gestures are another type of direct guid-

6-3 With the help of other teachers, you can learn more about the children in your center.

## DIRECT GUIDANCE PRINCIPLES

1. Use simple language.
2. Speak in a relaxed voice.
3. Be positive.
4. Offer choices with care.
5. Encourage independence and cooperation.
6. Be firm.
7. Be consistent.
8. Provide time for change.
9. Consider feelings.
10. Intervene when necessary.

6-4 These direct guidance principles outline the verbal and nonverbal skills you will need for effective guidance.

ance. Putting your arm around a child is one form of direct guidance. Your words are also a form of direct guidance.

Direct guidance principles are shown in 6-4. Following these principles will help you develop direct guidance skills.

### Use simple language

Using simple language is important. Young children have limited vocabularies. In order to communicate clearly, use language they can understand. Consider the ages of the children. Adjust your vocabulary to fit those ages. For instance, two-year-olds usually learn "big"

before they learn "large." Therefore, use "big" with these children. Working with three-year-olds, you could probably use "large." This depends, however, on their level of development. With four- and five-year-olds, again adjust the level of your vocabulary. With these children, you might use "huge."

### Speak in a relaxed voice

Speak in a calm, quiet, relaxed tone of voice. Children will listen to this type of voice. Save loud voices for emergencies. At those times, you will gain the children's attention with a loud voice. If you raise your voice during the normal course of the day, children will become used to this level. When an emergency occurs, you may not be able to gain their attention. In addition, when you raise your voice, the children will also raise their voices. The classroom will become a very noisy place.

### Be positive

Be positive. Guide the children by telling them what to do, as opposed to what not to do. Children will feel more comfortable with a positive comment. For example, instead of saying, "Don't put that puzzle on the floor," say, "Put the puzzle on the table." See 6-5.

### Offer choices with care

New, unskilled teachers sometimes confuse offering a choice with giving a direction. For

## USING POSITIVE GUIDANCE

| Negative | Positive |
|---|---|
| "Do not put the puzzle on the floor." | "Put the puzzle on the table." |
| "Do not touch anything!" | "Place your hands in your pockets." |
| "Do not run." | "Please walk." |
| "Quit screaming." | "Use your indoor voice." |
| "Do not drip paint." | "Wipe your brush on the container." |
| "Do not get paint on your clothes." | "Put on a painting smock." |
| "Do not rip the pages." | "Turn the pages carefully." |
| "Do not walk in front of the swing." | "Walk around the swing, please." |
| "Do not use your fingers." | "Use your fork." |

6-5 Be aware of negative comments you make and try to replace them with positive comments.

example, when it is lunchtime, the teacher may say, "Do you want to go in for lunch?" By asking this question, the child is given a choice. If the child is not interested in eating lunch then, he or she may answer by saying, "No."

Children should be offered a choice only when you want them to have a choice. In this case, a better direction would be, "It is time for lunch now," or, "We need to go inside for lunch now." The younger the children, the more simple the language used for giving directions.

### Encourage independence and cooperation

Give children the least amount of help they need. In this way, they will have opportunities to learn independence. For instance, encourage children to dress and feed themselves. Encourage them to share responsibility for keeping the classroom clean and orderly.

Some children begin school dependent on others. At home, these children have an adult or sibling to attend to their needs. As a result, they come to school expecting the teacher to dress them, pick up after them, and take care of their business with other children.

Encourage independence from the start in order to change this behavior. For instance, when Eugene reports that Tommy is teasing him, ask Eugene how he feels when this happens. If he says that he does not like it, tell him to share his feelings with Tommy. Likewise, if Talia does not want to share her clay, Eugene needs to tell Talia that he is mad because she will not share.

Children only become independent if allowed the opportunity. Many people are surprised at the competence of three-, four-, and five-year-old children who are provided the chance to do for themselves. See 6-6.

These children also must learn to help each other. Encourage children to work with and help each other. When Toby tells you he cannot zip his coat, say, "Ask Joanne if she can help you." If Marlene cannot tie her shoe, say, "Ask John to help you tie it." These experiences will also help the children to learn to work as a group.

### Be firm

Be firm when disciplining children. At the same time, speak in a quiet voice. Some children are very demanding. When you tell them that they cannot put a metal truck in the watertable, they may cry. Some may even throw temper tantrums. You cannot allow such behavior to persist. In this case, stand firm. Remove the truck yourself if necessary.

When a child throws a temper tantrum, you may wish to give in. But if you do, the child will likely use the same method again when he or she wants his or her own way. Effective guidance requires firmness.

6-6 Even young children can do for themselves, if given a chance.

### Be consistent

Children are good at testing adults. If they feel an adult is not firm in disciplining, they will repeat their bad behavior. In fact, they may want to find out what will happen if they continue to repeat their bad behavior. For this reason, discipline and approval should be given consistently. For instance, do not discipline children one day and praise them the next for running to the door at playtime.

### Provide time for change

Young children need time to change activities. It is important to provide them with ample time for change. Without this time, children can become confused. By allowing time, you will provide children with an adjustment period. For instance, when children are preparing to go outside during cold weather, allow them time to put on their coats, hats, and mittens. This time will allow them to prepare themselves for new activities and new surroundings.

### Consider feelings

Although it is not always included in daily lesson plans, learning about feelings and emotions is an important part of any day at the center. Children need to recognize, understand, and express their feelings.

Young children often have strong feelings. These feelings often center around control of their environment. Such feelings often relate to their bodies, siblings, eating, friendship, and toileting.

Feelings are best discussed in small group settings or alone with a child. For some children, talking about feelings and emotions is difficult. It is your responsibility to help them understand their feelings. See 6-7.

Facing someone else's pain is also difficult for young children. You will observe that children do not know how to deal with the pain of others. When a new child begins school and cries over separation from parents, the other children do not usually get involved. Some may pretend to not see or hear the child. Others may have a pained look on their faces. This shows sensitivity. Although they may feel sympathy,

they tend not to get involved. Usually, if a child is bleeding, only then will they get involved. They will bring the child to you for a bandage. However, they will not usually console the child.

Modeling is the best way to help these children. For instance, if Patrick is crying, put your arm around him. By doing this, you will teach the children a way to comfort each other. They will learn that crying can be mended with a hug.

Young children also need to learn how to handle mistakes. When a child spills milk or breaks a toy, do not overreact. Instead, show the child how to handle the mistake. The child will then know not to fear mistakes. See 6-8. For example, remind the child who spilled the milk that the milk must be cleaned up. Show the child how to do this. Depending on the situation, you may wish to help clean up.

### Intervene when necessary

To be an effective teacher, you will need to know when to intervene. Allow children to explore on their own. Interrupt only when you

6-7 Many children do not know how to handle their feelings. They may require your help in order to feel good about themselves.

6-8 Spilled crayons may seem like the end of the world to these children. Help them learn how to handle these mistakes.

can add to their knowledge or promote their safety. For example, if a four-year-old says, "Cows give eggnog at Christmas," clarify this statement. Unless you intervene, children who are listening may believe this comment.

Safety intervention will often require words and action. If James is not careful climbing up the slide, you will need to walk over and review the rules with him. Make clear the dangers of falling.

You may also need to intervene for health purposes. Remind children to dress properly for outdoor play in the winter. Encourage children to cover their mouths when they cough. When cooking, remind children not to lick the utensils.

Children need to learn to be friends with all the children. Thus, do not allow children to be excluded from play because of age, race, or sex. Children who are excluded feel awful. When Erica says, "Only girls can come into the playhouse," it is important for you to intervene.

One way to handle this is to say, "This school is for everyone." By doing so, you will give the children the words they need to defend their right to participate.

You must also intervene when children are impolite. Sometimes you will hear a child say, "I do not like you," or, "You are ugly." When this happens, you need to intervene. Point out to the child that such words can hurt another's feelings. With young children, that may be sufficient to end the behavior.

Property arguments may also require intervention. Center property does not belong to the children, but to the school. Therefore, the children must share it. During a property argument, remind the children to share. If this does not work, give the equipment to one child for a set time period. Then give it to the other child for another time period. For instance, tell Manny that he may play with the truck in the morning and Mark may play with it in the afternoon. Then make sure each child has his turn.

It is important for children to learn that they cannot grab materials from others. No matter how strong the child's feelings, others have rights, too. Children need to take turns painting at the easel, participating in cooking activities, and watering plants, 6-9. While children learn and develop, you will need to intervene. That is why in many early childhood classrooms, you will hear a teacher saying many times a day, "You can have a turn tomorrow," or, "After Mitchell is finished you can paint."

## INDIRECT GUIDANCE

You will recall that indirect guidance involves outside factors that influence behavior. The physical set-up of a center is a form of indirect guidance. It can indirectly influence both the children's and teacher's behavior. For example, a well-planned facility makes supervision easier. The fact that you can supervise properly will help you to feel relaxed and in control. The children will feel safer knowing they are being protected.

In order to carefully supervise young children, an open classroom is best. Stand with

6-9  These children have learned that they must take turns as they participate in cooking activities.

your back against the classroom wall. You should be able to view the entire room. Such a set-up will allow you to observe and give help when needed. It will also reduce your own fatigue, since you will not have to run back and forth between areas.

A healthy, safe environment can be promoted through the physical set-up of the facility. In one large room, you will be able to see everything that happens, 6-10. Therefore, you can step in when dangerous situations arise. For instance, the behavior of two-year-old children needs close monitoring. Many two-year-olds will hit another child instead of saying, "I do not like that." This threatens the security and safety of the entire group. With the proper physical set-up, you can see such situations occuring and step in immediately.

Young children, and especially two-year-olds, often do not have well-developed large motor skills. They often stumble, trip, and/or fall. To reduce the number of these accidents,

large, open areas are best. Shelving units should be placed around the outside walls of the room.

Children's independence can also be encouraged through the physical set-up of the facility. Independence should be a learning objective of every early childhood program, no matter the ages or abilities of children in the program. For example, you should encourage toddlers to use the washroom if they have developed control of their bowels and bladders. For this reason, the washrooms should be easy to find and use. Sinks, toilets, and hand dryers should be set at the children's level.

Children can also be encouraged to hang up their own coats and assist with clean up. To encourage this, provide low hooks for hanging coats and hats. Low shelf units and sinks will encourage children to help with clean up.

Through these arrangements, you will save time and energy assisting the children. This will allow you more time to observe and work with the children and plan meaningful activities.

6-10 These teachers can see all the children as they sit in this large room.

## TECHNIQUES FOR EFFECTIVE GUIDANCE

As an early childhood teacher, you will teach children acceptable behaviors. Likewise, the children in your classroom will also teach each other. Whatever effect you have on the children's behavior, the children, in turn, will affect others.

Children's behavior can often be molded by setting consequences for certain behavior. For instance, if you thank a child for holding the door, the child will most likely hold the door again. You have provided a positive consequence. Repeated reward will result in repeated behavior.

Negative consequences are also important in molding children's behavior. If Brad drives his scooter into Lawrence over and over, warn him to stop. If he does not, he must give up his turn on the scooter. Thus, Brad will learn that driving into others is not acceptable behavior.

Teachers sometimes reward children for

unacceptable behavior. This is called **negative reinforcement.** For instance, laughing at a child who is acting silly at group time is a negative reinforcement. This reaction is seen by the child as a reward. It encourages the child to repeat the behavior.

Specific techniques for guiding children's behavior include praising, suggesting, prompting, persuading, redirecting, modeling, listening, ignoring, and warning.

### Praising

*Praising* involves recognizing children's accomplishments. Young children thrive on praise. When you say, "I like the way you helped, Cedric," you tell the child he is important. This is a form of verbal praise. See 6-11. Nonverbal praise can also be used successfully. A smile, wink, or pat on the back are all types of nonverbal praise. Displaying a child's work on a bulletin board is also a form of praise. Some teachers paste a star or sticker on paperwork or artwork that a child has done. This is also nonverbal praise.

When praising young children remember the following:
- Make praise age appropriate.
- Give praise immediately. It is most effective to praise children while they are still in the act.
- When praising, always establish eye contact.
- Do not overuse praise. If you do, it will not be as effective.

### Suggesting

*Suggesting* means placing thoughts for consideration into children's minds. This, in turn, often leads to action. For instance, after Candy spills her milk at the table, you may have to suggest she clean it up. To do this, say, "Candy, here is a sponge." This will likely be enough to encourage Candy to wipe the spill. If not, you may have to add, "You need to wipe up the milk." Or, during snack time, you may suggest to the children that they try a new fruit. This can be done directly or indirectly. Simply stating, "This fruit is delicious," is enough to encourage some children to try the food. A more direct approach may work for other children. For example, you may say, "Tammy, try this fruit today. It is delicious."

Always make suggestions positive. Lead children's thoughts and feelings in a desirable direction. If you tell the children to listen carefully to the story, they will probably follow your advice, 6-12. However, if you tell the children that they are noisy and behaving poorly, they will probably continue to act this way. Negative suggestions usually produce negative behavior.

Effective teachers use suggestions many times each day. You will have many daily opportunities to mold behavior through suggestion. For example, Darlene may forget to put the blocks back on the shelf. A suggestion may work here. Or Corinna may drop her coat on the floor as she enters the room. A suggestion may work here, also.

### Prompting

Children often need prompting either to stop an unacceptable action or start an acceptable one. Prompting can also be used to prepare

Ways to Say "Good for You!"

| | |
|---|---|
| "Wonderful!" | "Marvelous." |
| "I love it!" | "Thank you." |
| "Beautiful." | "Lovely!" |
| "You are a good listener." | "Super!" |
| "I like the way you listen!" | "I like the way you work." |
| "Good work!" | "I like the way you try." |
| "I am proud of you." | "I like the way you help each other." |
| "I am pleased." | "You are a good worker." |
| "Congratulations!" | "Let me show your work to others." |
| "Perfect!" | "You do that very well." |
| "Fantastic!" | "I can tell you are trying!" |
| "Terrific!" | |

6-11 Opportunities for praising young children are limitless.

6-12 This boy's teacher suggested he sit on his carpet square and listen to a story.

children for transitions. *Prompting* differs from suggesting because a response is required of a prompt. Examples of verbal prompting include:

- "Jody, is a napkin placed on your lap at lunchtime?"
- "Susie, do you remember where we keep the play dough?"
- "Glenda, what is our rule when riding bikes?"
- "Michelle, do you remember where we put our painting?"

Prompting can also be nonverbal. You may place a finger over your lip at group time to signal, "Quiet, please!" Rules printed on a poster board are nonverbal prompts. Frowning can show your disapproval. Even turning a child around to attend to group activities is a form of prompting.

Generally, make prompting simple and noncritical. Prompt in a calm, impersonal manner. You may ask a child, "What are you supposed to be doing?" or, "What should we be doing before we have snack?"

Prompting may need to be repeated often before acceptable behavior is developed. A child who is new to the center may need to be prompted for several days to hang his or her coat on the hook before this behavior is developed. Once the child complies, praise this behavior.

## Persuading

By *persuading,* you encourage children to act or behave in a certain way by appealing to their basic wants and needs. Seeing things from their point of view will give you an idea on the best way to approach a situation.

Link behavior with the children's feelings. For instance, a child who hangs back from an activity might be persuaded to join by appealing to his or her need to belong. You might say, "We are having such fun, Elizabeth. Will you join us?"

A child who interferes with another child's activities also needs to be persuaded. You can persuade the interfering child by helping him or her understand the other child's feelings. For instance, you may say, "Kenny, Joanie is afraid that if you keep jumping over here, you will knock her building down."

## Redirecting

Children often need *redirecting* to a substitute activity. That is you will need to divert, or turn, their attention in a different direction. One way to redirect is through distraction. A child who cries when his or her parent leaves may have to be distracted. Choose a concrete object to distract the child's interest. In this case, an interesting toy or book may be helpful.

Redirection encourages children to express themselves in more socially acceptable ways. For example, an active child may constantly push around other children. To help this child release energy, provide activities that are physically demanding. Playing with a punching bag, carpentry tools, or play dough will provide an outlet for extra energy. The key to redirecting is providing an appealing substitute.

## Modeling

Children learn by imitating others. Every time that you speak or move, you are *modeling.* Thus, modeling involves both verbal and nonverbal actions. A variety of modeling examples are shown in 6-13.

6-13 Modeling can be used in many situations at the center.

## Listening

*Listening* involves giving children your full attention. One type of listening is called *active listening.* Through active listening, you first listen to what the child is saying to you. Then you respond to the child by repeating what was just said. This lets the child know that you have heard what he or she said and that you accept it. It does not mean, however, that you solve the problem. See 6-14.

For instance, Jeanine was playing in the housekeeping area. She wanted to use the broom that Sherry was using. She asked Sherry, "May I have the broom?" Sherry responded, "No, I am using it. Besides, I had it first." Jeanine got angry. She ran over and shared the incident with the teacher's aide. The aide listened carefully to what Jeanine was saying. Then the aide repeated what Jeanine had just said to make certain she heard correctly. The aide said, "You are angry because Sherry will not let you use the broom." Jeanine learned that people will listen to her and her feelings will be accepted. However, she will have to solve the problem herself.

## Ignoring

Do not encourage inappropriate behavior. When a child is able to gain your attention by whining, crying, or throwing a temper tantrum, you have reinforced the child's behavior. The child will likely continue this behavior rather than control it.

If a child's inappropriate behavior is not dangerous, avoid giving the child attention. Do not look directly at the child. Avoid acknowledging the behavior. This is called *ignoring.* On the other hand, praise the child when he or she models acceptable behavior.

Changing a young child's behavior is usually not a quick process. It is important to use patience. Unless you ignore unpleasant behavior 100 percent of the time, it is likely to reoccur.

## Warning

When children fail to follow a classroom rule, you must remind them that they are misbehaving and will be punished if they continue. You are *warning* the children. Warn only once. If the behavior continues, proceed with

6-14 Active listening is a nonverbal skill that helps children develop self-esteem.

the consequences. Effective warnings contain only two parts. First, state the misbehavior. Then state the consequences. Examples include:

- "Joel, sand needs to be kept in the sandbox. If you throw it again, you will lose your turn."
- "Mandy, guns are not toys. If you use the block as a gun again, you will leave the block area."

When warning children, use a firm voice. Your voice should reflect your displeasure with the child's behavior.

## SUMMARY

Effective guidance skills are necessary for effective teaching. Direct skills can be built by following several guidance principles. These include:

- Use simple language.
- Speak in a calm, quiet, relaxed voice.
- Be positive.
- Offer choices with care.
- Encourage independence and cooperation.
- Be firm.
- Be consistent.
- Provide time for change.
- Consider feelings.
- Intervene when necessary.

Indirect guidance skills can be built by paying attention to outside influences that affect behavior. One important factor that indirectly affects guidance is the physical set-up of the classroom.

Guidance techniques will help you put your guidance skills to work. Specific techniques you may wish to use include praising, suggesting, prompting, persuading, redirecting, modeling, listening, ignoring, and warning.

## to Know

active listening
direct guidance
guidance
ignoring
indirect guidance
listening
modeling
negative reinforcement

observation
persuading
praising
prompting
redirecting
suggesting
warning

## to Review

Write your answers on a separate sheet of paper.

1. Guidance:
   a. Is used to help develop socially acceptable behavior in children.
   b. Consists of direct and indirect actions.
   c. Should produce growth or desired change in children.
   d. All of the above.
2. Studies show that _____ teachers have more hyperactive, disruptive, and bored students.
3. Why do children of permissive teachers often exhibit aggressive and attention-seeking behavior?
4. List the materials and steps for making a proper observation.
5. Give three examples of actions used in direct guidance.
6. Use positive guidance statements to rewrite the following:
   a. Do not scream!
   b. You are getting paint on your dress.
   c. Do not spill the milk.
   d. Quit running!
   e. You are talking too fast.

7. Name the direct guidance principle being used in each of the following examples.
   a. Penny was disciplined yesterday for running through the cooking area. When she ran through the cooking area today, she was again disciplined.
   b. The children are playing in the art area. It will be lunchtime in 10 minutes. Their teacher says to them, "Children, it is almost time for lunch. Please start cleaning up the area."
   c. Henry is running from one end of the teeter-totter to the other. His teacher comes over to him and says, "Henry, stop that. You might hurt yourself."
   d. A teacher says to her children, "On Friday, we will be eating lunch outdoors. You can choose to have either a hot dog or a hamburger for lunch."
8. _____ _____ involves outside factors that influence behavior.
9. Give an example of how the physical set-up of the classroom can be used to encourage independence in the children.
10. True or false. Children's behavior can be molded by setting certain consequences.
11. When a child is rewarded for unacceptable behavior, this is called _____ _____.
12. True or false. Praise should be given immediately.
13. How does a prompt differ from a suggestion?
14. The key to _____ is supplying an appealing substitute.
15. Explain the process of active listening.

## to Do

1. Observe a teacher interact with children for one hour. Record all incidences of verbal guidance.
2. Practice verbal guidance techniques by showing a friend how to use a puzzle.
3. Have two children play a game while you practice making and recording observations.
4. Discuss situations in which a teacher may have to intervene in the classroom.

# Chapter 7

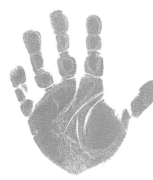

# Handling Daily Routines

After studying this chapter, you will be able to:
- ☐ Explain the importance of routines.
- ☐ Guide children successfully through five daily routines.
- ☐ Demonstrate the development of children's eating skills.
- ☐ Discuss the processes for solving various eating problems.
- ☐ List guidance steps for toilet training.
- ☐ Explain four types of transitions.

*Routines,* such as dressing, undressing, eating, napping, toileting, and changing activities, are everyday experiences. Routines reassure children by providing a structure to each day. The children know that after breakfast, they play. Then there is lunch and a washroom break. After this is nap time. After nap time, snacks are served. Then the children get dressed to go outside. After outdoor play, the children's parents come for them.

Daily routines also provide opportunities for children to develop independence. Young children feel great satisfaction in doing things for themselves. Remember to provide them with as little help as they need. This allows the children the opportunity for growth. See 7-1.

Like other aspects of the center, daily routines also need your guidance. Without guidance, routine activities may become time-consuming and frustrating. Learning to handle routines helps your classroom run smoothly and the children will be relaxed and happy.

## DRESSING AND UNDRESSING

As a teacher, tell the children what you expect of them. This is important. When four-year-old Frankie hands you his coat, refuse to help him put it on. Instead, tell Frankie he is able to dress himself. If needed, give him some verbal instruction. Once his coat is on, do not forget to praise him for his accomplishment. This will help him enjoy becoming independent. See 7-2.

Children should also be responsible for hanging up their own coats. You may notice that many of the children simply lay their coats in their lockers. Do not allow this to happen. For instance, if you see Eileen lay her coat in the locker, say, "Eileen, you need to hang your coat on the hook." If she does not understand, show her how to hang it on the hook. Then take the coat off the hook and let Eileen hang it up herself.

Label lockers so children can find their own spaces. The labeling method you use will vary

7-2 Letting children know they are capable of dressing and undressing themselves helps children build independence.

with the ages of the children. Names are usually written on the lockers for infants. This helps both teachers and parents. For two-year-olds, use a picture of the child. Names and symbols are helpful to three-year-olds. If children cannot recognize their own names, they can find the symbol they know is their own. Remember to give each child a different symbol. Most four- and five-year-olds can recognize their own names. If not, they can be taught.

**Suggestions for parents**

Dressing can be time-consuming and frustrating for teachers and children. For this reason, some centers provide parents with a list of clothing suggestions for the children. The list usually includes the following:

- Send an extra set of clothing for children to keep at school. These can be used in case of an emergency. For instance, a child might fall in mud, rip a pair of pants, or have a toileting accident.

7-1 Teaching children how to buckle their shoes allows them to be more independent.

- Attach labels to the inside of children's clothing. It is common for several children to have the same style and size of clothes. Labeling helps prevent confusion.
- Select clothing for your child with large zippers, buttons, snaps, etc. This makes dressing easier for children who do not have well-developed small motor skills.
- Make sure children's boots slide on and off easily. Make certain the boots fit well.
- Consider buying elastic-waist slacks and shorts instead of snap or button types. They are easier for children to handle during toileting.

### Demonstrating

Buttoning, zipping, pulling on boots, tying shoes, and putting fingers in gloves are all actions that can be demonstrated. *Demonstrating* means showing the children how to do a task. Demonstrating at the child's eye level is the most effective. Sometimes, verbal guidance is all that a child needs. At other times, you may need to start an action. Allow the child to finish the process. He or she will feel a sense of accomplishment.

**Tying shoes.** Tying is a skill that requires advanced coordination. As a result, most children do not learn this task until five years of age.

There are several methods for teaching children how to tie shoes. One method is to place the child on your lap. From this angle, the child can observe the process. For most children, the easiest technique to learn is to loop each string like a bunny ear. Tie these loops into a double knot. Encourage the child to repeat this process.

Some children will have shoes that clasp with Velcro® instead of tie with laces. Bring shoes with ties to the center to teach these children how to tie. Let them use these shoes to practice. This will help them learn tying skills. Or you can let them practice on a shoelace box, 7-3.

**Boots.** If you teach in an area that receives snow and/or rain, you will need to work with boots. This can be a difficult situation. This is especially true when children are wearing boots that are too small. When this happens, place a plastic bag over the child's shoes or feet.

This will help the boot slip on and off more easily.

Some centers store a box of boots. When a child is wearing boots that are too small, the teacher can make an exchange. Boots from this box are also handy if a child forgets to bring boots from home. This is common for children who are driven to school.

Children can practice putting on and taking off their own boots. Or they may practice using the extras in the box.

**Coats.** To demonstrate putting on a coat, lay the child's coat, button or zipper side up, on the floor. Have the child kneel at the collar end. Tell the child to place his or her hands into the sleeves. Then tell the child to put it over his or her head. Using your own sweater or jacket, demonstrate this technique to the children. See 7-4.

### EATING

Centers vary in terms of meal provisions. Some centers serve only lunch. Others may also

7-3 A shoelace box is useful for teaching tying to children.

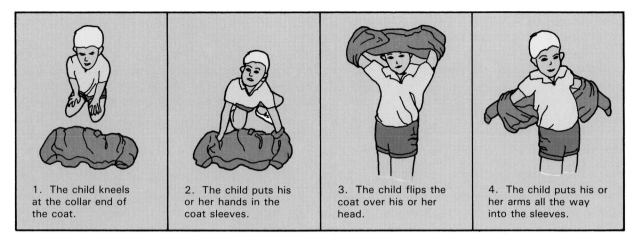

| 1. The child kneels at the collar end of the coat. | 2. The child puts his or her hands in the coat sleeves. | 3. The child flips the coat over his or her head. | 4. The child puts his or her arms all the way into the sleeves. |

7-4 This technique can be used by children to help them learn how to put on a coat.

serve breakfast. Some centers require that children bring their own bag lunches. And while most centers provide older children with meals, they require that parents send infant formulas.

As a teacher, you will have many concerns during mealtime. A main concern is serving nutritious meals that children will like. This concern is addressed in Chapter 12, "Planning Nutritious Meals and Snacks."

Making mealtime pleasant and orderly is another concern of teachers, 7-5. This means making meals appropriate for the ages, abilities, and interests of children. It also means teaching and enforcing rules of etiquette during meals.

### Development of eating skills

You will notice that children's appetites change. Children's appetites are influenced by a number of factors. Included are illness, stage of development, amount of physical activity, and a body's individual chemical needs. Emo-

7-5 Proper manners and order contribute to a pleasant meal.

tions can also affect appetite. For example, if Lila has cried since her parents dropped her off this morning, chances are she will not be hungry at lunchtime. Appetite changes will require you to be flexible in the ways that you treat children during meals.

**Infants.** Infants have definite food likes and dislikes. It is not unusual for infants to spit out or refuse foods they do not like. On the other hand, they will eagerly eat foods they enjoy.

Cup feeding may begin as early as six to seven months of age. At first, children may take only a few swallows. Spilling will occur for several months. Later, children will enjoy using cups by themselves. To help these children, many stores sell spill-proof cups.

Once children become mobile, their interest in food often changes. During this stage, some children are too interested in moving to sit still very long. Even if placed in a high chair or feeding table, they may try to get out.

Provide finger foods to infants whenever possible. By picking up small bits of food, the child will develop fine motor skills and hand-eye coordination.

Interest in self-feeding using spoons may occur between 15 and 18 months of age. You will need to be patient with children who are learning to feed themselves. You may have to help them fill their spoons. Since spilling occurs often, the children should wear bibs. Also expect food to be spilled on the feeding tray, high chair, and floor. Wipe up the spills immediately so others do not slip on them.

**Two-year-olds.** Two-year-old children become increasingly skilled at handling cups and spoons. Provide these children with child-sized spoons and small, unbreakable cups. Fill the cups only halfway. Then if a drink is spilled, there is less to clean up.

Use small, 16 ounce milk or juice pitchers with two-year-olds. Encourage the children to fill their own cups. Watch carefully and provide support. For instance, Molly may be able to pour her own cup of milk, but Daphne may need help. See 7-6.

**Three-year-olds.** By the age of three, children have distinct food preferences, 7-7. They may refuse to eat certain foods because of their

7-6 Supervise two-year-olds as they pour their own drinks. They may need help handling the pitcher.

7-7 Pizza is a favorite food among children.

98

color, shape, or texture. Your attitude will help children accept these foods. Other children can also influence food preferences. Some children who flatly refuse to eat vegetables at home may enjoy eating them with their peers.

Three-year-olds are old enough to assist with mealtime. Ask them to set the table. To help them do this properly, make placemats with outlines of the plate, glass, fork, and spoon. Provide forks and spoons to help the children develop handling skill. Use glasses with weighted bottoms to help prevent spills. Use pitchers with lids and pour spouts. Shallow bowls allow the children to see what is in the bowls.

Have children serve themselves. As a rule, tell children to fill their milk glasses only halfway. Keep portions small. If children want more food, they may ask for second portions.

Keep a wet sponge on the table for spills. When children spill, accept this as a normal occurrence. Avoid scolding the child. Rather, guide the child in wiping up the spill.

**Four- and five-year-olds.** Four- and five-year-olds like to help at mealtime. They may ask to set the table, serve, and assist with after-meal clean-up. They may also enjoy helping to prepare the meal. As the teacher, encourage them to do so. For a classroom activity, have them prepare pudding, rolls, or other simple foods, 7-8. Later, serve these foods for snack or lunch.

Older children enjoy talking at the table. You may wish to help them begin conversations. Mention activities they have seen, heard, or done. They will begin talking with each other and naturally move on to other subjects.

## Rules

Rules for eating depend on the ages of the children. However, general rules should include the following:
- Serve small portions. The rule of the thumb should be one tablespoon of food for each year of age.
- Children are to assist with serving and clean-up.
- All foods must be tasted before seconds of food or milk are served.

7-8 Children enjoy helping prepare foods they will eat later.

- Children must remain at the table until everyone has finished.
- Children must wipe up their own spills.

## Eating problems

Studies show that eating problems are common during the preschool years. At three years of age, these problems usually reach a peak. Eating will remain a problem for 25 percent of four- and five-year-olds. In most cases, problems will end somewhere around the sixth birthday.

Food refusal, dawdling, pica, and vomiting are all eating problems. They can become serious.

**Food refusal.** Food refusal problems are related to a lack of interest in food. Food refusal often begins between one and two years of age. At this time, children's need for food decreases. Some children may need only one meal a day. Refusing food because it is not needed is not a problem. But children who do not eat even when they need food have food refusal problems.

Lack of exercise or energy, excess energy (hyperactivity), and/or illness can all cause a lack of interest in food. These fairly common problems sometimes cure themselves. There are steps you can take, however, to help children with food refusal problems.

To encourage children to eat, serve small portions, 7-9. Avoid pushing the children to eat. Instead, talk with the parents of children having problems. Find out what these children eat at home. Despite mealtime refusal at the center, these children may be getting proper nourishment at home.

Do not provide between-meal snacks to children who refuse to eat breakfast and lunch. If you provide these children with food throughout the day, they will never be hungry at mealtime.

**Pica.** *Pica* is a craving for unnatural foods. Cravings include paper, soap, rags, and even toys. This condition is fairly uncommon in most preschool children.

If you think that a child may have this problem, ask other staff members to observe the child. Compare your observations. Discuss the problem with the center director. You may want to schedule a conference with the parents to discuss the problem. A combined effort between parents, medical professionals, and teachers may solve the problem.

**Dawdling.** While one child eats only one or two teaspoons of food, the other children may have finished an entire meal. It is common to have several children who eat slowly in a group of preschoolers. This is called *dawdling.* Some may hold food in their mouth for a long time, failing to chew or swallow it. Others are so busy talking at the table that they fail to take the time to eat. These children lack interest in food.

Many times dawdling is an attempt to gain attention. Therefore, do not urge or threaten dawdling children. Instead, provide these children with small portions of food. After being given a reasonable amount of time to eat, clear the table without comment. Children will

7-9 Children with small appetites are more likely to eat if they are given smaller portions.

learn that if they want to eat, they must do so in a timely fashion.

**Vomiting.** Young children are able to *induce* (to produce on purpose) vomiting. If a child in your class vomits often, without other signs of illness, he or she is probably inducing it.

If you are sure a child is not sick, ignore repeated vomiting. Clean up the mess quickly, without emotion. If the child notices any concern, he or she may begin vomiting to get your attention.

You should, however, share the child's behavior with the parents. Find out if this behavior also occurs at home during or right after a meal. If it does, you will need to work with the center director and parents to solve the problem.

## NAPPING

"Will my child be required to take a nap?" This question is asked often by parents who are thinking of enrolling their child in a center. The answer you give depends on state licensing requirements.

Most states require all children under a preset age be allowed nap time, 7-10. A center can also expand that requirement if they wish. For instance, a state requires all children under the age of five to be allowed nap time. A center is allowed to expand that rule to require all enrolled children to take naps. In any case, check your state's guidelines for requirements.

Most day care centers have a set nap time. At the end of this time, most children are awake. If not, they are gently woken.

You may note that a certain child needs to be woken every day. If this happens, the child may not be getting enough rest at home. This needs to be discussed with the parents. Check with your center director to find out who is responsible for talking to the parents. If you are asked to contact the parents, use a positive approach. Share your observations with the parents. Try to arrive at a solution together.

## Nap time rituals

Lack of rest can cause irritability in young children. Most preschool children, tired or not, can postpone sleep at nap time. Younger children may simply cry. Older children, however, may make repeated demands for your attention. They may request to go to the washroom or have a drink of water. In most cases, these are only pleas for attention.

Plan ahead to prevent children from making too many demands at nap time. First, have the children use the bathroom and have a drink of water before they lie down. Ask if anyone needs a tissue. After this, begin to cover them. Do not be surprised, however, if a child still asks for another drink of water or trip to the bathroom. These rituals seem natural to most two- and three-year-old children. They sincerely believe their needs are real. But if you allow these children to meet these needs before nap time, they will have an easier time getting and staying settled. See 7-11.

Schedule quiet activities prior to nap time. Children often enjoy hearing a story at this time. Select stories that will soothe the children.

7-10 Naps are required in many states.

7-11 Allow children to remove shoes and socks at nap time. They will be more comfortable and relaxed.

Four-year-olds may like to look at the book until they fall asleep.

Not all children will fall asleep at nap time. It is common for some of the five-year-olds to remain awake. Five-year-olds will cooperate, however, if nap time limits are stated clearly and enforced.

Children who do fall asleep may tell you they had bad dreams while sleeping. Others may cry out in their sleep. When this happens, calmly approach the child. Let the child know you are near. One way to do this is to hold the child's hand or straighten the covers.

## TOILETING

The toileting needs of infants are met through the use of diapers. That is because infants cannot control *elimination* (bowel and bladder release). For them, elimination is a reflex action.

The first few weeks after birth, infants eliminate many times each day. They may cry when it happens. The number of eliminations will decrease as the infant gets older. However, the volume increases. By 28 weeks, a child may remain dry from one to two hours. When they do eliminate, however, the diaper is usually soaking wet. It may leak unless it is changed immediately. Diapers need to be checked often and changed when wet to prevent diaper rash.

The toileting needs of older children are met through toilet training. Some centers require that older children be toilet trained before they can attend the center. However, this is not always the case. This is because children differ in their toilet training schedule. Some children are toilet trained as early as eighteen months. Others may not have full bladder and bowel control until two and one-half to three years of age. For some children, toilet training will take just a few days. Other children may require several months.

### Toilet training timetable

Children cannot be taught to perform toilet functions until their central nervous systems are ready. As a rule, this does not occur until about two years of age. At this age, most children will express their need to use the toilet. Some may pull down their pants and sit on the toilet. Others will tell you they have to use the bathroom.

Each child in the center will have his or her own toilet training timetable. Never force children to learn before they are ready. Instead, observe and praise them as they become better at keeping themselves dry. Controlling elimination is one step toward independence. It is a real accomplishment for young children.

### Guidance

As a teacher, maintain a matter-of-fact attitude in toilet training. Shaming and scolding have no place in helping a child develop control. Instead, provide children with the facilities and encouragement to stay dry.

Have toilet seats or potty chairs available. If you provide a seat for the toilet, also provide a step stool to help the children reach the toilet. Not all children like to sit on the toilet. Some are afraid they will fall in the toilet and be flushed down. These children will prefer the potty chair.

Children often provide clues when they have to use the toilet. Some start wiggling. Others cross their legs. When you notice these signs, provide reminders to the child. You can remind the child by saying, "It is toilet time again," or "Louis, do you need to use the toilet?" After children use the toilet, also remind them to wash their hands. See 7-12.

---

| TIPS FOR GUIDING TOILET TRAINING |
|---|
| • Each child has his or her own toilet training timetable. Never force children to learn before they are ready. |
| • Maintain a matter-of-fact attitude. |
| • Praise children as they become better at keeping dry. |
| • Do not shame or scold. |
| • Make toilet seats or potty chairs available. |
| • Watch for clues that children provide when they need to use the toilet. |

7-12 Remember these rules for effective toileting guidance.

7-13 Putting away toys helps prepare children for the next activity.

## TRANSITIONS

*Transitions* are changes from one activity to another and/or moves from one place to another. They occur many times during the day. Children may go from self-selected activities to using the bathroom to snack time to outdoor play in just a few hours. Transitions must be carefully planned to help children get through the daily routine without a fuss.

There are four basic methods for making successful transitions. You may use concrete objects, visual signals, novelty, or auditory signals. You may use several types of transitions in one day. Remember to be consistent. Young children respond better if they know what to expect. Therefore, it is best to use the same transition for individual activities. For instance, play the same clean-up song on the piano every day to let the children know it is clean-up time.

### Concrete objects

Using concrete objects as a form of transition involves children moving items from one

place to another. This technique directs a child's attention from one activity to another, 7-13. Examples include the following:

- "Leon, please put your picture in your cubby." This will direct Leon from an art activity to a new activity.
- "Rose, hang up your coat." Rose will move from an outdoor activity to an indoor activity.
- "Joel, here is some play dough. Take it to the art table." Joel is directed toward starting an art activity.
- "Wendy, put these washcloths on the bathroom hook." This signals the end of clean-up.

### Visual signals

Using visual signals is another transition method. This method involves informing children of a change through signals they can see. For instance, when you show the children a picture of lunchtime, the children move to the lunch table. After story time, you might hold up a picture of outdoor play. This will serve as a signal to the children that it is time to put on outdoor clothing and wait at the door for you. See 7-14 for other examples of visual transitions.

The first few times you use visual signals, you will need to explain them to the children. After you use them several times, the children will know what to expect.

**Novelty**

*Novelty transitions* involve the use of unusual, new actions or devices to move the children from one activity to another.

Locomotion is one type of transition. The children use motion to make their transition. For instance, ask the children to pretend they are elephants. Have them walk like heavy elephants to the snack table. Or ask them to tiptoe lightly like tiny monkeys.

Using locomotion is limited only by imagination. Children can march, skip, or walk backwards. Before introducing a transition, however, consider the abilities of the children. For instance, do not ask a group of two- or three-year-olds to skip. They may not have developed this skill yet.

Transportation is another type of novelty transition. The children can move like freight trains, jets, buses, or cars.

Each time you introduce a locomotion or transportation transition, get involved with the children. Model the movement you want them to make.

Identification games are also used for novelty transition. For instance, you may direct the children from one activity to another by asking, "Who is wearing red today? You may go into the bathroom and wash your hands before we have our snacks." See 7-15. Continue using other colors that the children are wearing until every child has departed from the group.

Novelty transitions can also be made using the alphabet. Direct the children to another activity by asking, "Whose name starts with the letter T? You may go outside." Continue calling out letters until all of the children are outdoors.

USING VISUAL TRANSITION

| VISUAL TRANSITION METHOD | APPLICATION OF METHOD |
|---|---|
| Construction paper | Use to break children into small groups. Place a piece of blue, red, green, or yellow construction paper at each table. Divide children into four groups and assign each group one of these colors. Have groups find their tables. |
| Hand motions | Use on playground to motion children indoors or to a specific area. |
| Blinking lights | Use to gain children's attention or to warn children to finish up an activity. |
| Clock | Use with older children by telling them, "When the big hand is on the 12, it will be lunchtime." |
| Words | Use to dismiss children from a group. Make a name card for each child. Hold cards up one at a time. Children are dismissed when they see their names. |

7-14 Visual signals can be used many ways for transition.

## Auditory signals

*Auditory signals* inform the children of a change through the use of sound. A bell, timer, autoharp, tamborine, or piano can all inform children of a transition. Some teachers use a simple song or chord of music as a transition signal. For example, when Mr. Andrews plays "Mary Had a Little Lamb" on the piano, the children know it is time to clean up.

Auditory signals also need to be developed for individuals. There will be times when you may wish to signal only one child. For instance, you may quietly tell a child that he or she needs to clean up or go to the snack table. This is called an *individual transition.*

Auditory signals are quite useful for providing warning. For instance, a ringing bell tells the children that playtime will end in three minutes. At the end of the three minutes, they know it is time to clean up.

## SUMMARY

Routines provide structure to each day. They also provide opportunities for children to develop independence. Learning to handle daily routines allows the center to run smoothly.

Dressing, undressing, eating, napping, toileting, and making transitions are all daily routines. Each of these presents its own particular challenges and problems during the course of a day. For instance, asking children to remove and hang up their coats seems like a predictable activity. However, without the proper guidance, this task may take an hour to complete. Therefore, it is important that you learn about these routines and how they are best handled.

7-15 Using a color identification game helps catch children's attention when making a transition.

## to Know

auditory signals       novelty transition
dawdling       pica
demonstrating       routines
individual transition       transitions

## to Review

Write your answers on a separate sheet of paper.
1. Routines:
   a. Provide structure to each day.
   b. Provide opportunities for children to develop independence.
   c. Reassure children.
   d. All of the above.
2. True or false. Children should be taught to depend on their teachers for assistance in dressing.
3. Why do some centers ask that parents send a second set of clothing for children to keep at school?
4. Demonstrating at a child's _____ _____ is the most effective way of teaching tying, buttoning, and zipping.
5. Name four factors that may influence a child's appetite.
6. List three rules children must follow when eating meals.
7. _____ _____ problems are related to a lack of interest in food.
8. What is pica?
9. True or false. Urging dawdlers will help correct their dawdling.
10. When toilet training:
    a. Shame.
    b. Scold.
    c. Be matter-of-fact.
    d. None of the above.
11. _____ are changes from one activity to another.
12. List four types of transitions and explain one.

## to Do

1. Practice putting on your sweater or jacket using the technique outlined in the chapter.
2. From a sitting position, practice teaching tying, buttoning, and zipping to one of your peers.
3. Ask experienced teachers for their successful nap time techniques. Present this information as a report.
4. Observe children at nap time. Record the techniques used with the children. Discuss your findings with your classmates.
5. Ask parents what clues their children use when they need to use the washroom. Compare these to the clues you observe.

# Chapter 8

# *Guidance Problems*

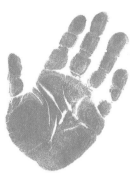

During your teaching career, you will likely have several children in your classes who will be difficult to control and teach. You will have *guidance problems* with these children. Many times, these problems will appear as disruptive behavior.

Disruptive behavior often is caused by tension. Overstimulation, changes in routine, and loud noise are just a few causes of tension in children. Because children do not know how to handle tension, they often react with disruptive behavior such as pushing and disturbing other children, running, and yelling, 8-1.

Helping children with guidance problems is an important job. You will need to understand situations and feelings that cause tension in children. You will need to know how to help children deal with this tension. And, finally, you will need to recognize behavior patterns that result from tension. With this information, you will be able to effectively guide and help these children.

## CAUSES OF TENSION

There are many causes of tension in children. These include certain situations and feelings children do not know how to handle. In addition, there are physical problems that can cause tension in children.

Being aware of situations and emotions that produce tension is important. This knowledge will allow you to avoid, or at least lessen the effects of, these causes.

## Overstimulation

Children can become overexcited, or *overstimulated,* by many things. For instance, simply playing with other children can overstimulate some children, 8-2. Usually, the larger the group of children, the greater the likelihood that overstimulation will occur. You may want to limit the number of children that can be in a certain area at any time. This will help prevent the chaos created when a large group of children play together. For example, post a sign in the blockbuilding area limiting space to four children at any given time. For younger children who do not read, make a simple sign showing four stick people. It will serve the same purpose. Similar signs can be posted in other areas of the classroom.

Some children become overstimulated when there are program changes. Holidays, such as Christmas and Valentine's Day, can be overstimulating times for children. Avoid making holiday plans too early. When this happens, the children may get keyed up long before the event occurs.

Overstimulation can also result from having too many activities planned. When this happens, some children have a hard time making choices. Instead of staying with one activity, they run back and forth between several. Their activity and excitement, in turn, can affect others.

## Breaks in routines

Routines are important to children. They let children know what to expect and when. If

8-1 Some children yell and become disruptive when they feel tension.

8-2 The combination of being outside and climbing on a jungle gym can cause overstimulation in some children.

routines are not followed, children become confused. Guidance problems can arise. For instance, Jimmy is put down for a nap at 12:30 on a regular basis. If this is not done, he may become overtired. This may result in disruptive behavior.

All children need consistent daily schedules. Quiet activities need to be followed by active activities. If children sit still too long, they may lose interest in the activity and become disruptive. Likewise, if children remain active too long, they may become overstimulated and disruptive.

## Noise

Noise affects children differently. Children with very sensitive ears are particularly upset by noise. For example, these children will cover their ears when a smoke alarm goes off. Likewise, if an ambulance drives by with its siren wailing, some children will cringe. While some children may try only to escape the noise, others may react by pushing or hitting others.

To avoid the problems caused by noise, control tape recorder and record player volume. Also pay attention to the volume of your own voice. In frustration, you may yell. Unfortunately, this causes a chain reaction. As the volume of your voice increases, the children's voices also become louder. This, in turn, will affect children sensitive to noise. The result will be chaos.

## Waiting time

Children often behave poorly when they have to wait for long periods of time. By nature, they are usually in motion. Therefore, if they are kept waiting too long for a story, they may start pushing or hitting. This behavior is not the child's fault. However, it will gain disapproval of the teacher. This will, in turn, contribute to the child's negative self-image.

Cut down on waiting time by being prepared, 8-3. If you are going to read a book for a large group, choose the book before you start and place it where it will be convenient. Likewise, prepare materials for all small and large group activities ahead of time. If you do not have a great deal of time to prepare, use the time when the children are involved in self-selected activities.

Manage your time effectively. This will reduce waiting time and resulting guidance problems.

## Frustration

Children sometimes feel they are not in control. They feel defeated or discouraged. These feelings are called *frustration*. They cause tension in children, 8-4. In order to control frustration, carefully plan each day's activities. The activities you choose should reflect the needs and interests of the children in the center.

Some children come to the center full of energy. These children need to be active. Provide wheeled toys for these children. Other children enter the center in quiet moods. These children prefer quiet activities such as looking at books, putting puzzles together, stringing beads, playing with dough, or just watching others for a while. Provide the proper toys for these children also.

Forcing any of these children into activities they are not prepared to join can result in frustration. A better approach is to allow the

8-3 Preparing visual aids before the activity helps reduce children's waiting time.

8-4 Being in control is important for young children. When they are not in control, they may become frustrated.

children to decide what is best.

Conflict over toys can also create frustration. Therefore, make certain that several kinds of toys are available to the children at all times. Always purchase several one-of-a-kind toys. For some reason, these toys have special appeal to young children. Wise teachers buy more than one wagon, scooter, fire engine, and car. As a result, they prevent constant conflicts over these particular pieces of equipment.

Select materials and equipment to match children's developmental level. This allows the children to feel success and an "I can do it" attitude. Working with mixed aged groups presents special problems. Include open-ended materials such as blocks, play dough, and sand. Children of all ages will play with these, but in different ways. See 8-5. Provide puzzles and books for a range of abilities.

When necessary, redirect children to materials that match their abilities. Repeated failures will cause frustration. Frustration may lead to anger. An angry child may pinch, hit, push, kick, or bite.

As an adult, you become angry when the children are uncontrollable due to frustration. When this happens, try to relax. Carefully watch your words and actions. If the children sense you are upset, they, in turn, will become more upset. They need to feel that you are calm and in control.

**Physical problems**

Poor health or other physical problems can cause tension and behavioral problems in

8-5 A sensory table and paints are materials that appeal to children of many ages.

children. One teacher, Miss Merde, had such a problem in her center. During Ethan's first day at the center, both Miss Merde and several other teachers observed Ethan. They feared he would be a behavior problem. He ignored all directions and suggestions made by Miss Merde. He also seemed to have a high anxiety level.

Ethan's behavior became a source of frustration for Miss Merde. More than once, she wondered whether Ethan should even be in the center. She feared that other children would copy his behavior. She was also concerned about her ability to handle Ethan's behavior. This concern continued for several weeks.

Miss Merde finally decided to ask the center director to observe Ethan's behavior. After observing Ethan for less than half an hour, the director determined a possible cause for Ethan's problem.

First, the director noted that Ethan did not respond to many of the verbal requests made by Miss Merde or other children. The director also noted that while interacting with others, Ethan closely watched their faces when they spoke. The director suspected that Ethan's hearing was poor. For added information, the director then picked up two wooden blocks, stood behind Ethan, and clapped them together as hard as she could. While several other children either jumped or turned to see what was happening, Ethan did not respond.

Before sharing these observations with Ethan's father, Miss Merde repeated the clapping incident. Ethan failed to respond. In addition, other staff members tried speaking to him when they were out of his field of vision. Again, each time he failed to respond. At this point, the center director shared these observations with Ethan's father. She encouraged Ethan's father to have his hearing tested.

Luckily for Ethan, his father, the staff, and other children in the center, the cause of Ethan's behavioral problems was pinpointed. After having his hearing tested, Ethan received a hearing aid. His behavior improved dramatically. At the same time, his speech also improved.

Children may be overly active or tense due to other health problems, 8-6. A child who is in constant pain due to lack of dental or medical assistance may act inappropriately.

Medications can also cause some children to behave poorly. This problem often has other symptoms you may watch for—dilated pupils, drowsiness, slurred speech, poor coordination, and general irritability. In many states parents are required to report to the staff when their children are on medication.

Prolonged or recurring illness can cause frequent absences from the center. When this occurs, some children are not able to maintain their friendships. Coming back to the center is difficult for them. Some of these children

8-6 Pain from this child's head injury may cause him to be tense and uncooperative.

may become *onlookers.* This means they watch others, but do not get involved. Other children may become aggressive. By acting out, they hope to gain the other children's attention.

Onlookers and aggressive children need your help. Carefully observe them. Focus on their needs.

An onlooker needs to get involved. Encourage this child by suggesting activities he or she might try. If the child does not respond, gently take the child by the hand, and walk him or her to an appealing activity. You may have to play with the child for a while or involve other children in the activity.

Aggressive children need a calming influence. Direct these children to activities in which they can release energy. For instance, direct the aggressive child to woodworking, sculpting, or water play activities.

Poor or inadequate nutrition can also affect behavior. Studies show that between one-fourth and one-third of preschool children do not receive the caloric intake recommended for them. Children who do not have the proper caloric intake or a proper breakfast may be inattentive and sluggish. Motor skills and motivation are also affected. To avoid this problem, breakfast is served at many centers.

## Stress

*Stress* is the body's reaction to physical or emotional factors. The reaction often takes the form of tension.

Occasional stress is not a problem. However, constant stress can cause many problems. This is because stress builds on itself. The stress created by one situation builds on the stress of another.

Stress can be caused by both negative and positive events. One negative event that can cause stress in children is the breakup of a family. Physical abuse, rejection, separation, and fights are also negative events that may cause stress.

Positive events that cause stress include birthday parties, overnight visits to friends' houses, new pets, and/or births of new brothers or sisters.

Common signs of stress are listed in 8-7. These signs might also signal problems other than stress. How do you determine, then, if children are suffering from stress?

First, observe children's behavior. Children who remain apart from other children may be feeling stress. Likewise, children who are easily irritated or excessively lazy or aggressive may also suffer from stress.

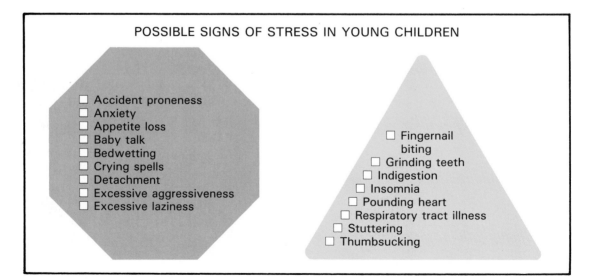

POSSIBLE SIGNS OF STRESS IN YOUNG CHILDREN

☐ Accident proneness
☐ Anxiety
☐ Appetite loss
☐ Baby talk
☐ Bedwetting
☐ Crying spells
☐ Detachment
☐ Excessive aggressiveness
☐ Excessive laziness

☐ Fingernail biting
☐ Grinding teeth
☐ Indigestion
☐ Insomnia
☐ Pounding heart
☐ Respiratory tract illness
☐ Stuttering
☐ Thumbsucking

8-7 The problems shown in this list may signal stress.

Second, watch closely for changes in habits or behavior. For example, Barry has always been a friendly, but quiet, child. You have noticed that recently Barry has been fighting with his friends. Barry may be suffering from stress. If you are aware of the normal behavior of each of the children in your class, you will also be aware of changes in their behavior.

Children can feel stress in the same way adults feel stress. Unlike adults, however, children lack the skills needed to understand and control these pressures. As their teacher, you are in a position to help these children.

What should you do when a child's normal behavior changes? First, accept the child's behavior. Scolding a child for thumbsucking will not stop the behavior. Likewise, forcing a child to eat will not make the child eat. When you notice unusual behavior, remain close to and comfort the child. Reassure the child that you care about him or her.

To help reduce stress, promote a positive environment. Praise children for the good things they do. Help them see themselves as positive, worthwhile people. Listen to them. Help them clarify their feelings. Correct any misconceptions they may have about themselves or their feelings.

## REACTIONS TO TENSION

Young children often behave in a socially unacceptable way when they are tense. Negativism, theft, anger, biting, exploration of the body, thumbsucking, and fear are all unacceptable reactions to tension.

These reactions remind us children are people, too. You must deal with and guide their behavior, just as you would an adult.

### Negativism

Preschool children can be negative, particularly between two and three years of age. See 8-8. It is not unusual for a child of this age to oppose every request you make. For instance, you may say, "Pick up the block." The child might look at you and say, "No."

A negative child cannot be hurried. If he or she is hurried, opposition will be stronger.

Given time, children outgrow this stage of development.

**Guiding.** Accept a young child's negative behavior. However, keep in mind all health and safety regulations. For example, children must wash their hands before eating. If a child refuses to do this, take the child's hands and wash them. Tell the child, "You need to wash your hands." Let the child know, through your voice and body language, that you expect cooperation.

### Stealing

Preschool children do not understand the difference between "mine" and "yours." When children under three years of age take something, they are not stealing. At this age, children do not understand the concept of stealing.

Small objects, such as toy cars and puzzle pieces, may vanish from the classroom. When you notice these items missing, warn the other teachers. Ask them to closely observe the children.

**Guiding.** If you see a child take something, do not ask the reason he or she stole it. Likewise, do not lecture about stealing. Instead, make the child return it. Otherwise, the child may keep taking things from others. Remember that preschoolers do not understand ownership.

A useful way to teach children about owner-

8-8 Young children may resist your requests for them to take part in different activities.

ship is to respect their property rights. That is, before trying Jodi's new puzzle, ask her permission to use it. If you see another child looking at Jodi's toy, say, "Why don't you ask Jodi if you can use it?"

## Anger

A child's anger serves a useful purpose. Anger draws attention to something that annoys the child. You can then help that child learn to deal with anger. The greatest number of tantrums typically occur at about 18 months of age. After this age, there is a sharp decline. Age also affects how a child will project anger. Young children often use the whole body to express anger. By age two, children may hold their breath for as long as they can. Screaming, kicking, hitting, pounding, and hitting one's head against a wall are other ways these children express anger. By the time children turn three, verbal abuse is more common, while four-year-olds often engage in name calling.

If children are able to get attention or gain control through outbursts, they will keep using this behavior. For example, if Toby cries and yells for another cookie and then receives one, she will cry and yell again. On the other hand, if she does not receive the cookie, she will learn that her outburst is unacceptable.

**Guiding.** Young children should not be allowed to hit each other. However, they will try. When they do, stop them immediately. Say, "I am sorry, but Jeff does not like that." At the same time, you might have to hold the child's hand. The child may try to hit you. Stop that action also.

Ignoring outbursts is also a successful technique when dealing with an angry child. Of course, ignore this behavior only if there is no threat to the health and safety of the children.

You can also redirect anger through activities such as finger painting, modeling with clay, punching a punching bag, hammering, and playing at the sensory table, 8-9. All of these activities involve use of children's hands, arms, and/or legs. Their anger will be redirected into physical movements. Remember to have enough supplies for these activities. Use a minimum of rules.

Surprisingly, noise can also help relieve aggression. Yelling, beating drums, dancing to loud music, crying, and making animal noises can all relieve anger. Remember, however, that noise can be catching. If several children make too much noise, the rest of the group may also become noisy.

Whenever possible, catch children before they react angrily. For instance, if you see that Billy is going to kick over Tommy's blocks, stop him. Then say, "Would you like Tommy to knock over your blocks?" Billy will be forced to think about what he was going to do.

## Biting

Young children often bite when they are upset. This is not unusual behavior, particularly with two-year-olds. For many of these children, biting is only a temporary problem. They may bite because they cannot express themselves using words. For them, biting is a form of body language.

**Guiding.** You need to help children who bite. Start by keeping playtime simple for these children. Limit the number of playmates they may have at any time. Large groups often create stressful situations. Therefore, biters become nervous and then bite.

Do not forget the child who is being bit. This child also needs to feel secure. To provide security, observe constantly. Stop biters, whenever possible, before they bite.

Never allow a child to bite back. Biting back does not prevent biting. It only creates more aggressive behavior.

Isolation of a biter sometimes helps to curb this habit. When the child bites another, say, "Paula does not like that." Then say, "I am sorry, but you must sit down over here." Make the child sit for a few minutes, but no longer than five. Then, allow the child to return to the play area.

## Exploring the body

Children begin to explore their bodies early in life. It is common for one-year-olds to explore their genitals during diaper changing. As children begin to gain control of their body functions, interest in the genital area grows. By three years of age, children are aware of sex differences. Boys may, in fact, become concerned because girls do not have penises. By age four, children who have to use the bathroom may hold the genital area. When this occurs, remind the child that he or she needs to use the bathroom. By five years of age, children may begin to manipulate their genitals. They may do this by rubbing pillows between their legs, or even squeezing their thighs together tightly. Some children may begin to rub their genitals in an effort to reduce irritation caused by tight clothing.

**Guiding.** Exploration of the body is normal behavior in development. However, it is not considered proper to engage in such behavior in public. Therefore, it is important to guide children away from public display of exploration of the body.

During nap time, you might see children touching themselves. Children sometimes rub their genitals while trying to get to sleep. When this occurs, never shame or threaten the child. Remember, whenever possible, use a positive approach when guiding young children. This can be done by firmly telling a child that this behavior is impolite in public.

## Thumbsucking

Like adults, children feel certain tensions. To relieve the tension, some children may suck their thumbs.

Many parents are concerned about thumbsucking. Reassure them that usually there is no need to worry about this behavior. Encourage them to accept this behavior as a normal stage of growth.

Studies show that almost half of all infants suck their fingers or thumb. By 18 months, thumbsucking usually reaches its peak. Then the behavior becomes less frequent, especially during the day. By four or five years of age, children who suck their thumbs usually only do so before they go to bed. Children of this age will sometimes engage in thumbsucking if they are tired. Most children outgrow thumbsucking by six or seven years of age.

**Guiding.** Parents' major concern over thumbsucking is often about children's facial appearance and/or damage to teeth. Dentists

8-9 Children can release energy through physical activity.

8-10 Teachers need to be prepared for fears on field trips that may be caused by unfamiliar sights or sounds.

claim, however, that there is no cause to worry if thumbsucking stops before permanent teeth erupt.

Children's urge to suck may be satisfied by supplying a pacifier. One advantage of a pacifier is that it does not place pressure on the roof of the mouth or the jaw. In addition, most children give pacifiers up between one and two years of age. In fact, some children may have an intense sucking need for only the first few months of life. When these children stop using their pacifiers, they can be taken away permanently. If, however, a child reverts to sucking fingers or thumbs, return the pacifier.

Attending day care may help curb thumbsucking for some children. At the center, the child will find many new interests and friends. As a result, you may not notice thumbsucking. Or, perhaps, children will only suck their thumbs when they lie down for naps or are tired.

If you notice a child thumbsucking, do not pull the thumb out of his or her mouth. This guidance will not be successful. In some cases, it might cause the child to increase thumbsucking.

It is important to remember that during the first three years, the harder you try to stop thumbsucking, the stronger it becomes. Instead, accept and ignore the behavior. In this way, children will usually stop thumbsucking between 4 and 5 years of age.

## Fear

Every child experiences fear. By three years of age, most children have many kinds of fear. Some fears will be real. Others will be imaginary. As the child grows, real fears will be kept. Imaginary fears will be outgrown.

Common childhood fears include falling from high places, putting faces in water, thunder, the dark, people in uniforms, fire engines, ambulances, and animals.

Fear of the unknown is also common in young children. You may see this fear on the first day of school. Children may cry, cling, and refuse to leave their parents. As the teacher, be prepared for this fear. Inform parents in advance about this common fear.

**Guiding.** Understanding children's fear is important in guiding young children, 8-10. For example, fear of the dark is quite common among young children. You may notice this fear at nap time or when a filmstrip is being shown. Understand that this behavior is due to unfamiliar surroundings. These children cannot sleep or concentrate on filmstrips. Instead, the children may focus on scary images formed by the shadows. Help these children by keeping a small light turned on during these times. Then the room will not be totally dark. Also, allow children to keep a familiar stuffed toy or blanket near them.

Accept children's fears. For young children, even the silliest fear is real. When a fire engine passes the play yard and a child cries, give the child immediate attention. You may wish to hold the child's hand, kneel down and put your arms around the child, or hold the child on your lap. When you do this, you are meeting the child's immediate needs. After the crisis, talk to the child about the fear.

Children may need to act out situations in order to conquer their fears. See 8-11. For instance, Toby's grandmother died in the hospital. When Toby came back to the center, he asked two other children to play hospital with him. Toby played the role of a doctor while one of his friends played the nurse. This was Toby's way of handling the fear he felt when his grandmother died at the hospital.

Talking with children can also help them control fear. For example, Mark visited his cousin Chris. When he returned to school, Mark told his teachers that the house had ghosts. As a result, Mark said that he was never returning. Mark's teacher was observant. He talked to Mark about his visit with Chris. He explained that sleeping in strange places is often frightening because it is new.

Jennifer was afraid of the new bunny. Fortunately for Jennifer, her teacher was understanding. She helped Jennifer face her fear by introducing her to the bunny in gradual steps. First, she asked Jennifer to place a carrot in the cage. Then she encouraged Jennifer to watch the bunny eat. The next day she encouraged Jennifer to touch the bunny's fur.

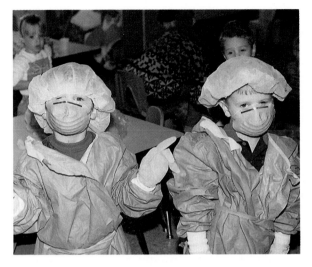
8-11 Playing hospital helps many children deal with their fears of hospitals and doctors.

Jennifer continued this for about one week. Her teacher did not rush Jennifer. Finally, she asked Jennifer if she wanted to hold the bunny. Jennifer said yes. Jennifer's teacher carefully and slowly took the rabbit from the cage and placed it on Jennifer's lap.

When children feel unsafe or strange, they may reject a person or situation. For example, a child may greet a new aide with, "Go away, I hate you." If this happens, do not scold the child. Telling the child that he or she likes the aide will not help either. Instead, accept the child's feelings. You may say, "Miss Brown is our new teacher. When you get to know her, you will learn to like her."

Children sometimes will hit others when they are afraid. For instance, a resource person visited a group of four-year-olds. This person brought a large snake to show the children. When Janice saw the snake, she began to act aggressively. She hit Susan and Peggy. The teacher then stepped in. She explained to Janice that her friends might be frightened, too. She then explained to Janice that this type of snake was not dangerous. There was no need to fear the snake.

## TIME OUT

*Time out* is used when a child's behavior cannot be ignored. The teacher moves the child to a place where he or she must sit quietly. This is a form of punishment. Not all teachers agree with its use. Some feel that children are negatively reinforced with this technique. These teachers feel the technique should be used seldom, if at all.

To be effective, tell children in advance what behaviors will result in time out. Limit the time to three minutes. Do not let the time exceed five minutes. Young children do not have a good sense of time. Thus, three minutes and five minutes seem equally long.

If you decide to use time out, carry it out in an unemotional, direct way. Simply say, "Time out." Be consistent using time out. If you tell a child that time out will be used, follow through. When a child's behavior requires time out, take quick action.

Some children may not sit quietly. If this happens, start the time period again. Make sure the child obeys the time out rules before leaving the area. If you do not follow through, the children will not take you seriously.

Time out can be an effective guidance tool for some children. Four- and five-year-olds usually understand the purpose better than younger children. By this age, most children have the ability to understand their behavior can have negative consequences.

## SUMMARY

Guidance problems occur with children who are difficult to control and teach. These children often behave disruptively. You must learn to identify and work with such children. The result will be a classroom in which all the children can learn and grow.

A great deal of disruptive behavior is caused by tension in children. There are several common causes of tension in children. Recognizing these causes and children's reactions to tension wil help you guide them to proper and productive behavior.

# to Know

# to Review

Write your answers on a separate sheet of paper.

1. Why do children react disruptively when they experience tension?
2. Tension can be caused by:
   a. Overstimulation.
   b. Change of routine.
   c. Frustration.
   d. All of the above.
3. True or false. Usually, the larger the group of children, the greater the likelihood that overstimulation will occur.
4. _____ let children know what to expect and when to expect it.
5. True or false. Noise affects all children in the same way.
6. Name two ways to cut down on waiting time.
7. Describe frustration and list two causes of frustration in children.
8. Frustration can be prevented by:
   a. Supplying the same materials to all children.
   b. Letting children choose which play activities they would like to do.
   c. Forcing children to play with certain materials, regardless of their abilities.
   d. Planning only one or two activities per day.
9. Symptoms of children under medication may include:
   a. General irritability.
   b. Dilated pupils.
   c. Drowsiness.
   d. All of the above.
10. _____ are children who watch others participate, but do not participate themselves.
11. Stress:
    a. Is the body's reaction to physical or emotional factors.
    b. Is not a problem if it is occasional.
    c. Builds on itself.
    d. All of the above.
12. Name two steps you can take to help a child deal with stress.
13. What will happen if you hurry a negative child?
14. Explain how you would effectively guide the children in the following situations.
    a. Philip gets angry whenever you announce clean-up time.
    b. Joanne bites a nearby child whenever George takes a toy from her.
    c. Martin cries whenever he hears thunder.
15. True or false. Exploration of the body is a natural stage in development.
16. What is time out and when should it be used?

# to Do

1. Prepare a checklist of ways to avoid overstimulation of children.
2. Discuss teacher strategies for reducing waiting time.
3. Visit a day care center. Observe children for any signs of stress. Note what signs you see. Discuss your findings when you return to class.
4. Discuss the advantages of thumbsucking from the child's point of view.
5. Invite a child psychologist to talk to your class about children's fears.
6. Invite a panel of parents to discuss with your class problems that they have guiding children.

# part *3*

# Creating a Safe and Healthy Environment

Your highest priority as a day care worker is to keep children safe and healthy. Creating a safe, healthy environment requires careful planning and preparation.

As you read this part, you will discover how to arrange the space in a center to promote safety as well as learning and fun. You will also learn criteria for choosing toys and equipment that will safely help meet your program goals.

This part gives safety objectives to help you prevent accidents and illness. It also makes you aware of your responsibilities in detecting and reporting child abuse and neglect.

Guidelines for planning and serving nutritious meals and snacks are given in this part. Also, procedures are given for handling such medical emergencies as wounds, burns, and fevers.

# Chapter 9

# Arranging Space

After studying this chapter, you will be able to:
- [ ] List reasons for the importance of planned space.
- [ ] Name the basic center areas, along with the functions of each area.
- [ ] Outline factors to consider when choosing playroom furniture and color schemes.
- [ ] Discuss factors that affect space organization.
- [ ] Organize basic activity areas of the classroom and outdoor play yard.

Jimmy is running. Susie is hiding. No one saw Mary take the fish out of the bowl. There is no place for Joe to play with the blocks. The behavior of children in this classroom is affected by the way the space is arranged.

In another classroom, the space is carefully organized. All the children are involved in constructive play. There are few, if any, behavior problems. Heather is smiling. Fred is looking at books in a quiet corner of the classroom. At the same time, Joel and his friends are building a large block structure.

The way a classroom is arranged provides clues about expected behavior. A well-planned setting usually promotes interesting play, provides children with choices, and lessens behavior problems. Well-planned space is arranged based on the children's developmental needs, interests, and program goals.

Children need space to build, move, sort, create, pretend, spread out, work, and interact with friends. They need a place to be quiet, to be active, to talk, and to move. Space affects the activity level of children. The choices children make and the way they carry out their

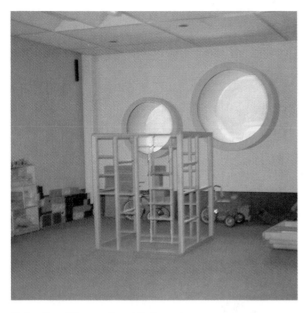

9-1 Quality early-childhood programs have ample space for children and teachers.

choices are also affected by space. Space can even affect the length of time children will remain with one activity. Therefore, space should be arranged according to children's needs and interests. But the space should also be convenient for the staff. See 9-1.

## VALUE OF PLANNED SPACE

The early years are crucial for the intellectual development of children. Before arranging a classroom, review the developmental objectives of the program. For example, two-year-old children do not have refined large motor skills. To promote safety and motor development, they need large, open spaces. The classroom should be planned with these goals in mind.

An attractive, well-arranged classroom prompts children to use materials. It also molds their behavior. Boundaries found in this type of classroom make the children more responsible. They know where to find classroom materials. They also know where to return them when they are finished.

Safety is an important concern in planning

space. Open spaces must be provided so adults can see the entire room. The ratio of caregivers to children also affects safety. If the number of caregivers is low, the room arrangement should be simple to make supervision easier.

Studies have shown that the arrangement of space greatly affects teachers' behavior as well as childrens'. In centers with well-planned space, teachers were more friendly, sensitive, and warm to children. These teachers taught their students to respect other's rights and feelings. In centers with poorly-planned space, teachers were often more insensitive to their students.

The goals for a well-planned space include:
- Providing a physically safe environment for the children.
- Providing children with areas for cognitive, emotional, social, and physical growth.
- Providing adults with a space that is easy to supervise.
- Providing space that is pleasing to the eye for both adults and children.
- Providing easy access to materials when needed so children are able to direct themselves, 9-2.
- Encouraging children to take part in activities.

## PHYSICAL SPACE

The physical space of a center may be divided into seven main areas. These basic areas include the following:
1. An entrance.
2. The director's office.
3. An isolation area.
4. A kitchen or kitchenette.
5. A staff room.
6. Bathrooms.
7. A playroom, also known as a classroom.

### Entrance

The entrance to the center should attract and appeal to children and adults, 9-3. Plants, children's artwork, and a bulletin board for parents will enhance the appearance. If space permits, chairs and a sofa are welcome additions for parents who need to wait.

### Director's office

The director's office should be just inside the center's entrance. School records, children's records, and public relations material can be stored here. This office can also be used for parent interviews and conferences. Some directors also have a small table in their offices for teachers' meetings and planning sessions.

### Isolation area

Most states require centers to provide a special room or space for children who become ill or show signs of a communicable disease. This room, often called an *isolation area,* should contain a cot and a few toys. If the space is not available, a cot may be put up in the director's office when needed.

### Kitchen

The size of a center's kitchen depends on how much food preparation is done. Even if meals are not served, most centers have a small area with a sink, refrigerator, and stove. Regardless of the kitchen's use, the local health department personnel should inspect it. They can tell you if all legal requirements are being met.

Floor coverings in the kitchen should be easy to clean. Vinyl coverings, ceramic tile, and wood are all good floor coverings for the kitchen.

### Staff room

To provide quality instruction for young children, adults need an area for their own use. A *staff room* should contain a locked storage space for personal belongings. A coat rack, sofa, and tables and/or desk also should be available for the staff. Most caregivers also enjoy a telephone, professional journals, and curriculum guides. A coffeepot or appliance that can boil water is also useful. Privacy is important for the staff area. This is because the area may be needed to meet with parents or other staff members.

9-2 Low shelving units in the small manipulative play area provide this child with the opportunity to choose her own activity.

9-3 The entrance to this center helps children feel welcome.

## Bathrooms

Most states require a certain number of toilets and sinks for a group of young children. Some states require at least one toilet for every ten children. However, a higher ratio is more convenient. There are many times during the day that several children may have to use the bathroom at the same time.

The size of the toilet fixture will vary with the size and age of the children. A group of two-year-old children would be comfortable with toilet fixtures ten inches from the floor. Five-year-old children would find thirteen-inch toilet fixtures more comfortable.

If small toilets are unavailable, a wooden step can be used for smaller children. This same wooden step can be used in front of the sinks that are too high for children to reach.

For safety purposes, the water heater that supplies water to the children's bathroom should be set on low heat. Only tepid water should be available in this area.

The flooring in the bathroom should be easy to clean. Also, it should not be too slippery.

## Playroom

The playroom should be on the ground floor. A rectangular room is the best shape for a classroom. This shape allows for many more arrangements than other shapes.

Good early-childhood programs have enough space for the children and for a variety of materials and equipment. The recommended amount of space varies from state to state. It can range from 35 to 100 square feet of indoor space per child. The National Association for the Education of Young Children recommend at least 35 square feet of free indoor space per child. This amount should not include hallways or space taken up by equipment and toilets.

**Walls.** All walls should be durable and washable. Many teachers like to attach bulletin boards to the walls. This provides space to hang artwork and papers and also absorb sound, 9-4.

Chalkboards can also be attached to walls. They should be installed at the children's eye level.

Instead of bulletin boards and chalkboards, some centers use audio-visual boards. An *audio-visual board* can serve as a bulletin board, chalkboard, and movie screen. It is usually white, off white, or beige. The disadvantage of the audio-visual board is that magnetic strips must be used to hold up objects when used as a bulletin board. These strips can be costly.

**Floors.** A recent trend for playroom floor coverings has been carpeting. Carpeting is easy to maintain. It also provides a sound cushion.

**Windows.** Windows in the playroom should be placed so that children can see outside. Screens should be installed outside the windows. As a fire precaution, all windows should open.

Drapes or blinds may be used to help control light. They also add interest and color to a room. Drapes or blinds reduce glare, heating bills, and noise. The disadvantage of hanging drapes is that they become dirty easily. This is caused by children brushing by them with dirty hands or art supplies.

For a softer effect than drapes, you might wish to use a ruffle above the window. It can

9-4 A brightly decorated bulletin board is a welcome addition to any classroom.

be a nice addition to a classroom if the colors complement the decor. If you use a ruffle instead of drapes, also use window shades to reduce glare.

**Doors.** Doors should be lightweight. To guard against injury, the doors should push out to open. Doorknobs should be low enough so children can reach them.

**Acoustics.** Studies show that noise affects children's behavior. For this reason, make an effort to use materials that will cut down or eliminate some noise.

*Acoustic material* is used to deaden or absorb sounds. Carpets, drapes, bulletin boards, pillows, stuffed toys, and sand are examples. Due to the physical makeup of these materials, noise can be deadened or eliminated. For instance, carpeting will absorb the sound of footsteps. Carpeting can also add comfort, warmth, and softness to a room.

If the classroom is still noisy after the addition of draperies, carpeting, and bulletin boards, acoustical tile may need to be installed on the classroom ceiling. Whenever possible, the ceiling should range from 10 to 12 feet high to relieve noise and provide a feeling of spaciousness.

**Temperature.** Temperature and humidity are important in planning a comfortable environment for young children. They cannot attend to or process information in an uncomfortable environment.

Usually a temperature range of 62 to 68 degrees Fahrenheit will be comfortable. When vigorous physical activities are planned, the temperature should be decreased. In order for children to be comfortable, adults may have to wear a sweater.

**Humidity.** Humidity, like temperature, influences the comfort of the environment. Usually a 40 to 60 percent relative humidity range is considered comfortable. Typically a temperature of 70 degrees Fahrenheit with a relative humidity of 60 percent would be comfortable. If comfort is to be maintained, the relative humidity should be decreased as the temperature rises.

**Electrical outlets.** For safety purposes, electrical outlets should be above the children's reach. When outlets are not being used, safety caps should be inserted for protection. Many times a room arrangement will be influenced by the location of electrical outlets. For example, the music area would be located near an outlet so a record cassette or player could be used. For the safety of the children and staff, do not use long cords. These can cause someone to trip and/or fall. Because of this danger, many states do not allow long cords to be used in the classroom.

## PLAYROOM FURNITURE

Playroom furniture should be durable, washable, and stackable. Tables and easels should be adjustable. Then they can be adjusted to fit each child who may use them. To check if an easel is the proper height, have the child stand next to it. Ask the child to touch the middle of the easel pad. If the child has to bend or reach to touch the middle of the pad, adjust the easel.

Chair and table heights are checked in a different manner. Ask the child to sit on a chair. Then push it under the table. If the table and chair are suited to the child, there will be room between the bottom of the table and the child's knees. The child should also be able to place his or her feet flat on the floor.

### Chairs

Children's chairs are often used in the art, dramatic play, and dining areas. Chairs should always be the proper height for the children. Plastic, stackable chairs are preferred by most teachers. Plastic chairs have other advantages. They are light enough for the children to move. And they do not require refinishing. An adult-sized rocking chair may be used by children in the library or dramatic play area. The chair may also be used by adults as a special place to hold and/or comfort a child.

### Tables

Classroom tables should be hard, smooth, and washable. The tables should be light enough to move. Most preschool teachers prefer tables that are large enough to seat four to six children. Rectangular tables are often preferred over round tables. The rectangular shape allows children to have their own space. This reduces the chance for aggression. Low round tables are sometimes used in the library and dramatic play area.

## Storage units

Blocks, books, art supplies, games, and other classroom materials are kept in storage units, 9-5. For flexibility, all storage units should have casters. Then they can be moved easily. For units without casters, the hardware can be bought and easily installed. Keep in mind that pegboard or corkboard can be attached to exposed sides and backs of units. These can serve as bulletin boards.

Storage units should match to the height of the children. They must be able to reach the materials. Therefore, choose small, lightweight sections of cabinets.

If doors are needed on the storage units, sliding doors are best. Swinging doors can cause safety hazards.

## Lockers and cubbies

Children can learn responsibility for their own belongings when they are given well-planned storage space. Each child enrolled in the program should be assigned a locker, 9-6. Most lockers for preschool children are 10 to 12 inches wide and 10 to 15 inches deep. Each locker should contain a hook for hanging a coat.

The primary purpose of the locker is to store the children's clothing. Finished artwork, library books, parent letters, and other valuable items must also be stored. For storage of these items, many lockers have a top section. These are often called *cubbies*. If the lockers do not have cubbies, five gallon ice cream containers can be stacked to store the children's belongings. See 9-7.

Lockers and cubbies should have a coat of varnish or paint. This coating will prevent staining from muddy boots, wet paints, etc. If lockers are painted, use a washable enamel.

Lockers should be placed near the entrance. This will save parents time when picking up

9-5 Paper and other art supplies are well-organized on this shelving unit.

9-6 Use symbols on lockers to help young children identify their space.

9-7 Empty ice cream containers can be used to store children's small personal belongings.

children. It will also save the class from being disrupted when someone must go to their locker. And it will save clean-up time during bad weather.

## COLOR

Color affects how teachers and children feel about their classroom. Because of the emotional appeal of color, select colors carefully. The goal should be rooms that look pleasant and feel spacious. This can be done using *cool colors*. These colors, such as blue, green, and purple, make a room appear larger. They create a feeling of openness. *Warm colors* make a room seem smaller. These shades include reds, yellows, and oranges. Studies show that children prefer warm colors until about age six. After the age of six, they start to prefer cool colors.

Several other factors affect color selection. These include the amount of available light in the room, room size, and amount of time spent in the room. For example, if the room does not have much light available, a light, cool color will help the room appear brighter.

### White

White is a good color for classrooms. Children respond well to white. White rooms are perceived as clean and cool. White is a good color for the eating, isolation, administration, and reading areas. It is also a good color for the bathroom.

### Light blue

Light blue is often used in preschools. Children respond to this color by feeling comfortable, soothed, and secure. Therefore, light blue is useful in the nap, reading, eating, and isolation areas.

### Light green

Light green, like light blue and white, creates a positive response. It makes children feel calm, refreshed, peaceful, and restful. It is useful for isolation, nap, reading, and eating areas.

### Yellow

Yellow makes people feel happy and cheerful. It is a good color in art and music areas.

### Orange

Orange is a welcoming, forceful, energetic color. Its use should be limited. Clearly, an orange room can be overwhelming. However, orange can be used effectively in small areas, such as an entrance.

### Red

As with orange, the use of red should be limited, 9-8. Overuse of red can be too stimulating for children. Children may become overactive. Red is best used on indoor gross motor equipment, outdoor equipment, and teaching aids designed to stimulate children.

### Purple

The color purple can have a mournful effect on children. It is best used only as an accent color on equipment, bulletin boards, and teaching aids. When used as a wall color, limit its use to reading areas.

## FACTORS THAT AFFECT SPACE ORGANIZATION

An organized classroom can inspire children to take part in the activities of the day. The space should be arranged to define the scope and limits of activities. Therefore, the space must provide for proper learning experiences.

As teachers plan the classroom, many factors must be considered. These factors greatly affect how the classroom is organized. They include licensing requirements, group size, scale size, and traffic patterns.

### Licensing requirements

Most states have licensing requirements for day care centers. You will need to know these requirements before you begin to plan classroom space. Requirements vary from state to state. However, some common requirements include that a certain number of fire extinguishers be installed, that all exits are clear, that entrance doors open to the outside, and

9-8 The use of red on this decoration creates interest without being over-powering.

that a certain number of square feet of space be available for each child.

### Program goals

A program's goals should be based on the needs and interests of the children. The goals a teacher selects should represent the major stages of development and growth. (These stages were discussed in Chapters 2, 3, and 4.) The environment, as well as planned classroom activities, should stimulate growth and development.

Caregivers concerned with all developmental areas might select the following program goals:
- To promote independence.
- To promote a positive self-concept.
- To promote problem-solving skills.
- To promote small muscle coordination.
- To promote large muscle coordination.
- To promote self-control.
- To promote language skills.
- To promote social skills.

After the goals for the children are listed, review each goal. Decide how each goal will be supported by the classroom environment. For instance, most teachers set a goal to develop independence in children. The arrangement of the room can help this goal be met. Materials, locker hooks, and shelving units should all be within easy reach for the children. This will encourage children to act without help from adults in many cases. Chart 9-9 lists a number of ways to meet various program goals.

Program goals should also reflect state licensing requirements. Therefore, if the state requires that children receive one meal and two snacks each day, a program goal might state that children receive nutritious meals and snacks.

## Group size

Group size is an important factor to consider when arranging space. A large number of children crowded into a small area will cause problems. Children are likely to cry and fight more when crowded. Likewise, a small number of children with too much space will also cause problems. Too much open space encourages children to run. You must strive to create an arrangement that will be the proper size for the group.

The more children, the more empty space is needed. Also, the room arrangement needs to be fairly simple. Children will feel safe and secure in this arrangement. A good rule of thumb is to plan between one-third and one-half of the classroom for open space.

Arrange shelving units and other furniture with group size in mind. A good arrangement allows teachers and children to move easily through the room. It also allows for teachers and children to see and be seen easily. This will promote a relaxed setting.

## Scale

The preschool environment must be scaled to the size of its occupants. Child-sized furniture should be purchased or built. Bulletin boards, toilets, water fountains, sinks, pictures, and other items should all be at the children's level. One method to judge if the setting is scaled for children is for an adult to walk on his or her knees through the entire classroom. Anything positioned too high for the children should be noted and adjusted.

## Traffic patterns

The arrangement of a classroom centers around the *traffic pattern.* This is the way people move through the classroom area. Furniture should be arranged to create a useful traffic pattern. For instance, children should be able to walk from the art area to the block-building area without going through the middle of the library area.

Program activities will affect traffic patterns. For example, most day care centers provide breakfast and lunch. These meals may be prepared on site or contracted. Whichever plan is used, the food will likely be made in or delivered to a kitchen. For this reason, the kitchen should be near a delivery door and near the eating area of the classroom.

## ORGANIZING BASIC ACTIVITY AREAS

Classrooms arranged according to activity allow children to make their own choices. Each activity area should clearly convey to children what their choices are. For example, the art area should have an easel, art supplies, and block play supplies. Display these materials so children are aware of all that is available to them. This gives them the chance to choose what they will do.

Each activity area is a space of its own. And each area supports the program goals. Each area should be defined, but flexible space. Areas can be set off using shelves placed in U or L shapes. These are defined, but the shelves can be moved when the shape of the space needs to be changed.

Arrange activity areas by function. Think carefully of each area as wet or dry, active or quiet, 9-10. Wet and dry activities should be placed far away from each other. Sensory and science activities are examples of wet/active activities. Art, eating, and cooking are types of wet/quiet activities.

Active activities should take place far from

| GOAL | HOW GOAL IS SUPPORTED BY ENVIRONMENT |
|---|---|
| To promote independence. | Similar materials are stored together.<br>Drawers, shelves, and containers are labeled with outlines of contents.<br>Materials and equipment are easily accessible to children.<br>Coat hooks are low enough for children to hang their own clothing.<br>Individual storage is provided for each child. |
| To promote a positive self-concept. | Equipment is correct for developmental stage.<br>Children's work is displayed.<br>Unstructured materials are available in each area.<br>A variety of materials are available for children to choose. |
| To promote problem-solving skills. | Equipment is correct for developmental stage.<br>Open-ended materials, such as blocks, are available.<br>A variety of materials are available for children to choose.<br>Materials are rotated to create interest. |
| To promote small muscle coordination. | A classroom area is devoted to manipulative equipment.<br>Enough material to maintain children's interest is available.<br>Materials are easily accessible to children.<br>Materials are changed frequently to create interest. |
| To promote large muscle development. | A classroom area is devoted to large development.<br>An adequate amount of space is provided for play.<br>The traffic flow does not interfere with the children's use of materials.<br>The area is located away from quiet activities. |
| To promote self-control. | Enough space is provided for children to use materials in each classroom area.<br>The classroom traffic flow permits children to work without interruption.<br>Noisy areas are located away from quiet areas.<br>Sufficient variety and quantity of materials are available in each area. |
| To promote language skills. | A book display space is placed at children's eye level.<br>Classroom materials are labeled.<br>A wide variety of materials, including books, puppets, and records are available. |
| To promote social skills. | Boundaries between areas are defined with low shelving units.<br>A sufficient amount of materials is available to encourage cooperative play. |

9-9 Defining program goals is the first step toward well-organized space.

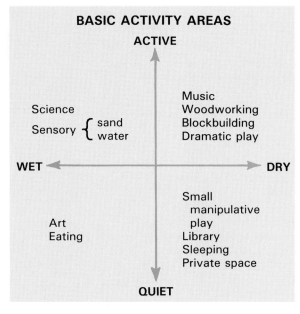

## BASIC ACTIVITY AREAS

**ACTIVE**

Science

Sensory { sand / water

Music
Woodworking
Blockbuilding
Dramatic play

**WET** ← → **DRY**

Art
Eating

Small
manipulative
play
Library
Sleeping
Private space

**QUIET**

9-10 Planning space requires that you consider each activity as it relates to other activities that take place in the same area.

quiet activities. Woodworking, blockbuilding, music, and dramatic play are all active activities. Each of these could disrupt a quiet activity. Sleeping, reading, and small manipulative play are all examples of quiet/dry activities.

Most teachers prefer to map out two or three possible area arrangements. This helps them see what will work best and why. Some room arrangement principles are shown in 9-11.

### Introducing activity areas

Children require an introduction to the activity areas in the classroom. They need to learn what materials are in each area. They need to learn what activities take place in that area. They also need to learn the safety and clean-up rules of the area. In programs that run for nine month sessions, the children can be introduced to the areas at the start of the session. In programs that run throughout the year, children can be introduced to each area on their first days. Children who have been in the program for a time may help the teacher introduce the areas to new students.

To help children feel comfortable in using and moving about the areas, use labels and signs, 9-12. Labels and signs direct children's attention. This then helps children become self-directed learners. Labels and signs also encourage children to return materials to storage areas.

### Blockbuilding area

Blocks give children practice sorting, grouping, comparing, arranging, making decisions, cooperating, and role playing. Therefore, this ares should be well-equipped and well-defined. See 9-13.

The best area for blockbuilding is a carpeted area. This keeps the noise level down. Define the area with low cabinets. Allow enough room for building. Children will need room to build structures that go around, up, and out.

In addition to blocks, provide other items in the blockbuilding area. Include plastic zoo and farm animals, people, traffic signs, wheeled toys, pulleys, and boxes.

Use the low cabinets that define the area for storage of materials. Make sure there are enough shelves to arrange the blocks according

---

### PRINCIPLES OF ROOM ARRANGEMENT

* Whenever possible, arrange areas around the edges of the room. This allows the center of the room to be used for traffic flow.
* Arrange shelving units so the teacher can clearly view the entire room.
* Store objects together that are used together.
* Place the art area near a water source.
* Place quiet activities far away from active activities and traffic areas.
* Place dry activities far from wet activities.
* Provide open space for blockbuilding and group activities.
* Define areas by arranging storage units into U or L shapes.
* Provide a private space where children can be alone.

9-11 Keep these principles in mind when planning space. Would you add any guidelines to this list?

9-12 With the help of labels and signs, children will learn to move around their environment easily.

to shape. Place all blockbuilding materials at the children's eye level and within their reach.

Large, heavy blocks (and other heavy materials) should be placed on a bottom shelf or on the floor to avoid accidents. Save higher shelves for lightweight items. Label each shelf with the shape of the block that can be found there. You can use paint or contact paper to label the shelves. Labels help children return the blocks to the correct shelf. Labels also provide matching practice and speed clean-up time. See 9-14.

### Art area

Place the art area near a water source. Arrange the space so either groups or individuals can use the area. Use tables, chairs, easels, drying racks, and shelving units that are easy to clean and maintain. See 9-15. Label the shelves with the materials found there.

### Dramatic play area

The dramatic play area is also known as the home living or housekeeping area. This area needs to be arranged to look like a real home. A stove, refrigerator, table, chairs, sink, and

9-13 Blockbuilding areas are very popular. Make sure this area is well-equipped and spacious.

9-14 Promote independence by labeling storage areas for materials.

9-15 Make efficient use of space by placing a drying rack for artwork overhead.

doll bed are basic furniture you may wish to provide. Other props may be added. For instance, you may wish to provide dolls, kitchen utensils, cleaning tools, and dress-up clothes. Place the dramatic play area in the active area of the classroom.

**Sensory area**

The key piece of equipment in the sensory area is the *sensory table*. It is also known as a water or sand table. The size of the table will depend on the amount of space available and the age of the children. Two- and three-year-old children love the sensory appeal of water and sand, 9-16. A sensory table can give the children practice in social situations.

Not all centers have sensory tables. Some centers use plastic wading pools or washtubs. Whatever container is used, it should be placed near a water source. Children and teachers

9-16 The sensory table can hold the attention of children for extended time periods.

enjoy adding water to the sand to change the feeling.

Other items are often used in the sensory table. Provide rustproof spoons, shovels, sand pails, measuring cups, funnels, strainers, old pots, and other kitchen items. Place shelving units near the table for storage. If shelves or other storage are not available, use a plastic clothes basket for storage.

### Woodworking area

After building wood sculptures, many children wish to paint them. So locate the woodworking area near the art area. For the children's safety, place this area outside the line of traffic.

Items you may wish to provide at the woodworking bench include tools, wood scraps, and styrofoam pieces. Hang a pegboard next to the wood bench, within children's reach. It can be used to hold tools. To encourage the return of tools, paint outlines of the tools on the pegboard. The children can replace tools by matching them with outlined shapes.

### Sleeping area

Most preschool children rest or nap after lunch. Not all programs, however, have separate sleeping areas. For those that do not,

a flexible room arrangement is key. Such an arrangement can be quickly and quietly altered during or immediately after lunchtime into a sleeping area. Allow sufficient space for sleeping. Some states require that two feet of open space exist between cots. Check your state's regulations.

### Small manipulative area

The small manipulative, or small motor, area is located in a dry, quiet area of the playroom. Table blocks, puzzles, plastic building pieces, parquetry blocks, stringing beads, board games, sewing cards, and color cubes with pattern cards are some items you may wish to provide. Many teachers also include math materials and equipment in this area. A table, chairs, and shelving unit are also useful in this area.

### Library area

The library area should be placed in the quietest part of the classroom. In addition to books and magazines, you may wish to supply language arts equipment. For example, to promote writing skills, supply pens, pencils, and paper. You may wish to place it next to the manipulative area. Shelving units, a table, and chairs are all useful in this area. See 9-17.

9-17 Display books at the children's eye level in the library area.

For comfort, pillows and beanbag chairs may also be used. Many centers also carpet this area or add an area rug.

### Music area

Rhythm instruments, records, and a record player are found in almost all music areas. When space permits, some centers have a piano. If a lack of money or space exists, some centers will use an autoharp.

### Private space

Provide an area in the classroom where children can be alone. Children then have the option of limiting contact with others when they choose. This reduces the pressure of being around others when they do not wish. Set a classroom rule stating that children who go to the private space will not be disturbed by others.

A loft is one unique way to provide private space, 9-18. In programs where a wooden loft is not in the budget, large cardboard boxes and wooden crates can serve the same purpose.

9-18 Children sometimes like to be alone. This loft provides a perfect setting.

The private space should be small, allowing room for only one or two children to use at a time. The children in the private space should not be visible to other children in the room. However, the teacher must be able to see into the private space.

### Science area

Place the science area in the wet, active area of the classroom. Most science areas contain at least one table. If needed, a shelving unit may also be placed in this area. For more information on guiding science experiences, refer to Chapter 19.

### Eating area

When space is available, provide a separate eating area. This area should be located near the kitchen. This allows for easy service and clean-up.

If space is limited, have children sit at tables in other areas of the classroom. The daily schedule will have to be arranged to allow for this.

Chart 9-19 summarizes each classroom area and the furniture, materials, and equipment you may wish to supply in each.

### Displaying children's work

The work of the children should be displayed throughout the activity areas. Bulletin boards, wall hangings, clothesline, or appliance boxes can all be used for display purposes. All display areas should be placed at the children's height. Then they are able to mount and view their own work.

A wall hanging can be made from a 36- or 52-inch wide piece of felt, burlap, or sailcloth. The length of the hanging can vary. Each end of the hanging is hemmed. Then a piece of dowel is inserted through each hem.

Colored yarn or a piece of clothesline can also be used to display work. Colored plastic clothespins can be used to clasp work to the line.

A large appliance box can provide a free-standing display area. The advantage of this type of display is that it is portable. It can be used in any area of the center. And even after it is assembled, it can be moved.

| CLASSROOM AREA | FURNITURE | MATERIALS AND EQUIPMENT |
|---|---|---|
| **Blockbuilding** | labeled shelving units | large hollow blocks<br>solid unit blocks<br>wheeled toys<br>small, toy people of various ethnic backgrounds<br>small, colored wooden blocks<br>zoo animals<br>farm animals |
| **Art** | easel<br>shelving unit(s)<br>tables<br>drying rack | pencils<br>crayons<br>chalk<br>ink markers<br>paper<br>tempera paint<br>scrap paper and fabrics<br>tape<br>glue<br>brushes<br>scissors |
| **Dramatic Play** | child-sized refrigerator,<br>  stove, sink, cupboard,<br>  and doll bed<br>trunk or tree to hold clothes | telephone<br>mirror<br>dishes and cooking utensils<br>dress-up clothes |
| **Sensory** | sensory table<br>shelving unit (optional) | funnels<br>pitchers<br>spoons<br>sponges<br>containers<br>strainers |
| **Woodworking** | woodworking bench | saw<br>screwdrivers<br>hammers<br>vice<br>nails<br>screws<br>scraps of wood and styrofoam<br>glue |
| **Sleeping** | cots<br>mats | blankets<br>pillows |

*Continued.*

9-19 Providing materials and equipment for activity areas
is a thought-provoking process. Many everyday
materials can be used for learning.

| CLASSROOM AREA | FURNITURE | MATERIALS AND EQUIPMENT |
|---|---|---|
| **Small Manipulative** | shelving units<br>table (optional depending on space)<br>chairs (optional depending on space)<br>shelving unit | blocks<br>puzzles<br>plastic forms for joining<br>parquetry blocks<br>stringing beads<br>board games<br>sewing cards<br>colored cubes with pattern cards<br>bingo games<br>rods and blocks of different sizes<br>flannel board numerals<br>number puzzles<br>wooden numbers<br>magnetic numbers<br>measuring containers<br>scale<br>rulers |
| **Library** | table<br>chairs<br>rug<br>soft pillows (optional)<br>bean bag (optional)<br>shelving<br>shelving unit<br>flannel board<br>chalkboard | picture books<br>children's magazines<br>child-authored books<br>charts<br>games<br>alphabet letters<br>felt pens<br>typewriter (optional)<br>pencils<br>felt tip markers<br>paper<br>chalk<br>tape recorders |
| **Music** | piano (optional)<br>shelving unit<br>record player | rhythm instruments<br>records<br>silk scarfs for dancing |
| **Private space** | loft<br>TV box<br>wooden crates | pillows |
| **Science** | table<br>shelving unit | scissors<br>measuring instruments<br>jars and other empty containers<br>collections of related objects such as leaves, nuts, rocks, and insects |
| **Eating** | tables<br>chairs | vases and centerpieces<br>placemats<br>plates<br>eating utensils<br>cups |

*9-19 Continued.*

136

Recognize the work of all the children when putting displays together. To make displays interesting, set a time limit for each display. Change the work often.

## OUTDOOR PLAY AREA

Children need to take part in both indoor and outdoor activities. Many classrooms do not have the proper amount of space for large motor development activities. Other activities such as science, water and sand play, social studies, art, and music can all take place outdoors during pleasant weather. The outdoor play yard can fill these needs, 9-20.

The location and shape of the play yard should allow for proper supervision. If possible, the play yard should be directly outside the classroom. This helps teachers supervise. They can move between the classroom and play yard without losing sight of the children.

The best shape for a play yard is a rectangle. Such a play yard can be seen from end to end. U or L shaped play yards are more difficult to supervise and arrange, 9-21.

In outdoor areas, the required number of square feet per child varies from state to state. The numbers usually range from 75 to 200 square feet per child.

### Planning the play yard

The play yard, like indoor space, needs to be studied in terms of use and then broken into areas. A well-planned play yard usually has empty space and a visible, broad path. These two items aid movement through the yard.

A path divides the activity areas of the play yard. This path creates space between areas and makes moving about easier. Without a path, children may constantly be bumping into each other.

To determine where a path should be laid, the teacher should kneel down to be at the children's eye level. The path should be wide and clear enough so children can see all areas of the play yard, even when outside school grounds.

Empty space should be located in the center of the yard. Activity areas can be placed around the outside of the yard, around the empty

9-20 The play yard is an exciting and fun place for children.

9-21 This play yard is not completely visible at this angle. This makes supervision difficult.

**Arranging Space 137**

space. You may also need to leave empty space around some pieces of equipment. For instance, children may wish to use wooden planks and crates to extend their play at the jungle gym. Therefore, extra space will be needed around the equipment to allow for this.

To best use play yard space, follow these guidelines. First, equipment should be far enough apart so a child using one piece of equipment cannot touch a child using another piece of equipment. Second, all equipment should be visible to the teacher from any spot in the yard or classroom. Third, children should not have to walk through one area to get to another. For example, the children should be able to get to the slide without walking through the sandbox. And fourth, between one-third and one-half of the yard should be used for play equipment. As with indoor space, the open space is needed so children can move around the areas.

In addition to paths and empty space, there are other factors to consider when planning an outdoor play yard. Among items to be considered are fences, the play yard surface, landscaping, storage, wheeled toy paths, stationary equipment, water, and animals and their shelter.

**Fencing.** Most states require play yards be fenced for safety of the children. Fences prevent children from wandering away from the play yard area. This makes outdoor supervision easier for teachers.

Selecting the proper fence requires careful thought. The goal is to purchase a fence that can keep children safe. The fence should fasten securely at the gate. There should be no sharp metal pieces or splintered wood to hurt children.

Two types of fences are commonly found in play yards: chain link and wood. Each type of fence has its good and bad points. For instance, because chain link is an open design, it is possible to see to the other side of the fence. This gives the play yard an open feeling. However, some children are able to climb chain link fences. This can be dangerous. In addition, many people feel that chain link fences are not very attractive.

Wood fences that complement the center design are very pleasing to the eye. However, the fence must also be designed with the children's safety in mind. Children should not be able to climb over or through a well-designed wood fence. The boards should be sanded to prevent children from getting splinters.

**Surfaces.** For safety, the best play yard surface is loose material such as bark nuggets, shredded bark, or sand. When children fall on such material, they receive fewer and less severe injuries than when they fall on hard surfaces. Four to six inches of loose material provides a good cushion.

The drawback to loose materials is that they tend to pile up in one spot. They shift under weight placed on them. In high traffic areas they will thin out and pile up around the edges of the area. Therefore, the material must be raked or shoveled back into position fairly often.

**Landscaping.** A well-landscaped play yard makes for pleasant surroundings. In addition, landscaping can also be used as part of the science program by encouraging observation skills. Trees, shrubs, and flowers in a variety of sizes, colors, and growing cycles will interest children. Trees are also a good source of shade and sound control. A well-landscaped yard gives children a place to be alone, as well as corners for play. And hills in the yard can be used to develop large muscle skills.

Before choosing flowers or shrubs, consult with a landscape architect. Some plants are poisonous. Any landscape architect can tell you which plants to avoid. The architect can also recommend shrubs and flowers from a number of growing cycles. This will ensure that children will always have a seasonal plant to study and view.

**Storage shed.** Tricycles, wagons, scooters, shovels, rakes, balls, plastic wading pools, and gardening tools are just some of the items you may want to keep in a storage shed. See 9-22. The materials stored will vary with the climate of the area. For instance, in a warm climate, many indoor activities can be conducted outdoors throughout the year. If this is possible in your area, and the funds are available, you may wish to purchase duplicates of some equipment. Then you will not need to move classroom materials. Dramatic play, art, and science activities are ideal for outdoor play.

Storage space should be arranged so children can put everything away themselves. Painted lines on the floor of the shed can be used to outline parking spaces for wheeled toys. Large barrels or baskets can be used to store many types of materials. Rakes and shovels can be hung on hooks from the wall.

**Wheeled toy paths.** A path that children can use to push or ride wheeled toys is key for two reasons. The first reason is safety. A path with one-way traffic will prevent children from riding into each other. And a path gives

## SUGGESTED CONTENTS OF A STORAGE SHED

| Water and Sand Play | Science |
|---|---|
| rakes | gardening tools |
| shovels | seeds |
| scoop trucks | worm jars |
| cooking utensils | garden hose |
| water hoses | animal feed |
| empty cans with paint brushes | butterfly nets |
| funnels | bird feed |
| strainers | binoculars |
| containers | magnifying glasses |
| wading pool | **Wheeled Toys** |
| sponges | wagons |
| **Carpentry** | scooters |
| | tricycles |
| carpentry bench | road signs |
| hammer | **Dramatic Play** |
| saw | dress-up clothes |
| vise | puppet stage |
| clamps | puppets |
| nails | folding table and chairs |
| brushes | cardboard appliance boxes |
| sandpaper | blankets |
| styrofoam pieces | |
| **Art** | **Construction** |
| easel(s) | cable spools |
| paint | packing crates |
| brushes | large wooden blocks |
| paper | saw horses |
| scissors | wooden boxes |
| paste | wooden planks |

9-22 The contents of storage sheds varies from center to center.

children a place to ride so they do not destroy grassy areas. Set limits regarding the use of wheeled toys and paths and enforce these rules.

The path should be joined to the storage shed. Children can then drive their toys directly into or out of the shed. The path should have curves instead of sharp right angles. Children can make easy turns on curves, keeping them from tipping over on sharp turns.

**Stationary equipment.** Jungle gyms, slides, and tree houses are all *stationary equipment.* This equipment must be set permanently in the ground for stability, 9-23. For added appeal, place large pieces of stationary equipment in different corners of the play yard.

**Sandbox.** Children will play in sandboxes for long periods of time. If the sandbox is in a sunny area, children are at risk for sunburn. Therefore, place sandboxes in shady areas. If there is little or no shade in the play yard, build a roof over the sandbox. Also, place the sandbox near a water source. By adding water to

dry sand, children can build more detailed structures.

To prevent cats from using the sandbox as a litter box, build a cover for the sandbox. When the sandbox is not being used, place the cover over it, 9-24.

**Water.** Water play is very pleasant for children during warm weather. For this reason, some centers have wading pools built into the ground. Other centers use plastic, above-ground wading pools.

A garden hose is also useful in the play yard. Attach it to a sprinkler so the children can play in the water during hot weather. The hose can also be used to water gardens and other plants.

**Animal shelter.** Play yards for young children often have a number of animals. What type of animals a center may have is determined by city laws.

To shelter animals, use cages. The cages should be large enough for the animal, have a mesh floor to keep the cage tidy between

9-23 These stepping logs are a type of stationary equipment. They are firmly secured in the ground.

thorough cleanings, and have a quality padlock to protect against vandals. Place the cages where animals will be safe from excess wind, sun, and rain.

## SUMMARY

Well-organized space is a key ingredient of a well-run center. It defines expected behavior for children. Well-organized space frees the children to play without interruption. They stay with activities for longer periods of time, increasing their attention spans. Well-organized space also provides children with choices.

Space should reflect children's developmental needs and interests, as well as program goals. In such a space, children are more relaxed and positive. They feel good about themselves. As a direct result, teachers can spend more time teaching and less time disciplining.

9-24 This sandbox can be covered with sheets of plywood when not in use.

# to Know

acoustic material
audio-visual board
cool colors
cubbies
isolation area

staff room
stationary equipment
sensory table
traffic pattern
warm colors

# to Review

1. Well-planned space is arranged based on:
   a. Children's developmental needs.
   b. Children's interests.
   c. Program goals.
   d. All of the above.
2. True or false. Teachers are also affected by the arrangement of space in their classrooms.
3. List four goals for well-planned space.
4. What is the purpose of an isolation area?
5. A _____ room is the best shape for a classroom.
6. An audio-visual board can serve as a:
   a. Movie screen.
   b. Chalkboard.
   c. Bulletin board.
   d. All of the above.
7. Acoustic materials include:
   a. Brick walls.
   b. Sand.
   c. Tile floors.
   d. Stone.
8. Storage units should be selected based on the _____ of the children.
9. The top part of a locker is often called a _____.
10. Until about age six, children prefer:
    a. Warm colors.
    b. Cool colors.
    c. Plaid.
    d. All of the above.
11. What color can have a mournful effect on children?
12. Organized space should define the scope and _____ of activities.

13. List two ways to promote:
    a. Self-control through the classroom environment.
    b. Social skills through the classroom environment.
14. Are problems created when a small group of children have too much space? Why or why not?
15. _____ _____ are the paths people follow through an area.
16. Activity areas are best defined by arranging storage units into _____ or _____ shapes.
17. What activities should be placed in the active/dry area of the classroom?
18. True or false. Children do not need to spend time alone.
19. A _____ in the play yard divides activity areas and makes moving about easier.
20. The best play yard surface is:
    a. Bark nuggets.
    b. Shredded bark.
    c. Sand.
    d. All of the above.

# to Do

1. Draw a room arrangement for each basic activity area. Include a center of interest for each area.
2. Read your state's licensing requirements as they apply to classroom space. For instance, how many square feet of space is required per child? How many toilets are required for a group of 40 children?
3. Interview teachers about space arrangement. Ask them what they like best about their classroom space. Ask them what they would like to change.
4. Plan a color scheme for a classroom. Be prepared to explain the reasons you chose the colors you did.

# Chapter 10

# *Selecting Toys and Equipment*

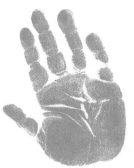

After studying this chapter, you will be able to:
- ☐ Discuss and explain the importance of guidelines to follow when planning selection of toys and equipment.
- ☐ Distinguish between developmental and physical age.
- ☐ Outline the procedure for reporting unsafe toys.
- ☐ List sources and methods for purchasing toys and equipment.
- ☐ Discuss guidelines for purchasing play yard equipment.

Children learn when they have chances to interact with and affect their world. Toys play an important role in this learning process. For instance, children can learn speech and dressing skills while playing with toys. Children can test the world and learn how they feel about others through the use of toys. When playing with toys, children are drawn to interact with each other. When children play with toys they make choices, solve problems, and apply some control over their environment, 10-1.

Simple toys like building blocks can promote intellectual growth. If children do not build a strong foundation on their block building, the building will topple. Thus, they learn physics concepts. If they join two semi-circular pieces, they make a circle. In this way, they learn math concepts.

## PLANNING SELECTION

In early childhood programs, selecting toys and equipment for children is the teacher's responsibility. And as you can see, this is an important job. Careful planning is required. Questions you will have to ask yourself include the following:

1. Does the toy support program goals?
2. Does the toy add balance to existing toys and equipment?

10-1 Toys help children build many skills. By playing together, these children learn important social skills.

3. Can the toy be used in available classroom space?
4. Does the toy require a great deal of supervision?
5. Is the toy easy to maintain?
6. Is the toy durable?
7. Can the toy be purchased in needed quantities?
8. Does the toy require the involvement of the child?
9. Is the toy proper for the developmental stage of the children who will use it?
10. Is the toy nonviolent?
11. Is the toy nonsexist?
12. Is the toy multi-cultural?
13. Is the toy safe?

Guidelines for answering these questions are discussed in the following sections.

### Program goals

Classroom toys and equipment should reflect program goals. If a program goal is to have the children develop language skills, then language materials should be placed in the classroom. Books, pictures, tape recorders, cassettes, records, alphabet cards, puppets, pencils, and paper can all be used to promote language skills.

Write your program goals on paper. Then make a list of items that promote each goal. Review the goals and lists. Take count of items you already have in the classroom. Then decide in which areas more toys and equipment are required. You may find a planning sheet helpful for this task, 10-2.

### Balance

Examining goals helps you decide what toys and equipment might be purchased. Before buying, however, review each item to decide if it will add balance to the items already on hand. Can it be used with other toys? Will it help children reach goals that are not being met sufficiently with other toys?

### Space

Keep in mind the space and storage needed for any new items you are thinking about buying or building. This is especially true for large pieces of equipment. For instance, an indoor jungle gym is a useful item in many centers. However, if the space for storing it is not available, it is a poor investment. It may end up being stored in another part of the building. If the location is inconvenient, the jungle gym will not be used very often.

### Supervision

Supervision is a key consideration when selecting toys and equipment. You must think about how each item will affect your ability to properly watch over children. You will have to consider each item individually. For example, a teacher may want to buy swings for the play yard. The state may require one adult supervisor for every ten children. The teacher can comply with state guidelines for ratios. But the teacher could feel that more supervision is needed for safety. The teacher may decide, in this case, that the swings would be an unwise purchase.

Consider the developmental stages of children when choosing toys and equipment. This will affect the amount of supervision required.

| TOY SELECTION PLANNING SHEET | | |
|---|---|---|
| **Program Goals** | **Available Toys** | **Toys Needed** |
| To encourage sensory exploration. | water table, shovel, cups, clay, egg beaters, feely box, harmonica, kazoo, guitar | bells, drum, texture matching games, pumps, funnels |
| To promote large muscle development. | low climber, wagon cart, large rubber balls, planks, boxes, jungle gym | low slide, balance boards, bicycle |
| | | |

10-2 Committing program goals to writing can make the selection of proper toys an easier task.

For instance, many five-year-old children can use blunt-nosed scissors with some guidance. However, four-year-old children require much more supervision for the same task.

## Maintenance

All toys and equipment require maintenance. The care required varies with the type of toy or equipment and the amount of use. For example, an aluminum swing set needs less upkeep than a wooden swing set because aluminum is weatherproof. A wooden set would require a coat of paint each year. Otherwise it might rot. Such upkeep can become costly.

## Durability

Children's toys need to be durable. Children drop, stand on, sit on, and lie on toys. When angry, they may even throw toys. And broken toys can pose a danger to children. A broken hard plastic toy can have sharp edges that cut. A broken wood toy may splinter. In addition to the danger posed by broken toys, children can also feel guilty if a toy breaks in their hands. To avoid these problems, it is usually best to buy toys and equipment that are built well.

Wood and cloth are two materials that are durable, 10-3. Wood toys can withstand many

years of use by many children. When buying wood toys, look for those made of hardwoods such as maple. The toys should also be split-resistant. And the corners of the toy should be rounded.

## Quantity

The quantity of toys can be as important as the quality. In most classrooms, it is common to find two or more children playing with the same toys. To promote this type of coopera-

10-3 Wooden toys can take a great deal of rough play from children.

tion, supply an ample amount of toys and materials for children. Be certain that any toys you wish to add to the classroom can be bought in the needed amounts.

Variety should also be considered along with quantity. Is the item you wish to add to the classroom similar to other items already there? Studies show that children who have been exposed to a wide variety of toys are more imaginative and creative. In order to provide variety, rotate toys and equipment regularly.

The chart in 10-4 lists toys and equipment for a classroom of fifteen. These items make up a well-supplied and varied group of toys and equipment.

## Child involvement

Choose toys that will actively involve children. Toys should move children to explore, manipulate, and create. In this way, children do and learn for themselves. They learn to share and use their imaginations.

*Spectator toys* such as battery-powered cars and talking dolls require little action on the child's part. Try to avoid using these types of toys. Besides being costly, their appeal with children is quite often brief. Children will leave these toys for others that involve more imagination.

Choose simple toys, 10-5. Too much detail limits imagination. Open-ended materials free

### SUGGESTED EQUIPMENT AND SUPPLIES FOR A CLASS UNIT OF 15 CHILDREN*

| TYPE OF MATERIALS AND EQUIPMENT | SELECT |
|---|---|
| Indoor blockbuilding | • 400 hardwood unit blocks, including such shapes as units, half units, double units, quadruple units, pillars, large and small cylinders, curves, triangles, ramps, Y switches, X switches, floorboards, roof boards |
| Floor play materials | • 24 cars, airplanes, boats, fire engines, wagons, tractors, trains of assorted sizes<br>• 30 rubber, plastic, or wooden figures of farm and domestic animals; community workers: policemen, firemen, postmen; family members: mother, father, boy, girl, baby, grandparents<br>• 1 rocking boat |
| Household and dramatic play | • 8-10 rubber dolls; doll clothes; chest for doll clothes<br>• 2 doll carriages<br>• 1 doll bed, big and sturdy enough for a child to crawl into<br>• 1 smaller doll bed or crib<br>• Blankets, mattresses, pillows for doll beds<br>• Furniture for household play: wooden stove, cupboard for dishes, sink, small table and chairs<br>• Kitchenware: plastic dishes, tea set, small cooking utensils, silverware<br>• Housekeeping equipment: broom, mop, dustpan, brush, iron, ironing board, clothesline, clothespins<br>• Full-length mirror<br>• Dress-up clothes: men's and women's shoes, pocketbooks, jewelry, hats, belts<br>• Supplies for other dramatic play: office equipment, telephones, cash registers, firemen's hats, badges, play money, stethoscope, doctors' bags and white coats, nurses' hats |

*Continued.*

10-4 The toys and equipment in this list comprise a well-stocked classroom. You may have ideas for further additions.

| TYPE OF MATERIALS AND EQUIPMENT | SELECT |
|---|---|
| Table activities | • 12 wooden inlay puzzles of varying degrees of difficulty<br>• 1 puzzle rack<br>• Pegs and peg boards<br>• Matching games<br>• Sets of small blocks (cubes, parquetry, interlocking, snap-in)<br>• Large table dominoes: picture sets, number sets<br>• Nested blocks<br>• Color cone<br>• Pounding peg board<br>• Cuisenaire rods; counting frames; abacus<br>• Hammer and nail sets with celotex boards |
| Art activities | • 2 easels<br>• 24 easel paint brushes with 1/2 in. and 3/4 in. handles<br>• 75-100 quarts liquid tempera paint of various colors<br>• 8000 sheets white manila paper<br>• 4000 sheets newsprint 24 in. by 36 in.<br>• Paste and paste brushes<br>• 20 packages finger paint paper or glazed shelf paper<br>• 24 packages construction paper of various colors<br>• 4 clay boards, 2 plastic covered pails for storing clay, and clay<br>• 100 lb. flour and 40 lb. salt for dough<br>• 18 blunt scissors, including some left-handed scissors<br>• 5 aprons or smocks<br>• Miscellaneous supplies: orange juice cans, baby food jars, drying rack, florist wire, pipe cleaners, armature wire, colored toothpicks, macaroni pieces, transparent colored paper<br>• 5 dozen crayons |
| Music | • Phonograph and records<br>• Autoharp<br>• Xylophone<br>• Drums, triangles, tambourines, cymbals, tom-toms<br>• Sleighbells for hands and feet, shakers, maracas, rhythm sticks<br>• Balls, hoops, scarves |
| Woodworking | • 1 sturdy, low workbench with 2 vises<br>• Tools: four 7 oz. claw hammers, two 12'' crosscut saws, 1 hand drill, 1 rasp, 1 file, 2 screwdrivers, assorted nails with large heads, screws, 2 large C clamps<br>• Soft wood scraps, doweling<br>• Sandpaper<br>• Miscellaneous: buttons, washers, corks, wire, nuts, hooks and eyes, spools, bottle caps |
| Furniture | • 15 chairs 8 in. to 12 in. in height<br>• 3 tables 18 in. to 22 in. in height for snacks, meals, and tablework activities<br>• 2 room dividers<br>• 15 mats or throw rugs for resting in half-day programs<br>• 15 lockers for hanging coats, hats, rubbers, extra change of clothes |

*10-4 Continued.*

*Continued.*

| TYPE OF MATERIALS AND EQUIPMENT | SELECT |
|---|---|
| **Science and special projects** | • Bar and horseshoe magnets<br>• Magnifying glass<br>• Large indoor and outdoor thermometers<br>• Tape measure, yardstick, rulers<br>• Scales<br>• Measuring cups and spoons<br>• Dry cell batteries, flashlight bulbs, electric wire<br>• Pulleys and gears<br>• Hand mirrors<br>• Hot plate and electric frying pan<br>• Aquarium and terrarium<br>• Cages for pets<br>• 1 typewriter for the children to use |
| **Water play (indoor and outdoor)** | • Small pitchers, watering cans, measuring cups, bowls of various sizes, plastic bottles, medicine droppers<br>• Funnels, strainers, egg beaters, ladles, straws, lengths of hose, brushes<br>• Soap and soap flakes |
| **Outdoor equipment** | • Sandbox, cans, buckets, spades, spoons, small dishes, colander<br>• Jungle gym<br>• Ladder box<br>• Horizontal ladder<br>• 5 tricycles<br>• 3 four-wheeled cars or "horses" manipulated by a child's feet<br>• 2 sturdy doll carriages<br>• 2 sturdy wooden packing cases (42 in. by 30 in. by 30 in.)<br>• 2 sturdy wooden packing cases (35 in. by 23 in. by 16 in.)<br>• 24 hollow wooden blocks (5 1/2 in. by 11 in. by 11 in.)<br>• 12 hollow wooden blocks (5 1/2 in. by 11 in. by 22 in.)<br>• 12 low sawhorses<br>• 8 small wooden kegs<br>• Wooden ladders<br>• Walking boards and flexible jumping boards<br>• Lengths of sturdy rope and garden hose<br>• Automobile and airplane tires and rubber inner tubes<br>• Rubber balls of different sizes; bean bags |
| **Literature** | • 25 picture storybooks appropriate to the age and special interests of the children; books should include a range of poetry and prose, humor, fiction, and non-fiction |
| **Audio-visual aids** | • Tape recorder<br>• Slide projector<br>• 8mm loop<br>• 16mm movie projector and screen |

*Project Headstart. *Equipment and Supplies—Guidelines for Administrators and Teachers in Child Development Centers.* (Washington, D.C.: Government Printing Office, 1967), pp. 3-8.

*10-4 Continued.*

10-5 These toys can be the source for a variety of unstructured play. What is done with them is limited only by a child's imagination.

children to use their minds and express their creativity.

Blocks, play dough, paint, sand, and construction sets all are open-ended toys. Using these items, children build structures, make designs, and play games. The limits of such toys are endless.

Use the checklist in 10-6 to define what skills can be learned from a specific toy. This task will help you see in what ways a toy will affect children. This knowledge can then be used when deciding on a purchase.

### Developmentally appropriate toys

Children's physical age and developmental age are often quite different. *Physical age* is an age determined by a birthdate. It is also known as *chronological age. Developmental age* refers to a child's skill and growth level compared to what is thought of as normal for that physical age group. For example, Kathy may be four years old physically but only functions as an eighteen-month-old child. A child who functions as a four-year-old would be able to string beads. However, Kathy would only be able to do those tasks and activities that an eighteen-month-old child can do. She lacks the eye-hand coordination needed to string beads.

As you choose toys, remember the difference between physical and developmental age, 10-7.

Toys help children build self-esteem. Toys that suit children's developmental ages help them build positive self-concepts. For instance, Leon will feel power as he learns to drive a scooter, or as he pushes a wagon up a hill. As he masters this skill, he gains a sense of control and builds an "I can do it" feeling.

Toys that are wrong for children's developmental age can cause frustration. This does little for a child's self-concept. Lack of success with a toy can have a negative effect on a child.

### CHECKLIST FOR SKILLS LEARNED FROM TOYS

| Will the children learn or improve: | YES | NO |
|---|---|---|
| auditory discrimination? | | |
| balance? | | |
| color concepts? | | |
| counting? | | |
| eye-hand coordination? | | |
| hearing-doing skills? | | |
| language concepts? | | |
| large muscle development? | | |
| matching? | | |
| number concepts? | | |
| patterning? | | |
| seeing-doing skills? | | |
| self-concept? | | |
| self-image? | | |
| sensory discrimination? | | |
| sequencing? | | |
| social skills? | | |
| small muscle development? | | |
| space perception? | | |
| strength? | | |
| throwing-catching skills? | | |
| visual discrimination? | | |

10-6 What other skills might you add to this list?

For instance, it is not likely that a two-year-old child would be able to put together an eighteen piece puzzle. The child may make a number of attempts at the puzzle. However, the child will soon become frustrated and move on to a toy that is more rewarding.

Chart 10-8 lists a number of toys and equipment pieces that are appropriate for various age groups. The ages on the chart refer to developmental ages. Keep this in mind as you scan the list.

### Violence and toys

Children should not be taught to handle conflict with aggression or violence. Instead, they need to find useful ways to vent their feelings. One way to prevent aggressive behavior is to avoid giving children monster toys, toy guns, and war games. Children learn very little from these toys. The play that revolves around such toys is most often aggressive and destructive.

For instance, when a child plays with a toy gun, he or she does little more than pull the trigger and play in a threatening way. In addition, research shows that violent behavior is increased by the mere sight of a toy gun. Children who played with toy guns were more likely to destroy other children's work.

Many parents and teachers are opposed to the use of these toys in the classroom. Therefore, it is best to simply avoid buying these toys.

### Equality and toys

Nonsexist toys provide children with the opportunity to explore many nontraditional roles. They are not locked into play that is common of their sex. For instance, boys can be nurses, preschool teachers, and stay-at-home fathers. Girls can be airplane pilots, truck drivers, and plumbers. This type of play will also help children form early ideas about careers.

10-7 Toys that are appropriate for children's developmental ages are challenging for those children.

| Age Group | Block and Dramatic Play | Large Muscle Equipment | Housekeeping | Transportation | Creative Art and Books | Classroom Furnishings | Miscellaneous |
|---|---|---|---|---|---|---|---|
| **Six months-one year** | foam blocks soft animals | | soft dolls | wagon stroller | | infant seat crib | soft ball cradle gym mobiles standard crib and mattress music boxes |
| **One-year-old** | | toddler stairs driving bench large foam blocks toddler barrel tire swing | Add: doll bed doll blankets doll mattress unbreakable doll wooden telephone | Add: small solid cars ride-a-stride animal cars and trains for pushing | large crayons hard books cloth books records record player | Add: clothing lockers storage shelves | Add: stacking and nesting toys pull toys pop beads stacking cones pegboards |
| **Two-year-old** | Add: unit blocks wooden figures | Add: doll wagon hollow blocks rocking boat small size jungle gym simple climber and slide tricycle | Add: simple doll clothes doll carriage child-sized furniture: sink, stove, pots, pans aprons | Add: tractor and trailer kiddie car big cars and trucks for hauling and riding | Add: books | Add: bookcase block cart play table and chairs | Add: simple puzzles large wooden threading beads small cots rest mat rest mat cover sheet |
| **Three-year-old** | Add: doll house small dolls furniture | Add: walking board large wooden nesting boxes scooter | Add: ironing board iron rocking chair broom, dustpan | Add: airplanes | Add: easels paints brushes blunt scissors | Add: work and library tables and chairs sand and water play table | Add: wooden puzzles portable screens (room dividers) cots plants |
| **Four-year-old** | Add: puppets puppet theater more unit blocks | Add: planks wheelbarrow swings slide shovel, pail, and rake triangle set coaster wagon large climber and slide | Add: chest of drawers washbasin clothesline and pins basket aprons, ties, etc. Child-sized bed/cradle, carriage, wardrobe | Add: riding train | Add: clay | Add: storage cart work and library tables and chairs chalk/peg and bulletin boards | Add: aquarium pets |
| **Five-year-old** | Add: derrick | Add: balls roller skates | Add: tepee | | | Add: woodworking bench tool cabinet tools | Add: giant dominoes construction sets |

These items are only possibilities. You must decide if each item fits available space and particular circumstances of each child.

*"Criteria for Selecting Play Equipment," *Community Play Things*, 1981, pp. 36-37.

10-8 Plan toy selection well. In this case, the toys from one age group
blend into the next age group.

*Multicultural toys* are those toys that represent a variety of racial and ethnic groups. These toys are as important in the classroom as nonsexist toys. When choosing hand puppets, puzzles, and dolls, include a wide range of backgrounds. Pictures and books should also be chosen with this in mind, 10-9.

Your attitude about toys will affect what children learn about sex roles and other cultures. Make a conscious effort to use or suggest a variety of toys to all children. At the same time, however, be matter-of-fact. For instance, you might suggest to Omar that he try playing in the kitchen. You can explain to him that there are many fun things to do in the kitchen.

It is important that you also use a variety of toys. When putting on a puppet show, use puppets representing many races and ethnic groups. Read storybooks that use a wide variety of cultural groups.

### Safety and toys

To promote safety, choose toys carefully. Serious injuries can be the result of poor judgement when purchasing toys. The safest toys are not those that appeal most to adults. Rather, the safest toys are those that meet the standards outlined so far in this chapter. And perhaps the most important of these standards in terms of safety is that toys be age appropriate. Small stringing beads can be a useful toy for many four-year-old children. In the hands of a two-year-old, however, they can be dangerous.

**Sources of safety information.** There are several sources of safety information for toys. Consult these as you go through the list of toys and equipment you may like to purchase.

*Consumer Reports* often contains results of tests they have conducted on any number of toys and play equipment. Always consult the latest issue that contains the information you need. Older issues may have outdated information.

The Toy Manufacturers of America, the National Safety Council, and child protection laws have all set standards for choosing toys. These standards include the following guidelines:

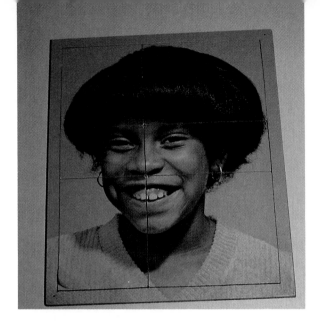

10-9 Include multicultural toys and materials in all areas of the classroom.

- Fabric products such as puppets and doll clothes should be made of nonflammable materials.
- Electrical equipment including tape recorders and record players should have the Underwriter's Laboratory (UL) seal on them.
- Washable, hygienic, nonflammable materials should be used as fill for stuffed toys.
- Nontoxic paint should be used on all painted items, including classroom furniture and equipment.
- Avoid plastic infant toys with squeakers.

**Reporting unsafe products.** If you have a safety problem with a toy or piece of equipment, report the item. This will help keep other children safe from the same danger.

To report an unsafe toy or piece of equipment, write to the United States Consumer Product Safety Commission, Washington, D.C. 20207 or the Standards Development Service Section, National Bureau of Standards, Washington, D.C. 20234. Both of these groups work to guard against items that can be harmful to children.

The Child Protection Act was passed in 1966. This law requires stickers or tags be placed on items that present possible danger. It also permits seizure of items that do not conform to the standards set forth in this law. The law also allows *injunctions* to be placed on manufacturers who break this law. This means the manufacturer must refrain from making the item until a decision is reached. Criminal charges can be brought against manufacturers who do not comply with these standards.

In 1969, the Child Protection and Toy Safety Act was passed. This act expanded the federal government's authority to include all mechanical, electrical, and thermal items designed for children's use.

### Sources for toys and equipment

Before you begin looking for new toys and equipment, take inventory of toys and equipment that are on hand. After this is done, compare the inventory with program goals. For example, you may note that there are too few manipulative toys. These then should be at the top of the list for purchase.

Using your list, browse through catalogs to find items you need. Take time to look through all the catalogs at the center. Catalog prices can vary a great deal. Consider all costs before ordering. For instance, does shipping cost for an item make the purchase price too high? Some companies will not charge a shipping fee if the order is large.

Equipment can also be bought through a co-op. A *co-op* is a group of people or groups who join together so they have more buying power. Co-ops are sometimes formed by directors of several small centers. The goal of the co-op is to purchase toys and equipment at the lowest cost. Companies will often give some type of discount on large orders. The directors in turn share the savings with all those making purchases.

If time is available, you may wish to visit flea markets, garage sales, and discount stores. Materials can often be purchased at discount prices.

Toys can also be designed and built at the center, 10-10. Senior citizens, Girl Scout and Boy Scout troops, and others may volunteer to help. Many of these people are skilled in making puppets, doll clothes, dramatic play clothes, and wooden toys.

*Buying consumable supplies.* Clay, paper, paint, paste, and other art materials are called **consumable supplies.** In most cases, once a consumable supply is used, it cannot be used again. In order to save money, some centers order these materials only once or twice a year. There are many ways to purchase these supplies.

If the order is large, the center may ask vendors to make bids on the sale. *Vendors* are the people who sell the supplies. Their bid is the price at which they will sell the items.

The center might also contact a vendor when placing a large order and ask for a ten percent discount, plus free shipping. Many directors are surprised to learn that this can be done. This is very useful for stretching the center budget.

Another approach is to make a list of the supplies needed. Mark those items that could be donated, 10-11. Note who is in charge of securing what items. For example, the head teacher may be in charge of getting newsprint.

10-10 This outdoor equipment was built by volunteers. Building your own toys can save a great deal of money.

Another teacher would be in charge of getting wallpaper. In some centers, the director is solely responsible for securing all donations.

## SELECTING TOYS

The best toys for young children are safe, durable, and developmentally appropriate. These toys teach children new skills, offer problem-solving opportunities, and foster imagination. Toys should help growth in all four areas of development: physical, social, emotional, and intellectual.

### Guidelines for selecting safe toys

Safety is a key consideration when buying toys. Many hazards cannot be seen at a glance or with normal use. Because of this, study each item thoroughly before buying. Keep in mind that young children often take things apart. Small pieces of large toys can be dangerous. Ask these questions before buying:

- Can the toy be swallowed?
- Are there small parts that could be placed in ears or mouth?
- Is the toy easy to clean?
- Are there sharp points or edges on the toy?

Remember that a toy can be fine in the hands of one child but a danger in the hands of another. To protect children, avoid buying the following:

- Hard plastic toys that break easily. Once broken, the sharp edges are a safety hazard.
- Balloons. Children often place them in their mouths to suck or chew. If swallowed they can cause choking.
- Stuffed animals or dolls with button eyes. These eyes can be pulled off and placed in the mouth. Choking and damage to the throat can result.
- Electrical toys such as stoves, ovens, and irons. Burns, fires, or electrocution are some hazards.

In addition to the guidelines listed here, there are other hazards.

**Dolls.** On a store shelf, a doll may appear safe. This may not be the case if a child changes its hairstyle, removes a leg or arm, changes its clothes, or holds it near a flame. Many times straight pins are used to attach clothing or to hold hair in place. Once removed, these pins can pose danger to a child. Sharp wires may be used to hold the doll's arms and legs together. These can also be hazardous. Danger also exists if the doll is made with flammable materials.

Before buying any doll, always read the label on the toy. Check that only nonflammable materials are used. Also make sure pins are not used to fasten hair. And finally, make sure the arms and legs are securely attached.

## CONSUMABLE SUPPLIES

| Quantity | Item | Purchase | Solicit Donation | Source | Person Responsible |
|---|---|---|---|---|---|
| 1 roll | Newsprint | | X | Dunn County News | Anna |
| 10 cans | Red tempera paint | X | | ABC School Supply | Jodi |
| 10 cans | Yellow tempera paint | X | | ABC School Supply | Jodi |
| 5 rolls | Wallpaper | | X | Menomonie Paint Store | Anna |
| 2 buckets | Sawdust | | X | Peterson Lumber Co. | Anna |
| 4 gallons | Dried corn | | X | Hardy's Elevator | Jodi |
| 4 yards | Fabric scraps | | X | Northwest Fabrics | Anna |
| 2 gallons | Paste | X | | ABC School Supply | Jodi |
| 1 box | Styrofoam packing pieces | | X | James Jewelers | Anna |
| 24 boxes | Crayons | X | | ABC School Supply | Jodi |

10-11 Many groups are often eager to donate materials to worthy programs such as day care centers.

**Plastic and metal toys.** Buy only toys that are durable and free from sharp edges. Hard plastic toys may appear safe. However, once broken, jagged edges become hazards. Sharp edges on metal toys are also very dangerous. Before buying or putting a metal toy out for children to use, run your fingertip along the edges. If any edges are rough, use a flat file to file the edge.

**Party favors.** Avoid buying or letting children bring small party horns or balloons to school for special events. Mouthpieces on horns can be removed, placed in the mouth, and swallowed.

Balloons are one of the most dangerous toys for young children. Children often chew or suck on deflated balloons. They might then swallow and choke on the balloon.

**Pull toys.** Inside many pull toys are small, ball-like objects. If these toys are broken, the objects can fall out. Placed in the mouth, they can cause choking or may be swallowed.

**Stuffed animals.** Check ears, paws, and tails of all stuffed animals to see that no sharp wires are used to stiffen them. Also check the eyes. Make sure they cannot be pulled off. Eyes are small enough to lodge in a child's windpipe, ears, or nostrils.

**Toy vehicles.** Avoid buying toy vehicles with small parts. Once removed, these parts can be put in the mouth. As a result, a child may choke on or swallow them.

**Electrical toys.** Never keep electrical toys in an early childhood classroom. Poor wiring can cause fires and electrocution. High heat produced by electrical toys can cause fires and burns.

## SELECTING PLAY YARD EQUIPMENT

It is important to have a wide variety of equipment for children to use in the play yard. Children need equipment on which they can push, pull, balance, and slide, 10-12. For

10-12 Equipment such as this allows children to do a variety of activities.

instance, studies show that outdoor equipment that can be used only for climbing is not used very often. Children climb on this equipment for a short period of time, then become bored. At that point, they move on to something else.

When shopping for play yard equipment, keep in mind the children's height as compared to the piece of equipment. Equipment should not be more than two times their height. This can, however, be hard to apply with a mixed age group. A jungle gym that is a good size for most four-year-olds will be a hazard to many two-year-olds. You may need to purchase separate equipment designed for two size groups.

Many play yard mishaps occur on slides. To prevent such injuries, buy slides that are low and wide. Several children can use this type of slide at one time. High narrow slides, on the other hand, can be dangerous for many children. Some children do not realize how high the slide is until they reach the top. Then they may decide to crawl back down. The danger of falling exists. If other children are also on the ladder, this increases the chance for a mishap.

High slides can also be dangerous for confident children. Bored with just sliding down, children may decide to explore other ways of using the slide. They may even be bold enough to try sliding down while standing.

All ladders should be slanted. Rungs should be close together. This will help prevent children from slipping. Ladders made of steel are easier to maintain. Wooden ladders, after being weathered, may splinter. Steel ladders can get cold in winter climates. However, they do not require sanding and painting every few years.

Ropeways, rocking bridges, and swings are very popular with children. They enjoy the sensation of speed, dizziness, and spinning that the movements on this equipment provide. By feeling these movements, children will learn to overcome fear of speed and heights.

Swings are not found often on playgrounds designed for young children. This is often because swings require a greal deal of supervision. Without thinking, some children will walk in front or back of swings. They may get bumped, bruised, or even knocked over. And more confident children will try swinging too high.

## Equipment safety

Did you know that at age five, children are most likely to be hurt on playground equipment? Jungle gyms, merry-go-rounds, and swings cause most of these injuries. Therefore, be careful when buying outdoor equipment. Avoid buying on impulse. Supervise play and repair broken equipment.

The most frequent play yard injuries come from falls off climbing equipment and slides. Children are also hit quite often when they walk in front of or behind a moving swing or tricycle. Injuries are also sustained from protruding bolts, rough edges, and from fingers and toes getting caught in equipment. Chart 10-13 contains a list to use for evaluating outdoor equipment.

Besides these dangers, the United States Consumer Safety Commission reports there are nine basic play yard equipment dangers. These can be avoided if you are careful when buying equipment and watching over the play yard.

**Pinch-crush parts.** The pinch-crush parts on seesaws and gliders are included in the nine safety equipment dangers. Check this type of equipment before making any purchases. If this equipment is already on the play yard, check it for this hazard. If you see it, remove the equipment.

**Rings.** Exercise rings on swing sets are another equipment danger. Rings between five and ten inches in diameter can trap a child's head. Remove and discard rings of this size.

**Open end S-rings.** Open end S-rings are often found on swing sets. They can catch clothing and/or skin. To avoid problems, do not buy swings with this type of hardware. If the hardware is on swing sets in the play yard, pinch the rings shut with a pair of pliers.

**Wooden swing seat.** Wooden swing seats can strike a dangerous blow to children who walk in the path of them. Replace any wooden swing seats on the playground. Replace them with lightweight seats made of plastic or canvas.

**Inadequate spacing.** Inadequate spacing is another equipment danger. To prevent injuries, place play equipment at least six feet away from other equipment or buildings. Space for sandboxes, wheeled toy paths, fences, and sidewalks needs to be planned so they are not too close to play equipment.

**Screws and bolts.** Exposed screws and bolts on outdoor equipment can scratch and/or cut children. Most equipment comes with plastic protective caps. However, with use they can break and fall off. Check all the equipment from time to time. If caps are missing, apply tape to all the bolts and screws.

**Hard surfaces.** Hard surfaces can also cause injuries. Play equipment should never be installed over blacktop, brick, or cement. Instead, place equipment in grassy or sandy areas.

**Sharp edges.** Some play yard equipment has sharp edges where pieces fit together. Using your hands, carefully wipe over all equipment edges. Cover all sharp edges with tape. After the tape has been applied, check often to see if the tape is still in good condition.

**Anchoring.** Play yard equipment should be properly anchored below ground level. This keeps the equipment steady during use. To illustrate, if the legs of a jungle gym are not set in concrete, the jungle gym could tip. To prevent this problem, anchor all new equipment before children are allowed to use it.

## SUMMARY

Selecting toys and equipment is an important task. Many guidelines must be followed before purchases are made. Three key guidelines are that toys and equipment be safe, durable, and age-appropriate.

Once guidelines are reviewed, purchases can be made. The teacher must know where and how to make these purchases. In this way, the teacher will be able to use the center budget wisely.

### EVALUATING OUTDOOR EQUIPMENT

| | YES | NO |
|---|---|---|
| 1. Is the construction durable? | | |
| 2. Is it an appropriate height? | | |
| 3. Does it complement existing equipment in function? | | |
| 4. Are the exercise rings over 5 inches in diameter? | | |
| 5. Are there open "S" rings? | | |
| 6. Are there wooden seats on the swings? | | |
| 7. Are there exposed nuts and bolts? | | |
| 8. Are there sharp edges? | | |
| 9. Can the equipment be properly anchored? | | |
| 10. Is the equipment easy to maintain? | | |

10-13 Evaluation of play equipment aids the teacher in locating problem areas and possible hazards.

## to Know

chronological age      multicultural toys
consumable supplies     physical age
co-op                   spectator toys
developmental age

## to Review

1. True or false. Toys can promote the development of specific skills.
2. List six questions to ask when planning selection of toys for young children.
3. Classroom toys and equipment should reflect and work with _____ _____.
4. How does available space affect toy and equipment selection?
5. True or false. Maintenance is not an important factor in choosing equipment.
6. Toys must be durable because:
    a. Children will sit on, stand on, and drop them.
    b. Broken toys can be dangerous.
    c. Children may feel guilty if they break a toy.
    d. All of the above.
7. Studies show that children who are exposed to many types of toys are more _____ and _____.
8. _____ toys require little action on the part of children.
9. Explain the difference between physical and developmental age.
10. Toys that are wrong for a child's developmental age can cause _____.
11. Play that revolves around violent toys is often:
    a. Constructive.
    b. Aggressive and destructive.
    c. A good learning experience.
    d. None of the above.
12. What are multicultural toys?
13. True or false. The safest toys are those that appeal to adults.
14. List three safety guidelines drawn up by the Toy Manufacturers of America and the National Safety Council.
15. What is a consumable supply?
16. Name the dangers of each of the following:
    a. Rings.
    b. Wooden swing seats.
    c. Screws and bolts.
    d. Anchoring.

## to Do

1. Break into groups and make a basic list of equipment needs for a classroom. Consider program goals, safety, durability, and expense of each item.
2. Discuss favorite childhood toys and the value of each.
3. Ask an early childhood program director to discuss the specifics of toy and equipment maintenance.
4. Using equipment catalogs, make a list of toys and equipment that could be made with a minimum of time and money.
5. Cut pictures of toys from equipment catalogs that would be safe and appropriate for most two-year-old children.
6. Visit a day care center. Make a list of toys and equipment available to the children. Decide which items are open-ended. Make a list of other toys that may be added.
7. Compare the prices of slides, jungle gyms, and wagons from three catalogs. Discuss the reasons for the cost differences.

# Chapter 11

# Guiding Children's Safety

After studying this chapter, you will be able to:
- [ ] List objectives for maintaining a safe environment in the center and explain their importance.
- [ ] Describe guidelines to follow for selecting and caring for various equipment used at the center.
- [ ] Name the types of fires and the fire extinguishers used to fight them.
- [ ] Outline the procedures for treating poisonings.
- [ ] Recognize the signs of child abuse.
- [ ] Design games that teach children how to resist child abuse.

"Please give me that broken toy," Mrs. Goldstein said to a child. She immediately saw the danger of the unsafe toy. At the same time, Mrs. Hernandez, the center director, was checking the art supplies. In the kitchen, the cook was filling out the monthly safety and sanitation checklist. All these staff members were showing their concern for the children's safety by checking the safety of their surroundings.

Dangers can be found everywhere in a preschool center, 11-1. Electrical outlets, cleaning supplies, woodworking tools, outdoor climbing equipment, and cooking tools can all cause injuries. Staff members must closely watch for and remove these dangers. Failure to do so may result in accidents. And most of these accidents can be avoided.

Children can also be put in danger through abuse. Teachers must be aware of the signs of physical and emotional abuse. By law, teachers must protect their pupils from abuse.

As an early childhood teacher, you will need to be alert to any dangers that threaten the safety of your pupils. In addition, the center must have safety rules and procedures. The staff must be aware of their legal responsibilities for protection of children in their care.

## SAFETY OBJECTIVES

The staff is responsible for providing a safe environment for children. Basic objectives toward this safety goal are:

- Be aware of your liability as a preschool teacher.
- Supervise the children at all times.
- Develop safety rules.
- Maintain (at least) the minimum staff/child ratios as required in your state.
- Check to see that center vans, buses, and/or other vehicles have safety door locks installed.
- Practice operating fire extinguishers.
- Post evacuation procedures.
- Practice fire drills.
- Plan an environment that minimizes falls, cuts, and poisonings.
- Read emergency procedures for poisoning.
- Report any suspected cases of child abuse.
- Provide children with protection education.

## LIABILITY

By law, young children are not expected to care for themselves. This is the primary role of the staff at the center. The staff must ensure their safety and health. Education is a secondary function.

Center directors are responsible for the acts of their employees. The extent of their liability may vary, however. As a result, only those who are quite safety and health conscious should be employed, 11-2. Once hired, the director needs to watch these people to ensure that they use good supervision techniques.

11-1 Young children are active and adventurous. They can get themselves into dangerous situations in seconds. Supervision is necessary at all times.

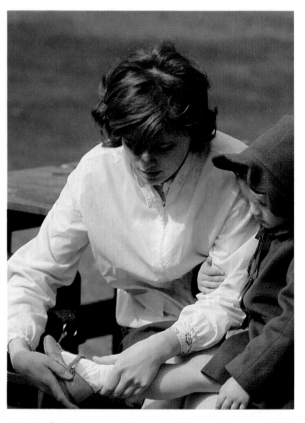

11-2 Safety conscious staff members watch for danger in all situations.

## Types of liability

Day care staff can be held responsible for failing to follow state licensing rules and regulations. Center staff can be liable for not doing the following:

- Obtaining a signed health form from a licensed physician for each child.
- Requiring a staff member to have an approved physical before working with children.
- Providing safe indoor and outdoor equipment.
- Operating a center with the required number of adults.
- Providing proper supervision.
- Providing proper food storage.
- Maintaining fence and door locks in proper condition.
- Providing staff with information on children with special needs. This includes visual problems, hearing problems, allergies, epilepsy, emotional problems, or family problems.
- Refraining from corporal (physical) punishment.
- Providing a safe building.
- Removing children who lack self-control and are a hazard to themselves as well as others.
- Covering electrical outlets.

Center directors and staff should keep constant watch over the center environment. They must ensure that it is safe as well as healthy. New teachers need almost constant support from the staff and director. As new teachers learn the importance of safe surroundings, support can decrease.

## Supervision

"It happened so fast—I just left them for a moment or two," said a preschool teacher. This teacher did not understand that children cannot be left alone, not even a moment. A teacher who is responsible for a group of children should supervise constantly. Preschool teachers must protect children until they can protect themselves.

Young children are unpredictable. They are quick, fearless, and not able to care for themselves. As a result, they lack judgment. They may bite, throw, push, or shove. All of these actions are hazards to others as well as to themselves.

Proper supervision of a group of children requires the teacher's back to face the wall. Your eyes should always face the classroom. The entire room should be visible. Move closer to an area if there appears to be confusion on classroom rules, danger, or children who need assistance.

**Staff/child ratios.** Staff/child ratios are important to safety. Usually, younger children are supervised in small groups. Therefore, younger children require more staff. Chart 11-3 outlines the staff/child ratio and maximum group size requirements of a Midwestern state.

At least the minimum number of staff members set by your state's licensing rules must be present at all times. Failure to comply may result in the center's license being revoked. Remember, too, if a child is injured, and staff/child ratios are not being met, center staff may be held liable.

## SAFETY RULES

Safety rules protect the children in the classroom. Make rules clear, simple, and easy to understand, 11-4.

| | Maximum Number of Children in a Group | Minimum Number of Staff to Children |
|---|---|---|
| Infant to one year | 8 | 1 to 4 children |
| One to 2 years | 8 | 1 to 4 children |
| Two to 3 years | 16 | 1 to 8 children |
| Three to 4 years | 20 | 1 to 10 children |
| Four to 5 years | 24 | 1 to 12 children |
| Five and over | 28 | 1 to 14 children |

11-3 These are the staff/child ratio requirements of a Midwestern state. The number of children in a group and ratios vary among states. Obtain your state's licensing regulations for local requirements.

11-4 Use bulletin boards to teach children about safety.

Some rules that will protect children include:
- Walk indoors. Do not run.
- Cover your mouth when you cough or sneeze.
- Use blocks for building, not for hitting.
- Wipe up spills right away.
- Wash your hands before eating.
- Tell the teacher when equipment breaks.

Remind children about rules. Otherwise, they may ignore or forget them. For example, John may walk directly to the lunch table, forgetting to wash his hands. When this happens, say, "John, we wash our hands before eating." Usually, this will be enough. If John still fails to comply, you may have to say, "John, you need to wash your hands." Do not allow John to eat lunch until his hands are washed.

Teach children to cover their mouths when coughing or sneezing. Always keep at least one box of tissues on hand. Put them in a spot that the children can reach. When children forget to cover their mouths, remind them. Likewise, it is important to praise children who remember. Say, "Lizzie, I am so pleased you covered your mouth when you coughed."

## SAFETY GUIDELINES

Closely watching children and setting safety rules for them to obey helps create a safe center.

However, this is only part of the process. You must also keep watch for other hazardous situations. Fire, playground equipment, and even household cleaners can pose danger to children.

### Equipment selection

Equipment selection is important to safety of young children. Refer to Chapter 10, *Selecting Toys and Equipment,* for information about choosing safe toys for children.

There are a few general rules to remember. Beware of stuffed toys that may have button or glass eyes. These can be pulled off easily by some children. Once removed, children may place the small objects in their mouths and swallow them. This could cause choking. Stuffed toys can also be unsafe for children with allergies to certain fabrics.

Never buy balloons for classroom use. They are easily popped. Once broken, some children may chew or suck on them. The balloon can be swallowed and suffocation can result.

Use of plastic rattles must be carefully observed. Many contain small pellets. Others are made from hard, brittle plastic. These rattles can break easily. If the rattles break, children may place the pellets or broken plastic pieces in their mouths. Choking can result.

Remember, a toy can be safe for one child, but dangerous for another. For instance, five-year-old children love to play with large marbles. But these same marbles can be dangerous for infants, one-year-olds, and even most two-year-old children. Younger children may place the marbles in their mouths, swallow them, and choke.

### Playground equipment

Playground equipment needs to be checked often for dangers: slivers, sharp edges, unstable equipment, rusted parts, frayed or stressed ropes, etc. See 11-5. Some centers use checklists to check equipment weekly.

Contact the child welfare or social services department to learn your state's safety codes for equipment. Using the code, prepare a safety checklist. Make a habit of filling out the checklist weekly. Report any problems to the center director.

Playground surfaces should be soft, if possible. A child is less likely to be cut falling on grass than on blacktop. A hard surface is needed for wheeled toys. However, most of the playground can have a softer surface. To prevent injuries from falls, place sand, bark, or grass under climbing devices, swings, and tree houses.

## Center vehicles

Vans, buses, and other vehicles owned by the center should have safety door locks and seat belts installed. For younger children, car seats that meet standards for the appropriate age should be installed. While riding in any center vehicles, children should be seated and buckled in. When a number of children are riding in

11-5 Maintaining outdoor equipment ensures the children's safety.

a vehicle, extra adult supervision may be required.

## Fire safety

To promote fire safety, check the center regularly for fire hazards. Each day care center also needs several fire extinguishers. Place one fire extinguisher in or next to the kitchen. Place another extinguisher in or near each classroom. Place a third extinguisher in the laundry area.

**Fire hazards.** The best protection against fires is to prevent them from happening. For instance, keep matches away from children. Then they cannot accidentally start fires. As a teacher, you need to find and correct fire hazards. A fire safety checklist is shown in 11-6. Study this list so you will be able to spot hazards and take action quickly.

**Fire extinguishers.** Not every fire extinguisher is useful for every fire. There are three classes of fires and four types of extinguishers.

*Class A fires* involves ordinary combustible materials, such as common plastics, fabrics, paper, and wood. *Class B fires* involve flammable liquids, including gases, grease, paints, and solvents. *Class C fires* are electrical fires.

*Water-type extinguishers* are designed for use on Class A fires. They should not be used on any other types of fires. In fact, they can make Class B and C fires worse.

Water-type extinguishers have three disadvantages. First, their usefulness is limited. Second, the water in the extinguisher will freeze unless it is treated with an antifreeze. Third, water-type extinguishers usually weigh over 20 pounds.

*Purple K dry chemical extinguishers* are used to fight Class B and C fires. They are slightly more useful against Class B fires. *Standard dry chemical extinguishers* are also designed for Class B and C fires.

*Multipurpose dry chemical extinguishers* are the only type able to put out all three classes of fire.

Contact the local fire department before buying any fire extinguisher. The fire chief can recommend an extinguisher best suited for your purpose. The fire chief can also provide maintenance information and instructions for restoring a charge after an extinguisher has been used.

**Staff in-service.** Schedule an in-service on fire extinguisher use prior to the first day of work. Some directors prefer to have a local firefighter conduct this in-service. After this orientation, update all staff members yearly on fire extinguisher use.

**Fire drills.** Most state licensing rules and regulations require fire drills. Most states also recommend drills be scheduled on a regular basis, such as once a month. These drills will prepare staff and children for a real fire.

Every center, no matter what its size, needs to have well-planned evacuation procedures. The evacuation procedures should be posted.

An example of the procedures to be used is shown in 11-7.

If a fire is discovered in the center, sound the alarm immediately. Evacuate children from the building at once, even if you do not see flames. Smoke, not fire, is responsible for more deaths. Leave the classroom lights on. Lights allow firefighters to see better in a smoke-filled structure.

Call roll as soon as the children and staff have cleared the building. When the fire truck arrives, inform the officer whether anyone is still in the building or it is all clear.

When making evacuation plans, remember that infants are more difficult to remove than older children. This is because infants cannot

## FIRE SAFETY CHECKLIST

|  | Yes | No |
|---|---|---|
| 1. Exit passageways and exits are free from furniture and equipment. | | |
| 2. Locks on toilet doors can be opened from the outside, and can be opened easily by center staff. | | |
| 3. Protective covers are on all electrical outlets. | | |
| 4. Permanent wiring is used instead of lengthy extension cords. | | |
| 5. One wall outlet contains no more than two electrical appliances. | | |
| 6. A fire evacuation plan is posted. | | |
| 7. Fire drills are conducted monthly. | | |
| 8. Flammable, combustible, and other dangerous materials are marked and stored in areas accessible only to staff. | | |
| 9. Children are restricted to floors with grade level exits (no stairs). | | |
| 10. The basement door is kept closed. | | |
| 11. There is no storage under stairs. | | |
| 12. Fire extinguishers are in place and checked regularly. | | |
| 13. Smoke alarms and fire alarms are checked weekly. | | |
| 14. Matches are kept out of the reach of children. | | |
| 15. Toys, chairs, tables, and other equipment are made of flame-retardant materials. | | |
| 16. Carpets and rugs are treated with a flame-retardant material. | | |

11-6 A fire safety checklist may include many items. Would you add any items to this checklist?

EVACUATION PROCEDURES
1. Sound fire alarm.
2. Evacuate the building.
3. Turn on all lights when leaving the building.
4. Call roll as soon as the children are together in a safe place.
5. When the fire truck arrives, report whether all children and staff are or are not out of the center.

11-7 Review evacuation procedures with children. Post the procedures in a noticeable place.

walk. Most adults cannot carry more than two infants at one time. Therefore, when ratios are higher than one caregiver to two infants, a careful plan needs to be made. Some centers practice by placing several babies in a crib and rolling it out of the building.

**Building safety**

Many accidents that occur in centers involve the building and building fixtures. Windows, floors, and stairs all may cause injuries.

Keep windows closed at all times, unless gates or sturdy screens are in place. Keep floors dry. If wax is used, use a nonslip type. Cover stairways with carpet or rubber treads. Install railings at the children's level on both sides of the stairs, 11-8.

Sliding patio doors, doors with glass panels, and storm doors are all dangerous. The Bureau of Product Safety estimates that over a quarter of a million people are injured by glass each year. To protect the children, use only safety glass. Decals applied to sliding glass doors at eye level warn children of glass they might not otherwise see.

**Poisonings**

Studies show that children under five years of age account for almost two-thirds of poisonings that occur each year. Nearly any substance can, under certain conditions, be poisonous. The National Safety Council claims that the average residence contains over 40 poisonous products. Chart 11-9 lists many of these poisonous products.

Children eat many things adults would not think of placing in their mouths. There may be times when you are not sure whether a child has eaten something. For instance, you see a child playing with an empty aspirin bottle. The child has powder around the mouth. When in doubt, always assume the worst. If the child has eaten the aspirin, failing to act may result in great harm.

If you suspect that a child in your classroom has eaten something poisonous, remain calm. If the substance came in a container, check the container for instructions to treat poisoning. Follow the instructions.

If there are no instructions or no container, telephone the nearest poison control center. If your area does not have a poison control center, call the nearest emergency room. Ask for instructions on treating the child.

11-8 Instruct children to hold on to the hand railing when they climb or descend stairs.

**Emergency procedures for poisonings.** Check Chart 11-9 for the number of the correct procedure. If the substance is not listed, or you do not know what the substance is, follow Procedure 3. Do not give the child anything by mouth if the child is not fully conscious. Instead, get the child immediate professional medical attention.

Making a child vomit is not always useful. When vomiting is advised, tickle the back of the child's throat with your finger. If this fails, give the child an *emetic.* This is a substance that, when swallowed, will induce vomiting.

The safest emetic is ipecac syrup. If you do not have this syrup, give the child a solution of one cup warm water mixed with one teaspoon baking soda, salt, or dry mustard.

In Procedure 1, induce vomiting if the child has not already vomited. If tickling the child's throat does not work, give an emetic. Rush the child to the nearest emergency room if he or she does not vomit within 10 to 15 minutes.

Keep the vomit if the child does vomit. Call the child's doctor or the poison control center.

Report the odor and appearance of the vomit. Ask for further instructions.

In Procedure 2, follow the same steps outlined for 1. But, if the child does not vomit immediately, rush him or her to the nearest poison control center or emergency room.

In Procedure 3, do not give the child anything by mouth or try to induce vomiting. Instead, check the child's lips and mouth for burns. If you find any burns, apply ice to help relieve the pain. Then rush the child, along with the poison container, to the nearest emergency room.

In Procedure 4, do not induce vomiting. Rush the child to the nearest hospital for emergency treatment. Call an ambulance if you do not have transportation. Remember to take the poison container with you.

Have a staff member call the hospital immediately for any instructions. If the ride to the hospital is over fifteen minutes, they may tell you to give the child milk to drink.

Procedure 5 is similar to Procedure 4 with one exception. Give the child an acid substance

---

**POISONOUS SUBSTANCES\***

| | | |
|---|---|---|
| After-Shave Lotion (1) | Glue (1) | Paint, liquid (3) |
| Ammonia (5) | Lemon Oil (1) | Paint Thinner (4) |
| Anacin™ (1) | Matches, Safety (1) | Perfume (1) |
| Ant Poison (2) | Matches, Sulfur (3) | Plant Food (1) |
| Battery Acid (4) | Medication, contents | Reducing Pills (2) |
| Bleach (4) | unknown (6) | Shampoo (1) |
| Candle Wax (1) | Mistletoe (2) | Shoe Polish (2) |
| Cold Pills (1) | Moth Repellent (2) | Soap (1) |
| Crayons (3) | Mouthwash (2) | Spot Remover (3) |
| Dishwasher Detergent (3) | Nail Polish (2) | Suntan Lotion (2) |
| Dishwashing Liquids (1) | Nail Polish Remover (2) | Toilet Cleaner (4) |
| Drain Cleaner (5) | Nose Drops (2) | Vitamin Pills (1) |
| Flowers (1) | | |

\*The number following each substance indicates what procedure should be used if a child has consumed this poisonous substance.

11-9 These common household items are all poisonous and should be kept out of the reach of children.

such as diluted vinegar, lemon, or grapefruit juice instead of milk.

For Procedure 6 poisonings, call the drugstore listed on the label of the container. Give the identification number. Explain the problem. Ask the name of the medication. Then contact the poison control center and request instructions.

### Accident report forms

Every center should have a standard accident report form. Any information recorded on this form is useful if legal action is brought against the center. Parents also appreciate having the details of a child's accident. A sample form is shown in 11-10.

### CHILD ABUSE

Doctors, social workers, school administrators, and teachers must report suspected cases of child abuse. This is the law. These people are also required to follow the privacy laws of their state.

ACCIDENT REPORT FORM
CHILD AND FAMILY STUDY CENTER

Name of injured child:_____

Time of injury: _____

Date of injury: _____

Person(s) notified of accident:                    Time of notification:

_____          _____

_____          _____

Person supervising child at the time of the accident:

_____

Description of incident: (Include specific information such as where the child was playing, with whom, with what, etc.)

Child's reaction to injury:

Description of injury:

First aid given:

Person administrating first aid:

11-10 The information in an accident report form is useful for parents and teachers.

Information concerning your legal responsibility is contained in your state's *statute.* This statute is a formal document drawn up by elected officials. It outlines the law. To receive a copy of the statute, contact the district attorney's office, state attorney general's office, social services department, city attorney's office, or a law enforcement office.

There are four types of child abuse: non-accidental physical injury, neglect, emotional abuse, and sexual abuse. Be aware of the signs of each type of abuse.

### Nonaccidental physical injury

The most visible type of child abuse is *nonaccidental physical injury.* This is physical abuse inflicted on purpose. Children being abused in this way often come to school with bruises, bites, burns, or other injuries.

Physically abused children often refuse to discuss their injuries. This may be because their abusers threaten them with further harm if they tell someone.

### Neglect

When children are not given the basic needs of life, they suffer from *neglect.* Neglect takes many forms. A neglected child may be deprived of proper diet, medical care, shelter, and/or clothing. Neglect may or may not be intentional on the part of the abuser. But it may still harm the child.

Children who wear clothing that is too small or dirty may be neglected. Neglected children may also wear clothes that are inappropriate for the weather. Children who are poorly groomed may also be neglected.

Other signs of neglect may appear in a child's health. Neglect may result in children who are too thin or malnourished. Constant fatigue or illness may be other signs of neglect.

### Emotional abuse.

*Emotional abuse* is abuse of a child's self-concept. This can cause mental harm to that child. Emotional abuse can take the form of insufficient love, guidance, and/or support from parents or guardians.

Children who are emotionally abused may repeat certain behavior over several months. Look for the following signs:
- Refusal to talk.
- Unusual or unpredictable behavior.
- Excessive clinging or crying.
- Withdrawn behavior.
- Destructive behavior.
- Poor motor coordination for age.

### Sexual abuse

Rape, fondling, incest, and indecent exposure are all forms of *sexual abuse.* Each of these acts involve adults using children for their own pleasure.

### Reporting child abuse

Report suspected abuse cases immediately by telephone. Call your county's child welfare agency. Report the facts that led you to your suspicion. After the telephone conversation, confirm your report in writing. Keep a copy for your own files.

If the case results in a trial, you may have to testify in court. Do not let this keep you from reporting suspected abuse. As a teacher, you are immune from liability if the report is made in good faith.

### Privacy law

The *privacy law* is designed to protect children. It states that a child's records cannot be given to anyone other than parents, without the parents' permission. Give a child's records only if the parents have made the request in writing. After receiving the request, the materials must be released within 45 days. A form that can be included in each child's file is shown in 11-11.

Parents are given unlimited access to all of their child's records kept by the center. Included may be screening information, developmental evaluations, and parent meeting planning sheets and summaries. Many teachers share all of this information during parent meetings. These meetings will be discussed more in Chapter 25, *Parent Involvement.*

### Protection education

Planning for children's safety goes beyond the classroom. Children need to learn how to deal with dangers outside the classroom. They must learn about child abuse, especially sexual abuse. And they must learn how to protect themselves from it.

**Teaching children about sexual assault.** Warning children about strangers has been a common practice for some time. However, only 10 to 15 percent of child abusers are strangers to the children they abuse. The other 85 to 90 percent are people known to the children. These people may be neighbors, relatives, friends of the family, scout leaders, siblings, or parents.

Most offenders are men. However, women are also reported.

Before age 8, 30 to 46 percent of all children are sexually assaulted. About 10 percent of these children are assaulted by the time they are five-years-old. Girls are abused more often than boys. Studies show that race, intelligence, family income, and social class do not appear to affect the occurrence of sexual assault.

Teach children to resist sexual attacks. Encourage them to "yell and tell." To do this, they must first resist the offender by saying, "no."

THE INFORMATION CONTAINED IN THIS FILE IS CONFIDENTIAL AND IS NOT TO BE CIRCULATED OUTSIDE OF THE CENTER WITHOUT THE PRIOR WRITTEN CONSENT OF THE CHILD'S PARENTS

Under Public Law 93-380: Parents have access to all educational records. According to this law:

(1) You are not allowed to provide the information contained in this file to anyone without the written consent of the child's parent or guardian.

(2) You must advise parents of their rights concerning their child's file.

(3) Parents have the right to read and review the file. Moreover, they may request a revision of information in their child's file.

(4) Within forty-five (45) days, you are required to respond to a parent's request.

FILE REVIEWED BY:

| Name and Title | Address | Reason | Date |
|----------------|---------|--------|------|
| | | | |
| | | | |
| | | | |
| | | | |
| | | | |

11-11 Use a form such as this to record reviews of children's files.

Then, they must tell a trusted friend or relative about the attack. Role play this process with the children. Give them useful phrases to use if they find themselves in trouble. For example:

- If someone tries to give you a wet kiss, shake hands instead.
- If someone tries to get you to sit on his or her lap and you do not want to, say, "No, not now."
- If someone wants to give you a hug and you do not want it, say, "No thanks."
- If someone tries to touch your genitals, say, "Stop, that is not okay."
- If someone rubs or pats your bottom, say, "Do not do that."

Children can also learn by playing "What if" games. To play, ask such questions as:

- "What if a stranger asks to give you a ride?"
- "What if a stranger offers you candy?"
- "What can you do if a neighbor gives you a sloppy kiss?"
- "What can you do if a relative pats you on the bottom?"
- "What if someone places a hand under your clothes?"
- "What if someone tries to place you on his or her lap?"

- "What if the babysitter told you to take off your clothes and play with or look at your genitals?"
- "What if a neighbor invited you into his house to play a secret game?"

Children also need to learn how and who to tell if someone assaults them. Use puppets, charts, movies, or other materials to teach children this lesson. For instance, you might develop a "Who would you tell?" game using puppets.

Remember, as a teacher, it is important to believe comments made by children. Children do not lie about child abuse. If a child relates an attack to you, believe the child. Report the incident to your administrator and/or the proper law enforcement officials.

## SUMMARY

Providing a safe environment for children requires a great deal of time and attention to details. Danger can be found in every corner of the center. These dangers can threaten both the physical and mental well-being of children. Protecting children from these dangers is the most important job of a teacher.

# to Know

class A fire
class B fire
class C fire
emetic
emotional abuse
neglect

nonaccidental physical
  injury
privacy law
sexual abuse
statute

# to Review

1. Which of the following is not a basic safety objective?
    a. Develop safety rules.
    b. Supervise children at playtime only.
    c. Practice fire drills.
    d. Report suspected cases of child abuse.
2. What is the primary role of the staff at a center?
3. List three unsafe situations for which a center is liable.
4. True or false. Most accidents in a preschool center can be avoided.
5. Usually, younger children require _____ staff supervision than older children.
6. What safety hazards can be caused by:
    a. Stuffed toys?
    b. Balloons?
    c. Plastic rattles?
7. Name three ideal places to keep fire extinguishers in a day care center.
8. Classify the following fires. Name the type (or types) of fire extinguisher you would use to fight the fire.
    a. A burning toaster.
    b. A burning plastic milk carton.
    c. A burning pan of cooking oil.
    d. A burning painting done on paper.
9. True or false. Smoke, not fire, claims more lives.
10. Applying _____ at eye level to glass doors makes glass visible to children.
11. True or false. Nearly any substance, under certain conditions, can be poisonous.
12. What is an emetic?
13. What poisoning treatment procedures do not require induced vomiting?
14. What procedure would you use for each of the following?
    a. Drain cleaner.
    b. Vitamins.
    c. Flowers.
    d. Mouthwash.
15. Name the four types of child abuse.
16. List 3 behavior patterns exhibited by emotionally abused children.
17. True or false. Parents are allowed limited access to records kept by the center concerning their child.

# to Do

1. Design an evacuation chart for the classroom.
2. Review procedures for treating poisonings. Discuss the procedure to use for the following substances: glue, medicine, liquid paint, toilet bowl cleaner, ammonia.
3. Arrange a visit to a center to learn about their safety objectives. Ask to view any safety checklists they might use.
4. Ask the local fire chief to address your group concerning the proper use of fire extinguishers.
5. Arrange a visit to the emergency room of a local hospital. Ask the doctor on duty to discuss emergency procedures used for poisonings.
6. Create a puppet play using phrases that children may use if ever faced with sexual abuse.

# Chapter 12

## Planning Nutritious Meals and Snacks

After studying this chapter, you will be able to:
- [ ] List some goals for a good nutrition program.
- [ ] Explain how nutrition maintains the body and how lack of nutrition harms the body.
- [ ] Describe functions of and sources for the nutrients found in food.
- [ ] Name the food groups, along with the sources and nutrients of each group.
- [ ] Plan nutritious meals and snacks.

It was lunchtime at the Happy Time Day Care Center. Nidda asked for a second serving of spinach, a food being served for the first time. Maria said the potatoes were "yummy." Geneva said her mother was sending oranges for her birthday treat. Throughout her meal, the teacher talked with the children and ate portions of the foods served.

The lunchroom was decorated with twelve large paper ice cream cones. Each cone represented one month of the year. The children's names and birthdays were written on paper scoops of ice cream. These scoops were placed in the cone that matched their birthday month.

On the other side of the lunchroom was a large carrot cut out of tagboard. A cloth measuring tape was pasted down the center. Each child's height was marked next to the tape.

In this classroom, children learn about nutrition. They learn both directly and indirectly. For instance, the variety of foods served and the teacher's comments about the food are direct learning experiences. Children learn about many types of food and that mealtime is a pleasant time. The positive attitudes and pleasing surroundings of the lunchroom are indirect learning experiences. By watching friends and teachers, they develop good habits and attitudes about food.

Teaching about nutrition is an important job of the teacher, 12-1. Proper nutrition is needed for children's health, growth, and development. Behavior and learning ability may be related to proper diet. Some studies suggest that young children who have learned proper nutrition concepts may experience lifelong good health. Thus, teaching nutrition concepts is a major job of the preschool teacher.

Teaching nutrition concepts requires a good nutrition program. A good program centers on the needs of the children, including their ethnic backgrounds. These nutrition concepts should be integrated into all subject areas. Program goals should include:

• Providing nutritious meals and snacks.
• Introducing new foods that are nutritious.
• Encouraging good eating habits.
• Involving children in meal activities.
• Providing nutrition information to parents.

To meet these goals, the teacher must understand how food is used by the body. In addition, the teacher must know the various nutrients and their sources. Meal plans and food experiences for the children are also needed to meet program goals.

## NUTRITION

*Nutrition* is the science of food and how the body uses it, 12-2. Proper nutrition is needed to build a strong body and mind. It also provides the body with energy. Each type of food has its own energy value. This value is measured in Calories. Without proper nutrition, energy decreases. Energy from food maintains body functions such as breathing and blood circulation. It also maintains vital organs: the heart, lungs, liver, and kidneys. Energy from food also maintains body temperature.

The real amount of energy a person needs depends on age and activity level. Children need more energy than adults, in relation to body weight. For instance, a four-year-old boy weighing 42 pounds needs about 1,800 Calories

12-1 Teachers can greatly influence the nutrition habits of young children.

12-2 Knowledge of nutrition is needed for planning healthy snacks.

per day. A 45-year-old man weighing 160 pounds needs about 2,700 Calories per day. Thus, the child needs about 43 Calories per pound while the man needs about 17. Children's physical growth is greater than adult's growth. Children are also very active. All their physical activities use a great deal of energy.

Undernutrition and overeating are two problems that affect children's health and development. In order to plan balanced, nutritious meals and snacks, you need to know the effects of these problems.

### Undernutrition and malnutrition

*Undernutrition* is a lack of proper nutrients in the diet. It is caused by not eating enough food in an otherwise well-balanced diet. *Malnutrition* is a lack of nutrients. It is caused by the inability of the body to use the nutrients in the food. Malnutrition can occur even in children who eat the proper amounts of food. Children with these problems often are shorter than their peers. Long-term deficiencies can slow, or even stop, growth.

Other signs of poor nutrition include irritability, bowed legs, sunken eyes, decaying teeth, and/or fatigue.

### Overeating

*Overeating* is the intake of more food than is needed by the body to function properly. This can cause many health and emotional problems. A major health problem caused by overeating is obesity. *Obesity* is a condition in which body weight is 20 percent above the "normal" weight for a given height. Fourteen percent of children under age six are obese. Studies show obese children tend to be obese adults.

Obesity can lead to many other health problems in adult life. These include hypertension (high blood pressure and related problems), diabetes, and heart disease.

Obesity can also cause emotional problems. Many obese children have poor self-concepts. Some of these children become loners due to their low self-concepts.

Obesity is easier to prevent than to treat. First, note the activity level of any heavy children. Encourage them to join in large motor play. Second, discuss your concerns about a child's nutrition with staff and parents.

### Nutrients and their sources

The chemical substances found in foods are called *nutrients*. There are six nutrients needed for growth and maintenance of health. These are proteins, carbohydrates, fats, vitamins, minerals, and water. Chart 12-3 contains a list of nutrients, their functions and sources.

### The Daily Food Guide

To ensure good nutrition, children need to eat a variety of foods. One easy way to plan a well-balanced diet is to use the *Daily Food Guide*. This guide contains the following five food groups:
1. Milk and milk products.
2. Breads and cereals.
3. Meats and meat alternates.
4. Fruits and vegetables.
5. Fats and sweets.

| NUTRIENT | FUNCTIONS | SOURCES |
|---|---|---|
| **Proteins** | Build and repair tissues.<br>Help build antibodies, enzymes, hormones, and some vitamins.<br>Regulate fluid balance in the cells.<br>Regulate many body processes.<br>Supply energy, when needed. | High quality proteins: Meat, poultry, fish, eggs, milk and other dairy products, peanuts, peanut butter, lentils.<br>Low quality proteins: Cereals, grains, vegetables. |
| **Carbohydrates** | Supply energy.<br>Provide bulk in the form of cellulose (needed for good digestion).<br>Help the body efficiently digest fats. | Sugar: Honey, jam, jelly, sugar, molasses.<br>Fiber: Fresh fruits and vegetables, whole grain cereals and breads.<br>Starch: Breads, cereals, corn, peas, beans, potatoes, pasta. |
| **Fats** | Supply energy.<br>Carry fat-soluble vitamins.<br>Protect vital organs.<br>Protect the body from shock and temperature changes.<br>Add flavor to foods. | Butter, margarine, cream, cheese, marbling in meat.<br>Nuts, whole milk, olives, chocolate, egg yolks, bacon.<br>Salad oils and dressings. |
| **Vitamins**<br>**Vitamin A** | Helps promote growth.<br>Helps keep skin clear and smooth.<br>Helps keep mucus membranes healthy.<br>Helps prevent night blindness. | Liver, egg yolk, dark green and yellow fruits and vegetables, butter, whole milk, cream, fortified margarine, ice cream, cheddar-type cheese. |
| **Thiamin**<br>**(Vitamin B-1)** | Helps promote normal appetite and digestion.<br>Helps keep nervous system healthy.<br>Helps body release energy from food. | Pork, other meats, poultry, fish, eggs, enriched or whole grain breads and cereals, dried beans, brewer's yeast. |
| **Riboflavin**<br>**(Vitamin B-2)** | Helps cells use oxygen.<br>Helps keep skin, tongue, and lips normal.<br>Helps prevent scaly, greasy areas around the mouth and nose.<br>Aids digestion. | Milk, all kinds of cheese, ice cream, liver, other meats, fish, poultry, eggs, dark leafy green vegetables. |
| **Niacin**<br>**(a B-vitamin)** | Helps keep nervous system healthy.<br>Helps keep skin, mouth, tongue, and digestive tract healthy.<br>Helps cells use other nutrients. | Meat, fish, poultry, milk, enriched or whole grain breads and cereals, peanuts, peanut butter, dried beans and peas. |

*Continued.*

12-3 Each nutrient performs a specific
function and can be found in several sources.

| NUTRIENT | FUNCTIONS | SOURCE |
|---|---|---|
| **Vitamin C** | Helps keep gums and tissues healthy. Helps heal wounds and broken bones. Helps body fight infection. Helps build cementing materials that hold body cells together. | Citrus fruits, strawberries, cantaloupe, broccoli, green peppers, raw cabbage, tomatoes, green leafy vegetables, potatoes and sweet potatoes cooked in the skin. |
| **Vitamin D** | Helps build strong bones and teeth in children. Helps keep adult bones healthy. | Fortified milk, butter and margarine, fish liver oils, liver, sardines, tuna, egg yolk, sunshine. |
| **Vitamin E** | Acts as an antioxidant although exact function is not known. | Liver and other variety meats, eggs, leafy green vegetables, whole grain cereals, salad oils, shortenings, and other fats and oils. |
| **Vitamin K** | Aids in blood clotting. | Organ meats, leafy green vegetables, cauliflower, other vegetables, egg yolk. |
| **Minerals Calcium** | Helps build bones and teeth. Helps blood clot. Helps muscles and nerves function properly. Helps regulate the use of other minerals in the body. | Milk, cheese, other dairy products, leafy green vegetables, fish with bones. |
| **Phosphorus** | Helps build strong bones and teeth. Helps regulate many body processes. | Protein and calcium food sources. |
| **Iron** | Combines with protein to make hemoglobin. Helps cells use oxygen. | Liver, lean meats, egg yolk, dried beans and peas, leafy green vegetables, dried fruits, enriched and whole grain breads and cereals. |
| **Water** | A basic part of blood and tissue fluid. Helps carry nutrients to cells. Helps carry waste products from cells. Helps control body temperature. | Water, beverages, soups, and most foods. |

*Fig. 12-3 Continued.*

The first four food groups must be included in a child's daily diet. Foods in the fifth group should be limited. Chart 12-4 lists foods that are included in the Daily Food Guide, along with recommended serving sizes for children.

**Milk and milk products.** Children need a minimum of four to six servings from this group daily. The most important nutrient provided by this group is calcium, 12-5. Riboflavin, protein, and phosphorous are also provided. Fortified milk and milk products also provide vitamins A and D.

Milk is considered the best source of calcium in this group. But milk products such as cheese,

## FOOD GROUPS, SOURCES, AND DAILY NEEDS

| FOOD GROUP | SOURCES | NUMBER OF SERVINGS NEEDED BY CHILDREN | CHILD-SIZED SERVINGS* |
|---|---|---|---|
| **Meat and meat alternates** | Beef, veal, lamb, pork, fish, shellfish; variety meats such as heart, kidneys, and liver. | 3 or more | 1 egg<br>1 ounce lean meat, poultry, or fish<br>2 tablespoons of peanut butter<br>1 frankfurter<br>1/2 cup dried beans, peas, lentils<br>1/4 cup canned fish |
| **Milk and milk products** | Milk: whole, 1%, 2%, skim, buttermilk, evaporated, and non-fat dry; cheese, ice cream, yogurt. | 4 to 6 | 1/2 cup milk<br>1/2 cup yogurt<br>1/2 cup baked custard<br>1/2 ounce cheese<br>1 cup ice cream<br>3/4 cup cottage cheese |
| **Vegetables and fruit** | Vitamin C: orange, grapefruit, tomatoes, cabbage, green pepper, potatoes, strawberries, cantaloupe, broccoli<br>Vitamin A: Brussel sprouts, broccoli, cantaloupe, carrots, spinach, pumpkin, sweet potatoes. | 4 or more<br>Serve one Vitamin C rich food every day.<br>Serve one Vitamin A rich food every other day. | 1/4 cup juice<br>1/4 cup cooked fruit or vegetable<br>1/2 apple, banana, potato |
| **Breads and cereals** | Baked goods from enriched flour, cereals, crackers, flour, macaroni, noodles, rolled oats. | 4 or more | 1/2 slice of bread<br>1/4 cup cereal, macaroni, noodles, rice, or spaghetti<br>1/2 cup ready-to-eat cereal<br>3 crackers<br>1/2 cup rolled oats |

*Larger servings are needed as children grow older.

12-4 Nutritious meals can be planned using the Daily Food Guide.

12-5 The calcium found in milk helps build strong bones. This is very important for the body of a growing child.

yogurt, and ice cream are also good sources. Whole milk is preferred for most preschool children. Physicians sometimes recommend that overweight children be provided skim or low-fat milk. If you serve milk other than whole milk, be sure that it is fortified.

**Breads and cereals.** A child's diet should include four or more servings of breads and cereals daily. Carbohydrates, iron, and B-vitamins are the chief nutrients in these foods.

Foods in the breads and cereals group include whole grain and enriched breads. Also included are pancakes, pastas, crackers, and hot and cold cereals. Only whole grain and enriched products should be served to children. Most bread and cereal products are whole grain or enriched. However, check labels on products to be sure. Also, if you make bread products at the center, be sure to use whole grain or enriched flour.

**Meats and meat alternates.** Three or more servings from this group should be included in a child's daily diet. Protein is the most important nutrient supplied by foods in this group. Meats are also good sources of B-vitamins, iron, and phosphorous.

Animal products in this group provide the highest quality of protein. These include beef, pork, veal, lamb, eggs, seafood, and poultry. But dried beans, dried peas, and nuts are also included in this group. The proteins in these foods are not as high-quality as the proteins in animal products. But they are good sources, especially if they are served with milk, milk products, breads, or cereals.

**Fruits and vegetables.** Preschool children should receive four or more servings from this group daily. Foods in this group are major sources of vitamins C and A, 12-6.

Rich sources of vitamin C include citrus fruits such as lemons, limes, oranges, and grapefruits. Green pepper, Brussel sprouts, broccoli, tomatoes, and strawberries are other sources. Rich sources of vitamin A are found in deep yellow and dark green fruits and vegetables. Apricots, cantaloupe, carrots, pumpkin, and winter squash are examples of deep yellow fruits and vegetables. Spinach, broccoli, and asparagus are deep green.

When planning meals for children, be sure to include sources of vitamin A and vitamin C. At least one source of vitamin C should be served daily. A good source of vitamin A should be included at least every other day. Fruits and vegetables should be served raw or cooked as little as possible. This is because cooking in water can lower the vitamin A and C content of foods.

**Fats and sweets.** Foods in this group do not have very high nutritional value other than providing Calories. Such foods as butter, margarine, jellies, syrups, and salad dressings are included. So are pastries, candy bars, doughnuts, and many other sweets and snack items.

12-6 Serving a fruit or vegetable at snack time gives children one of the four servings they require.

Eating large amounts of fats and sweets can lead to weight gain and obesity. And if children fill up on fats and sweets while refusing other foods, they can be deprived of needed nutrients. That is why it is important to limit offering foods from this group. Instead, offer such items as fresh fruit or crackers with cheese for snacks. Of course, it is okay for children to have foods from this group from time to time. But be sure that you offer enough servings from the first four food groups for that day.

## PLANNING ENJOYABLE MEALS AND SNACKS

Nutrition is the most important part of a well-planned menu. However, many other factors also contribute to a well-planned menu. For instance, scale servings to the children's appetites. A usual child's serving is about one-half of an adult's serving. Children manage best with small servings. Their appetites often vary from day to day. Suggested serving sizes for specific age groups are listed in 12-7.

### Food appeal

Children should also be able to enjoy what they are eating. Texture, flavor, color, form,

| FOOD | AGES | | |
|---|---|---|---|
| | 1 | 2-3 | 4-6 |
| Milk | 1/2-1 cup | 1/2-1 cup | 3/4-1 cup |
| Bread | 1/2 slice | 1/2-1 slice | 1-1 1/2 slice |
| Cereal | 1/4 cup | 1/3 cup | 1/2 cup |
| Vegetable | | | |
|   Vitamin A Source | 2 tablespoons | 3 tablespoons | 4 tablespoons |
|   Other | 2 tablespoons | 3 tablespoons | 4 tablespoons |
| Fruit | | | |
|   Vitamin C Source | 1/4 cup | 1/3-1/2 cup | 1/2 cup |
|   Other | 2 tablespoons | 3 tablespoons | 4 tablespoons |
| Meat, lean cooked | | | |
|   without bone | 1/2 ounce | 1-1/2 ounce | 1 1/2-2 ounce |
| Egg | 1 | 1 | 1 |
| Dried Peas or | | | |
|   Beans, cooked | 1 tablespoon | 2-3 tablespoons | 3-4 tablespoons |
| Peanut butter | 1 tablespoon | 2-3 tablespoons | 3-4 tablespoons |
| Cheddar cheese | 1/2 ounce | 1-1 1/2 ounce | 1 1/2-2 ounce |
| Cottage cheese | 1 tablespoon | 2-3 tablespoons | 3-4 tablespoons |
| Butter or Margarine | 1/2 teaspoon | 1 teaspoon | 1 teaspoon |

12-7 Consider the age of children as you plan meals and snacks.

temperature, and food preferences all affect how much a child enjoys a meal.

When considering each of these aspects, keep in mind that children also like variety. A meal with all the same texture or color could be boring for children. Children also enjoy trying new foods. A new food should be added with a meal of familiar and well-liked foods. This is because children may be overwhelmed if given too many new foods at once.

**Texture.** Soft, hard, chewy, mashed, chopped, crisp, creamy, and rough are all textures. It is wise to combine textures when planning meals and snacks for young children. This makes the meal more interesting for the children. For instance, at mealtime, serve one soft food, one crisp food, and one chewy food. See 12-8. Combine contrasting textures for a pleasing effect. This also provides you with an opportunity to include language concepts during meals and snacks.

Dry foods are hard for children to eat. Serve dry food only in combination with two or more moist foods. Cream sauces or gravy poured over dry food makes the food more pleasing to young children.

12-8 Bananas covered with peanut butter combine the textures of soft, chewy, and creamy.

Meat is difficult for young children to chew. Their teeth cannot grind meat as easily as adults' teeth. Because of this, children usually prefer frankfurters and hamburgers. Chili, spaghetti, and casseroles are other ways of serving meat with varied textures.

**Flavor.** In general, children prefer mildly seasoned foods. One rule of thumb is to use only half as much salt as noted in a recipe.

Whenever possible, enhance the natural flavor of the food. This means that only small amounts of sugar and spices should be added.

**Color.** Children enjoy color in their meals. If the foods you are serving are not very colorful, add color to one or more of the foods. For example, tint the applesauce pink. For St. Patrick's Day, you might color pudding green.

**Food forms.** Serve most foods in bite-sized pieces. Children have poorly developed fine motor coordination skills. They find it difficult to use spoons and forks well, 12-9. Therefore, slice cooked carrots and other vegetables in large pieces rather than dicing them. Or, add diced vegetables to another food. For instance, add diced carrots to mashed potatoes.

Soup is also difficult for many young children to eat. They become tired from spooning. Children may get frustrated if they spill on clothing or the table.

Two methods can be used to make soup easier to eat. One method is to thicken the soup. This can be done by adding solid ingredients or a thickener, such as flour. The second method is to let the children drink the soup from a cup.

Whenever possible, prepare foods so they can be eaten with the fingers. For example, serve chopped raw vegetables instead of a tossed salad.

**Temperature.** Children are more sensitive to hot and cold than adults. Therefore, they prefer foods close to room temperature. Serve hot dishes warm. Fruits, salads, and other cold foods should not be frozen or very cold. They should be cool.

### Food preferences

A child's home environment affects food preferences early in life. Family habits and

12-9 The large pieces of fruit in this salad will be easy for children to pick up with forks or spoons.

12-10 Children will accept new foods more readily when they are made occasionally.

culture affect food preferences. For instance, Mexican-Americans may prefer more spicy foods than Americans of European background.

Family income influences food preferences, too. Lower income families tend to eat less costly cuts of meat, such as hamburger, chicken, and variety meats. They also tend to eat more starchy foods, such as breads and pastas. High income families are more likely to buy more fresh fruits and vegetables, dairy products, and costly cuts of meat. They also are more likely to eat convenience foods, such as frozen entrees.

Consider the children's backgrounds as you plan meals. Offer foods that are familiar to them. Then add foods from other cultures from time to time for variety. See 12-10.

## SERVING MEALS

Licensing requirements exist that outline how often and how much food must be provided for young children in day care centers. These requirements vary from state to state. As a rule,

the number of hours a child spends at a center governs the number of snacks and meals served. In most states, children who attend less than four hours must be served a fruit juice or milk and a snack item. Children who attend five to eight hours must be served both a meal and a snack.

The decision to serve breakfast is often based on two factors. These are the length of the school day and the distance the child travels to reach the center. Centers that provide full-day care usually serve breakfast. Centers with children who travel long distances also often serve breakfast.

### Breakfast

The purpose of breakfast is to break the 10 to 14 hour overnight fast. Breakfast provides energy for morning activities. Studies show that children who eat a nutritious breakfast perform better mentally and physically.

A good breakfast should include foods from at least three of the four required food groups. The United States Department of Agriculture

(U.S.D.A.) Child Care Food Program recommend:
- Fruit or juice.
- Protein rich food.
- Milk.
- Bread.
- Butter or margarine.

or
- Fruit or juice.
- Cereal.
- Milk.

Fruit drinks or punches are not juice subtitutes, even when fortified with vitamin C. Fruit juices have fewer additives and less sugar.

**Self-serve breakfasts.** Self-serve breakfasts are popular with center staffs. This is because children can eat their breakfasts as they arrive. And they can choose what and how much to eat, based on their own appetites.

The self-serve breakfast gives children the chance to prepare their own breakfasts. Some ideas for breakfasts children can help make are shown in 12-11.

Many prepackaged breakfast foods come in child-sized servings. These include dry cereals (variety packs), yogurt packs, and muffins. Juices and milks are also available in child-sized servings.

**Snacks**

Most children eat small amounts of food at one sitting. They may not be properly nourished by just eating three meals a day. Therefore, provide snacks between meals. Snacks satisfy hunger and help meet daily food requirements.

In most centers, snacks are served mid-morning when their is no breakfast program, and again in mid-afternoon. Snacks should not

---

### BREAKFAST FOODS CHILDREN CAN EASILY MAKE

Fresh squeezed juices
Egg sandwich
Deviled eggs
Tomato stuffed with scrambled eggs
Eggs-in-a-basket of bread
Eggs-foo-yung
Omelets with infinite fillings
Hashed brown potatoes with a poached egg on top
Cheesy mashed potatoes
Potato pancakes
Pizza or Breakfast Pizza
Tacos or burritos
Soups
Sandwiches: toasted cheese
            peanut butter and jelly waffles or french toast
            egg salad with lettuce and tomato
            hamburgers
            hot dogs
            tuna salad with cheese
Fish sticks
Pigs in a blanket
Meatballs
Grits, mush, scrapple

Hot cereal topped with fruit, ice cream, or yogurt
Surprise muffins with different fillings
Salads: carrot raisin
        fruit salads
        vegetable salads
Baked apples with raisins and nuts
Stuffed fruits
Raisin-peanut mix
Yogurt with fruit and granola
Milk shakes, milk/fruit or juice blends
Bread, rice, pumpkin, egg noodle puddings/custards
Pancakes with fruit faces
Cottage cheese pancakes
A change from syrup for pancakes and waffles:
    applesauce
    fruit sauces (a thin cranberry sauce is especially good)
    sliced and slightly sugared fruits
    thin custard sauce or pudding
    scoop of ice cream
    chopped nuts
    peanut butter
    cheese spreads
    creamed, hard-cooked eggs
    creamed chicken, chipped beef, etc.

*Smell, Touch, Listen, Look—Kids Learn, Kids Cook,* Project funded under U.S. Department of Agriculture, University of Wisconsin-Stout.

12-11 Remember to plan breakfast foods that are nutritious as well as easy to make.

interfere with a child's appetite for meals. Because of this, it is best to schedule snacks at least 1 1/2 hours before meals.

Snacks should include one or more of the following: milk, fruit, vegetable, juice, or protein rich food. In addition, a snack may include a bread or cereal product.

Choose snacks according to the Daily Food Guide. Plan a snack based on the menu for the day. Consider the nutrients, colors, and textures of the meals. Then choose snacks that complement the meals. Avoid fats, sweets, and highly salted foods such as potato chips, pretzels, and corn chips. Children usually enjoy simple snacks they can eat with their fingers. Suggestions for snack ideas are shown in 12-12.

## SNACK IDEAS

**Milk and milk products**
Dips (yogurt, cottage cheese)
Cheese (balls, wedges, cutouts, faces)
Milk punches made with fruits or juices
Yogurt

Conventional cocoa
Cottage cheese with vegetables or pancakes
Cheese fondue (preheated, no open flame
 in classroom)

**Meats and meat alternates**
Meat strips, chunks, cubes
Meatballs, small kabobs
Meat roll-ups (cheese spread, mashed potatoes,
 spinach as stuffing
Meat salads (tuna, chicken, turkey, etc.)
Sardines
Hard boiled eggs
Deviled eggs
Egg salad spread
Red beet or pickled eggs

Beans and peas mashed as dips or spreads
Bean, pea, or lentil soup
Roasted soybean and peanut mix
3-bean salad
Chopped nut spreads
Nut breads
Peanut butter on, in, around, over, or with
 anything

**Fruits and Vegetables**
Fruits (use variety): pomegranates, cranberries,
 apricots, pineapples, tangerines, kiwi
Vegetables (with or without dips): sweet and white
 potatoes, cherry tomatoes, broccoli, cauliflower,
 radishes, peppers, mushrooms, zucchini, squashes,
 rutabagas, avocados, eggplant, okra, pea pods,
 turnips, pumpkin, sprouts, spinach
Kabobs and salads
Fruit and vegetable juices and juice blends

Fruit muffins, yogurts, and milk blends
Stuffed dates, prunes, etc.
Dried fruits (raisins, currants, prunes, apples,
 dates, figs)
Vegetable soups
Stuffed celery, cucumbers, zucchini, spinach,
 lettuce, cabbage
Vegetable spreads

**Breads and cereals**
Granola
Slices of rice loaf
Dry cereal mixes (not presweetened)
Seed mixes (pumpkin, sunflower, sesame, poppy,
 caraway)
Roasted wheat berries, wheat germ, bran as roll-ins,
 toppers, or as finger food mix
Popcorn with grated cheeses, flavored butters, or
 mixed nuts as toppers
Variety of breads (tortillas, pocket breads, crepes,
 pancakes, English muffins, biscuits, bagels,
 popovers) and grains (whole wheat, cracked wheat,
 rye, cornmeal, oatmeal, buckwheat, rolled wheat,
 wheat germ, bran, grits)

Toast (plain, buttered, with spreads, cinnamon)
Homemade yeast and quick breads
Waffle sandwiches
Whole grain and spinach pastas
Pasta with butter and poppy seeds
Cold pasta salad
Lasagne noodles cut for small sandwiches

12-12 Plan snacks to coordinate with the Daily Food Guide.

## Lunch

The U.S.D.A. recommends the following pattern be used to ensure children receive the proper nutrients:

Protein rich food (main dish).

- Vegetable and/or fruit (two different kinds).
- Bread (whole grain or enriched rice or pasta).
- Butter or margarine as needed.
- Fluid milk.
- Dessert.

Desserts are optional. They need not be served with every lunch. Plan desserts carefully. Many are high in fat and sugar and low in nutrients other than Calories. For example, plain cookies and cakes have little nutritional value, but are high in Calories. Instead, plan to use carrots or pumpkin in recipes to provide vitamin A. Custards and puddings are considered good desserts since they contain calcium and protein.

When included, desserts should be part of the meal, like the vegetable or bread. They should not be treated as a special part of the meal. Never tell children they must eat everything on their plates in order to get dessert. This will only make desserts appear special.

Chart 12-13 contains sample daily food plans for one meal and a snack. Note how the meals and snack complement each other.

## SUMMARY

Teaching children about nutrition is an important job. Children who learn proper nutrition concepts can use the information their entire lives. And proper nutrition helps children grow and develop properly.

In order to teach about nutrition, the teacher must first understand how food is used by the body. The teacher must also understand how nutrients and their sources fuel the body. The teacher can then use this information to plan nutritious meals and snacks.

## SAMPLE DAILY FOOD PLANS FOR ONE MEAL AND SNACK

(Other foods may be used to add nutrients and to meet the varied Calorie needs of children)

| PATTERN | I | II | III | IV | V | VI |
|---------|---|----|-----|----|----|----|
| **SNACK** | Orange juice<br>Whole wheat<br>  bread<br>Butter | Apple wedge<br>Cheese | Milk<br>Banana | Hard cooked<br>  egg<br>Tomato juice | Celery stuffed<br>  with liver<br>  sausage<br>Apple juice | Milk<br>Peanut butter<br>  and cracker |
| **LUNCH** | Ground beef<br>  patty<br>Peas<br>Carrot strips<br>Enriched roll<br>Butter or<br>  margarine<br>Milk | Roast turkey<br>Broccoli<br>Mashed<br>  potatoes<br>Whole wheat<br>  bread<br>Butter or<br>  margarine<br>Milk | Fish sticks<br>Scalloped<br>  potatoes<br>Stewed<br>  tomato<br>Whole wheat<br>  bread<br>Butter or<br>  margarine<br>Milk | Black-eyed<br>  peas with<br>  ham<br>Mustard<br>  greens<br>Purple plums<br>Corn bread<br>Butter or<br>  margarine<br>Milk | Scrambled<br>  eggs<br>Spinach<br>Fried apples<br>Biscuit<br>Butter<br>Milk | Oven fried<br>  drumsticks<br>Corn-on-the-<br>  cob<br>Sliced tomato/<br>  green pepper<br>  rings<br>Whole wheat<br>  bread<br>Butter or<br>  margarine<br>Milk |

| PATTERN | VII | VIII | IX | X | XI | XII |
|---------|-----|------|----|----|----|----|
| **SNACK** | Apple juice<br>Cheese toast | Milk<br>Raisins and<br>  peanuts | Grapefruit<br>  juice<br>Finger-size<br>  pieces of<br>  leftover<br>  meat | Raw carrots,<br>  celery, green<br>  pepper with<br>  cottage<br>  cheese dip | Tomato juice<br>Flour tortilla<br>  with melted<br>  cheese | Fresh fruit in<br>  season<br>  (strawberries,<br>  melons,<br>  tangerines<br>  etc.) |
| **LUNCH** | Meat loaf<br>Green beans<br>Baked potato<br>Carrot strips<br>Enriched bread<br>Butter or<br>  margarine<br>Milk | Tuna sandwich<br>  on whole<br>  wheat bread<br>Tomato juice<br>Raw cabbage<br>  (small pieces)<br>Apricots<br>Milk | Pinto beans<br>  with melted<br>  cheese<br>Chili peppers,<br>  chopped<br>Tomato,<br>  onion,<br>  lettuce<br>Flour tortilla<br>Milk | Meatballs in<br>  tomato sauce<br>  over<br>  spaghetti<br>Zucchini<br>Peaches<br>French bread<br>  heated with<br>  butter or<br>  margarine<br>Milk | Liver fingers<br>Sweet potato<br>Apple, banana<br>  and orange<br>  salad<br>Rye bread<br>Milk | Swiss steak<br>  cubes<br>Cauliflower<br>Cooked<br>  carrots<br>Whole wheat<br>  roll<br>Butter or<br>  margarine<br>Milk |

12-13 Planning menus is the first step toward teaching nutrition concepts.

## to Know

## to Review

Write your answers on a separate sheet of paper.

1. True or false. Children have learned proper nutrition concepts may also experience lifelong good health.

2. List four goals of a good nutrition program.

3. Define nutrition.

4. The energy value of food is measured in _____.

5. Describe the difference between undernutrition and malnutrition.

6. _____ is a condition in which the body weight is 20 percent above the normal weight for a given height.

7. True or false. The chemical substances found in foods are called nutrients.

8. True or false. A well-balanced diet provides the body with the six types of nutrients it needs: fats, proteins, vitamins, minerals, carbohydrates, and water.

9. The function of protein is to:
   a. Build and repair tissue.
   b. Supply energy when needed.
   c. Help make antibodies.
   d. All of the above.

10. Good sources of _____ include cream, olives, egg yolks, and nuts.

11. List three functions of carbohydrates.

12. Milk is a good source of:
   a. Calcium.
   b. Riboflavin.
   c. Niacin.
   d. All of the above.

13. What are the five food groups in the Daily Food Guide?

14. What are the chief nutrients found in breads and cereals?

15. A good source of vitamin _____ should be served every other day, and a good source of vitamin _____ every day.

16. Why should food be served to children in bite size pieces?

17. List the recommendations for a nutritious breakfast outlined by the U.S.D.A.

## to Do

1. Plan a breakfast, lunch, and snack menu for one week for a group of three-year-old children.

2. Ask a nutritionist to discuss the importance of a well-balanced diet with your class.

3. Observe a group of children at lunchtime. Describe their food preferences. Make notes of what is or is not lacking in their diet.

4. Prepare a list of nutritious desserts. List the nutritional information for these desserts. Are they really nutritious? Why or why not?

5. Discuss reasons why obesity is easier to prevent than treat.

# Chapter 13

## Guiding Children's Health

After studying this chapter, you will be able to:
- ☐ Develop a workable health policy for a day care center.
- ☐ List steps for controlling transmittable illness and disease.
- ☐ Explain the importance of first aid training.
- ☐ Identify various wounds and outline procedures for treating them.
- ☐ Explain treatment for emergency situations such as burns, choking, and insect stings.
- ☐ Discuss your responsibility when caring for children with special illnesses such as diabetes and epilepsy.

Johnny's health affects his performance, ability to learn, and behavior. Johnny has a constant inner ear infection, and he is having trouble hearing. This hearing loss may affect his development of language skills, contact with peers, and general behavior.

A child's health is a key concern when planning, preparing, and maintaining a classroom environment, 13-1.

A healthy environment for young children starts with health policies. Stress hygiene and food preparation to avoid the transmission of disease. Plan for emergencies such as control of head lice. Also plan for sudden illnesses. In addition, have the knowledge and skill to provide first aid treatment.

### OBJECTIVES FOR GUIDING HEALTH

It is your responsibility to protect, maintain, and improve children's health. Thus, you will need to create a healthful environment:
- Develop center health policies.
- Review the children's health records to ensure that they receive immunizations.
- Recognize ill children when making daily health observations.

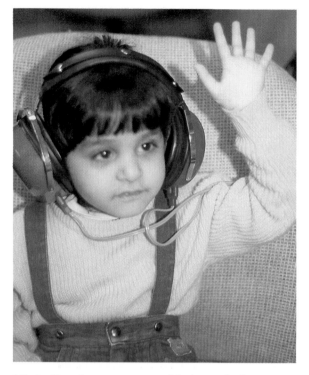

13-1 Hearing tests, provided yearly by many centers, are an important health service.

- Isolate children who may have an illness from the group.
- Contact parents on health issues when appropriate.
- Plan a safe environment to prevent accidents.
- Provide first aid treatment.
- Take part in health-related in-service training.
- Include health in the children's curriculum.

## HEALTH POLICIES

A *policy* is a course of action that controls future decisions. It is important for your center to have health policies. These policies will help you make consistent decisions regarding the health of students and classroom.

In most states, child care is controlled by licensing rules and regulations. The purpose is to protect young children. These rules and regulations address only the basic requirements.

In addition to these health policies your center may have rules that are more detailed.

### Medical examination

Require all children to have a preadmission medical examination. This exam will help you learn:

- Whether the child is free from *communicable diseases.* (These are illnesses that can be passed on to other people.)
- If the child has had all needed immunizations.
- Whether the child has any known allergies.
- If the child has any special health problems that would affect his or her enrollment.

To provide the best environment for children, the staff must also be in excellent physical, mental, and emotional health. They should have an examination prior to their first day of work. A record of these examinations should be maintained in the employees' files.

### Immunizations

To protect all children, each child attending the center must have the proper immunizations. Chart 13-2 shows the immunizations required for each age. See 13-3 for the Day Care Immunization record used in Wisconsin.

**IMMUNIZATIONS FOR PRESCHOOLERS**

| Age | Immunization |
|-----|--------------|
| 2 months | Oral Polio and DPT (Diphtheria, Pertussis, and Tetanus) |
| 4 months | Oral Polio and DPT |
| 6 months | Oral Polio and DPT |
| 15 months | Measles, Mumps, and Rubella |
| 18 months | Oral Polio and DPT (Booster) |
| 4-6 years | Oral Polio and DPT (Booster) |

13-2 Proper immunization is a health policy required by most states.

PLEASE PRINT/TYPE      **CERTIFICATE OF CHILD HEALTH EXAMINATION**

(INFORMATION ON THIS FORM MAY BE SHARED WITH APPROPRIATE PERSONNEL FOR HEALTH AND EDUCATIONAL PURPOSES)

PUPIL'S NAME: _____ BIRTHDATE _____ SEX ☐ M ☐ F   GRADE LEVEL: _____

      LAST         FIRST      MIDDLE        MO DAY YR

ADDRESS: _____ PARENTS TELEPHONE: _____ / _____ SCHOOL: _____

    STREET   CITY   ZIP CODE      HOME      WORK

PARENT OR GUARDIAN: _____ ADDRESS: _____

## MEDICAL HISTORY

TO BE COMPLETED BY PARENT

CHICKEN POX . . . . . . . . . . .YEAR: _____

SCARLET FEVER/STREP . . . .YEAR: _____

T.B. / T.B. CONTACT . . . . . .YEAR: _____

CONGENITAL DEFECTS . . . . . _____

DIABETES. . . . . . . . . . . . . _____

EPILEPSY. . . . . . . . . . . . . _____

HEART DISEASES . . . . . . . _____

FREQUENT EAR INFECTION . . . _____

INJURIES/ACCIDENTS . . . . . .YEAR: _____

   RESULTS _____

PERMANENT DISABILITY . . . .YEAR: _____

   TYPE _____

   RESULTS _____

SURGERY (OPERATIONS). . . . .YEAR: _____

   TYPE _____

   RESULTS _____

ALLERGIES (LIST) _____

ROUTINE MEDICATIONS (LIST) _____

OTHER _____

PARENT'S SIGNATURE _____ DATE

**IMMUNIZATION:** PLEASE PROVIDE THE MONTH DAY AND YEAR FOR EVERY DOSE ADMINISTERED. THE DAY AND MONTH IS REQUIRED IF YOU CANNOT DETERMINE IF THE VACCINE WAS GIVEN PRIOR TO THE MINIMUM INTERVAL OR AGE.

| DOSE | 1 MO DAY YR | 2 MO DAY YR | 3 MO DAY YR | 4 MO DAY YR | 5 MO DAY YR |
|---|---|---|---|---|---|
| DIPHTHERIA, PERTUSSIS AND TETANUS (DPT) . . . . . . . . . . | | | | | |
| DIPHTHERIA AND TETANUS (Td) OR (TD) . . . . . . . . . . . . . | | | | | |
| ORAL POLIO . . . . . . . . . . . . . | | | | | |
| COMBINED MEASLES/MUMPS/ RUBELLA (MMR) . . . . . . . . . . . | | | | | |
| COMBINED MEASLES AND RUBELLA (MR) . . . . . . . . . . . . . | | | | | |
| RUBEOLA (RED MEASLES) LIVE VIRUS VACCINE . . . . . . . . . | | | | | |
| RUBELLA (3DAY OR GERMAN MEASLES). . . . . . . . . . . . . . | | | | | |
| MUMPS . . . . . . . . . . . . . . | | | | | |
| *TB SKIN TEST. . . . . . . . . . . | | | | RESULTS | |

*MANDATED FOR CHILD CARE FACILITIES

HEALTH PROVIDER SIGNATURE (PHYSICIAN, SCHOOL HEALTH PROFESSIONAL OR HEALTH OFFICIAL) (VERIFYING THAT IMMUNIZATIONS WERE GIVEN)

SIGNATURE _____ DATE

SIGNATURE _____ DATE

SIGNATURE _____ DATE

1. CLINICAL DIAGNOSIS IS ACCEPTABLE IF VERIFIED BY PHYSICIAN.

MEASLES _____

   MONTH   DAY   YEAR

MUMPS _____

   MONTH   DAY   YEAR

2. LABORATORY CONFIRMATION OF ANY DISEASE IS ACCEPTABLE.

DISEASE _____

   MONTH   DAY   YEAR

LAB RESULT _____

PHYSICIAN'S SIGNATURE _____ DATE

## PHYSICAL EXAMINATION

TO BE COMPLETED BY PHYSICIAN

**EVALUATION:**

| | NORMAL | ABNORMAL | (REQUIRED) FOLLOW-UP – COMMENT |
|---|---|---|---|
| HEIGHT ____ WEIGHT ____ | | | |
| SKIN. . . . . . . . . . . . . | | | |
| EYES . . . . . . . . . . . . | | | |
| EARS . . . . . . . . . . . . | | | |
| NOSE . . . . . . . . . . . . | | | |
| THROAT . . . . . . . . . . . . | | | |
| THROAT/DENTAL. . . . . . . . | | | |
| CARDIOVASCULAR B/P ____ | | | |
| RESPIRATORY. . . . . . . . . . | | | |
| GASTROINTESTINAL . . . . . . . | | | |
| GENITO-URINARY. . . . . . . . . | | | |
| NEUROLOGICAL. . . . . . . . . | | | |
| MUSCULAR SKELETAL. . . . . . | | | |
| SCOLIOSIS SCREENING . . . . . | | | |
| NUTRITIONAL STATUS. . . . . . . | | | |
| OTHER _____ | | | |

**(STRONGLY RECOMMENDED)**

| | DATE | NORMAL | ABNORMAL RESULTS |
|---|---|---|---|
| HEMOGLOBIN . . . . . . . | | | |
| HEMATOCRIT . . . . . . . | | | |
| URINALYSIS. . . . . . . . | | | |
| LEAD SCREENING. . . . . | | | |
| SICKLE CELL. . . . . . . | | | |

MEDICATIONS _____

DIET RESTRICTION/NEEDS _____

SPECIAL EQUIPMENT NEEDED _____

ALLERGIES _____

OTHER _____

GENERAL COMMENTS _____

INTERSCHOLASTIC SPORTS (FOR 1 YEAR) ☐ YES ☐ NO

PHYSICAL EDUCATION ☐ YES ☐ NO

ON THE BASIS OF THIS EXAMINATION ON THIS DAY I APPROVE THIS CHILD'S PARTICIPATION IN: IF NO, PLEASE ATTACH EXPLANATION.

PHYSICIAN'S SIGNATURE _____ DATE: _____

ADDRESS _____ TELEPHONE: _____

## VISION AND HEARING SCREENING DATA

THIS SECTION TO BE COMPLETED BY I.D.P.H. CERTIFIED SCREENING PERSONNEL – IF PRE-EXISTING APPROVED FORM BY I.D.P.H. IS NOT AVAILABLE.

PRE-SCHOOL – DURING FIRST YEAR OF ENROLLMENT    SCHOOL AGE – DURING SCHOOL YEAR AT REQUIRED GRADE LEVEL

| | | | | | | | | | | | | |
|---|---|---|---|---|---|---|---|---|---|---|---|---|
| DATE | | | | | | | | | | | | |
| GRADE | | | | | | | | | | | | |
| | R | L | R | L | R | L | R | L | R | L | R | L |
| VISION | | | | | | | | | | | | |
| HEARING | | | | | | | | | | | | |

CODE

P – PASS
F – FAIL
R – REFERRED

ILLINOIS DEPARTMENT OF PUBLIC HEALTH
ILLINOIS STATE BOARD OF EDUCATION
ILLINOIS DEPARTMENT OF CHILDREN AND FAMILY SERVICES
ILLINOIS HIGH SCHOOL ASSOCIATION

IDPH ● ISBE ● DCFS ● IHSA ● 001.2 ● 10/80

**13-3** This form supplies written proof that a child is properly immunized. Parents or legal guardians and the child's physician must sign the form.

## Attendance

For the safety of all children, centers need a policy stating when an ill child should be kept at home. For example, your policy might state that a child should be kept at home if he or she shows any of the following symptoms:

- A temperature over 99 degrees, unless the child's normal temperature is above the average.
- Intestinal upset along with diarrhea or vomiting.
- Sore or discharging eyes.
- Profuse nasal discharge.

It is also advised that a child should be kept home for a period of 24 hours after a fever. Instruct parents to report all sicknesses to center personnel.

## Medication

To protect staff against lawsuits, most centers have a policy on steps for using medication. These policies must adhere to, but can exceed, your state's licensing requirements. For instance, your state may require that only doctor-prescribed medication may be given to a child. You must follow this rule. Likewise, if the state requires a record of the child's name, time, date, and amount of medication given, you must keep these records.

## Napping

One health policy that is needed to help prevent the spread of illness is related to napping. Children should not share cots or beds. Rather, each child should be provided with a washable cot or bed and clean sheets. See 13-4. Clean sheets should be provided on a weekly basis. At times, it may be necessary to change sheets more frequently, such as when a child is ill, has perspired a great deal, or has soiled the sheets.

## Daily health inspection

To protect children's health, conduct an informal health inspection each day. This inspection is best conducted as soon as each child arrives at school. Observe for rashes, changes in appearance of eyes, runny noses, flushing of skin, coughing, sneezing, and/or a sweaty appearance.

Even after the health inspection at arrival time, observe the children from time to time for symptoms of illness. Throughout the day watch for irritability, frequent trips to the bathroom, sleepiness, vomiting, and uncommon aggressiveness. Also watch for symptoms of infection, 13-5. If a child appears sick, contact the parents.

Preschool children are prone to communicable diseases. These include chicken pox, conjunctivitis (pink eye), influenza, and measles among others. Observe for symptoms of each of these diseases. Make this information known to all staff. Post a communicable diseases chart in the staff room, 13-6.

## Contacting parents

Children may arrive at the center in good health, but later show symptoms of illness or

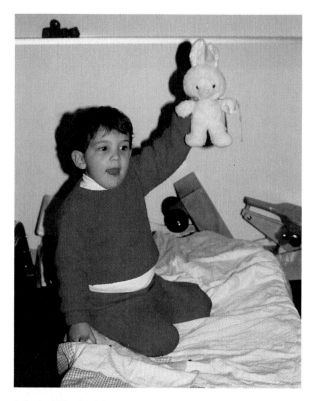

13-4 Washable cots, sheets, and blankets allow the sleeping area to be cleaned on a regular basis.

190

## INFECTION SYMPTOMS

- A sensation of heat.
- Puss, either draining from a wound or beneath the skin.
- Fever.
- Redness of affected area.
- Red streaks leading from wound.
- Swollen lymph glands.
- Tenderness in affected area.
- Throbbing pain.

13-5 Infections are very dangerous and sometimes even fatal. Be aware of the early signs of infection.

infection. When do you decide to contact a parent to pick up a sick child? The answer to this question varies from center to center. The need to contact parents mainly depends on program resources, along with instructions from the parents. Some programs have a sick bay and a flexible staff. When a child becomes ill, the child is moved to the sick bay and the parent is contacted. An adult stays with the child until the parent arrives.

Always contact parents when a child shows signs of illness. Describe the symptoms to the parent. If the child is very ill, the parents should be responsible for picking the child up within a reasonable amount of time. Some programs have this clearly stated in their policy.

**Emergency information.** In case of an emergency, all telephone numbers should be easy to find. To prevent a delay, post all emergency numbers by the center telephone. Include the numbers of the fire station, police station, hospital, poison control center, and ambulance.

Each child's folder should contain emergency information. Record parents' or guardians' home and work telephone numbers. Also note phone numbers of the family doctor and dentist. An example of an emergency information sheet is shown in 13-7.

Some staff members prefer to keep each child's emergency information in a small metal box next to the telephone. You may wish to do the same. This could save time in an emergency, especially if another staff member or volunteer needs to call during an emergency.

### Personal hygiene

Personal hygiene is a chief part of a healthy environment. Programs that stress personal hygiene provide healthy environments. Fewer children and staff suffer illnesses caused by poor hygiene.

Stress the importance of cleanliness to all new employees, as well as volunteers. This can be done through an in-service or employee handbook. Each person should follow basic habits of cleanliness:

- Bathe or shower on a daily basis.
- Use deodorant daily.
- Keep hair clean. Wear a hairnet while working in the kitchen.
- Refrain from smoking in the kitchen or any rooms used by children.

## CONTROLLING DISEASES TRANSMITTED BY FOODS

Small living organisms, called *bacteria,* can cause food-borne illnesses. These are illnesses transmitted through food. The bacteria vary in shape and size. They can only be seen using a microscope. Most bacteria prefer nonacid foods. Examples include eggs, fish, meat, milk, and poultry.

Many food-borne illnesses can be traced back to the staff. Because of this, all new employees should be required to have a complete physical exam. A chest x-ray or tuberculosis test should be included.

Bacteria and viruses can cause many diseases: colds, influenza, measles, mumps, pneumonia, septic sore throat, and scarlet fever. Viral hepatitis Type A, several types of dysentery, and typhoid fever are all diseases traced to the intestinal tract.

### Food poisoning

An infection may occur in the gastrointestinal tract from eating food with a high bacterial count. This is called *food poisoning.* Common

## COMMUNICABLE DISEASES

| DISEASE | INCUBATION PERIOD (TIME FROM EXPOSURE TO FIRST SIGNS) | SIGNS AND SYMPTOMS | PERIOD OF COMMUNICABILITY PRECAUTIONS AND RESTRICTIONS | GENERAL INFORMATION |
|---------|------------------------------------------------|---------------------|-----------------------------------------------|---------------------|
| Chicken pox (Varicella) | 2 to 3 weeks, commonly 13 to 17 days. | Sudden onset, slight fever, lesions often appear first on scalp, then on face and body. Successive crop of lesions remain 3 to 4 days, leaving crusts. | Keep patient home until all lesions are crusted over, usually 5 to 6 days after onset of rash. | Mild disease in children. May be more severe in adults and in children with cancer, leukemia and other high risk conditions. |
| Conjunctivitis (Pink Eye) | 24-72 hours. | Redness in the white of the eye. May or may not have pus discharge. Eye irritation. | The communicable period depends on the cause, but is usually while inflammation or drainage is present. Keep patient home during communicable period, and refer for medical diagnosis and treatment. | Most infections are viral by cause; some are bacterial. May spread person to person through hand to eye contact. Also an early symptom for measles. Some symptoms may be an allergy, and are noncommunicable. |
| Viral Hepatitis Type A (Formerly Infectious) | 15-50 days. Average 25 days. | Usually abrupt onset with fever, fatigue, loss of appetite, nausea and abdominal pain. Jaundice is less common in children than in adults. | Most communicable during first week of illness and up to 1 week after jaundice. Keep patient home and no food handling or patient care while communicable. | Vaccine not available. May be confused with Hepatitis B. Differential diagnosis is important for prevention and control. Careful handwashing is essential. Household contacts should be given immune serum globulin as soon as possible. |
| Influenza | 24-72 hours. | Rapid onset with fever, chills, headache, lack of energy, muscle ache, sore throat, cough. | Communicable for 3 to 7 days after clinical onset. Keep home until symptoms disappear. | Vaccine is available and should be given to persons with greatest risk of serious complications from the disease: the chronically ill and the elderly. |
| Measles (Rubeola) | 8-13 days. | High fever (101 °F or more), with cough, runny nose and/or conjunctivitis. Blotchy rash appears 3 to 5 days after early signs, beginning on face and becoming generalized, lasting 4 or more days. | Communicable from onset of respiratory illness until 4 days after appearance of the rash. Keep patient home until 5 days after the appearance of rash. | A very serious, highly contagious but vaccine preventable disease. |
| Mononucleosis, Infectious | 2-6 weeks. | Characterized by fever, sore throat, and inflamed posterior lymph nodes. | Keep patient home, at the discretion of physician. | In children the disease is usually mild and difficult to recognize. |
| Mumps | 12 to 26 days, commonly 18 days. | Fever, pain and swelling about the jaws involving one or more salivary glands. Many infections occur without symptoms. | Keep patient home until salivary gland swelling has subsided, or other symptoms have cleared. | Infectious early. May cause complications in adults. Vaccine available. |

*Continued.*

13-6 Awareness of the symptoms and treatment for communicable diseases and illnesses is important in order to control the spread of sickness through the center.

| DISEASE | INCUBATION PERIOD (TIME FROM EXPOSURE TO FIRST SIGNS) | SIGNS AND SYMPTOMS | PERIOD OF COMMUNICABILITY PRECAUTIONS AND RESTRICTIONS | GENERAL INFORMATION |
|---|---|---|---|---|
| **Pediculosis (Lice)** | Eggs hatch in a week; reach maturity in about 2 weeks. | Excessive scratching of head or other parts of body. Light gray insects lay eggs "nits" in the hair, especially at the nape of the neck and around the ears. | Keep patient home until treated (should not need to miss more than 1 day of school). | Avoid sharing personal belongings such as clothing, head gear, combs and brushes. |
| **Ringworm (scalp, skin, feet)** | Variable, 1-3 weeks. | Scalp: Scaly patches of temporary baldness. Infected hairs are brittle and break easily.<br>Skin: Flat, inflamed ringlike sores that may itch or burn.<br>Feet: Scaling or cracking of the skin, especially between toes or blisters containing a thin watery fluid. | Communicable as long as active lesions are present. Keep patient home until adequate treatment is begun. | Preventative measures are largely hygienic. All household contacts, pets, and farm animals should be examined and treated if infected. Ringworm is spread directly by contact with infected person or animal or indirectly by contact with articles and surfaces contaminated by such infected persons or animals. |
| **Rubella (German Measles)** | 14-21 days. | Mild symptoms, slight fever, rash lasting about 3 days, enlarged head and neck glands common (particularly in back part of neck, behind ears). | Keep patient home until 4 days after appearance of rash. | Highly communicable, but vaccine preventable disease. Complications are mild except in pregnancy when fetal infection or damage may occur. If contacts include a pregnant woman, she should consult her physician immediately. |
| **Pertussis (Whooping Cough)** | 5 to 10 days. | Begins with upper respiratory symptoms and an increasingly irritating cough develops with a characteristic "Whoop" and frequently occurs in spasms accompanied by vomiting. | Keep patient home for 21 days from beginning of "Whoop," or 5 to 7 days after onset of appropriate therapy. | Most dangerous to pre-school children. Immunization is not recommended for children over 6 years of age. Susceptible contacts should be treated and observed for respiratory disease. |
| **Scabies** | 4-6 weeks with first infections several days with reinfection. | Small raised reddened areas or lesions with connecting grayish-white lines. Marked itching. Most commonly found in the folds of the skin, finger webs, wrists, elbows, thighs, beltline, abdomen, nipples, buttocks. | Keep patient home until under adequate treatment and no open lesions can be observed. | All cases, family members, and other close physical contacts should be treated for scabies simultaneously. |
| **Streptococcal Infections including Scarlet Fever (Strep throat)** | 1 to 3 days. | Fever, sore throat; tender swollen glands with a fine, red rash present in Scarlet Fever. | Keep patient home for 7 days from onset if untreated; with adequate medical treatment, 24 hours. | Medication for symptomatic patients is recommended because of possibility of complications, including rheumatic fever. Culture survey rarely recommended. |

*13-6 Continued.*

**EMERGENCY INFORMATION**

**CHILD AND FAMILY STUDY CENTER**
**SCHOOL OF HOME ECONOMICS**
**UNIVERSITY OF WISCONSIN-STOUT**

CHILD'S NAME _____ BIRTHDAY _____

HOME ADDRESS _____ HOME PHONE _____

MOTHER'S NAME _____ | FATHER'S NAME _____

PLACE OF EMPLOYMENT _____ | PLACE OF EMPLOYMENT _____

PHONE NUMBER _____ | PHONE NUMBER _____

IN CASE OF EMERGENCY, WHO SHOULD BE NOTIFIED?

NAME _____ PHONE _____

NAME _____ PHONE _____

FAMILY DOCTOR _____ PHONE _____

FAMILY DENTIST _____ PHONE _____

13-7 Always have the information needed to contact parents in an emergency.

symptoms are vomiting and diarrhea. Other symptoms include chills, cramps, fever, headache, muscular pain, nausea, and weakness.

The effect of the bacteria's toxin varies. The types and numbers of bacteria and the person's reaction to the bacteria affect the strength of the illness. Commonly, the larger the number of bacteria, the more severe and quick the onset of illness. Young children, the elderly, and the sick are most likely to have a severe reaction.

People can transmit bacteria to food in several indirect ways. Chief among these methods are unclean cooking equipment and utensils. To help prevent food poisoning, thoroughly wash all kitchen equipment, 13-8. Replace kitchen towels daily. Do not allow classroom pets to eat from dishes used by people. After playing with classroom animals, tell the children to wash their hands.

13-8 A refrigerator that is clean and in good working condition helps control transmission of food-borne illness.

To prevent food contamination, practice the following habits:
- After each visit to the restroom, adults and children should thoroughly wash their hands.
- Hands need to be washed after coughing, sneezing, rubbing the nose, or handling handkerchiefs.
- Only disposable tissues should be used.
- Once used, tissues should be discarded.
- The mouth should be covered when coughing or sneezing.

Foods need to be properly handled, prepared, stored, and served to prevent bacterial growth. Serving temperature should be below 40 °F or above 150 °F. Bacteria grow most rapidly at warm temperatures. At temperatures below 40 °F bacteria will remain inactive. At temperatures above 40 °F, bacteria become active and start multiplying. Very high temperatures (150 °F or more) will destroy most harmful types of bacteria, 13-9.

Set policies for proper preparation, storage, and service of food. Examples of rules you may wish to use are shown in 13-10.

## FIRST AID

In every preschool injuries and illness occur. Sometimes, it may just be a scratch or bumped knee. At other times, it may be a sudden high temperature.

First aid training provides the knowledge and skill needed to handle emergency medical care. With the proper training, you will know how and when to treat illnesses and injuries. You will also know when professional medical help is required.

### First aid in-service

All employees in child care should be certified by the American Red Cross. This certification may have been acquired through prior course work or past employment. If an employee is not certified, he or she should be required to obtain certification in order to be employed.

Conduct a first aid in-service training session for all center personnel each year. Include

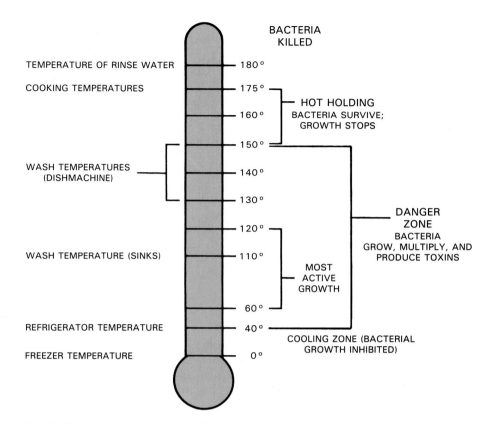

BACTERIA
KILLED

TEMPERATURE OF RINSE WATER — 180°

COOKING TEMPERATURES — 175°
— 160°
HOT HOLDING
BACTERIA SURVIVE;
GROWTH STOPS

— 150°

WASH TEMPERATURES
(DISHMACHINE) — 140°
— 130°

DANGER
ZONE
BACTERIA
GROW, MULTIPLY, AND
PRODUCE TOXINS

— 120°

WASH TEMPERATURE (SINKS) — 110°

MOST
ACTIVE
GROWTH

— 60°

REFRIGERATOR TEMPERATURE — 40°

COOLING ZONE (BACTERIAL
GROWTH INHIBITED)

FREEZER TEMPERATURE — 0°

13-9 Study this chart for information on
proper temperatures at which to prepare,
store, and serve food.

---

### SAFETY RULES FOR AVOIDING FOOD CONTAMINATION

- Do not allow staff with infected sores or respiratory illnesses, such as colds and sore throats, to prepare or serve food.
- Never use home-canned foods.
- Quickly chill foods and keep refrigerated.
- Hold hot foods at above 150°F.
- Wash hands before preparing food and eating.
- Thoroughly wash equipment and hands after working with raw meat.
- Thoroughly cook pork.
- Control flies, insects, and rodents.
- Cool foods in the refrigerator, instead of at room temperature.
- Discard cans with dents along side seams, swells, or off odors.
- Discard meats with off odors or slimy surfaces.
- Thaw foods in refrigerator.
- Prepare perishable foods just prior to serving.

13-10 Children often have severe reactions
to food poisoning. Help ensure their health by
setting and enforcing policies such as these.

secretaries, janitors, cooks, and bus drivers in the training session. Training should focus on updating personnel on first aid procedures of the American Red Cross.

## First aid kits

Most drugstores, department stores, and school supply catalogs sell first aid kits. You may also purchase your supplies separately and put them together in a kit.

Store all first aid items in one area. Keep them out of children's reach. But do not keep first aid supplies in a locked cabinet. During an emergency you may not have time to search for a key.

Each month, check the contents of the first aid kit. Check the contents against a list, 13-11. Many programs have one person responsible for this duty. Replace any supplies that have run out. After checking the kit, submit a form to the director for purchase of replacements.

## WOUNDS

A *wound* is damage to the surface of the skin or body tissue. Basically, there are two types of wounds. A *closed wound* is an injury to the tissue directly under the skin surface. It does not involve a break in the skin. An *open wound* is a break in the skin.

---

### FIRST AID KIT INVENTORY

Date _____ Staff Signature _____

| Quantity | Item | Complete | Replacement needed |
|----------|------|----------|--------------------|
| 15 each | Individual adhesive bandages in 1/2 inch, 3/4 inch, and round sizes. | | |
| 10 | 2 x 2 inch sterile first aid dressings, individually packaged for burns and open wounds. | | |
| 10 | 4 x 4 inch sterile first aid dressings. | | |
| 1 roll | Gauze bandage, 2 inches by 5 yards. | | |
| 2 rolls | Adhesive tape, 1 inch wide. | | |
| 1 bar | Mild soap, for cleaning scratches, wounds, etc. | | |
| 1 pair | Tweezers for removing splinters. | | |
| 1 pair | Blunt tipped scissors, for cutting tape and bandages. | | |
| 1 bottle | Calamine lotion, for insect bites. | | |
| 1 bottle | Ipecac, for use in poisonings. | | |
| 1 | Flashlight. | | |
| 1 | Thermometer, strip-type that can be used on the child's forehead. | | |
| 1 package | Absorbent cotton balls. | | |
| 1 bottle | Antibacterial skin cleaner. | | |

13-11 Make sure the first aid kit is well-stocked at all times.

### Closed wounds

Children usually get closed wounds from falling, being struck, or running into some object. Most closed wounds involve the soft tissues under the skin. The most common type of closed wound is a bruise.

Common signs of a closed wound are tenderness and pain in the damaged area. To help control the pain, apply a cold cloth or pack to the injured area, 13-12. This will also help reduce swelling.

### Open wounds

Cuts and scrapes that break the skin are called open wounds. Two first aid problems are caused by open wounds. First, there may be rapid blood loss. If this is the case, the injured child may go into shock. Second, exposed body tissue may become contaminated and infected.

Some open wounds bleed freely. This reduces the danger of infection. Other wounds bleed very little. These are more likely to become infected.

Open wounds on the top skin layer require simple treatment. To clean the wound, wash it with soap and water. If the wound is deep or does not stop bleeding in a short amount of time, seek medical attention.

**Abrasions.** An *abrasion* is a scrape that damages a portion of the skin. Children usually get abrasions from falling and handling rough objects. It is common to have several children in a classroom with skinned knees, scratched arms, or rope burns.

Bleeding from an abrasion is often limited to blood flow from broken *capillaries* (small veins). However, bacteria or dirt may still enter the wound. Infection can still occur. Dirt particles may actually slow down the healing process. Sometimes, abrasions heal around the particles, forming a permanent scar.

**Cuts.** Cuts, or incised wounds, on body tissues are often caused by broken glass, metal, or sharp edges. Bleeding can be heavy if a blood vessel has been cut. Nerves, muscles, or tendons can also be damaged if the cut is deep enough.

**Puncture wounds.** Puncture wounds are made by sharp objects such as nails, splinters, thumbtacks, and even sticks. In order to puncture the skin, the force at which the object meets the skin must be strong. Bleeding is often light. As a result, the wound is not flushed out. Infection may set in. Harmful bacteria such as tetanus organisms may grow in the presence of moisture and warmth. This can then be carried within the body.

**Bites.** Bites are a type of puncture wound. They can be inflicted by humans and animals. In the case of a mild human bite, you may need only to thoroughly wash the injured areas. However, if the skin is broken, consult a doctor at once. This is especially important if the bite was from an animal. This is because there is a danger of an infection such as rabies.

**Rabies.** *Rabies* is a disease caused by a viral infection of the nervous system and brain. Humans who are infected are not able to swallow. This is a result of the tightening of throat muscles.

Rabies is transmitted through the saliva of a rabid animal. It can be contracted by a human when animal saliva enters an open cut. The infection is most often spread to humans when the rabid animal bites and breaks the skin.

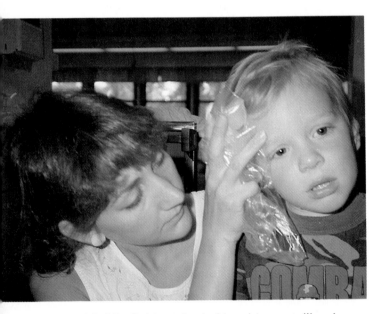

13-12 Cold packs help reduce swelling in closed wounds.

Call a doctor at once if a child is bit by an animal. Report the animal's size and color to the police. If the animal cannot be caught and tested for rabies, the child will need to undergo rabies immunization. This is a very painful series of shots. Without the immunization, the child can die.

All animal bites are dangerous. They carry great risk of infection. Most animals carry a wide variety of bacteria in their mouths, not the least of which is rabies. For that reason, it is important to take immediate action when a child is bit by an animal.

### Open wound care

As the teacher, you can usually treat minor wounds such as abrasions and small cuts. First, wash the area with warm water. Then, as you apply a bandage, bring the wound edges together. This will help prevent a scar from forming.

The following open wounds will require medical attention:

- An animal or human bite that has broken the skin.
- Bleeding that cannot be stopped despite all effort to control it.
- A cut on the face or some other part of the body where scar tissue will be noticeable.
- A wound that goes deeper than the outer layer of skin.
- Wounds with foreign objects such as dirt deep inside the tissue.
- A wound with foreign matter that cannot be removed.

Assume that any loss of blood is harmful to the child. To control severe bleeding place a sterile gauze over the wound. Press on the wound with the palm of one hand. The object is to control the bleeding by pressing the blood vessels against something solid such as a bone or muscle.

If there is no sign of a fracture, elevate open wounds of the leg, arm, neck, or head. To elevate, raise the injured area above the level of the child's heart. The force of gravity will help reduce blood pressure in the injured area, thereby slowing blood loss.

## BURNS

A *burn* is an injury caused by heat, radiation, or chemical agents. Burns vary in size, depth, and severity. Burns are generally classified by degree or depth. There are three classes: first-degree burns, second-degree burns, and third-degree burns. A burn victim can have more than one type of burn resulting from a single accident.

Children are commonly burned by hot liquids, cooking and electrical equipment, open fires, matches, chemicals such as strong detergents and acids, and overexposure to the sun. See 13-13.

### First-degree burns

*First-degree burns* are burns to the top layer of skin. They are the least severe of all burns. They may result from brief contact with hot objects, overexposure to the sun, or scalding by hot water or steam. Common signs include redness or mild discoloration, pain, and mild

13-13 Care must be taken to keep children safe around items that cause burns.

swelling. Healing is normally rapid because the burn does not go deep.

Special medical treatment is not needed for first-degree burns. Applying cold water to the burn may help relieve some pain.

### Second-degree burns

*Second-degree burns* cause damage to underlying layers of skin. These burns are more serious than first-degree burns. They are caused by extreme overexposure to the sun, contact with hot liquids, and contact with flash fires from gasoline, kerosene, and other products.

Second-degree burns are marked by pain, blistering, swelling, and discoloration. Over several days, the burn is likely to swell a great deal. Due to the severity of these burns, they require medical treatment. Do not treat the burn by breaking blisters or by placing an ointment on the burn. This may cause infection. If infection arises in the wound, a second-degree burn can quickly become a third-degree burn.

### Third-degree burns

*Third-degree burns* destroy the skin layer and nerve endings. They can be caused by open flames, burning clothing, immersion in hot water, contact with hot objects, and contact with live electrical wires.

Third-degree burns are very serious. They require prompt medical attention. An ambulance should be called at once.

### Sunburn

Children can get first- or second-degree burns from exposure to the sun's ultraviolet rays. There is usually a 3 to 12 hour lapse in time between exposure and development of sunburn. Sunburn commonly does not require a hospital stay. However, sunburn can cause a child to be out of school several days due to swelling, pain, headache, and fever.

## SPLINTERS

Children often get splinters. It will be your job to remove them. A pair of tweezers is the best tool for this process. Remove splinters at the same angle they entered the skin.

If you cannot remove a splinter, consult a doctor. Do not put any ointment or antiseptic on it. Instead, clean the area with soap and water. Then cover with a sterile bandage until a doctor can see it.

## INSECT STINGS

Wasps, bees, hornets, yellow jackets, and fire ants are all stinging insects. The stings are painful to all children. And for children who are allergic to insect stings, a sting can be fatal. React quickly when a child has been stung. Most deaths from insect stings occur within two hours of the incident.

A rash or swelling is usually the sign of a mild allergic reaction. A condition called *anophylactic shock* results from an extremely allergic reaction.

Shock symptoms develop quickly. These symptoms include weakness and collapse. Other signs include problems breathing, a drop in blood pressure, and severe itching. Abdominal cramping, which may be followed by vomiting, can also occur. Watch the child closely. If you notice any of these signs get prompt medical help.

Children who are allergic to stings and have been stung before may have their own medication and injection equipment. Make sure that it is available for emergencies. When you leave the school grounds, take the equipment.

## CHOKING

Young children, especially those under four years of age, often put small objects in their mouths. Young children may also put too much food in their mouths at one time. In either of these cases, the object or food can get lodged in the windpipe, causing choking.

The best way for the child to get rid of the blockage is to cough it up. If the child can cry or talk, it may be best to wait and see if the child can dislodge the object on his or her own.

If, however, you see that the child is not able to breathe or speak, take immediate emergency steps. The procedure often used in choking emergencies is called the Heimlich Maneuver or the obstructed airway maneuver, 13-14.

# First Aid For Choking

**1**

- **ASK: Are you choking?**
- If victim cannot breathe, cough, or speak...

**2**

- **Give the Heimlich Maneuver.**
- Stand behind the victim.
- Wrap your arms around the victim's waist.
- Make a fist with one hand. PLACE your FIST (thumbside) against the victim's stomach in the midline just ABOVE THE NAVEL AND WELL BELOW THE RIB MARGIN.
- Grasp your fist with your other hand.
- PRESS INTO STOMACH WITH A QUICK UPWARD THRUST.

**3**

- **Repeat thrust if necessary.**

**4**

- **If a victim has become unconscious:**
- Sweep the mouth.

**5**

- Attempt rescue breathing.

**6**

- Give 6-10 abdominal thrusts.
- Repeat Steps 4, 5, and 6 as necessary.

American Red Cross

**LOCAL EMERGENCY TELEPHONE NUMBER:** _____

Everyone should learn how to perform the steps above for choking and how to give rescue breathing and CPR. Call your local American Red Cross chapter for information on these and other first aid techniques.
Caution: The Heimlich Maneuver (abdominal thrust) may cause injury.
Do not *practice* on people.

13-14 The Heimlich Maneuver can save the life of a choking child.

## DENTAL EMERGENCIES

Dental emergencies include toothaches, cut or bit tongues, lips, or cheeks, knocked out permanent teeth, and broken teeth. With any of these problems, take quick action and remain calm.

### Toothache

If a child complains of a toothache, help the child rinse the affected area with water. Apply cold compresses if the face is swollen. Urge the parents to take the child to a dentist.

### Cut or bit lip, tongue, or cheek

Apply ice to the injured area. If you see blood, hold a clean gauze or cloth over the area. Gently apply pressure. Contact the child's parents if the bleeding does not stop in fifteen minutes. If the cut is severe, arrange to take the child to an emergency room for treatment.

### Knocked out permanent tooth

To provide emergency care for a knocked out permanent tooth, first find the tooth. Pick it up by the crown, not the roots. If the tooth is dirty, rinse it. However, avoid unnecessary handling. Keep the tooth moist. If the tooth is not broken, put it back in its socket. Some children may refuse to let you do this. In that case, place the tooth in a cup of water. Call the child's parents right away. In order to save the tooth, the child must see a dentist at once.

### Broken tooth

If a child breaks or chips a tooth, report it to the parents. The parents can decide whether a dentist should be consulted.

## HEAD LICE

To maintain a healthly environment, you will need to recognize head lice. *Head lice* are small bugs that make their home on the hair and scalp. They grow small round eggs, called nits that feed on human blood. In roughly one month, head lice complete their life cycle. But each generation will multiply, and create a new group of lice. During its thirty day life, the head louse can produce as many as six eggs per day. As a result, hundreds of lice may be produced from one louse.

Head lice are small, about one-tenth to one-eighth of an inch in length. They have no wings and do not fly. They have six pairs of hooks in their mouth. With these hooks, they attach themselves to the hair shaft. Short legs and large claws help them keep their grip on hair.

Head lice can spread from one infected person to another person through direct contact with the hair. Combs, brushes, hats, and beddings are key sources of transport.

It is difficult to see head lice with the naked eye. However, there are several signs you can recognize. See 13-15.

The best way to get rid of head lice is to seek medical help. Most physicians prescribe a medical shampoo. They suggest the shampoo be used in the manner outlined in 13-16.

Doctors also suggest boiling or dry cleaning all personal items such as hats, combs, brushes, clothing, and bedding.

If one child in your classroom has had lice, it is likely that other children will get it too. In some areas, a county or city nurse will conduct daily inspections at a center that has had an outbreak.

Send notices home to all parents if even one child has been infected with head lice. An example of a notice is shown in 13-17. Provide space to include the child's name, illness exposed to, and date.

---

### SIGNS OF HEAD LICE

- A constant itch of the scalp. Often the child will also have infected scratches or even a rash on the scalp.
- Small, silvery eggs attached to individual hairs. Usually a hand lens, or magnifying glass, will help reveal these.
- In severe cases, swollen lymph glands may appear in the neck or under the arm.

13-15 These signs can help you identify cases of head lice.

## STEPS FOR TREATING HEAD LICE WITH MEDICATED SHAMPOO

1. Apply about two tablespoons of the medicated shampoo to the hair.
2. Apply a small amount of warm water.
3. Work the shampoo into a good lather for a minimum of four minutes.
4. Rinse the hair thoroughly.
5. Using a clean towel to avoid reinfestation, dry the hair.
6. Thoroughly comb the hair with a clean, fine-tooth comb.

13-16 Medicated shampoo and proper shampooing techniques help eliminate head lice.

## VOMITING

Children often vomit when ill. After the child has vomited, he or she will need a place to rest and keep warm. The child may request foods and drinks. However, only provide sips of water. Any other foods may prompt more vomiting.

Record the number of times the child vomits and the amount thrown up. At the same time, remove the child from the group. Always report any continued vomiting to parents.

## TEMPERATURE EMERGENCY

The human body normally maintains a constant internal temperature of 98.6 °F. Normal temperatures range, however, from 97 °F to

Dear Parent:

This is to notify you that your child, _____ was exposed to _____ on _____ at the Child and Family Study Center.

Signed_____
(Head Teacher)

Date _____

13-17 It is important that you inform parents when their children have been exposed to head lice or any other communicable disease.

just under 100 °F. For this reason, it is important to have each child's normal temperature recorded on a health form.

A slight change in a child's temperature is a signal that the body is preparing against illness. A temperature at least two degrees above normal is significant. Most, but not all, young children will run a higher fever than adults.

A child may have a slight rise in temperature for several reasons. For example, the presence of infection raises a child's temperature. Too much physical activity will also raise a temperature. Temperature also may vary depending upon the time of the day. Temperatures are somewhat lower in the morning than the evening.

Call the parents right away if a child has a fever. Report any other unusual behavior.

## ISOLATION AREA

An isolation area or room is needed in every early childhood center. Some states require that centers have isolation rooms. Whenever a child becomes ill, he or she should be moved into this area at once.

Due to a lack of space, some centers do not have a special room for this purpose. Instead, a cot in the director's office is used for these emergencies.

## SPECIAL HEALTH CONCERNS

If a child with a special physical condition is enrolled in the program, you will need to make special plans for this child's health and well-being. Begin by discussing the child's condition with the parents. Be certain you understand what the condition is and what type of emergencies may arise. Find out what approach the center needs to take. Does the child require a special diet? Medication? Specific exercise? Also discuss with the parents how you can help the child feel comfortable.

### Diabetes

*Diabetes* is a disease in which the body cannot properly control the level of sugar in the blood. Having too much or too little blood sugar can cause serious health problems.

Children with diabetes cannot produce enough insulin. *Insulin* is a hormone that is needed to keep sugar in the blood at a proper level. As insulin is released, the blood sugar level drops. Healthy people produce insulin when blood sugar level gets too high. But diabetic children do not. To correct this problem, diabetic children are given insulin injections. But they must also balance food intake and exercise. If these are not balanced, an insulin reaction may occur.

Symptoms of an insulin reaction vary. Hunger, irritability, headaches, confusion, fatigue, crying, sweating, and drowsiness are all symptoms. With severe reactions, the child may pass out. If this happens, take the child to an emergency room or call a doctor at once. This condition is dangerous.

To avoid an insulin reaction, space the child's meals and snacks throughout the day. Glucose levels will remain constant when this is done. On days when the child exercises a great deal, food intake must be increased. This is because exercise decreases the amount of insulin needed and lowers glucose levels. Keep a supply of candy, soft drinks, and juice for the child to eat in case of an insulin reaction.

### Epilepsy

*Epilepsy* is a condition in which a person has periodic seizures. There are two types of seizures. *Grand mal seizures* consist of repeated convulsions, or jerking, over the entire body. *Petit mal seizures* are milder than grand mal. The person may have a few muscles twitch briefly or may become confused with the surroundings.

Most seizures can be prevented with proper medical care. If a child in your program has epilepsy, discuss treatment with the parents. You may be required to give medication or take other action.

If a child has a grand mal seizure, your main duty is to make sure the child does not injure himself or herself. Clear the area around the child. Make sure the child stays lying down and keeps breathing. Do not place any object in the child's mouth during the seizure. Watch the child until the seizure is over. Then loosen any tight clothing around the child's neck. Take the child to a quiet place. Let the child rest on a cot or bed.

Contact the child's parents or doctor after any seizure, even a petit mal. The doctor may want to know what was happening before the seizure. This information may help the doctor find new ways to prevent further seizures. Therefore, try to record as many facts as you can about the time right before the seizure, as soon as you have a chance.

## SUMMARY

Children's health can be protected, maintained, and improved in many ways during each day at the center. This is a very important part of the job as a teacher.

The best way to begin guiding children's health is by setting health policies. Policies might include requiring all children enrolled to have medical exams and immunizations. Contacting parents might also be addressed in your health policy.

The second step in guiding health is having knowledge of various illnesses and diseases. You will need to know how to control transmittable illnesses and diseases. You also will need to know what steps you should take in an emergency.

Protecting, maintaining, and even improving health is a major responsibility of the job of a teacher. The teacher is trusted with the well-being of many children.

# to Know

abrasion
anophylactic shock
bacteria
burn
closed wound
communicable diseases
diabetes
epilepsy
first-degree burn
food poisoning

grand mal seizure
head lice
insulin
open wound
petit mal seizure
policy
rabies
second-degree burn
third-degree burn
wound

# to Review

1. What will a preadmission medical exam help you learn about a child being enrolled?

2. List the immunization(s) needed for preschoolers at the following ages:
   a. 2 months.
   b. 4 months.
   c. 6 months.
   d. 15 months.
   e. 18 months.
   f. 4-6 years.

3. True or false. Each child should be provided with a washable cot or bed and clean sheets for napping.

4. During a health inspection observe for:
   a. Coughing.
   b. Runny nose.
   c. Rash.
   d. All of the above.

5. What are six signs of infection?

6. True or false. Parents should be contacted whenever a child shows symptoms of illness.

7. What emergency numbers should be posted by the center telephone?

8. What are the signs and symptoms of conjunctivitis (pink eye)?

9. The incubation period for influenza is from _____ to _____ hours.

10. Mononucleosis is communicable for how long?

11. True or false. The hygiene of staff does not affect the occurrence of food-borne illnesses.

12. Bacteria prefer (acid, nonacid) foods.

13. What is food poisoning?

14. To prevent diseases transmitted by food:
    a. Use home-canned food.
    b. Store hot food at 120°F.
    c. Thaw food in a refrigerator.
    d. Cook slimy meats immediately.

15. In order to prevent the growth of bacteria, keep foods at a temperature above _____ or below _____ °F.

16. Check the contents of the first aid kit:
    a. Whenever it is used.
    b. Once a month.
    c. Once a year.
    d. Twice a year.

17. A _____ is damage to the surface of the skin or body tissue.

18. True or false. Most closed wounds involve the soft tissue under the skin.

19. An _____ is a scrape resulting in damage to part of the skin.

20. What is the most serious burn?

21. How can the pain of a first-degree burn be relieved?

22. Signs of shock from an insect sting may include:
    a. Weakness.
    b. Severe itching.
    c. Vomiting.
    d. All of the above.

23. What is the best way for a child to get rid of blockage in the windpipe?

24. List two symptoms of head lice.

25. _____ is a hormone that keeps sugar in the blood at a proper level.

26. What is epilepsy?

# to Do

1. Invite a first aid instructor to give a demonstration on the Heimlich Maneuver.

2. Prepare a handout listing the health policies of a center for preschool children.

3. Stage a panel discussion on ways of promoting a healthy environment for young children.

4. Do a research paper on diabetes or epilepsy. Explain the illness itself and dispel any commonly believed untruths about the illness. Explain various treatments for the illness.

# part *4*

# Learning Experiences for Children

Providing a variety of learning experiences helps children learn and grow in many ways. As you read this part, you will learn techniques for guiding the following types of experiences:
- Art.
- Storytelling.
- Sociodramatic play and puppetry.
- Manuscript writing.
- Math.
- Science.
- Social studies.
- Food.
- Music and movement.
- Field trips.

Each chapter will give you guidelines for planning and supervising activities. You will read many ideas for specific activities to try with children. You will also discover what types of supplies and resources you will need to conduct these activities.

# Chapter 14

# Guiding Art Experiences

After studying this chapter, you will be able to:

☐ Discuss how art experiences affect physical, social, emotional, and intellectual growth.

☐ Outline at least three ways to guide art experiences.

☐ Explain the stages of art skill development.

☐ Compile a list of art supplies needed for a well-stocked classroom.

☐ Make tempera paint, paste, and play dough using recipes.

☐ Describe a variety of painting activities.

Preschool children are curious about their world. They love to learn about it through hands-on activities. For them, art activities can be learning opportunities. These children can think, plan, and create their own ideas. Art experiences provide children the pleasure of working with and molding materials. And art fulfills children's need for movement, self-expression, and achievement.

Art promotes physical, social, emotional, and intellectual growth in children. Physical growth is promoted through the movements done in painting, coloring, drawing, and even scribbling, 14-1. All these motions improve small muscle skills. When children mold clay, they gain control of their fingers and hand muscles. All art activities foster motor and hand-eye coordination. This in turn helps growth in other areas.

Social growth is also promoted by art. Children learn responsibility. For example, they learn that they must put on their smocks before painting. They also learn that they must put their work in a safe storage space when they are finished. Children also learn to work and share with others, 14-2. In many programs, several children will share one container of paint or a box of crayons. And they learn to respect the property of others.

Art experiences also promote emotional growth. Through a creative activity, children are allowed to express emotions. For example, pounding at the woodworking bench, hitting play dough, or scribbling with crayons allows angry children to express their frustrations in an acceptable way. Children also have the chance to choose their own activity. For instance, during a painting session children decide what they will paint. Their choice—painting a pet, a friend, or a flower—are often expressions of their feelings.

Finally, intellectual growth is promoted through art experiences. Children explore and experiment with many materials and tools. Through this process they learn important concepts such as color, size, texture, and shape. Skills such as cutting and drawing are also learned through manipulation and control of tools. Rolling, smelling, rubbing, pounding, and tearing all use visual and tactile senses. *Tactile senses* are those that relate to touch.

## TECHNIQUES FOR GUIDING ART EXPERIENCES

As a caregiver, you must be creative in your approach to art. You must observe in order to find new ways to expand children's learning experiences. Creative growth is promoted through careful choice of age-appropriate activities. A good art program allows children to express their ideas. It also provides them with time to experiment and explore. These experiences should involve all five senses: sight, smell, taste, touch, and hearing.

Helping children during art sessions is an important task. If done properly, children will accept your help. If done improperly, however, children will come to think of you as an intruder. For instance, Rudy had just started cutting out paper shapes. Her teacher came by at that time and finished cutting one of the shapes for her. Rudy walked away from the table. She did not need the teacher's help at that time. She preferred to do the cutting herself. Tasks done for or forced on children often cause tension and displeasure.

14-1 Children improve hand-eye coordination during art activities that use small muscles.

14-2 Cooperation is an important skill learned during art activities.

To foster independence, start each session by telling the children what supplies are available that day. Encourage them to use the supplies, 14-3. For instance, if they have never worked with cotton balls, tell them, "I think you will enjoy painting with cotton balls. They are very soft."

As you walk through the class, observe what the children are doing. However, it is best not to ask them what they are making. They might just be experimenting with different tools and supplies. In this case, they do not know what they are making. Keep in mind that some children lack the language skills needed to explain their artwork. Asking questions may make them uneasy.

Let children decide when their work is finished. Take them at their word. Do not urge them to fill up space or add to their work. This decreases their pride and confidence.

Always remember to praise the children's work. However, avoid singling out one child's work as being the best. Instead, use praise that invites everyone to respect everyone else's work. For instance, you might say, "Mary loves red and blue," or "Mark's colors are happy colors."

### Stages of art skill development

Children move through three distinct stages as they build art skills. These stages are scribbles, basic forms, and first drawings. Knowing these stages helps child care workers plan activities that reflect children's skill level.

**Scribbles.** The first stage in art skills most often occurs between 15 months and 3 years of age. Children's motor control and hand-eye coordination are not well developed yet. However, they can make zigzags, whirls, and circles. In the scribble stage, children do not make the connection between the marks on the paper and their own movements. The scribbles that are made are by-products of the experience.

To help children in this stage, make them aware of their movements. Comment on how hard they press their pencils, how fast they move their arms back and forth, or how large they make their movements. Such remarks help children make the connection between their actions and the art they make.

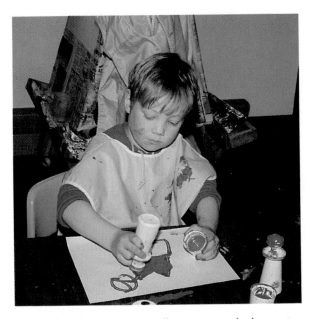

14-3 Devise new supplies to use during art sessions and show children how to use them.

Comments about the look of children's artwork are also helpful. For example, you may say, "This is a long line," or "This line has a curve." As you speak, trace some of the lines with your finger. The children's attention will focus on what they have made.

**Basic forms.** The second stage in art skill development of children is basic forms. This often occurs between ages three or four. Children learn basic forms such as ovals, rectangles, and circles. They now have more control over their movements and better hand-eye coordination. As a result, they can control the size and shape of a line.

At this stage, children also begin to see the connection between their movements and the marks they make. Before this time, children's scribbles were the result of the sheer pleasure of moving arm and hand. Now children connect those motions to their artwork. Children may even begin to name their drawings at this stage.

As in the scribble stage, you can help the children understand and talk about their work by commenting on their movements. For example, say "You are moving your arm in big circles." Or you might describe the end product. Say, "You have drawn a big picture."

**First drawings.** The third stage of art development occurs during the fourth and fifth years, 14-4. During this stage, children produce their first real drawings. They attempt to mimic their own view of the world. Using their skill with basic forms, they begin to create symbols of objects and events that they know. The drawings are often large. Objects are randomly placed. Color is unrealistic. Crudely drawn human figures with straight lines for arms and legs are common. Later, children often add animals, trees, houses, cars, boats, and airplanes to their artwork.

**Color selection.** In preschool children's artwork, color does not play an important part. The artwork is more important than the color. Often there is no relationship between the colors chosen and the objects in the artwork. Children choose colors they like as opposed to colors that mirror real life. An apple may be painted bright pink or an elephant red.

Studies show children do have color preferences. Beautiful colors, according to young children, include yellow, blue, orange, and green, 14-5. Brown, white, and black are labeled ugly. You may wish to keep a large supply of preferred colors on hand.

## ART SUPPLIES AND TOOLS

You have the option of buying or making your own art supplies and equipment. Most teachers need to purchase the basic tools: scissors, paint brushes, cookie cutters, easels, and paper punches. Most of these items can be purchased at thrift stores or garage sales. Other places you might wish to look for supplies and tools include:

- Clothing factories (discarded spools, trimmings, fabric scraps).
- Newspaper or print shops (scrap paper).
- Garage and rummage sales.
- School supply and stationery stores (bulk quantities of paper, paint, glue, tape, paste, and clay).

14-4 First drawings represent a child's view of the world. Colors are often unrealistic. Notice the sun is blue.

14-5 Children prefer painting with such colors as yellow and green.

- Hardware stores (sandpaper, woodworking tools).
- Paint and decorating stores (paint chips, wallpaper books).
- Drugstores (tongue depressors, cotton balls, peppermint oil, used packing materials, pipe cleaners).
- Grocery stores (toothpicks, shelf paper, food coloring).

You might also wish to secure donations of these items from parents or from the stores themselves.

### Tempera paint

Tempera paint is used in many child care centers. It has a slight odor and tastes chalky. When dry, tempera tends to crack and peel. It can be purchased in both liquid and powdered form. Many teachers prefer powdered paint over liquid because powdered is cheaper. Powdered tempera paint is *water soluble*. This means it can be dissolved in water. Thickness of the mixed paint varies from a sticky paste to runny fluid. To avoid drips and runs, mix the paint to the consistency of thick cream. Consistency will also affect color.

To reduce costs, many teachers add bentonite, a thickening agent, to powdered tempera paint. *Bentonite* is a clay product. It can be purchased through landscape and gardening stores. Adding bentonite to powdered paint can save about eighty percent of paint costs.

Some teachers mix enough paint to last for a week or two. Others mix the paint each day. Whichever you prefer, remember to put the powdered paint in the container before you add the liquid. To avoid paint that is too thin, add only a small amount of liquid to the tempera while stirring constantly. This will make a very thick paste. Then slowly add more liquid until you get the thickness you want.

To prepare a large quantity of one color of tempera paint, use the recipe in 14-6. Some teachers do not wish to prepare a large amount of one paint color because they are not able to store it. Instead, they make a basic paint/bentonite mixture that can be mixed with any color. The recipe for this mixture is given in 14-7. You will notice that in this recipe, the powdered

paint is added to the liquid. This method differs from mixing tempera with a plain liquid (either water or pure bentonite).

### Brushes

Provide children with a number of paint brushes. They should range in size from 1/2 to 1 inch wide. The youngest children use the widest brushes. As their small muscle coordination improves, they can be given smaller brushes. Pieces of string, cotton swabs, and feathers may be used as paint brushes by older children.

### Easels

Sturdy, adjustable easels should be provided as a place to paint. Brushes and paint should be placed in an attached tray. Clamps or hooks

---

**TEMPERA PAINT**

7 to 10 tablespoons bentonite
A large bowl or jar
One-pound can powdered tempera
2 tablespoons soap flakes or detergent
3 cups liquid starch
Water

Place bentonite into large bowl or jar. Add to this entire contents of powdered tempera. Stir in soap flakes/detergent and liquid starch. Add water until desired consistency is obtained.

14-6 This recipe will yield a large amount of one color of tempera paint.

---

**BASIC BENTONITE**

3/4 cup powdered detergent
1 cup powdered bentonite
2 quarts water

Mix all ingredients using a beater or wire whip. Place mixture into crock or plastic container. Let stand for two or three days. When you are ready to mix paint, remove some basic bentonite from container and add enough tempera to make desired color.

14-7 Use this recipe to make bentonite, a paint extender.

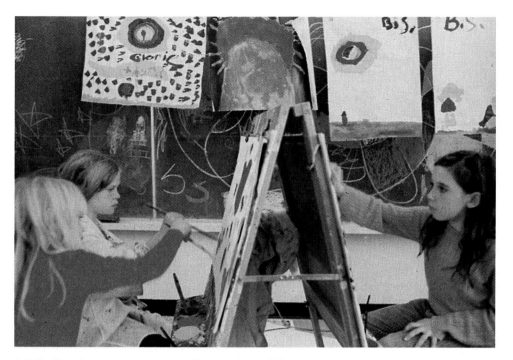

14-8 Easels are a space saving and useful supply. They can be used to hold paper for painting or drawing activities.

at the top of the easels should be used to hold the paper in place, 14-8. The sides of the easel should be adjusted so that they are angled or slant outward. This reduces the dripping and running of paint.

**Crayons, chalk, and felt markers**

Children enjoy using crayons, chalk, and felt markers. However, these items are harder to use than paint. As a rule, these tools need to be pushed hard with small muscles that are not well-developed in young children. Paint, however, flows easily.

Crayons come in regular and kindergarten sizes. Kindergarten size crayons are round, large, and flat on one side. These crayons do not break easily, nor do they roll off tables or other surfaces. Crayons can be stored in bowls, baskets, or boxes.

Chalk is available both in an art and blackboard form. Art chalk comes in a variety of sizes. As with crayons, chalk can be purchased in large, fat sticks. Choose basic colors that are clear and brilliant. Be careful that children do not use art chalk on a blackboard. Marks from art chalk cannot be erased from a blackboard. Store chalk in baskets, boxes, trays, or bowls.

Felt markers come with washable or waterproof inks. Always buy washable ink markers for use in day care centers, 14-9. Be sure that any markers you buy have tight caps. This prevents the markers from drying out. Remind children to replace the caps after use.

**Paper**

There are many types of paper that can be used successfully for art activities. Included are newsprint, manila paper, construction paper, wallpaper, cardboard, and old newspaper. Other types of paper not often considered for art activities are listed in 14-10.

The least costly paper is newsprint. It is durable and easy to use. Roll ends of newsprint

14-9 Children enjoy using markers. This can be a messy activity; make sure the ink is washable.

can be bought at little or no cost from local newspaper printers. Cut the large sheets into the size sheets you want. To determine the size of the paper remember younger children have poorer muscle control. As a result, they need large surfaces on which to paint or draw. A good size for easel painting is 18- by 24-inch sheets.

### Coloring books

Studies show that coloring books have a negative effect on children's creativity. The value of art as a way to express emotion is lost when children are confined to pages of a coloring book. Children become self-conscious and doubtful about their art talents. For example, Sara colors in the outline of a kitten in a coloring book. The next time she is asked to draw something, she recalls the perfect kitten from the coloring book page. She knows she

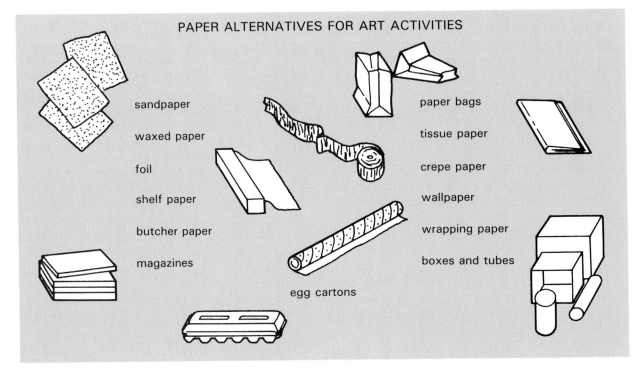

PAPER ALTERNATIVES FOR ART ACTIVITIES

sandpaper

waxed paper

foil

shelf paper

butcher paper

magazines

egg cartons

paper bags

tissue paper

crepe paper

wallpaper

wrapping paper

boxes and tubes

14-10 Paper for use in art activities comes in many forms. Some of these types of paper can be obtained for little or no cost.

could not draw that perfect kitten. She says, "I cannot draw very well." Lacking confidence in her own talents, Sara may not attempt to make many of her own drawings.

Some teachers see no harm in using coloring books. Coloring books are easy to buy and keep on hand. Some teachers also feel that their children enjoy working in coloring books. However, coloring books do not enhance art skills. For more enriching art experiences, rely on materials that allow children to explore.

## Paste

Paste can be made or bought. Many teachers prefer to buy paste by the gallon which is more economical. Other teachers prefer to make their own paste, 14-11.

## Glue

Glue is more permanent than paste, and often more costly. If purchased by the gallon, it is a better bargain. Many building supply stores carry gallon containers of glue.

Glue is difficult to remove from clothes, carpeting, and art tables. Therefore, wipe up spills immediately.

## Clean-up tools

Keep clean-up tools in the art area. Include small buckets, sponge mops, and various sizes of sponges. Keep supplies within children's reach. Cut mop handles down so they are child-sized. This will encourage children to be responsible for cleaning up.

## Space and storage

Well-planned space is needed to encourage children to use art areas. Storage and display areas for artwork are part of a well-planned space. Bookshelves can be used to store **staple supplies.** These supplies include paper, scissors, paste, glue, collage materials, crayons, watercolor markers, chalk, tape, and paint.

Containers are needed to store paint, paste, scissors, and collage materials, 14-12. Baby food jars, plastic cups, and plastic bowls are often used to store tempera paint. Shallow dishes, including empty meat trays and frozen food containers, can be used in the art area to hold paint during painting activities. After use, the paint can be covered for storage.

Paste containers may be small enough for one child or large enough for a group to use. The size will depend on the activity. Empty catsup or mustard squeeze bottles and baby food jars are useful for individual activities. Foil or small plastic dishes are useful for several children to use at one time.

Scissors should be stored within easy reach. Special scissor holders may be bought. They

---

> **PASTE**
>
> 1 cup cold water
> 1 cup flour
> 2 1/4 cups boiling water
> 1 teaspoon powdered alum
> 3/4 teaspoon oil of wintergreen (optional)
>
> Mix the cold water with the flour, stirring until smooth. Continue stirring while adding boiling water. Cook mixture on low heat in a double boiler until smooth. At this time, the mixture should look slightly bluish-gray and shiny. Remove from heat and add oil of wintergreen for an interesting smell. Store in a cool place.

14-11 Making paste is easy and can be a source of budget savings.

14-12 Store paint in well-marked, see-through containers.

can also be made by the staff. Egg cartons, turned upside down, are often used to hold scissors.

Collage materials need to be well-organized to appeal to children. They should be sorted and placed in clear plastic boxes, shoe boxes, plastic dishpans, or baskets. Place these containers on a shelf within eye level of the children.

## PAINTING ACTIVITIES

To learn what painting means to young children, listen and watch. You will note that most children find their work pleasing. The artwork of a two-year-old is different than that of a four-year-old. Children's paintings change from simple dots and strokes to crude figures as they move through art development. Some children enjoy moving the tools. Other children enjoy the feelings and visual aspects, 14-13.

Consider some of the children you might meet. Noah, a two-year-old, seems to be fascinated by the painting process. He dips his brush and paints, making large circles over his entire paper. His friend, Renee, delights in moving her brush back and forth. When she dips her brush into different colors, she ignores the cleaning process.

Mark, an active three-year-old, makes large dots and zigzags all over his paper. He pays little attention to the paint color but carefully watches his strokes. Heidi, another three-year-old, paints different colors on top of each other. As a result, her paper becomes soaked. At this point, she uses her hand to feel the paint. Then she proceeds to remove her painting from the easel. During this process, it tears. This does not bother Heidi. Like most three-year-olds, she is interested in the process, not the product.

Jon, a highly verbal five-year-old, is comfortable handling the brush. He paints a man by making a circle face. Then he paints straight lines to represent legs. He uses a smaller circle for a mouth, two large round dots for eyes, and a V-shaped figure for a nose. As he paints, he keeps renaming his

14-13 Many children enjoy the feel of paint.

figure and inventing related stories. First, he tells the child standing next to him that the figure is a police officer. Later, he claims the same figure is a fire fighter.

Children like Jon are not unusual. Some comment to themselves as they paint. They appear to be carrying on a conversation with their painting. These comments are useful. They tell you what the child feels and thinks. Sometimes children are eager to discuss their artwork; other times, they are not.

There are many types of painting activities that children will be eager to do. Included are easel, finger, string, texture, salt, mono, spice, and chalk painting. Children may also like to paint using vegetables. This process is called vegetable printing. From these experiences, children learn to apply the correct amounts of paint and to recognize color and shapes.

### Easel painting

Easel painting should be a daily activity in all early childhood programs. Provide an easel, paper, brushes, and paint. Easels should be adjusted to the correct height for the children. Brushes with long handles (about twelve inches) in a variety of sizes should be provided on the easel tray. The size of the paper you give the children will depend on the activity being done and age of the children. For young children, provide large sheets of newsprint. Sheets of this size will encourage the use of large muscles. On special occasions, you may wish to provide colored paper and white tempera.

To ensure success in easel painting plan the session ahead of time. Provide only a small amount of paint since children do spill. Pour in only enough paint to cover the bottom of the container. This will save clean-up time. Make only one color of paint available for early experiences. When a second color is added, provide a brush for each container.

Permit only one child to use each easel. Encourage children to wear smocks, 14-14. Push sleeves above elbows to prevent paint from getting on clothing.

Teach young children how to use the paint brush. Gently dip the brush into the paint con-

tainer. Then wipe the brush on the side of the container. This will rid the brush of extra paint. As children gain skill, give them smaller brushes and pieces of paper to work with. Wash brushes after use. Until they are used again, place them with handles down in a storage container. This allows the bristles to dry.

**Finger painting**

Finger painting is a sensory experience. It promotes expression and release of feelings. It is one of the most satisfying experiences for young children. Some may resist their first experience because they fear getting dirty. These same children, after having the chance to observe, may begin painting with one finger. Later, when they become comfortable, they will use their hands and arms as brushes.

Finger painting requires more supervision than most other painting activities. For this reason, work with no more than four children at a time. Children need to stay at the table until they are finished painting. Hands must be washed immediately after painting.

Finger paint recipes are given in 14-15.

Finger paint may also be made from instant pudding, soap flakes whipped with water, partially-set jello, and instant shaving cream. Children enjoy using a variety of paints.

**String painting**

To prepare for string painting, cut several pieces of heavy yarn or string. Place a tray, or trays, of colored tempera paint and paper on the table. Show the children how to slide the yarn through the paint and across the piece of paper. Another technique is to place the string in a folded piece of paper and pull it out.

**Mono painting**

A mono painting starts with a regular finger painting. After this, an 8 x 12" piece of paper is placed over the finger painting. The papers are patted together, then pulled apart.

**Chalk painting**

To make chalk paintings, dip chalk into water and draw on construction paper. Use chalk at least one inch thick. Choose construc-

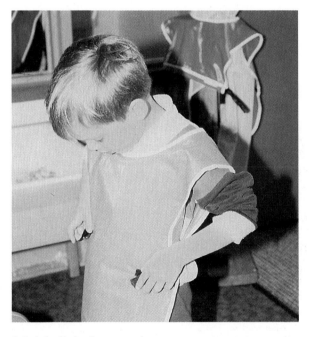

14-14 Painting can become very messy so children should wear smocks.

## Speedy finger paint

1 cup of laundry starch
3 cups of soap flakes
1 cup cold water

Mix all ingredients together. If colored finger paint is desired add food coloring or colored tempera.

## Blender finger paint

One pound powdered tempera paint
1/4 cup liquid starch
1/3 cup water
1 tablespoon of powdered laundry detergent

Place in blender. Mix until finger paint is blended well.

## Cornstarch finger paint

One cup of dry starch
1/2 cup water
1 1/2 cups boiling water
3/4 cup powdered laundry detergent

Mix starch and 1/2 cup water in heat-resistant bowl. Add 1 1/2 cups boiling water while stirring rapidly. Blend in 3/4 cup powdered laundry detergent until smooth.

14-15 Using recipes allows you to make the type and color of finger paint you need.

tion paper based on the color chalk being used. Add vinegar to the water to deepen the color of the chalk.

## Texture painting

Make paint for texture painting using liquid tempera or mixing powdered tempera with liquid starch. To this mixture, add sand, sawdust, or coffee grounds. For best results, the paint should be thick.

## Salt painting

Materials needed for salt painting include construction paper or cardboard, paste or glue, cotton swabs or tongue depressors, and salt mixed with colored tempera in shakers.

Have the children spread paste or glue on the paper. Then have them shake the salt mixture onto the glue or paste. Shake off excess paint and set aside to dry.

## Spice painting

Spice painting results in a scented painting. Prepare the mixture by adding a small amount of water to liquid glue. Give each child enough glue to spread over their piece of paper. They can use their fingers to do this. Then have them shake spices onto the paper. When it dries it will look as interesting as it smells.

Cinnamon, onion powder, garlic powder, and oregano all make aromatic paintings. For texture, use bay leaves, cloves, or coffee grounds. The center budget may dictate which and how many spices you can use. In addition, consideration must be given to any policies toward the use of food. Some directors tend to discourage this type of food use.

## Vegetable printing

*Vegetable printing* involves dipping a mold into paint and then pressing the mold onto a surface. See 14-16. This makes a print. The molds in vegetable printing are made from vegetables. They are washed and dried, then cut in half. Place the cut vegetables on the table, along with trays of paint. Children dip the vegetables into the paint and then press them onto paper.

If school policy limits the use of food for art activities, common household items may also be used. Try using spools, clothespins, pieces of oddly shaped wood, pine cones, and jar lids.

## MOLDING

Play dough and clay are materials that can be molded and formed. Dough has a softer texture than clay. Children enjoy the tactile appeal of these materials. They may roll, pound, feel, squeeze, and tear the material. They will often use pans, cookie cutters, and rolling pins to make pies, cookies, and other baked goods from these materials.

**Clay.** Clay must be bought. It is difficult to make. Mixed properly, it should be stored in a plastic bag to prevent drying. Clay can be used on large pieces of tile to save clean-up time.

**Play dough.** Play dough is soft and pliable. It offers little resistance to pressure. Children's play with this material reflects their level of development. Two-year-old children pull, beat, push, and squeeze play dough. When children are about three years of age, they make balls and snake-like shapes. By age four, children can make complex forms, some of which they name. By age five, children will announce what they are going to make before they begin.

Each type of play dough has different features. Provide the children with a number of types by using the recipes in 14-17. You can vary these play doughs even further by adding rice, corn meal, pebbles, sand, oats, and coffee grounds.

## CUTTING

Children need time, supplies, and space each day for cutting. Young children learn to cut because they enjoy working scissors. At first, children just snip in a straight line. Provide strips of construction paper or wrapping paper. The paper should be long enough so the children may hold fast to one end of it. Avoid heavy wrapping paper, corrugated paper or vinyl paper. Children do not have enough small muscle strength to cut through these materials. As children progress they may wish to cut in curves. This requires good hand-eye coordination.

14-16 Children like to make prints using vegetables and other objects.

---

**PLAY DOUGHS**

**Refrigerator play dough**

1 cup salt
2 cups flour
1 tablespoon alum (optional, a preservative)
1 cup water
3 tablespoons oil
Food coloring or tempera

Mix salt, flour, and alum. Add oil, water, and coloring, if desired, and mix. Check the consistency. If sticky, add more flour. Store in a tightly covered container in the refrigerator.

**Sawdust dough**

3 cups flour
2 cups sawdust
1 cup salt

Mix the three ingredients together. Add water as needed to form a soft dough.

**Cooked play dough**

1 cup salt
1/2 cup flour
1 cup water

Mix ingredients together in a pan. Cook over medium heat, stirring constantly. Remove the mixture from the heat when it becomes thick and rubbery. After cooling, the mixture will not be as sticky. Store in an air-tight container.

14-17 Varying the types of play dough you make helps give children a variety of sensory experiences.

Have children work with one type of paper. This allows them to master handling one type of material and tool. To avoid failure, give children quality scissors. Provide left-handed children with proper scissors. Mark these scissors with colored tape. All scissors should have rounded tips.

## COLLAGES

Collages are arrangements of many materials. Making collages gives children the chance to make choices. They decide what material will be placed where. Collages also introduce many materials of contrasting colors and textures to children. Materials that can be used in collages are listed in 14-18.

The base material for collages should be heavy. Construction paper or cardboard are ideal. Arrange collage materials in attractive containers. Children can go through these containers choosing items for their collages.

Remember to provide paste or glue. Glue is best because it can hold heavier objects, such as buttons. To add interest, tint the glue with food coloring or tempera paint.

Provide good scissors. Children can then change the shape of materials. Also provide felt pens, chalk, and crayons.

## SUMMARY

For young children, art sessions are great learning experiences. Through their own creativity, children can learn how to express their emotions and ideas. They also grow physically and emotionally.

The teacher has an important job in guiding art experiences. The teacher will decide what types of activities will be done and how. A variety of materials and techniques should be used. Knowing how to carry out this task so children benefit from the experience is important for the teacher.

**OBJECTS FOR COLLAGES**

| | | |
|---|---|---|
| buttons | suede | leaves |
| corks | leather | tree bark |
| yarn | plastic | pebbles |
| shoelaces | felt | seeds |
| feathers | fabric | shells |
| sponges | netting | twigs |
| straw | styrofoam packing | cotton balls |
| tin foil | material | paper plates |
| paper of all kinds | magazine pictures | egg cartons |
| paper cups | paper bags | |
| doilies | baking cups | |

14-18 The types of items used in collages are nearly limitless. Several items are listed here. What other interesting things could be used?

## to Know

## to Review

1. Art promotes _____ growth in children.
   a. Physical.
   b. Social.
   c. Emotional.
   d. Intellectual.
   e. All of the above.
2. _____ _____ relate to the sense of touch.
3. True or false. Helping children during art experiences should be avoided.
4. Name the stages of art skill development. Explain one stage in detail.
5. Which of the following colors do young children consider to be beautiful?
   a. White.
   b. Brown.
   c. Orange.
   d. All of the above.
6. List the art supplies and tools that can be found at the following businesses.
   a. Hardware stores.
   b. Print shops.
   c. Drugstores.
   d. Clothing factories.
7. _____ _____ comes in liquid and powdered form, has a slight odor, and tastes chalky.
8. _____ is a thickening agent that can be added to powdered paint.

9. True or false. As children progress in art skills, paint brushes should become more narrow.
10. Why are chalk, markers, and crayons more difficult for children to use than paint?
11. Coloring books have a _____ effect on children's creativity.
12. _____ is more permanent than paste.
13. The greatest amount of supervision is required during:
    a. Easel painting.
    b. Finger painting.
    c. String painting.
    d. None of the above.
14. _____ is difficult to make.
15. True or false. Level of development is reflected in the way children play with play dough.
16. Base materials for collages should be _____.

## to Do

1. Collect children's drawings. Determine what stage of development each drawing represents. Give reasons for your conclusions.
2. Make a list of materials that could be collected through donation for use in art activities. Indicate how each item could be used.
3. Make a list of objects that could be used for printing activities.
4. Prepare and use each of the finger paint recipes. Discuss which has the best texture. Suggest methods for storing the paint.
5. Prepare each of the play dough recipes. Compute the cost to make each recipe. Compare these prices to the price of store-bought dough.

# Chapter 15

# Guiding Storytelling Experiences

After studying this chapter, you will be able to:
- ☐ Explain some advantages of storytelling.
- ☐ List the four types of children's books.
- ☐ Discuss the process of choosing children's books.
- ☐ Outline the steps to follow when reading aloud to children.
- ☐ Explain a variety of storytelling methods.

The words "once upon a time" contain magic for young children. The art of storytelling has delighted millions of children throughout the ages. By inviting children to share in a make-believe world of adventure, the storyteller provides a strong educational tool.

As a child care worker, *storytelling* is an important task. It involves reciting a story or reading from a book. In most centers, storytelling is routine. It is included every day in the schedule, 15-1. Fortunately for children, it is a valuable experience. They develop a love for both stories and books as a result of daily storytelling sessions. This in turn enhances language development.

## ADVANTAGES OF STORYTELLING

Storytelling helps children with many skills. Among these skills, storytelling helps young children:
- Understand other people.
- Develop an enjoyment of books.
- Build correct concepts of objects and ideas.
- Form new ideas.
- Present information properly.
- Develop an appreciation of beautiful things.

- Increase their vocabulary.
- Desire to read.

Carefully chosen stories are a key part of the storytelling experience. Stories that draw on children's backgrounds help them understand themselves better. Children learn the words that describe feelings and experiences they have. They learn to think about familiar situations in new ways. Stories invite children to explore and wonder about their world.

Carefully chosen stories also provide models of acceptable behavior and positive social relationships. When exposed to a variety of characters, children learn that other people often feel the same way that they do. They learn how these people express their feelings. They become more understanding of the needs of others.

Storytelling also helps children learn reading skills. For example, as a teacher reads aloud from a book children learn to follow the pages from left to right and top to bottom. Watching the storyteller read, children learn the relationship between spoken and printed words. They also learn to listen. Books help children learn letters and language.

Storytelling is also a good form of relaxation, 15-2. Listening to a story is a quiet activity. Children are not moving about or interacting with other children.

## BOOKS AS A SOURCE OF STORIES

Children's books are an important source of stories. Most can be divided into two main groups: picture books and storybooks. Storybooks are often categorized as family life stories, animal stories, and fairy tales. *Picture books* have single words or simple sentences and simple plots. These are usually the first books shared with young children.

After picture books, *storybooks* are introduced. These books also contain pictures. But they have more words and more complex plots than picture books. Most of these books are built around themes of achievement, love, and reassurance. For instance, a book that uses all three themes is *Peter Rabbit*. In the story, Peter has an adventure but safely returns home (achievement). His mother tucks him into bed and gives him tea (love and reassurance). Examples of other such stories include *Little Bear, Mike Mulligen and His Steam Shovel,* and *Little Tim.*

*Family life stories* contain the theme of social understanding. The children in these stories

15-1 Storytelling is an enjoyable time for teachers and children.

15-2 Because storytelling requires children to sit and listen, it is a good form of relaxation for children.

have their problems. Some problems may be funny; some serious. But all problems are resolved with love and concern. The purpose of these stories is to help children develop social understanding by sharing the problems, troubles, and feelings of others. Examples include *Johnny Crow's Garden, My Dog Is Lost, My Grandpa, Timid Timothy,* and *Will I Have a Friend?*

Young children also enjoy *animal stories.* In these stories, animals are given some human qualities. Usually, the animal hero has some unusual success or ability. Examples of these stories include: *Little Brown Bear, All About Dogs, Dogs, Dogs, Nothing But Cats, Cats, Cats,* and *Angus and the Cat.*

Fairy tales are another type of book enjoyed by older children. *Fairy tales* have a theme of achievement. The characters or heroes of these stories must perform difficult tasks in order to succeed. They must confront giants, witches, and glass hills. In these tales, kindness and goodness supported by courage and good judgment win out over evil. *Three Billy Goats Gruff, Three Little Pigs,* and *Cinderella* are popular examples of fairy tales.

## STORYTELLING STORIES FOR CHILDREN

Storytelling is an art that requires study and practice. The key to a good story is selection. A story is only good if children enjoy it. If the story is to be a good classroom activity, the teacher should also enjoy and value it. Otherwise, sharing it in an interesting way will be difficult.

Selecting storybooks is often hard for the new child care workers. Public libraries have many useful lists and descriptions of books. These are called *reviews.* Reviews will help you find titles, authors, and publishers of books. Reviews can also be ordered from the American Library Association Children's Service.

When choosing books for children, study the story content, illustrations, vocabulary, durability, and length.

### Fictional content

Stories should match children's developmental level and experiences. Familiar objects, people, and situations make stories more interesting to children. Stories about children, activities, and backgrounds similar to children's own are special favorites.

Most preschool children cannot separate fact from fiction. Therefore, it is important to look for realistic stories. Until children are about five years old, they are often not ready for fantasy, 15-3. Books in which animals or lifeless objects, such as trees and flowers, behave as humans should be avoided.

### Illustrations

Illustrations are used to create interest and to arouse children's imagination. The pictures in a book for young children should almost tell the story by themselves. Children will be more interested if they can "read" the story by looking at the pictures.

Pictures should be easy to recognize. Too much detail and shading or a lack of color will confuse young children. Instead, children respond best to brightly colored pictures with large, clearly defined objects. Illustrations should:
- Be large, colorful, and plentiful.
- Represent the written word.
- Reflect actions.
- Avoid unneeded detail.
- Be realistically and attractively colored.

### Vocabulary

A good children's book uses words that can be understood by most children of a certain age. Only a few new words are introduced in a story. Repetition of certain words will increase the children's enjoyment. This rhythm of certain word sounds is one major reason why children so enjoy stories such as Mother Goose tales.

### Durability

Children should be allowed to hold, carry, and turn the pages of books. Therefore, covers and pages must be sturdy. Covers made of strong, washable material are best. Pages should be easy to handle. The page surface should be dull to prevent glare. The book's binding should lay flat when the book is open.

15-3 Younger children may become confused or even frightened by fantasy stories.

## Length

Appropriate book length varies with the age. Infants and toddlers may stay with a book for only a few minutes. Their books are often only a few pages long. Two-year-olds will remain interested in a book for five to eight minutes; three-year-olds, from six to ten minutes; four-year-olds from eight to twelve minutes; five-year-olds from ten to fifteen minutes. This interest is reflected in the number of pages in the book.

## Selecting books based on age

Age plays an important part in choosing books for children. Chart 15-4 outlines some factors to consider for different ages.

Infants and toddlers need durable picture books. These books may be made of washable cloth or thick cardboard. The pages need to be thick to allow for easier handling. Pictures should be large and clearly outlined. Simple items in children's surroundings should be represented in the pictures.

Two-year-olds enjoy books about things that they do, enjoy, or know. Animals and small children are the preferred subjects. These books should still be quite durable with plenty of large, clearly outlined drawings. Actions and

## CONSIDERATIONS FOR CHILDREN'S BOOKS

| Infant | 2-year-old | 3-year-old | 4-year-old | 5-year-old |
|---|---|---|---|---|
| Thick pages. Pictures of simple objects. Large, clearly outlined pictures. | Imitate familiar sounds. Repeat children's own experiences. Contain large pages with big pictures. Include the familiar. | Include things and people outside of the home. Explain the who's and why's. Interpret the child's own experiences. Contain repetitive sound words. | Include humor in reality. Contain new words. Explain the how's and why's. Include exaggeration. | Add something to their knowledge. Take them beyond the here and now. Contain new information and relationships between familiar facts. |

15-4 Children of different ages each have their story preferences.

sounds in the pictures should be familiar. The colors should be realistic. For example, goats should not be purple, or some children may believe they really are that color.

Three-year-old children enjoy stories about familiar subjects, such as small children and animals. But they also enjoy learning about people outside the home. They enjoy stories about community helpers such as police officers, mail carriers, and garbage collectors. Three-year-olds want to know what these people do and why. Pictures should be realistic, simple, and clear. Sentences on each page should be limited to a few.

Four-year-old children are less self-centered than the younger group. These children are becoming more curious about the world about them. They want to know how and why things work. At this age they can enjoy simple, short stories that use exaggeration. Four-year-olds are often silly and enjoy pranks in books.

Five-year-old children like stories which give them added knowledge. They prefer stories that take them beyond here and now. These children want new information and relationships along with familiar facts. Fantasy trips beyond the confines of their world are now enjoyed. Examples of these books include *Little Red Riding Hood, Peter Rabbit,* and *Goldilocks and the Three Bears.*

### Children's stories

Children learn a great deal from stories. You have learned it is important to choose age-appropriate stories. It is also important to select stories that are not based on stereotypes. *Stereotypes* are preset ideas about people based on one characteristic such as sex, nationality, or religion. Most stereotypes are unfair. Therefore, they should be avoided.

**Sexism.** Children's stories whether selected for infants or five-year-olds, need to be free of sexism. *Sexism* is any action, attitude, or outlook used to judge a person based only on the sex of that person. For instance, many books do not show women who possess a full range of interests and skills.

In the past, most children's books showed women wearing aprons and doing housework.

Girls were passive and helped their mothers around the house. Boys, on the other hand, were active and adventurous. Doctors, lawyers, police, as well as many other important workers, tended to be men. Also, few men were shown in roles of teachers and nurses.

Read stories carefully and study illustrations before using a story. Sexism is sometimes easier to find in pictures. Pictures should be studied closely as they have more impact on children than words.

Study the ratio of men to women in the illustrations. As a rule there should be as many men as women or girls as boys. Notice how female characters are described and what kinds of activities the pictures show them doing. See 15-5. Books that avoid sexism will describe women and girls as lively people who do interesting things. Likewise men and boys will be shown as people who are interested in homes, families, and friends.

**Racism.** Through books, children can gain an understanding of people who have different skin coloring, food preferences, and languages. Children must learn that because people are different from them, those people are not bad.

15-5 Books that show men involved with their families and women in interesting jobs do not promote sexism.

Both illustrations and text should depict all races and nationalities in a positive way.

**Ageism.** Ageism is stereotyping of the elderly. Search stories for this type of problem. Children should be given a real and positive picture of elderly people. Children should learn to enjoy and know the elderly members of their community. Stories should describe warm, pleasing relationships between elderly people and children.

## READING ALOUD TO CHILDREN

Good oral reading takes time and effort. Three steps need to be taken before reading stories to young children. First, choose stories that both children and you will enjoy. Then, become familiar with the story. Finally, decide how you will present the story. The success of the story lies in your ability to be interesting and enthusiastic.

### Preparing to read

Read the story several times so you know it well. Then a quick glance at the page will remind you of the text. This leaves your eyes free for contact with the children. No one way is best for learning stories. Each person has his or her own method.

Oral reading skills are important when storytelling. One way to build these skills is to practice reading in front of a mirror. Another method is to record yourself as you read. Using these methods, you can correct any problems you notice. For example, tape yourself and then ask the following:
- Did I convey enthusiasm about the story?
- Did I keep the tempo lively?
- Did I suggest different voices for different characters?

After you are familiar with the book, decide whether you want to read or tell the story. Reading the story has its advantages when working with young children. They can look at the drawings as they listen to the story. Reading stories may also get some children interested in reading. Watching you, the children will also learn the link between printed and spoken words. The advantage to telling a story is you are able to better dramatize action and characters.

A comfortable setting is required for a successful reading time. Children must be free from distractions. They should sit in a group to listen. Some teachers like to have children sit on carpet samples or pillows. A colorful quilt may also be used. Such seating arrangements prevent children from moving around and help them focus more on listening.

Story groups should be small, 15-6. You may wish to divide children into two or more groups, based on age and interest. This also allows the children more interaction.

Most children need a settling down time. To help children get ready to listen, some teachers recite a fingerplay. Another technique is to talk to the children using a puppet. Other teachers simply discuss the events of the day.

### Introducing the story

Begin stories by setting the mood. Ask questions, make personal comments, or show a book to get children involved in the story. For example, you can set a humorous mood by asking, "How many of you like to laugh?" You

15-6 In small groups, children are free to interact with the teacher.

might hold the book up and show the cover. The picture on the cover should suggest the story content. Setting the mood should be brief. A few sentences or less is most often enough.

A personal comment is another way to introduce a story. You may share where you learned about the story. For example, "This is a story that my grandmother told me as a child."

Props are also good for introducing stories. Any items that relate to the story and would attract children's attention could be defined as props. To introduce *Peter Rabbit,* for example, you may bring in a live rabbit, a stuffed rabbit, or a picture of a rabbit. See 15-7.

Store props in a storytelling apron. As you introduce a story, pull props out of the apron pocket one at a time. A storytelling bag can be used in the same way. The bag is also useful for storing books in the reading area.

Before you begin the story, explain any words that the children do not know. For example, before reading *The Gigantic Elephant,* define the new word "gigantic."

Before you start, create a feeling that something special is about to be shared. This feeling can be created by the enthusiasm in your voice as you introduce the book. Your facial expression can also create enthusiasm.

## Reading the story

Read stories with enjoyment and feeling. Maintain eye contact with the children. Pause before introducing a new character or idea.

Read the story in a normal speaking voice. Speaking too softly or at a high pitch may cause the children to lose interest. Think of your voice as a tool. To add interest, you can whisper or shout when appropriate. You may mimic a sound, or speed up or slow down the pace. The pitch of your voice can also be changed. An example would be the story of *Goldilocks and the Three Bears.* Use a high pitch for the baby bear. Use a low pitch for the papa bear.

## Handling interruptions

Interruptions happen often when telling stories to young children, 15-8. The children

**PROPS FOR INTRODUCING STORIES**

| | | |
|---|---|---|
| | A red balloon | *The Red Balloon* |
| | A red apple | *The Apple is Red* |
| | A doll | *William's Doll* |
| | A black stuffed cat | *The Tale of the Black Cat* |
| | A purple crayon | *Harold and the Purple Crayon* |

15-7 Well-chosen props will grab children's attention.

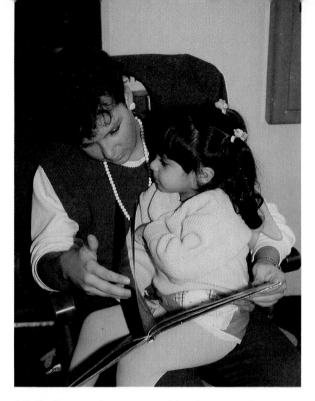
15-8 Do not be annoyed by interruptions. Young children like to ask questions and make comments on stories they are hearing.

will ask such questions as, "Why is baby bear brown?" Accept these interruptions. Patiently answer their questions. There may be children who continue to ask many questions. If this happens, say, "Mark please save your questions until after the story."

Wiggling children can distract other children. Do not make an issue of this. It is best to ignore the wiggling and keep reading. A positive response is to praise children who sit still. For example, you may say "Joellen, I like how quietly you are sitting." This will strengthen Joellen's actions. It will also encourage wigglers to sit still.

## Maintaining interest

Children's interest in a story can be seen in their laughter, stillness, and faces. If children do not appear to like a story, talk faster. You might also use more expression or skip over some details. You can also restore interest by asking the children simple questions about the story. To quiet a bored or disruptive child, ask "Louis, what color is baby bear?" At times, no matter what you do, a book does not have holding power. If this should happen, end the story. You may say, "Boys and girls this is not the right story for today."

## Ending stories

Ending a story is as important as introducing it. The children need to know when you are finished. Therefore, the ending should be clear. You may ask a question about the story such as, "What did you like best about the story?" Or you may ask a question about the characters, the plot, or setting.

At times, a simple "thank you for listening" may be enough. You may also wish to give the children something to take home after some stories. This is done most often for special occasions, 15-9.

Be prepared to read the same story over and over again. You will be pleased to hear, "Mr. Andrews, tell us that story again." This request tells you the children enjoyed the book.

## Evaluating your performance

After reading a story, you will need to evaluate your methods. Children's reactions are good feedback. As a rule, the more children respond to a story, the better your methods. If children lose interest, you may have talked too fast or slow. Or you may have spoken so carefully that you forgot to add expression and vary tone.

### ITEMS TO PASS OUT AFTER STORIES

| ITEM | STORY |
|------|-------|
| Vegetable seed | *The Carrot Seed* |
| Pumpkin seeds | *The Magic Pumpkin* |
| A flower | *The Story of Ferdinand* |
| Pebbles | *Sylvester and the Magic Pumpkin* |
| Balloons | *Winnie the Pooh* |
| Blueberries | *Blueberries for Sal* |

15-9 After ending a story, you may wish to give the children an item to take home. This item should relate to the story.

Note your strengths as well as your weaknesses. When children smile, laugh, and watch you closely, you have used methods that hold their interest. Build on your strengths as you read stories in the future.

## ACHIEVING VARIETY IN STORYTELLING

In addition to reading stories aloud, there are other methods of storytelling. Guidelines for these methods are like those for reading aloud. First, decide whether you will read from a book or make up your own story. Next practice the story using a tape recorder or in front of a mirror until you know it well. After this you are ready to introduce the story and perform as a storyteller.

Younger children in particular will stay interested longer when several methods are used during story time. As a child care worker, you will need to learn a number of storytelling methods.

### Draw and tell

*Draw and tell,* or *chalk talk* as it sometimes called, is one storytelling method. Drawings are made on chalkboard, tagboard, or an 18- by 24-inch newsprint pad as the story is told. Textbooks containing draw and tell stories can be purchased from school supply stores or catalogs. Some child care workers prefer to find a storybook and adapt it. Illustrations may be deleted, combined, and added. A general rule is no more than five sheets of paper should be used.

If you do not have good drawing skills, you may want to use an opaque projector to prepare the stories. Find a book and place it on the projector. Tape a piece of cardboard or paper on the wall. Project drawings from the book onto this paper or cardboard. Lightly trace the drawings with a pencil. Then as you tell the story, use brightly colored markers to retrace the lines.

Draw and tell stories may be prepared so they can be used more than once. Cover original light tracings with clear laminate. Use grease pencils to draw in the outline and fill in the color. After the story is done, clean the clear laminate by wiping it with a piece of felt. Window cleaner may also be used for cleaning.

### Story records

Story records have appeal for young children. *Story records* contain sound effects and music. Records telling many popular stories are available. Examples include:
- *The Carrot Seed*
- *Muffin in the City*
- *Andy and the Lion*
- *Make Way for Ducklings*

### Filmstrips

Filmstrips can hold the interest of most children. See 15-10. Some classic children's stories are available on filmstrip. One disadvantage of filmstrips is that children may have already seen them on television. Filmstrips may be purchased from school supply stores and catalogs. Popular titles include: *Stone Soup, Cinderella, The Little Engine That Could, The Snowy Day,* and *Where the Wild Things Are.*

### Tapes

Purchased or teacher-made tapes may be used for storytelling. Tapes may be purchased through school supply stores or catalogs.

15-10 Filmstrips offer children a different way to hear stories.

To save money, some child care workers prefer to make their own tapes. To do so, you will need a tape recorder, cassette tape, and story. As you make the tape, read the story clearly. Pause after each two-page spread. At this point, insert a signal. You may want to hit a spoon against a glass or play a piano key. This signal will tell children listening to the tape to turn the page in their book, 15-11.

## Puppets

Puppets have always appealed to young children. Having puppets tell a story is a useful change of pace. Use a puppet as a listener who remarks and asks questions about the story. Puppets can be made from tin cans, tongue depressors, socks, and other inexpensive materials. Stuffed animals can be used in the same manner. For example, a brown teddy bear could be used to tell the story of *Little Brown Bear*. A mitten also makes a good puppet. Cut eyes, a nose, and a mouth from construction paper and paste onto the mitten. Use the mitten puppet with the story *The Lost Mitten*.

After you tell the story, place the puppet in the library area. The children will enjoy playing with it. (Refer to Chapter 16, "Sociodramatic Play and Puppetry Experiences," for more information.)

## Individual or group stories

Given the chance, children can be clever storytellers. After a field trip, visit from a guest, or other special event, ask children or small groups of children to record a story about that special time. See 15-12. Or, write down the children's ideas as they tell you their story. You could write the ideas on a piece of tagboard paper or the chalkboard. Seeing their own words helps children understand the link between spoken and written words.

## Flipcharts

*Flipcharts* are stories drawn on large tagboard cards. If you lack drawing skills, you will find the opaque projector helpful.

After you finish drawing, tracing, and coloring the cards, number the back of each card. This will help you keep the cards in correct

15-11 Even young children who do not yet read can follow along in a book while listening to a tape.

15-12 Stories created by children add special interest to story time.

order for storytelling. You may also wish to print the story for each drawing on the back of each flipchart. To protect the flipchart, cover it with a plastic film.

After telling the story, you may wish to place the flipchart in the book area. Then the children have an opportunity to use the flipchart themselves and retell the story. Some children also enjoy arranging the cards in order of the story.

### Slide stories

Slide stories usually center around pictures taken on field trips or during classroom events like holiday parties. You might start a slide story at the beginning of the year. Then at the end of the year the slide story can be told. Slide stories involving the children are also enjoyed by parents at special events.

### Flannel boards

*Flannel board,* or *felt board,* storytelling uses characters and props cut out of felt and placed on a felt background, 15-13. Flannel boards may be purchased from school supply stores and catalogs or made by the teacher. To make a board, you will need a piece of styrofoam in-

sulation board, 27 by 17 and one-half inches. This material can be bought at a lumber supply company. To prepare the board, cover it with two contrasting pieces of felt, 29 by 19 and one-half inches. The two pieces provide different colored backgrounds for felt figures.

Pieces of paper, cardboard, or felt are used to show major characters. These may be cut out of storybooks, hand drawn, or bought. Flannel board books contain many stories. They often also contain patterns for characters and props. These can be bought from school supply stores.

A quick way to make figures is to use a non-woven interfacing fabric. Hold the fabric in place and trace over the patterns with a black felt pen. Fill in the areas you wish to brighten.

Felt figures may also be made from a story-book pattern. Place a piece of carbon paper behind the paper and on top of a piece of card-board. Trace over the drawing with a paper clip. This transfers onto the cardboard. Cut out the cardboard figures to use as patterns. The patterns can be placed on felt and traced. If you need larger figures, use the opaque pro-jector to enlarge the drawings.

## DISPLAYING BOOKS

An important area of a classroom is the book area. Books, flannel boards, tapes, and other storytelling equipment are located in this area. The books should be arranged in an appealing manner. The book covers should be visible to attract the children's interest, 15-14. Books should be arranged so they will not fall after one is removed.

The book and reading areas should be located away from traffic. They should also be separated from the rest of the classroom by dividers. This provides a quiet atmosphere. Scissors, crayons, and painting should not be allowed here. These limits should prevent the books from being misused.

The books for the reading area should be carefully chosen. Each child's developmental needs should be considered. You may wish to include books on topics facing children in the group, such as divorce, death, and illness. Some

15-13 Let children place the felt figures when using a flannel board.

15-14 Displays that show book covers encourage children to look at books on their own.

books, such as the children's favorites, can remain in the area for a long time. Other books can be rotated frequently. Fun books should always be available. Add new books often to stimulate children's interest and enthusiasm. You may want to borrow books from the public library, friends, and parents.

## SUMMARY

Done well, storytelling is a useful learning tool for children. Through storytelling, children can learn many skills. Some of these skills include developing an enjoyment of books, learning to form new ideas, and increasing vocabulary.

Stories must be selected with care. Content must match the developmental levels and experiences of the audience. In addition, content must be free of stereotypes.

Illustrations should spark interest and be pleasant. The vocabulary and story length must match children's skills. Finally, the books must be durable.

Before reading to children, it is important to prepare ahead of time. There are several ways to present a story. Draw and tell, story records, and filmstrips are a few options.

## to Know

ageism
animal stories
draw and tell
fairy tales
family life stories
flannel boards
flipcharts

picture books
racism
reviews
sexism
storybooks
story records
storytelling

## to Review

1. Stories that draw on children's _____ help them understand themselves better.

2. True or false. Storytelling is a good form of relaxation.

3. Which type of books are usually the first books shared with young children?
   a. Picture.
   b. Fairy tales.
   c. Animal.
   d. Family life.

4. What theme is used in family life stories?

5. In _____ _____ kindness and goodness win over evil.

6. True or false. It is not important if a teacher cares for a story, as long as the children enjoy it.

7. _____ are used to create interest and to arouse children's imagination.

8. The appropriate length of a book will vary with the _____ of the child.

9. What is sexism?

10. True or false. Teachers should choose books that show all races and nationalities in a positive way.

11. Name two ways to build oral reading skills.

12. Introduce stories by:
    a. Asking a question.
    b. Making a personal comment.
    c. Using a prop.
    d. All of the above.

13. The _____ of a story must be clear.

14. Explain one storytelling method.

## to Do

1. Using one of the storytelling methods explained in the chapter, prepare a children's story. Share it with the class.

2. Prepare a bibliography of children's books you might use in storytelling. Divide the books into groups based on age: infants, two-, three-, four-, and five-year-olds.

3. Create an introduction for a story to read. Use props in your introduction.

# Chapter 16

# Guiding Socio-dramatic Play and Puppetry Experiences

After studying this chapter, you will be able to:
☐ Explain the growth promoted by socio-dramatic play.
☐ Discuss the types of play and stages of material use through which children progress.
☐ Determine childrens' age groups based on their play themes.
☐ List skills needed by teachers in order to promote socio-dramatic play.
☐ Make puppets and use them in a puppet story.
☐ Describe three types of puppets.

Young children love to pretend and play make-believe. Such fantasy play provides opportunities for growth and development. Young children are actors without stage fright. They say what they feel and feel what they say.

*Dramatic play* is a form of play in which a child imitates others. *Socio-dramatic play* is social play in which several children play together as they imitate others, 16-1. It is the most complex form of play seen in child care settings. But it is seldom observed before age three. Themes vary. Children may play as doctors, nurses, and patients, or as spacemen and monsters. As one child plays the role of a beautician, another plays the role of the customer.

Puppetry is another type of play that allows a child to imitate others. A child's puppet may become a wolf, police officer, or even a witch. Through this play, a child may share his or her inner world. The child places feelings and emotions he or she feels onto the puppet. This is known as *projection.*

## SOCIO-DRAMATIC PLAY

As children engage in socio-dramatic play, they mimic adult roles. They may play at being a wife, husband, mommy, daddy, doctor,

16-1 Socio-dramatic play involves at least two children as they role play. These girls are role playing workers in a restaurant.

or police officer. This is called **role playing.** Role playing gives children a chance to try out a variety of roles, 16-2. In this play they grow physically, socially, emotionally, and intellectually.

Physical growth is promoted through the play actions of children: sweeping floors, dressing dolls, and pretending to paint furniture. Building structures that enhance socio-dramatic scenes also helps develop physical skills.

Social and emotional development are promoted through socio-dramatic play. Sometimes negative feelings and situations that disturb children are acted out. At other times, children may seek attention. During these times, children learn a great deal about human relationships. They learn what kind of behavior upsets another child. They learn how to get along with others. They discover important social skills. As a result, they gradually learn how to balance their play so everyone is content.

While engaging in socio-dramatic play, children try out different social roles. They express their dreams and fears. At the same

time, they learn to bare emotions such as anger, aggression, and hostility.

Intellectual development is also built through socio-dramatic play. Children's roles range from babies to parents to bears to astronauts. Their imaginations allow them to act out what they cannot yet be in real life. During this type of play, children need to make decisions and choices. By doing so, they learn problem-solving skills, 16-3. Language concepts are also developed as children engage in play. They learn new names for equipment. Children also gain new ideas from other children.

## Types of play

Children go through several stages of play before they are able to take part in socio-dramatic play.

Toddlers are *egocentric* (concerned only with themselves). They are not able to understand other people's needs. As a result, they play alone. This play is called **solitary play** or independent play. That is, their play does not involve other children. They most often play by themselves.

*Parallel play* is the next stage of play. A room with two-year-old children will show parallel play. In this type of play, children play by

16-2 This child is role playing a nurse.

16-3 Running a refreshment stand gives these children the chance to build intellectual as well as social skills.

themselves, but stay close by other children. All the children may be involved in similar activities, but play between and among the children does not exist. Children in this age group focus more on using play materials on their own.

Children under 3 years of age engage in *personification.* This means giving human traits to non-living objects. For instance, children may talk to dolls or puppets. They act as if the toys can hear what they say. Many everyday situations are acted out. A child may say, "Mommy is going to feed you now." Or, while speaking to a puppet a child may say, "You're going to go for a walk now."

As children grow socially and emotionally, they begin playing with their peers for short time periods. Gradually they learn to respect the property rights of others. This is a clue they are gaining social skills, 16-4. At the same time, they may also grasp that permission is needed to use some materials.

16-4 Children learn social skills such as cooperation in socio-dramatic play.

*Cooperative play* is play between two or more children. It is at this stage that socio-dramatic play begins. As children take part in cooperative play, they become more interested in social relationships. As this occurs, they learn how to develop and maintain peer relationships. From this grows socio-dramatic play.

Children who are aggressive and uncooperative may have problems building and keeping peer relationships. These children will need help. To be successful in cooperative play, they will need to learn to give affection, use friendly and social behavior, and submit to other children's wishes. They will also need to understand the viewpoint of others. Only through practice and help from the teacher will they learn to use proper social skills.

Children engaged in cooperative play often give specific instructions for roles. A child might say, "You be the doctor, and I'll be the little girl." Conditions are also common. For example, a child may say, "I'll play, but I have to be the bus driver."

## Use of materials

Children move through three stages of material use in their play. Not all young children, however, will reach the second or third stages.

The first stage of material use is called the *manipulative stage.* A child at this stage handles props. For instance, when given a baby bottle, children in the manipulative stage will screw and unscrew the cap.

The second stage is called the *functional stage.* During this stage, the child will use the prop as intended while playing with other children. Using the doll bottle as an example again, the child will pretend to feed a doll.

The third, and final stage, is called the *imaginative stage.* Children in this stage do not need real props, 16-5. They are able to think of substitutes. Instead of feeding the doll with a bottle, they may use their finger. Or, they might use a stick, clothespin, or pencil. Likewise, if a broom is needed to sweep a floor, a yardstick may be used.

While you observe children in socio-dramatic play, you will see that some children have a hard time getting involved in a role because there are no real props. In a restaurant scene, for instance, some children will play the roles of servers. A child not at the imaginative stage will say he or she cannot play the role because there is no paper and pencil. A child who has reached the imaginative stage might just raise up his or her hand for the paper and use a finger as a pencil. Remember, not all young children will be able to move to the imaginative level.

Many times children at the imaginative level will model an unusual approach to their socio-dramatic play. Their imaginations are shown when they use a toy to represent a dinosaur, a doll carriage for a grocery cart, or a paper bag as a chef's hat. Children at this stage are able to deal with abstract ideas. As a result, they are able to make up their play as they progress. When dramatizing a restaurant theme, they may make paper money to buy food.

## Play themes

The themes of play often focus on everyday situations children experience, 16-6. Children may try on life by imitating auto mechanics fix-

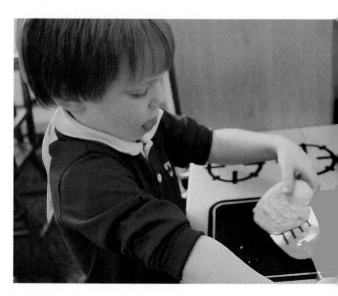

16-5 Making a hamburger out of play dough is a sign of imaginative play.

238

ing cars, chefs making dinner, or painters working on a house. Teachers will often provide props that complement a unit of study, as well as the children's interests. Examples might include doctors, fire fighters, fast food restaurant, bakery, or grocery store.

Themes change with age. Toddlers have no theme. They love to fill, empty, and release objects. Their play reflects intense exploration of objects. Blocks are piled high and then knocked down.

Three-year-old children's play stresses process. There is no preplanned plot or theme. Real and pretend are still not firmly separated. So the child becomes what he imitates. Routines are important. Many three-year-old children always begin their day with the same activity.

Four-year-old children are more likely to take part in socio-dramatic play. Their play no longer centers around the home. Play now involves management of aggressive feelings.

Four-year-olds like to imitate ghosts, monsters, or aggressive TV heroes. As you watch the socio-dramatic play, you will often notice feminine and masculine traits exaggerated. For example, to role play a mother, children need all the props: gloves, hats, purses, high heels, and scarves.

Themes in the play vary. One moment a child may be a career woman, and the next she may be a helpless baby. Children are included in or excluded from play based on sameness and difference. Sex, color, and kind of clothes worn may all be factors.

The socio-dramatic play of five-year-olds reflects games with rules, as well as fears and hostile feelings. At this age, the child usually can tell the difference between reality and fantasy. As a result, you may hear the child say, "This is just pretend."

Real life roles as well as folk heroes are part of five-year-olds' socio-dramatic play, 16-7.

## THEMES FOR DRAMATIC PLAY

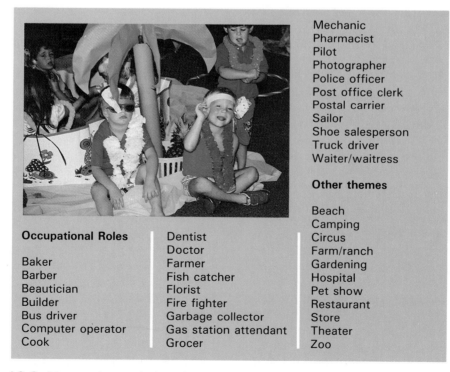

**Occupational Roles**

| | | |
|---|---|---|
| Baker | Dentist | Mechanic |
| Barber | Doctor | Pharmacist |
| Beautician | Farmer | Pilot |
| Builder | Fish catcher | Photographer |
| Bus driver | Florist | Police officer |
| Computer operator | Fire fighter | Post office clerk |
| Cook | Garbage collector | Postal carrier |
| | Gas station attendant | Sailor |
| | Grocer | Shoe salesperson |
| | | Truck driver |
| | | Waiter/waitress |

**Other themes**

Beach
Camping
Circus
Farm/ranch
Gardening
Hospital
Pet show
Restaurant
Store
Theater
Zoo

16-6 Many roles and situations can become the theme of play.

16-7 Five-year-olds enjoy playing roles they see every day.

Queens, kings, cowboys, nurses, teachers, brides, doctors, and characters such as Big Bird and Batman are all frequent themes. At the same time, children are quite interested in romance. Thus, they like to act out fairy tales such as *Cinderella*.

## Teacher's role

Once started, play often needs encouragement to continue. Thus, the first role of the teacher is to act as a resource person who provides materials and space.

Studies show that in classrooms where theme-related props were provided, children spent more time in socio-dramatic play. The location of the play area is important. Studies also show that children spend more time in socio-dramatic play when the area is in the center of the classroom. Small areas tend to promote quiet, solitary play. Large, open areas promote more socio-dramatic play.

The quality of toys and activities in the classroom will also affect the time spent in socio-dramatic play. Provide interesting materials. Real materials will also enhance play. That is, instead of supplying small plastic fire fighter hats, provide real hats from a local fire station. Change materials often to maintain interest.

## Teaching skills

Coaching, modeling, and reinforcing are all skills teachers need to build and support socio-dramatic play. *Coaching* requires that the teacher provide children with ideas for difficult situations. For instance, a child may not want to be a baker because there is no baker's hat. The teacher may then suggest that the child use a paper bag as a hat. Another child may be hitting a classmate. In this case, the teacher should tell the child to stop because the other child does not like to be hit. The teacher might also remind the child that others will stop playing if the experience is not pleasant.

In *modeling,* the teacher shows correct behavior for children during their socio-dramatic play. In a shoe store scene, a child may not know how to sell shoes. The teacher can then say, "Would you like to buy some shoes today?" Watching the teacher, the child has a chance to model this correct behavior to other children.

Verbal guidance is helpful. Comments and suggestions need to be made many times by the teacher who remains outside of play. See 16-8. For example, Mr. Domingo sees a child unable to get involved in play. Mr. Domingo comments to the child, "Your son looks hungry. Shouldn't you go to the store and buy some food?" This statement may encourage the child to take the role of the parent. It should also get the child involved in dramatization with the children who have set up the grocery store.

Children's correct behaviors during socio-dramatic play should be reinforced. Comments may be made directly to the children who are using the desired behavior. If Sally just gave

Sam a turn to use the cash register in their fast food restaurant, say, "Sally, I like the way you are giving Sam a turn."

**Anecdotal records.** *Anecdotal records* are notes kept by the teacher concerning children's play. These records may be tape recorded or written down. Record the roles and themes that interest each child. Make notes about the quality and extent of play. A study of these records should reveal the types, duration, and content of the children's play. It should also provide an overview of trends and patterns children's play follows. This will be helpful in determining what types of props to provide.

**Scheduling.** Dramatic play is best scheduled during the play period. These periods must be long enough for the children to carry out their ideas. Many preschool programs allow about one hour in the morning for free, or self-selected, play.

Avoid scheduling too many activities. This affects the number of children who take part in and remain with socio-dramatic play. If few children are playing, too many activities have been scheduled. Reduce the number of activities. Schedule only activities that complement each other. Blocks, woodworking, puppets, and arts would all promote dramatic play.

## Equipment and setup for socio-dramatic play

Good equipment, set up in a useful manner will greatly improve the quality of socio-dramatic play.

**Prop boxes.** Extend children's play by providing prop boxes. A *prop box* contains materials and equipment that foster playing of a certain role. Boxes that are the same size, clearly marked, and made of lightweight cardboard can be stored and carried with ease.

Prop box themes might include a secretary, shoe shop owner, painter, beautician, post office clerk, baker, or carpenter. Each prop box should contain materials for one role, 16-9.

You might also make prop boxes for use in the sand box. One box might contain small vehicles. Another box might contain molds for use in building sand castles or in baking. Add small animals and rubber figures of people for variety and interest.

**Costume corner.** Every dramatic play area should have a costume corner. Rotate costumes to complement current studies. For instance, if the theme of the week is community service, provide clothing to reflect this. Include clothing for fire fighters, nurses, doctors, and post office clerks. If Halloween is the theme, provide a variety of Halloween costumes.

16-8 Teachers sometimes need to encourage children to become involved in socio-dramatic play.

## BEAUTY SALON PROPS

| | |
|---|---|
| hair dryer | clear nail polish |
| combs | aprons |
| empty shampoo, | emery boards |
| conditioner, and | newspapers and |
| hair spray bottles | magazines |
| mirrors | cosmetics |
| rollers | play money |
| towels | |

16-9 A prop box for a beauty salon might contain some of these items.

Store these costumes after use. Lightweight, cardboard boxes are good for storage. Mark each box clearly so they are easy to locate.

**Housekeeping area.** Every early childhood classroom should have a housekeeping area. Dramatic and socio-dramatic play often occurs in this area. Supply child-sized furniture and equipment. Kitchen utensils, furniture, and other household items that complement current studies should be included. Rotate this equipment often.

**Outdoor play area.** The outdoor play area needs equipment that promotes socio-dramatic play. Include a jungle gym, sand box, housekeeping items, toy cars and trucks, sawhorses, wooden boxes, planks, and boards. Accessories such as tents, large blankets, and hats are also useful. With these materials, children can build forts, houses, and ships.

## PUPPETRY

*Puppetry* involves the use of puppets in play. A *puppet* is a figure designed in likeness to an animal or human. Puppets come in a number of sizes and shapes. People make puppets move. Most puppets can be moved using fingers, hands, and wrists.

Puppets are powerful learning tools for young children. With a puppet, a self-conscious child can act out feelings and thoughts such as anger and love. While using the puppet, the child often becomes the character and loses himself or herself. All children can learn how to communicate feelings and thoughts using puppets, 16-10. And by listening, teachers may learn what makes children angry, sad, happy, or joyful.

For the teacher, a puppet can be a teaching aid. Often, puppets are used to motivate children, to open up thoughts, and to spark ideas. Puppets can be used effectively in almost every area of the curriculum. Chart 16-11 points out some of the values of puppets.

### Making puppets

Many teachers make their own puppets using store-bought or self-designed patterns. After cutting the fabric, the mouth, eyes, ears, nose, and other parts should be sewn on. It is quicker to attach these parts with glue. However, this method is not durable. In fact, many times the parts will fall off once the glue has dried. Children may also pull at parts. As a result, poorly fastened parts will come off.

All seams on a puppet should be sewn with the same color. White or black thread is most

16-10 Children can use puppets to express their feelings.

## PUPPETS AND CURRICULUM

| Curriculum area | Value of Puppets |
|---|---|
| Art | • Offer emotional release<br>• Provide sensory stimulation<br>• Promote large and small muscle development<br>• Encourage problem-solving and decision-making<br>• Provide for exploration of materials |
| Math | • Encourage thinking through problem-solving<br>• Introduce concepts<br>• Practice classification skills<br>• Encourage measuring, ordering, and counting skills |
| Social studies | • Promote communication<br>• Model sharing and cooperation with others<br>• Model critical thinking |
| Language arts | • Encourage development of language skills<br>• Encourage listening and talking skills |
| Dramatic play | • Offer emotional release<br>• Promote listening skills<br>• Encourage problem-solving<br>• Promote decision-making<br>• Promote self-expression and creativity<br>• Provide opportunities to gain self-confidence as group members<br>• Provide opportunities to express feelings |
| Science | • Classify food into food groups<br>• Discover the value of the five senses<br>• Observe changes in texture shape and sizes<br>• Evaluate ideas<br>• Identify food groups through the five senses |

16-11 Puppets can be used as a learning tool in many areas of the classroom.

often used. Provide a seam allowance of 1/4". Unless noted, all seams on a hand puppet should be on the outside of the puppet. To make sure the stitches are secure, backstitch at the beginning as well as the end of each seam. Chart 16-12 contains a list of materials for making puppets.

## Types of puppets

Puppet types include hand, mascot, and me puppets. The value of each type depends upon the interest of children as individuals and as a group.

**Hand puppets.** Hand puppets are the easiest type of puppet to make. They are also the

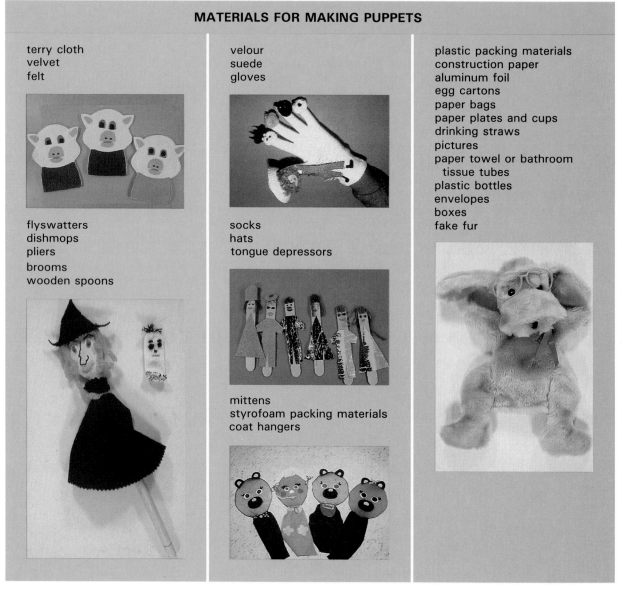

**MATERIALS FOR MAKING PUPPETS**

terry cloth
velvet
felt

flyswatters
dishmops
pliers
brooms
wooden spoons

velour
suede
gloves

socks
hats
tongue depressors

mittens
styrofoam packing materials
coat hangers

plastic packing materials
construction paper
aluminum foil
egg cartons
paper bags
paper plates and cups
drinking straws
pictures
paper towel or bathroom
  tissue tubes
plastic bottles
envelopes
boxes
fake fur

16-12 Items that can be used to make puppets are limited only by imagination.

easiest to use since no strings or rods need to be worked. The best way to work a hand puppet is to place the second and third fingers in the puppet's head. In this position the hand is more relaxed and the puppet's entire body can be spread open. The thumb should be placed in one of the puppet's arms, the fourth and fifth finger in the other arm.

Hand puppets can be held in front of the face or over the head. This allows the puppeteer to work the puppet from a sitting, standing, or kneeling position.

**Mascot puppets.** Some teachers choose to have a mascot puppet in their classroom. A mascot puppet usually remains in the classroom all year. Therefore, it should be well made to withstand handling from the teacher and children.

Mascot puppets can be used in many classroom routines. It can "help" introduce new activities and class members. The puppet can also be used as a teaching tool. It can model proper classroom manners. For this reason, the puppet should be given an expressive face and a strong personality.

The mascot puppet can also be used to teach classroom rules. If a child neglects a rule, the teacher may have the mascot puppet provide a reminder. For example, if Larry yells indoors, the puppet may tap Larry on the shoulder and whisper, "We use soft voices indoors."

**Me puppets.** Children can also be taught how to make puppets using their own hands. These are me puppets. To do this, collect nontoxic, washable marking pens, felt pieces, fake fur, or construction paper, and double stick tape.

Using the materials, first demonstrate on your own hand for the children. Line the inside opening between the index finger and thumb with a red marking pen. This line will be the puppet's lips. Using another colored marker, add the puppet's eyes. Use a piece of construction paper or fake fur for the hair. With double stick tape, attach the hair to the top of your knuckle.

Show the children how the puppet can open and close its mouth and talk when you move your thumb. Urge the children to make a variety of puppets, including people and animals.

Older children (those in after school programs) may enjoy making me puppets on the first day of school. After making their puppets, each child can share something about himself or herself. They might tell their age, hobby, grade in school, favorite stories, or whatever else they feel like sharing.

**Writing puppet stories**

Not all puppet stories are found in books. In fact, most puppet stories are written by teachers. These stories are often contemporary and designed to fit the children's needs and interests.

**Themes.** Begin writing a puppet story with a theme. A theme provides unity. It is the subject of the story. Using a theme will also help you decide in what order the story will be.

Using friends, relatives, or other people as the theme of a story is helpful for most teachers. Personal experiences are another useful theme, as are manners, safety, friendships, vacations, holidays, and school experiences. A puppet story is quite easy to write based on such themes, 16-13.

**Developing a plot.** Developing a plot is the most challenging aspect of writing a puppet story. Be flexible and open to exploring different ideas. Many times, several ideas have to be tried.

The children must be able to follow the action of the plot. Begin with the theme and

---

**THEME IDEAS FOR PUPPET STORIES**

Johnny's Broken Tooth
My Dog Heidi
Kelsi's Hamster
My Cousin Dorothy
Jesse's Grandmother
Bobby's Friend Eric
Christmas at Aunt Sharese's
My Favorite Gift
A Trip to the Zoo

16-13 Children do not require complex themes for stories. Simple, familiar experiences are more interesting to them.

include the story events and problems. Remember, it is the problems that add interest and tension to the story. Then end the story by resolving the conflict.

The events of a story should occur in a logical manner. The flow of events is important if the children are to follow the story. The flow of events should be meshed smoothly.

In a story, *conflict* can be best described as two or more forces that oppose each other. Conflict adds interest. When developing scenes of conflict, think in terms of synonyms and antonyms. Make a list of opposites. For example, opposite pairs might include: ugly—beautiful; poor—rich; weak—strong; soft—hard; kind—mean.

**The ending.** The ending of a puppet story finishes the picture for the children. The ending should make clear that the story is over. And it should leave children with the story's most important point.

### Working puppets

When using a puppet in the classroom, hold it in your hand. The puppet should always model proper communication skills for the children. When the puppet speaks, it should move and face the children. When children or you speak, the puppet should be held still, facing the speaker.

Three basic types of movements can be modeled with hand puppets. The fingers, wrists, and arms may be moved. The fingers can create small movements in the puppet's arms and head. Waist movements can be made using the wrist. Arm movements can be used for locomotion movements.

**Finger movements.** The puppet's head can nod "yes" by moving fingers up and down inside the puppet's head. This movement can also mean, "I understand," or "I can do it."

The idea of "me" or, "This is mine" can be expressed by pointing the fingers inside the puppet hands toward the puppet.

The puppet can gesture, "Come over here" by waving one hand toward the body. Clapping can express joy or enthusiasm. Jumping up and down also can create these feelings. Pointing can convey such ideas as "you" or

"over there." Waving can be used to say, "goodbye" or "hello." Rubbing the puppet's hands together can mean the puppet is cold or thinking of doing something sneaky.

Thinking can be expressed in a number of ways. The puppet can cross its hands or tap its head lightly. The fingers can also be used to mimic sneezing, crying, and snoring. Soft snoring, for instance, is shown by moving the puppet's head up and down slightly.

**Wrist movements.** Sitting, bowing, reading, looking, and lifting are all made with wrist movements. Rotating the puppet back and forth, a "no" movement can also be expressed.

To show a seated puppet, pivot the wrist, changing from a front to a side view. After this, the wrist needs to be bent, allowing the puppet to rest on a seat. See 16-14.

A puppet can also be bowed from the waist using the wrist. To do this, bend the wrist down. At the same time, use the finger to make the puppet point toward itself.

The puppet should model left to right progression skills when reading a book. The wrist must pivot to mimic this action. At the same time, slowly move the fingers in the puppet's head to show reading action.

Move the wrist back and forth to make a puppet look. Using some arm movement, the puppeteer can make the puppet look to the sides of the stage and above and below it.

Lifting is a rather simple motion to mimic. It involves hand and finger movements. Bend the wrist down like in bowing and grasp objects with the hands. When the puppet straightens up, it looks as if it has lifted something.

**Arm movements.** Running, walking, hopping, flying, fainting, and falling are all made with arm movements. To mimic running, move the wrist up and down in a rapid, choppy motion. At the same time, move the puppet quickly across the stage.

A puppet can be made to walk by holding it upright and straight. As the puppet is moved across the stage, move its arms up and down.

Although a puppet can hop across the stage, each hop needs to be deliberate. For variety, have the puppet hop in circles, returning to the ground as the last motion for each hop.

16-14 Simple wrist movements can be used to make a puppet appear to sit down.

Broad arm movements can mimic flying. The puppet should always face the direction that it is flying.

A broad arm movement can also create fainting or falling movements. The puppet should land on its back. The speed at which the puppet lands depends on the desired effect. The best effect is acquired by freezing the puppet's movements for a few seconds before falling. The rhythm of a fall is created by this puppetry technique.

### Telling a puppet story

The puppets are prepared and you are comfortable working them. It is now time to tell a puppet story to the children. This will involve creating the setting, preparing the children, and acting out puppet characters.

**Creating a setting.** The room should set the mood for a story. For a circus theme, you might place colorful balloons next to the storyteller. A Valentine's Day event might include a valentine box set next to the storyteller. Likewise, a Halloween story could be enhanced with dimmed lights. The purpose of this preparation is to put the children in the proper frame of mind for enjoying the presentation.

**Preparing children.** The first few minutes of a puppet story set the tone of the story. Make a special effort to gain the children's attention. This may be done using recorded music, slamming doors, or a song the children sing. However, keep some surprises for later in the story. Novice storytellers should build these techniques over a period of time. Experienced storytellers often scatter these elements throughout the story.

### Puppet voices

Since puppets are not people, their voices should not be similar to human voices. Pitch is important. If there are two puppets being used, one should have a low-pitched voice and the other a high-pitched voice.

Puppet voices need to be *audible*. That is, the children should be able to hear the voices clearly. Voices should also be constant. The puppet should have the same voice throughout the story. If the puppet begins with a high-pitched voice, it should finish with one.

The voice should also match the puppet's size and character. A huge tiger should have a booming voice. On the other hand, a spider should have a tiny voice. A puppet of an elderly person may have a slower voice than that of a child.

### Puppet stage

A puppet stage is not always needed. However, most classrooms have a lightweight, portable stage, 16-15. The puppet stage should be easy to fold and store. In fact, a cardboard cutting board is an excellent puppet stage. These can be bought at fabric shops. If the board is too tall for children, it can be cut to the correct height. To make the stage more interesting, the cutting board can be painted, wallpapered, or covered with a contact paper.

**Guiding Socio-dramatic Play and Puppetry Experiences   247**

A tension rod can also be used as a puppet stage. When covered with a gathered curtain, the rod can be placed across a door as a temporary stage. Use a simple curtain in a solid color that will not be distracting.

Puppet stages can be ordered through most equipment catalogs. Generally, they are made of wood. As a result, they are often quite heavy. Teacher-made puppet stages have the advantage of being more portable and less expensive.

## SUMMARY

Socio-dramatic play and puppetry experiences are two types of make-believe in which children like to take part. Each offers its own advantages to children's growth.

Socio-dramatic play allows children the chance to try out many roles. Through this play, children grow physically, socially, emotionally, and intellectually. With correct teacher guidance, socio-dramatic play can be an excellent form of play for children.

Puppetry experiences give children the chance to explore emotions, thoughts, and situations they might not be familiar or comfortable with. Children can work through these areas by projecting their feelings onto puppets. Teachers can help children learn how to handle these emotions and situations in a constructive way through puppetry experiences.

16-15 A low shelf can be used as a puppet stage.

# to Know

| | |
|---|---|
| anecdotal records | parallel play |
| coaching | personification |
| conflict | projection |
| cooperative play | prop box |
| dramatic play | puppet |
| functional stage | puppetry |
| imaginative stage | role playing |
| manipulative stage | socio-dramatic play |
| modeling | solitary play |

# to Review

1. Define socio-dramatic play.
2. _____ _____ gives children the opportunity to try out a variety of roles.
3. True or false. Socio-dramatic play is the simplest and first type of play used by children.
4. Play in which children play by themselves but stay close by other children is called:
   a. Cooperative play.
   b. Solitary play.
   c. Parallel play.
   d. None of the above.
5. Children in the _____ stage of material use will screw and unscrew the cap on a baby bottle.
6. True or false. All children reach the imaginative stage of material use.
7. Indicate what age groups use the following play themes:
   a. Imitation of ghosts and monsters.
   b. No preplanned themes.
   c. Real life roles as well as folk heroes.
   d. Filling, emptying, and releasing objects.
8. True or false. Studies show that in classrooms where theme-related props were provided, children spent more time in socio-dramatic play.

9. _____ requires that teachers provide children with ideas for difficult situations.
10. In _____ the teacher shows correct behavior for children during their socio-dramatic play.
11. Of what worth are anecdotal records?
12. A _____ _____ contains materials and equipment that foster playing of a certain role.
13. True or false. With a puppet, a self-conscious child can act out feelings and thoughts such as anger and love.
14. These puppets are easiest to make and use:
   a. Hand puppets.
   b. Me puppets.
   c. Mascot puppets.
   d. Animal puppets.
15. _____ puppets are made using the puppeteer's hand.
16. A _____ is the subject of a puppet story.
17. What is the most challenging aspect of writing puppet stories?
18. What three types of movements can be used to model movement in hand puppets?

# to Do

1. Brainstorm a list of prop box materials for a secretary, painter, baker, and carpenter.
2. Design a hand puppet.
3. Invite a puppeteer to speak to the class about his or her occupation.
4. Write a puppet story.
5. Create a portable puppet stage that is lightweight and easy to store.
6. Visit a local day care center and observe the socio-dramatic play area. What types of play did you notice? What stages were the children in?

# Chapter 17

## Guiding Manuscript Writing

After studying this chapter, you will be able to:

☐ Define manuscript writing.

☐ List reasons for encouraging manuscript writing skills in preschool setting.

☐ Explain activities that help children develop manuscript writing skills.

☐ Make letters following the Zaner-Bloser writing system.

☐ Outline the sequence children follow in learning alphabet letters.

☐ Discuss guidelines to use to help children build proper writing skills.

"Writing before starting kindergarten?" asked a concerned visitor. "Preschool children can't even read yet." These people are not aware that formal writing instruction is not usually given in preschool settings. Correct spelling, form, and style are given only secondary attention during the preschool years. Rather, the emphasis is on a readiness to develop needed skills and attitudes for writing.

Some preschool children may have mastered these writing and readiness skills. However, most have not. Children who are ready for writing need proper beginning writing tasks. Children who are not ready for writing must be introduced to proper activities to prepare for these tasks.

*Manuscript writing,* or print script, is a simple form of calligraphy. It does not require the sustained muscle control that cursive writing does. This writing involves unconnected letters that are made of simple, separate strokes. Included strokes are vertical lines (|), horizontal lines (−), diagonal lines (/), and circles (O). These simple strokes can be made easily by children who do not have well-developed small muscle coordination. Because of the separate strokes, this process is also slower to complete than cursive writing. These simple strokes look like the printed words seen in most books. As a result, reading is encouraged by the writing process.

Manuscript writing is not taught formally in the preschool setting. Most young children are not developmentally ready for this task. It is included in this book only to introduce readiness activities and the sequence by which children should learn manuscript. It is also included to teach caregivers of young children correct letter formations. All teacher-made materials should be done using proper manuscript writing techniques, 17-1. Your work will then serve as a model for children. It may also stimulate some children, particularly four- and five-year-olds, to write.

## OBJECTIVES FOR WRITING

There are many reasons to encourage writing in the preschool, especially with children who are ready for the task. These reasons include:

- To develop children's skills in seeing differences in letters. These skills are necessary for reading.
- To teach the letters of the alphabet.
- To learn that words are made up of letters.
- To learn that letters stand for sounds.
- To learn letter/sound associations.
- To learn that the spelling of words is related to their sound.

Four elements are needed if children are to meet these objectives. Included are interest, enthusiasm, clear instructions, and support given by you to each child.

## PRE-WRITING SKILLS

Two skills are needed before children are able to perform manuscript writing. These include small muscle coordination and hand-eye coordination. Children need enough small muscle coordination to hold a pencil and make basic strokes. They also need their hands and eyes to work together to make basic strokes. Caregivers need to include activities that promote these skills in the daily routine to ensure children learn the basic skills needed to learn manuscript writing.

### Small muscle activities

Small muscle activities are those that encourage children to use the small muscles in their hands and fingers. Materials used in these activities are listed in 17-2.

17-1 Teacher-made materials must be good enough for children to use as a model. This game board shows proper letter formation and size.

## MATERIALS USED IN SMALL MUSCLE ACTIVITIES

play dough
clay
sand
building blocks
puzzles
finger paints

small, wheeled toys
snap beads
threading beads
buttons and buttonholes
easel paints

17-2 Using these materials will require use of small muscles, thus promoting their growth.

Observe the children's interest and success with these materials. Practice should provide them with small muscle coordination needed for manuscript writing.

### Hand-eye coordination activities

*Hand-eye coordination* is muscle control that allows the hand to do a task in the way the eye sees it done. Activities that promote this type of coordination are listed in 17-3. These activities will promote writing skills. Therefore, they should be available for use at all times.

## MANUSCRIPT WRITING SYSTEMS

There are a number of manuscript writing systems available for teachers to use. The differences in these systems are small. They deal

### ACTIVITIES THAT IMPROVE HAND-EYE COORDINATION

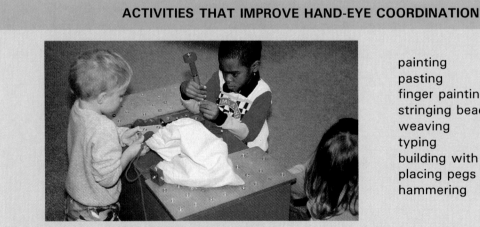

painting
pasting
finger painting
stringing beads
weaving
typing
building with blocks
placing pegs in pegboards
hammering

17-3 Eye-hand coordination activities help train the eye and hand to work together to accomplish a task.

with directions in which strokes are made and the shapes of the letters. Research does not support one system over another. Whatever system is used, you need to be skilled and consistent in its use.

Zaner-Bloser is perhaps the most widely used system. It is the system introduced in this book, 17-4. It was selected because of its common use and the ease by which children can learn to print using it.

**Materials**

Preschool children do not have the muscle control or hand-eye coordination to use lined paper. Use large unlined pieces of paper, such as newsprint instead. As children increase their muscle control and skill with writing tools, reduce the size of the paper. Writing tools for the children include chalk, crayons, watercolor markers, colored pencils, and lead pencils. Oversized lead pencils are not the best tools for

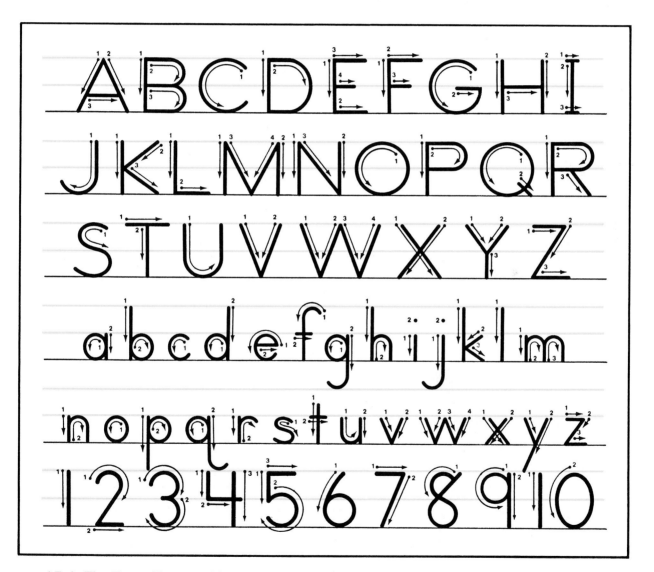

17-4 The Zaner-Bloser writing system is easy for children to use and for teachers to teach.

young children. They are hard to handle. Provide regular-sized pencils.

## Manuscript sequence

There is a sequence in how children learn alphabet letters. First, children recognize whether a line is curved or straight. Next, they learn to distinguish round letters (O, C) and curved letters (S, D). Then they learn to recognize curved letters that have intersections, such as B and R. Finally, letters with diagonal lines (K, X) and horizontal lines (L, H) are recognized.

Certain letters are easier than others for children to form. The sequence recommended in the Zaner-Bloser method follows the similarities in lower case letters. This is because lower case letters are used more often. Zaner-Bloser's recommended sequence is as follows:

litoadcefgjqusbhprnmvywkxz

1, 2, 3, 4, 5, 6, 7, 8, 9, 10

LITEFHOQCGPRBDUSJANMVWYKXZ

The easiest letters are those made of straight lines or circles. You can follow this sequence as you design written materials.

## BUILDING WRITING SKILLS

Proper writing skills are based on a few basic guidelines. Children must learn the importance of letter size, proportion, spacing, and line quality. The teacher must be able to guide them through common problems, such as letter reversal. And the teacher must be able to work through unique situations faced by left-handed children.

## Size and proportion

To provide useful models for children to imitate, you need to perfect your own writing skills. You must use the correct letter size and proportion. Lower case letters are always half the size of upper case, or capital, letters. This rule holds true no matter how small or how large the writing, and no matter where the writing appears (name tags, charts, chalkboard, games).

The size of the children's writing is based on their individual muscle development. First

writings are typically large. The letters vary in size and proportion. As the children's coordination skills mature, their writing forms decrease in size. Within any given classroom, there will usually be a wide range of skill. Look at the writings in 17-5. Kathryn's writing is mature for a four-year-old child. Her letters are all of a similar size and proportion. Amy's writing does show some variation in both size and proportion. Given time, she will develop the skill to make letters of proper proportion and size. Jena's writing almost looks like a scribble. Even though she is the same age as Kathryn and Amy, she still does not have the skills needed to write her name so it can be read. Jena needs many more hand-eye coordination and small muscle activities before she attempts writing.

## Spacing

Achieving proper spacing between letters and words is difficult for many beginning writers. Proper spacing requires more control than most preschool children are able to use. One technique to help them gain this control is to tell the children to leave enough space to write the

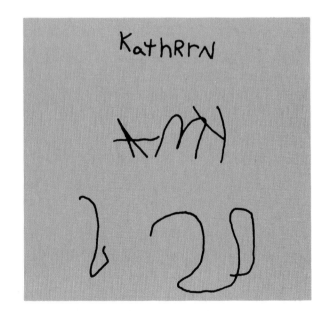

17-5 Three levels of writing skill. Jena requires extra practice to bring her skills up to a higher level.

letter "O" between words. However, this may still be too difficult for some preschool children. If so, direct them to place their index finger on the paper after the word. Then have them write the first letter of the next word to the right of their finger. Unless a child's fingers are unusually large, this technique should produce proper spacing.

### Line quality

Observe the line quality of children's writings. If a line wavers, this could mean immature coordination. Wavering lines can also result from writing too slowly or moving only fingers but not the pencil. In this case, the writer is trying to draw rather than write. Most often, wavering lines are a sign that the child lacks enough muscular control to apply constant pressure to the writing tool. To remedy this, have children use more arm action and relax their grips. Illegible writing is another common problem. Pencil lead that is too fine or too hard may be the cause of illegible work.

### Reversals

In the early stages of writing, children often reverse letters. For instance, one letter becomes another letter. A child will print b when he or she intends to write d. Some letters are written backwards. A J may have the tail reversed (ᒐ). Children may also write the letters of a word in the reversed order. For instance, Mark may write his name kraM.

You can guide children with reversal problems by pointing out differences in direction. If the child confuses the letters b and d, say, "b, line, then circle." This tells the child that a b contains a straight line first and then a circle. If the child is having a problem writing a d correctly, say, "d, circle, then line." You will find that after being given these directions some children will repeat them aloud when writing d or b.

### Practice

Children need many opportunities for writing practice. Be selective in what you provide for these times to promote this skill. Be careful that these practices do not become meaningless drills. For instance, when children are required to write a line of ten letters, they can become bored and tired. The result can be that the last letter is not formed as well as the first. Since children usually use the last letter they wrote as a model, any errors are repeated.

During practice with writing tools, show children how to hold the writing tool properly. First, ask children to watch the way you pick up a pencil. Place the pencil between your first finger and thumb. Lightly rest your index finger on the top of the pencil. Show the children how the index finger controls the heaviness of the letter. See 17-6.

### Left-handed children

About 10 percent of all children are left-handed, 17-7. A series of activities can assist you in learning a child's preferred writing hand. One of the simplest is to ask children to pick

17-6 By holding this pencil properly, this child is successful in the writing activity.

17-7 Work with left-handed children to make sure they are comfortable with writing. This child has been correctly seated with her left arm towards the left end of the table.

17-8 Introduce writing activities by helping children learn to recognize the letters of their name.

up a piece of paper, throw a ball, pick up a fork or spoon, and/or place pegs in a pegboard. To avoid stressing the use of one hand over the other, center objects in front of children. If a child repeatedly uses his or her left hand, he or she has shown a preference for that hand. Left-handed children should be placed so that their left arm is at the left end of a table for eating and work. Such placement prevents the problem of bumping arms with a right-handed child.

## EARLY EXPERIENCES IN WRITING

Early experiences often determine whether children like or dislike an activity. For this

reason, start slowly and provide activities children will not find frustrating.

Begin by encouraging children to copy their first names, 17-8. Most children have had experience writing or watching adults write their names. Early childhood teachers should stress that children learn the proper letter forms. Otherwise children can become confused if they see their name written differently at school than at home. Therefore, do not capitalize all the letters. For instance, the name "Tom" should be written using an upper case T followed by lower case o and m.

### Techniques for encouraging writing

Some children will learn to recognize their own names, classmate's names, and other words in their environment. To encourage this skill, you will need to use many teaching tools. See 17-9.

Provide children with copies of their names. Then make a bulletin board containing the children's pictures. Under each picture, place the correct name.

Other practices to encourage writing include using place mats at mealtime. Print the child's first name on the place mat. Also print names in the upper, left corner of all papers.

Writing can also be encouraged by printing labels for classroom materials and furniture. Label tables, windows, doors, clocks, sinks, shelves, and curtains, as well as other items.

Make children aware of printed names other than their own in the classroom. Do this by printing names on cards for transition times. Print all the children's names on tagboard cards. Place all of the cards in a small basket. Then draw one name at a time, allowing the children to identify the name.

Encourage children who are ready to print their name on their artwork. To prepare them for the left to right progression required in reading, tell children to print their names in the upper, left corner of their artwork.

When working with children who are having trouble writing a particular letter, try *skywriting*. Stand beside the child. Demonstrate the correct way to make the letter by writing it in the air in front of you. Have the child observe your motion, hold up his or her writing hand, and follow the strokes. Observe the child to ensure that he or she is making the correct letter.

Always use the correct terminology. For example, when writing capital letters call them capital, or upper case, letters. Do the same for lower case letters.

Provide children with letters cut out of sandpaper and mounted on tagboard. By feeling a letter, the children learn its form and shape. Another technique is to print the manuscript letters on paper, cover the paper with clear acetate sheets, and give children grease or china marking pencils. Let the children trace the letters. Their markings can be removed with a piece of felt or window cleaner spray. The acetate sheets are reusable. You might also develop puzzles that require children to match upper case letters with the proper lower case letters.

**Group experiences**

There are many group situations in which writing can be encouraged, 17-10. Have children dictate an invitation, letter, or thank you note to you. As they dictate, record their

17-9 Letter blocks provide an opportunity to trace and match letters. This helps children become familiar with all letters.

17-10 Write poems out on poster board using imaginative lettering methods. In this poem, children are shown the connection between the word "apple" and the item itself.

message in print. Follow the correct manuscript format. Call attention to the use of an upper case letter at the beginning of a sentence, a question mark or a period at the end, and an upper case letter at the beginning of names of people.

### Space for writing

A writing center has particular appeal for four- and five-year-olds. It can be developed for the classroom setting. By providing this type of center, you are saying writing is important.

This space should be separated from other areas of the classroom by bookshelves, screens, or mobile bulletin boards. This allows the privacy and quiet required for writing. Provide a variety of writing tools such as crayons, pens, pencils, and watercolor markers. Provide many sizes of unlined paper, picture dictionaries, and models of the alphabet. See 17-11.

Teachers also need to display materials that encourage printing. These materials include alphabet models, sandpaper letters, and sandboxes. Using a sandbox, children can practice tracing various alphabet letters with their index fingers. A large chalkboard can also be a useful display. On chalkboards children can make free, large movements. These movements give writing a smooth quality. Charts and other label materials throughout the classroom can be useful displays for the children to copy.

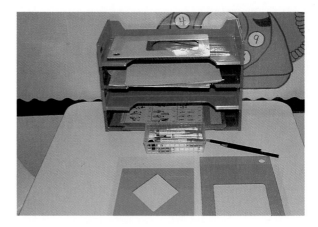

17-11 The basics of a writing center include a variety of paper types and writing tools.

Watching children's writing progress by using these materials will be exciting as well as rewarding.

### SUMMARY

In the preschool setting, children can be taught manuscript writing skills. This type of writing involves unconnected letters made of simple, separate strokes. These skills are an excellent basis for the more advanced writing done at later ages. Taught properly, children can also build basic reading skills.

## to Know

## to Review

1. Manuscript writing:
   a. Is a simple form of calligraphy.
   b. Is slower to complete than cursive writing.
   c. Does not require the sustained muscle control that cursive writing does.
   d. All of the above.
2. True or false. Manuscript writing should be taught formally in the preschool setting.
3. List three objectives for encouraging writing in preschool.
4. In order to meet these objectives, the teacher must provide _____, _____, _____, and _____ to each child.
5. What two activities should be provided to encourage children to build skills in manuscript writing?
6. True or false. The differences in writing systems are small.
7. Why should lined paper be avoided for young children's writing activities?
8. Arrange the following letter groups in the order in which children learn to recognize them.
   a. Curved letters with intersections (B, R).
   b. Round letters (O, C).
   c. Straight and curved lines.
   d. Letters with diagonal lines (K, X).
9. True or false. Upper case letters are always half the size of lower case letters.
10. What is another name for upper case letters?
11. A common writing problem for young children is _____.
12. List three items that can be placed in the writing area to encourage printing.

## to Do

1. Collect, compare, and discuss writing samples from a group of five-year-olds.
2. Practice making the letters following the Zaner-Bloser writing system.
3. Practice writing a letter using manuscript writing. When you finish, check your letter for line quality, spacing, and letter formation.
4. Prepare a set of tracing alphabet cards that children can use.
5. Brainstorm a list of all equipment and fixtures in the classroom that could have labels attached. Prepare the labels.

# Chapter 18

# Guiding Math Experiences

After studying this chapter, you will be able to:
- [ ] List objectives of early math experiences.
- [ ] Use two basic assessments to determine math skills of students.
- [ ] Recognize a variety of items that can be used to promote math experiences.
- [ ] Identify math experiences that promote the development of key math concepts.
- [ ] Design math experiences that stress specific math concepts.

"One, three, five, two," and similar phrases can often be heard from young children. They are searching for meaning as they echo these words. Reciting numbers is a key step in learning math concepts.

Early math experiences for children should focus on exploration, discovery, and understanding. Unlike in elementary schools, math concepts are not formally taught in early childhood classrooms. Instead, math concepts are taught informally in day-to-day activities. Math concepts can be taught during many activities. These include art, cooking, games, dramatic play, stories, and storytelling, 18-1.

Through art activities or by playing with blocks children may learn shapes, color, and order (logic) concepts. Cooking activities teach how quantities are related and ordered. For instance, you might tell a child, "Beat the eggs first, add the sugar second, and add the vanilla last." Classroom games can teach the concepts of first and last, as well as high and low numbers. If dice are used in games, addition concepts can be taught to the older children. Dramatic play offers all kinds of teaching opportunities. For example, as children play store, they can learn about money, 18-2. Songs, stories, and fingerplays can contain numbers and math words.

Other ways to include math concepts in the daily routine include asking, "Are there enough chairs?," "Is everybody here today?," or, "Is there a cookie for each child?" Math concepts can be used in any appropriate situation. For example, you may introduce counting concepts by remarking, "Kelsie brought three kittens to school."

Transitions (time between scheduled activities) are a good opportunity to present new math concepts. For example, you might say, "It's two o'clock and time to go to the library." At clean-up time one-to-one relationships can be taught if there is one puzzle for Mark, one for Kris, and one for Wendy to put back on the shelf. Or, after group time, you may have the set of children wearing red use the bathroom first.

18-1 Cooking activities help children learn many math concepts.

## GOALS OF EARLY MATH EXPERIENCES

Well-structured settings provide play experiences that also help form math skills. These math experiences should help form concepts such as color and shape recognition, classification, measurement, counting, time, temperature, space, and volume concepts. The math experiences should stress:

- Observing and describing concrete objects.
- Recognizing colors and shapes.
- Comparing objects and using terms that describe quantity, such as "more than" and "lighter than."
- Classifying objects.
- Copying patterns.
- Recognizing and writing numerals.
- Counting.
- Using logical words such as "all," "none," and "some."

## ASSESSING MATH ABILITY

Before planning math activities for children, first determine the children's skill levels. In

18-2 As children play store, they start to form concepts about money.

order to do this properly, children need to be assessed individually. There are two common forms of assessment: observation and specific task assessment. The information obtained from these processes will help you better know children's skills and needs. It will also help you plan developmentally appropriate math activities.

### Assessment by observation

*Observation* involves informal viewing of a child during self-selected activities, 18-3. Specific behaviors to watch for include:
- Sorting objects.
- Setting a table correctly.
- Pouring liquids and carefully watching the amount poured.
- Counting all fingers.
- Writing numerals.

Through observation, you will be able to determine a child's needs. If you notice a child cannot sort objects, you will need to provide sorting activities. Specific sorting activities are outlined later in this chapter.

18-3 Observation assessments are made by noting children's math-related actions as they play.

### Specific task assessment

*Specific task assessment* involves giving children set activities to determine skill and/or needs. Examples include:
- Present a child with crayons and say, "Tell me the colors." After the child has replied, say "Now count these for me."
- Show a child two groups of pennies: one of four pennies and one of seven pennies. Then ask the child, "What group has more pennies?"
- Present a child with circle, triangle, diamond, square, and rectangle shapes. Say, "Find the square." Then have the child identify each of the remaining shapes.
- Show a child four different sized balls. Ask: "Which is the smallest ball?," and "Which is the largest ball?"
- Lay 10 blocks in front of the child. Ask, "How many blocks do I have here?"

As with observation, the information provides information for use in planning math activities.

## MATH EQUIPMENT

Provide the children with a variety of materials that promote physical and mental activity. These items should encourage counting, observing, creating, sorting, discussing, constructing, ordering, developing patterns, and comparing. From these activities, children can develop math concepts and learn written symbols for numbers. Chart 18-4 lists many materials for learning math concepts. If these materials are in the classroom for use, children can explore and discover many math concepts.

## MATHEMATICAL ACTIVITIES

Math activities for preschool children should aid in the development of many skills. For example, children should learn to identify, to classify, and to understand the concept of a set. Children should also learn to count and recognize numbers and understand the concepts of space, size, volume, and time. The art of curriculum design is matching children's needs to their interests. This requires good observa-

## SUPPLIES FOR MATH ACTIVITIES

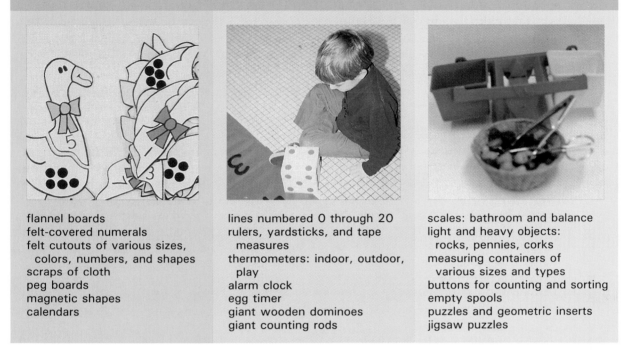

flannel boards
felt-covered numerals
felt cutouts of various sizes,
  colors, numbers, and shapes
scraps of cloth
peg boards
magnetic shapes
calendars

lines numbered 0 through 20
rulers, yardsticks, and tape
  measures
thermometers: indoor, outdoor,
  play
alarm clock
egg timer
giant wooden dominoes
giant counting rods

scales: bathroom and balance
light and heavy objects:
  rocks, pennies, corks
measuring containers of
  various sizes and types
buttons for counting and sorting
empty spools
puzzles and geometric inserts
jigsaw puzzles

18-4 Many items can be used to stress math experiences.

tion skills and a good knowledge of child development.

### Color concepts

Color is considered a math concept since it helps children learn to discriminate (tell the difference) among objects. Using color, children can classify, pattern, and sequence, 18-5. Identifying colors also seems to help language development. It requires the skill to recall a name and associate it with a visual image. Then, as the children's language skills grow, their skill at naming colors improves.

According to studies, children learn to identify colors before shapes. However, it is not uncommon for a preschool child to confuse color and shape. For example, you may ask a child to name a shape, and the child will answer with the name of a color.

Infants as young as four to six months begin to distinguish color hues, according to research.

18-5 The color in this bulletin board helps children see differences between the circles, crayons, boy, and girl.

Red, yellow, and blue (primary colors) are recognized more quickly than green, violet, and orange (secondary colors).

By age two, many children can match a color to a sample. However, some three-, four-, or five-year-old children may not be able to match colors. This problem may be caused by color blindness. This problem can be discovered through careful observation as children try to learn colors. Children who are color blind see shades of green and red as grayish brown. They may even see all colors as gray. If you notice that a child has a problem, report it to the center director. Often the director can discuss the problem with the child's parents. The parents can then decide if their child should be tested for color blindness.

Color concepts can be taught formally or informally. You can teach children to name colors using different colored blocks. Hold up a red block and ask for the name of the color. Continue by asking the children to point out other red objects around the room. Repeat these steps using the rest of the blocks.

Color recognition can also be taught at transition times. For instance, at the end of story time you may say, "All the children who are wearing red may go to the bathroom." Repeat this, using different colors, until all of the children have been excused.

Sorting objects by color can also be used to teach color concepts. Provide each child with a small bag containing several colors and shapes, including squares, rectangles, and circles, cut from tagboard. The children can be directed to sort by color and then by shape.

Charts are also a good way to teach color concepts. Charts also teach children the usefulness of graphing. An example would be a chart labeled "eye colors." Divide a piece of tagboard into four even, vertical sections. Then divide the tagboard into enough horizontal sections for every child in the class. Then have each child in the class look at the chart and determine their eye color. (You may need to help some children determine their eye color.) If the children are able, encourage them to write their name under the color that matches their own eyes. See 18-6. If the children cannot write,

give them pictures of themselves or round faces cut out of tagboard. After all of the children are done, ask, "Which eye color is the least common?" Then ask, "What eye color is the most common?" This same activity can be done using hair color.

Colored shapes can also be graphed on charts. For example, cut triangles, squares, circles, and rectangles from colored tagboard. Using a felt tip marker or pencil, divide the tagboard into four equal horizontal sections. Then divide the tagboard vertically into five or six sections. In the first vertical column glue different shapes in each box. See 18-7. Then give the children shapes to match.

A feely box or bag is useful for teaching color. Place colored buttons, paper, felt strips, or blocks into the box or bag. Select children to draw an object from the bag and identify its color.

Color hunts in the classroom are a fun way to teach color concepts. To conduct a color

| EYE COLORS | | | |
|---|---|---|---|
| Brown | Blue | Green | Hazel |
| Pablo | Mark | Sandy | |
| Sally | Chris | | |
| Shawnna | | | |
| Tom | | | |
| | | | |
| | | | |
| | | | |
| | | | |
| | | | |
| | | | |
| | | | |

18-6 This chart can be used to help children understand the concept of eye color.

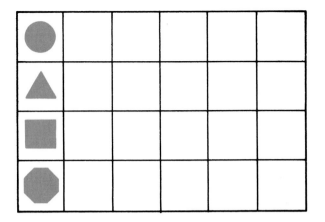

18-7 This chart helps children learn to identify shapes.

hunt, ask a child to choose a color. Then have other children point out objects of the same color found in the classroom.

Discussing colors also helps children learn to recognize them. Have a child choose a color, then ask the child to describe what the color makes him or her think of. One child may choose red and say, "Red makes me think of fire trucks and valentines." Another child may choose blue and say, "Blue makes me think of the sky."

Other activities you can conduct to teach color concepts include the following:

- Hold up a piece of green construction paper. Ask children wearing green to stand up. Repeat using different colors each time. To add interest for four- and five-year-old children, give more complex directions. For instance, say, "If you are wearing blue stand on one foot."
- Pour all of your crayons into a basket or box. Then set out several empty baskets or boxes for each color crayon. Encourage the children to sort the crayons by color.
- Using a flannel board, display several identically colored shapes. Then add one that is the same shape, but a different color. Ask the children, "Which one does not belong?" This activity can also be done using different shapes.
- Play "I Spy" with a group of children.

First, note a brightly colored classroom object. Then say, "I spy something red." Encourage the children to take turns guessing what object you are thinking about. If they cannot guess it, give them more clues. The next game is started by the child who guesses correctly.

**Shape concepts**

Children are often confused by shape. At first they will say circles and squares are the same figures because both have closed boundaries. Over time they will become aware of the features of the boundaries themselves.

The skills needed to identify and draw shapes do not develop at the same time. Children can most often name shapes before they can draw them. When copying shapes, circles are easiest for children, followed by squares, then rectangles and triangles. Most children cannot copy shapes other than circles until they are about five years of age. Before this, their copies have round corners and distances of uneven length.

To learn basic shape concepts, use a number of activities that stress touching, holding, and matching of shapes. Each activity should stress that shape. *Shape* is defined by what "goes around the outside," or the outline of the object, 18-8. To help the child grasp this concept of shape, have them trace around the outside of the shape.

Some teachers prefer to use *parquetry blocks*

18-8 Children need to focus on the outlines of these triangles before they can identify the shape.

to teach shape concepts. These blocks are geometric pieces that vary in color and shape. When the children are familiar with the blocks, hold up a shape and ask the children to find a similar shape. Next, build a simple design with three or four blocks. Ask the children to copy it.

Other activities to encourage the identification of shape include the following.

- Cut geometric shapes, including squares, rectangles, circles, and triangles out of one color of tagboard. Ask children to name and sort the shapes.
- Place a circle on a flannel board. Ask the children to name an object in the classroom of that shape. Repeat this activity using squares, rectangles, and triangles.
- Using jump ropes, masking tape, or chalk, make shapes on the floor. Ask children to name the shapes as they walk, march, or walk backwards on the figure.
- Give each child a shape cut out of tagboard. Then have the children move around the classroom to find another child with the identical shape. This activity is most useful with four- and five-year-old children.
- Another game that teaches shape is called "It's in the bag." The objective of this game is to help children name shapes by touch. Place a variety of shapes in a paper bag. Hold up a duplicate of one of the shapes. Ask a child to feel in the bag to find the matching shape.
- Plan a treasure hunt. Instruct children to find shapes around the room. For example, a round clock can be pointed out as a circle.

Do not attempt to teach shape and color concepts at the same time. Wait until color concepts are well-understood. Otherwise, some children may confuse color names with shape names.

Shape concepts are harder to teach than color concepts. Perhaps this is because color descriptions are used more often in everyday conversation. For example, children often hear phrases such as a black puppy, yellow socks, red shirt, and green room.

## Classification

Classification is one of the first skills displayed by young children. *Classification* is the process of mentally grouping objects or ideas into categories or classes based on some unique feature. If the object belongs to a class, it has one or more features in common with another object. Classification allows people to cope with large numbers of objects.

*Matching* is a form of classification. It involves putting like objects together, 18-9. *Sorting* also involves classification. It is the process of physically separating objects based on unique features.

Children begin to learn classification skills in their first weeks of life. By two months, children begin to classify experiences as pleasant or unpleasant. Eating applesauce may be pleasant. Sitting in an infant seat may be unpleasant.

Infants gather information to make classification using their senses through repeated experiences. This makes them able to relate past and present experiences. This process is known as *recognizing.* Recognizing allows children to join a new experience with a similar, earlier experience. Recognizing is a simple form of classification.

First classroom experiences with classification should involve only one feature. Often this feature is color, size, or shape, 18-10. Provide

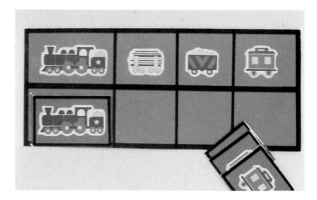

18-9 The simplest matching activities involve putting two objects that are exactly alike together.

items with obvious differences. For young children, this might include size, length, height, shape, color, or thickness.

Some useful classification tasks for young children include the following:

- Provide children with a set of black and red buttons. Have them sort the buttons into piles by color.
- Give children kitchen and bathroom items. Have them sort the items based on use.
- Provide children with a set of toys with and without wheels. Have them sort the toys into two piles based on whether or not they have wheels.
- Give children pictures of known and unknown objects cut from old magazines. Ask them to sort the pictures into "I don't know the name of" and "I know the name of" piles.
- Give children a bucket of household items. Fill the water table. Have them sort the items into "float" and "sink" piles.

As children build classification skills, increase the number of common features in the activities, 18-11. This can be done in two ways: increase the number of items to be classified or increase the number of groups into which items can be sorted.

Advanced activities include giving children a set of fabric squares. Ask the children to sort the materials into piles of striped, plaid, polka-

18-11 This sorting game involves the use of a spinner and familiar classroom objects.

dotted, and solid fabrics. Or have children classify classroom items according to function. For example, some items are used for listening, some for talking, some for writing, etc.

Notice that after children learn classification skills, they begin to watch and describe features of objects. First, a child may say an apple is round and red. Later, the child may classify it as good food. Finally, the child may say the apple belongs to a group of foods known as "fruit."

## Sets

Before children learn to add and subtract in elementary school, they need to understand sets. A *set* is a group of objects that are alike in some way and, therefore, belong together.

A key objective of early math activities is to have children learn to organize objects. Objects belonging to a set are its members. A set can have a few or many members. A set with no members is called an *empty set*. A set of glasses is often a certain number such as four, six, eight, or twelve. A set of tires for a small airplane is usually two.

18-10 These cards are designed to be classified only by shape.

In order to understand the concept of set, children first need to learn about sets that have like members. This is best taught in small groups. Items needed are sets of objects having like members, such as puzzle pieces, blocks, crayons, and squares of colored paper. See 18-12. Introduce one set of objects at a time. Say, "What are these? These are all blocks. We call them a set of blocks." Then introduce the remaining sets. Repeat the process. Stress the concept of set. To conclude the activity, ask, "What are some other sets in the room?"

The concept of set can be strengthened by asking a small group of children to divide themselves into a set. First divide the children into sets of light- and dark-haired children. Encourage them to regroup themselves into different sets. They might divide by sex, color of clothing, color of eyes, types of footwear (street shoes, tennis shoes), age, or type of hair.

Teach the concept of an empty set during snack time. Provide each child with a plate holding a banana sliced into five pieces. Tell the children to eat one piece of banana. Explain that they now have a set of four banana pieces. Tell the children to eat another piece. Ask the

children how many pieces remain. Tell them that is the number of members still in the set. Keep going until all the pieces are eaten. Then explain that a set without any members is called an empty set. To strengthen this lesson, ask the children to name other empty sets in the room. For example, the set of tables without legs, or the set of children with beards are empty sets.

Another way to explain the empty set is through experience. To do this, use five empty jars. Leave the first jar empty. Place a penny in the second jar. Place two pennies in the third jar, three pennies in the fourth jar, and four pennies in the fifth jar. Then ask the children to observe and compare the number of objects in each jar. (Self-sealing plastic bags could be used instead of jars for this activity if preferred.)

## Counting

Counting is a basic math skill. It needs to be included in the curriculum because it is a key problem-solving tool. Many people believe counting is taught at home. This is not always true. Therefore, it does need to be taught at school. Most children can count up to their age. Two-year-olds can often count to two. Three-year-olds usually can count to three. Of course, some children can count higher. Many four- and five-year-old children can count beyond their age.

Children are often first exposed to counting by an adult who counts the children's toes or fingers. After they hear this routine enough times, children will begin to count along. This same technique is used to count other objects, such as beads, puzzle pieces, and blocks. Only after children learn the spoken number do they learn the written numbers (two) and the numerals (2).

The ability to count occurs in two stages: rote and rational counting. Rote counting is learned before rational. Rote counting is recitation of numbers in order. This skill involves memory, not understanding. *Rational counting* involves attaching a number to a series of grouped objects, 18-13. For example, a child has a box of crayons sitting on the table. If you ask the child for some crayons, he or she may

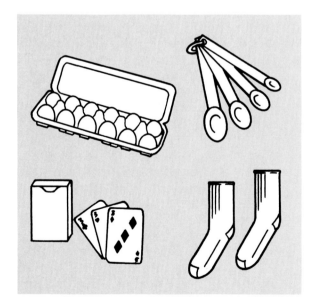

18-12 Many common items can be used to teach the concept of set.

place them on the table one at a time. As the child places each crayon, he or she assigns it a number in sequence.

Many children you teach will be able to recite numbers in their correct order. However, they will often not understand their meaning.

Three-year-old Tammy has typical number skills. The following activities illustrate her understanding:

- The teacher places seven pennies on the floor and asks Tammy to count them. She counts from one to nine before she fingers the last penny.
- The teacher then arranges the pennies in a circle. Again she asks Tammy to count them. She becomes confused several times and has to begin again.
- Next, the teacher places seven pennies in a pile and spreads out seven pennies more. When asked which pile has more pennies, Tammy points to the pennies that are spread out.

Children should always be exposed to rational counting using concrete objects. The simplest way to do this is through physical guidance. Lay the objects in a straight line. Then take the child's hand as he or she counts, touching each object as it is counted. At first, you may have to help the child count aloud.

After children have had many counting experiences, test their understanding. Send a child to get four crayons, two pieces of paper, or three blocks.

18-13 Rational counting involves attaching a number to a series of objects.

## Identifying numerals

In order to read and write, children must first recognize written numbers and their symbols. This skill develops as children are exposed to written numerals. Group time is a good time to emphasize numbers. Have children help you keep a record of daily attendance and daily temperature. Discuss the calendar.

A good activity for teaching number symbols is to have the children take part in a number walk. To do this, collect ten sheets of 9- by 12-inch paper. Number the sheets from 1 to 10. (To increase the durability of these sheets, cover them with clear adhesive sheets.) Then place the papers in a circle on the floor at random. Play some familiar music and ask the children to walk through the path of numbered pieces. Tell them when the music stops they will each get to tell the name of the number on which they are standing.

Another way to teach symbols is to set up a grocery store in the dramatic play area. Collect empty food containers and attach stickers with price tags from one to five cents. This activity can also include a toy store or drugstore.

A number line is yet another way to teach numbers. This teaching aid is based on units of length, instead of objects.

Children should also have the opportunity to write numerals in their symbol form. You may have children write in numerals on calendars or charts.

Children often find numerals hard to form. You may see many reversals. These problems are common and usually are self-correcting in time. You may be surprised to learn that children often prefer to write numbers over alphabet letters.

## Space concepts

Describing positions of objects in space is an important part of early math experiences. Space concepts can be taught during cleanup time, art time, blockbuilding, and other activities. Space concepts that should be introduced are listed in 18-14.

Some experiences for teaching space concepts include the following:

## SPACE CONCEPTS

before, after
high, low
up, down
here, there
far, near
above, below
in front of, in back of, between
inside, outside
top, center, bottom

18-14 These word groups stress space concepts.

- Play the game "Simon Says." Use the words listed in 18-14. Give directions to the children such as, "Place your finger on top of your head," and "Raise your right hand." Using simple concepts often works well, even with two-and-a-half and three-year-old children. When using a new concept, you may have to model it for the children.
- Place several picturs of fruit on a flannel board. Then ask, "Which piece of fruit is below the orange?" "Which piece of fruit is above the grapefruit?" "Which piece of fruit is below the grapes?"
- Give each child three different items such as a block, a poker chip, and a button. Then give the children verbal directions using space words: "Place the poker chip on top of the block." "Place the button under the block." "Pick up the block with your right hand."
- Using a small animal puppet, such as a monkey, tell the children the puppet's name is Marvin. Explain to the group that Marvin is going to tell them what to do. They must listen closely. Disguise your voice and have Marvin model a number of space concepts. After two or three examples, ask the children to stand and follow Marvin's directions. Marvin might make these statements: "Put your hand on top of your head." "Point your finger up

high." "Place one foot above the other." "Sit down." "Stand up."
- Give each child a crayon, a small box or empty can, and a button. Again, have the puppet give directions: "Place the crayon on top of the box." "Place the crayon behind the box." "Place the crayon beside the box." To get the children more involved, allow them to take turns using the puppet and giving directions.
- Use familiar circle games such as "Hokey Pokey" to teach space concepts.
- Place five familiar items, such as a penny, stick, rock, clothespin, and puzzle piece, top to bottom on a table. Then ask the children questions about the items: "What item is at the top?" "What item is at the bottom?" "What item is in the middle?" A stack of colored blocks or puzzle pieces can also be used to teach the concepts of top, bottom, and middle.

Remember that to maintain any skill children need frequent review. Unlike adults, children do not tire as easily from repetitive experiences. Your enthusiasm and support is important.

### Size concepts

Children develop size concepts only through experience. Introduce and stress the words listed in 18-15 to teach children about size. These words can be used throughout the day.

### Volume concepts

An early childhood program should offer many opportunities to explore volume. The sand and water table is a piece of equipment that is useful for this task. Provide many containers of varying volumes and shapes for measuring. During the children's play with these materials, introduce volume concepts such as a lot, much, empty, full, little, and some. When children use these concepts, they think about their world in terms of quantity.

### Time concepts

"Is yesterday Christmas?" Molly, a four-year-old, asked one of the other children. Molly's question is common of a young child. Time is a difficult concept for children to

big, little
large, small
long/tall, short
wide, thin
big, bigger, biggest
small, smaller, smallest
inches, feet, pounds
smaller than, bigger than

18-15 Use of proper terms, along with visual aids, will help children grasp size concepts.

understand. Part of the reason for this is because it can stand for so many situations: past, present, future, tomorrow, soon, in no time, etc.

Studies suggest that young children have only a vague concept of time. In fact, the average five-year-old child knows only the difference between afternoon and morning, night and day. Children usually cannot read the time on a watch or clock until about age seven.

You can use routines to teach time concepts to young children. For example, you might say the following: "After lunch, we take naps." "Your mother will come to pick you up after outdoor playtime," "Before large group, we need to put our toys away."

You can also offer time experiences to children by using the correct time words. Include words such as those listed in 18-16.

Children should also learn about the passing of time. For example, you may ask, "Do you remember the clown that came to school?" Or you may ask, "How did we make the play dough last time?"

There are many activities for teaching children time concepts. Included are the following:
- Provide children with a large, month-long calendar. Use the calendar each day during a large group activity. Review the days of the week, and use such words as yesterday, tomorrow, last week, and next week.
- Encourage children to play with a toy alarm clock.

## TIME CONCEPTS

| | |
|---|---|
| day, night | yesterday, tomorrow |
| before, after | early, late |
| minute, second | spring, summer |
| now, later | new, old |
| morning, afternoon | autumn, winter |

18-16 Use terms such as these to describe time. This reinforcement will help children understand time concepts.

- Hang a large classroom clock at the children's eye level.
- Use a cooking timer during cooking experiences. Some teachers also use a cooking timer to give children a warning before they change activities. For example, the teacher may say as the timer is set, "In five minutes, it will be time to clean up."
- Provide time recording equipment, such as a stopwatch, alarm clock, wristwatch, hourglass, etc. Place these items on a table where children will feel free to explore them.

### Temperature concepts

Cooking and outdoor activities help introduce temperature concepts. (Many ideas for cooking activities are given in Chapter 21.) To teach these concepts, include such words as thermometer, hot, cold, warm, and cool.

### SUMMARY

Math experiences in the early childhood setting should stress exploration, discovery, and understanding. Children of this age require these broad, basic experiences. With such a foundation, they can build more advanced math skills as they get older.

For younger children, math experiences can be informal in nature. Many daily events and routines lend themselves to informal math experiences. Play experiences can also be a setting for math experiences.

## to Know

classification    recognizing
empty set    set
matching    sorting
parquetry blocks    specific task
rational counting    assessment

## to Review

1. Early math experiences should focus on:
   a. Exploration.
   b. Discovery.
   c. Understanding.
   d. All of the above.
2. List four objectives of early math experiences.
3. Name and describe the two common forms of assessment used to determine math abilities.
4. True or false. Math materials and equipment should consist of only traditional items such as an abacus and flash cards.
5. Why is color considered a math concept?
6. Which do children learn to do first—to identify or draw shapes?
7. _____ defines what "goes around the outside."

8. Is it a good idea to teach shape and color concepts at the same time? Why or why not?
9. _____ is the process of mentally grouping objects based on some unique feature.
10. What is the difference between sorting and matching?
11. A _____ is a group of objects that are alike in some way, and therefore, belong together.
12. _____ is a difficult concept for children to develop because the word represents the past, present, and future.
13. List three vocabulary words that can be used to teach temperature concepts.

## to Do

1. Review a school equipment catalog and make a list of any equipment that can be used to teach space concepts.
2. Discuss methods to use to help young children understand size concepts.
3. Make a list of activities parents or guardians can use to teach counting.
4. Find a recipe that could be used for a cooking activity to teach temperature concepts.
5. Discuss activities that could be used to teach children the concept of set.

# Chapter 19

# *Guiding Science Experiences*

After studying this chapter, you will be able to:
- ☐ Explain what is meant by science.
- ☐ Discuss reasons for studying science.
- ☐ Outline the procedure for planning science activities.
- ☐ List a variety of science supplies and sources for these supplies.
- ☐ Explain the role of the teacher in guiding science experiences.
- ☐ Identify methods for developing children's understanding of their senses.
- ☐ Name and explain various ways to teach science concepts.

Kelly's first contact with a butterfly was accidental at about age two. Her study of the bug was brief but intense. It involved mainly her senses of sight and touch. Quickly she picked the butterfly up and said, "What's dat?" Her mother replied, "It's a butterfly." This experience opened the world of natural science to Kelly. Later, whenever she saw a butterfly or moth, she repeated her new word, "butterfly."

Much of what children learn relates to science concepts. Their first learnings are often simple, but meaningful. You can help form children's science concepts by making science experiences a part of your curriculum.

## WHAT IS SCIENCE?

*Science* is the study of natural processes and their products. It is a way of viewing the universe. In order for children to understand their world, they must actively explore and question. For this reason, early childhood experiences should use the hands-on approach for both process and products. The hands-on approach gives children the chance to be involved in and think about sights, sounds, and smells of the world around them.

274

Science is a creative field of study. It requires the development of curiosity and imagination. As children watch, study, wonder, or ask questions, they learn about science. Therefore, science activities should relate to the children's daily experiences.

Science is also a way to gain understanding of why events happen the way they do. Studying science inspires children to be aware of and involved with their surroundings.

Science involves observing, exploring, measuring, comparing, classifying, predicting, and discovering. The focus for young children should be on observing and exploring, 19-1. Young children are good observers and explorers because they see the world from a fresh point of view. They have no preformed ideas of how the world and nature work.

All attempts to gain information about our surroundings begin with observation. With their keen observation skills, children notice new items in their surroundings.

Using all the senses to observe is the start of discovery. Using their senses, children begin to see relationships between different events. They start to group their information and begin to make generalizations.

**Why study science?**

Studies show science activities enhance the curiosity of children, 19-2. Children also build skill in picking out similarities and differences. Vocabulary improves. This enhances reading readiness. Children improve their language skills and general knowledge as concepts such as round, triangular, rectangular, big, and small are discussed.

Small muscle development and hand-eye coordination improve as children measure items, collect samples, and handle objects. By weighing seashells and counting rocks, math skills are also enhanced.

## PLANNING SCIENCE ACTIVITIES

Some of the most successful science experiences will be unplanned. For instance, you might bring in a small snake you found on the

19-1 This child is learning to observe and explore as she watches for this egg to be hatched.

19-2 Watching plants grow often enhances the curiosity of young children.

way to the center. This can be the starting point to discuss snakes. Or a spider may move across the floor. You can watch, study, and talk about the spider. If the wind rises suddenly, blowing debris around the play yard, you can discuss the wind.

However, most science projects need to be planned. You will need to schedule events, prepare materials, and arrange the science area. You will find that science activities mesh well with other daily activities. You may plan a water, food, or sensory activity that teaches a science concept. Fingerplays, stories, field trips, math activities, physical activity, and art projects can all be the basis of science concepts.

Give children time to play with, examine, and try the science materials and equipment, 19-3. Science activities should offer children the chance to:

- Observe.
- Note differences and likenesses.
- Solve problems.
- Collect samples.
- Develop new interests and skills.
- Listen to sounds and records.
- View filmstrips.
- Look at books.
- Collect pictures.

### Science area

The science area is often set apart from other classroom areas. Tables, shelves, and/or storage cabinets can be used.

The science area is best located near a kitchen. This allows access to both heat and water sources. These sources are quite important for many science projects.

An outdoor science area may also be used. This area may contain a garden space and an area for conducting weather tests. Small animals, such as chickens, rabbits, and birds may be raised. Store garden tools, insect nets, and water tubes in an outdoor shed to encourage children to use the outdoor area.

### Equipment and materials

Equipment and materials for a science area need not be costly. Most items can be secured free or at little cost. Two factors must be given

19-3 Having the chance to play with, examine, and use science equipment will promote children's growth in science knowledge.

some thought during the selection process. First, consider whether the item you are thinking about buying is safe. Then decide whether the children have the skills needed to use the item. See Chart 19-4.

Many child care centers have a *science table,* 19-5. This table is used to display items related to the science area. The teacher often obtains the items to be placed on the table. However, children should be encouraged to bring their own items for the table. Collections children often enjoy include leaves, nuts, rocks, weeds, moths and other insects, bird's nests, cocoons, and seeds.

Children should feel motivated to explore the science table on their own. Therefore, the material on the science table should be changed often. If the collections remain on the table too long, children become bored and their interest in the table decreases. It also helps to house collections in an appealing way. You might display items in a tent, store setting, cave setting, booth, trailer, push cart, or wagon.

The science table should sit away from walls. This allows children to move about the table freely. They will feel comfortable touching, smelling, hearing, tasting, and observing as they explore.

Centerpieces at the snack or lunch table also promote children's interest in nature. A bowl of pine cones or gourds, a bouquet of flowers, or a pumpkin bring the world of science indoors.

Playground equipment can also be used to teach science concepts. For example, pedaling a bike makes the energy needed to move a bike.

## SCIENCE SUPPLIES

**School supplies**

| | |
|---|---|
| globes | scissors |
| paints | paste |
| clay | string |
| chalk | blocks |
| straws | measuring instruments |
| colored paper | |

**Scrap items**

| | |
|---|---|
| discarded clocks | airplane and automobile parts |
| sawdust | funnels |
| locks and keys | |

**Classroom pets**

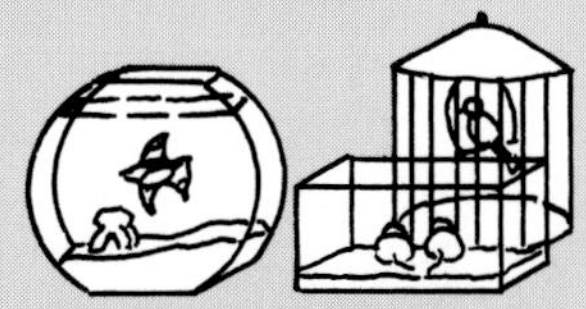

| | |
|---|---|
| hamsters | gerbils |
| snakes | spiders |
| frogs | fish |
| birds | mice |
| rabbits | guinea pigs |

**Construction tools**

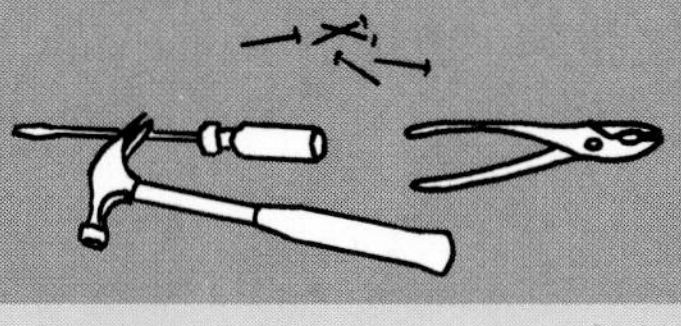

| | |
|---|---|
| hammers | screws |
| nails | bolts |
| rulers | vice |
| saws | pliers |
| screwdriver | |

**Household items**

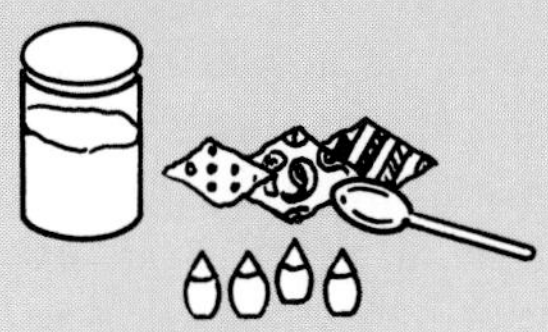

| | |
|---|---|
| jars | spoons |
| strainers | empty containers |
| food coloring | cloth pieces |
| salt | wood scraps |
| sugar | plastic meat trays |
| metal scraps | |

19-4 Materials and equipment that can be used in science experiences are nearly endless.

19-5 This science table has many interesting items for children to explore: photographs, magnets, plants, etc.

19-6 Teachers direct science experiences, but they must also know when to step back and let children do for themselves.

Using a teeter-totter demonstrates the laws of balance.

## ROLE OF THE TEACHER

As the teacher, your role is to direct activities and projects, 19-6. You must know when to let children work alone and when to step in. At times, a simple suggestion or hint can help a child who is frustrated. On the other hand, unneeded input can sometimes stifle curiosity. This can destroy the desire to keep experimenting.

The activities you plan should include materials for all children. Children should have ample hands-on activities in which they work with materials. This process allows children to discuss relationships and concepts among themselves.

Activities should promote development of the five basic process skills. These skills are:

1. Observing objects using the five senses: seeing, feeling, tasting, smelling, and hearing.
2. Drawing conclusions from observations based on knowledge gained in past experience.
3. Classifying objects into sets based on one or more observable properties.
4. Comparing sets of objects by measuring and counting.
5. Communicating by describing objects, relationships, and occurrences.

Provide many chances for children to practice being careful observers. Children enjoy watching and wondering. Going on field trips, viewing filmstrips, looking at pictures, and viewing objects on the science table are all good ways of helping children build powers of observation.

To encourage children to explore, use effective questioning techniques. Asking a great deal of questions is not always a useful technique. Instead, ask fewer questions that require more thought. *Open-ended questions* promote discussion and require decision-making skills. *Close-ended questions* (sometimes called *single-answer questions*) demand few decision-making skills and are most often answered with yes or no. See 19-7. Poor questioning techniques encourage children to guess.

Children need time to respond to open-ended questions. And, at least for a short time, they need their answer accepted. Positive response should be given. When a "better" answer is offered, the teacher can explain how the new answer adds to other answers. Children also need to be heard. Listening on the teacher's part strengthens their wish to participate.

The caregiver or teacher always sets the tone for learning science in the classroom. A simple rule is to base activities on children's questioning. Do not give answers to questions children have not asked. Let the children "do" science using process skills as well as listening, watching, or reading about science. Teachers who control the learning activity do little to promote questions. To create the right climate, provide materials for all children, study their interaction with the materials, and listen to them talk to each other. Finally, ask only those questions that add to the child's knowledge.

## DEVELOPING THE CHILD'S UNDERSTANDING OF SENSES

As children learn more about their senses, they become aware of how to explain their surroundings. One way to help children learn to focus on how they use their senses is to pop popcorn. During the experience, children can see, hear, and smell the popcorn popping. After it is popped, they can feel and taste the popcorn.

From popping corn, children can learn the following concepts: we see with our eyes; we hear with our ears; we smell with our noses; we feel with our skin; we taste with our tongues.

### Feeling

Feeling is a fun and important sense to explore in science studies for children. Whenever time permits, provide opportunities to feel a number of objects in the classroom. A *feely box* can be made by cutting a circle in a box large enough for the children to put their hands in. (A *feely bag* can also be used. It should be opaque and easy to reach into without exposing the contents.) See 19-8. Put different objects and materials inside the box. Let each child

19-8 Children can concentrate on the sense of touch when they feel objects in a feely box.

### OPEN-ENDED AND CLOSE-ENDED QUESTIONS

| Open-Ended | Closed-Ended |
|---|---|
| What are you observing? | What color is it? |
| How could you classify these? | Can you classify these by shape? |
| What happens to hamburger when it is fried? | Has the hamburger changed color? |

19-7 Can you think of other pairs of open-ended and close-ended questions?

reach in the box and try to identify an object. If they have a hard time, give clues. For example, if the item is a spoon, you may say, "It is something we use to eat cereal with in the morning."

Children can also build the sense of touch using fabric samples of varying textures. These may include velvet, leather, flannel, knit, burlap, felt, and cotton. Encourage the children to explain what each piece feels like. You might add other materials such as fur, sandpaper, glazed paper, sponge, pebbles, and cork. To add variety, place the materials on the science table where the children can sort them based on like textures.

### Smelling

Preschool children need to learn that objects can be named by their smells. One method for teaching this is to collect items in the classroom that have distinct odors such as tempera paint, markers, crayons, play dough, bar soap, sawdust, gerbil food, and glue. Place a small amount of each item in a container such as a small paper cup. Explain to the children that the game you will be playing involves naming items by smell.

Food can also be used in the smelling activity. For example, place catsup, mustard, applesauce, chocolate syrup, orange juice, and other common foods in containers and repeat the same steps.

### Seeing

Experience using sight is just as important as smelling. One game that has been used in early childhood centers is "I See Something." For example, you may say, "I see something green. It is small and round. It is in the art area." After you speak, pause to allow the children to guess. If the children are not able to guess, provide more clues.

An activity that helps children build visual memory skills is naming what is missing from a group. Collect common classroom objects such as crayons, blocks, puzzle pieces, paint brushes, and toy cans. Gather four children, show them the objects, and explain that you will remove one object. Instruct the children

to close or cover their eyes. Remove one object, then have them open their eyes and tell you what object is missing.

There are many variations to this game. You may increase the number of objects. Or you might place three or four objects in a sequence and ask which objects are out of sequence. Or you may remove two or three objects from the group and have the children name what is missing.

### Hearing

Hearing is another sense that helps children explain their surroundings. To help children become more aware of this sense, use a tape recorder.

Teach the concept that each person's voice sounds differently from any other. Record the voice of each child. To encourage the children to talk, ask each child to tell you about a family member, a favorite person, or a story. After you have taped all the children in the classroom, play the tape to the group. Ask the children to place each child's voice with the correct child.

### Tasting

Tasting skills can be built through the use of food. Plan a tasting party using a number of common foods. Blindfold a child and give him or her a small sample of some food. Ask the child to name the food. Repeat the activity with all of the children in the group. Some teachers prefer to do this as a group activity, providing a sample of each food for all of the children at the same time.

## USING COLOR TO TEACH SCIENCE CONCEPTS

Color is a part of science that children observe daily. Naming colors is one way children describe their world. Color also serves as a basis for grouping. The primary colors red, blue, and yellow can be introduced to the children in the science area. Using red, blue, and yellow boxes, encourage the children to match toys, such as beads or blocks with similarly colored boxes. The secondary colors, purple, green, and orange can be introduced next. Again, using toys, have the children match the color of the toy to the container.

Some teachers have special "color days." For example, Monday may be orange day. To prepare for this day, send a note or letter to parents or guardians. Ask that children wear the color of the day. This may be in the form of a hair ribbon, pin, barrette, or any article of clothing.

Snacks may be coordinated with the color of the day. For example, orange slices, carrots, or cantaloupe may be served on an orange day.

Mixing colors is another way to teach color concepts, 19-9. Mixing primary colors to make secondary colors, the children learn how colors are made. Thus, as children learn color concepts they become more aware of their surroundings. One way to show mixing of colors is to overlap colored cellophane. Another way is to set up jars or clear plastic glasses in the science area. Have the children fill the jars with water. Using food coloring, have the children place drops in each container. Stress color comparisons by using terms such as "lighter than," "darker than," or "same color as."

## USING WATER TO TEACH SCIENCE CONCEPTS

Water delights almost all children. As young children play with water and accessories, they learn about science concepts. Some concepts taught with water include:
- Water flows when poured.
- Water makes objects wet.
- Some containers hold more water than others.
- Some items float on water.
- Water dissolves some foods.
- Some materials soak up water.

### Equipment and accessories
In programs without watertables, large washtubs, sinks, photographic developing trays, or plastic swimming pools can be used. A table can also be made, 19-10.

Supply watertable accessories. Include funnels, spoons, sprinkling cans, nesting cups,

19-9 Food coloring can be used to teach children the concept of color mixing.

19-10 A watertable can be made using wood scraps and a plastic liner.

plastic containers, egg beaters, measuring cups, strainers, corks, sponges, plastic tubing, soap, and food coloring.

To avoid excessive cleanup, put down a shower curtain or plastic tablecloth to protect the floor. Plastic aprons may be used to protect the children's clothes.

Fill the container with water based on the children's experience and age. (Younger children only need two or three inches.) Provide the children with accessories and allow them to experiment freely.

### Activities

Freeze water for the children. From this, the children will learn that ice is frozen water; ice can melt; melted ice is called water; ice can be picked up; and ice melts in warm places.

Teach the children that some materials absorb water. Use sponges, terry cloth, tissues, paper towels, cardboard, plastic wrap, wax paper, newsprint, finger paint paper, and plastic. You may wish to make a chart listing the materials and noting whether they absorb water. From using these materials, children should learn that some materials soak up water.

Water can teach children about floating. Fill the watertable half full of water. Provide items such as wooden blocks, pencils, paper, plastic alphabet letters, metal spoons, large nails, and aluminum foil. Record each item that floats on a chart. Children will learn that some items float on water.

Children can also learn, through observation and participation, what materials dissolve in water. Fill several small pitchers with water. Then have each child fill several small baby food jars or plastic glasses. Provide each child with a material that dissolves in water such as salt, sugar cubes, or baking soda. Also supply items that will not dissolve such as cooking oil, rice, or margarine. Then let each child stir the mixture. Ask the children, "What happens when you add (salt, rice, etc.) to water?" Encourage the children to discuss the results as each item is added to the water.

Painting with water is an activity best suited to the outdoors. Provide the children with cans of water and wide paint brushes. Have them paint surfaces such as a cement sidewalk. Then ask them what happens to the water. Try this in different types of weather. Children will see that on hot days the water evaporates and on cold days it freezes. Select a cement area that will not be used for walking to avoid accidents.

## USING FOODS TO TEACH SCIENCE CONCEPTS

Science experiments that can be eaten are both fun and educational. Watching foods as they cook, children learn how solid materials can change. Some foods become softer and some firmer as they are heated. Heat may also change the color and blend the flavors of many foods. Many guidelines for using foods in classroom experiences are given in Chapter 21.

Baking bread is a science project that involves both a process and a product. In order to have baked bread, a process must be followed. This process involves:

- Reading the recipe.
- Collecting all of the ingredients, pans, and utensils.
- Mixing the correct amounts of ingredients.
- Setting the correct oven temperature.
- Checking when the bread should be removed.

A number of other cooking projects can be used. Some teachers prefer to tie these experiences to weekly themes or units. For example, they may have a unit on fall, Halloween, and/or Thanksgiving. Cooking experiences can focus on pumpkins, squash, apples, or cranberries. Activities should include:

- Preparing food in different ways (boiling, baking, broiling).
- Using many kitchen tools (mixers, food processors, blenders).
- Examining the insides of foods (peeling a potato, slicing an apple).
- Observing the way products change during preparation.

Foods that can be prepared easily in the center are listed in 19-11.

Children can learn that food varies in size, shape, and color. Some foods are heavier than others. One way to teach these concepts is to supply children with carrots, celery, apples, bananas, oranges, and grapes for snacks. Have them discuss the differences among these foods.

## USING THE CHILD'S OWN BODY TO TEACH SCIENCE CONCEPTS

Children go through rapid physical changes during the preschool years. These growth changes are often more obvious to parents and teachers than to the children themselves. One way to help children understand their own bodies is through science experiences. Using photographs and drawings of the children is quite effective.

**FOODS CHILDREN CAN PREPARE**

| | |
|---|---|
| ice cream | scrambled eggs |
| cookies | cocoa |
| pumpkin bread | butter |
| jelly | popcorn |
| applesauce | ice pops |
| bread | pudding |

19-11 Making food items such as these will give children the chance to both proceed through a recipe and see the finished product.

One science concept to introduce is that people can be recognized by the way that they look. To teach this, take pictures of each child using an instamatic camera. After the picture is developed, show it to the child. Encourage the child to tell you about the picture. If he or she does not respond, ask specific questions about the photo, such as, "What are you wearing in the picture? What color eyes do you have? What color hair do you have?"

You may have some children who find it hard to link a photo with themselves. For instance, one teacher had a very difficult time with twins. Each time the twins saw themselves in a mirror or a picture, they identified their sibling. Experiences like these are helpful for showing children they have special physical traits.

A body outline is another activity that will help children understand their bodies, 19-12. You will need crayons and a large sheet of paper to trace the body outline. Have one child at a time lie down on a piece of paper so that you can trace his or her body. After you have finished, have the children draw their facial features and clothing on their body outlines.

19-12 Body outlines help children understand their own bodies better.

Encourage parents to get involved by sending home their child's body outline along with a parent letter. In the letter, explain how the parents can assist the children in cutting out the figures and filling in the clothing and features. When the body outlines are returned to school, display all of them.

A growth chart can be used to teach the concept of measurement. A chart can be made by outlining and cutting a shape such as a carrot from a piece of tagboard. Use orange for the carrot and green for the stem. Glue a tape measure vertically down the center of the carrot. Hang the carrot to a door, wall, or bulletin board. Have each child stand next to the tape. Record their heights on the tagboard. (Other shapes, such as a banana or stick of celery, can be used for the chart.)

A chart recording each child's weight can be used to teach the concept of weight. You may want to record weight at the start of the year and again at midyear to show this concept to the children.

## USING GARDENING TO TEACH SCIENCE CONCEPTS

The study of gardening and seeds helps children build an interest in growing things. Most children, by five or six years of age, can identify common seeds such as watermelon, apple, and peach seeds. Yet not many of these children know they are eating seeds when they eat bananas. Not many children know walnuts, pecans, rice, and peas are seeds, also.

### Seeds and food

Science experiments using seeds can be done at snack time or lunchtime. Talk about only one type of seed at a time. For example, ask the children, "What color is the orange? What is inside the orange?" Then give each child an orange that you have begun to peel. Show them how to peel the rest of the fruit. Then show them how to pull the orange apart. Encourage the children to look for seeds. Ask questions about the orange seeds such as, "How many seeds are there in your orange? Are the seeds the same size? How do the seeds look? How do the seeds feel?" When they are through, have them place their seeds on the science table.

Introduce new seeds at other snack times or lunchtimes. Use the same steps. Compare the seeds from different fruits in terms of size, color, and texture. Again, collect the seeds. Place them on the science table. Collect seeds from a number of fruits to display on the science table.

**Seed party.** Have a seed party to teach children that some seeds must be shelled before they are eaten. Collect a number of nuts that can be eaten: peanuts, walnuts, pecans, and a coconut. Ask the children to help you crack the seeds and remove the meat. As they sample the meat from each seed, discuss the flavors and talk about which seeds are grown underground.

Pumpkin, sunflower, mixed nuts, and soybean seeds, as well as mixed nuts and popcorn, may also be used. You may want to roast and sauté some of the seeds. During the roasting period ask questions such as, "Which seeds are labeled nuts? How does cooking change the taste?"

### Observing seeds

A nature or seed walk is another way to teach children that seeds come from fruits of plants. Before leaving on the walk, give each child a paper bag. Label each bag with the child's name. Then walk to a park or other area where seeds are plentiful. When the group returns to the classroom, ask the children to each choose three seeds to add to the science table. Save the rest of the seeds for an art display.

Put magnifying glasses on the science table with the seeds, 19-13. Encourage the children to use the glasses to view the shapes, sizes, colors, and textures of the seeds. This should help the children become aware of the seeds' differences and similarities.

### Planting seeds

Planting seeds is another way to teach children about plants and growth. Have children plant bean, corn, and radish seeds in individual containers, 19-14. Use paper cups, tuna cans, milk cartons, or clay pots. Put the children's names on the containers. Give the children soil to use for planting. The best mixture for growth is garden soil, or loam. It supplies nutrients for the plant and provides good moisture and drainage control. After the soil is in the can, let the children choose the seeds they will plant. Show them how to use their fingers to make holes in the soil. Add the seeds and cover with soil. Then, using a watering can, show them how to lightly dampen the soil.

19-13 This child is using a magnifying class to study the shape, size, color, and texture of the seeds from a gourd.

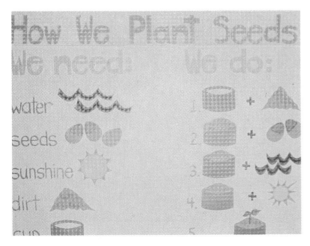

19-14 Use a chart to show children how to plant seeds.

Most seeds will grow when given proper moisture and temperature. When the seedlings emerge from the surface of the soil, place the containers where they will receive sunlight. Encourage the children to check the containers daily. Ask questions such as, "What seeds sprouted first? Do all plants have similar leaves? How many leaves does each plant have?" From this experience the children should learn:

- Seeds planted in soil and given water, warmth, and sunshine grow.
- As plants grow, their size changes.

**Dish garden.** Make a dish garden using pineapple, turnip, carrot, or beet tops. First, cut off the tops about one and one-quarter inch below the leaves. Then place the tops in clear, shallow dishes with water and sand. Put the dish on the science table where the children can watch the growth.

**Vase garden.** Collect an onion, yam, sweet potato, or avocado pit and a jar large enough to hold the vegetable. Suspend the vegetable on toothpicks, 19-15. You may have to add small amounts of water from time to time. As

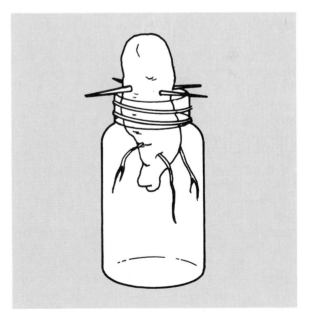

19-15 Many vegetables grow with little care if suspended in this way.

the vegetable sprouts and evaporation takes place the water level will decrease. Students can observe the roots and stems as they grow.

## USING AIR TO TEACH SCIENCE CONCEPTS

Every day children have experiences with air. They watch airplanes and birds, blow up balloons, and fly kites. They feel the wind blow against their bodies.

### Teaching about air

To help children understand the concept that air takes up space, inflate some balloons. Do this activity in a group. Start by showing the children a deflated balloon. Then tell them to watch closely as you blow up the balloon. After the balloon is inflated ask, "What is inside the balloon?" Pass out balloons to all the children. Encourage them to fill the balloons with air. After the activity, collect all the balloons.

Bubble solutions are another way to teach children that air takes up space. You can buy a prepared solution or use the recipe in 19-16.

After you have mixed the solution, give each child a straw and a paper cup. Make a hole, using a pencil point or an ice pick, about one inch from the bottom of the paper cup. Have the children place a straw in the hole. Then have them dip the open end of the cup in the bubble solution. Finally, ask them to remove the cup from the solution and, with the cup in an upside down position, blow.

Encourage the children to blow bubbles, 19-17. Ask them, "What is inside of the bubbles? How did you get air inside of the bubble? How can you make the bubble larger? How can you make the bubble smaller?"

Use a clear container, such as an aquarium or glass mixing bowl, to conduct another experiment. Fill the container with water and pass straws to each child. Tell the children to place their straw in the container and blow. Ask, "What happens when you blow air through the straw into the water?"

### Teaching about wind

To teach the concept that the wind makes things move, use thin strips of newsprint or

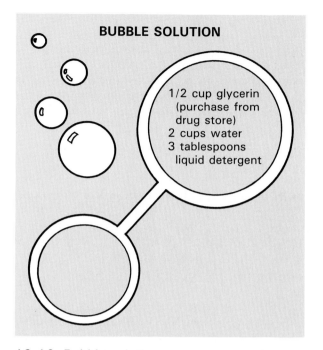

**BUBBLE SOLUTION**

1/2 cup glycerin (purchase from drug store)
2 cups water
3 tablespoons liquid detergent

19-16 Bubble solutions are very easy to make.

19-17 As children blow bubbles they become aware that the bubbles, and therefore air, take up space.

286

crepe paper streamers. For this activity to work, you need to introduce it on a windy day. Take the children outside and hand out the streamers. Show them how to hold the streamers. Ask, "What happens to the streamer when the wind blows? What direction is the wind moving in? What happens when you run fast?"

## USING MAGNETS TO TEACH SCIENCE CONCEPTS

Children are intrigued by magnets. Concepts about magnets are best learned through a combination of teacher guidance and hands-on activities, 19-18. Therefore, teachers need to buy quality magnets. These can be bought through science equipment or school supply stores. Buy a variety of magnets including horseshoe magnets, ceramic magnets, U-magnets, bar magnets, disk magnets, and rod-shaped magnets.

As children work and play with magnets they will observe:
- Magnets pull some things, but not others.
- Some magnets are big; others are small.
- Some magnets are stronger than others.
- Magnets pick up objects made of iron.

To aid in building these concepts, place several magnets on a table. Collect objects that magnets will pick up and others they will not. Types of objects magnets attract include scissors, metal screws, staples, nails, paper clips, and other small metal objects. A magnet will not pick up objects that do not have an iron content. Such objects include paper, cloth, wooden pencils, crayons, shoelaces, and aluminum dishes.

Place a variety of horseshoe and bar magnets in a small box. In a second box, place chalk, toothpicks, paper, nails, paper clips, plastic spoons, and other objects. Have the children name the objects and tell whether the magnets can lift each item.

Children also enjoy making magnet faces. To do this, draw a face on a piece of heavy tagboard. Place iron filings on the tagboard. Then cover with a sheet of clear plastic and seal the tagboard and plastic with tape. Show the children how to move the magnet under the tagboard, making hair, eyebrows, and mustache.

## USING WHEELS TO TEACH SCIENCE CONCEPTS

Children see wheels every day. They may ride in a car or truck to their child care center or preschool. There they see wagons, tricycles, scooters, and other toys with wheels. At home they see a vacuum cleaner, a machine with wheels. Perhaps on a trip to the airport they have even seen people pulling suitcases with wheels. All these experiences with wheels should help them learn about the uses of wheels.

Children can learn concepts about wheels such as:
- Wheels are round.
- Wheels roll.
- Wheels usually turn on an axis.
- Wheels make work easier for people.

To learn these concepts, children need to be exposed to many types of wheels. You might demonstrate these concepts using wagons and wheelbarrows.

To help children learn to identify a wheel, use a feely box or bag. Place cubes, balls, wooden blocks, and rubber wheels in the box.

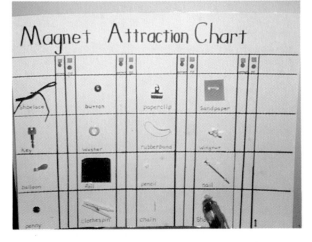

19-18 Charts are also useful for learning magnet concepts.

Ask one child at a time to feel in the box and find the wheel.

Another way to teach children about wheels is to cut out and hang pictures of wheels from magazines. Include fire engines, cars, trucks, tractors, wagons, airplanes, golf carts, scooters, and roller skates. Then cut out and hang pictures of other types of transportation. These might include motorboats, sailboats, skis, rafts, sleds, ice skates, donkeys, elephants, and horses. When you have finished, place the cardboard forms in front of the children. Then ask them to point out the pictures with wheels.

## USING FIELD TRIPS TO TEACH SCIENCE CONCEPTS

Field trips promote curiosity, supply opportunities for discovery, and encourage interaction with the environment. During field trips children can observe how machines make work more easy, precise, and orderly. For example, on a trip to the fire station point out the pole for sliding, the fire alarm system, the ladder, the axe, the hose, and the fire extinguisher.

Chart 19-19 lists field trip locations and things to observe there.

A "technology walk" in the neighborhood is also a type of field trip. It can provide children with chances to see machinery, including computers and typewriters, being used.

## USING ANIMALS TO TEACH SCIENCE CONCEPTS

Some animals can be used as classroom pets. Science concepts can be taught to young children using these pets. For example, children can learn how different animals look and feel, what they eat, how they should be handled, and how they respond to their environment. Pets can help teach respect for all kinds of life. After having the opportunity to observe and compare animals, children can draw conclusions from their experiences.

### Care of animals

All animals brought into the classroom should receive humane care and treatment. Children should always see animals being

## SCIENCE FIELD TRIPS

| Location | Science Concepts Studied |
|---|---|
| Lumber company | Nature of wood and sawdust. |
| Automobile and bike shops | Workings of motors, gears, chains, wheels; use of tools. |
| Grocery stores | Forms of foods. |
| Vacant land | Insects, plant life, animal shelters. |
| Print shop | Mechanics of the printing process. |
| Commercial laundry | Effects of cleaners, heat, starch. |
| Produce market | Nature of fresh fruits and vegetables. |
| Interior decorating shop | Nature of fabrics, use of colors. |
| Television and radio studios | Production and transmission of images and sounds. |
| Fire department | Mechanics of trucks, engines, ladders. |
| Animal hospital | Care of pets. |
| Toy shop | Nature of toy materials such as plastic, wood. |
| Excavation site | Nature of soil, rocks, building materials. |
| Zoo | Birds, insects, animals. |
| Botanical gardens | Plant life. |
| Museum | Rocks and other geological formations. |

19-19 Field trips can be used to teach a variety of science concepts. For instance, a trip to a fruit market can teach children about plants and seeds.

handled and cared for properly. Make every effort to provide for the basic needs of classroom animals. These needs include food, water, light, air, proper space for movement, and exercise.

## Value of animals

Experiences with animals should teach children the following concepts:

- Animals, especially pets, require care.
- Pets depend on humans for proper care.
- There are many kinds of animals; some are small and some are large.
- Animals need water, proper food, shelter, and exercise.
- Animals have different kinds of body coverings, 19-20. Some have feathers, some have scales, some have hair, and some have smooth skin.
- Animals move in different ways. Some fly, some swim, some walk, some run, some crawl or creep, and some hop.
- Animals are fun to watch.
- Animals have different numbers and kinds of legs. Some have two legs, some four, some six, some eight, and some have none.
- Animals make different sounds.
- Animals can be identified by their sounds.

## Animals as classroom pets

Many animals can be used as classroom pets, 19-21. Hamsters, snakes, toads, frogs, rabbits, and guinea pigs have all been used in early childhood programs.

**Hamsters.** A healthy hamster is chubby and has a shiny coat and bright eyes. Buy hamsters only from pet stores that handle healthy

19-20 Children are often surprised to find how oily a lamb's fleece feels.

19-21 Having classroom pets gives children a chance to observe, care for, and learn about pets as a part of their daily routine.

animals. (One strain of hamster spreads a form of meningitis.)

Hamsters should be housed in a wire, rust-proof cage. The cage should have an exercise wheel. Since hamsters are able to chew through many materials and escape through small holes, a wire cage prevents escape. Wood shavings or sawdust should be spread on the floor for cage litter. This litter should be replaced daily. Newspaper should also be placed in the cage for the hamster to shred for nesting. Because hamsters have two pairs of gnawing teeth, they also enjoy having a piece of soft wood for gnawing. Gnawing also helps keep the hamster's teeth at a healthy length.

Provide hamsters with nutritious food. This includes one or two large dog pellets or one and one-half teaspoons of grain. Hamsters also enjoy almost all greens such as lettuce, clover, alfalfa, and grass. Provide them with fresh water in a special bottle purchased from a pet store. This bottle prevents spilling and ensures that the animal has a constant supply of water.

Generally, hamsters have been found to be quite friendly with children if they are treated gently and fed regularly. When they are handled roughly or exposed to loud voices, they have been known to bite. For this reason, you need to make rules for handling the hamster. Supervise this activity closely.

**Snakes.** Harmless snakes make good classroom pets. They require little care and, when handled properly, rarely bite. Having a snake in the classroom can also prevent or dispel any fear the children might feel.

Aquariums are good housing for snakes. Spread newspaper on the bottom of the aquarium. Then cover the newspaper with gravel and a small piece of wood. For privacy, build a cave in one corner with small rocks. Add a small dish of water. To prevent the snake from wandering off, cover the top with a secure screen.

Different types of snakes require different foods. Your local pet shop salesperson or conservation authority worker can help you determine the snake's dietary needs. As a rule, small snakes can exist on insects, worms, and meat. Frogs and mice are required by the larger species. Some teachers prefer to arrange for their local pet store to feed large snakes.

**Toads and frogs.** Toads and frogs are common classroom pets. They can be housed in an aquarium. To avoid odors, clean the housing often. Water should be changed at least twice a week. You will notice that frogs often sit in their water. They do this to moisten their bodies. This is necessary in order to survive.

Toads and frogs enjoy eating small earthworms or insects. They will accept raw or chopped beef, or canned dog food. Children enjoy watching these animals use their sticky tongue to catch food such as bugs.

**Fish.** Fish are an ideal pet for some teachers because they can be left without attention longer than most other pets. If you would like fish as classroom pets, you will need to decide whether to buy tropical or freshwater fish. Freshwater fish are less costly and have easier care requirements.

Fish should be housed in an aquarium. Most teachers prefer 20 gallon aquariums. They are easier to maintain than smaller tanks. Also, children can see the fish more easily. Maintain a water temperature between 70° and 80°F at all times. To ensure this range, purchase a thermometer and a self-regulating aquarium heater.

The pH balance of the water is important. It should be kept close to neutral. This is especially important if you wish to breed fish. If the pH is acidic, it can be corrected by adding sodium biphosophate or sodium bicarbonate. Either of these products can be purchased at a pet store. You might also buy a kit to test the water.

Fill the tank with water and allow it to settle. Wait one week for the water to reach the correct temperature and pH balance. Then add the fish. There should be a half gallon of water for every inch of fish in the aquarium.

Talk to the salesperon at your pet store to find out exactly what, how much, and how often to feed your fish. Chances are a prepared fish food and/or shrimp brine will be recommended.

**Rabbits.** Rabbits have always been a favorite pet of young children and their teachers, 19-22. However, not all teachers enjoy having a rabbit indoors. This is because rabbits must be cleaned quite often.

Rabbits are often kept in large wire cages that allow plenty of room for movement. For shelter, place a wooden box at one end of the cage. Wood shavings or straw should also be placed in the bottom of the cage for bedding.

You may prefer to keep the rabbit outdoors to prevent classroom odor. Make sure that the cage is placed so it is sheltered from the wind and sun. If your play yard is enclosed, you may let the rabbit exercise outside of the cage for short periods.

Because rabbits are hearty eaters, they require large amounts of food and water. Green or leafy vegetables, including lettuce, cabbage

19-22 Rabbits are popular with teachers and children.

and celery tops, are preferred. You may wish to omit cabbage and other strong-smelling vegetables from their diet. This will help control the unpleasant odor of strong-smelling urine.

**Guinea pigs.** Most early childhood teachers agree that guinea pigs make good pets for young children. They are easy to handle and they do not bite. Also, guinea pigs are very gentle. They enjoy being held and cuddled by children. In addition, children can easily observe, care for, and handle these animals. These pets have heavy bodies and tight skins. So they can be picked up easily by placing a hand under the pig's body.

Wire cages provide good housing for these animals. Recommended cage sizes are about two and one-half to three feet in length, one and one-half feet deep, and one and one-half feet wide. Doors on cages need to fit tightly to prevent the animals from escaping. A space to hide, exercise, and sleep should be included. A small cardboard box can be placed inside the cage for sleeping.

Food for a guinea pig is similar to that of rabbits. They enjoy pellets or grains including corn, wheat, and oats. Grass, alfalfa, clover, and carrots can be added to their diets for variety. Most teachers who have guinea pigs for classroom pets recommend pellets as the most convenient type of food.

## SUMMARY

The nature of modern life makes studying science important. Young children can be introduced to study at the center through simple experiences.

In order to guide these experiences, teachers must know the objectives of studying science. They must also know how to help children reach these goals. This will require planning.

With a solid plan, teachers can then design a variety of activities to teach science concepts. Many methods and items can be used to teach these concepts, including colors, water, food, bodies, gardens, air, magnets, wheels, field trips, and pets.

## to Know

close-ended questions    science
feely box    science table
open-ended questions

## to Review

1. _____ is the study of natural processes and their products.
2. Science is creative. It requires the development of children's _____ and _____.
3. Science involves the process of:
   a. Observing.
   b. Measuring.
   c. Comparing.
   d. All of the above.
4. List three reasons why science should be studied.
5. True or false. All science projects need to be planned in detail.
6. During their science experiences, children should have many opportunities to:
   a. Observe.
   b. Solve problems.
   c. Collect samples and pictures.
   d. All of the above.
7. Why should the science area be located near the kitchen?
8. What is a science table?

9. True or false. Unneeded teacher input can sometimes stifle children's curiosity, thereby harming their desire to continue experimenting.
10. List the five basic process skills.
11. _____ -ended questions promote discussion, but _____-ended questions tend to require only one word answers.
12. Name four ways to teach science concepts. Of these four methods, explain one in detail.

## to Do

1. Develop a collection of items that could be placed on the science table. Explain how the collection would contribute to the science experiences of young children.
2. Brainstorm a list of centerpieces for the snack or lunch table that would help develop science concepts.
3. Draw a sketch of a science area as you would design it. Include placement of equipment.
4. Review a recipe book. List examples of cooking activities that would involve a process and product.
5. Develop a recipe file of foods that can be prepared by the children in an early childhood setting.
6. Make a dish garden using a pineapple, turnip, carrot, or beet top. Document the amount of time it takes for each to sprout.

# Chapter 20

# Guiding Social Studies Experiences

After studying this chapter, you will be able to:
- ☐ Explain what subject areas are involved in the social studies curriculum.
- ☐ Discuss the importance of social studies.
- ☐ Outline the role of the teacher in designing and guiding social studies experiences.
- ☐ Explain how social studies concepts are developed in children.
- ☐ Discuss ways to teach many social studies concepts, including self-concept, multicultural concepts, intergenerational concepts, governmental concepts, ecology concepts, change concepts, and geography concepts.

Young children approach classroom social life eagerly and positively. They are interested and question the events around them. For example, Johnny may ask, "Why does Kimberly get two cupcakes? What does your mother do?" Sally may question, "How does the butcher help me? Where do babies come from? When do plants die?" Many of these questions arise naturally during daily classroom activities. Children's questions might be about social skills, cultures, careers, holidays, current events, geography, or change. These questions all revolve around the area of social studies.

The field of social studies includes many distinct subjects. History, economics, geography, current events, and career education are all vital parts of the social studies field.

Studying social studies provides children with the chance to learn social skills, 20-1. These skills will help them get along with others in many situations. Social studies helps children learn useful group living skills. Children learn how a society works. They learn how to accept themselves and get along with others. This, in turn, will help them learn to act, feel, and think. These skills are needed in order to become useful members of society.

Young children build social studies concepts as they move through the world around them.

For example, children learn key social studies concepts when they build an airport with blocks or walk around the neighborhood. Social studies concepts can also be built by looking at many types of housing. Role playing doctors, mail carriers, grocers, or mothers also promotes an understanding of social studies. So does the process of making and eating ethnic foods or hearing a story about community helpers. By taking part in tasks for maintaining the classroom, children learn social studies concepts. Watering flowers, feeding classroom pets, putting blocks away, and wiping up spills teach children about getting along in their world.

## IMPORTANCE OF SOCIAL STUDIES

Children need to understand how other people live. They need to learn about their neighbors' living styles, languages, and viewpoints. Social studies helps children acquire skills for living. Children should:
- Develop self-respect and a healthy self-concept.
- Develop self-control and independence.
- Learn to share ideas and materials, 20-2.
- Develop ways of relating to and working with others.

20-2 Learning to share ideas helps children build communication skills.

- Develop respect for other peoples' feelings and ideas.
- Learn about the roles people have in real life.
- Learn to appreciate the past and its relationship to the present.

The value of the social studies curriculum, then, is that it makes children better able to understand their world and their place in it.

## THE TEACHER'S ROLE IN SOCIAL STUDIES

The key to a good social studies program is the teacher and the knowledge he or she brings to the classroom, 20-3. The interests of each teacher determine the degree to which social studies will be included. To prepare for this role, teachers need thorough training and interest in the social sciences and child development. A well-trained teacher will understand the need to use community resources, chance learnings, themes, group participation, observation, checklists, and evaluation to enrich the social studies program.

To provide this quality of learning, teachers need to make daily observations. These routine checks should provide data about children's in-

20-1 Through social studies experiences, children learn to accept themselves and get along with others.

20-3 Teachers play a crucial role in quality social studies programs.

terests, abilities, developmental levels, attitudes, and knowledge. From this data, teachers can determine what children need to know and what behaviors need to be changed. Thoughtful programs reflect children's interests and abilities.

**Observations**

Observe young children to note behavior that is displayed in different situations. Do not draw conclusions. Instead, make observations based on the goals of the social studies program. To do this, record behavior at the following times:
- Free choice experiences.
- Group time.
- Eating and dressing.
- Discussions.
- Outdoor play.

Every group of children brings a wide variety of interests to the classroom. Some children may be interested in airplanes, trains, or geography. Others may prefer to study community helpers. To determine children's interests you can:
- Observe them at play, noting the type of play and their use of materials, 20-4.
- Interact with them in a casual way. Ask them what they prefer to do or learn more about.

20-4 Children have many interests. To determine individuals interests, playtime is an excellent time to observe.

- Ask children's parents what their interests are at home.
- Observe the children's choice of books.

Like interests, the skills of every group of children should influence the social studies program. In any given classroom, there will be many levels in intellectual, physical, social, and emotional development. Some children will put 23-piece puzzles together. Others will have difficulty in completing a six-piece puzzle.

As a teacher of young children, you will need to match materials with each child's ability level. If the materials are too difficult for a child to use, he or she may become frustrated. This may lead to boredom, stress, or pressure. Boredom can also result, however, from too little challenge.

Determine children's ability levels in these ways:
- Observe children's social skills as they play with others children.
- Review the children's records of physical and health growth.

- Structure a variety of tasks for each child to complete and take note of their success.

There is no shortcut to gathering data to determine children's skill levels. Gathering takes time. The information, however, will secure successful planning.

### Developmental characteristics

Developmental characteristics are key to designing a social studies program. These traits can be used as a starting point for planning social studies activities. Characteristics and their implementations are listed in 20-5.

### Checklists

Checklists can be used to assess children's progress. Checklists can be designed with special goals or objectives in mind. Chart 20-6 shows a checklist for a group of four-year-olds.

You may prepare your own checklists. To do so, refer to the appendix on child development or other child development resources. On a piece of paper, list common social behaviors

## ACTIVITIES RELATED TO CHILDREN'S CHARACTERISTICS

| CHARACTERISTICS | IMPLEMENTATIONS |
|---|---|
| Interest centered on immediate environment. | Provide opportunities to explore the school, home, and neighborhood. |
| Enjoys opportunities for self-expression. | Provide small group opportunities whenever possible. |
| Shows interest in people with whom he or she is acquainted. | Share resource people with whom the children have indicated an interest. |
| Learns best through direct experiences. | Provide concrete materials. |
| Enjoys pretending. | Provide many opportunities and props for dramatic play. |
| Tends to be egocentric (self-centered: I or me) | Provide consistent guidance in respecting other's right. |

20-5 Watch for children to show these characteristics. Social studies activities can be implemented to either enhance or discourage such traits.

for the age groups you are teaching. Then observe and record the occurrences of the listed behaviors.

## Developing curriculum

Encourage children to take part in planning. This process will help them organize their thoughts, express their ideas, and experience the results.

During the planning process, allow children to make important choices. Involve all children in the group. You may find that some may be quite shy. These children may feel better if given an opportunity to plan on their own or in a small group.

Young children are able to plan these aspects of their activities:
- Materials to work with.
- Who to play with.
- Materials needed for a project.
- Places to visit.
- People to invite to the classroom.
- How to celebrate birthdays and holidays.

**Themes.** Many teachers use themes when planning a social studies program, 20-7. One

20-7 A pet theme can be the basis for teaching many social studies concepts.

### CHECKLIST FOR FOUR-YEAR-OLDS

| Name: | | Date: | |
|---|---|---|---|
| Behavior | Always | Sometimes | Never |
| • Plays cooperatively with other children. | | | |
| • Calls attention to own actions. | | | |
| • Demonstrates interest in other people by asking "why" questions. | | | |
| • Understands the idea of taking turns. | | | |
| • Participates in clean-up. | | | |
| • Dresses by lacing shoes and buttoning clothing. | | | |

20-6 Checklists are a concrete method for observing and assessing children's skill levels and growth.

theme can be used to combine the learning opportunities of many different activities. Therefore, varied experiences help children learn concepts. (See Chapter 24 for additional information on themes.)

**Using community resources.** Look closely at community resources for a variety of learning opportunities. Use a small tablet or file folder for noting topic ideas. Record the names of stores, museums, art galleries, community services, community workers, and housing groups that may be of use. The people in these groups might also have suggestions for objectives and goals.

**Tools.** Many teaching tools can be used to introduce and teach social studies concepts. These include bulletin boards, puppets, field trips, and games. Tool choice will depend on the developmental level of the children and how the tool will be used. Some materials may be more useful for the total group. Others may be useful to small groups of children.

### Incidental learnings

Structure the classroom to promote *incidental learnings*. These are learning experiences that happen during the course of a normal day. You might set up incidental learnings by keeping the cap off the paint container, letting a plant die, placing pictures on the library table, or adding dramatic play props to the housekeeping area. These situations cause children to question and learn on their own.

Every classroom makes its own incidental learning experiences. You will need to mentally or visually record and plan for them. Topics that might come up in the course of any day include:

- Classroom and playground repairs.
- Classroom rules.
- The roles of school workers such as the janitor, bus driver, or the secretary.
- Handling an argument.
- Happenings in the local community.

### Evaluation

Evaluation is a key part of planning the social studies curriculum. The evaluation process will help you see if goals have been met,

what new goals are needed, and whether any current goals need modification. This process can be done with the children. For example, you may ask the children the following questions:

- What did you like best?
- What did you learn?
- What do you want to learn more about?
- What would you like to do again?

## BUILDING CONCEPTS

Young children want to find out about their world. They touch, taste, smell, see, and hear in an attempt to learn. They form perceptions from such activity. *Perceptions* are ideas formed about a relationship or object as a result of what a child learns through the senses. Repeated experiences form a set of perceptions. This gives rise to concept formation. For instance, a young child sees a black and white cow with four legs. Later, the child sees a black and white dog and calls it a cow. Given proper feedback, the child will learn to tell the difference between a dog and cow.

Concepts help children to organize, group, and order experiences. Concepts help them make sense out of the world. Concepts become ingredients for thinking. Once learned, concepts help children communicate with each other.

Personality, experiences, language skill, health, emotions, and social relationships all affect the formation of accurate concepts. Many varied experiences help form more concepts. Children with well-formed language skills form useful concepts. Good physical and mental health help children form proper sensory concepts. Experiences are affected by feelings and emotions. Therefore, children who have contact with others learn to view other ways of thinking.

## SELF-CONCEPT

*Self-concept* can be defined as the qualities a child believes he or she possesses. It is a result of beliefs, feelings, and perceptions a child has of himself or herself as part of the world, 20-8. Children's self-concepts reflect the feelings

20-8 A child with a healthy self-concept is not afraid to explore new and different types of play.

others have for them. Self-concepts also reflect feelings of confidence children do or do not feel about themselves.

Children's self-concepts can be observed in their behavior, 20-9. A child who lacks confidence may reveal feelings of inadequacy. For instance, the child may not be willing to try new activities, may withdraw from an experience, show little curiosity, or appear overly anxious or overly independent. This child may also be hostile, seek attention, or perform poorly.

Children with positive self-concepts perceive themselves as able and important. They accept and respect themselves as well as others. These children are often able to judge their own skills and cope with problems they confront very well. Typically, they are more objective and understand other people's behaviors.

The teacher can promote or undermine a healthy self-concept. In many subtle ways, a teacher will affect how a child feels about himself or herself. Your reactions may give children the feeling that they are bad or annoying. For instance, you may need to ask children to be quiet. Consider the message the children will receive. If you ask them to be quiet because they are too noisy, they may feel that they are bad people because they make too much noise. If you ask them to make less noise because it is disturbing you, the children see that they can help you by being quiet. They do not feel that they are bad, noisy people.

If a child spills juice, do you call the child clumsy? Do you react negatively by scowling? Or do you accept this as common behavior for a young child and help wipe up the spill? Caring adults are able to separate children's needs from their own. Clearly, they are able to see the difference between adult needs and children's.

Every day you provide the subtle messages in the form of verbal and nonverbal feedback. These signals can either enhance or decrease children's sense of self-worth. You can make children feel appreciated, worthy, loved, and secure by being accepting, concerned, and respectful. Also, provide children with experiences with which they will have success. You can make children feel unworthy or unloved by being critical of and unconcerned with them. Research shows that before children can accept and understand others, they must respect and understand themselves.

Helping young children grow to respect themselves, as well as others, is not easy. Caring adults must always watch the subtle ways they interact with children, 20-10. The following teaching techniques encourage children to develop a positive self-concept:
- Listen to each child.
- Use every child's name each day.
- Use encouraging statements.
- Acknowledge both attempts and successes at tasks.
- Say only positive things about children.
- State directions in a positive manner.
- Provide materials to encourage social interaction between and among children.

# CHECKLIST FOR EVALUATING A CHILD'S SELF-CONCEPT

|  | YES | NO |
|---|:---:|:---:|
| Does the child speak positively about him/her self? | ☐ | ☐ |
| Does the child appear to feel proud of his/her appearance? | ☐ | ☐ |
| Is the child proud of accomplishments? | ☐ | ☐ |
| Does the child accept failure? | ☐ | ☐ |
| Is the child willing to try new experiences? | ☐ | ☐ |
| Does the child make decisions on his/her own? | ☐ | ☐ |
| Is the child independent? | ☐ | ☐ |
| Does the child share his/her possessions? | ☐ | ☐ |
| Is the child willing to vocalize thoughts? | ☐ | ☐ |
| Is the child naturally curious? | ☐ | ☐ |
| Does the child usually appear calm and controlled? | ☐ | ☐ |

20-9 Observation is an important tool in social studies.
Not only is it used to determine skill level, it can
also be used to evaluate a child's self-concept.

## TEACHER CHECKLIST FOR PROMOTING A POSITIVE SELF-CONCEPT

☑ Am I an open-minded person?

☑ Do I recognize and value differences in children?

☑ Do I constantly strive to gain more knowledge about the world and share it with the children?

☑ Do I provide the children with choices so that they may become independent decision makers?

☑ Am I constantly trying to increase my human relations skills?

☑ Do I encourage parents to share their attitudes with me?

☑ Do I avoid showing favoritism?

☑ Do I listen to the children?

☑ Do I plan developmentally appropriate activities?

☑ Do I permit enough time to complete activities?

☑ Do I call attention to positive interactions between and among children?

☑ Do I make expectations clear?

☑ Do I acknowledge the child's attempts at tasks as well as accomplishments?

20-10 The teacher's behavior can promote or hinder development of a positive self-concept.

### Activities

There are many activities that promote the development of a positive self-concept. These activities focus on making children feel good about themselves and their abilities. Thus, choose activities that are developmentally appropriate. As you use these activities, your role will be to enhance the self-concept of each child with whom you come in contact.

Self-concept classroom activities are many and varied. Several are outlined in Chart 20-11.

### MULTI-CULTURAL CONCEPTS

Social scientists use the word culture to describe all the aspects of people's lives. This includes a group's ideas and ways of doing things. It includes traditions, language, beliefs, and customs. *Culture* then is learned patterns of social behavior.

A child's culture is a lens by which the child judges the world. Culture influences feelings, thoughts, and behavior. It imposes order and meaning on all experiences. Culture provides children with a lifestyle that defines what foods are eaten and when. In fact, culture is so much a part of a person that he or she does not realize that behavior might be different from behaviors in other cultures.

A multi-cultural perspective is very important in planning a social studies curriculum. Studies show that children's attitudes toward their own identity and other racial groups begin to form during preschool years. They are aware of race and color as early as three years of age.

## Goals for a multi-cultural perspective

The goals of a multi-cultural perspective are to help each child develop:

- Respect for oneself as a worthwhile and competent human being.
- Acceptance and respect for others' similarities and differences.
- The skill to attack tasks, expecting to succeed.

### BUILDING POSITIVE SELF-CONCEPTS

- After an outing, make an experience chart. Include children's names and their exact words.
- Provide a special chair and crown for each child on his or her birthday. Take an instant snapshot of the child.
- Make a slide show of the children in action: on a field trip, at a party, at a play, or at the end of an ongoing project. Present the slide show to the children.
- Record children's stories from sharing and telling time on a large piece of posterboard titled "Our News."
- Make charts of children's likes. For instance, you might chart children's favorite colors or animals.
- Make charts of hair and eye color to reinforce concepts of similarities and differences among people.
- Tape record children telling their own stories.
- Make height and weight charts.
- Add a full-length mirror to the room.
- Label children's lockers and artwork with their names.
- Make a mobile or bulletin board with the children's pictures or names.
- Provide children with family face puppets. Encourage children to act out imaginary family situations using the puppets.
- Outline children's bodies on large sheets of paper for the children to paint or color and display.
- Provide dramatic play kits to encourage children to try new roles and roles that they find interesting. For example, a carpenter kit could include a hat, an apron, a hammer, nails, and boxes or scraps of wood.
- Display pictures of the children at eye level.
- Use children's names frequently in songs and games.

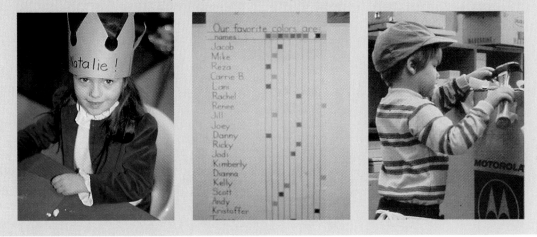

20-11 These activities are quite useful for helping children build positive self-concepts.

- An appreciation of one's own racial and ethnic background.
- The skill to interact positively with other children.
- An understanding that there are many ways to do things.

To meet these goals, stress parent involvement, selection and preparation of learning tools, curriculum, and teacher behavior.

**Parent involvement.** Parents can play a key role in meeting multi-cultural goals for children. Teachers need to study the background of each child. Parents or other family members are the best resources for this task. These people can provide information on their culture's child rearing techniques. Meeting and talking with parents can provide knowledge of the family and their needs, concerns, and hopes. Parents can also share their heritage by taking in classroom activities, 20-12. They can share stories, games, songs, dances, foods, and holiday observances related to their culture.

**Selecting and preparing materials.** Teachers must learn to examine materials for their appropriateness in teaching social science concepts. If biases exist in any materials, they must

be noted. Then teaching methods must be developed to overcome the bias.

*Stereotyping* means showing people in a rigid, traditional way. Stereotyping ignores individual differences. Take care when choosing games, books, filmstrips, films, and visual aids. For instance, in the area of career choices, both males and females should be shown in diverse occupations. The elderly should be shown as physically active. Children should be portrayed in positive, competent roles.

Omission is another bias found in some teaching materials. *Omission* implies that some groups have less value than other groups in our society. This is done by omitting a group's presence in the material. All groups must be included and respected in teaching materials, 20-13. To build self-esteem in children, show them strong role models from all cultural backgrounds.

### Activities to encourage a multi-cultural perspective

Reflect the ethnic heritage and background of all children. The following list includes items that are useful for reaching this goal:

20-12 Encourage parents to become involved in promoting multi-cultural perspectives in their child's classroom.

20-13 Play materials should represent the racial make-up of society.

- Common cooking utensils.
- Flags.
- Weavings.
- Traditional games.
- Ethnically diverse children's books.
- Musical recordings.
- Pictures.
- Slides.

Special activities can be planned to focus on similarities and differences. For example, schedule a "special day" for a particular child. During group time, the child may share his or her favorite toy, food, and/or color. Or, ask each child to bring in family photographs. They can use these photos to compare similarities and differences. Cooking a variety of cultural foods is another way of stressing multi-cultural concepts.

Social interaction is seen as one key method for helping children to explore relationships. As children take part in classroom chores and activities, they learn others' points of view. Often these views conflict with their own. As a result, children learn there are many points of view.

Special needs children can also be included in the classroom. By their presence, young children learn about the needs of others. This helps them understand social responsibility.

## INTERGENERATIONAL CONCEPTS

Young children's concepts of the aged, or elderly, are not always positive. When a group of preschool children were asked about aged adults and growing older, their comments included:

"Well, they sure have a lot of extra skin."
"My grandpa fixes my bike."
"They walk slow and have to sit a lot."
"They're sick."
"You get bald if you are old."
"They help you make cookies."

Such responses show the need to include intergenerational concepts in the early childhood program.

The number of aged persons in American society is steadily increasing. With this growth, there is a great need to inform all people about the many problems the elderly face. For many children today, the only contact they have with the aged is with their grandparents. This may lead to one-sided views and ideas of the aged. Therefore, young children need to learn from and about the aged.

Negative stereotyping is one of the greatest problems faced by the aged. These thoughts about growing older have also been noted in children. Studies have found that some young children have already accepted society's stereotypes of the aged.

There is a great deal of information that shows attitudes are formed early in life. These feelings and thoughts remain a strong force in a person's life. Children's attitudes toward the aged are based on the way their families feel. These attitudes can be changed, if need be, through contact with the aged. Education and information from the radio, television, and newspaper can also change these attitudes.

Studies show that negative stereotypes of the aged may be caused by lack of knowledge. Another reason may be little or no contact with older people. To change this attitude, early childhood teachers can invite the elderly to take part in the classroom. Intergenerational contacts can benefit both the young and old.

### Goals for children

Include intergenerational concepts in the program to encourage children to view the aged more positively. Contact with the aged will affect the formation of positive concepts of aging persons. The goals for such a program are listed in 20-14.

The program must support these goals. Interacting with the aged should be included. Books, filmstrips, and pictures used in the classroom should all portray the aged without bias. These materials should show the varied interests, abilities, mobility, and health of the aged.

### Curriculum

The curriculum must contain concepts of the aged that will foster positive ideas of the aged. There are many themes where these concepts can be used, 20-15. For instance, using the theme "Me, Myself," children could focus on their own aging. Pictures of the children as babies could be brought to school. These could serve as a basis for a talk about growth and development. You might also discuss other changes to come. Height and weight records could be compared. Children could then guess what other changes will occur as they continue to grow. The children could also make booklets telling of things they liked to do when they were younger, things they enjoy doing now, and the things they think they might like to do when they are older.

If constant direct contact is not possible, provide opportunities for this contact. Arrange field trips to visit elderly neighbors, a retirement home, or a senior citizens' center. You might arrange to do seasonal activities, such as singing Christmas carols or making May Day baskets. Other classroom activities include having the children use drawings or pictures cut from magazines to form a large collage or mural depicting the aged in positive, active roles (swimming, jogging, skiing, nurturing). A caption such as "It can be fun to be older," can be added to the collage.

### Educational materials

There are increasing numbers of resources for teaching gerontology to young children. (*Gerontology* is the study of the aged.) Use care

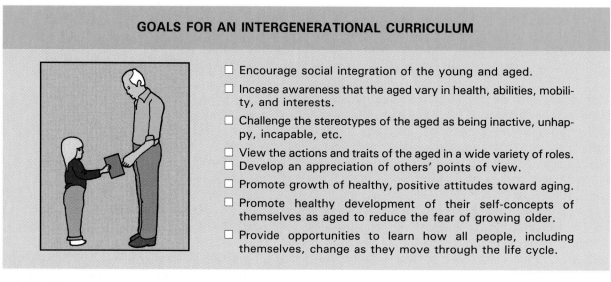

**GOALS FOR AN INTERGENERATIONAL CURRICULUM**

☐ Encourage social integration of the young and aged.
☐ Incease awareness that the aged vary in health, abilities, mobility, and interests.
☐ Challenge the stereotypes of the aged as being inactive, unhappy, incapable, etc.
☐ View the actions and traits of the aged in a wide variety of roles.
☐ Develop an appreciation of others' points of view.
☐ Promote growth of healthy, positive attitudes toward aging.
☐ Promote healthy development of their self-concepts of themselves as aged to reduce the fear of growing older.
☐ Provide opportunities to learn how all people, including themselves, change as they move through the life cycle.

20-14 The goals of an intergenerational program should include these items.

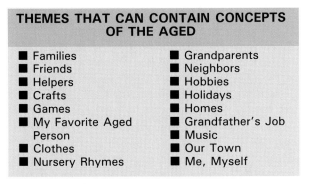

20-15 Can you think of activities that would revolve around these themes?

when choosing them. Books and other materials should depict the aged positively. Pleasing relationships between the children and aged should be shown.

If materials are limited, use your imagination to design your own. Cut pictures from magazines. Take slides. Then combine several pictures or slides and use them to tell stories.

### Contact with the aged

The aged can make useful contributions to the classroom. For example, they may work with children who are in need of special attention, help with projects, or direct small groups of children. The roles taken by older adults depends on the needs of the teacher(s), children, and the aged persons.

Intergenerational programs that focus on developing positive concepts of the aged also must focus on the needs of the aged. Like other programs using volunteers, careful planning is required for a successful program. Consider the following guidelines:

- Ensure that each aged person has a definite role to play in the classroom.
- View each aged person as an individual, using his or her special talents, interests, and training.
- Maintain close communications between the administration, teachers, and the volunteer.
- Design and provide training and sharing opportunities for the aged person.

- Maintain a low ratio of aged persons in the program. This allows for personal bonds to be developed.

Intergenerational programs benefit adults as well as children. Both often enjoy the growth of caring relationships. Adults have the chance to observe children's interest as they share their special talents with them. The children gain understanding of and appreciation for the elderly.

### GOVERNMENTAL CONCEPTS

Before age five, children's concepts of the government are based on the information they receive from the media, home, and school. By this age, children can point out the flag and pictures of the president. They can also recognize the National Anthem and the Pledge of Allegiance.

### Activities

To help children learn governmental concepts, you will need to design group activities based on the function of a democracy. Such activity will help children understand the purpose of rules and laws. The following list contains sample activities that help build governmental concepts:

- When your class gets a new pet, let the children vote on its name.
- During cooking experience, let the children vote on what type of food to make.
- When a new toy arrives, let the children outline rules for its use.
- Encourage the children to suggest field trips they would like to take.
- Let children plan the type of sandwiches they will have on a picnic, 20-16.

### ECOLOGY CONCEPTS

*Ecology* is the study of the chain of life. It focuses on water, land, air, grass, trees, birds, and insects. In order to develop ecology concepts, children need good observation skills. Using these skills, they can build an appreciation of their environment. They can also learn about the interdependency of all life on the

20-16 Choosing the type of sandwich for an indoor picnic helps children learn about planning.

planet. As a result of these activities, children will learn a social concern for the environment.

**Activities**

In the daily schedule, activities that focus on ecology include:

• Taking children on a trip around the block. As you walk, point out plants, trees, shrubs, and birds.
• Keeping many plants and animals, 20-17.
• Providing magazines that children may use to cut out pictures they feel are beautiful. Let each child explain the beauty of a picture.
• Supplying each child with a paper bag and taking a "trash hike" around the play yard. Encourage children to pick up trash and place it in their sacks.

## CHANGE CONCEPTS

Children need to learn that change affects their lives in many ways. Change is constant. To help the children learn this concept, use nature and the family. Taking part in these experiences will help children learn to accept change.

By observing nature, children learn to understand the concept of change. Plan a nature walk. During the walk, point out the cherry trees budding, the leaves turning colors, flowers blossoming, and fruit ripening. Each of these experiences should help the child understand that all things change.

People are always changing. To help children understand how they have changed, include concepts about changes they have experienced:

• Show a film on babies.
• Record children's height and weight at the beginning of the year, at mid-year, and at the end of the year. Discuss with the children how they have changed.
• Collect a variety of baby clothes and toys. Place these items on a table where the children can explore them.
• Make a bulletin board of new and old houses.

## GEOGRAPHY CONCEPTS

Young children are geographers as soon as they become mobile. They explore space, play in water and snow, and dig in dirt. They note

20-17 Giving children their own plants helps children learn the importance of caring for the environment.

differences in wet and dry sand and begin to form some concepts about the earth.

The earth is home to many people. The relationship of humans to the earth is important for children to understand. They need to learn that man's food, shelter, and raw materials are provided by the earth. Since these concepts are quite complex, formal lessons are most often first introduced in elementary school. There are, however, some informal activities to use with younger children. For instance, allow children to dig in a sand box or a garden area, and play in a sand box with cars, trucks, pails, shovels, etc. See 20-18. You might also play readiness games that use symbols which can prepare children to read maps. Finally, design a bulletin board that maps out the neighborhood surrounding the center. Children can study this board and then help "navigate" a field trip through the neighborhood.

## SUMMARY

Social studies concepts help young children learn how to function in the world around them. A well-planned social studies program teaches children about people different from themselves. Children learn to appreciate and get along with these people. A useful social studies program also teaches children about their environment: how it works and how we make use of it.

20-18 Playing with sand helps children form concepts about the earth.

## to Know

## to Review

1. The field of social studies includes:
   a. Current events.
   b. Career education.
   c. History.
   d. All of the above.
2. True or false. Studying social studies provides children with the chance to learn how a society works.
3. List three skills children should learn in a social studies program.
4. True or false. The key to a quality social studies program is the teacher and the knowledge he or she brings into the classroom.
5. Describe four ways to determine children's interests.
6. A _____ can be used to assess children's programs.
7. What aspects of their activities are children capable of planning?
8. _____ _____ are experiences that happen during the course of a normal day.
9. The _____ process will help you see if goals have been met, what new goals are needed, and whether any current goals need modification.
10. Ideas formed about a relationship or object as a result of experiences are called:
    a. Concepts.
    b. Perceptions.
    c. Learnings.
    d. All of the above.

11. Define self-concept.
12. True or false. Children's self-concepts can be observed in their behavior.
13. List three teaching techniques that encourage children to develop positive self-concepts.
14. _____ is learned patterns of social behavior.
15. List the goals of a multi-cultural perspective.
16. _____ involves portraying people in a rigid, traditional way.
17. True or false. Omission is a type of discrimination found in some teaching materials.
18. _____ stereotyping is one of the greatest problems faced by the aged.
19. True or false. Intergenerational programs benefit only children.
20. _____ is the study of the chain of life.

## to Do

1. Make a list of activities that promote self-concept. Add these activities to your file.
2. Brainstorm a list of community resources. Include museums, art galleries, stores, and services that are available.
3. Use the checklist found in the chapter to evaluate your skills for promoting positive self-concepts in children. Record your responses on a separate piece of paper.
4. As a class, choose a theme and brainstorm a list of activities that could be used in various subject areas.

# Chapter 21

# *Guiding Food Experiences*

After studying this chapter, you will be able to:
- ☐ Conduct relaxed, useful food experiences for children.
- ☐ Discuss ways to work with parents to best serve children's nutritional needs.
- ☐ List nutritional concepts to teach in the young childhood setting.
- ☐ Outline the procedure for conducting cooking experiences.
- ☐ Name and make simple recipes for children to use in early cooking experiences.
- ☐ Discuss various eating problems encountered in young children.
- ☐ Teach children to set a table.

Food experiences involve many activities: eating meals and snacks, cooking, setting tables, and cleaning up. These activities provide learning experiences children will use for their entire lives. Many of these activities will require their help and effort. This builds feelings of responsibility and worthiness. These activities also provide opportunities for teaching nutrition concepts. This will help children build good eating habits.

The key to an effective food program is to present activities in a positive way, 21-1. It is quite easy for food experiences to become tense and unproductive. There may be children who will not eat. Other children may not wish to help with the tasks. Still other children may eat too much or help to a point where others cannot take part. Keep in mind several simple rules to promote happy, relaxed food experiences:
- Schedule quiet, relaxing activities just before mealtimes.
- Provide child-sized tables, chairs, and serving tools.
- Encourage children to serve themselves.
- Expect some accidents. Children will spill and drop things. Be prepared by having sponges handy in all food areas. Encourage children to clean up their own messes.

21-1 Food activities tend to go well when you have a positive attitude about them.

## WORKING WITH PARENTS

Parents need to be aware of how they can and do influence their children's eating habits. These influences can be direct or indirect. For instance, the snacks they provide their children are a direct influence. The atmosphere of the home at mealtime is an indirect influence. Several methods are useful for working with parents in this key area of child development.

Many centers have lending libraries. These libraries are a good way to share nutrition information with adults. Parents and guardians may check out pamphlets, magazines, and books to learn or update their nutrition knowledge. Recipes may also be shared in such a setting.

Parents' meetings, workshops, and discussion groups are also useful methods for interacting with parents. Here, parents, guardians, and teachers can discuss reliable information on nutritional needs of children, suggestions for dealing with common mealtime problems, and resources in the community for food.

Some centers find that a weekly or monthly newsletter is a good way to keep parents and guardians informed and involved. Such a newsletter can contain a great deal of useful information: home food activities that reinforce concepts learned at the center, suggestions for menu planning, serving, and stressing good nutrition, etc. A center menu is also a useful addition. Parents can use this to coordinate home meals.

## NUTRITION CONCEPTS

Nutrition knowledge is useful throughout life. Teaching nutrition, then, is an important part of guiding food experiences. For instance, children learn that a wide variety of foods are available to meet the needs of their bodies. This concept can be taught by introducing children to many foods during snack and mealtime. These experiences can also teach children that foods can be eaten in a number of ways. For example, apples can be eaten raw or cooked. They can be made into applesauce, apple bread, apple pancakes, apple pies, apple juice, and apple dumplings. Chart 21-2 highlights other nutrition concepts to include in a young childhood setting.

## COOKING EXPERIENCES

Children enjoy cooking experiences. These promote language, math, and science learning. Words such as stirring, measuring, pouring, and grating are added to their vocabularies. Basic concepts such as shape, size, number, texture, and temperature change can be taught. In addition, the children can learn how food is prepared.

By taking part in food experiences, children learn how to use cooking utensils. See 21-3. They learn how to use can openers, vegetable peelers, and egg beaters. Children learn left to right progression skills as the teacher helps them read recipes. Cooking is also a natural way to learn how to follow directions.

21-2 Young children need to learn simple nutrition concepts.

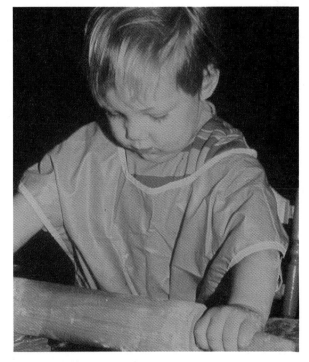

21-3 Food experiences help children learn how to use such items as a rolling pin.

## The "Cook's Corner"

Most teachers know the value of cooking experiences. These teachers often have a corner set aside in the classroom for this purpose. To increase learning and decrease safety and health hazards, follow these actions:

- Use a plastic cloth covering with a flannel backing to protect tables. The flannel backing will help prevent the tablecloth from slipping.
- Limit the number of children taking part in an activity. Four to six children is usually best.
- Place the recipe, ingredients, clean-up supplies and utensils on a tray before the activity begins.
- When using recipe cards, write short, clear, instructions in order. Food labels, picture symbols, numerals, short phrases, and single words make recipes easy for young children to "read," 21-4.
- Have all cooks wash their hands in warm, soapy water and wear aprons for health protection.

### First Experiences

First cooking experiences should revolve around simple recipes that can be served at snack time. Have the children shake cream to make butter or make instant pudding. Measure ingredients before the experience. This will help insure a successful experience. Success is important. Then children will want to take part in future activities. Several recipes are given at the end of this chapter.

**Guiding Food Experiences   313**

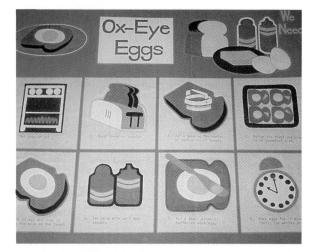

21-4 Even young children can follow recipes that are written using picture symbols.

21-5 Small groups work best for cooking activities.

**Planning.** Plan a series of cooking experiences that gradually become more complex. Make the same food a number of times. Each time add something new. For example, add flavoring or berries to instant vanilla pudding.

As you select recipes, be aware of any food allergies children may have. Common culprits include milk, milk products, and orange juice.

Limit the number of children who will take part in any activity. Usually no more than four to six children can be involved, 21-5. Therefore, children may have to take turns. Some teachers schedule cooking during small group time. In that way, the number of children is naturally limited.

Collect enough tools and equipment for all children involved. Plastic bowls and blunt tools are best. Each child should have a tool when activities such as peeling apples are scheduled.

**Cooking.** Place the ingredients, tools, and other equipment on a low table so all children can watch. If possible, use portable appliances such as hot plates rather than a stove. To prevent accidents, turn pan handles away from children. Remind children of safety rules.

Start the activity by telling the children what you are going to make. Then have them wash their hands. After all the children return,

explain the sequence of steps you will use. If you do not have a chart made, write the steps on a blackboard or large piece of paper.

As the children move through the steps, remain with the experience. Encourage children to talk about what is being done. Include science, math, language arts, and social studies concepts if they mesh with the lesson. Name any new foods, processes, and equipment.

Cleanup is an important part of the experience. Children should be involved in the process. Dishes and ingredients will have to be returned to the kitchen. Table and dishes will have to be washed.

### Tasting experiences

After cooking, tasting helps children learn about new foods. New foods can be compared with familiar foods. For example, a lime can be compared with a lemon, or a sweet potato can be compared with a white potato. Food temperature and texture can be discussed. Many teachers use these activities as part of an interest center. This limits the number of children who can be involved at any given time.

### EATING HABITS

No doubt you will find that some children have poor eating habits. Often, these habits are learned from others. If parents, relatives, and peers have poor eating habits, chances are that the young children will have them also.

You can use food experiences to model and encourage good eating habits. By tasting all foods in front of children, you will encourage them to do the same. You also can model appropriate attitudes toward eating. Offering constructive comments is another way to improve eating habits. For instance, you might say, "Seth, I'm glad you tried the peas today. Aren't you glad you found out how good they taste?"

### Changing appetites

Children do not always eat the same amount of food every day, 21-6. If a child is very active on a certain day or has a light breakfast, the child will likely have a big appetite. If the weather is hot or a child has just eaten before

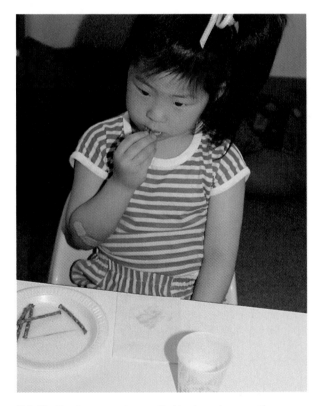

21-6 Earlier meals, activity level, weather, and health all affect a child's appetite.

coming to the center, he or she probably will not be very hungry. Fatigue and illness can also cause a change in children's appetites. When children do not feel like eating, do not force them.

If a child's lack of appetite continues for a length of time, observe the child. Ask these questions:
- Is the child getting enough nutrients?
- Is the child eating too much at snack time?
- Is the child paying attention at mealtime?
- Is the child being properly reinforced at mealtime?
- Is the child always tired at mealtime?

After observing the child, you may notice one of these problem areas. For instance, if the child is eating too much at snack time, limit the amount of snacks the child is allowed to eat. If the child is always tired at mealtime, provide him or her with a quiet period before eating. Then at the table reinforce the child when he or she accepts food. You may do this with praise.

If the problem continues after these observations, you may wish to contact the child's parents.

### Refusing foods

There will be times when some children refuse to eat certain foods. They may do this for a number of reasons. They may have seen other adults and peers refuse to eat these foods. Or the food may not be prepared in the manner they are use to.

Serve these children small portions of the food. Also, be certain you eat all of the food you have on your plate.

### SETTING THE TABLE

Children should be expected to set tables. This routine provides experiences in counting and in space relationships. Have children take turns performing this routine. Teachers often list this task on a chart, along with other tasks to be done around the classroom.

Begin teaching children to set the table by explaining rules. Before the table is set, the children must wash their hands. Then they must wash the table with soapy water and a sponge or cloth. At this time, they may set the table.

Place mats that show the positions of eating utensils, plates, and glasses are quite helpful for beginners. These mats also help children learn the space relationships of eating utensils.

Teach children to place the plate on the middle of the place mat. Then have them place the fork on the left side of the plate. Place the napkin next to the fork. After this, the knife is placed on the right side of the plate (if you are using knives). The spoon is placed next to the knife. Finally, the glass is placed at the tip of the knife.

Small centerpieces are a nice addition to the dining table. Those made of unusual materials can become the focal point of conversations. Centerpieces may be something a child has brought from home or something the class has made.

### Serving and eating

To foster independence, children should serve themselves and others. Place serving dishes on each table. They should be the proper weight and size for young children to handle. Provide small pitchers so children can pour their own milk, juice, or water, 21-7.

Begin a meal encouraging children to try a small amount of each food. This will be about one or two serving spoons. If a child eats all the food on his or her plate, allow the child to have another serving.

The meal should begin with a glass of milk. Some children prefer liquids to solid food. They will often drink their milk right away and then ask for more. Remind these children that more milk will not be provided until all other foods are tasted.

**Cleaning up.** Cleaning up is also part of the eating routine. Children should learn how to clean up after themselves.

Place a utility cart or small table next to the eating area. After the main meal is completed, have the children take their plates to the cart. If dessert is being served, they may keep their eating utensils and glasses. When dessert is finished they should then take all their dinnerware and eating utensils to the cart.

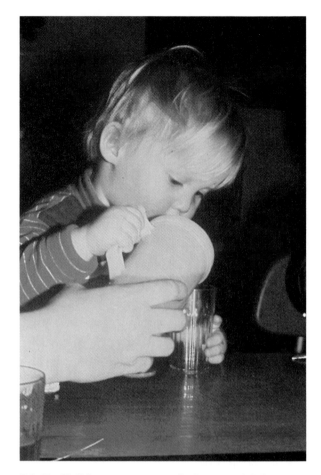

21-7 Children can pour their own drinks from small pitchers.

## SUMMARY

Guiding food experiences includes many tasks. It requires planning cooking experiences, teaching basic nutrition concepts, setting tables, and eating. The skills children learn in this area will be used their entire lives.

Food experiences also involve a great deal of movement and activity. Children get excited and require extra supervision. For this reason, the experiences must be well planned and structured.

Guiding food experiences will require extra effort from you as a teacher. Done correctly, these experiences can be very useful and enjoyable for you and the children.

## Pizza Popcorn

12 cups prepared popcorn
1/2 cup margarine
small amount of garlic salt
1 teaspoon of oregano
3 tablespoons of Parmesan cheese

Melt margarine in a saucepan. Add garlic salt and oregano to the melted margarine. Pour over the popcorn, mixing well. Toss with cheese.

## Banana Pops

Peel one banana for every two children. Cut bananas lengthwise. Dip each banana in orange juice. Roll in crushed corn flakes, chopped peanuts, or granola. Insert a wooden stick in the center. Banana pops can be served frozen or at room temperature.

## Apple Pinwheels

Core one medium sized apple for each child. Stuff the opening with cheese spread, cream cheese, or peanut butter. Slice crosswise and serve.

## Easy Nachos

14 taco shells, cut into quarters
2 to 3 cups refried beans
2 cups of shredded cheddar cheese

Spread refried beans on each taco quarter and then sprinkle with grated cheese. Bake or broil until the cheese melts.

## Carrot-Raisin-Cheese Spread

1 cup plain yogurt
1 1/2 cup raisins
2 cups grated carrots
1 1/2 cups cottage cheese

Blend or mix together until well combined.

## Yogurt Shake

10 medium bananas
5 cups yogurt
4 cups apple juice

Place all of the ingredients in a food processor. Blend for 20 seconds. Makes approximately 20 servings.

## Watermelon Ice Pops

1 medium sized watermelon

Cut the rind off the watermelon. Remove all of the seeds. Place the fruit in a food processor and blend. After the fruit has been blended, pour into forms or fill 6 ounce juice cans half full.

## Peanut Butter

2 pounds unsalted shelled peanuts
vegetable oil
salt

Have the children remove the shells from the peanuts. Place the peanuts in a blender with 2 teaspoons of vegetable oil. Blend until smooth. If necessary, add an additional teaspoon of oil.

Serve on crackers, bread, or raw vegetables. Recommended are celery sticks filled with peanut butter.

## Yummy Peanut Butter Balls

2 cups peanut butter
1 1/2 cups dry milk
1 cup raisins
1/2 cup honey

Mix all the ingredients. Roll into small balls. For variety, substitute granola, coconut, or sesame seeds for the raisins.

## Eggnog

1 large egg, well beaten
2 tablespoons sugar
1 cup milk
1/4 teaspoon vanilla
nutmeg

Beat the egg and sugar together. Add the milk and vanilla. Sprinkle lightly with nutmeg and serve cold. (Serves two children.)

## Cheese Fondue

1 ounce cheese per child
1 loaf French bread
individual paper cups

Cut the bread into chunks. Melt the cheese and pour into individual cups. Dip bread into cheese.

## Milkshakes

1 cup cold milk
fruit flavoring
ice cream, if desired

Blend all of the ingredients together. This recipe can be modified:
Orange Milkshake: Add 1 cup orange juice.
Prune Milkshake: Add 1/2 cup prune juice.
Strawberry Milkshake: Add 1/4 cup crushed sweetened berries.
Banana Milkshake: Add 1/2 mashed banana. (Serves two children)

## Fruit or Vegetable Kabobs

Cut any of the following fruits and vegetables and thread on a stick or skewer in desired combinations. For fresh fruit, dip chunks into lemon, orange, or pineapple juice to keep from darkening.

Vegetables:
asparagus spears, broccoli florets, carrot sticks, celery sticks, green pepper sticks, radish roses, cucumber slices, cherry tomatoes, mushrooms, turnip sticks

Fresh fruits:
apples, apricots, bananas, berries, cherries, grapefruit, grapes, melon, nectarines, oranges, peaches, pears, pineapple, plums, tangerines
For variety, add cheese or meat chunks.

## Cottage Cheese Pudding

1 pint cottage cheese
2 cups applesauce
1 can coarsely chopped apricots
1 1/2 teaspoon of cinnamon
1 cup raisins

Combine all ingredients and chill. Any fruit may be substituted for the apricots.

## Vegetable Dip

1 cup small curd creamed cottage cheese
1/3 cup milk
1 tablespoon lemon or lime juice

Place all of the ingredients into a blender. Blend until smooth. Serve with fresh, raw vegetables or fruits.

## Butter

5 pints cold whipping cream
dash salt
one small baby food jar (with lid) for each child

Fill each jar half full of very cold whipping cream. Let the children shake the containers until butter forms. Remove the excess milk. Encourage the children to spread the butter on individual crackers.

## Dill Dip

1 cup sour cream
1 cup mayonnaise
1 tablespoon dried minced onion
1 tablespoon dill weed

Combine and chill. Serve with a variety of raw vegetables.

## Guacamole

1 ripe tomato, chopped
1 ripe avocado
1/4 cup mayonnaise
1 teaspoon lemon juice
salt and pepper

Peel and mash the avocado. Add the chopped tomato, lemon juice, and mayonnaise. Salt and pepper to taste.

# to Review

1. List four rules that promote relaxed food experiences.

2. Name three methods for working with parents regarding their children's nutrition. Explain one method.

3. True or false. Nutrition knowledge is useful only for adults who make their own food choices.

4. Cooking experiences provide children with the opportunity to:
   a. Develop language skills.
   b. Learn basic concepts about shape, size, texture.
   c. Learn how to use cooking utensils.
   d. All of the above.

5. When using _____ _____, write short, clear instructions using food labels, picture symbols, and simple phrases.

6. True or false. Meeting with success is not very important in first cooking experiences.

7. How can you avoid the problems that result from having to limit cooking experiences to only a few children?

8. Where do many children learn their poor eating habits?

9. If a child constantly refuses to eat a certain food:
   a. Ignore the behavior.
   b. Scold the child.
   c. Give the child large portions of the food.
   d. None of the above.

10. To promote independence, have children _____ themselves and others.

# to Do

1. Design a newsletter to be sent out to parents. Determine columns and special features you would include.

2. Choose one nutrition concept from Chart 21-2. Design a brief lesson for teaching this concept.

3. Make up a simple recipe to use with young children. Write the recipe out, making it understandable to the users.

# Chapter 22

# *Guiding Music and Movement Experiences*

After studying this chapter, you will be able to:
- ☐ Explain the benefits of music experiences.
- ☐ Design a useful music center.
- ☐ Outline the teacher's role in music experiences.
- ☐ Discuss the use and purpose of rhythm instruments in the program.
- ☐ Name a variety of rhythm instruments.
- ☐ List considerations of scheduling music activities.
- ☐ Plan a variety of music activities.
- ☐ Explain how to teach various movement activities.
- ☐ Discuss useful movement activities.

On a rainy afternoon, Mrs. Kohler noticed the children in her classroom were restless. They needed some activity. She decided to guide them in a movement activity using a piece of music designed to promote movement.

The children were told to listen closely. Then Mrs. Kohler told them to move the way the music made them feel. Watching them she saw that fast music made them quickly hop up and down. Slow music made them tiptoe, taking tiny steps.

After the activity, Mrs. Kohler felt she had met her goal. The children gained practice in listening. They also released pent up energy and played well with each other. The activity Mrs. Kohler designed used both music and movement.

Music is a form of communication, 22-1. It is an important form of communication between adults and children. Adults often rock babies to sleep with lullabies. And adults play musical games with children, such as ring-around-the-rosy, London Bridge, and pat-a-cake. As adults play with children, adults convey messages. They communicate feelings to children. They pass on culture. They teach language skills. And they teach music basics.

Teachers use music with young children for many reasons. Music:

- Provides a pleasant background for playing, eating, and sleeping.
- Releases tension and energy.
- Calms angry feelings.
- Can be used to express feelings through movement and dance.
- Creates a festive holiday or birthday feeling.
- Makes learning fun.
- Teaches listening skills.
- Teaches language skills.
- Helps build an understanding of musical concepts, including loud/soft, high/low, fast/slow, up/down.
- Helps build an appreciation of cultural background.

## BENEFITS OF MUSIC EXPERIENCES

Music experiences can build creativity when children are urged to experiment, explore, and express themselves. Music can also enhance expression of feelings and thoughts. And music helps children build an awareness of other's feelings.

Language skills build as children take part in activities. As children listen and sing, they learn new words and sounds.

Music activities help children grow intellectually. They memorize words to songs. They learn to sing musical notes. And they learn to compare concepts: loud/soft, fast/slow, etc.

Children grow physically as they move in rhythmic activities and play instruments. Their small and large muscle control refines.

Music experiences also can help children build positive self-concepts. As children learn about their culture and learn new skills, they learn to like themselves. Children also learn to respond to moods expressed by music. They become more at ease with their emotions.

Music should be a natural part of daily routine. Music experiences should be spontaneous and casual. Likewise, music time should not be at a set time every day.

Children respond to and enjoy many forms of music experiences. They delight in listening to music and stories about music. They enjoy singing and moving to music. They enjoy making simple rhythm instruments. With their instruments, children enjoy making sounds, 22-2. Four- and five-year-old children at times might even make up their own songs.

22-1 Music can be used many ways as a form of communication.

22-2 Children enjoy using gourds as musical instruments.

## A MUSIC CENTER

Design a music center to encourage use by children. Place it in an open section of the classroom to allow room for movement. The active section of the room is best. Creative play will be stressed if housekeeping and block-building areas are nearby.

Display instruments on a table or open shelf, 22-3. The children should feel free to use these. Include drums, guitars, tonettes, and recorders on the shelf or table.

When buying instruments look for quality. Quality instruments produce the best sounds.

Instruments and other supplies can be bought through local music stores. Consult the Yellow Pages for names, addresses, and telephone numbers. These businesses are listed under such headings as school supplies, music instruments, music, piano, music dealers, or records.

Parents are a good source for instruments. Often they are happy to lend or give instruments to the schools. Instruments of different cultures many times are supplied by parents.

The music center should also contain pictures of dancers, instruments, and singers. Local record music stores may be happy to supply you with these. See 22-4.

## THE TEACHER'S ROLE

The teacher's role is to encourage musical expression. To do this, children need surroundings in which they feel free to explore, sing, and move to music.

It is common for novice teachers to be shy about singing before a group of children. This fear is needless. Young children are not critics. They enjoy hearing their teachers sing.

Enthusiasm is the key factor in conducting a useful experience, 22-5. Your delight in music will be catching. Remember to smile and enjoy yourself. If you do, you will see children smiling and enjoying themselves also.

When singing with or to children, use a light, pleasant singing voice. Children find it easier to match the tones of human voices rather than pianos or instruments. Therefore, with children

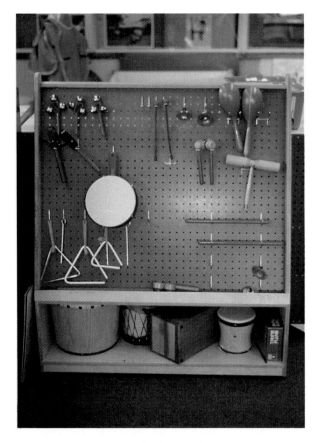

22-3 This inviting display of instruments encourages the involvement of children.

| CONTENTS OF A MUSIC CENTER |
| --- |
| Autoharp |
| Variety of records |
| Quality three-speed record player |
| Tape recorder and cassettes |
| Pictures of dancers, instruments, and singers |
| Rhythm instruments |
| Sound-producing objects (clocks, containers filled with pebbles) |
| Songbooks |
| Scarves, crepe paper streamers |
| Piano, guitar (optional) |

22-4 The contents listed here are part of a useful music center. What other items might you add?

22-5 This teacher's enthusiasm is more important to the children than the instrument she is playing.

- How can you make a different sound?
- How was this sound different?
- Can you make a faster sound?
- Can you make a slower sound?
- Can you make a louder sound?
- Can you make a softer sound?

You may also increase music awareness by asking children to listen to each other play instruments. You might place four of five instruments on a table during free play periods. Or you could introduce them at group time. A comment like, "Here are some instruments that you may wish to play," may be all that is needed to start the children playing.

To encourage the children, comment on their efforts. Such statements as, "You are making some interesting sounds," "Your sounds are beautiful," or "You found a new way," build positive self-concepts. You may also encourage children by prompting. For example, you may say, "Show me how you did that."

### Encouraging nonparticipants

In every group of young children there are some children who prefer to observe. These children prefer to listen and watch the group. Nonparticipating children generally need more time to take part in music activities. Such children should be handled with patience, 22-6. Try to stand next to such children during movement activities. Slowly take their hands and swing to the rhythm. A skilled assistant can also help encourage children who do not want to take part.

### Selecting songs

When choosing songs for young children, give thought to children's developmental level and interests. The best songs for young children:
- Tell a story.
- Have frequent repetition.
- Have a proper vocabulary.
- Have a strongly defined mood or rhythm.
- Have a range of no more than one octave. Most children are comfortable with the range from C to A or D to B.
- Have moods that children know or can mimic.

through age three, use instruments as little as possible.

Do not push children to take part. Singing alone or in a group takes some courage. When children feel ready to take part, they will. Meanwhile, try to make music an enjoyable experience for them. Your enthusiasm will be catching. Children's natural creativity will blossom.

Music does not have to be used at a set time and place. It should occur throughout the day. For instance, children respond better to musical directions than spoken. For this reason, many teachers use music to make announcements, provide transitions, and direct clean up. It is also important that the surroundings promote and support music. Records, record players, cassette recorders, rhythm instruments, and singing all invite children to share music.

### Encouraging discovery

Another role of the teacher is to promote children's interest in instruments and their sounds. This helps children grow in awareness. To promote children's interest, you must also show interest. For example, during a group play activity, you may ask one of these questions:

- Relate to children's level of development.

Choose songs that you also enjoy. To arouse children's interest, you must convey enthusiasm for a song. For instance, you may ask children to clap the "words" of favorite songs. Children will not tire of a well-loved song. They will repeat it over and over again once they know it.

Most children enjoy many types of songs. Songs about familiar things and families, lullabies, holiday songs, and songs with actions are all enjoyed by children. Some songs are best for older children. Others, because of their content, are best for young children, such as "Twinkle, Twinkle, Little Star."

Children's songbooks are available at music stores. These books can be used to find new songs. Or the books may be used along with the piano, guitar, or autoharp. If possible, keep several of these books on hand.

### Creating songs

An easy to follow tune can be used with many songs. The best way to make a song is to use a known melody with new words. For example, "Baa, Baa, Blacksheep," "Twinkle, Twinkle, Little Star," and "A, B, C, D" are all tunes that can be used for other songs. You will find that changing words to these tunes is a good way to teach language skills.

### Teaching songs

The teacher's attitude about music influences children's responses. If you, as a teacher, are thrilled by and enjoy music, the children will likely also enjoy music. Try to sing clearly, using expression, proper pitch, and rhythm. The children will learn by imitating your voice. There are three methods for teaching songs: the phrase method, the whole song method, and the phrase/whole combination method.

The *phrase method* of teaching is used with longer songs and younger children. First, prepare the children by telling them what to listen for. For example, say "I'm going to sing you a song about a dog named Wags. I want you to listen carefully and tell me what Wags does."

After this introduction, sing the entire song.

22-6 Children who avoid taking part in music activities can be helped through individual contact with the teacher.

Then stop and talk about the song. Next, sing short sections and have the children repeat these sections after you. Keep singing, increasing the length of the sections until the children know the song. After the children appear comfortable, drop out. This will prevent them from depending on you to lead songs.

The *whole song method* is used to teach songs that are short and simple. Tell the children to listen to you. After they have listened to you sing the song once, ask them to sing with you. Repeat the song a few times, to be sure the children know the words.

The *phrase/whole combination method* is done by teaching key phrases. Sing a key phrase and have the children repeat it. Continue until you have introduced a few key phrases in the song. Then sing the whole song and have children join in when they can. Repeat the song until children have learned all of the words. Stress key phrases with rhythmic movement or visual props to make them more meaningful, 22-7. An example would be "Johnny Pounds with One Hammer." As the song is sung, both you and the children can mimic a pounding action.

### Accompanying singing

Many early childhood teachers like to play the piano, autoharp, or guitar while children

22-7 This prop for "Five Green Speckled Frogs" helps children learn and remember the song.

sing. Whether this is done depends in large part on the instruments available and the teacher's playing skill. Remember, though, your enjoyment of the music is much more important than flawless playing.

Some teachers do not use instruments even if they are skilled. They believe that playing instruments detracts from the total experience. Children's attention tends to wander. To avoid this pitfall, use the autoharp or guitar. With these instruments, facial expressions and lip movements can be seen by the children. They will feel your involvement in the activity.

**Piano.** A piano has a clear sound and can be used to play melodies as well as to accompany singing. Advanced playing skills are not needed for successful music experiences. Children seldom notice missed chords or bad notes. Instead, they notice enthusiasm and delight.

**Autoharp.** An *autoharp* is a simple chording instrument that can be used to accompany singing. The autoharp is more useful than a piano for a number of reasons. An autoharp is not as costly as a piano. An autoharp can be carried to different places. It can be taken to class picnics, on field trips, and out on the play yard. And it is a simple instrument to learn to play. In fact, within a few hours, many early childhood teachers can learn to play the autoharp using a self-instruction book.

Learning to play the autoharp is quite simple. Place the instrument so you can read the identification bars. Use the left hand to press the chord bars. Strum the strings with the right hand. Strum one chord for each beat.

**Guitar.** The guitar is a string instrument. It is more difficult to learn to play than the autoharp. Like the autoharp, it is portable. It can be moved to the play yard or taken on a field trip. For this reason, it is often a favorite of many early childhood teachers.

## RHYTHM INSTRUMENTS

Rhythm instruments can be used by children to take part in music activities. By playing rhythm instruments, children can express their feelings. Children who have expressed little in-

22-8 Children can have fun with rhythm instruments without worrying about their musical talents.

terest or skill in singing may respond to musical instruments, 22-8.

Rhythm instruments can be used to:
- Accompany the beat of a sound or recording.
- Emphasize music or mood.
- Encourage children to make rhythmic sounds.
- Experiment with sounds.
- Build listening skills.
- Develop classification skills by learning the difference between quiet and loud, hard and soft, and other sounds.

Rhythm instruments can be store-bought or made by teachers, parents, volunteers, and sometimes even children. Handmade instruments will not have the same quality as store-bought instruments. However, handmade instruments serve a purpose by exposing children to many sounds.

## Introducing rhythm instruments

Rhythm instruments can be used during individual or group experiences. Before giving children instruments to play, set rules. The following guidelines are suggested for using rhythm instruments in a group:
- Quietly hand out the instruments. This prevents children from getting too excited and becoming disruptive. One method that works well is to choose one child to hand out the instruments. This prevents children from struggling with each other in an attempt to get their favorite instruments. Some teachers prefer setting the instruments in a circle to prevent crowding.
- If you have a variety of instruments, introduce only one at a time. It is recommended that the number of instrument types be limited to two, three, or four to keep the volume lower.
- Explain to the children that the instruments must be handled with care and that instruments will be taken away from children who abuse them.
- After the children have instruments in their hands, allow them a few minutes to experiment. Most children will want to play their instrument right away. Use a signal such as beating a drum, raising your hand, or playing the autoharp to have the children stop.
- Rotate instruments after children have had time to experiment. This gives each child a chance to play all of the instruments.
- After the activity, have the children return their instruments to the box, table, or shelf where they belong.

## Building rhythm instruments

Some teachers have the time and resources to make rhythm instruments. Directions are included for making sandpaper blocks and sticks, bongo and tom-tom drums, rattlers and shakers, rhythm sticks and bells, and coconut cymbals.

**Sandpaper blocks.** Sandpaper blocks can be used by children of all ages. For this reason, they are often the first rhythm instruments used in the classroom. Some classrooms contain one pair of sandpaper blocks for each child.

Sandpaper blocks can be used for sound effects. They make a soft, swishing sound and are played by rubbing the two sandpaper blocks together. See 22-9 for instructions on making sandpaper blocks.

**Sandpaper sticks.** Purchase rough sandpaper and wooden doweling one inch wide and twelve inches long for each stick. To construct the sticks, wrap and glue sandpaper around each of the dowels. Leave a small section for use as a handle. Then sand the end of the sticks smooth. Direct the children to scrape the

dowels back and forth across each other to make a sound. These sticks, like the sandpaper blocks, will need to have the sandpaper replaced from time to time.

**Bongo drums.** Bongo drums are a favorite of many preschool children. With a drum they can make many tones by hitting the drumhead near the rim, in the center, and elsewhere.

To construct bongo drums collect a pair of scissors, string, an automobile tire tube, an empty shortening can with both ends removed, a hammer, and a large nail.

Use the plastic lid from the shortening can to trace two circles on the tire tube. Allow an additional inch to pull over the edges. Cut the circles out. Take the hammer and large nail, and punch holes around the outside edge of the circle. After the holes have been punched, place each of the rubber circles over an end of the can. Then lace the rubber circles to each other using string.

**Tom-tom drums.** Making tom-toms can be a group project for the children. You will need oatmeal boxes (with lids) and tempera paint, watercolor markers, or construction paper. One way to get all the empty oatmeal boxes needed is to ask parents to send them from home. To make the tom-toms, tell the children to tape the lid on the box. After this, give them tempera paint, watercolor markers, or colored construction paper and paste to decorate their tom-toms. A rhythm stick can be used for a drum stick.

Tin can tom-toms can be made with large empty coffee cans. Use the plastic top to cut three sheets of wrapping paper 2 inches larger than the top of the tin for each tom-tom. Glue the three sheets together. Stretch the glued paper over one end of the coffee can. Secure the paper with a large rubber band or string.

**Rattlers.** Making rattlers is a simple activity in which the children can take part. To make the instruments, ask parents to send a round salt box to school with their children.

To make the rattlers, give each child a handful of dry beans, corn kernels, or rice. Have the children pour them into the box. Then give each child a strip of tape to seal off the pour spout on the box.

## SANDPAPER BLOCKS

**Materials**

2 blocks of soft pine, 5 by 3 by 1 inches in size
Several sheets of coarse sandpaper
Colored enamel paint
Thumbtacks or staples
Strong glue (epoxy based)
2 straps of leather or flexible plastic, 4 to 4 1/2 inches long
Scissors
Hammer

**Procedure**

1. Sand the wood to remove all rough edges.
2. Paint the blocks a bright color to make them attractive and to prevent the wood from becoming soiled.
3. Glue the handles to each block:

4. Cut the sandpaper to fit the bottom and sides of each block:

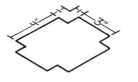

5. Attach the sandpaper to the blocks with thumbtacks or staples. (As sand is rubbed off the paper, replace with new sandpaper.)

22-9 It takes just a little effort to make these inexpensive sandpaper blocks.

After the box has been filled and the spout taped off, the children can decorate their rattlers. Give the children tempera paint, washable markers, crayons, colored construction paper, and paste. After the rattlers have been decorated, put them on display. Encourage the children to explore the variety of sounds made by the different materials.

**Shakers.** Collect empty toilet tissue and paper towel tubes. Tape one end of the tube shut with paper fastened by masking tape. Pour small pebbles, dried corn, dried beans, or rice into each tube. Tape the open end shut. If desired, cover each shaker with construction paper or enamel paint.

Children delight in using shakers. They are most useful with light, fast music. Shakers should be held at face level and shook briskly.

**Rhythm sticks.** Rhythm sticks are always made in matching pairs. Wooden doweling from 3/4 to one inch in diameter is needed. Cut the doweling into 12-inch lengths. Sand each end of the doweling. Add a protective coat of shellac or enamel paint.

Rhythm sticks can also be made from bamboo. This type of wood will produce a hollow sound. A good source for bamboo is a local carpet dealer. To make the rhythm sticks, cut the bamboo into 10 to 12 inch pieces. Tape each end of the stick with library tape to prevent splinters.

Teach the children to play rhythm sticks holding one stick in each hand. One stick should be held steady while it is struck near the top with a second stick. See 22-10.

Jingle sticks are rhythm sticks with bells attached to each end. The bells can be attached with a small cup hook. After placing the bell on the hook, use a pliers to force the cup hook closed. You may wish to paint the sticks bright colors. This may make them appealing to children.

**Rhythm bells.** Materials needed to make rhythm bells include strips of elastic, 1/2 to 3/4 of an inch wide and five inches in length. Five to six bells are needed for each strip of elastic. A needle and thread are needed to sew the bells to the elastic.

Sew the ends of the elastic together by over-lapping the ends. This can be done by hand or on a machine. On one side of the loop, sew on five or six small bells. Vary the size of the bells on the loops for a variety of sound. The children will then learn that the sounds made by bells of different sizes vary.

**Coconut cymbals.** Cymbals made of coconut halves offer many sounds. They can sound like horses galloping when clapped together. They can also be hit with a rhythm stick to make fast, light music.

To make coconut cymbals, buy several large coconuts at the supermarket. Each coconut will make a pair of cymbals. Cut each coconut in half with a sharp saw. Drain the milk and remove all the meat. Sand the outside and inside edges of the shell until smooth. After this, shellac or paint both sides of the shell.

### Buying rhythm instruments

Many teachers do not have time to make all the instruments needed for their programs. As a result, some instruments will have to be bought.

Buy instruments that are sturdy, 22-11. For instance, buy maracas that are constructed in

22-10 Children quickly learn to play rhythm sticks properly.

328

22-11 Center instruments get much use, so they need to be durable.

one piece. Otherwise the handles may come loose. Triangles should hang from sturdy holders. If the holder is not strong, the instrument may twirl around when a child is trying to strike it. Jingle bells should always be attached to elastic. This makes them flexible enough to use as either wrist or ankle bracelets. Check drum and tambourine heads to make sure they are fastened firmly. The skins should not have any cuts or holes.

Try to buy instruments in a number of sizes. This allows for a good mix of tones. Usually, smaller instruments have higher tones. Larger instruments have deeper tones.

## SCHEDULING MUSIC

Music should be scheduled throughout the day. It fits in well after a story, at the start of the day, after a snack, and during free playtime. It can be used during waiting times, such as the end of the day, a bus ride on a field trip, or before and after lunch. It can also be used to remind children of rules they may have forgotten. For instance, if Sam and Gail did not hang up their coats, you may sing, "At school we hang up our coats, hang up our coats."

In addition to these impromptu uses of music, music should also be scheduled as a group activity for four- and five-year-old children. This should occur at the same time every day.

### Using group music

Group music activities are useful in building group feelings and pride. A group setting is a good way to introduce new songs and new instruments. These activities should focus on the group, not the individual.

Group time should be fairly brief. At the start of the program, schedule seven to ten minutes in half-day programs. You may later extend the period up to 15 minutes for four- and five-year-old children. Some centers that operate all day schedule two short music periods. Day care centers may have to adjust their music time to meet the attention spans and developmental levels of the children.

**Suggestions for group music.** The group needs to be well-organized for a successful music period. The following suggestions may help:
- Always be prepared. Make sure you have all the needed instruments, music, and other accessories.
- Use the same signal for calling the children together for group music time. This signal may be a song, an autoharp chord, a beat on a drum, or a piano tune.
- Have the children sit in a circle or semi-circle. Then the children can see you and you can see them. To help children sit in the proper places, mark the floor with chalk, tape, or carpet squares.
- Require all adults in the classroom to take part. Their support encourages children to obey. These adults can also sit on the floor near the children and help them learn words and responses to the music.
- Switch between active and quiet music activities. Children may get bored if they are always required to listen to music.

Likewise, they may tire quickly from or become too excited by activities that involve a great deal of movement.

- Reward children for positive behavior. Tell them what type of behavior you expect: sitting quietly, waiting for their turns, holding instruments correctly, singing clearly at the proper volume. Ignore disruptive behavior if it is being done by only one child. If the child continues, despite being ignored, ask another adult in the group to remove the child. Children who act up when they are together should also be separated during group time.
- Include familiar songs that use fingerplay every day. Such songs are favorites because children find it easy to take part.

### Using individual music

Group music activities tend to stress conformity. Children are not as free during these times to express their creativity. For this reason, individual music activities are also an important part of the music experience.

During individual activities, encourage children to interact with music. Play records during this period. Make rhythm instruments, the piano, and a tape recorder available during these times, 22-12. It is also a good idea to station a teacher or other adult in the music area. An adult's presence will encourage children to enter the music area.

## MUSIC ACTIVITIES

Listening, singing, playing rhythm instruments, and moving to rhythm are all music activities. A good program contains all of these activities.

### Listening

All music activities involve listening. The ability to listen is important for learning. Good listening skills help children build proper speech habits, an extended attention span, and reading readiness skills.

Listening to music can enrich the imaginations of young children. It also can help them relax and release pent-up feelings. Listening can

22-12 Many children love to spend time alone at the piano.

take place when singing or when playing rhythm instruments, the piano, the phonograph, or a tape player.

Children need to be taught how to listen. You, as a teacher, need to give them reasons for listening. For example, you may say, "Listen to this music and tell me how it makes you feel." After playing the music, let the children express their feelings. The games in 22-13 can help young children develop listening skills.

Fingerplays are another useful method for teaching listening skills. Choose fingerplays based on developmental levels. For example, a fingerplay for two-year-olds should be short and contain simple words.

Teachers who enjoy fingerplays may wish to order their own fingerplay books. These books

## LISTENING GAMES

### What's the Sound?

Tape sounds from different parts of the home. These may include running water, flushing toilets, ringing telephones, closing doors, or sounds made by scissors, egg beaters, doorbells, electric washing machines, radios, and electric garage door openers. Play each sound back to the children and ask them to name the object making the noise.

### Instrument Sounds

Provide the children with a box or basket of rhythm instruments to explore. Then ask the following questions:
- What instrument sounds like jingle bells?
- What instrument sounds like a church bell?
- What instrument sounds like the tick of a clock?
- What instrument sounds like thunder?
- What instrument has a loud sound?
- What instrument has a quiet sound?

### Body Sounds

Tell all of the children that you are going to play a body sound game. Tell them to close their eyes or cover them with their hands, and to listen carefully. Then using your body, stomp your feet, snap your fingers, slap your thigh, smack your lips, and clap your hands.

### Guess the Instruments

Let the children become familiar with the classroom instruments. Then, based on developmental level or age of the child, choose a few instruments to use in a game called ''Guess the instrument.'' With two-year-old children, choose only two instruments. These should have very different sounds. As the children progress, add more instruments. To play the game, tell the children to cover their eyes and listen to the sound made by the instrument you are playing. Then they can guess what instrument you are playing. After children are familiar with the game, older children may want to play the teacher's role. In this event, you, too, should cover your eyes and take part.

22-13 Children have fun and develop their listening skills while playing these games.

can be ordered through a local bookstore, bought at a professional conference, or bought from a local school supply store.

Some teachers prefer to file fingerplays under certain units of study. For example, "Two Little Apples" could be filed with units on apples, fall, or nutrition. "Roll Them" could be filed in units on transition, movement, or body concept. Size concept or numbers would be good units for using "Here's A Ball." "Lickety-Lick," a childhood favorite, is often filed and used for teaching science concepts during cooking experiences. See 22-14.

### Singing

Children's best musical instrument is their voices. Their voices are always with them. Children learn to sing at birth. Cooing and crying sounds are musical. These tones vary in strength and pitch. Voice control is learned as children grow.

After children babble, tonal patterns emerge. By age two most children can sing. They often sing as they dress, eat, and play. By this time, singing is a meaningful activity.

Children's singing skills vary a great deal. In a group of two-year-olds, there may be children able to sing in tune and make up tunes. Other children may not be able to master these skills until they are three or four years old.

You may notice that children who stutter often sing clearly. Speech skills can be improved through singing, 22-15.

**Mouthing.** Children's mouths can be used to make coughing, gurgling, sipping, kissing, and hissing sounds. Animal, train, plane, machinery, and traffic sounds can also be made with the mouth. As children compare these sounds, they will learn that some are fast, others slow, some loud, and some quiet. Thus, exploring mouth sounds can add to knowledge. As children explore these sounds, they learn others. Joining a variety of sounds can produce unique music.

To encourage children to make sounds, bring pictures to a group activity. For instance, collect pictures of large, medium, and small dogs in a number of poses. The dogs might be barking, showing their teeth, or playing with

## FINGERPLAYS

### Two Little Apples

Two little apples hanging high in the tree.
*(Place arms above head.)*
Two little apples smiling at me.
*(Look up at hands and smile.)*
I shook that tree as hard as I could.
*(Make a shaking motion.)*
Down came the apples. Mmmmmmm, so good.
*(Make a falling motion with arms. Hold hands to mouth pretending to eat.)*

### Roll Them

Roll them and roll them. *(Roll hands.)*
And give your hands a clap. *(Clap hands.)*
Roll them and roll them. *(Roll hands.)*
And place them in your lap. *(Place hands in lap.)*

### Here's A Ball

Here's a ball
*(Make a small circle with thumb and index finger.)*
And here's a ball
*(Make a large circle by using both thumbs and index fingers.)*
A great big ball I see.
*(Make a huge circle with arms.)*
Shall we count them? Are you ready? One, two, three.

### Lickety-Lick

Lickety-lick, lickety-lick.
*(Make a big circle with the left arm by placing hand on hip. Place the right hand inside the circle.)*
The batter is getting all thickety-thick.
*(Stir with the right hand.)*
What should be bake? What shall we bake?
*(Gesture by opening hands.)*
A great big beautiful cake.
*(Extend arms to show a big cake.)*

22-14 How would you file these fingerplays?

their owners. Show the children each picture. Ask them to mimic the sounds a dog would make in each instance. You can use pictures of other animals, people, machines, cars, trucks, and other objects. These activities will help children become sensitive to sounds.

**Chants.** Chants are an important form of early childhood song. A *chant* is a song that has word patterns, rhymes, and nonsense

22-15 Singing along to music helps many children correct speech problems.

syllables in one to three tones repeated in a sequence. "Teddy Bear, Teddy Bear, Turn Around" is a chant. Mother Goose rhymes are also chants.

## MOVEMENT EXPERIENCES

Movement provides opportunities to pretend. Children can walk like elephants, crawl like worms, build houses, type, cry. Children nearly always enjoy these experiences, 22-16.

Movement activities should provide children with the chance to:
- Explore the many ways their bodies can move.
- Practice combining movement with rhythm.
- Discover that many concepts and ideas can be expressed to others through movement.
- Learn how movement is related to space.

Some children will take naturally to movement activities. Other children may feel self-conscious or embarrassed. To help these children, begin with some short, simple movement activities. Knowing what type of responses to expect can help you prepare.

### Children's responses

Studies show that two- and three-year-old children's responses to movement varies. Most two-year-old children actively respond to rhythm, but at their own tempo. Their response may be to repeat the same basic movement through the entire activity. For example, a two-year-old may simply jump up and down during an entire song.

By age three, children have gained greater motor coordination. As a result, they have more control of rhythmic responses. Three-year-old children will use many responses. That is, they will circle with their arms, run, jump up and down during the same recording.

Between ages four and six, muscular coordination keeps improving. At the same time, their interest in movement and space increases. If you watch children at this stage, you will notice they skip, run, climb, and dance to music. These movements are now done to the beat of the music. If the beat is fast, their movements are fast. If the beat is slow, their movements are slow.

### Teacher preparation

To prepare for movement activities, first select your activity. Chart 22-17 lists many movements. Then stand in front of a full-length mirror and practice the movements. Do each movement in the activity. If possible, repeat the movements several times.

In the classroom, children learn best when they can see and hear. Rather than simply explain, you may have to act out certain movements. In the fingerplay "Two Little Apples," for instance, during the line, "way up high in the sky," place your hands high above your head.

### Teaching movements

In most movement activities, children should be encouraged to explore and express their own way of moving. A tambourine can be used to capture children's interest before and during the activities. Tambourines are very useful. They can be played loud or soft, slow or fast. They can represent a galloping horse or a frightened kitten.

For successful movement activities you will need to follow certain guidelines:
- Choose a time when the children are well rested.

22-16 Children like to discover what their bodies can do through movement activities.

**BODY MOVEMENTS**

| Finger Movements | Hand and Arm Movements | Whole Body Movement |
|---|---|---|
| Cutting | Carrying | Bending |
| Folding | Clapping | Bouncing |
| Holding | Dropping | Climbing |
| Pinching | Grabbing | Crawling |
| Pointing | Lifting | Creeping |
| Poking | Punching | Dancing |
| Patting | Pulling | Galloping |
| Petting | Reaching | Hopping |
| Pulling | Sweeping | Jumping |
| Rolling | Slapping | Scooting |
| Rubbing | Stretching | Shaking |
| Smoothing | Waving | Shuffling |
| Tickling | | Skipping |
| Typing | | Sliding |
| Touching | | Swaying |
| | | Rocking |
| | | Rolling Over |
| | | Running |

22-17 These movements can be included in a variety of movement activities.

- Define space limits. There needs to be enough open, clear space. If space is limited, move chairs and furniture to the side.
- Tell children they need to stop when the music stops.
- For variety in movement experiences, provide props such as paper streamers, balloons, balls, and scarves, 22-18.
- Use movement activities involving records, rhythm instruments, and verbal instructions.
- Allow children to get to know activities by repeating many of the experiences.
- Stop before fatigue sets in.

You may want children to be involved in planning some movement activities. Ask the children to suggest movement activities and to bring in their favorite records. After the group experience, records can be placed in the music center. This will give children the chance to listen to the music again.

**Body percussion activities.** Early movement activities should be simple. Stomping feet, clapping hands, patting thighs, and snapping fingers are all simple movements. These are called *body percussion.* All of these movements involve using the body to make rhythm. Body percussion can be used to learn to do more than one movement at a time. Body percussion also helps children build *auditory discrimination skills*—the ability to detect different sounds by listening.

Stomping feet to music has always been a favorite action of young children. To stomp correctly, children should bring their legs back and stomp down and forward.

Children should be taught to clap with one palm held up steadily. You should refer to this palm as the instrument. The other hand serves as the mallet. Children should clap with arms and wrists relaxed and elbows out.

The thigh slap is easy to teach. Relax your wrist for modeling the thigh slap. With arms relaxed, move your hands to slap your thigh.

When teaching children to snap their fingers, hold your hands high. Tell the children to follow you. Snap once. Have the children repeat this action. After they have mimicked

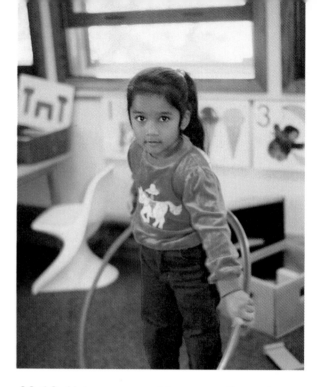

22-18 Using props adds a new dimension to movement activities.

your action, have them do two snaps, and then three snaps. Keep this up as long as they are able to repeat your action.

After children have learned to stomp, clap, slap, and snap, you can have them combine two actions. They might "snap, snap, snap," and then "clap, clap, clap." Depending on the skills of the children, you may gradually introduce all four levels of body percussion during one experience.

## MOVEMENT ACTIVITIES

One of the first movement activities should focus on listening to a drum beat. A drum is the only instrument needed for the activity. First, tell the children to listen to the drum. For two-year-old children, provide one steady beat. With older children you may vary the rhythm: fast, slow, heavy, soft, big, small. Then ask them to respond. Encourage them to run, crawl, roll, walk, hop, skip, and gallop. After experiences using the drum, many more movement activities can be used.

334

### Partners

This activity is best for four- or five-year-olds. Instruct the children to choose partners. You will also need a partner to demonstrate. With your partner, move under, over, and around each other. Then have the other children mimic your movements.

### Time awareness

Use a drum to provide a beat that tells the children to run very fast. After they have done this well, tell them to run very slowly. Then tell them to jump on the floor quickly. Again, follow this request by having them jump slowly.

### Space awareness

Have the children stand in front of you. Make sure that there is enough space between each child so movements can be made freely. Stress your instructions with actions as you tell them to do the following:
- Lift your leg in front of you.
- Lift your leg backwards.
- Lift your leg sideways.
- Lift your leg and step forward.
- Lift your leg and step backwards.
- Lift your leg and step sideways.
- Reach up to the ceiling.
- Reach down to the floor.
- Stretch to touch the walls, 22-19.
- Move your arm in front of you.
- Move your arm behind you.

### Weight awareness

Children can learn differences between light and heavy using their own body force. To begin this activity, give verbal directions and demonstrate the actions. Tell the children to focus on the weight of their bodies as they make the movements. Give the following instructions:
- Push down hard on the floor with your hands.
- Push down softly on the floor with your hands.
- Lift your arms slowly into the air.
- Lift your arms quickly into the air.
- Walk on your tiptoes.
- Stomp on the floor with your feet.

22-19 Reacing helps make children more aware of the space around them.

- Kick your leg as slowly as you can.
- Kick your leg as hard as you can.

### Organizing movement into dance

Combining time, space, and weight movements, children can learn to form their movements into dance. To teach this concept have the children do the following:
- Walk around quickly in a circle on the floor.
- Walk around slowly in a circle on the floor.
- Tiptoe slowly around the circle.
- Tiptoe quickly around the circle.
- Jump hard around the circle.
- Move your arms in a circle above your head.
- Move your arms in circles everywhere.

### Word games

Word games can help children move in ways that express feelings. To play word games, tell the children to move the way the words you say might feel. Use such words as happy, sad, angry, sleepy, and lazy. After they have moved to these words, remind them to use their bodies and faces. Keep repeating the words.

## Moving shapes

Four- and five-year-old children enjoy the moving shapes game. As with other movement activities, children will need ample space. Give children the following instructions:
- Try to move like something big and heavy: an elephant, tugboat, bulldozer, airplane.
- Try to move like something small and heavy: a fat frog, a bowling ball, a brick.
- Try to move like something big and light: a cloud, a beach ball, a parachute.
- Try to move like something small and light: a snowflake, a flea, a feather, a butterfly, a bumblebee.

## Pantomiming

*Pantomiming* involves telling a story. It is best for use with four-, five-, and six-year-olds. Begin by telling the children they are going to get presents. Tell them to show you how big their box is. The children should show you a shape made by outlining with their hands. Continue with the following statements:
- Feel the box.
- Hold the box.
- Unwrap the present.
- Take it out of the box.
- Put it back into the box.
- Rewrap the present.

Another pantomime children enjoy is acting out an occupation. Tell the children to think about an occupation. Then have them show how the worker acts. Sometimes this is fun to do one by one. Have one child act out his or her occupation while the rest of the class tries to guess it.

## Pretending

Pretending is an activity best used with older children. Tell the children to pretend they are crying, singing, boxing, driving, cooking, laughing, typing, scrubbing, painting, playing an instrument, flying, playing cards, or building a houses. See 22-20. There are many songs that children can act out as they sing. Classics in-

clude "Here We Go Around the Mulberry Bush" or "This is What I Can Do." The music to "Peter and the Wolf" provides the same opportunity for drama.

Another pretending activity involves telling the children to imagine there is a box in front of them. Then tell them they are outside the box and they should crawl into it. After they have crawled into the box, tell the children to crawl out of it. Continue by telling them to crawl under and beside the box.

## SUMMARY

Music is a form of communication. It can be used to teach many skills. Through music, children learn about emotions and feelings, their culture, and sound. For these reasons, teaching music is an important part of a preschool program.

Movement provides children with opportunities to pretend and exercise. Movement activities can be easily combined with music activities for meaningful experiences.

22-20 Older children can pretend to show such expressions as laughter.

336

# to Know

auditory discrimination skills
autoharp
body percussion
chant

pantomiming
phrase method
phrase/whole combination method
whole song method

# to Review

1. List four reasons teachers use music with young children.
2. True or false. Music experiences help children build positive self-concepts.
3. A music center should:
    a. Be in an open section of the classroom.
    b. Have instruments displayed on a table or shelf.
    c. Should encourage use by children.
    d. All of the above.
4. _____ is a key factor in conducting useful music experiences.
5. True or false. Nonparticipants should be pushed into taking part in music activities.
6. The best songs for young children should:
    a. Have little or no repetition.
    b. Have a vocal range of two or three octaves.
    c. Tell a story.
    d. None of the above.
7. Name three methods for teaching songs. Explain one method.
8. Why do some teachers not use instruments to accompany singing?
9. An _____ is a simple chording instrument that can be used to accompany singing.
10. Rhythm instruments can be used to:
    a. Accompany the beat of a sound or recording.
    b. Emphasize music or mood.
    c. Experiment with sound.
    d. All of the above.
11. _____ music activities are useful in building feelings of togetherness.
12. State five useful suggestions for conducting group music experiences.
13. True or false. All music activities involve singing.
14. _____ are songs that have word patterns, rhymes, and nonsense syllables used in sequence with one to three repeated tones.
15. List four objectives for movement experiences.
16. For successful movement activities, you should:
    a. Choose a time when children are well rested.
    b. Define space limits.
    c. Stop before children get tired.
    d. All of the above.
17. _____ _____ activities involve stomping feet and clapping hands.
18. What is auditory discrimination skill?
19. _____ involves having children act out a story as it is told.

# to Do

1. Watch a teacher during a music experience. Note the methods used to teach songs. Share these methods with the class.
2. Design a music center. Start by reviewing equipment catalogs. Make a list of instruments and equipment to include. Draw up a budget for this center.
3. Select a movement activity and demonstrate it to your class.
4. Select a song and teach it to your class.
5. Build two or three types of rhythm instruments. Plan a music activity using these instruments.

# Chapter 23

# *Guiding Field Trip Experiences*

After studying this chapter, you will be able to:
- ☐ Discuss the importance of field trips.
- ☐ Explain points of consideration for first field trip experiences.
- ☐ Describe the process for selecting a field trip.
- ☐ Explain various types of theme walks.
- ☐ Plan a field trip, from pre-trip planning to follow-up activities.

"Apples grow on trees," announced Karla after a recent field trip. Christopher replied, "I know that, and I know something else. Apples are grown in special places called orchards." Hearing the conversation, Robbie added, "Orchards can have red, green, or yellow apples." These children, by going on a field trip, have broadened their concept of an apple.

Mr. Smith, after hearing the children's comments, promoted further learning by saying, "It sounds like you know a lot about apples." All the children agreed. Mr. Smith then suggested that they write a story about the trip.

First, Mr. Smith found a large sheet of paper and a grease pencil. He then asked the children to tell him about their trip to the apple orchard. This is what he recorded:

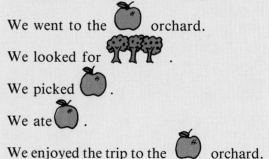

From the field trip the children learned many concepts related to apples. They learned about color, size, shape, and plant growth. Mr. Smith's goals for the children when planning the field trip were to expand their concepts and to have a good time. Both goals were met.

## THE IMPORTANCE OF FIELD TRIPS

Young children have limited understanding of the world. Many of their experiences with the world come from books, pictures, television, and movies. These media help children understand their world. However, they do not take the place of real experiences. To fully understand their world, young children need to use all their senses. They need to see, hear, feel, taste, and smell, 23-1. The more senses are involved, the more likely they will learn.

Children can gain these firsthand experiences during field trips. They are able to look at, listen to, touch, and feel their world. As the children connect words and concepts with real objects and places, vague concepts become clearer to them. Field trips also help children:

- Build keener observation skills.
- Build vocabularies.
- Clarify concepts as new information is learned.
- Learn about their community.
- Take part in sensory experiences.
- Gain new insights for dramatic play.
- Learn about their environment.
- Practice following directions in a group.

## FIRST FIELD TRIPS

For young children, first field trips can be a very new experience. They may not be used to such activity. As a result, they may be uneasy about such trips. For this reason, design first trips to be short and nonthreatening. For instance, a first trip could be a simple walk around the block taken during the first few weeks of the session, 23-2. Some children may be hesitant to leave the building. They may fear

23-1 While children often learn about animals through books and filmstrips, contact with live animals further enhances their learning.

23-2 First field trips should involve familiar surroundings.

their parents will come for them while they are gone. Reassure these children that this is not the case.

To calm other fears, remind children of their daily routine. Say, "First we are going to walk around the block. When we return, we will have a story. Then it will be snack time. After that we will play outside, and then it will be time to go home." Knowing a familiar routine will help calm many fears.

After taking a few trips around the neighborhood, field trips may be taken to familiar places. A visit to a local grocery store is often a good trip. Here, children can see and talk about things that are well-known to them.

First field trips can build or hinder children's confidence. Therefore, first trips need to match children's developmental needs. Plan trips in which children will meet with success.

## SELECTING TRIPS

The trips you select will depend on the location of the center and the money available for trips. Centers located within walking distance of many potential sites will take more trips than centers located in more isolated areas. Centers located in large cities have the option of using public transportation.

Field trips are sometimes selected based on the season or weather. A trip to a pumpkin patch or an orchard can be taken in the fall. Trips that require walking, like a trip to a zoo, need to be taken during warm weather. Substitute days should be set up in case of bad weather.

Field trips are sometimes chosen based on themes being studied. For instance, a trip to a farm may be chosen while children are studying about farms, food, or machinery. While learning about clothes, a trip to a tailor shop, shoe repair shop, or clothing store may be chosen. Chart 23-3 lists many field trip suggestions based on themes.

### Theme walks

Simple field trips that can be taken in and around the center and are based on a theme are called *theme walks*. Most children enjoy walk-ing and the exercise is good for their bodies and minds. Theme walks also provide an opportunity to sharpen children's observation skills.

Theme walks may center on many things: numbers, colors, people, occupations, buildings, flowers, trees, or cars. For best results, focus on only one theme during each walk.

Before starting a theme walk, talk about what children might observe. For instance, if the theme is buildings, tell the children to observe types of buildings they see. They may see houses, office buildings, stores, and service stations.

Color is a good concept for a theme walk. Choose one or more colors children should watch for throughout the walk. Two- and three-year-old children should be asked to look for only one color. Older children, especially five-year-olds, may enjoy looking for many colors. In fact, a fun walk for these children would be to record as many colors as they can.

A shape walk is a way to teach children about shapes. Before leaving the classroom, review with the children what shape(s) they are to observe. As with colors, the number of shapes children are to observe depends on their ages.

Shapes can be seen everywhere. Tires are round; most sidewalk slabs are square; doorknobs may be oval or round. As children are encouraged to use their eyes to recognize shapes, they will also be busy using their minds.

Theme walks based on numbers and letters may also be useful learning experiences. As children walk, they will see numbers and/or letters everywhere. They are seen on license plates, street signs, store windows, billboards, passing trucks, and houses. Determine the number of numbers or letters to observe based on children's ages.

People walks can teach many social study concepts. The children will see that people may be tall or short and have different colored hair and eyes. Children will also notice that some people wear glasses, some have beards, and some have long hair.

Two-year-olds may be able to identify a baby, man, lady, boy, or girl. Three-year-olds may be able to distinguish differences among these people. Four- and five-year-olds may be

## FIELD TRIP SUGGESTIONS

| Field Trip | Related Themes |
|---|---|
| Airport | Air transportation or airplanes |
| Bakery | Foods, community helpers |
| Barber shop | Health, "I'm Me—I'm Special" |
| Beauty shop | Health, "I'm Me—I'm Special" |
| Bird sanctuary | Birds |
| Butcher | Foods, careers |
| Car dealer | Transportation, car, truck, wheels |
| Car wash | Cars, trucks |
| Carpenter's shop | Careers, construction |
| Children's homes | "My Friends," "Our Neighborhood" |
| Construction site | Buildings, construction |
| Dairy farm | Food, farm animals, machinery |
| Dentist's office | Health, careers |
| Doctor's office | Health, careers |
| Fire station | Community helper, fire safety |
| Garage | Tools, careers, machines |
| Greenhouse | Plants, spring |
| Grocery store | Food, community helpers |
| Hatchery | Animals |
| Hospital | Health, careers, people and places |
| Laundry | Health, careers |
| Library | Community helper, books |
| Newspaper office | Books, careers, communication |
| Pet shop | Pets, animals |
| Photography studio | Communication, careers |
| Planetarium | The universe, planets |
| Police station | Community helper |
| Potter's studio | Careers |
| Poultry farm | Food, farm animals |
| Print shop | Books, careers, communication |
| Radio station | Communication, careers |
| Television studio | Communication, careers |
| Train station | Transportation, careers |
| Veterinarian's clinic | Pets, animals, health, careers |
| Zoo | Animals |

23-3 In your community there are most likely even more field trip sites that can be related to a theme.

able to describe the actions of people they have observed.

During occupational walks children observe what people are doing. They may see a bus driver, truck driver, bank teller, street sweeper, or a house painter.

A building or architecture walk may be of special interest to older children. As you approach buildings, note their purposes. When children see a gas station-garage combination, discuss why large windows and large doors are part of the architecture. (Large windows are needed to see customers; large doors are needed for cars and trucks.) You may also encourage children to imagine what is inside of the building.

To gain the most on these theme walks, carry a note pad and pencil. Record observations that may later be discussed in the classroom. These observations make good discussion topics for lunch, snack, or group time. Listening to the children's discussions, you will be able to note their interests. To promote further learning, you may want to invite to class those people the children showed the most interest in. Or you may take the children on field trips to visit the people. These guests or field trip hosts are called *resource people,* 23-4.

**Resource people.** Parents, grandparents, aunts, uncles, neighbors, siblings, and friends are some of the best resource people. Ask them what interests and hobbies they have that they would be willing to share. This can be done personally or through a questionnaire. Select only those people who enjoy children. They should represent many cultural groups and both sexes. Compile a list of these people, along with their interests and hobbies. Place the list on file. During the year, select people from the list that fit in with your studies.

To be the most useful, resource people need an orientation before meeting the children. Tell the resource people the number of children in your group, their interests, and the length of their attention spans. Suggest questions that they may ask the children. Let them know their presentation must be simple.

If possible, suggest to resource people that the children be allowed to have a "hands-on

23-4 Fire fighters are nearly always at the top of the list of interesting resource people.

activity," 23-5. For example, if a grandmother is willing to demonstrate how she dyes Easter eggs, encourage her to let the children try dying eggs, too. Or, if a person demonstrates playing the drums, ask that each child have the chance to hit the drum.

After a resource person has visited the classroom or hosted the field trip, always send a thank-you note or some other token of thanks, 23-6. You may write a personal note. Or children who can write may wish to express their own thanks. Younger children may choose to dictate thank-you notes to you. Other forms of thanking people include sending children's artwork or freshly baked cookies.

Appreciation may also take other forms. The children may go caroling at the fire station during the holidays. In February, handmade valentines may be mailed to all resource people who took part in the program during the year. Taped thank-you notes or songs on a cassette are one more thoughtful way to say thank-you to resource people.

23-5 Hands-on experiences help make vague concepts more concrete for children. After holding this goat, the children will have a real experience to remember when they see goats in a book or hear about them in the classroom.

Dear Fire fighter:

Thank you for showing us your truck. Thank you for showing us the truck's parts. Thank you for sounding the siren. Thank you for showing us a fire fighter's clothing.

Love,

Ron Smith's Class

23-6 Build a positive image of the center in your community with a thank-you note to resource people.

## PLANNING A FIELD TRIP

Field trips for young children need to be carefully planned. Consideration must be given to suitability, costs, scheduling, adult-child ratio, behavioral expectations, educational goals, and the children's preparation. As a teacher, you need to think about all of these factors. A good way to do this is to take a pre-trip to the field trip site.

### Pre-trip

The success of any trip depends upon preparation. After setting goals, always make a pre-trip if you have not been to the site before. This visit will give you a chance to:

- Describe to the tour guide the goals you have set and the developmental level of the children.
- Explain the children's interests and their need to use a number of senses.
- Prepare the tour guide for the types of questions the children may ask.
- Locate bathrooms.
- Check for any potential dangers.
- Ask about parking (if necessary).
- Watch for teaching opportunities.
- Revise trip goals, if necessary.

Keep a field trip file. In some centers, teachers maintain their own files, 23-7. In other

23-7 A field trip file provides "at a glance" information about various field trip sites.

centers, the director maintains a file for use by all personnel. This file may be a notebook, a folder, or an index card file box. As a rule, information to note for each trip includes:

- Name of site.
- Telephone number.
- Address.
- Contact person (tour guide).
- Costs.
- Distance from center in blocks or miles.
- Dangers.
- Special learning opportunities.

Before the trip, plan what you will need to take along. Paper tissues and a first-aid kit are a must. Depending on the length of the trip and the weather, you may want to take snacks and refreshments for the children.

In hot weather children often get thirsty. Make sure water or some other nutritious drink is on hand. Gallon insulated jugs are a good way to transport liquids.

Permission slips, signed by parents, must be on file for each child before a trip, 23-8. For convenience, many center directors use one

**BROWN'S DAY CARE**
**FIELD TRIP PERMISSION FORM**

Child's Name _____

Parent(s) Name _____ Business Phone _____

_____ Business Phone _____

Home Address _____ Home Phone _____

In consideration of _____'s
(child's name)

acceptance as an enrollee in Brown's Day Care Center, I hereby give permission for my child to participate in any walks or field trips planned and supervised by the staff. I understand that various modes of transportation may be used for these trips.

_____        _____
(Parent's Signature)                    (Date)

23-8 Permission slips from parents, such as this one, are a necessity when planning a field trip.

form for all trips and walks. This form is filled in and signed at enrollment time. This saves the time and energy of sending home permission slips for each trip. Busy parents will also benefit from this timesaving method.

## Suitability

Before choosing a trip ask yourself, "How suitable is this trip for the children?" Consider the developmental level of the children. For five-year-olds, a trip to a television studio may be both fun and educational. This same trip would not be appropriate for two-year-olds. Two-year-olds are more interested in those things closer to their immediate surroundings. For example, pets, animals, babies, mothers, daddies, and grandparents are topics which capture the interest of two-year-olds.

Field trips for children from birth to 24 months are often simple walks around the neighborhood. For safety purposes, use strollers for these children. Many centers purchase double strollers. To provide extra seating space, some strollers allow for additional seats to be attached to the back. This allows one teacher to handle from two to four children at one time.

When planning field trips for young children, avoid crowds. Crowds may overwhelm some children. It is also difficult to watch children in a crowded setting. Trips to the zoo and the circus will involve large groups of people. In these cases, during your pre-trip ask what days are least crowded. Parent volunteers may be needed to help when crowds cannot be avoided.

Choose trips that provide learning through participation. Children enjoy touching and doing things. When planning a trip to the farm, ask if the children can pet the animals, assist in milking the cows, and help collect the eggs, 23-9. Likewise, a trip to the apple orchard could provide children with opportunities to pick and taste apples.

## Costs

When planning a field trip, always figure the costs. This helps you decide if the trip is the best use of your resources. You may feel that

23-9 Petting farm animals can be an enjoyable experience for children who are developmentally ready.

the cost of chartering a bus to the zoo is more than your budget allows. You may decide that the money needed for that trip could be more wisely spent on something else. If most of the children have already had this experience, you may want to use the money for two or three less costly trips. This would give the children new experiences.

Most field trips involve little or no expense, particularly if the site is within walking distance. In some cases, the only costs are admission and/or transportation. If there is an admission fee, call in advance and ask if group rates are available for day care centers. At times, you may get a generous discount or free admission.

**Transportation.** Costs for transportation vary greatly, depending on the type used, 23-10. For centers that own their own vans, the costs of most field trips are minimal. To cut costs, some centers ask parents and teachers to drive their own cars. This type of arrangement is not recommended. In case of an accident, many legal problems can arise, and the driver and/or center could be sued for damages.

Public transportation, such as the city bus or subway, is most often less costly than a chartered bus. However, it does have some disadvantages. Trains are often crowded and noisy. These two combined conditions are stressful for children. There is also the danger of children being hurt or lost during the course of the trip. Thus, some teachers elect not to use public transportation for their children.

If you decide to use a chartered bus, call several companies and request prices. State where you intend to go, the length of your stay, and the number of passengers. Ask them to send you the price quote in writing. After you receive all the quotes, compare to find the company that will provide the best service for the least amount of money. By thoroughly checking costs for a field trip, you will prevent unplanned spending of your resources.

### Scheduling

If possible, schedule field trips for midmorning. Midmorning works best for several reasons. First, children are usually well rested at this time. They will find it easier to listen, observe, and follow instructions. Second, not all children arrive at the same time in the morning. Some parents may bring their children to the center at 7 a.m. Others may not bring their children until 8 or 9 a.m. If you schedule the trip too early, some children would be deprived of the field trip. Also in colder climates, early morning temperatures can be rather cool for the children. This is a key consideration for trips that require walking.

Afternoon field trips are also difficult to plan. Most preschool children need to take a nap at this time. Also, children may be deprived of the trip if their parent picks them up early in the afternoon.

Field trips should begin after a quiet activity. This helps children avoid excess excitement or overstimulation during the trip. Overstimulated children are very active and difficult to manage.

One question often asked is, "What is the best day for a field trip?" The answer to this question depends on the group and attendance. First, study the behavior and routine of the group. Some groups are always tired and restless by Friday. You may want to choose a day early in the week for such a group. Second,

23-10 Children can travel to nearby field trip sites in wagons.

consider the days children attend. Some children may be deprived of trips if they are always scheduled for a day they do not attend.

The right day for a field trip may also depend on the field trip. If the trip requires formal arrangements to be made, ask the contact person to suggest a day. Many resource people prefer a midweek day. This allows time early in the week to prepare for the visit.

Carefully plan around the children's needs, children's schedules, and resource person's schedules. This takes time. However, a well-planned field trip produces the greatest amount of learning and pleasure for the children.

### Adult-child ratio

The best adult-child ratio is based on the number of children in the group, the nature of the field trip, and the dangers involved, 23-11. Walks around the neighborhood can often be handled well using the center staff. More adults may be needed for trips using public transportation or for visits to places with potential dangers.

For most field trips, a ratio of one teacher for every four to six children is sufficient. This allows for close supervision and communica-

23-11 A trip to a farm can have many hidden dangers. For this reason, extra adult supervision is required.

tion. However, if some children need to be closely watched, this ratio should be adjusted. Allow for a higher adult ratio. Many times children are grouped based on their temperaments. For instance, if Sam and Frank behave badly when together, they should not be in the same group.

When more adults are needed for field trips, parents may be contacted. Many programs maintain lists of parents and other volunteers interested in helping on field trips. When the need arises, give these people at least one week's notice.

### Behavioral expectations

Behavioral expectations need to be planned and discussed with children before the trip. *Behavioral expectations* are trip rules which children are expected to follow. They vary with the children and nature of the trip. Some rules apply to all trips and some rules do not.

For best results, state all rules in a positive way. Tell the children exactly what they are expected to do, rather than what they should not do. For example, instead of telling the children not to touch anything in the store, tell them to place their hands at their sides or in their pockets.

Regardless of the type of trip, rules are most often the same in most early childhood programs. First, the children must wear their name tags at all times. Name tags should be durable so that they can be reused. They should be worn on all field trips. The child's name, school name, and school telephone number should be on the tag. This information is helpful in case a child wanders from the group.

The second rule for field trips is that children must speak softly. To ensure this, teachers need to set a good example. Talk should be low key to avoid overstimulation.

The third rule is that the children must remain with their assigned adult supervisor on field trips. In this way, adults know where each child is, 23-12.

Many teachers prefer to have children follow the "hold-your-partner's-hand" rule. However, this rule is not always useful. It is unfair to interested children to have partners whose at-

23-12 Correct trip behavior includes staying with adult supervisors.

tention is not focused on the learning experience. Also, constant physical contact can result in stress for some children.

Instead of holding hands, children can hold on to a rope to keep them together as a group. To make this rope purchase clothesline, allowing 2 to 2 1/2 feet per child. Before the trip tie the line in a knot at 2 to 2 1/2 foot intervals. Show the children how to hold on to the knot during the trip.

### Educational goals

For the most benefit on a field trip, educational goals must be carefully planned. For example, a trip to a local service station may have a number of goals:
* To observe mechanics at work.
* To learn about the care of cars.
* To see how machinery works.
* To learn vocabulary words: mechanics, gas pump, nozzle, and hoist.

During the pre-trip visit, these goals need to be discussed with the resource person.

### Children's preparation

Preparation for children may begin a few days before the trip. Introduce the trip by putting up displays, reading a book, sharing a filmstrip, looking at pictures, or simply talking about the trip.

On the day of the trip tell children what to observe (educational goals) and how to behave (behavioral expectations). Give name tags to each child. Assign children to their adult guides. After this, encourage children to use the bathroom. Explain that a bathroom is not always available on walks or some field trips.

### Parent preparation

Parents should always be informed in advance of field trips. A newsletter, calendar, or notice posted on a bulletin board are all useful methods, 23-13. Inform the parents of the location, the address, and exact times you will be leaving and returning. This will help parents plan to drop off and pick up their children on time and schedule care appointments for their children.

Before leaving on a field trip, post a sign on the classroom door. Note where you have gone and when you will return. This will also serve as a trip reminder for the parents.

Share trip goals with children's parents. This information may help them plan home experiences such as discussions and books.

### Follow-up activities

To help children clarify their learning, plan follow-up activities, 23-14. Once you return to the center, talk about what they saw and did.

23-13 Placing this notice on a center bulletin board helps remind parents of an upcoming field trip.

348

field trip
to
**Perkin's Pumpkin Farm**
23 Half-day Road,
Streamwood

Tuesday, September 23

We will leave the center
at 10:00 am
We will return to the center
at noon

23-14 After a trip to a pumpkin patch, a class made this bulletin board.

Plan an activity that reinforces the learning that occurred on the trip. Recall the classroom scene after the trip to the apple orchard. Apples were discussed at lunch. Then the experience was used as a basis for writing a story. Or after a trip to a bakery, children could bake bread or cookies. Ice cream could be made after a trip to a local creamery. See 23-15.

## SUMMARY

Field trips can be a useful learning experience for children. Through field trips, children gain firsthand knowledge of the world around them. This learning can involve new experiences or enhance previous knowledge.

Field trips require planning. Children must be prepared for the experience. Their preparation includes conducting pre-trip talks and activities and explaining rules for children to follow.

The teacher must also be prepared. This preparation includes selecting a trip, taking a pre-trip, setting goals, obtaining permission from parents, arranging transportation, and sending thank-you notes to helpful individuals.

**FOLLOW-UP ACTIVITIES**

| Trip | Activities |
|------|-----------|
| Apple orchard | • Taste a variety of apples.<br>• Make applesauce or apple muffins.<br>• Read stories about apple orchards.<br>• Serve apple butter, baked apples, or some other form of apple. |
| Fire station | • Place puzzles and stories related to the role of fire fighters in the classroom.<br>• Read stories about fire fighters.<br>• Place fire fighters clothing in the dramatic play area.<br>• Act out fire safety procedures. |
| Print shop | • Provide rubber stamps, ink pads, and paper to print on.<br>• Place a typewriter or computer in the classroom.<br>• Make games using alphabet letters. |
| Beauty shop | • Provide a prop box containing hair rollers, combs, brushes, and a hair dryer with the cord removed.<br>• Place dolls with hair and combs in the dramatic play area.<br>• Hang up a mirror and have children compare the ways they wear their hair. |

23-15 Follow-up activities based on field trips can be simple or complex.

# to Know

behavioral expectations
resource people
theme walks

# to Review

1. List four benefits children experience from field trips.

2. Design first field trips to be:
   a. Long and unique.
   b. Short and nonthreatening.
   c. At unfamiliar places.
   d. None of the above.

3. True or false. The location of the center and the budget are two factors that affect what field trips you will select.

4. _____ _____ are simple field trips that can be taken in and around the center and the neighborhood.

5. People who visit class to teach children about a hobby, job, or skill they have are called:
   a. Teachers.
   b. Tour guides.
   c. Friends.
   d. Resource people.

6. List four opportunities a teacher is given by conducting a pre-trip.

7. When planning trips for young children, avoid _____.

8. What are the disadvantages of using public transportation to reach your field trip site?

9. What is the best day for a field trip? Explain your answer.

10. _____ _____ are also known as trip rules.

11. List three basic rules for field trips involving young children.

12. What is the purpose of follow-up activities?

# to Do

1. Start a file of field trip ideas that could be taken by young children in your community.

2. Make a list of pre-trip and follow-up activities for a field trip to a bakery.

3. Invite a center director to speak to your group about successful field trips he or she has conducted.

4. Plan a field trip for your class. Go through the same steps that you would for a group of young children.

# part 5

# The Importance of Planning

Good planning helps you meet your goals in the most efficient ways possible. You can save time and effort while being assured of meeting children's needs by planning carefully.

In this part, you will learn appropriate methods of developing and writing program curriculum. You will also learn strategies for involving parents in your program.

351

# Chapter 24

# *The Curriculum*

After studying this chapter, you will be able to:

☐ Discuss who is involved in curriculum development and in what way.

☐ Explain the process-centered approach to curriculum development.

☐ Develop program goals.

☐ Discuss the use of themes as a basis for selecting activities.

☐ Develop a theme using a flowchart.

☐ Select a balance of activities that reflect the curriculum.

☐ List and explain various learning styles and learning characteristics.

☐ Write a block plan and lesson plan for one week of a program.

Reading a story, feeding a bunny, singing songs, and playing outdoors are all parts of the curriculum. Cooking applesauce, scribbling on paper, building with blocks, and playing in the dramatic play corner are also parts of the curriculum. The curriculum also includes materials and equipment, 24-1. Pictures used in displays and on bulletin boards are part of the curriculum. Even room arrangements can reflect curriculum.

A good curriculum in an early childhood program consists of a wide range of experiences and materials designed to meet the developmental needs of a group of children. This includes their social, emotional, physical, and intellectual needs. A good curriculum also focuses on children's interests. It includes all learning experiences, both direct and indirect.

*Direct learning experiences* are planned with a specific goal in mind. For instance, a carpentry activity may be planned to promote fine motor skills and to teach the use of safety goggles. And the room arrangement may be planned to foster the independence needed for this task.

*Indirect learning experiences* occur on the spur of the moment. For example, while watching Janet, Dwayne may learn how to button his coat. Shelly may learn how to paint by

24-1 Children's physical needs are as important to the curriculum as their emotional, social, and intellectual needs.

watching Mark. Or, while mixing paint, Kelsie may learn that adding red paint to blue paint makes purple paint.

A good curriculum requires detailed plans in addition to knowledge of child development. This chapter will outline the steps to follow when planning a curriculum.

## RESPONSIBILITY

Curriculum development can involve one person or a few staff members. In some centers, a wide range of people are involved in the process. Directors, teachers, aides, parents, and in some cases even the center cook may all be included. Each of these people can add to the quality of the program in a unique way.

A curriculum specialist is sometimes hired by large organizations. However, in most small centers, the head teacher is most often the person in charge of planning the curriculum, 24-2.

The day care director also usually plays a key role in curriculum development. In most centers, the director is in charge of supervising all center activities. As a result, the director's job almost always includes curriculum supervision. In some centers the director alone does the actual planning. In other centers, the director works with the staff.

Some for-profit day care chains provide the director with a preplanned curriculum. In this case, the director introduces the curriculum to the staff. After modifying it to fit the children's needs, the teachers are expected to use the curriculum.

A preplanned curriculum has advantages and disadvantages. For staff with little training or experience, a preplanned curriculum can be helpful. Activities, procedures, and suggestions are often outlined in detail. Having these curriculum ideas at their fingertips saves time and energy.

A preplanned curriculum also has disadvantages. As a rule, teachers are more likely to feel enthusiastic about a self-planned curriculum. Experienced teachers may feel stifled or limited by a preplanned curriculum. Because of their experience, they are more likely to observe a

24-2 Using a self-planned curriculum allows teachers to create their own games for the children.

mismatch between children's needs and the curriculum, should it occur. If this happens, experienced teachers are likely to feel frustrated.

## APPROACHING CURRICULUM

There are a number of approaches to curriculum development. One popular method is the *process-centered approach.* Learning is seen as a constant process of exploring and questioning the environment. A hands-on curriculum is stressed. All four areas of child development—social, emotional, physical, and intellectual—are included. A wide range of age appropriate materials, supplies, and experiences are used to enrich the environment, 24-3. Materials and equipment are matched to the children's readiness and development.

Basic learning materials are a key part of the process-centered curriculum. These materials are chosen by the teacher. They may include puzzles, games, blocks, sand, water, books, records, and supplies for dramatic play and science study.

Once the physical environment is planned and prepared, the children choose most of their own activities. The use of time, space, and equipment is largely determined by the children. However, the environment always needs to be carefully planned. It should reflect children's developmental needs and interests.

## DEVELOPING PROGRAM GOALS

*Program goals* are broad statements of purpose that reflect the end result of education. They state what is important. Some people describe goals as the "why" of the curriculum.

In an early childhood program, the program goals outline the philosophy of the center. They state what is to be achieved through the program. Program goals based on child development focus on the "whole child." Possible goals for children in an early childhood setting might include the following:
- To develop a positive self-concept.
- To develop independence.
- To develop problem-solving skills, 24-4.

24-3 In this process-centered environment, a child learns more about fire fighters by trying on a fire fighter's outfit.

24-4 Bulletin board activities are a good method to teach problem-solving skills.

354

- To develop language skills, both listening and speaking.
- To develop fine motor coordination.
- To develop large motor coordination.
- To develop a curiosity about the world.
- To develop positive social skills, including cooperation and interdependence.
- To develop respect for one's own rights as well as the rights of others.
- To develop self-expression skills.

Each of these goals is broad. The goals include all four areas of development. A good program has curriculum that addresses each of these areas.

## Meeting goals

Teachers, activities, and the environment all influence whether goals will be met. For example, if one of the goals is to create independence, provide children with a minimum of help. This gives children many opportunities to grow in independence. Classroom activities should require little involvement on the part of the teacher. Children should be able to carry out most activities without an adult's help. The activities, then, will need to match children's skill levels.

The classroom environment, including room arrangement, can also foster development of independence. Coat hooks, paper towels, tables, chairs, and equipment placed within children's reach is helpful. The children can act on their own, 24-5. They do not have to depend on teachers for help at all times.

## THEMES

Themes, or units, are used to mesh activities with classroom studies. The environment and learning experiences are planned to complement the theme. For example, a theme on apples may include a trip to an apple orchard. A bulletin board with three different colors of apples might also be planned. Books such as *Johnny Appleseed* could be read to the children at group time.

An apple theme lends itself to cooking. Applesauce, baked apples, apple muffins, apple bread, and apple butter could all be made. An art activity might involve making apple prints from sponges cut in the shape of apples. Lotto games could be made using three different colors of apples: red, yellow, and green. Apples of various sizes and colors could be placed on the science table. These can be cut apart and studied under a microscope. Chart 24-6 lists examples of themes.

## Theme ideas

Sources of themes can be endless. Since most successful themes take the children's interests into consideration, theme sources vary from one program to another. As a rule, however, certain themes appeal to certain age groups, 24-7. Very young children's interests center on their immediate surroundings. As children grow, their circle of interests becomes larger,

24-5 The low work surface and child-sized utensils for this activity allow this child to feel confident about working on her own.

## EXAMPLES OF THEMES

| | | | |
|---|---|---|---|
| The Five Senses | *The Family cont.* | Puppets | Friends |
| Zoo Animals | Grandfather | Art | Travel |
| Pets | Aunts | Brushes and Brooms | The Circus |
| All About Dogs | Uncles | How I Care For Myself | All About Measuring |
| The Farm | Sisters | Hats | Money |
| Colors | Brothers | Scissors | Directions |
| Music | Watches and Clocks | Our Town | Gestures |
| Flowers | Foods | Water Animals | Camping |
| Health | Vegetables | Wheels | Shapes |
| Weather | Fruits | Transportation | Bugs |
| Water | Breads | Land | Plants |
| We Create | Meats | Water | Exercise |
| We Dance | Dairy Products | Air | The Garden |
| We Sing | Seasons | Signs and Pictures | Hospitals |
| We Act | Summer | Police Officers | Telephones |
| Toys | Fall | Fire Fighters | Safety Signs |
| Safety | Winter | Garbage Collectors | Fairy Tales |
| Emotions | Spring | Truck Drivers | Sounds |
| Fantasy and Reality | Shadows | Carpenters | The Newspaper |
| The Family | Homes | Doctors | Nature |
| Mother | Holidays | Nurses | The Library |
| Father | Clothes | Mechanics | Computers |
| Grandmother | Community Helpers | Temperature | Machines |

24-6 Themes can come from all segments of children's environments.

## A SPIRAL CURRICULUM

### Themes for Two- and Three-Year-Olds

| | | |
|---|---|---|
| All About Me | Concepts I'm | |
| I'm Me, I'm | Learning | |
| Special | Big/Little | |
| My Family | Up/Down | |
| My Friends | Soft/Hard | |
| My Home | Wet/Dry | |
| My Toys | Things That Go | |
| My Senses | Cars | |
| Foods I Eat | Trucks | |
| Colors in My | Boats | |
| World | Airplanes | |
| Shapes I See | Animals in My | |
| Circles | World | |
| Squares | Dogs | |
| Triangles | Cats | |
| Rectangles | Farm Animals | |
| Hearts | Zoo Animals | |

*Continued.*

24-7 Children's interests widen as they get older. Study this chart for evidence of the spiral curriculum concept.

# A SPIRAL CURRICULUM

## Themes for Three- and Four-Year-Olds

People in My World
  My Family
  My Friends
  Police Officers
  Fire Fighters
  Bakers
  Meat Cutters
  Librarians
  Printers
  Medical Doctors
  Nurses
  Pharmacists
  Ambulance
    Attendants
  Bankers
  Chefs
  Waiters and
    Waitresses
  Musicians
  Hair Stylists
  Photographers

  Secretaries
  Computer
    Programmers
  Clerks
  Sanitary
    Engineers
  Pilots and Flight
    Attendants
  Gas Station
    Attendants and
    Mechanics
  Painters
  Carpenters
  Plumbers
  Farmers
  Florists
All About Me
  My Senses
  My Feelings
  My Home
  My School

## Themes for Four- and Five-Year-Olds

My Body
  Good Health
  Exercise
  Nutrition
Communication
  Speaking
  Listening
  Puppets
  Acting
  Writing
  Radio
  Television
My World
  Pets

  Plants
  Flowers
  Insects and
    Spiders
Transportation
  Air
  Land
  Water
Tools
  Garden
  Carpenter
  Mechanic
  Dentist
  Beautician

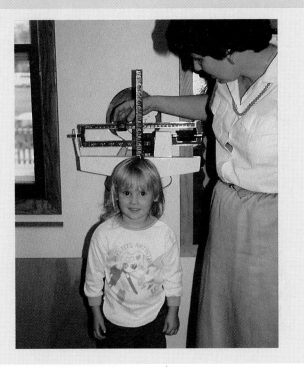

*24-7 Continued.*

like a spiral. A curriculum based on this concept is called a *spiral curriculum.*

Two-year-old children are interested in their immediate world. Themes such as sight, sound, touch, taste, and smell often meet with success. Families, colors, shapes, pets, farm animals, and foods are also good themes for two-year-olds. Plan plenty of activities that relate to the theme you choose. This will keep the young children interested.

Three-year-old children are also interested in their families. However, they are often becoming interested in their neighbors and their community. Themes based on the supermarket, bakery, library, and post office are of special interest to these children. Their interests are growing in the spiral outside of their immediate surroundings.

Themes related to animals are also enjoyed by three- and four-year-olds. These themes can be broken down to deal with certain groups of animals. Groups might include farm, forest, and zoo animals. Bugs and birds can also have appeal for these young children.

Four- and five-year-old children enjoy themes related to a wider variety of topics. Themes can be grouped into a few broad categories. For instance, broad themes might include "My World," "Things I Like to Do," and "Things that Move."

These categories could be broken down to contain a few sub-themes. "My School," "My Home," "My Feelings," and "My Family" are just a few examples of sub-themes in "My World."

**Holiday themes.** Be careful when planning holiday themes for children. Preschool children do not have a firm understanding of time. If a holiday theme is introduced too early, children may become too excited. For instance, if Halloween is introduced the first week of October but does not actually happen until four weeks later, children will become confused. They will not know when to expect Halloween.

The activities planned around holiday themes are also often quite stimulating for children. If this excitement goes on for four weeks, behavior problems could arise. More guidance will be needed.

## Theme length

Children's attention spans and available resources are the two major factors affecting theme length. For example, if children are interested and resources are available, a Valentine's theme could go on the entire week of Valentine's Day.

Some themes can be carried out for a month or two. A community helpers theme could go on for quite some time. Many community helpers could be used as bases for themes.

## Developing themes

A good method for developing themes is to use resource books. To make this possible, many centers have a set of encyclopedias. The staff can refer to these books for background information. After using this resource, a flowchart can be drawn, outlining major concepts to be covered.

**Flowcharts.** Drawing a flowchart is a simple method for listing concepts to cover in a theme. For example, when developing a theme on puppets, consult a resource. List all concepts you might include, 24-8. The major headings in a puppet flowchart could be vocabulary, movement, types, stages, materials, and characterization.

Chart 24-9 shows a flowchart on hats. After drawing up a flowchart, writing goals is the next step. Study the flowchart for goals that can be developed. For instance, based on the flowchart in Chart 24-8, children might be expected to:

- Identify the five types of puppets.
- Develop skill in moving puppets with rods, wires, strings, and hands.
- Enjoy a puppet show.
- Learn new vocabulary words: marionette, shadow, and dummy.
- Construct puppets from a variety of materials.
- Express their own thoughts and feelings using puppets.
- Practice using a puppet behind a puppet stage.

Using the same process, goals can be developed for a hat theme. Review the flowchart on hats. Theme goals could include the following:

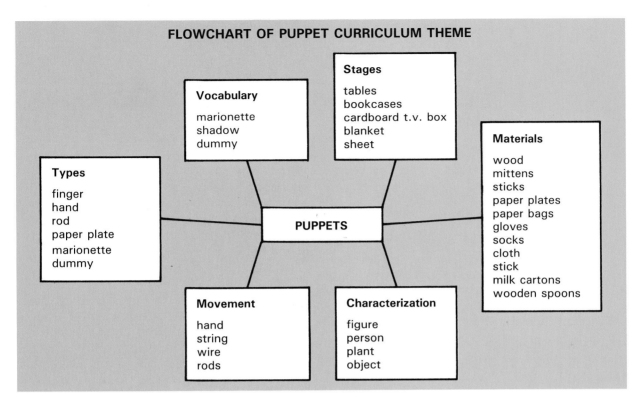

**FLOWCHART OF PUPPET CURRICULUM THEME**

**Vocabulary**

marionette
shadow
dummy

**Stages**

tables
bookcases
cardboard t.v. box
blanket
sheet

**Materials**

wood
mittens
sticks
paper plates
paper bags
gloves
socks
cloth
stick
milk cartons
wooden spoons

**Types**

finger
hand
rod
paper plate
marionette
dummy

**PUPPETS**

**Movement**

hand
string
wire
rods

**Characterization**

figure
person
plant
object

24-8 Flowcharts can be developed using resources such as encyclopedias.

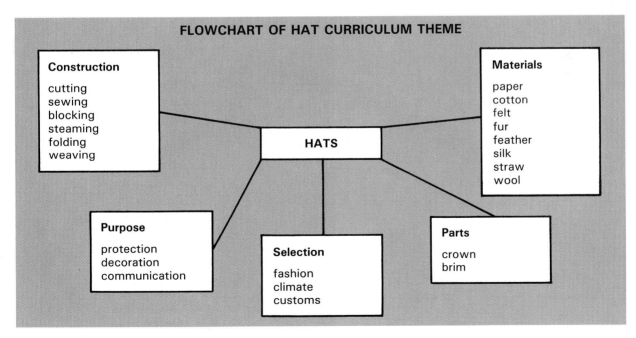

**FLOWCHART OF HAT CURRICULUM THEME**

**Construction**

cutting
sewing
blocking
steaming
folding
weaving

**Materials**

paper
cotton
felt
fur
feather
silk
straw
wool

**HATS**

**Purpose**

protection
decoration
communication

**Selection**

fashion
climate
customs

**Parts**

crown
brim

24-9 A basic item like a hat can be the source of many useful activities.

- To learn how to construct a hat from paper.
- To observe many types of construction materials for hats.
- To identify the parts of a hat.
- To learn the three purposes of hats—protection, decoration, and communication.

## ACTIVITIES

A good curriculum contains a balance of activities. These activities must be chosen with care. Activities that keep children busy are not always the best activities. Likewise, just because children prefer a certain activity does not mean it must be kept in the curriculum. Instead, it is important that children's time be used wisely. This means the value of a single activity cannot be overlooked. You must evaluate each activity to be sure it is right for the children.

### Selecting activities

Before you plan proper curriculum, you must know how to evaluate activities. Three basic questions can help you do this. These questions must be answered whether you are planning curriculum with or without a theme. Included are:

1. Is the information gained worth knowing?
2. Is the information testable by the children?
3. Is the information developmentally appropriate for the children?

First, consider the question, "Is the information worth knowing?" In order to answer this question, think about the cultural context. In some societies a certain learning outcome may be important. Ask yourself, "Will the outcome help the child better cope with his or her surroundings?"

Children in the United States at some point must learn to read. Our culture places great importance on reading. As a result, children are read many stories in day care centers. Through listening, children learn to enjoy and appreciate literature. In an illiterate society, these skills would not be needed. Other skills important to that culture would be stressed.

A second question needs to be answered: "Is the information testable?" In other words, the child should be able to see firsthand that the information is true, 24-10. Many times, teach-

24-10 Information on cows is testable if children can see and touch a cow.

ers choose activities based on personal appeal. They like the activity. For instance, activities related to dinosaurs have long been included in the curriculum of many day care centers. Think about the activity based on this question. Will children ever see a live dinosaur? This activity is not testable. Another activity would be more appropriate. Instead of reading a book about dinosaurs, choose one about an animal children know about or may have a chance to see at the zoo.

Here is another example. If you were going to do a unit on foods, making butter would be a testable activity. To begin this activity, tell the children that cream can be made into butter. Then show the children the consistency of cream. After this, give each child a container filled with whipping cream. Show them how to shake the container. Tell the children to keep shaking until the mixture becomes thick. After the cream has turned to butter, let each child taste the butter. This will help them test their knowledge.

The third basic question concerns the developmental appropriateness of an activity. An activity that requires giving scissors and paper to three- and four-year-olds is appropriate. Children this age can use scissors properly. This activity would be inappropriate for children 18 to 24 months old.

Reading the book, *Little Red Riding Hood,* might also be inappropriate. You may find that even some five-year-olds may not be ready for this book. Many preschool children cannot separate fantasy from reality. As a result, this book could produce fear. It could also teach false concepts. For instance, wolves do not talk, although in the book they do.

### Balance of activities

A good curriculum includes a balance of activities. Structured as well as unstructured activities should be included. Examples of unstructured activities include blockbuilding, collages, water play, and sand play. Children should spend most of their time in unstructured activities.

Structured, or close-ended, activities also need to be included. These activities indirectly prescribe children's actions. Stringing beads, working puzzles, and cooking are all examples.

Whenever possible, also plan a balance of indoor and outdoor activities, 24-11. The climate in your area will determine whether this is possible. During extremely hot and cold weather, the children should be kept indoors. When this happens, provide children with indoor large motor activities.

In warmer climates, weather permitting, many indoor activities can be moved outdoors. Painting, water play, and story and music time can all be done outdoors.

Active and quiet activities must be balanced. Planning too many active activities in a row may overstimulate some children. The result can be chaotic. To prevent this, follow active activities with quiet ones. For example, outdoor activity followed by a story and small group would be a good balance.

Too many quiet activities in a row also have a drawback. Children will get restless. The results can be just as chaotic as too many active

24-11 Outdoor activities allow children to get fresh air and work off excess energy.

activities. Children may lose interest in the activities and begin to wiggle and talk out of turn.

### Theme activities

The number and types of activities will vary with the theme. Very seldom do the majority of the activities relate to the theme. Some themes will have more resources than others. The only two activities that nearly always relate to the theme are stories and bulletin board displays.

Once you have set goals, you can develop activities. This is best done through brainstorming as a group. In some centers one staff member may set the goals. Whichever process is used, the result should be a list of activities related to the theme, 24-12.

### Learning styles

When planning activities for young children, consider individual learning styles. Basic learning styles include field-sensitive, field-independent, visual learner, and auditory learner. You

**ACTIVITIES FOR A PUPPET THEME**

**Fine Motor Development**

Handling puppets.
Making puppets.
- Paper bag puppets.
- Peanut puppets.
- Sock puppets.
- Paper plate puppets.
- Stick puppets.
- Milk carton puppets.
- Spoon puppets.

**Art**

Designing and making puppets

**Social Studies**

Attending a marionette show.

**Language, Storytelling, and Dramatic Play**

Telling a story using a puppet.
Putting on a puppet show.
Telling a shadow puppet story.
Learning new vocabulary related to puppets.
Looking at pictures of puppets at group time.
Setting up a puppet stage with a variety of puppets.

**Sensory Table**

Provide a variety of puppets made from different materials.

24-12 A brainstorming session among several teachers yielded this list of activities for a puppet theme.

may find that learning styles vary from program to program. That is, last year more children might have been field-independent, while this year more children are field-sensitive. The number of children who are primarily visual learners may also vary from year to year. This information is important for planning a program that relates to the children's learning styles.

**Field-sensitive.** *Field-sensitive* children like to work with others, 24-13. In a group setting, they are helpful. They will volunteer and assist others in picking up blocks, setting the table, and finding a place for a puzzle piece. Field-sensitive children will also try to gain your attention.

When introduced to a new activity, field-sensitive children want a model to follow. Or they may say, "Show me how." If there is not a model or demonstration, they may wait. When someone else begins, they will observe. After this observation, they will begin their work.

**Field-independent.** *Field-independent* children like to try new activities. They enjoy discovery. These children do not have to be urged to try new activities. In most cases, they will be the first to try new activities.

Field-independent children prefer to work on their own, 24-14. However, they enjoy competition as well as individual recognition. Field-independent children are also task orientated. When engaged in an activity, they generally do not notice what is going on around them.

Children who are field-independent will rarely contact the teacher for help. They enjoy engaging in new tasks without directions or assistance from the teacher.

**Visual learners.** *Visual learners* depend a great deal on the sense of sight. These children notice small changes in the environment. When a plant is added to the science table, they are the first to notice. Looking at books and other objects are activities that this type of learner enjoys.

**Auditory learners.** *Auditory learners* are those who learn best through hearing. These children are the first to hear a fly in the classroom or a snow plow outdoors. You will

24-13 Field-sensitive children enjoy playing in the dramatic play area with others.

24-14 Field-independent children enjoy working alone.

find that auditory learners enjoy listening. To meet their needs, records, stories, and poems need to be included in the curriculum.

Most children use a combination of senses. That is, they use both visual and auditory input to learn. To provide for these children's needs, plan activities that involve several senses, 24-15. For example, while reading a book, also show the pictures. Using this method, children should retain more knowledge. They will also find activities more satisfying.

### Learning characteristics

Each classroom has children with a wide range of learning characteristics. Some children work slowly, others quickly. Some children are attentive. Others are easily bored. Some are quick decision makers, while others are cautious.

You must evaluate children's learning characteristics in relation to your own. If you work quickly, keep this in mind as you plan the curriculum. When demonstrating for children, slow down so they can understand concepts. Be careful not to read or talk too fast.

Group assignments are also important. If Joey works extremely slow and Tommy works quickly, being in the same group may be frustrating for both. It is better to place children with others who work at the same pace.

24-15 Showing snowflake patterns while talking about December weather appeals to both visual and auditory senses.

Some children have long attention spans. They are able to pay attention and sit still for long periods of time. Other children, however, are easily distracted. To hold the interests of these children, plan novel and interesting group activities. For instance, during story time use a variety of teaching methods. During one week, use at least three types of media. Flannel board figures, flip charts, puppets, draw and tell charts, and filmstrips could all be used to tell a story.

Children also make decisions in different ways. Some children are quick to make decisions. This type of decision making is called *impulsive.* When given the chance, impulsive decision makers act immediately.

Other children are slower to make decisions. This type of decision making is called *cautious.* These children approach a new activity carefully. They study the environment before they begin.

Remember that not all children complete activities in the same amount of time. Children move and learn at different rates. As a teacher, you will need to be aware of individual learning styles and characteristics when planning the curriculum.

## WRITTEN PLANS

After considering your curriculum approach, theme, goals, and activities, written plans need to be developed. Many centers require two types of written plans to be developed. A *block plan* is an overall view of the curriculum. It outlines the general plans. A *lesson plan* is more detailed than a block plan. It outlines specific actions and activities that will be used to meet goals.

### Block plan

A block plan is key to planning an appropriate curriculum. Without this written block plan, curriculum areas may be overlooked. You may think these areas were covered, but without a written record, you cannot be sure.

A good block plan usually includes days of the week, time periods, and scheduled activities. Charts 24-16 and 24-17 show two sample block plans.

**WEEK** August 27-31  **MORNING SESSION — 2 YEAR OLDS**  **THEME** My School  Yvonne Libby

| | 9:00-10:10 Free Play/Centers | 10:10-10:25 Large Group | 10:25-10:40 Snack | Small Groups #1 | 10:40-11:00 Small Groups #2 | #3 | 11:00-11:30 Outdoors |
|---|---|---|---|---|---|---|---|
| **MONDAY** | * water colors<br>* H₂O + toys in sensory table<br>* tunnel<br>* tennis shoes color match game | <u>My Nursery School</u> story cards / "If You're Happy + You Know it" | crackers & cheese spread<br>milk | Stringing Beads | Table Blocks | Stringing Beads | * sand toys |
| **TUESDAY** | * crayons and markers<br>* "goop" in sensory table<br>* driving wheel<br>* "tuff" blocks | * Short Walk Around the Neighborhood | chex mix<br>milk | Table Blocks | Stringing Beads | Table Blocks | * balls |
| **WEDNESDAY** | * playdough<br>* styrofoam pieces in sensory table<br>* balance beam<br>* color clowns | "Little Red Wagon" song / <u>My Nursery School</u> | honey nutters<br>milk | book: <u>Where Is It?</u> by Tana Hoban | puzzles | feely box: exploring things around in the classroom | * painting with water |
| **THURSDAY** | * Ivory snow finger painting<br>* H₂O in sensory table<br>* rocking boat | Tour of school / "Little Red Wagon" | veggies & dip<br>milk | feely box | <u>Where Is It?</u> book | puzzles | * bubbles |
| **FRIDAY** | * roller painting<br>* sand in sensory table<br>* crawling cubes | "If You're Happy and You Know It" / Tour of school | peanut butter cookies<br>milk | puzzles | feely box | <u>Where Is It?</u> | * rocking boat |

24-16  This block plan is for a group of two-year-olds. Notice the theme and the large group activities related to it.

**AFTERNOON SESSION — 4 YEAR OLDS**

Yvonne Libby

WEEK  October 15-19          THEME  My Friends

| | 1:00-2:25 Free Play/Centers Snack | 2:25-2:40 Large Group | 2:40-3:00 Snack | 2:40-3:00 Small Groups Rhonda | Cathy | Diana | 3:00-3:30 Outdoors |
|---|---|---|---|---|---|---|---|
| **MONDAY** | *crayons, chunk crayons (Traci) *Soybeans on the sensory table *Beauty shop (Sheila) *listening center—"It's a Small World" | *"Here We Are Together" *"Downright, Upright..." song with puppet | Chex mix Milk | Paper Bag Puppets *cutting & pasting | Parachute Fun! | We're Very Good Friends, My Brother and I – book | *Game – "Grey Squirrel" |
| **TUESDAY** | *art rubbings (Sherry) *Orange H₂O and utensils in sensory tub *Drying wheel (Tammy) *cooking; making mini-pizza! | *"Downright, Upright..." *"Cobbler, Cobbler, Mend My Shoe" | Mini-pizzas Milk | We're Very Good Friends, My Brother and I – book | Paper Bag Puppets *Cutting & pasting | Parachute Fun! | *rakes! Jumping in piles of leaves |
| **WEDNESDAY** | *colored glue and styrofoam pieces *leaves in the sensory table (Sheila) *toothpick structures (Jaci) *tumbling mat | *"The Clown's Smile" story cards | | Parachute Fun! | We're Very Good Friends, My Brother and I – book | Paper Bag Puppets *cutting + pasting | *trikes |
| **THURSDAY** | Fieldtrip to Connell's Apple Orchard | | | | | | |
| **FRIDAY** | *painting with roller paints (Mary) *Bubbles! in sensory table *Apple tasting! *Twister! *"Showing" center | *Discussion of Apple Orchard *Goodbyes to Rhonda and Cathy... | Cheese & Crackers Milk | Show and Tell | | | *Chalk on sidewalk |

24-17 Notice the theme for this group of four-year-olds. It focuses on an outside interest—friends.

Block plans should be kept on file. They can be used as a reference to review what has happened during the year. The plans also contain a variety of activities that may be used in future years, if appropriate.

To write a block plan, follow these steps:

1. Review your program goals.
2. Review children's developmental needs using developmental charts if necessary.
3. Review children's interests.
4. Select a theme.
5. Plan theme goals.
6. Select activities and record them on the block plan. Make certain you have a balance of activities using all developmental areas.

It is not uncommon to learn that a group of children need more help in one area than another. For instance, children may have good large motor skills but poor language skills. If you notice this, include as many language tasks as possible.

## Lesson plans

Lesson plans are more detailed than block plans. While a block plan gives just the title of a book, a lesson plan provides step-by-step directions for sharing the book. Lesson plans contain the following:

- Activity goals.
- Behavioral objectives.
- Materials needed.
- Motivation.
- Procedures.
- Closure/transition.
- Evaluation.

Chart 24-18 contains a sample lesson plan.

**Activity goals.** Activity goals are statements that tell the "why" of the activity. They are more specific than program goals. Examples of goals for cooking applesauce with a group of four-year-olds are shown in 24-18.

To write goals for a lesson plan, think carefully about each activity. Ask yourself, "What can the children learn from this experience?" Then write the lesson plan, as outlined above, including all the learning involved.

**Behavioral objectives.** *Behavioral objectives* describe the expected outcomes of an activity.

Objectives can be used to plan teaching strategies.

There are three parts to behavioral objectives. These parts are:

- The conditions of performance.
- The behavior.
- The level of performance.

Chart 24-19 includes examples of each part of the behavioral objective.

The *conditions of performance* list what tools the child will use. Included could be puzzles, paper, scissors, beads, or any other materials and/or equipment found in early childhood settings. The conditions of performance can also include what the child will be denied. For example, they may need to work a puzzle without the aid of a teacher.

*Behaviors* refer to any visible activities done by the child. It tells what the child will be doing. When choosing behaviors, avoid words that are open to many interpretations. To know, to understand, to enjoy, to believe, and to appreciate are all words that can mean many things. For instance, how will you judge if a child understands? Useful words for objectives are listed in 24-20.

The *level of performance* states the minimum standard of achievement. It should note how well you want the child to do. Unless working with children who have special educational needs, the level of performance many times is understood. Therefore, it is not always included as part of the objective.

**Materials.** Under the materials section of the lesson plan, list everything that is needed for the activity. For example, if you are going to make instant pudding, include milk, box of instant pudding, bowl, wire whisk, spoon, scraper, and measuring cup. Or, if you are going to do a finger painting activity, list paint, paper, aprons, and wet sponge.

You will find a materials list helpful for gathering supplies. As you get each item, check it off on the lesson plan. This preparation will ensure a successful activity.

**Motivation.** *Motivation* describes how you will gain the children's attention. The best devices are items that interest the children. A picture of a cat may be used as motivation

# A SAMPLE LESSON PLAN

**DATE:** 9/21      **TIME:** 10:00 A.M.
**GROUP:** 4 YEAR OLDS
**ACTIVITY:** COOKING EXPERIENCE — APPLESAUCE
**GOALS:**

- To practice following directions.
- To practice using a knife as a tool.
- To develop cooking safety habits.
- To learn the parts of an apple: seed, core, flesh, skin, and stem.
- To observe the changes in texture and color when heat is applied to the apples.
- To practice personal hygiene by washing hands before the cooking experience.
- To taste the ingredients in applesauce.
- To taste cooked apples.
- To observe the beauty of an apple.

**Behavioral objectives:**

Given apples, knives, measuring cup and spoons, a bowl, a mixing spoon, a microwave oven, sugar, cinnamon, and a recipe chart, the children will help peel apples and measure the ingredients to prepare applesauce.

**Materials needed:**

| | |
|---|---|
| 6 peelers | measuring cup and spoon |
| 12 apples | kettle |
| recipe chart | bowl |
| water | mixing spoon |
| 2 cups of sugar | microwave oven |
| 3 tablespoons of cinnamon | |

*Continued.*

24-18 Lesson plans contain much more detail than block plans. Notice all the details that go into making applesauce.

**Motivation/introduction:**

Set up the housekeeping area with recipe chart, cooking utensils, and tray with food. Ask, ''What can we make from apples?'' Listen to responses. Tell the children, ''Today we are going to make applesauce.''

**Procedures:**

1. Tell the children to wash their hands.
2. Review the recipe chart step by step.
3. Cut an apple in half. Show the children the parts of an apple—seed, core, flesh, skin, and stem.
4. Demonstrate how to use a peeler as a tool, stressing safety.
5. Pass out apples and peelers, again explaining safety.
6. Encourage children to observe and feel the apples.
7. Peel apples.
8. When apples are peeled, focus children's attention back to recipe chart. Proceed by following directions step by step until the mixture is ready for a heat source.
9. Discuss each ingredient, allowing children to taste them, if they wish.
10. Ask individuals to measure the sugar, cinnamon, and water.
11. Direct children's attention to the applesauce as it cooks. Clarify the porcess by asking questions such as, ''How do you the apples look different?''
12. Serve the applesauce as a snack.

**Closure/transition:**

Assign clean-up tasks to the children. Tell children they will get to eat the applesauce at snack time. Then tell the children that it is time to go outside.

**Evaluation:**

*24-18 Continued.*

## BEHAVIORAL OBJECTIVES

**CONDITIONS OF PERFORMANCE:** States the conditions under which the child will perform.
  Given a three-piece puzzle . . .
  Given crayons and a pencil . . .
  Given a set of blocks . . .
  Without the aid of a teacher . . .
  Given farm animals . . .
  Within a five minute time limit . . .

**BEHAVIOR:** States what the child will be able to do.
  . . . the child will cut . . .
  . . . the child will draw . . .
  . . . the child will construct . . .
  . . . the child will sing . . .
  . . . the child will match . . .
  . . . the child will climb . . .
  . . . the child will jump . . .
  . . . the child will skip . . .
  . . . the child will stack . . .

**LEVEL OF PERFORMANCE:** States the minimum level of achievement.
  . . . four inches . . .
  . . . all . . .
  . . . at least three feet . . .
  . . . two out of three times . . .
  . . . within a five minute period . . .

24-19 Studying these parts of behavioral objectives will help you write effective objectives.

before reading a story about cats. Motivation may include the following:

- Pictures.
- Puppets.
- Alphabet letters.
- Records.
- Resource people.
- Cards.
- Sticks.
- Artwork.
- Photographs.
- Animals.
- Stuffed toys.
- Clothing.
- Hats.
- Masks.

**Procedures.** The procedures section resembles a cookbook. Simple, step-by-step directions should be provided. The directions should be in order. Number each step to help you remember the order.

Each of the activity's goals should be included in the procedures. For example, if a goal is to have each child taste the ingredients, this should be a step in the procedures.

Examples of procedures for two activities are included in Chart 24-21. The sample lesson plan also contains procedures.

## BEHAVIORS FOR OBJECTIVES

| | | | |
|---|---|---|---|
| ask | feed | point | tap |
| answer | find | pour | taste |
| blow | follow | print | tell |
| button | jump | remove | touch |
| catch | lace | replace | throw |
| climb | locate | return | tie |
| collect | mark | roll | turn |
| comb | move | run | wait |
| color | nail | say | wash |
| clap | name | separate | wipe-off |
| cut | paint | sit | weigh |
| grab | paste | sing | write |
| group | pick | skip | zip |
| hit | peel | solve | |
| hoop | place | stand | |

24-20 Learn to use concrete terms such as these when stating behavioral objectives.

## PROCEDURE CHARTS FOR ACTIVITIES

---

**ACTIVITY: Visual perception** (This type of activity encourages children to see fine differences between and among objects.)

1. Place individual cards face down on the table.
2. Provide each child with one game board.
3. Demonstrate how to play the game, stressing the importance of taking turns.
4. Ask one child to begin by choosing a card from the middle of the table.
5. After the child has drawn the card ask, "Do you have an object like that on your board?"
6. If the object does not match, instruct the child to return the card to the center of the table, face down.
7. Continue with the next player until one child has filled all of the game board spaces.

---

**ACTIVITY: Story—*The Very Hungry Caterpillar***

1. Introduce the new vocabulary word chrysalis.
2. Read the story.
3. After the story, ask questions and encourage the children to answer in full sentences. Include questions such as:
   - What were some of the things that the caterpillar ate?
   - Can real caterpillars eat all of those things?
   - What is a chrysalis?
   - What happens to the chrysalis in the story?

---

24-21 Using a procedure chart, you should cover each step of an activity.

**Closure/transition.** *Closure* refers to how an activity will end. *Transition* refers to the movement from one activity to another. In some cases, closure and transition are the same task. For example, at the end of a creative drama activity, you may ask the children to walk like heavy elephants to the snack table.

**Evaluation.** A staff that offers a quality early childhood program often does evaluations daily. In some centers, time is set aside every day for this purpose. Many day care centers, however, do not have the resources to do this with the entire staff. Instead, staff members will evaluate the activities they conducted on their own. This process involves three steps: (1) evaluating the learning experience; (2) evaluating the children and their responses; and (3) evaluating your own teaching strategies.

When evaluating the learning experiences, ask yourself whether the activity was proper for the age group. If, for example, children had trouble cutting paper there could be several reasons for the trouble. Were the scissors in good repair? Scissors with dried glue on the cutting edge will not cut properly. Left-handed children need left-handed scissors. Paper thickness could also be a problem. Children who are learning to cut need lightweight paper and proper tools.

Successful activities give children the chance to test their knowledge. For example, children will learn more about making applesauce by taking part in the activity than if they only watched an adult make it.

Your skills working with young children only have meaning if the children learn. So it is important to study the children and their responses to activities and to you. First, see that the children reach the objective. If they do not, think through the activity. Ask yourself, "What could I have done differently?" Likewise, if there were behavior problems, try to find the cause.

Lack of organization, you will find, can affect the outcome of an activity. If you forget some of the ingredients for a cooking activity, leaving the group to gather them could affect outcomes. During your absence, some child may start to mix the ingredients. The product may not turn out if the ingredients were not measured properly. To illustrate, packaged pudding only requires two cups of milk for four servings. If a child pours in a whole quart of milk, the pudding will not thicken properly.

Chart 24-22 includes a sample evaluation form for an activity. To help in the evaluation process, you may want to duplicate several copies of this form. After using it a few times, you will find that you can remember the three parts of the form, including the specific questions. At this point, you may want to start writing your evaluations on index cards. In time, you will be able to go through this process without paper and a pencil.

## A SAMPLE EVALUATION OF AN ACTIVITY

**ACTIVITY:** Story—*NEVER TALK TO STRANGERS*
**GROUP:** Five-year-olds

### I. THE ACTIVITY: SELECTION AND DEVELOPMENT

A. **Was the content (concept) worth knowing?**
*The content is valuable for five-year-old children since it deals with personal safety. With the increased incidence of child abuse, this is an important topic.*

B. **Was it developmentally appropriate?**
*Although fantasy was involved in the story, almost all of the children were able to understand the content.*

C. **Was it interesting to the children?**
*All of the children but Don listened and responded. During the repetitive sentences, the children repeated, ''Never talk to strangers.''*

D. **Did the activity include opportunities for the children to use or ''test'' their knowledge?**
*After the story the children were asked questions. These included:*
* *Is your grandmother a stranger?*
* *Is your neighbor a stranger?*
* *Is a man you never saw before a stranger?*

E. **What would you suggest as a follow-up experience?**
*Children's books related to child abuse will be read tomorrow. The game ''Good Touch and Bad Touch'' will also be introduced.*

### II. THE CHILDREN: RESPONSES

A. **Did all of the children reach the objective(s)? If not, why?**
*With the exception of Don, all of the children reached the objective.*

B. **Were there behavior problems? If so, do you have any insight as to what caused them?**
*If Don and Ben were separated during the story, Don may have paid attention. Likewise, Ben found Don's behavior disturbing. He tried to move away from him, but another teacher made him sit down.*

### III. THE TEACHER: STRATEGIES

A. **Were you well organized?**
*Yes, the book was placed so I could easily find it. During the outdoor play period, an individual carpet square was laid out for each child. Approximately ten inches were left between each square. This spacing probably helped maintain group control.*

B. **Were you satisfied with the effectiveness of your teaching strategies in reaching the learning objective? If not, why?**
*I should have practiced the story beforehand. In addition, I should have held the book so that all of the children could view the pictures.*

C. **Did you effectively guide or manage the group?**
*Yes, with the exception of Don, I managed the group effectively.*

D. **Did you introduce the concepts in a stimulating manner?**
*The cover of the book appealed to the children. After the story, two children asked to have it read again.*

E. **Did you involve the children in the closure of the activity?**
*Yes, I did. The children were involved through a series of questions. Concepts of strangers and safety were both discussed.*

F. **What strategies would you change if you were to repeat this activity?**
*First, I would separate Don and Ben. I would also practice reading the book to myself several times before sharing it. This would make me less dependent on the story lines. As a result, I would feel confident enough to share the pictures with the children.*

24-22 Evaluation is the final step in the curriculum development process. It can be used to determine how well your curriculum worked.

At first, you may find the evaluation process time consuming. You will learn, however, that it is a useful process, 24-23. With constant evaluation you will improve your teaching skills as well as the curriculum.

## SUMMARY

Planning and carrying out a curriculum is an important and time consuming task. It is the basis for all that is done in an early childhood program. Starting with curriculum approach, program goals are set and themes are developed. Then activities are selected based on the curriculum you have planned. And, finally, a written plan is drawn up.

Your curriculum will go through constant changes. As you note that one activity does not work, you will substitute another. While this may seem like an overwhelming task, with practice you will develop skill at curriculum planning.

24-23 A well-planned curriculum gives you more time for interacting with students.

# to Know

auditory learner
behavioral objectives
behaviors
block plan
closure
conditions of
  performance
direct learning
  experience
field-independent
field-sensitive

indirect learning
  experience
lesson plan
level of performance
motivation
process-centered
  approach
program goals
spiral curriculum
transition
visual learner

# to Review

1. _____ learning experiences are planned with a specific goal in mind while _____ learning experiences occur on the spur of the moment.

2. True or false. Curriculum development involves only the teacher who is responsible for the group.

3. List two advantages of a preplanned curriculum.

4. Describe a process-centered approach to curriculum development. Explain how materials and environment relate to this approach.

5. What are program goals?

6. Name three factors that influence whether program goals are met.

7. True or false. The environment and learning experiences do not need to complement the theme.

8. Explain the meaning of spiral curriculum.

9. A _____ is a very useful method for developing a theme.

10. A good curriculum:
    a. Contains activities that keep children busy at all times.
    b. Has a balance of activities.
    c. Contains those activities the children like to take part in.
    d. All of the above.

11. List three questions to ask when selecting activities.

12. _____-_____ children like to work with others and often volunteer to help.

13. _____-_____ children like to try new activities and work on their own.

14. (Visual, auditory) learners enjoy looking at books and other objects.

15. (Visual, auditory) learners enjoy activities involving records, stories, and poems.

16. True or false. The majority of children use a number of senses in learning.

17. What are the six steps in writing a block plan?

18. A lesson plan should include:
    a. Activity goals, behavioral objectives, materials needed.
    b. Motivation, procedures.
    c. Closure, transition, evaluation.
    d. All of the above.

19. How do activity goals and program goals differ?

20. Name the three parts of behavioral objectives. Explain one of these parts.

21. The _____ section of the lesson plan resembles a cookbook.

22. True or false. Evaluations are not important to the overall curriculum.

# to Do

1. Ask a day care teacher to talk to your class about curriculum planning.

2. Invite a chain day care director who uses a preplanned curriculum to talk to your class about curriculum planning.

3. Take a poll in your community to learn the number of early childhood programs that use preplanned curriculums. Ask the teachers what they feel are the advantages and disadvantages of this approach.

4. Divide into four groups. Each group should prepare a flowchart on a different theme. Compare your flowcharts.

5. Write a lesson plan for cooking grilled cheese sandwiches.

6. Write and share with your classmates five behavioral objectives.

7. Discuss strategies for meeting program goals listed on pages 354 and 355.

# Chapter 25

# *Parent Involvement*

After studying this chapter, you will be able to:
- [ ] List objectives for parent involvement.
- [ ] Cite advantages and disadvantages of various methods for involving parents in the school program.
- [ ] Design a newsletter about an early childhood program.
- [ ] Write a letter to parents.
- [ ] Plan, conduct, and follow up a parent/teacher meeting.
- [ ] Explain how to conduct a discussion group.

***Parent involvement*** refers to those activities parents do related to their roles as parents. Included are such activities as volunteering in the classroom, assisting with fund raising activities, home teaching, supplying classroom materials, and attending parent meetings. This involvement is a key factor in the success of a program, the students, and the teachers, 25-1.

It is unfortunate,then, that little information has been written about the parent-teacher relationship. Quite often, teachers and parents do not view each other well. In the past, teachers have not called parents to praise their child's efforts and accomplishments. Likewise, parents have not always let teachers know they are appreciated.

As a teacher, you will need to build good relationships with parents. Begin by noting a child's strengths. Communicate these strengths to the parents. Parents will then be more accepting when you have to share a child's weaknesses.

Always welcome parents at school. Whenever possible, include them in program functions. Parents may be observers, resource people, volunteers, or guests at special celebrations. There should be a friendship between parents and teachers. Studies show that teachers who are confident of their skills and

25-1 A parent's involvement in a child's school program reaps many benefits for both child and parent.

abilities are more inclined to include parents in program functions. Likewise, studies show that good relationships with parents affect a teacher's feelings of self-esteem and competence.

## OBJECTIVES

The purpose of parent involvement is to help parents:
- Develop an understanding of child growth and development.
- Gain confidence in their parenting roles.
- Learn about their children's experiences at school.
- Understand their children by watching other children.
- Learn new ways of interacting with their children, 25-2.
- Become informed about community resources.

- Understand how the center and home work together in helping children.

Parent involvement can be encouraged using a number of methods. These include written communication, parent-teacher meetings, and discussion groups.

## WRITTEN COMMUNICATION

Two popular forms of written communication are newsletters and letters. *Newsletters* most often include information concerning a variety of subjects. They are shared on a regular basis. *Letters* most often address only one subject and are sent out on an "as needed" basis.

Written communications are popular for one important reason. These forms of communication require less time and energy for the teacher

25-2 Being exposed to other parents and children means adults can find new ways to work with children.

than meetings or telephone calls. If a letter is sent out regarding an upcoming event, the teacher need only type one letter and then send copies of that letter to all parents.

Parents also like written communication for the same reason. A newsletter can be read over a weekend, during lunch hour, or while commuting. This saves parents time and energy, also.

### Writing style

The first step in developing a newsletter or letter is to choose a writing style. There are some important points to remember.

Use the active, not passive, voice. Active verbs provide more enjoyable reading. The active voice states the subject did something. The passive voice says the subject was acted upon. For example, the active voice would say, "John read books and painted pictures." The passive voice would say, "Reading books and painting pictures were John's main activities."

Another factor to keep in mind is the educational level of the parents. Your writing style should match this level. A good rule of thumb

is to keep your communications short, clear, and simple for all parents. Short messages are appreciated by busy parents. And simple, clear writing prevents misinterpretation of the message.

### Newsletters

A newsletter serves as a link between home and school. In most centers, the newsletter is produced and sent out on a regular basis, 25-3. At one center, staff sends out newsletters on the first Monday of each month. Other centers, depending on budgets and resources, send out newsletters on a daily, weekly, or bi-weekly basis.

A newsletter may include a variety of information:
- Review of special classroom activities.
- Special activities for children to do in the home.
- Upcoming special events at the center.
- Short articles of interest.
- Summaries of books or articles related to parenting.
- Nutritious recipes.

25-3 A newsletter can be written quickly using a word processor.

- Child development information.
- A want ad section.
- A help-wanted section, asking for parent volunteers.
- Upcoming community events of interest to young children and their families.
- A "meet the staff" section.
- Recognition for parent contributions.
- Suggestions for helping children at home.
- A parent exchange section.
- Reminders of school policies.
- Helpful hints on child rearing.

The design of a newsletter can also allow for a blank section. This section can be used by the teacher to write a brief, personal note. This should be a positive note about the child. For instance, a teacher may write, "I'm so pleased with James; he has learned how to tie his shoes."

Another section could also be provided for parents. After reading the newsletter, the parents might write their comments and/or thoughts. Perhaps they could respond to the newsletter. Or they could submit ideas or information for future issues. Thus, the newsletter can be a two-way communication tool.

### Letters

Letters are another useful written communication tool. Letters can be used to touch base with one parent or an entire group of parents. Letters are often one or two pages long and sent on a weekly basis. Thus, parent letters can supplement parent newsletters.

The first letter sent to parents should introduce the teachers and staff to parents. This letter can also address classroom goals, rules, and expectations. The first letter should also welcome parents to observe and/or take part in the classroom.

After the first letter, subsequent letters should include the theme of the week. Special center activities should be noted, along with the goals for the week. New songs and fingerplays should be written out with the accompanying music or actions that go with the play. Field trip sites, dates, and times should be included. Parents should also be thanked for any favors. Home learning activities for the parents to do

with their child should be shared. Include with these activities a rationale for their use. Thus, parents will feel involved in their child's education. An example of a parent letter is shown in 25-4.

Families always enjoy reading about their children. On some occasions, you might wish to mention the children in a parent letter. When doing so, be sure to include each child in the classroom. For example, if the class has vegetables for its theme, ask each child to share his or her favorite vegetable. Report this information in a parent letter.

At times you may choose to send home a special letter during the week. This letter should outline something special the children did on a special day. It may be an event, such as a field trip, or an activity within the classroom, 25-5. This letter can promote a learning experience between parent and child.

## PARENT-TEACHER MEETINGS

Parent-teacher meetings are one way to involve parents in their children's school program. Meetings help both the parent and you understand their child. Parents will share what the child is like at home. As the teacher, you will share what the child is like in the center. When these two viewpoints are shared, everyone gains, especially the child, 25-6. You can then plan to meet the child's needs.

There are three phases to parent-teacher meetings. The first phase is planning. This phase includes setting basic rules that will help you work successfully with the parents. The second phase is the individual meeting. The final phase is the follow-up. This involves touching base again with the parents to make sure actions agreed on in the meeting are being followed. It should also include a report of the progress made since the meeting.

### Planning

Before the conference, spend time planning. A good meeting does not just happen. It needs to be carefully planned if you are to win the respect of the parents. Thus, responsibility for success lies largely on you as the teacher.

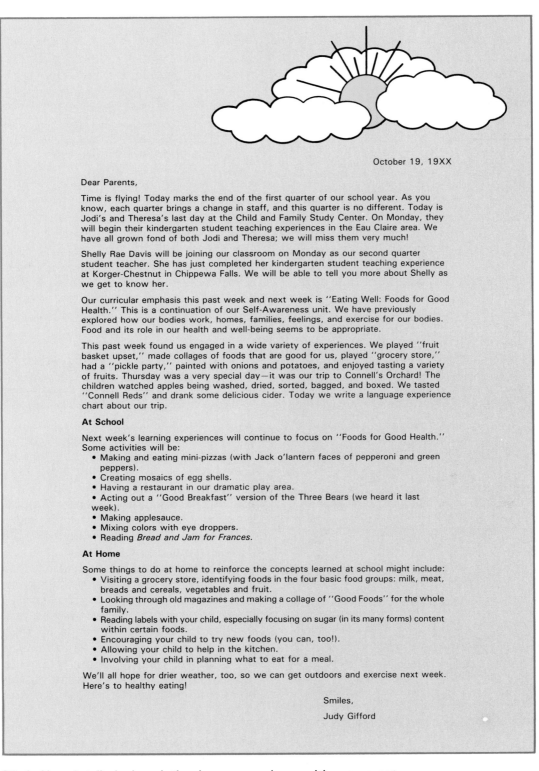

October 19, 19XX

Dear Parents,

Time is flying! Today marks the end of the first quarter of our school year. As you know, each quarter brings a change in staff, and this quarter is no different. Today is Jodi's and Theresa's last day at the Child and Family Study Center. On Monday, they will begin their kindergarten student teaching experiences in the Eau Claire area. We have all grown fond of both Jodi and Theresa; we will miss them very much!

Shelly Rae Davis will be joining our classroom on Monday as our second quarter student teacher. She has just completed her kindergarten student teaching experience at Korger-Chestnut in Chippewa Falls. We will be able to tell you more about Shelly as we get to know her.

Our curricular emphasis this past week and next week is "Eating Well: Foods for Good Health." This is a continuation of our Self-Awareness unit. We have previously explored how our bodies work, homes, families, feelings, and exercise for our bodies. Food and its role in our health and well-being seems to be appropriate.

This past week found us engaged in a wide variety of experiences. We played "fruit basket upset," made collages of foods that are good for us, played "grocery store," had a "pickle party," painted with onions and potatoes, and enjoyed tasting a variety of fruits. Thursday was a very special day—it was our trip to Connell's Orchard! The children watched apples being washed, dried, sorted, bagged, and boxed. We tasted "Connell Reds" and drank some delicious cider. Today we write a language experience chart about our trip.

**At School**

Next week's learning experiences will continue to focus on "Foods for Good Health." Some activities will be:
- Making and eating mini-pizzas (with Jack o'lantern faces of pepperoni and green peppers).
- Creating mosaics of egg shells.
- Having a restaurant in our dramatic play area.
- Acting out a "Good Breakfast" version of the Three Bears (we heard it last week).
- Making applesauce.
- Mixing colors with eye droppers.
- Reading *Bread and Jam for Frances.*

**At Home**

Some things to do at home to reinforce the concepts learned at school might include:
- Visiting a grocery store, identifying foods in the four basic food groups: milk, meat, breads and cereals, vegetables and fruit.
- Looking through old magazines and making a collage of "Good Foods" for the whole family.
- Reading labels with your child, especially focusing on sugar (in its many forms) content within certain foods.
- Encouraging your child to try new foods (you can, too!).
- Allowing your child to help in the kitchen.
- Involving your child in planning what to eat for a meal.

We'll all hope for drier weather, too, so we can get outdoors and exercise next week. Here's to healthy eating!

Smiles,

Judy Gifford

25-4 Use detailed, descriptive language when writing a parent letter. It is an inexpensive way to keep all parents informed.

We went to the apple orchard today.
We rode in a big yellow bus.
We saw many trees with apples on them.
We observed the beauty of apples on the trees.
The guide showed us four parts of an apple—
    stem, skin, meat, and core.
We tasted green, yellow, and red apples.
Tomorrow we will make applesauce.

To: Parents
From: Miss Libby
Activity: Field Trip to the
    Apple Orchard

25-5 This letter is intended to promote discussion between parents and children.

25-6 Through parent-teacher meetings you and the parent can gain insight into how best to work with a child.

Begin the planning phase by gathering developmental data on the child. Gather records on the child's emotional, social, intellectual, and physical development. This information can most often be obtained from developmental checklists and from anecdotal records.

Anecdotal records should be kept in every classroom. To do this, set up a recording system. Many options are available. One option is to use a metal card file with large index cards. Another option is to use a standard size three ring notebook. Choose the system that works best for your needs.

Recall that anecdotal records contain only the teacher's observations, not interpretations. An observation may read, "Richard tried to string beads today. He first tried a red bead. It fell from his hands. After this, he tried a blue bead. Again, he dropped the bead as he tried to place the string through it. He made three more attempts and then went back to the blockbuilding area."

Note that the observation only noted Richard's actual behavior. No mention was made that Richard has poor hand-eye coordination. That would be an interpretation.

Some teachers use planning sheets to prepare for meetings. After reviewing all anecdotal records and developmental records, this information is recorded on the planning sheet. Included are the following:

- Routines.
- Types of play.
- Play media and activity preferences.
- Fine motor coordination.
- Large motor coordination.
- Social behavior.
- Relationships with children and adults.
- Intellectual development.
- Eating habits.
- Sleeping habits.

The planning sheet is divided into sections. For instance, one section might cover these routines: clothing, rest patterns, eating, and clean-up, 25-7.

Collect some of the children's artwork to share with the parents. Make sure that the child's name and date are on each piece. Tape recordings can also be useful. Ask each child to tell you a story about a picture. Record the story as the child speaks.

Video recordings are also becoming popular for use in parent-teacher meetings. A week or two before a meeting videotape each child alone. Allow three to five minutes per child. Review the tape before the meeting, and note the start and stop numbers for each child.

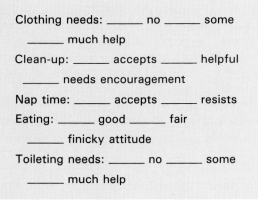

**ROUTINES**

Clothing needs: _____ no _____ some
_____ much help

Clean-up: _____ accepts _____ helpful
_____ needs encouragement

Nap time: _____ accepts _____ resists

Eating: _____ good _____ fair
_____ finicky attitude

Toileting needs: _____ no _____ some
_____ much help

25-7 If you use a planning sheet, you may wish to divide notes into sections.

**Preparing the parent.** A brief newsletter can be sent home explaining the purpose of the parent-teacher meeting. Include in the newsletter the date(s) the meetings will be held and the length of the meetings. In addition, tell parents they should feel free to use part of the time for questions they may have.

**First impressions.** The first impressions you make with a child's parent(s) are important. Be prepared. Have your notes outlined, including what you would like to discuss. Use your notes during the meeting. This will show the parents that you are well prepared.

As you think through the meeting, keep in mind that you will set the tone for the meeting. That is, if you are nervous and anxious, parents will feel the same. If you are calm, parents will be calm. Set the proper tone for a successful meeting.

**Questions.** You may ask parents questions during the meeting to help them think. For instance, ask them how their child acts at home; what the child's interests are. It is best to plan your questions before the meeting.

Ask open-ended questions if you want more than a yes or no answer. The "w" questions are many times the most successful. These include why, what, how, when, and where.

**The setting.** The meeting setting can greatly influence success. Find an area in the center that is private. No interruptions should occur during the meeting. To insure this, place a sign on the door that states a meeting is in session and must not be interrupted. If the meeting is scheduled in an office, take the telephone off the hook or arrange for messages to be taken.

When an office is used, set chairs around in a grouping. This will help create a feeling of a partnership. Likewise, avoid sitting behind a desk. This places you in the position of authority. This will decrease the feeling of a partnership.

**Scheduling.** Scheduling parent-teacher meetings can be a problem. Working parents are only available certain hours of the day. So, before you begin making plans, ask parents what time is convenient. Some teachers place a sign-up sheet outside the classroom door, 25-8. Parents desiring a meeting can sign up

25-8 Many parents are at the center daily picking up and dropping off children. A sign-up sheet outside the classroom door is a convenient method for scheduling meetings with these parents.

during the time that is best for them. You might find some parents who are not willing to sign up for a meeting. You may still feel a meeting with them would be helpful. When this occurs, call the parent(s) to set up an appointment.

Your schedule may also make scheduling meetings difficult. Time may be taken up by administrative duties. You might try scheduling meetings:
• During nap time. One teacher may use this time for conferences.
• Before or after program hours.
• By hiring a substitute for one day each month.

• By hiring a substitute over the noon hour, providing parents can come at this time.
• By dismissing center activities for a day every two or three months. This may not be an option if parents cannot find other care.

Parents' time must also be considered. If families have more than one child at the center, schedule successive meetings. This will prevent the parent from making several trips back to the center.

Plan a 10 minute break after each meeting. This will provide you with a chance to record any important information. It will also provide time for the meeting to run longer than planned.

Home meetings may also be scheduled when a school meeting is difficult to arrange. Dual career families may find this very convenient. This type of scheduling, however, is costly. It requires more time for travel. Transportation costs are also involved. As a result, not many centers offer this alternative.

A scheduled home visit can be valuable for the teacher. Seeing the child's home environment can provide a better understanding of the child. For instance, the teacher can observe parent-child interaction as well as the books and toys in the home.

**The meeting**

Always begin and end the meeting with a positive comment. Parents always enjoy hearing something positive about their child. As you share the comment, try to be relaxed. If you are tense, the parents will be aware of it.

Avoid making general statements. "Tommy is doing fine" or "Jodi is doing well in school" does not give parents much information. Rather, be specific. For instance, you might say the following:

"Johnny has really improved in the area of routines. He no longer needs assistance with his clothing when preparing to go outside. At transition time, he takes care of his personal needs in the bathroom. At nap time he accepts the center's rest pattern. Likewise, he no longer needs encouragement to help during clean-up. In fact, I am so pleased, for he is even encouraging other children to assist."

Watch how you word your comments. As you speak, put yourself in the parents' place. Try to imagine the effects of your remarks. You must evaluate the child's progress without being critical. To do this, always try to use a positive expression. See 25-9.

During the meeting, watch for signs of emotion. These signs may include gestures, changes in tone of voice, or expression. If the parent appears uncomfortable, provide reassurance that all information will be kept confidential.

**Questions parents ask.** "How is Wendy doing?" "Does Kelly behave at the center?" "Is Kris ready for kindergarten?" All of these questions are common for parents to ask. Each question can have several answers. When planning for the meeting, be prepared for these questions. Questions may be phrased differently, but they basically include:

- Is my child happy in day care?
- How can I help at home?
- Does he or she get along with others?
- Does he or she respect others' property rights?
- How long does he or she nap?
- Does he or she get a balanced diet?
- Does he or she eat everything given to him or her?
- Is he or she average in abilities?

### LANGUAGE EXPRESSIONS

| Negative Expressions | Positive Expressions |
|---|---|
| troublemaker | disturbs others at story time |
| below age | performs at his own level |
| lazy | is capable of doing more |
| stubborn | insistent in having his own way |
| mean | finds it difficult to get along with others |
| clumsy | is not physically well-coordinated yet |
| selfish | needs to learn to share with others |
| show-off | tries to get others' attention |

25-9 Practice using positive phrases when talking to others. Such phrases are much more acceptable than negative phrases.

- Who does he or she play with?
- Does he or she have any special abilities?

Be prepared to answer these questions with positive comments. Instead of labeling a child based on behavior, explain actions using positive expressions.

**Listening.** Most people can listen to 400 words per minute but only speak 125 words. Based on this difference, a good listener does not jump ahead of the speaker. Give parents time to finish their stories or thoughts.

While a parent is talking, show interest and alertness. Avoid preparing an answer while listening. The parent's last sentence may be a source of new information. This may put an entirely different slant on what was previously shared.

Never interrupt a parent. Also, avoid quibbling over words. Instead, focus intently on what the parent is trying to say. Also focus on areas of agreement. This will encourage more friendly, open communication from the parent.

**Working with parents.** Some parents are more difficult to work with than others. For example, a timid parent may be speechless at the start of a meeting. To reassure this parent, be friendly. As you speak, provide this parent with several sincere compliments. Second meetings are often much easier for timid parents.

The worried parent always needs reassurance. This parent can often be identified by hand twirling, handkerchief twisting, or finger drumming. To reduce this parent's worry, provide reassurance that the child is performing satisfactorily.

A parent who is egotistical often enters feeling self-confident and smiling. The parent will want to talk about what a wonderful child he or she has and what a wonderful parent he or she is. With this parent, it is very important to remember that the ego is a precious possession. Thus, comment on the parent's skills.

The critical parent can be hard to work with if not handled properly. This parent has expert opinions on teaching the children in the center. Be accepting. That is, do not show disapproval or surprise as the parent talks. Never argue with this parent or any other. Arguing only arouses resistance and bad feelings. Arguments will not benefit the child. Successful meetings depend on your relationship with parents.

**Professional behavior.** Always model professional behavior. If a parent makes a negative comment about another teacher, ignore it. Your attitude should always be positive toward your colleagues. Likewise, do not bring up or respond to negative comments about other children or parents.

**Ending a meeting.** Just as a conference should begin on a positive note, it should also end on one. Summarize major areas that have been discussed. Begin by repeating positive comments made at the beginning of the meeting. Note areas that may need attention, including the agreed upon action. Then restate what you will do at the center as well as what the parent(s) will do at home. End the meeting by again making a constructive, pleasant comment.

Invite the parents to visit the school any time. Thank them for sharing. Then walk them to the door. Leave them with a statement of encouragement or reassurance.

### Follow-up

A parent-teacher meeting should allow for a sharing of information. Just as parents will learn, so will you, the teacher. Specifically, you may learn answers to the following:

- The child's reaction to the center, including likes and dislikes.
- How the child spends time outside of the center.
- What home responsibilities the child has.
- Special interests the child has shown at home.
- The status of the child's health.
- Who the child prefers to play with in the home as well as in school.

Record meeting notes in the child's folder. Make a point of calling or sending a note to the parent(s), sharing any progress the child has made. Some teachers schedule time each week to contact parents. Each week they contact a few parents by phone or with a brief note. Over the course of a month, each parent hears from the teacher regarding their child.

## DISCUSSION GROUPS

Another method for involving parents in their children's education is group discussion. Through discussion, parents become familiar with child growth and development concepts. They also learn to notice some crisis points in the family cycle and learn to understand their own roles better.

When conducting discussions, remember that adults:

- Need to integrate new information with what they already know.
- Tend to take errors personally.
- Prefer self-designed learning experiences.
- Like straightforward "how-to" approaches.
- Must be physically comfortable.
- Learn a great deal from interacting with others.
- Enjoy learning when many senses are used.

Group discussions are useful for studying new ideas. Discussions allow several people to take part. And through discussion, individual thinking is challenged. As the group exchanges experiences during discussion, individuals have the chance to study and review their own experiences. They are made to think through their positions. Chart 25-10 lists techniques for helping parents relax in a discussion group.

---

| TECHNIQUES TO HELP PARENTS RELAX |
|---|
| • Place items of interest on the walls for parents to look at. |
| • Provide refreshments for parents to eat and drink. Play soft background music. |
| • Provide name tags on which parents can write their name as well as their child's name. |
| • Arrange the chairs in a circle. Greet parents individually as they enter. |
| • Introduce parents to each other. |

25-10 Parents are not immune to being nervous when visiting the school. Listed here are several methods for helping parents relax prior to a group discussion.

Group discussion also has disadvantages. First, it most often takes a long time. Other methods, such as a film or lecture, are generally faster. If the group is not handled properly, the discussion may wander. See 25-11.

### Preparation

Arrange the room so parents can easily talk face to face. A circle or horseshoe arrangement is usually best. Coffee, tea, punch, and/or water should be available for parents when they arrive. If all the parents do not know each other, hand out name tags. These tags should include the child's name under the parent's name. This will allow parents to identify parents of their children's friends. You may also ask the members to introduce themselves before the discussion begins.

To encourage the parents to talk, you may want to begin with a short filmstrip or cassette tape addressing the subject to be discussed.

You will need to be aware of problems that may arise. Some parents may not feel comfortable taking part. When this happens, ask a question that requires a response. For example, you may ask, "John, how do you feel?" Or, you can build on a previous comment by saying, "John, earlier you said you were opposed to physical punishment. Why do you think you feel this way?"

Another problem that occurs quite often is that small groups begin debating among themselves. If this happens, you will need to redirect the group's attention by asking them to share their comments with the whole group.

## OTHER METHODS OF INVOLVEMENT

There are many other ways to involve parents in their children's educations. These other methods are not as detailed as meetings and discussion groups. However, they are useful in their own way. These methods include a lending library, problem-solving file, bulletin boards, and sunshine calls.

### Lending library

A lending library is one way to share parenting information. If space is not available for a parent library, a few shelves in the director's office can be used. Books that relate to parenting needs should be included in the library. Available books can be mentioned during daily parent contacts, at meetings, in newsletters, and/or on the parent bulletin board.

### Problem-solving file

Some day care directors use a *problem-solving file* to help parents. This file contains information on problems parents may face. Reading materials, such as journal articles and newspaper clippings, related to each problem are filed in folders. Topics you may wish to include in a problem-solving file are listed in

## ADVANTAGES AND DISADVANTAGES OF DISCUSSION

| Advantages | Disadvantages |
|---|---|
| 1. Ideas can be carefully studied.<br>2. Many people can take part.<br>3. Parent educators can note if parents understand the discussion.<br>4. People are forced to think through their positions.<br>5. Disagreement is clarified or agreement is reached. | 1. It is time-consuming.<br>2. Parents may pool misinformation.<br>3. Parents expecting to be told what to do may dislike this method.<br>4. Parents can come to the wrong conclusion.<br>5. Tension and emotions may be aroused. |

25-11 Before you decide to schedule a group discussion, study the advantages and disadvantages. Will your concerns be best addressed by such a discussion?

| TOPICS FOR A PROBLEM-SOLVING FILE | |
|---|---|
| Allowances | Lying |
| Bedwetting | Mental retardation |
| Blended families | Nightmares |
| Childhood diseases | Play |
| Child abuse | Personality development |
| Children's clothing | Reading readiness |
| Crying | Selecting toys |
| Emotional development | Self-esteem |
| Death | Separation anxiety |
| Divorce | Small muscle development |
| Food | Social development |
| Gifted children | Stealing |
| Handedness | Speech problems |
| Identity | Teething |
| Intellectual development | Television |
| Language development | Thumbsucking |
| Large muscle development | |

25-12 Today, parents are concerned about many topics that affect their children. A problem-solving file is a useful resource for these parents.

25-12. The file can be publicized through newsletters and at parent meetings.

## Bulletin board

Making a parent bulletin board is a convenient way to communicate with parents. Put the board in a noticeable spot. Post meeting dates, newspaper clippings, and other center information, 25-13. Cover the board with paper or an attractive fabric. Use captions to communicate its use.

## Sunshine calls

Sunshine calls create positive parent-teacher relationships. A *sunshine call* is a telephone call made by a teacher to a parent to communicate praise and support for the child. The purpose of this call is to share with parents something outstanding or interesting the child has done recently. For instance, Mrs. Barr may call Mr. Ross to let him know his child has just learned to ride a tricycle, jump rope, or even tie shoelaces.

Some parents have had poor school experiences. When these parents were in school, a call from the teacher usually meant they had done

25-13 A parent bulletin board can be set up outside the classroom door to announce topics of interest and messages to parents.

something wrong. Such calls often focused on a social or learning problem. As a result, these parents may be alienated.

Done well, sunshine calls can help dispel some of these negative attitudes and help build good feelings toward the teacher and center. The goal of sunshine calls should be to build feelings of cooperation.

Sunshine calls are valuable for the parent, teacher, and child. For the teacher and parent, the value of sunshine calls lies in the two-way communication that occurs. For the child, the call is a pleasant event. The teacher has taken a personal interest in him or her. A sunshine call, however, should not replace regularly scheduled parent-teacher meetings.

There are several guidelines that must be followed when using the telephone:
- Plan the conversation by carefully choosing what to say.
- Keep the call to about five minutes in length.
- Begin the conversation by asking the parent if it is a convenient time to talk. If it is not, arrange a time to call back.
- Put the parent at ease immediately by telling the reason for the call.
- Share positive statements about the child.
- Whenever possible, also give the parent a word of praise or thanks.

Some adults are at ease with a telephone conversation. They are used to using the phone. Thus, the conversation may be quite relaxed. Also, many teachers and parents are more relaxed when they do not need to talk face-to-face.

## VOLUNTEERING

Parents want to be involved in their children's educations. Many parents feel a need to improve their relationship with their child's school. A large majority of parents also note they would like to take part in school committees. Thus, teachers and directors need to make an effort to involve parents. One way to do this is through volunteer programs.

Some teachers hesitate to include parents in their program plans. Their objections include:

- Parents do not have the time needed to devote to volunteer efforts.
- Parents may criticize the program.
- Parents may not have effective child guidance skills.
- Parents may want to take over classroom responsibilities.
- Children may act up when their parents are present.
- Parents may discuss confidential information outside of school.

These concerns are all worthwhile. However, most can be addressed by carefully recruiting and then training volunteers. These volunteers, in turn, will gain a great deal, including:
- Personal satisfaction.
- A better understanding of child development and child guidance.
- An understanding of how children learn.
- An understanding of what activities are appropriate for young children.
- An understanding of his or her own child by observing him or her playing with other children.
- An experience of being part of a teaching team.

### Recruiting

The best volunteers are those that have an interest in education. Perhaps they would have enjoyed teaching as a profession. Still others are interested in presenting the best experiences to their children. These people are interested in supporting the center and learning more about young children. Many parents have talents or interests that could be useful to your program. A letter that can be used to recruit parents is shown in 25-14.

Parent volunteers must be dependable, fond of children, and healthy. In order to take part in a program, parents need some type of orientation.

### Orientation

To get the most from volunteers, plan a training session. During this session, share staff expectations of them, including classroom limits and state licensing rules. As you discuss these duties, make the parents feel welcome.

In addition, prepare a list of guidelines for parent volunteers as shown in 25-15.

If you have not met any parents before the orientation session, be prepared to make a good impression. Studies show that first impressions are lasting impressions. The tone for an entire relationship is often set in the first four minutes.

First, begin by making the parents feel comfortable. Welcome them. Offer them chairs. Begin the orientation by explaining how important volunteers are in a center.

Parents feel good when you remember their name. As you meet each parent, pay attention to his or her name. If you do not hear it, ask the person to repeat it. Say the name to

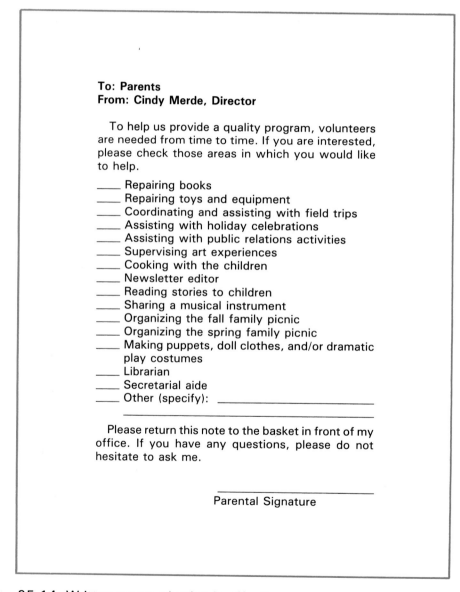

To: Parents
From: Cindy Merde, Director

To help us provide a quality program, volunteers are needed from time to time. If you are interested, please check those areas in which you would like to help.

_____ Repairing books
_____ Repairing toys and equipment
_____ Coordinating and assisting with field trips
_____ Assisting with holiday celebrations
_____ Assisting with public relations activities
_____ Supervising art experiences
_____ Cooking with the children
_____ Newsletter editor
_____ Reading stories to children
_____ Sharing a musical instrument
_____ Organizing the fall family picnic
_____ Organizing the spring family picnic
_____ Making puppets, doll clothes, and/or dramatic play costumes
_____ Librarian
_____ Secretarial aide
_____ Other (specify): _____

Please return this note to the basket in front of my office. If you have any questions, please do not hesitate to ask me.

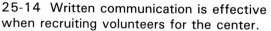
Parental Signature

25-14 Written communication is effective when recruiting volunteers for the center.

## SUGGESTIONS FOR PARENT VOLUNTEERS

**General participation.** Remember the children always come first. Share your interest in the child by:

1. Providing praise with such statements as "I like your painting," or "Thanks for hanging your coat on the hanger," or "You are good at helping with clean-up."
2. State your suggestions positively by telling what the child should do. For example, instead of saying, "Don't put the puzzle on the floor," tell the child where to place the puzzle.
3. When talking with the children, get down at their level by squatting or sitting. As the child speaks, give him or her your full attention.
4. Speak with other adults only when necessary.
5. Never do for a child what he or she can do for him or herself. That is, always stress independence. Let children put on their own coats, boots, etc. Assist only when absolutely needed.
6. Avoid discussing the children outside of the classroom.

**At story time**

1. Sit in the circle with the children.
2. Allow interested children to crawl on your lap.
3. Show your interest in the story by listening attentively.
4. If you are asked to read, hold the book so all the children can see.

**At the easel**

1. Children need to wear a smock while painting.
2. Only one child should use each side of the easel at a time.
3. Encourage the children to replace the brushes in the proper color. (There is one brush for each container of paint.)
4. Show an interest in the children's work, but do not interpret it for them. Likewise, do not ask children what they have made.
5. After children finish painting, write their names in the upper left-hand corners of their work. Capitalize only the first letter of each name.
6. Hang finished paintings on the drying rack.
7. At the end of the day, encourage the children to take their paintings home.

**At music time**

1. Participate with the children.
2. Reinforce the head teacher's actions.
3. Show your enjoyment of the music.

25-15 Parent volunteers need guidance when they begin their work at the center.

yourself. Memory experts claim that by repeating the name to yourself, you will improve recall by thirty percent. See 25-16.

Whenever possible, use the parent's name in conversation. This process is called ***reinforcement***. Through repetition, you will engrave the parent's name in your memory. Studies show people recall faces better than names. So another way to recall parent's names is to observe their faces. Concentrate on one trait such as the nose, eyes, or cheekbones. Then associate the name to the parent's face. By remembering the parents' names, you will make them feel important.

### Schedule

Parents will only return to the classroom if they feel needed. Post a parent helper schedule

25-16 Parents and teachers both benefit by wearing name tags. These help everyone learn names more quickly.

like the one shown in 25-17. This will help detail your expectations. You will also need to ask volunteers if there are any questions you can answer.

**Thank-you's.** Send each parent a thank-you after he or she has volunteered. This gesture will show your appreciation. It will also encourage parents to volunteer again.

## SUMMARY

Parents play the key role in the development of their children physically, emotionally, intellectually, and socially. Involving them in the school program, then, makes sense.

Involve parents in their children's school program by keeping in touch with the parents. Conduct meetings, during which you can get to know parents one-on-one. Hold discussion groups so all parents can share ideas and get to know one another. And communicate often, either over the telephone or through newsletters or letters.

Parents can assume many roles in the classroom as volunteers. With their help, the teacher can attend to those tasks that can be done only by a teacher.

## PARENT HELPER SCHEDULE

| Time | Teacher—Judy | Teacher—Lisa | Parent—Rita Ulesich | Parent—Georgia Smith |
|------|--------------|--------------|---------------------|----------------------|
| Before Class | Set up equipment for special free play activities. Welcome volunteers. | Set up equipment for activities other than dirt-and-water play; special, and paint activities. | Place paper on easels. Put out paint. | Fill water table. |
| 9:00 | Welcome children. Supervise free choice of activities. | Welcome children. Supervise free choice of play activities. | Supervise painting. | Supervise water table. |
| 10:00 | Serve snack. | Supervise handwashing. | Put away easels and join snack table. | Put away dirt-and-water play equipment and help with handwashing. Assist with snack. |
| 10:30 | Help with equipment or story as needed. | Read story. | Assist Judy in putting away equipment. | Assist with story and quiet time. |
| 10:45 | Help with special activity, or on alternate days, introduce it. | Introduce special activity, or on alternate days, help with it. | Assist with cooking activity. | Help with special activity. |
| 11:00 | Supervise movement activity. | Put away equipment from cooking activity. | Assist with movement activity. | Assist with movement activity. |
| 11:15-11:45 | Do dishes and pick up classroom. | Supervise play-yard. | Supervise play-yard. | Supervise play-yard. |

25-17 Have duties outlined for parent volunteers for the days they work.

## to Know

letters                problem-solving file
newsletters        reinforcement
parent involvement   sunshine calls

## to Review

1. List four objectives for involving parents in the school program.
2. Name two points to consider when developing a writing style.
3. Newsletters may include:
    a. A review of special classroom activities.
    b. Upcoming center events.
    c. Child development information.
    d. All of the above.
4. What are the three phases of the parent-teacher meeting?
5. True or false. Anecdotal records should include the teacher's interpretations.
6. The "w" questions are often the most successful for getting information from parents. What are these questions?
7. What is the purpose of scheduling a ten minute break after each parent-teacher meeting?
8. Always begin a parent-teacher meeting with a _____ _____.
9. Rewrite the following negative expressions as positive expressions.
    a. Selfish.
    b. Show-off.
    c. Lazy.
    d. Clumsy.
10. Avoid preparing an _____ while listening.
11. During a meeting, worried parents always need:
    a. To be ignored.
    b. Refreshments.
    c. Reassurance.
    d. None of the above.
12. True or false. Adults tend to take errors personally.
13. List two advantages of group discussions.
14. Disadvantages of group discussions include:
    a. Too many people can take part.
    b. The discussion may wander.
    c. Parents will take over the discussion.
    d. All of the above.
15. What is the purpose of a lending library?
16. A _____ _____ file contains information on difficulties parents with children may face.
17. A sunshine call:
    a. Is made by a teacher to a parent.
    b. Is made to share with parents something positive about their child.
    c. Can help dispel some negative feelings parents may have about school.
    d. All of the above.
18. How can teachers address their concerns about parent volunteers?
19. Who makes the best volunteer?
20. Using a parent's name often during conversation is called _____.

## to Do

1. Make a list of questions that parents most often ask teachers. Design answers for these questions, based on the contents of this chapter.
2. Discuss ways you might build a positive relationship with:
    a. A shy parent.
    b. A worried parent.
    c. An angry parent.
    d. An unconcerned parent.
3. Write a parent letter about an upcoming field trip to an ice cream factory. Use the active voice.
4. Collect parent newsletters from several centers. Analyze their design and content. Then, based on your analysis, design a newsletter for the "A-B-C Learning Center."
5. Invite a day care teacher to your class to discuss parent-teacher meetings. Be prepared with questions to ask of the teacher.
6. Brainstorm a list of discussion topics for a parents' group.

# part 6

# Other Children You will Meet

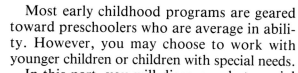

Most early childhood programs are geared toward preschoolers who are average in ability. However, you may choose to work with younger children or children with special needs.

In this part, you will discover what special qualities are needed by teachers in infant-toddler programs. You will learn special techniques for providing care and learning experiences for these children

This part also introduces you to the teaching concerns of children with special needs. You will understand how such needs as speech disorders, health disorders, and giftedness may affect your role as a teacher.

# Chapter 26

## Programs for Infants and Toddlers

After studying this chapter, you will be able to:

After studying this chapter, you will be able to:
- List the characteristics of a good infant-toddler teacher.
- State guidelines for proper infant-toddler care.
- Design useful, functional infant and toddler space.
- Discuss handling the routines of infants and toddlers.
- Choose toys that are safe and developmentally appropriate for infants and toddlers.
- Plan a curriculum for infants and toddlers.
- Design activity areas for use by toddlers.
- Develop an illness policy for an infant-toddler center.

Patti is learning how to walk. Sally and Tom have just said their first words. Working with infants and toddlers can be very exciting and rewarding, 26-1. For the young child, it is a time of wonder and discovery. Everything is new to the child. As the teacher, you will take pride in these children's achievements. You will marvel with them as they learn to crawl or take a few steps. You will be delighted when they learn to play peek-a-boo with you. All these events are major accomplishments for very young children. They learn so fast and are so eager to learn new skills.

## TEACHER CHARACTERISTICS

Teachers always control the environment in an infant-toddler center. As a teacher, your behavior will influence the behavior of the children. Children will react based on the ways you treat them. If you are warm and loving, the children will be warm and loving. If you are aloof to the children, they will also be aloof. Thus, positive teacher behavior is needed for a successful program.

In the program, touch, smile, make eye contact, and speak affectionately to children. Likewise, be patient and accepting while working with the children.

26-1 Infants and toddlers depend a great deal on adults as they learn about the world around them.

field. Read professional journals, books, and articles. Another way to stay informed is to discuss your observations and needs with other teachers and attend workshops. If possible, you may also want to enroll in advanced course work.

## GUIDELINES FOR INFANT-TODDLER CARE

In order to provide the most useful infant-toddler program, follow some general guidelines:
- Provide children with a safe and healthy environment, 26-2.
- Respect children for their ethnic and family identities.
- Design care to meet the unique needs of each child.
- Care for each child affectionately.
- Respond to children's distress or discomfort signals immediately.
- Follow a set routine in providing for children's needs.
- Encourage curiosity by providing many chances to explore.

As a teacher of young children, you must have energy, be healthy, and enjoy children. You must also be able to handle many situations and understand feelings. Part of your teaching responsibility includes helping children express feelings such as joy, love, anger, satisfaction, and sadness.

You will also have to be accepting of parents as an early childhood teacher. Show respect for all cultures, customs, and languages. Also, invite parents into the program to observe, take part, and share their hopes for their children.

Infants and toddlers need teachers who expect the same behavior each day. To provide this consistent environment, all center staff must be agreed on what is proper behavior. In most cases, having only a few rules for children increases the chances that rules will be consistently followed.

Finally, as a teacher of infants and toddlers, you need to be aware of new research in the

26-2 Toddlers can be very curious. For their safety, keep all poisonous materials well out of their reach in a locked cabinet.

- Avoid overstimulation. Too many new experiences at one time can overwhelm young children, particularly infants.
- Plan experiences so young children learn to master new skills.

## INFANT AND TODDLER SPACE

In order to follow the guidelines set forth, you will have to consider the many factors that make up a center for infants and toddlers. One important factor is space. Without proper space, all persons involved in the center are harmed. On the other hand, adequate, properly organized space is a benefit for all.

### Infant space

Space for infants should address their daily routines. Included are eating, diapering, sleeping, and playing.

The most convenient feeding area is near the entrance to the center. Parents arriving with baby food and bottles can place these items in the refrigerator at once. This area should be equipped with high chairs, feeding tables, a heat source, and comfortable, adult-sized chairs. A bulletin board can be placed in this area to post feeding charts and records. The floor surface must be washable.

The diapering area should be located next to a sink. As in the feeding area, the floor surface needs to be washable. This allows for easy cleaning and disinfection. To prevent back strain for adults, changing surfaces should be waist high. Place a mirror on the wall next to the changing surface so children can look at themselves. A bulletin board hung nearby can be used to post records of children's elimination patterns.

The sleeping area usually uses the most space because cribs take up a great deal of floor space. The ideal location for this area is joining the diapering area. Do not worry about light. Infants do not need a dark room in which to sleep. However, a dimmer switch can be installed in this area to control lights used in the diapering area.

Crawling babies need their own play area. They need to be out of the way of older children. To ensure safety, use low dividers to make a crawling area. A short pile carpeting should be on the floor for comfort and warmth.

### Toddler space

Toddlers need more open space than infants. They move most of the time. To prevent accidents, use a nonslip surface indoors for all space that toddlers use. Usually this space is divided into several convenient areas. Included are receiving, playing, napping, diapering, and eating areas. (Napping, diapering, and eating areas for infants can be shared by toddlers.)

The receiving area is located near the main entrance. This area should contain a bulletin board for parent information and lockers or hooks to hold children's clothing. When standing in the receiving area, you should be able to have a clear view of all other areas, most importantly the play area. Set up interesting equipment in the room to encourage children to play and help prevent separation anxiety.

Toddlers need a play area that allows them to move freely, 26-3. It is important to leave

26-3 As children become mobile, their need for play space increases.

one-third to one-half of the total space open. In crowded areas, some children may find it hard to play. As a result, they are more inclined to cry and fight. If adequate space is not provided, the children will bump into each other.

Although a tile floor is easier to maintain, some teachers prefer a carpeted floor in the play area. Carpeting has two advantages. First, it provides a cushion for falls. Second, it is warmer for crawling children. If carpeting is used, it should be washable.

In a section of the play area, there should be equipment that encourages large muscle development (climbing). Scaled slides and tunnels are two types of equipment that invite exploration and climbing. Cardboard boxes can also be fun for toddlers. Equipment should be arranged so all areas can be seen by the teacher.

The outdoor play area should connect to the indoor play area. This outdoor area should have a large, grassy area for running and crawling. Grass, like carpeting, helps cushion falls.

## CARING FOR INFANTS AND TODDLERS

As you work with infants and toddlers, you will notice each child has his or her own rhythm. Some will go about their routines quickly. Others move slowly. As a caregiver, you must adjust your own rhythm to each child's rhythm. You may find this hard to do. At times, if your rhythm simply does not mix with a child's rhythm, you may wish to switch responsibilities with another teacher. That teacher may be more compatible with the child.

All infants and toddlers, regardless of their differences, require their needs to be met promptly if they are to learn trust. A child who has been promptly and properly cared for is likely to be a happy person. To provide this attention to needs, you must provide consistent care. Through this care, children learn that they are special persons and develop trust.

### Observing

Infants learn a great deal, and set the stage for further growth, by observing their surroundings. This is a major task for them. Interesting shapes, objects, and colors give infants things to observe and focus on. Studies show that infants who have interesting things to observe tend to be more attentive and responsive.

Studies also show that infants can recognize faces before objects. For this reason it is important to pick up infants often and let them look into your face. When an infant looks at you, look back. After repeating this, those infants will learn to recognize you.

Once an infant starts to notice objects around a room, pick the child up and place him or her over your shoulder. This gives the infant the chance to look around and explore that portion of the environment that can be seen.

## HANDLING ROUTINES

With infants and toddlers, routines make up much more of the day than routines do with preschoolers. Much of your day will be spent soothing crying children, coping with separation anxiety, taking care of diapering and toileting needs, feeding, preparing for nap time, and preventing illnesses. See 26-4.

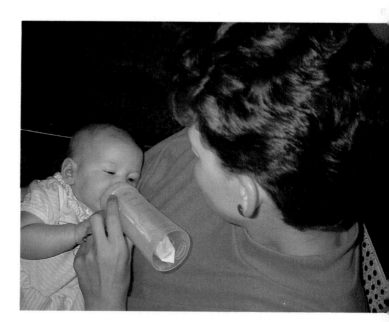

26-4 Routines such as feeding are an important part of caring for infants.

## Crying

Crying is often thought to be a distress signal. Infants cry in an attempt to control their worlds. There are many reasons why infants wish to control their worlds. They may cry to express needs, cope with frustration, or get attention. Regardless of the reason, you should never ignore crying. Always remember that the crying does have some meaning for the child.

Studies support the theory that an infant's crying should always be given prompt attention. According to these studies, when cries are answered promptly the frequency of the crying will be reduced.

You will notice that babies have individual differences in their crying behaviors. Some babies cry more often and with greater strength. Other babies may seldom cry. All babies have various reasons for crying. As a caregiver, you will have to learn the meaning of each child's cries. You will learn which cries indicate fussiness, hunger, soiled diapers, boredom, or discomfort related to being too cool or warm.

Always respond to a child's crying by first trying to solve the problem. If the baby is wet, change him or her. Likewise, if the child is hungry, feed him or her. If you cannot find an obvious reason for the child's crying, check the baby's daily care record. (This record is described later in the chapter.) Perhaps the baby is sleepy, teething, reacting to medication, or catching a cold.

Tired, crying babies can be comforted in a number of ways. Some enjoy being held; others love to be rocked. Often a child can be quieted simply by speaking or singing softly to him or her. Studies show that young infants are able to hear well. In the first few days of life, they become upset by loud noises. Infants will often turn their heads toward quiet talking. Studies also show that one method to calm an upset child is to speak in a soft voice. Familiar voices are very effective.

Remember that a crying baby creates an unpleasant environment. Sometimes crying can become contagious. One child's crying can cause other babies to cry. When this happens, the environment may become even more tense and unpleasant for the teachers and children.

## Separation anxiety

Often between nine to twelve months of age, some children will have difficulty separating from their parents. You may find that children experiencing this anxiety will cry each day when their parents leave them at the center. This is called *separation anxiety*. It is a sign that a child is learning and developing a special relationship with an individual, 26-5.

Parents may also have difficulty leaving children who feel separation anxiety. They do not enjoy seeing their children in distress. Some parents may even feel guilty for leaving their children. Other parents may unfavorably compare their children to those who are not crying.

When a child shows anxiety over separation, reassure the parent that this is normal behavior. Explain that the behavior may go on for several days or, in some cases, several weeks. During this time, it is important to relay any progress to the parents on a daily basis. This information may make the parents feel more comfortable and less guilty about leaving the child.

Whenever possible, allow infants and toddlers to visit the center with their parents before they enroll. This may help reduce some distress.

26-5 Between the ages of nine and twelve months many infants become aware of their parents and their need for their parents. At this time, separation anxiety can occur.

If time permits, children can stay a short time at the center the first day, perhaps an hour or two. Gradually the stay can be increased. It takes children about three to five weeks of regular attendance to adjust to the new setting.

Until the child adjusts, your support, patience, and understanding are required. You will notice that the infant or toddler may react to strangers, sudden movements, noise, and strange objects. To help support the child, let him or her explore at his or her own pace. Meanwhile, gradually expose the child to new objects in the center.

## Feeding

Young infants' lives consists of little more than sleeping and eating. Nutrition is very important at this stage of development. To provide properly for the infant, talk to the parents. Many infants are on special diets. You may also find that some mothers may wish to come to the center to breast-feed their infants. If this request is made at your center, provide the mothers with a quiet and comfortable place.

Just as important as the type of food is how the infant is fed. Most infants will need to be bottle-fed. In a good infant-toddler program, each infant is constantly cared for by one teacher. This allows for one-on-one attention and physical closeness. The assigned teacher should hold and cuddle the infant during feeding. This will help form a bond between child and teacher.

Infants vary in the amount and frequency of feedings. Some infants will drink only four ounces of milk at a feeding, while others will drink eight ounces. Some infants will need to drink every four hours, while others will demand food every two hours. Each of these infants' needs should be met. Infants should be fed when hungry, not when it is convenient for the teacher.

Whenever possible, toddlers should be served finger foods. These are easy for children to handle. Always provide many sizes and shapes so children can practice picking them up. Examples include cubes of raw apple, cooked green peas, raisins, chopped cooked eggs, banana pieces, and soft cheese.

For feeding, toddlers can be seated in high chairs, at eating tables, or on low chairs placed in front of a low table. They will need some table space on which to move their food. Children of this age love to explore their food. Before eating, they may smell, touch, and push around their food. This behavior should be encouraged. Exploring food can give children important sensory experiences that foster cognitive growth.

After eating, toddlers need to wash their hands. If child-sized sinks are not available, use a small pan of water at the table. In the beginning, you may have to assist the children in swishing their hands as well as wiping them on a paper towel or cloth.

## Diapering and toileting

Changing diapers is a routine that a teacher of infants and toddlers will repeat many times each day. For this reason, it should be a pleasant experience. Give the child all your attention. Look into his or her eyes. Smile, sing, and talk softly to the child.

A diaper checking routine is a useful policy to follow. To protect against serious rashes, and possibly infections, infants need frequent changes. A chart to record diaper changes should be hung in the changing area, 26-6. If infants are sleeping, do not waken them. Instead, mark an S on the chart to note they were sleeping. In addition to half-hour checks, infants should always be checked just before eating and sleeping.

Do not be shocked if, as a child grows older, he or she objects to having a diaper changed. Many times this objection occurs because the child is having fun playing and does not want to be interrupted. When this occurs, there is no harm in waiting a few minutes. Wait until the child finishes with an activity, and then gently guide him or her to the changing area. Many times this transition is easier if the child is allowed to carry a toy into the changing area.

If a child has a diaper rash, it is important to change the diaper right away when it is soiled. Always report any noticeable rash to the parent(s) on the day it is noticed. Ask them if there is any ointment they prefer. If they prefer

# DIAPER CHECK CHART

| | Sally | Peter | Mark | Tom | Sue | John | Sally | Kelsie | Kris | Erika |
|---|---|---|---|---|---|---|---|---|---|---|
| 7:00 | | W | | X | X | W | | | | BM |
| 7:30 | S | | BM | | | | X | S | X | |
| 8:00 | | BM | | W | W/BM | X | | | | X |
| 8:30 | S | | X | | | | W | W | W/BM | |
| 9:00 | | | | | | | | | | |
| 9:30 | | | | | | | | | | |
| 10:00 | | | | | | | | | | |
| 10:30 | | | | | | | | | | |
| 11:00 | | | | | | | | | | |
| 11:30 | | | | | | | | | | |
| 12:00 | | | | | | | | | | |
| 12:30 | | | | | | | | | | |
| 1:00 | | | | | | | | | | |
| 1:30 | | | | | | | | | | |
| 2:00 | | | | | | | | | | |
| 2:30 | | | | | | | | | | |
| 3:00 | | | | | | | | | | |
| 3:30 | | | | | | | | | | |
| 4:00 | | | | | | | | | | |
| 4:30 | | | | | | | | | | |
| 5:00 | | | | | | | | | | |
| 5:30 | | | | | | | | | | |
| 6:00 | | | | | | | | | | |

S = Sleeping      W = Wet
X = No change needed      BM = Bowel movement

26-6 Clean diapers are key to the health of infants. Keep track of the changing routine of infants and share this information with parents.

a certain brand, ask them to supply you with a tube. In some cases, parents may ask for your advice.

When diapering a child, certain steps should always be followed by all staff. First, always wash your hands with soap and water before and after diapering. Proper hand washing before and after diapering helps prevent the spread of disease. Therefore, all new staff should learn the proper procedures, 26-7. Included should be the choice of soap as well as step-by-step directions for cleaning the hands.

Liquid soap should be used because bar soaps, when wet and jellylike, harbor microorganisms. You will probably find that a soap dispenser is most convenient. Remember, though, that microorganisms may also grow in liquid soap. Therefore, clean the dispenser each time it is refilled.

If you have cracks in the skin of your hands, wear lightweight, disposable rubber gloves when changing diapers to avoid infection. Medical experts agree that it is nearly impossible to prevent microorganisms from growing in cracks within the skin.

After each change, wipe the diapering table or changing mat with a disinfectant solution. Then record this information on the chart located near the table. The time of the change and whether the child urinated and/or had a bowel movement all need to be noted and given to the parent at pick-up time. If the child had diarrhea, this should be noted along with the amount, color, and consistency. Any evidence of a diaper rash also needs to be recorded.

Some toddlers may be in the process of or show an interest in being toilet trained. For these children it is important that the home and center coordinate their efforts. Discuss with the parents the toilet training process. Explain that it will be an easier process for the child if the home and center routines are consistent.

Like diapering, toileting policies must be used for health purposes. After each use, the seat of the potty chair needs to be wiped with

a disinfectant solution. The container under the chair must be emptied and rinsed with the solution. Finally, you will need to wash your hands with warm water and soap.

## Nap time

All children need a certain amount of sleep. This amount varies from one child to another. Without adequate sleep, a child can become cranky and hard to handle. When this happens, other children in the center can become disruptive.

One consideration for planning a nap time schedule is to check parents' preferences. Some parents keep their infants up late and wake them early in the morning. They want their child to sleep at the center so he or she is awake and alert at the end of the day. Other parents, who may have to travel some distance to get home, prefer to have a sleepy baby at the end of the day. Their goal is to have the baby sleep on the way home.

Nap times may have to be staggered to meet the individual needs of the children. This type of scheduling will allow you time to feed and rock each child to sleep. Often this will require meshing individual needs with group needs. Once a schedule has been developed that fits individual needs, it is necessary to be consistent.

Other considerations for scheduling nap time are the amount of available space and the size of the staff. For most centers, space is not a problem. But if there are not enough teachers to supervise the nap room and play room at the same time, all naps may have to be scheduled at the same time.

## Preventing illnesses

As a staff member in a day care center, you will need to take steps to prevent illness. Disease-causing microorganisms grow in a damp, dirty environment. Play equipment, cribs, changing tables, strollers, floors, tables, high chairs, and feeding tables—as well as the children's hands—all need to be cleaned.

Since infants and toddlers explore with their mouths, it is important that all toys be routinely cleaned. Saliva forms a film on the surface of toys. Microorganisms grow on this film. As a

---

### SANITATION PROCEDURES FOR DIAPERING

1. Dispense enough soap to provide a good lather.
2. Add a small amount of water and rub back and forth, providing friction.
3. Work up a good lather.
4. Rinse hands.
5. Use paper towels to turn off the faucet and dry hands.
6. Diaper baby.
7. Examine the area under your nails for dirt. Remove any dirt with an orange stick.
8. Wash hands using steps 1 through 5.
9. Apply lotion to hands to prevent chapping.

26-7 Proper hand washing is vital to preventing the spread of disease from diapering.

result, any toys such as rattles and teething rings that go into the infant's mouth must be cleaned on a daily basis. If your center has a dishwasher, use it. Most small toys are dishwasher safe.

Clean by hand the toys that cannot be washed in the dishwasher. First, wash the toys in a hot, sudsy detergent and rinse well. Then mix a disinfecting solution of one gallon of water with one tablespoon of chlorine bleach. Wipe or spray each piece of equipment with the solution. Air or sun dry.

Depending on the frequency of use, cribs and strollers need to be cleaned on a daily or biweekly basis. This process should be similar to cleaning toys. First wash each piece with warm, sudsy water. Rinse well. Wipe or spray with a solution of disinfectant. Air or sun dry.

Floors, tables, high chairs, and feeding tables also need cleaning each day. Food left on any of these can grow microorganisms. In some centers, the floors are cleaned by the janitor. Your responsibility, then, is to make sure this is done on a daily basis. In addition, you will be responsible for washing the tables, high chairs, and feeding tables.

**Hand washing.** Contaminated hands are a common cause of the spread of illness in day care centers. To prevent illnesses, it is most important that you follow the hand washing procedures discussed under diapering.

Children's hand washing is also important. Many crawl on the floor and later use their hands to feed themselves. Before eating always wash infants' and toddlers' hands, 26-8. To do so, apply a small amount of a liquid soap to a dampened towel. Thoroughly wipe the child's hands. Rinse the hands with a clean towel, moistened with water. Finally, wipe the child's hands with a dry paper towel.

## TOYS

When choosing toys for the infant or toddler, safety is the number one consideration. Check each piece carefully for sharp edges or points. To avoid splinters, all wooden toys should be sanded smoothly. Small toys or toys with small parts should be avoided. Objects smaller than 2 1/2 inches in depth and 2 inches in diameter could be swallowed or cause choking.

Each year many infants and toddlers accidentally swallow small toys or parts. This can cause suffocation from choking on the object. Or a child may develop intestinal or respiratory problems as a result of swallowing a small toy.

Most plastic toys do not show up on X rays. Toy companies, therefore, are now adding a special plastic to children's toys. This plastic is known as *nontoxic radiopaque plastic*. Toys made with this material will show up clearly on an X ray. When you choose toys, check to see if this product is included on the label or package.

**Purpose**

Toys serve as sensory stimuli for young children, 26-9. By positioning an infant's toys, you can create an incentive for the child to use his or her memory or locomotive abilities. Even during the first few weeks of life, an infant can touch, see, and hear. As the child exercises these abilities, physical and mental development are fostered.

26-8 Older toddlers can sometimes wash their hands themselves.

26-9 Children's senses of sight, touch, and hearing are stimulated by many toys.

### Color

Studies show that traditional baby colors, light blue and pale pink, are not appealing to infants. Colors that are more likely to attract the infant's attention include shocking pink, shades of red, or the contrast of black and white.

### Sounds

Babies enjoy toys that make sounds. When a sound is made, grasping and reaching become more fun. Examples include bell bracelets, rattles, and mobiles. This type of toy is especially satisfying for an infant in a quiet room. Toys that make sounds also encourage infants to use their hands as tools.

### The developmental use of toys

Mobiles make excellent first toys for infants. They provide visual appeal and require a minimum of physical interaction. Select mobiles carefully. Avoid mobiles that are not sturdy. If your center has such mobiles, hang them out of reach. For the young infant, place toys 7 to 24 inches from the eyes. Studies show that a child of this age can best focus on objects which are 7 to 9 inches away from the eyes.

Between 1 1/2 and 3 1/2 months of age, infants will discover their hands. The hands then become a toy for the child. Infants will study their hands as they move them back and forth. Infants between three and six months of age will continue to watch their hands. Even when infants move objects to their mouths, they will continue watching.

Smiles begin to appear at about two months of age. Infants at this age also want to touch what they see. To provide stimulation for the child, place a mirror over the changing table. You will find it fun to watch the child smile at his or her reflections in the mirror.

Soon, infants begin touching objects within their reach. This behavior usually occurs between three and six months of age. As they do this, they gain information about the world and develop intelligence. Thus, provide a variety of toys for the child to touch. These may include soft rattles and soft, furry animals. Caution should be taken when selecting stuffed animals for young children. Facial parts should be securely attached. They should not be able to be removed.

To provide grasping exercise, infants need a variety of toys within reach, whether in the playpen, in the crib, or on the floor. Since the child is likely to place these toys in his or her mouth, choose only safe toys, 26-10. By placing objects in the mouth, babies learn about objects. Studies show that between six and ten months of age, nerve endings in an infant's mouth are very sensitive.

Rattles are important for the infant's development. When a rattle is handed to an infant, he or she goes through a specific process. The first step is to locate the toy with the eyes. After this is done, the child will move his or her hand toward the rattle. Just before contact, the infant's hand will open. In this process the child will be persistent. He or she will repeatedly try to pick up a small toy.

Observations have shown that infants follow a progression of hand movement skills. First, there are raking motions which appear to be somewhat random. Next, scissor motions are made. The child uses the whole hand to pick up an object. Finally, the child develops the

26-10 Large, clean, smooth toys are best for infants because they like to explore with their mouths.

pincer pick-up. Using this method, the infant is able to pick up objects using only the forefinger and thumb. A child using this method will usually shape the hand into the grasp before reaching for the intended object.

Toys will encourage the development of all of these hand movement skills. A variety of toys such as cradle gyms can be used to encourage raking motions. Scissor motions can be encouraged by providing small balls or figures that will fit into the hand. Finger foods, such as dry, ready-to-eat cereal, can be used to practice the pincer pick-up.

As the child develops, he or she begins to experiment with cause and effect. Up to this time the infant has been more interested in watching the hands than the objects that were touched. By five to eight months, the child is more intent on watching the effects of his or her actions.

Around this age, the child will enjoy dropping objects. He or she will often drop objects, including silverware and toys, from the high chair or feeding table. As the child does this, he or she will watch for the consequences of the actions. As the toy hits the floor, the infant may wince at the sound it makes. During this time, avoid hard plastic toys. They may break when hitting the floor.

At about the same time the child begins to enjoy dropping objects, he or she will become interested in simple gadgets in the environment. Electrical receptacles appear to be appealing. For safety purposes, it is important that these all be capped. Other appealing objects include light switches, cupboard knobs, door knobs, television knobs, fringe on rugs, locks, and any other small objects within their reach, 26-11. The manipiulation of these objects gives the child a sense of magic.

Once the child begins to crawl or walk, he or she will want to continually explore the environment. To encourage this curiosity, make the environment safe. Maintain large, open areas where the child can pull or push toys, straddle large trucks, or roll large balls.

Toddlers love to climb. Provide them with small slides, jungle gyms, and sets of stairs. Make sure that you closely watch toddlers when they use the large muscle equipment. Some children may try to walk up the slide. When this happens, you need to take their hand and direct them back to the stairs. Once they learn how to use the equipment, it is not uncommon for children of this age to use the equipment over and over again.

Small wagons, wheelbarrows, doll buggies, and strollers also appeal to toddlers. If you lack indoor space, limit the use of these toys to an outdoor area.

Paper and paper products are also appealing to the toddler. They love to scribble with large pencils and crayons. Large cardboard boxes can be fun toys. The children will open and close them as well as climb into them.

Toddlers love to play with water. Encourage this play by providing floating toys, spoons, sponges, and cups in a water play area. Demonstrate how to pour water, to sail a floating toy, and to squeeze a sponge. For interest, add color to the water.

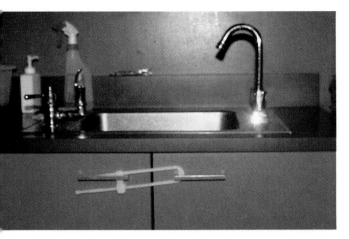

26-11 All accessible cabinet doors need to be equipped with a safety lock when toddlers are near.

Books are also of interest to toddlers. Since they enjoy turning pages, select books with thick pages that are easy to turn. Objects in the book should be recognizable. Book bindings should be strong and sturdy.

Puppets also appeal to young children. Children enjoy puppets that are soft and recognizable. Puppets made out of a fabric, instead of plastic or rubber, are the easiest for the children to work. Before buying puppets, ask if they are washable. It is not uncommon to find a puppet floating in the water table.

The most time consuming activity of toddlers is staring. Approximately one-fifth of their time is spent either sitting or standing and staring. They may stare at a picture, another child, a toy, or even at you. Therefore, always keep the room visually stimulating.

### Lack of interest in toys

Some children will lack interest in a particular toy. This is a sign of *overfamiliarity*. Children who are given the same toy day after day may become bored. Or once they are comfortable with a particular toy they repeat the same actions over and over again. When this happens, new skills do not develop. It is time to provide a different toy that offers new challenges.

Young children like to have a variety of toys. As the teacher, you should change some toys every other day.

### Toy inventory

Many infant-toddler centers maintain a toy inventory that lists all of the equipment available in the center. The inventory is subdivided into developmental sequences. For example, toys are grouped in the following categories:
- Looking toys.
- Reaching and grasping toys.
- Cuddling toys.
- Squeezing and manipulation toys.
- Kicking and hitting toys.
- Pull/push toys.
- Sound toys.
- Large motor toys.
- Small motor toys.

This list is quite helpful when planning activities for children. Since it is important to frequently change toys, the list will help you keep a record of the toys already used and toys that are available. Another advantage of keeping a toy inventory is that it is helpful when ordering new toys. See 25-12 for a sample toy inventory.

### CURRICULUM

A good curriculum is based on the needs of the children attending the center. It is also based on child growth and development principles.

Curriculum for infants or toddlers differs from that planned for older preschool children. Babies set their own goals. As the teacher, you support this growth. The curriculum consists of simple, basic activities. It includes physical activities: being fed, cuddled, held, bathed, rocked, diapered, and taken on walks. It involves both verbal and nonverbal communication: being sung, talked, and listened to; being smiled at and looked at.

Curriculum for toddlers requires more planning. Much of their day will involve activities that promote physical, emotional, intellectual, and social growth. Most of these activities can take place in various activity centers within the center.

# INFANT-TODDLER CENTER TOY INVENTORY

| | |
|---|---|
| LOOKING | —dog mobile<br>—farm animal mobile<br>—shape mobile<br>—metal mirror |
| REACHING AND GRASPING | —ring cradle gym<br>—musical cradle gym<br>—colored cradle gym<br>—colored rattles<br>—frog rattle<br>—car rattle |
| CUDDLING TOYS | —monkey<br>—black bear<br>—baby lamb (with chime)<br>—pink pig<br>—brown pony<br>—black puppy<br>—dolls |
| SQUEEZING/MANIPULATION | —fish squeaker<br>—pretzel squeaker<br>—mouse squeaker<br>—bunny squeaker<br>—pig squaker<br>—busy box<br>—plastic rings<br>—plastic rattles (various colors)<br>—snap beads<br>—chain of plastic discs |
| KICKING AND HITTING | —large rubber beach balls<br>—colored foam balls<br>—bouncing clowns |
| PULL/PUSH | —popper<br>—wooden train (makes a noise)<br>—wooden dog<br>—lawnmower<br>—wooden car<br>—wooden wagon |
| SOUND | —music box<br>—drum<br>—jingle bells<br>—phonograph and records<br>—xylophone<br>—squeaky animals |

*Continued.*

26-12  A toy inventory is useful for planning and buying.

## INFANT-TODDLER CENTER TOY INVENTORY

| LARGE MOTOR | —push toys<br>—animals on wheels<br>—small, light wagon<br>—wheeled train<br>—wheeled lamb<br>—climbing tunnel<br>—small gym<br>—toy trucks big enough to ride |
|---|---|
| SMALL MOTOR | —geometric form board<br>—blocks<br>—snap beads<br>—small cards<br>—nesting cups and boxes<br>—shape box<br>—strings of large beads<br>—sand toys |

*26-12 Continued.*

## Activity centers for toddlers

Similar activities can be grouped into centers around the room. Each center should contain equipment and material that suggests activity to the child. An interesting, well-equipped room invites children to take part. Areas that can be included in a toddler program include art, sensory, fine motor, gross motor, music, and language.

When planning to invite involvement, arrange each area so there will be few rules for children to follow. Try to provide many opportunities for success. Plan activities in which children can freely take part, without your help. Arrange furniture so there is plenty of open space. Place materials within the children's reach. Use materials that do not require your help to use. Plan activities so children can move freely from one activity to another as their interests dictate.

Foresight is the key to successful and safe activity centers. Anticipate and plan for problems. No setting can be entirely safe. However, to reduce hazards, always be alert and attentive to the environment. In addition, study the activity centers and ask yourself:

- Is there enough room for the children to play?
- Are the materials within the children's reach?
- Are the heavy toys stored on the bottom shelves?
- Are the toys developmentally appropriate?
- Are the children provided choices so they can pursue their own interests?
- Are a variety of toys presented including those for solitary play and those that encourage group play?
- Do the play materials respond to the children's actions?
- Are the toys checked frequently for sharp edges, loose pieces, and small parts which could be swallowed?
- Are small play materials picked up off the floor when not in use?
- Are toys rotated?

**Art.** A center for art activities can be fun for toddlers. Plan the area to encourage freedom and creativity. Art activities provide good opportunities for promoting small motor development. Chart 25-13 lists tips for art activities.

## TIPS FOR ART ACTIVITIES

- Provide only nontoxic materials. Young children tend to put materials in their mouths.
- For health reasons, discourage children from eating the materials.
- Allow plenty of space to prevent children from putting paint, chalk, or markers on each other.
- Cover the table and/or floor with a plastic cloth or newspapers to catch spills.
- Provide large plastic bibs to use as art smocks.
- Keep a cloth handy to clean children's hands as soon as they finish activities.
- Wipe spills as they occur to prevent children from slipping or getting dirty.

26-13 Plan safe, healthy art activities. Then toddlers will not need to remember a large number of rules.

Finger painting experiences are quite appealing to young toddlers. Tempera paint, shaving cream, and colored liquid soap can all be used for finger painting. As the children use these items, they learn to sense the different feel of each item.

Older toddlers also enjoy painting. Provide a variety of brushes for this type of experience. Regular art brushes, toothbrushes, small household brushes, and sponge staining brushes may all be used. You will need to mix paint with a thickener to help prevent dripping. Bentonite, starch, or a powdered clothes detergent usually work very well.

Toddlers also enjoy scribbling. Provide a variety of marking tools. Large crayons, chalk, and nontoxic watercolor markers can be used. To help children feel some control over their movements, give younger children larger tools. As their control improves, smaller tools can be used.

According to developmental principles, large muscle development precedes small muscle development. To accommodate large muscle movements, provide large sheets of paper for children to scribble or paint on. If paper is too small, drawings or paintings will run off the paper and onto the table or floor. This will require extra clean-up time.

**Sensory.** Sensory activities should stimulate many of the children's senses. Most involve at least seeing, hearing, and touching. Many teachers often add to some activities the sense of smell. Food flavorings and extracts which have unique scents may be added to some of the activities at the sensory table.

Chart 26-14 lists sensory materials that can be used for toddlers. Small objects that can be inhaled or swallowed should be avoided. Likewise, discourage toddlers from chewing or eating any of the sensory materials.

**Fine motor.** Most fine motor activities will revolve around toys. When choosing toys for these activities, avoid small toys that can be put in the mouth or swallowed. Stacking toys, building blocks, sorting boxes, puzzles, stringing beads, and play dough are all safe toys that promote fine motor development in toddlers. Most of these toys will also provide toddlers with problem solving opportunities. These toys may also provide for hand-eye coordination opportunities.

Rotate the toys in this area to foster interest. Rotate toys as they become less used and developmentally inappropriate.

## SENSORY MATERIALS

- Colored and/or scented water.
- Soap bubbles.
- Small plastic boats.
- Shaving cream, plain or with drops of food coloring.
- Dry or wet sand. Shovels, strainers, and/or small wheeled trucks.
- Wet or dry oatmeal.
- Snow.
- Ice cubes.
- Musical instruments such as drums, tambourines, bells on wrist bands, and cymbals.
- Common foods with strong smells such as peanut butter, popcorn, etc.

26-14 You will find that toddlers are most interested in simple, everyday objects.

**Gross motor.** Gross motor activities can take many forms. These may involve indoor equipment, outdoor equipment, or simple movement. As children crawl, walk, and run, they are developing their gross motor skills.

Much space is needed for gross motor equipment, both indoors and outdoors. Plenty of free space is needed around it. Allow enough space for active use by several children.

Balls, slides, tumbling mats, pull toys, small wagons, and large blocks can all be used to promote gross motor development. The development of the children's large muscles can also be promoted by having them run, crawl, or even chase bubbles outdoors.

**Music.** Young children love music. Background music from a tape or record player is quite enjoyable and soothing for many toddlers. Some toddlers will even move to the music. If they do not, you may want to dance with them. The toddlers may also enjoy hitting drums with their hands or clapping their hands.

**Language.** Although planned activities are not required, you should be encouraging language growth at all times. During play, diapering, bathing, dressing, or feeding, speak or sing to children.

Avoid using baby talk with infants and toddlers. Young children will often mimic your speech patterns. If they hear baby talk, chances are good they will speak baby talk. It is also important to use complete sentences and introduce new words. Use adverbs and adjectives to create colorful descriptions.

Puppets, unbreakable mirrors, books, pictures, posters, and dolls can all be placed on small shelves in the language area. These materials should be placed so the children can safely remove them from the shelves. See 26-15.

### Activity file

Many teachers maintain a file listing activities that have met with success. An activity file can be in index card file or notebook form.

Ideas can be collected in a variety of ways. First, note successful activities you have used. This will help you remember the best activities. Ask other infant-toddler teachers to share their favorite activities. Observe other teachers in your center. Make notes of useful interactions and activities. Attend conferences. Read textbooks and journal articles on infant-toddler care. As you do this, add to your file of good ideas. Record all of the ideas you collect for future use.

### Picture collection

You will also want to start your own picture collection. The best source for obtaining pictures is from calendars, children's books, magazines, and travel posters. Infants and toddlers enjoy large, simple pictures. People, animals, vehicles, and toys have the most appeal.

Before displaying a picture, mount it on a piece of colorful poster board. To frame each picture, leave at least a 1/2-inch border around

26-15 Encouraging children to play with dolls is one way to promote language development.

the entire picture. Since young children enjoy touching pictures, protect them by covering with clear contact paper or laminate.

Organize your picture collection in a large cardboard box. To store the mounted pictures, stand them on end. Use cardboard sheets as dividers to section off different categories.

## PARENT INVOLVEMENT

Keep the parents informed of how their child's day went. Also, encourage parents to inform you of the happenings in the home. When children are first enrolled, always find out their routines at home, food preferences, and favorite toys. You can use a form at enrollment time to record the information, 26-16. This information will help coordinate center and home activities.

To help you provide a quality experience for children, parents' goals and concerns need to be shared. It will also be helpful if any change in the home environment is shared. These changes can cause stress for children, such as a death in the extended family. Other changes may cause pleasure. Examples include a new family pet or a grandparent visiting. Parents should also let the teacher know about such home routines as toilet training.

From time to time you may wish to share reading materials with parents. Information on topics such as toilet training, separation anxiety, language development, and toy selection can be quite useful for parents. Parents also enjoy receiving information on developmental stages. Knowing and watching for stages of normal development can be reassuring to parents.

## RECORD KEEPING

Record keeping is an important part of an infant-toddler program. Such records should track children's eating, sleeping, and eliminating routines, 26-17. Also, keep track of new behaviors and skills as they occur and change over time.

Good records provide valuable information. Parents will be especially interested in their child's daily eating, sleeping, and eliminating patterns. Unusual patterns may signal illness or a need to change the child's diet.

By maintaining a record of the child's skills and behaviors, you will be able to note the child's progress and the start of any problems. Early detection is important for the child's development.

When reporting the child's daily routines to the parents, be objective and factual. Do not be negative or judgmental. Try to state comments in a positive manner. For instance, avoid remarks such as "Mark was very crabby and difficult to be with today." Rather say, "Mark's new tooth was causing him some pain today." This type of comment will leave the parent more open.

Whenever possible, provide the parent with comments in writing. Always make a carbon copy to keep in the child's files. These copies are quite useful when planning a curriculum to meet the child's individual needs.

## ILLNESS POLICIES

Sick children cannot be cared for in a center without endangering the health of other children. An environment for infants and toddlers needs to be healthy. As the teacher, it is your responsibility to maintain the best health conditions. In order to do this properly, you will need to have a center illness policy. This policy will help staff and parents decide whether a child is too sick to be brought to or remain in the center.

The policies you develop for your center must abide by your state's rules and regulations for running day care centers. Eye infections, temperatures, diarrhea, respiratory infections, rashes, contagious diseases, bronchitis, and vomiting all need to be addressed. In general, most centers restrict children with a fever of 101 °F orally or 102 °F rectally, contagious diseases, diarrhea, or vomiting other than spitting up after feeding.

Prior to enrollment, every parent should be given a copy of the center's illness policies. At this time, it should be stressed that a primary objective of the program is to protect the

## INFANT TODDLER CENTER

CHILD'S NAME _____ BIRTHDATE _____

HOME ADDRESS _____ HOME PHONE _____

-------------------------------------------------------------------------------

MOTHER'S NAME _____     FATHER'S NAME _____

PLACE OF EMPLOYMENT _____     PLACE OF EMPLOYMENT _____

PHONE NUMBER _____     PHONE NUMBER _____

-------------------------------------------------------------------------------

IF THERE ARE ANY SPECIAL FAMILY CIRCUMSTANCES SUCH AS DIVORCE, SEPARATION, REMARRIAGE, PARENTAL DEATH, ADOPTION, ETC., PLEASE INDICATE THEM.

_____

_____

IN CASE OF EMERGENCY, WHO SHOULD BE NOTIFIED?

NAME _____ PHONE _____

NAME _____ PHONE _____

DOCTOR OR CLINIC _____

### ENVIRONMENT AND EXPERIENCES

| Names of brothers and sisters | birthdate | school attending |
|---|---|---|
| _____ | _____ | _____ |
| _____ | _____ | _____ |
| _____ | _____ | _____ |

How does your child react when you leave him or her with someone other than a parent?

_____

Name any previous day care centers used _____

_____

What was your child's response? _____

*Continued.*

26-16 Stress to parents the importance of the information on this form.

**PHYSICAL DEVELOPMENT**

**Toilet Training:**

Is your child completely toilet trained now? _____

Does he/she usually stay dry all day? _____

**Eating Habits:**

In general, describe your child's attitude toward eating.

What are his/her special food likes?

What are his/her special food dislikes?

Does your child have any food allergies?

Are there any special characteristics or problems which the school should know about in order to be of most help to your child and your family? Include any vision, hearing, physical difficulties, and unusual abilities or disabilities of which you are aware.

**FAVORITE TOYS**

Describe your child's favorite toys.

*26-16 Continued.*

**DAILY CARE RECORD**

CHILD'S NAME  Susie Olm _____  DATE  Aug. 6th _____

TEACHER  Pat Denk _____

**Feeding Schedule**

|  | Time/Amount | Time/Amount | Time/Amount |
|---|---|---|---|
| Milk | 8:30/8 oz. | 12:15/6 oz. | 3 p.m./6 oz. |
| Food | 12:15  1 oz. carrots<br>1 oz. turkey<br>4:50  4 oz. apple | 3 p.m. 2 oz. custard | |
| Juice | juice | | |
| Water | 10 a.m.  2 oz. | 2 p.m. 3 oz. | |

**Diapering Check**  (W-wet, BM-bowel movement, X-no change needed)

A.M.      8:30            X            **NOTES**

9:15            W

10:15           X

11:00          W/BM

P.M.      1:00            W

2:00            X

3:00            W

4:00            X

5:00            W

**Sleeping Patterns**

10:45 a.m.  to  12:15 p.m.

3:15 p.m.   to  4:45 p.m.

_____  to  _____

_____  to  _____

26-17  Supply a copy of the daily care record to each
parent when they pick up their child from the center.

children's health. Thus, center illness policies are always adhered to. An example of a center illness policy is shown in 26-18.

## SUMMARY

Infants and toddlers are at a special stage in their lives. They are just learning about their world and yet they learn and grow quickly. The care they receive at this stage is quite important for later development.

Caring for infants and toddlers requires skill in areas unique to the age group. Stress is shifted toward care of daily routines such as eating, diapering, and sleeping. However, infants and toddlers also require interesting, but simple, activities.

---

**INFANT TODDLER CENTER ILLNESS POLICY**

To protect all the children's health, you must keep your child home when she/he has:
- An oral temperature of 101 °F or above or a rectal temperature of 102 °F or above.
- Diarrhea.
- Vomiting that extends beyond the usual spitting up.
- Bronchitis symptoms, including hoarseness and/or cough.
- A severe cold that is accompanied with a fever and nose drainage.
- A rash that has not been diagnosed by a doctor.
- Impetigo, chicken pox, mumps, measles, scarlet fever, or whooping cough.

26-18 An illness policy helps avoid misunderstandings when infants and toddlers are ill.

## to Know

overfamiliarity

## to Review

1. Characteristics of a successful infant-toddler teacher include:
   a. A positive attitude.
   b. Patience.
   c. Understanding.
   d. All of the above.
2. List three ways an infant-toddler teacher can stay informed of new research in the field.
3. Complete the following guidelines for infant-toddler care.
   a. Provide children with a _____ and _____ environment.
   b. _____ children for their ethnic and family identity.
   c. Avoid _____ caused by providing too many activities.
4. Space for infants should address their _____ _____.
5. What is the reasoning behind locating the feeding area near the entrance to the center?
6. True or false. The diapering area requires the most space in the center.
7. Name the five major areas in the toddler space.
8. True or false. If an infant's rhythm varies from your rhythm, you should train the child to function at your rhythm.
9. All infants and toddlers require their needs to be met promptly if they are to learn to _____.
10. Always respond to a baby's crying by:
    a. Ignoring the baby.
    b. Giving it a bottle.
    c. Trying to solve the problem.
    d. None of the above.
11. What is separation anxiety?
12. Describe how to feed an infant.
13. Should toddlers be encouraged to smell, touch, and push around their food before eating? Why or why not?
14. Why should liquid soap be used in the diapering area?
15. One consideration for planning a nap time schedule is to check _____ _____.
16. True or false. Contaminated hands are a common cause of the spread of illness in day care centers.
17. What toy colors are most likely to attract the attention of infants?
18. Name two advantages of keeping a toy inventory.
19. In terms of curriculum, babies should set their own _____.
20. Toddlers' days are largely taken up by activities that promote _____, _____, _____, and _____ growth.
21. Activities to include in an activity file can be collected by:
    a. Noting successful activities you have used.
    b. Asking other teachers to share their most successful activities.
    c. Attending conferences to learn more about designing activities.
    d. All of the above.

## to Do

1. Collect and compare illness policies from three day care centers.
2. Add 10 activities for toddlers to an activity file.
3. Practice directing the proper handwashing procedures using large, plastic dolls or classmates.
4. Design an infant space on a large piece of tagboard.
5. Visit a hospital. Ask about the care of infants in the hospital. Report your findings back to your classmates.
6. Invite a pediatrician to talk to your class about preventing illnesses in infants and toddlers.
7. Collect daily care records from several centers. Discuss the contents of each.
8. Interview several parents. Ask them the type of teacher characteristics they desire in an infant or toddler teacher. Share your findings with the class.

# Chapter 27

# *Guiding Special Needs Children*

After studying this chapter, you will be able to:
- ☐ Develop an individualized educational plan for a special needs child.
- ☐ Explain the role of the teacher in working with special needs children.
- ☐ Describe methods for identifying and working with special needs that may be encountered in the early childhood program: Hearing, speech, language, vision, physical, and health disorders.
- ☐ Describe methods for integrating special needs children into a typical program.
- ☐ Explain the special needs of gifted children and how they can be met.

Tommy, a lively four-year-old, has a hearing impairment. He can speak and understand only a few simple words. Rosie, an active five-year-old, is color deficient. She cannot identify the primary colors. Stephen has cerebral palsy. He needs special help to develop fine motor skills. Toby is a two-year-old who has taught herself to read. These children can be identified as having special needs.

By law, children who have special needs can be enrolled in a regular classroom. Since 1972, Head Start has mandated the enrollment of handicapped children if their parents desire to enroll them. In 1975, Public Law 94-142 was passed. This law requires that children with special needs be provided with a free, appropriate public education when they reach three years of age. A special curriculum should be designed to meet their unique needs.

*Mainstreaming* is the term used for placing special needs children in a regular classroom. This process allows children to learn in a less restrictive environment. It allows normal and special needs children to gain skills interacting with each other. In this type of environment, special needs children have "normal" children as role models. This interaction can lead to developmental imitation, 27-1.

There are many types of special needs. Communication needs are the most common. These usually fall into three categories: hearing, speech, and language problems. Visual, orthopedic, and crippling health are other types of special needs. Culturally distinct, gifted, and talented children also have special needs.

Assistants and volunteers can be most useful in mainstreaming. Instruct all staff members on the nature of the condition and how they are to help. Encourage adults to meet the special needs of the children in group settings if possible. To do this, the staff may have to adapt classroom materials, change expectations, and/or give extra help when needed.

Nonhandicapped children can also assist in mainstreaming by helping a handicapped child adjust to the environment. The nonhandicapped child might introduce the other child to the classroom setting. At times, the nonhandicapped child can help the child organize his or her materials or practice a new skill.

A word of caution is necessary when working with children with special needs. Sometimes the other children in the classroom will want to do too much for special needs children. They try to "help" by doing the special needs children's work for them or by helping them with their self-help skills. Remind the children that assistance should be provided only when needed. Encourage staff, volunteers, and the other children to be patient and give extra encouragement to special needs children.

## INDIVIDUALIZED EDUCATIONAL PLANS

Public Law 94-142 requires that Individualized Educational Plans (IEP's) be written for each handicapped child. Some special needs children will come to your center already identified. These children will already have IEP's. Usually an IEP is written for a 12-month period extending from October 1st to September 30th.

The purpose of an *Individualized Educational Plan* is to ensure that each special needs child has his or her own plan. By law, parents are allowed to take part in designing their child's program. This plan is jointly developed by the teacher, the parents or guardians, and experts on the particular handicap. A copy of the plan is given to the parent(s).

Each IEP needs six components. These components are:
1. A description of the child's current level of performance.
2. Annual goals for the child.
3. Short-term educational objectives.
4. A statement outlining the involvement of the child in the regular educational program.
5. Educational services that will be provided with a time line noting the dates services will begin and end.
6. Criteria that will be used to decide if educational objectives are met.

27-1 Playing alongside normal children helps special needs children gain confidence and learn new skills.

## TEACHERS' ROLES

Teachers' roles have changed since Head Start mandated including special needs children and Public Law 94-142 was passed. Now teachers need to:

- Take part in identifying special needs children.
- Work with speech clinicians, school psychologists, health professionals, and other resource persons to design individual programs.
- Deal with special needs children and normal children in the same classroom.
- Share information with parents and make suggestions for referrals.

First, as a teacher, you will need to learn how to identify special needs children. Then you will need to develop a basic understanding of the learning needs of children with hearing, visual, speech, physical, and health handicaps. With this knowledge, you can then adapt the curriculum and classroom environment to meet the special needs.

### Identification

Early identification of special needs is the key to a child's successful development, 27-2. Children who are not identified early may go through years of failure. This failure, in turn, can create a poor self-concept which can compound the disability.

Many young children's special needs are identified after they enter a preschool program. Often, identification is made by an adult who is not part of the family. You, as a teacher, may be the first to detect a speech, visual, or hearing problem. You also may be the first to note a cognitive, emotional, or physical handicap.

To learn to identify special needs, you need to understand normal, or average, development. When a problem is suspected, observe the child closely. Informal observation may be used for assessing a child's needs. These observations may be noted on cards or paper. When recording observations, mention those signs of behaviors that suggest a special need. Any unusual social, cognitive, emotional, or physical development could signal a possible special need.

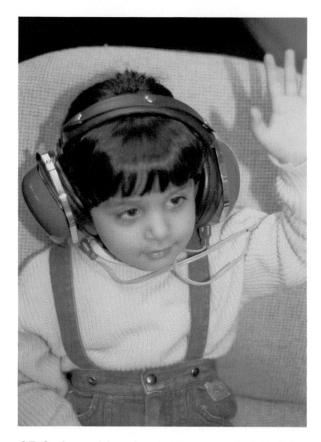

27-2 Annual hearing tests are a vital tool for identifying hearing problems early.

For instance, you may suspect a certain child has a special need. Developmentally, there appears to be something not quite normal. In this case, you observe the child closely. Make notes about any unusual behavior. If Terry cannot identify primary colors after studying color concepts a number of times, observe her closely. Ask yourself, "Could Terry be color deficient?"

A number of techniques can be used to collect data. You might study a child's work, 27-3. Photographs and video tapes are also useful. Scales or checklists that name skills children of certain ages should be able to perform can be helpful.

After you have made and confirmed your findings, alert the center director. The director may wish to confirm your observations. He or she may give other tests to measure the child's abilities. After this, a conference will likely be scheduled with the child's parent(s).

Begin the conference by introducing the suspected problem. Share your observations. Provide the parents with examples from your observations. Ask the parents if they have noticed any of these behaviors at home. If their observations confirm yours, suggest a formal diagnosis.

Some parents may not share your concern. If this is the case, keep making your observations and schedule more conferences. It sometimes helps to ask the parents to take part in structured observations in the home and school. Remember, any delay in diagnosis can hinder the child's development.

### Referrals

When the parent(s) agree a problem may exist, direct them to obtain a diagnosis. You may be able to suggest a professional they can take their child to see. This is called a *referral.* Vision or physical problems may first be referred to a county or school health nurse. Hearing, language, or speech problems may be referred to a speech clinician. Learning and behavioral problems are most often referred to a school psychologist or local agency.

Two other options exist for referrals. The parent(s) may choose to hire a professional on their own. Or, depending on the state, a referral may be made to the Department of Social Services.

### Labeling

Special needs children should not be labeled after the diagnosis. Labels usually focus on one aspect of a child, his or her disability. Labeling may lead to development of negative expectations by other children. They may describe the child by saying, "She is blind," or, "He is deaf." Labeling may also cause future teachers of a child to be biased. As a result, they may have lowered expectations of the child.

## HEARING DISORDERS

A hearing impaired child can be identified often by his or her lack of vocabulary compared to average children. This child may only

27-3 If a child's work is quite different from work of other children that age, this may indicate a special need.

speak a few simple words. Before you begin to alter your program, learn the extent of the child's hearing loss. This information can only be learned through a professional.

The child's hearing loss may range from mild to profound. With a mild hearing loss, the child's vocabulary will not be as large as that of his or her peers who have normal hearing. This child often also has difficulty during large group activities, stories, and field trips. The child may miss as much as half of what is being communicated.

A child with a moderate hearing loss will also have trouble in large group situations. This child has a limited vocabulary. To understand the child's speech, you should stand face-to-face. This will allow you to read the child's lips.

Children with severe, or profound, hearing loss have little understandable speech. These children must rely largely on their vision to communicate.

To make up for hearing losses, many children will wear either a hearing aid in their ear or a Y-shaped hearing aid over their chests. The advantage of the ear hearing aid is that it can be adjusted to compensate for the hearing loss in each ear. The Y-shaped aid is the most popular. It has one hearing aid with tubes going to both ears.

It is important that you understand the type of hearing aid used by a child. Ask the parents to tell you about it. If it falls out of the child's ear during program hours, you will need to replace it. You should also know how to check batteries. Keep a ready supply on hand.

The purpose of the hearing aid is to amplify and magnify all sounds. It will not perfect a child's hearing. In fact, most hearing aids are only useful within a 10-foot radius.

### Teaching suggestions

When approaching a hearing impaired child, get down to the child's eye level, 27-4. Then get the child's attention before speaking. Sometimes this can be done by lightly touching the child's hand or arm. With practice, you will learn how close you must stand in order to be understood. You should also follow these suggestions:

- Speak in a normal volume and speed.
- Use the same sentence structure as you would for other children.
- Pause and wait for a response after you speak.
- If the child does not understand you, repeat, rephrase, or demonstrate.
- Encourage other children to imitate you when they communicate with the child. That is, they need to get the child's attention, look into his or her eyes, and speak at a normal volume and speed.
- Whenever needed, use gestures to reinforce the spoken word.
- In a group situation, let the child sit in front of you. This will encourage him or her to watch your body language and lips as you speak.

In addition to using these teaching strategies, adapt the curriculum for the hearing impaired child. Before you begin making these changes, however, you may wish to consult a language and speech clinician.

Visual skills are important for hearing impaired children. Their finely-tuned visual skills make up for their lack of hearing. To provide for their needs, stress visual activities.

- Use concrete materials to demonstrate abstract concepts. For example, if you are

27-4 The key to working with hearing impaired children is to modify your teaching methods to meet the needs of the child.

talking about pumpkins, use a real pumpkin or a picture of a pumpkin. (Avoid drawing on the blackboard as you are talking. These children need to see your face as you communicate with them.)

- Provide a variety of classification games and puzzles for the child to practice visual perception skills.
- Label classroom furniture and materials.
- Select books with simple, large, and uncluttered illustrations. These children will rely more on vision than hearing during story time.
- Teach safety by using traffic signals with the wheeled toys in the play yard.
- Teach daily routines and transitions using a light switch. Flash the light to get the child's attention.
- Use a picture poster to point to the upcoming activity.

## SPEECH AND LANGUAGE DISORDERS

A child may come to school and refuse to talk. Another child may speak but cannot be understood by teachers or peers. Still another child may not be able to recall sentences correctly. These children have speech and language disorders.

### Identification

Before programs can be altered you must identify the problem. Informal observations are the most common method used to identify speech and language problems. Chart 27-5 contains a checklist to use when observing for these problems. You will need to listen carefully as the child speaks. Listen to both sounds and content.

When a child is having trouble pronouncing words, record those sounds causing the difficulty. Young children find the consonants p, b, m, w, and vowels the easiest to pronounce. Cr, bl, sh, ch, th, j, r, l, and z are more difficult sounds to pronounce and take longer to learn. Chart 27-6 contains the approximate ages at which most children use certain sounds.

Observe and listen to children in a variety of settings: on the play yard, in the housekeep-

---

### SPEECH OBSERVATION CHECKLIST

1. Do the sounds the child makes match those listed for his or her age group on a developmental chart?
2. Is the rate and fluency of the child's speech appropriate for his or her age group?
3. Is the child's speech understandable?
4. Does the amount of talking done appear to be normal?
5. Does the child recall and repeat sentences correctly?

27-5 If you suspect a speech disorder, observe the child, paying close attention to the items listed.

### DEVELOPMENTAL ORDER FOR SPEECH SOUNDS

| Age | Sounds | | | | | |
|-----|--------|--------|--------|--------|--------|--------|
| 1 1/2-3 1/2 | (p) | (m) | (h) | (n) | (w) | (b) |
| 2-4 | (k) | (d) | (t) | (n) | (g) | |
| 2 1/2-5 1/2 | (f) | (y) | | | | |
| 3-6 | (r) | (l) | (s) | | | |
| 3 1/2-7 | (ch) | (sh) | (z) | | | |
| 4 1/2-8 | (j) | (r) | | | | |

27-6 Keep these parameters in mind when observing a child you believe may have a speech disorder.

---

ing area, during lunch time, and as they converse with others. As you identify the problem, make notes and continue observing to collect information.

Based on repeated observations, you may conclude a child most likely does have a speech problem. Share your observations with your director. The director will determine whether a parent conference should be scheduled.

### Articulation disorders

The term "lazy tongue" and "baby talk" are frequently used to describe articulation problems. These terms focus on the child's tongue or developmental level as being the problem. Neither is true. ***Articulation problems*** are most often omissions, distortions, or substitutions of vowels or consonants or both. It is possible for a child to have one or more of these problems.

Certain speech sounds are left out in an omission error. This results in only a part of a word being said. For example, a child may say "oat" for "boat." Or, the child may say "had" for the name "Thad."

A child with a distortion problem sometimes has trouble identifying the intended sound. For example, instead of pronouncing an S, a child may suck air in between his or her teeth.

Substitutions involve speech patterns such as "thome" for "some" or "tate" for "cake." The most common sound substitutions include f for th, t for k, b for v, th for s, k for t, and w for l or r. A common substitution problem is a lisp. It involves substituting a "th" sound for the letter s.

After a child has been diagnosed as having an articulation problem, consult a speech clinician. Ask for advice on how to help the child.

As a teacher, your reaction to the child with articulation problems has a great effect. To help a child feel secure, always react positively. Ensure that the other children do, too. If the child does not respond verbally, do not demand a response. Instead provide the correct answer for him or her.

Model good listening skills and speaking skills with all the children. Give the children your total attention. Look directly into their faces as they speak. Verbally respond with interest to what the children are saying. If you do not understand, ask the children to repeat what they have said.

Children with articulation problems need to be encouraged to talk. Set an example by feeding in language when they take in activities. To illustrate, you may say to a child, "You are placing a large red block in the square hole," as he or she plays with a sorting box.

Use language that is proper for the child's developmental level. For example, the child may point to a large red car and say "far." You should then say, "That is a large, red car." This technique is called ***expansion.*** It involves taking the child's mispronounced words and correctly expanding them into sentences.

Some children are more comfortable talking about things that are special to them. One technique you can use is to have the child bring something special from home. Then have him or her tell everyone about the item.

Always provide a variety of activities in your classroom. The wider the variety, the more the children will have to talk about. Try to relate classroom activities to children's home experiences and cultural backgrounds.

Demand speech from all children, including those with articulation problems. Do this by asking open-ended questions. Instead of asking, "Did you like the book?" ask, "What did you like about the book?"

**Stuttering**

*Stuttering* in young children is often characterized by repetition, hesitation, and prolongation. Few young children stutter all the time. It is often only under certain conditions that some children stutter.

In the early stages of language development, many children experience stuttering. This most often occurs when they feel pressured, 27-7. Children function best in a warm, noncritical classroom. This type of environment helps all children speak with confidence.

If you have a stuttering child in your classroom, focus on creating good speaking conditions:
- Plan activities so all children will experience success.
- Provide the child with enough time to say what he or she has to say.
- Listen closely to what the child is saying, as opposed to focusing on the stuttering.
- Avoid rushing a child through a task.

Unfortunately, many well-meaning people try to provide directions to a stuttering child. "Stop and think," "Start over," and "Speak slower" are common examples. These suggestions often make the child feel even more fearful. A child's difficulty could continue as a result of this fear. An environment free of pressure is important.

422

### Voice (phonation) disorders

Voice characteristics include pitch, loudness, flexibility, and quality. The lowness or highness of the voice is the **pitch.** It is not uncommon for some children to use a pitch that is too low or too high.

Loudness is related to the amount of energy or volume used when speaking. The voice may be strong or weak. A strong voice will be loud and can be disturbing. A weak voice may be hard to hear and can also hinder communication.

A good speaking voice during routine conversation uses a variety of pitches and loudness levels. This is referred to as *voice flexibility.* Changes in pitch and loudness often reflect the emotions of the speaker.

Harshness, hoarseness, breathiness, and nasality are all voice-quality disorders. The harsh voice is often louder than normal. Hoarseness may indicate a problem in the throat. A breathy voice sounds like a whisper.

It is weak and not clearly phonated. Nasality is a condition in which sound passes through the nasal cavities instead of the throat.

To help prevent or correct voice disorders, promote voice control:

- Encourage children to use the correct voice volume during indoor play. You may need to say, "Teddy, you need to use your indoor voice in the building."
- Discourage children from screaming or yelling too much during outdoor play.
- Model good voice characteristics. Your own voice should be the proper pitch, loudness, quality, and flexibility.

## VISION DISORDERS

One of the smallest groups of special needs children is the visually impaired. Common vision problems include amblyopia, nearsightedness, farsightedness, and/or a color deficiency. Physically, children with visual impairments are similar to children with normal vision. However, this handicap can limit the motor abilities of these children as they take part in some physical activities. See 27-8.

27-7 Children who feel pressured are more likely to stutter than children who are relaxed.

27-8 Children with visual impairments often lack small muscle coordination. They need to experiment with an art medium to build these skills.

To understand visual impairments, you need to understand how a healthy visual system works. Despite young children's thinking, the eye does not actually see. The purpose of the eye is to take in light. After it has taken in light, the eye transmits impulses to the brain through the optic nerve. The brain then decodes the visual stimuli, and "seeing" takes place. Most defects of the eye itself are correctable. If the brain or the optic nerve is damaged, however, the impairment is not correctable.

## Early identification

Early identification of a visual impairment is important. Many day care centers have a volunteer from the National Society for the Prevention of Blindness, a county health nurse, or some other professional conduct a visual screening each year. Children who appear to have problems are given a referral for a complete exam by an eye specialist.

Classroom staff need to observe children closely to identify vision problems. Certain symptoms may suggest problems:
- Excessive rubbing of the eyes.
- Clumsiness and trouble moving around the classroom.
- Adjusting the head in an awkward position to view materials.
- Moving materials so they are close to the eyes.
- Squinting.
- Crossed eyes; crust on eye; swollen, red eyelids.

## Types of visual handicaps

There are a number of common visual impairments that young children may have. Amblyopia is likely a disorder you might note in your classroom. You may also find children with glaucoma, nearsightedness, farsightedness, a color deficiency, and some uncorrectable conditions.

**Amblyopia.** This disorder is often called *lazy eye*. *Amblyopia* is the result of a muscle imbalance caused by disuse of an eye. It is one of several visual conditions that can be corrected if found during early childhood. To force the use of the weaker eye, a patch is placed over the stronger eye. If this does not work, surgery may be required. If treatment of the amblyopia is not done by age six or seven, the child's vision may always be poor.

**Glaucoma.** *Glaucoma* is a condition caused by failure of the eye fluid to circulate in the proper way. The lack of fluid results in increased pressure on the eye. Over time, this pressure can destroy the optic nerve. This problem can be treated with eye drops if diagnosed early. This will prevent loss of vision.

**Nearsightedness.** Some children may be unable to see things that are far away. These children suffer from *nearsightedness.* The medical term for this visual disorder is *myopia.* It results when the eye focuses in front of the retina.

**Farsightedness.** Children who have a difficult time seeing objects that are close to them suffer from *farsightedness.* The medical term for this visual disorder is called *hyperopia.* It is caused by having the visual image focus behind the retina.

**Color deficiency.** *Color deficiency,* or *color blindness* as it is sometimes called, is the inability to see a color. This problem is hereditary. It mostly affects males and is caused by a recessive gene. You should be able to quickly identify children with color deficiencies. They are not able to recognize one or more primary colors.

**Uncorrectable conditions.** There are several visual disorders that cannot be corrected by glasses, surgery, or other means of treatment. Any damage to the optic nerve by disease or trauma is an example. After damage, signals do not get to the brain to provide the child with sight.

## Teaching suggestions

You may need to make changes in your classroom depending on the visual needs of the children. The following teaching suggestions may be helpful:
- Always create a need to see. For instance, if farsighted children refuse to wear their glasses, provide them with materials that have fine detail and print. The children will then realize the importance of wearing their glasses.

- Include a study unit on sight to help all the children understand vision.
- When ordering blackboards, purchase those with a dull finish. Glare can be very tiring for partially-sighted children.
- Hang all the children's work at their eye level.
- Safety is always important. To ensure a safe environment, blocks, cars, and other items should be picked up right after play.
- Auditory clues are important for children with visual impairments. Provide a comfortable environment by keeping the noise level low.
- In the reading area, always have a number of large print books with clear, simple pictures.
- Provide many tactile (touch), olfactory (smell), and auditory clues to structure the environment for the child, 27-9. For instance, use a piece of shag carpeting in the story area and a bubbling aquarium or fragrant flowers in the science area.
- Use auditory reminders for transition times. These may include singing a song, beating a drum, playing a piano, or hitting tone bells.
- During activities, always encourage children to describe what they remember using their senses.

Remember that children with visual impairments may need to learn some skills children with normal vision already have. For instance, children with normal vision acquire eating, toileting, and dressing skills by watching others. A visually impaired child, however, may not possess these skills when he or she comes to the center. You will need to teach these skills. You will also need to teach the child the classroom areas. Do this by repeatedly guiding the child from one area to another.

## PHYSICAL DISORDERS

Most preschool children can crawl, walk, run, climb, and move their bodies in different ways. A child with a physical impairment may only be able to crawl or walk. Due to this limitation, his or her experiences may vary from his or her peers.

### Types of physical disorders

Like other children with special needs, physically impaired children are grouped based on their ability to function. Impairments are classified as severe, moderate, or mild. Children with severe impairments usually cannot move from one place to another. Typically, they have to be carried, pushed, or moved about with the use of a wheelchair. Children with moderate impairments can do more for themselves, but they still require much help from staff members. Due to their lack of mobility, children with severe or moderate physical impairment are seldom enrolled in the typical day care center.

Children with mild physical impairments can often do what most other children do. These children may need to use a walker, crutches, or other devices to help them move about. As

27-9 Activities involving touch are especially important for children with vision disorders.

can be expected, they will need more time to move about or to do tasks.

The children you will meet in the typical day care center will be **ambulatory**. They will be able to move from place to place. You may elect, however, to work in a center that caters to special-needs children. In these centers you will observe a higher staff to child ratio. This is necessary to meet the special needs of these children.

### Cerebral palsy

*Cerebral palsy* results from damage to the brain. This damage can be caused by an infection or improper nutrition during pregnancy, physical injury to the brain during birth, or lack of oxygen during birth. It can also be acquired during the developmental years as a result of a tumor, head injury, or brain infection. Cerebral palsy is characterized by lack of control of voluntary movements.

Speech problems are often found in children with cerebral palsy. These problems are caused by the inability to control the muscles used to make speech sounds. If a child in your group has a speech disorder, consult with the parents and a speech clinician.

Cerebral palsy children also often lack fine motor skills. Many of their self-help skills are impaired. Eating utensils and other equipment may be difficult for them to use. A physical therapist and the child's parents can best advise what type of eating utensils, crayons, and other items are most useful. Modifications may be needed on equipment. For example, you may want to glue large wooden knobs on puzzles so the child with cerebral palsy can remove and insert the pieces.

### Spina bifida

*Spina bifida* is a condition in which the bones of the spine fail to grow together. The nerves are left exposed. This results in paralysis. This is a *congenital defect* (caused before birth but not hereditary), the cause of which is unknown. Children with this problem many times lack bowel and bladder control. They often cannot tell when they are wet because of lower body paralysis.

In order for a child with spina bifida to focus on learning activities, he or she needs to feel comfortable. You may need to ask such questions as, "Are you comfortable?" or, "Do you want to sit another way?" To provide the best environment for this child, discuss positions with the parents and physical therapist. They may suggest positions which will provide the child with a sense of balance. Specific questions you may want to ask them include, "Should learning activities be on the floor or table?" and "Should the classroom tables be modified?"

### Amputation

At some point, you may have a child in your classroom who is missing a hand, arm, or leg. Perhaps the severed limb resulted from an accident or cancer. Sometimes the limb is missing from birth. A child who is missing a limb is often fitted with an artificial limb called a **prosthesis**. Research has shown that it is quite easy for a young child to adjust to an artificial limb, 27-10.

In order to use a prosthesis, it must fit properly. To avoid frustrating the child, you, as a teacher, will need to know how the artificial limb works. Parents usually welcome a

27-10 With the help of artificial limbs, this child can take part in many of the same activities as other children.

teacher's questions related to the device. In fact, these questions assure them of your interest in providing the best care for their child.

## Teaching suggestions

Although it is difficult for some, movement is important for all children. Children with physical handicaps may have to crawl or move with special equipment such as wheelchairs and crutches. As a result, they need more time and energy to do small and large motor tasks. It takes them longer to go to the bathroom or to finish a project. To allow for this, you will need to provide time in your schedule. You may also have to make some adjustments in the facility:

* Modify chairs to accommodate the child.
* Provide space for a child's wheelchair, crutches, cane, walker, or cart.
* Provide ramps so the child has access to the classroom.
* Raise tables so wheelchairs fit under them.
* Glue knobs on puzzle pieces so the pieces are easy to remove and replace.
* Secure all carpeting or area rugs to the floor so the child does not slip or trip on them.
* Provide double handled mugs and deep-sided bowls rather than plates.
* Serve finger foods as often as possible at snack time.

## HEALTH DISORDERS

Some children miss school more often than others. These are often the children with chronic health needs. A *chronic health need* can be defined as an illness that persists over a period of time. For some children, a problem may last a lifetime, while for others, it may last a few months.

Children with health problems have cycles of good and poor health. Since health needs are the most common type of special needs, it is vital that you be aware of a variety of these disorders.

## Allergies

The most common health problem of young children is allergies. Studies note that up to 50 percent of all people have mild or severe allergies. An allergy may begin at any age. Studies also note that only a small percentage of children with allergies have been diagnosed.

An *allergy* is a sensitivity to something. This sensitivity may cause rashes, swelling, sneezing, or other reactions, 27-11. There are four categories of allergenic substances: inhalents, ingestants, contactants, and injectables. *Inhalants* are airborne substances that are inhaled. *Ingestants* are foods, drugs, or anything taken through the mouth. *Contactants* are things that make contact with the body through touch. *Injectables* are chemicals or drugs injected into the body.

Animal dandruff, dust, feathers, fungi spores, molds, and plant pollens are all types of airborne allergenic substances. If a child in your classroom has a severe allergy to animal dandruff, you may have to remove any hamsters, gerbils, or guinea pigs.

Beans, berries, chocolate, cinnamon, citrus fruits, corn starch, cola drinks, eggs, fish,

27-11 An allergic reaction to an insect bite may cause swelling and skin irritation.

shellfish, milk, tomatoes, and wheat are typical foods that the body reacts to. Fabric dyes and fragrances or colorings added to soaps and shampoos are contactants that may also cause reactions. Aspirin, penicillin, and sulfa drugs are common drugs that are offenders. It is important that you ask parents at the time of enrollment whether their child has any known allergies.

If a child has food allergies, you will need to plan accordingly. Try to plan menus which avoid foods to which the child is allergic. At times, you may have to offer the allergic child food substitutes. For instance, if a child has an allergy to milk, you will have to supply another type of milk or substitute. Many times parents will provide the substitute to make sure their child is not tempted to have cow's milk.

Cosmetics, some detergents, wool, and starch are all substances that may cause an allergic reaction when they come in contact with the skin. Common reactions include a red rash and itching. These symptoms are a warning that the child is to avoid contact with whatever substance caused the problem.

Some substances cause a reaction when they enter the body through the skin. Examples include the venom from bee stings and mosquitoes, and the drug penicillin. You need to be keenly aware of insect bites. For some children, these bites can be fatal.

Bee stings usually result in redness and swelling around the wound. This indicates only a mild allergy. With a severe allergy, the child may swell all over the body and have trouble breathing. If this should occur, promptly seek medical attention. Death can result if treatment is not received immediately.

Some symptoms of allergies may be related to the season. For example, a child who is allergic to tree pollens may sneeze often in the spring. There are three major pollen seasons: early spring with tree pollens, late spring or early summer with grass pollens, and late summer and fall with weed pollens.

You may be the first to suspect allergies in a young child. Allergy symptoms are listed in 27-12. If you suspect that a child has a problem, discuss it with his or her parent(s).

You may be responsible for following through on some aspects of treatment for children with allergies. There are three basic treatment methods for people with allergies. The sensitive person may avoid the offending item. For instance, if a child is allergic to chocolate, foods with chocolate should be taken out of the diet.

If the person cannot avoid the irritant, he or she may be *desensitized*. In this process, a doctor injects small amounts of the allergen into the body over a period of time. This builds immunities so the person is eventually able to withstand the irritant.

## ALLERGY SYMPTOMS

**Eyes**
- pink and puffy
- red from being constantly rubbed
- dark circles underneath
- burning feeling and much tearing
- lids may appear glued together by dry mucus

**Mouth**
- constant dry hacking cough
- mouth breathing more common than nose breathing
- wheezing
- canker sores

**Nose**
- running nose
- inability to smell
- nasal discharge
- frequent sneezing
- itchy nose

**Skin**
- frequent rashes
- lesions

**Throat**
- tickling
- enlargment of lymph nodes

**Body**
- chills
- fever
- sweating
- abdominal cramps
- vomiting

27-12 Allergies are quite common in young children. As a result it is vital that you recognize symptoms of more common allergies.

Finally, medication may be used to treat the symptom. For example, a person who has nasal congestion and blockage would use a medication to control this symptom.

## Arthritis

*Arthritis* is a condition brought on by inflammation of joints and surrounding tissues. The most common form of juvenile arthritis is called *rheumatoid arthritis.* General fatigue, loss of appetite, aching joints, and a stiffness of joints as they become tender from swelling are the first signs of the disease.

After 10 years, 60 to 70 percent of affected children are free from juvenile arthritis. Adults who acquire the condition have a much smaller chance of recovery.

Arthritic children often find it difficult to remain in one position for long periods of time. They also may require more time to move from one place to another. When the disease is in its active stage, the child will need more rest.

## Asthma

*Asthma* is a disease characterized by a recurrent shortness of breath. An annoying cough, wheezing, and whistling breathing also often occur with asthma. An attack may last for weeks or for just a few hours. Some people are never free from asthma.

Asthma is often caused by allergies. In some cases, an attack may be caused by overextension and excitement. An attack may be relieved using medication. The medication is most often either a pill or inhaler.

Many children with asthma are allergic to dust. To prevent their attacks, you may have to make some changes in the physical environment. You may have to remove stuffed toys, pillows, rugs, or curtains. If this is not possible, make sure that the room is cleaned well each day. It is best to have the room vacuumed in the evening. This will allow the dust to settle by morning when the children return.

## Cystic fibrosis

*Cystic fibrosis* is a hereditary disease that occurs almost from birth. This chronic condition involves persistent and serious lung infections, failure to gain weight, and loose, foul-smelling stools. Some of these symptoms are caused by a thick mucus produced by the sweat glands. This mucus interferes with the digestive and respiratory systems.

Seldom do children with cystic fibrosis enroll in early childhood programs. This is because they cannot risk developing lung infections such as pneumonia. Moreover, these children must be treated under the close supervision of a doctor.

## Diabetes

Diabetes is a hereditary disease. Common symptoms of diabetes include frequent urination, loss of weight, constant hunger, itching (especially around the groin), and slow healing cuts and bruises. However, it is also possible that some affected children will not show any obvious symptoms.

With *diabetes,* the body cannot make full use of the foods eaten, particularly carbohydrates. As a result, proper levels of insulin are not produced by the pancreas to burn or store foods as energy. Thus, the body's sugar content increases which, in turn, increases the blood's sugar level. When the blood passes through the kidneys, the sugar is excreted in urine. This loss of carbohydrates leads to the disease. If diabetes is not controlled, it can be fatal.

A special diet is the best way to treat diabetes. A balance of proteins, fats, carbohydrates, vitamins, and minerals needs to be included. The diet must also be constant in food value. In other words, the diet should not be high in carbohydrates one day and low the next.

Exercise and insulin, along with the proper diet, are also necessary to manage the disease. Insulin is vital in the treatment of most cases of juvenile diabetes. The type and exact dosage for each is determined by a doctor. Most diabetic preschoolers receive insulin injections from their parent(s). If the amount of insulin is not properly adjusted to the child's food intake and activity level, an *insulin reaction* may occur. A late meal or excessive exercise may cause a reaction. A child who has an insulin reaction becomes uneasy, nervous, weak, and hungry. The child becomes pale and sweaty. Trembling, dizziness, and headaches may occur. If left untreated, the insulin reaction will lead to shock. Feeding the child simple sugar sources will help counteract the reaction.

Several teaching suggestions are important when a diabetic child or children are enrolled in the program. These are given in 27-13.

### Epilepsy

*Epilepsy* is a convulsive disorder caused by damage to the brain. It affects about one percent of the population. As a result of this disorder, the electrical rhythms of the central nervous system are disturbed. Epilepsy is *not* a disease.

Epilepsy can cause varying degrees of reactions, or seizures. Two major types are petit mal and grand mal. *Petit mal seizures* result in reactions that many times go unnoticed. Often, the only visible signs are the fluttering of the eyelids, frozen postures, staring, and a temporary stop in activity. This type of seizure may be only five to ten seconds long.

As a teacher, you may not always notice a petit mal seizure. What you may notice is that the child's behavior is strange or that he or she may not be paying attention. During the seizure, the child may have only a brief lapse of consciousness.

Grand mal seizures are much more pronounced. During a *grand mal seizure,* a child will lose consciousness. He or she may also jerk, thrash, or become stiff. The child may also be injured by hitting objects or biting the tongue.

When the child regains consciousness, he or she may be confused. In fact, the seizure will not be remembered. Instead, the child may get up and continue with classroom activities.

Epilepsy is treated primarily with drugs. These drugs will either prevent or reduce the frequency of the seizures. Unfortunately, many drugs for epilepsy cause serious side effects, such as restlessness and lethargic behavior.

There may be times when you, as a teacher, may have to control a seizure. If a child falls, you should:

1. Let the child remain on the floor, clearing the area to provide him or her with ample room to thrash.
2. Remain calm.
3. Cradle the child's head in your lap. Avoid restraining movement. If possible, turn the child's body to the side, allowing saliva to drain from the mouth. This should help keep the child from choking.
4. If the child goes from one seizure to another, consult the child's parent(s) and physician.
5. After the child has regained consciousness, allow him or her to remain lying down. Place a blanket over the child and allow him or her to sleep.

### Hemophilia

*Hemophilia* is a genetic blood disease in which the blood cannot clot normally. Extreme *internal* (under the skin) bleeding may result from simply bumping against something. This causes joint problems and extreme pain that may require a stay in the hospital. The real threat, however, is death caused by internal bleeding of vital organs or by blood flowing into air passages.

With the help of the parent(s), decide what

---

**TEACHING SUGGESTIONS FOR DIABETIC CHILDREN**

1. Ask the parents how to handle emergencies. Ask them to put these recommendations in writing. File this information in the child's file.
2. Schedule snack and lunch at the same time each day.
3. Make sure that diabetic children have the same food values each day.
4. Keep quick sugar sources such as chocolate candy bars, soda, or orange juice on hand in case an insulin reaction occurs.
5. Take the child immediately to a hospital emergency room if she/he becomes unconscious.

27-13 Follow these suggestions to assure that a diabetic child receives proper care in your program.

equipment is safe for the child to use. You should also:

- Tag the outdoor and indoor equipment the child can use.
- Ask the parent(s) what to do if the child is injured.
- Carefully watch the child's play to prevent accidents.

## Leukemia

*Leukemia* is a form of cancer that affects the blood-forming organs and the blood. There is a sharp increase in the number of white blood cells in the bloodstream.

Leukemia is likely to be fatal. It is unlikely that a child with leukemia would enroll in a child care center. You may find, however, that a child currently enrolled may develop the disease. This child will have to be treated in the hospital. But when the disease is in remission, the child may want to come back and visit friends at the center.

If the parents elect to have a child with leukemia attend the center when in remission, you will need to discuss the disease with them.

Find out what goals the parents have for the child as well as implications of the disease.

## INTEGRATING SPECIAL NEEDS CHILDREN

There are no exact numbers stating the recommended number of special needs children that can be accommodated in a given classroom. Several factors must be considered: the teachers' training and experience, the ratio of adults to children, and the specific needs of these children.

Regardless of a child's needs, she or he should be grouped with others based on developmental level, not age. This requires careful observation of the child before grouping.

It is important for special needs children to enjoy the center, 27-14. Many of these children have not had a full range of home and neighborhood experiences. Others receive painful medical treatment. For these children, the center will provide a chance for companionship and education.

At times, to meet the individual needs of the children and to feel confident, you must ask

27-14 Encouraging a special needs child to try new experiences may help the child enjoy being at the center.

for help from a specialist. For example, if a child has a speech problem, a speech therapist can be most valuable. The therapist can also help you plan helpful activities for the child.

If the parent does not remain with a child on a first visit, provide the parent(s) with feedback on the progress of that time. Parents will be most interested in their child's adjustment to the school setting. Some teachers make a habit of either verbally sharing some positive experiences or writing a short note each day during the child's first week or two.

The children in your classroom should be prepared for a special needs child. Explain any changes that will need to be made in the classroom. As you talk to the children, be positive and focus on strengths. This will help your group of children focus on positive expectations.

Inform the other children about the special needs child. Some children are afraid of children with special needs. They fear the disorder or illness may be contagious.

Develop a few simple rules for classroom behavior. Stress to the children that the special needs child should be encouraged to be independent. Young children may want to be overly helpful. This type of behavior can cause dependence and prevent a child from growing. As children become more independent, they feel better about themselves.

As a teacher, your attitude toward the special needs child will set the classroom tone. To make yourself feel comfortable, study the disorder or illness before the child begins at the center, 27-15. Or, if the child is already enrolled and the condition has just become known, learn as much as you can about the condition. This process will help lessen any fears that you may have.

After you have learned about the disorder, arrange to have the child visit the classroom for a short period of time. This visit will reduce the fears of the child, the other children in the classroom, and perhaps the parents.

Parents of the special needs child may wish to remain with the child for the first, brief visit. This practice usually reduces the separation anxiety the child and parents may feel.

Remember that parents are the primary teachers of their children. Therefore, it is vital that parents take part in planning useful, proper learning experiences. Parents should always be involved in planning for the child's individual needs, as well as planning for complementary opportunities in the home.

## GIFTED CHILDREN

No one had prepared Yvonne Libby, a preschool teacher, for all the children she would meet in her first teaching position. Thad, a two-year-old child enrolled in the program, had taught himself to read. By 10 months of age, this same child had spoken in complete sentences. Thad is a minority in Miss Libby's classroom. He is a gifted child, and he needs help.

27-15 You will feel more comfortable working with a special needs child if you study the need in advance.

Often, gifted children are neglected in education. They often spend time doing things they already know. Only a small number receive instruction at the right level for their needs or abilities. These children need programs and services different from those provided in the "normal" classroom. This is vital since gifted children's skills vary more than other special needs groups.

**Giftedness**

*Giftedness* can be defined in many ways. Traditionally, giftedness was based only on intelligence quotient scores (IQ). Today scholars argue that there are many forms of giftedness.

People who are gifted can be defined as having exceptional skill in one or more of six areas:
1. Creative or productive thinking, 27-16.
2. General intellectual ability.
3. Leadership ability.
4. Psychomotor ability.
5. Specific academic aptitude.
6. Visual or performing arts.

About three to five percent of young children could be gifted. These children may be political leaders, artists, dancers, and scientists. These children need to be identified so they can receive the education they require.

**Identification**

Identifying gifted children is difficult. No single test, checklist, or observation will point out all types of giftedness. During the preschool years, observations are commonly made by parents and teachers.

A child's parents are often most familiar with his or her development, interests, and abilities. Because of this, they may be better able to identify their children as gifted.

Teachers are more aware of how the child's behavior compares with that of his or her peers. However, identification of gifted children by the teacher is not always the best method. Studies found that teachers who identified giftedness chose about one-third of the children incorrectly. In addition, over half of actual gifted children were not identified by their teachers.

There are certain characteristics that can be used to identify the gifted. Many gifted children have a constant curiosity about many subjects. Their social and emotional behavior equals or exceeds that of children the same age. They also are more independent and motivated. Chart 27-17 lists other characteristics of the gifted child.

**Teaching suggestions**

The needs of a preschool gifted child can be met by including acceleration and enrichment in the program. *Acceleration* is a process in which a gifted child is assigned to a class with older children. The objective is to move the child through activities at a faster pace than children with average ability. After spending a year with older children, the gifted preschooler may be ready for even older children.

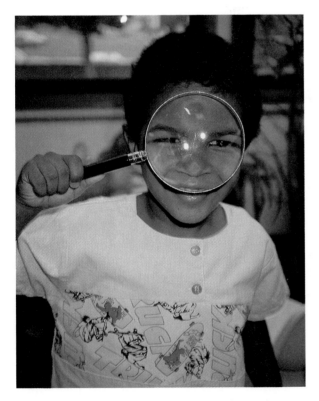

27-16 Children who are constantly curious and trying to figure out how objects work may be gifted.

## CHARACTERISTICS OF GIFTED CHILDREN

- Early speech.
- Advanced vocabulary for age.
- Keen observation skills: ''see more'' on field trips, in films or pictures than other children.
- Attention span is unusually long for age.
- Inquisitive nature: constantly is asking questions.
- Flexible: adapt easily to new situations.
- Persistent.
- Responsible for age.
- Self-critical.
- Strive toward perfection.
- Good memory.

27-17 Early identification of gifted children will promote further growth.

In *enrichment* the range of experiences is broadened to provide the child with a special curriculum. This process will help the child identify areas of interests.

Gifted children often receive enrichment through individual or small group instruction. You or a volunteer may use audiovisual materials, games, and field trips to promote learning. The key to a useful program for gifted children is to build educational experiences around student interests.

Provide open-ended learning activities for creative children, 27-18. They prefer loosely structured activities that give them the chance to express their own ideas and inquire and discover on their own.

Children who are gifted in a certain area, such as reading, should have instruction designed to match their skills. They should be provided with a variety of books related to their special interests. It also helps to have an adult who will take the time to listen to the child read and tell the child about the story.

Many small group activities should be planned to build leadership skills. These activities provide children with opportunities to learn to plan, organize, and make decisions.

As a teacher of gifted children, you need to understand the problems the gifted child faces.

These children tend to be self-critical. As a result, they tend to be too hard on themselves. To help them, you will need to provide guidance so they learn to accept failure.

Sometimes, because of a critical nature, the gifted child will not involve himself or herself with other children. You will need to help the child learn to be considerate of others. This will help improve their social skills.

## SUMMARY

Special needs children are, by law, entitled to a full, proper education. These children are now brought into the average program through mainstreaming. As a result, special needs children may be encountered at any time in your career.

Despite their presence in a typical center, special needs children still require Individualized Educational Plans. As a teacher, you will need to know how to identify a child with special needs. You will then need to know how to work with the child so he or she receives the most effective education possible.

27-18 Through open-ended learning activities, gifted children can be creative and learn on their own.

Part of your role as a teacher may involve
identifying and working with special needs
children. Careful observation will help you
gather helpful information about children
with special needs.

# to Know

acceleration

allergies

amblyopia

ambulatory

arthritis

articulation problems

asthma

cerebral palsy

chronic health needs

color deficiency

cystic fibrosis

desensitized

diabetes

enrichment

epilepsy

expansion

farsightedness

giftedness

glaucoma

grand mal seizure

hemophilia

Individualized
  Educational Plan

leukemia

mainstreaming

nearsightedness

petit mal seizure

pitch

prosthesis

referral

rheumatoid arthritis

spina bifida

stuttering

voice flexibility

# to Review

1. _____ needs are the most common special needs.

2. _____ is a term used for placing children in a regular classroom.

3. Each individual educational plan needs six components. Name them.

4. True or false. Labeling a special needs child may encourage negative expectations by other children.

5. A _____ _____ child does not have the same vocabulary as an average child.

6. True or false. A hearing aid will perfect a child's hearing.

7. What four consonants are easiest for children to pronounce?

8. Articulation problems usually take the form of _____, _____, and _____ of vowels or consonants or both.

9. The communication problem of _____ may increase when a child feels pressure.

10. Symptoms of vision problems may include:
    a. Excessive rubbing of eyes.
    b. Squinting.
    c. Swollen, red eyelids.
    d. All of the above.

11. _____ is the result of a muscle imbalance caused by disuse of the eye.

12. What is the difference between nearsightedness and farsightedness?

13. What actions might you need to take if a child with cerebral palsy is enrolled in your program?

14. _____ _____ is a condition in which the bones of the spine fail to grow together.

15. List four teaching suggestions for working with physically disabled children.

16. Which of the following is an allergy symptom?
    a. Runny nose.
    b. Wheezing.
    c. Fever.
    d. All of the above.

17. True or false. Epilepsy is a disease.

18. _____ is a genetic blood disease.

19. List six characteristics of a gifted child.

# to Do

1. Observe the activities in a day care center that works with special needs children.

2. Invite a speech therapist to your class to discuss stuttering.

3. Discuss the disadvantages of labeling children's special needs.

4. Interview an ophthalmologist (eye doctor) to learn how visual impairments are detected and treated.

5. Make a list of items found in a day care center that may cause an allergic reaction in children.

# part 7

# Exploring Careers with Young Children

A world of career possibilities is open to early childhood teachers. It's up to you to choose a career path that fits your goals and to find a job that will start you on your path.

In this part, you will read about a variety of early childhood programs. Family day care, Montessori schools, and parent cooperatives are some of the programs you will study.

This part also helps prepare you for your job hunt. You will read about how to prepare a resume and find available positions. You will also discover ways to make the best impression possible in an interview and land the job you really want.

# Chapter 28

# Types of Early Childhood Programs

After studying this chapter, you will be able to:
☐ List and describe the various types of early childhood programs available to parents and their children.
☐ Explain the advantages and disadvantages of each type of program.
☐ Name the types of sponsorship available to most early childhood programs.
☐ Explain steps a parent may take in choosing a child care center.

Why should children attend early childhood programs? Many parents cite one or two reasons for placing their children in these learning programs.

Studies show that children develop quickly during the first five years. They grow intellectually, socially, emotionally, and physically. In order to take advantage of this growth period, many parents enroll their children in an early childhood program. In this program, children can learn and take part in activities that will challenge this growth, 28-1.

Many parents of young children work. These parents provide care for their children by enrolling them in programs. This arrangement allows children to learn and grow as they receive care.

Distinct differences exist among the many types of early childhood programs. Some provide services for just part of the day. Others provide full-day care, including meals and a scheduled nap time. Some centers focus on children's physical and social growth while others focus on intellectual growth. Other differences are in terms of size, facilities, staff qualifications, parent involvement, ownership, and fees.

Some types of programs are more common than others. However, all of them serve a very important purpose by meeting the needs of young children.

## FAMILY DAY CARE

The most common type of day care in the United States is called *family day care.* In this type of program, child care is provided in a private home. Most states require these homes be licensed. This, however, is rather difficult to enforce. Some caregivers are not aware of licensing. Others ignore licensing rules.

### Program

Programs provided in a family day care center reflect state rules as well as the skills of the caregivers. Focus in some homes is on *custodial care.* With this type of care, the environment is kept safe and healthy for young children. Meals are usually provided.

In a home where the caregiver has received early childhood training, a developmental curriculum may be used. This involves planning and equipping an environment to relate to children's developmental needs and interests. For instance, a curriculum for two-year-old children would focus on language and large motor development and social and emotional growth. Ample space would be needed for these children to move around. Developmentally appropriate puzzles, storybooks, push and pull toys, large blocks, housekeeping equipment, and other toys would also be provided.

## DAY CARE CENTERS

Facilities that offer full-day children's programs are often called *day care centers* or *extended preschool centers.* This type of program provides a place for child care while parents and guardians are at work or school. The focus of most day care centers is to meet the child's basic nutritional, social, emotional, intellectual, and physical needs, 28-2.

28-1 A challenging environment can help children develop intellectually, emotionally, socially, and physically.

28-2 Many parents rely on the skilled staff of day care centers to provide for the basic needs of their children.

Most day care centers open early in the morning and remain open until six or seven o'clock in the evening. Some centers provide care for children 24 hours per day. For parents whose children need care during the evening or early morning hours, this service is most convenient.

### Program

Programs provided by day care centers depend a great deal on the skills of the faculty and state licensing rules. Like family day care, some centers simply provide a safe environment. Some stress intellectual growth.

Ideally, the program will provide for all needs. There is a balance of activities. The environment is safe and well supervised.

## MONTESSORI SCHOOLS

In the early 1900s, Maria Montessori developed her own method of education. Montessori was the first woman in Italy to receive a degree in medicine. Early in her career, she was an assistant doctor at a clinic that served mentally retarded children.

While working with retarded children, Montessori developed her theory of education. This theory stated that children learn best by being active and doing. Montessori soon learned that these methods could also be used with normal children. This led to the development of a school in Rome's slum district.

Montessori's methods became known all over the world. Because of her success, she was asked to speak in the United States. After her visit, a group of people formed the first Montessori Society. Interest, however, declined for the next 40 years. Then, in the 1950s, there was a rebirth of the Montessori approach. Magazines and television helped make the Montessori method known.

### Montessori approach

In her first schools, Montessori stressed proper diet, cleanliness, and manners. Children also worked with equipment she designed. See 28-3. These materials were self-correcting and required little adult guidance. The materials were organized from simple to complex. As the children worked through the materials, they learned motor and sensory skills, number concepts, and writing skills.

Montessori believed in self-education. Her primary goal was for children to "learn how to learn." This approach allowed the child to explore materials that were meant to instruct. Certain materials were given to the child by the teacher in a prescribed sequence. This sequence was related to the child's physical and mental development. Montessori felt that this approach would provide the child freedom within limits.

*Montessori schools* provide a rather structured approach. Each of Montessori's materials has a fixed method in which it is presented. After the teacher correctly presents the materials, the child is told how to practice. Sensory materials are presented first. Using these materials, the children build writing, math, and reading skills.

Experimentation with materials is not permitted. The proper use of materials is most important. Interaction between the child and materials is highly structured. Materials are

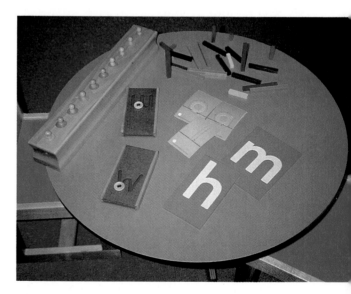

28-3 Materials used in a Montessori school are designed to help children learn with little adult guidance.

used only as intended. For instance, a child is not allowed to use puzzle pieces for building.

**Practical life experiences.** Independence is stressed in Montessori schools. Children must learn to care for themselves. Teachers provide little help. As a result, children learn to button, zip, tie, and put on coats and boots. These experiences are called *practical life experiences* in the Montessori curriculum.

**Sensory training.** The purpose of sensory training is to help children learn touch, sound, taste, and sight discrimination. One piece of equipment for this training is a set of sandpaper blocks that very in texture. The children are told to rub their fingers across the blocks. Their goal is to correctly match blocks with like textures. Musical bells with varying tones are used in the same way. Based on tone, children match like tones.

**Writing and reading.** Academics are also stressed in the Montessori program. But before a child is introduced to these experiences, sensory training must be mastered. Then, to teach letter recognition, sandpaper letters are used. After the teacher introduces a letter, children are encouraged to trace the letter with their fingertips. Numbers are taught in the same manner.

When a child demonstrates knowledge of and interest in letters, reading instruction may be started.

### Teacher's role

The Montessori teacher's role is passive compared to other early childhood methods. The basic role of the teacher is to determine children's needs, prepare the environment, and present the materials. Need is determined by observation. After need has been determined, proper materials are chosen. Each material is individually presented. During this time, the teacher silently shows the child how to do the task.

Unlike most preschools, there is little teacher talk. In fact, the teacher often does not even acknowledge the child's achievements. According to Montessori, children are motivated by inward satisfaction gained when a job is performed well.

## HEAD START

During the 1960s the federal government developed a program called *Head Start.* Its purpose was to strengthen the academic skills of children from low-income homes. To do this, the program was designed for the social, emotional, physical, and intellectual needs of these four- and five-year-old children.

The first Head Start programs were offered for eight weeks during the summer months. They met with great success and have since been extended to a full year program.

### Education

The curriculum in a Head Start program is designed to meet the needs of each child. Special considerations are given to cultural and ethnic backgrounds. The goal is to provide the child with a healthy self-concept.

A variety of learning experiences are designed for the children. All four areas of development are stressed in these experiences. Staff and parents work as a team to plan curriculum and teach children.

Studies have shown that the Head Start program has been successful. On preschool achievement tests, Head Start children perform equal to or better than their peers. Once they enter school, these children are more likely to be successful in school.

### Nutrition

Many children who take part in Head Start do not receive well-balanced meals at home. Nutrition then is a vital part of the program, 28-4. Federal rules require the center to provide at least one snack and one hot meal every day. Both breakfast and lunch are served in some programs. The goal of this program is to help the children build good eating habits they can use throughout their lives. Children also gain increased physical skills due to sound nutrition, medical attention, and learning activities.

### Health

All children who attend a Head Start program are given a total health plan. Dental,

28-4 A well-organized, sanitary kitchen is an important link in providing sound nutrition for children.

medical, and mental health services are provided. Prior to enrollment, many of these children have never been to a dentist. Children who have not already received childhood immunizations are given them while they are enrolled.

### Parental involvement

Head Start recognizes the parent as their child's primary teacher. Therefore, parental involvement is vital to the program. Parents are encouraged to help recruit new students, assist in the center, and take part in policy meetings. Thus, Head Start parents are able to influence administrative decisions.

## KINDERGARTEN

In 1837, the first kindergarten was opened by Frederick Froebel in Germany. The *kindergarten* curriculum stressed play. Froebel believed that self-development took place through creative activities such as play. The children in this kindergarten, like many today, engaged in painting, stringing beads, blockbuilding, and clay modeling. The children cared for pets, sang songs, and gardened.

The first American kindergarten was opened in Watertown, Wisconsin in 1856. It was held in the home of Margarenthia Schurz. This mother and teacher had studied under Froebel. Mrs. Schurz first opened the kindergarten for her own children and four of their cousins.

Today kindergartens are part of many public school systems. They are restricted to children who are at least four years old. In the past, these programs usually lasted a half day. Today, however, there are more options.

### Schedules

There are three basic scheduling patterns in kindergarten: half-day, full-day, and full-day/alternating day session. The half-day session usually runs from two and one-half to three and one-half hours per day. Full-day sessions run from six to eight hours per day. Full-day/alternating day programs vary. Some programs meet every other day. Others require children to attend on Tuesday and Thursday the first week, and on Monday and Friday the next week. Other alternating programs have children attend two full days and one half day. To illustrate, one group may attend all day on Monday and Wednesday, plus on Friday morning. The other group might attend all day on Tuesday and Thursday, as well as Friday afternoon.

### Goals

Goals for a kindergarten program permit variety. Basic objectives of most kindergarten programs include:
- Respect for the contributions, property, and rights of other children.
- Appreciation of objects of beauty.
- Growth in creative skills.
- Achievement of problem-solving skills.
- Development of a positive self-concept.
- Growth in language, social, and physical skills.
- Development of positive feelings about school.

The most common element in most kindergartens is emphasis on the growth of the whole child: physical, emotional, social, and intellectual.

## Curriculum

Kindergarten curriculum may vary from school to school. Some schools place a greater stress on certain pre-academic skills such as learning the names and sounds of alphabet letters. Other programs focus more on social development. These programs are less structured than those that stress pre-academics.

Kindergarten teachers, unlike most elementary teachers, have more freedom in planning curriculum. Studies show that in most kindergarten programs, about 50 percent of the day is spent on creative activities. Included are art, woodworking, blockbuilding, storytelling, and music. Free play, self-care, and rest fill the remaining time, 28-5. During these activities, the teacher includes social studies, mathematics, language, and science concepts.

28-5 Free play and creativity are important in kindergarten programs.

## LATCH-KEY PROGRAMS

*Latch-key programs* provide care during after-school hours for children. Children from five to ten years old most often attend. These children do homework, play games, cook, and take part in other creative activities. Latch-key programs are often sponsored by schools, churches, or day care centers.

An alternative to latch-key programs are called *checking-in services.* Many have been started on a trial basis. These services assign children to caregivers. Children do not go to their caregivers' homes, however. Instead, caregivers call the children to make sure there are no problems. To date, this program has met with success.

## PARENT COOPERATIVES

*Parent cooperatives* are formed and run by parents who wish to take part in their children's preschool experience. Parents draw up a budget, hire teachers, set policies, establish goals for the children, and perform other tasks.

Cooperatives provide developmental experiences for adults as well as children. Specifically, parents:
- Obtain guidance in their jobs as parents.
- Learn what children are like at different ages and stages.
- Gain several free mornings each month.
- Become familiar with creative materials and equipment.
- Gain a more objective picture of their child.

Due to all of these experiences, many parents have reported feeling a greater sense of personal worth.

### Advantages and disadvantages

There are many advantages to teaching in a parent cooperative. Since the parents make the administrative decisions, collect fees, and order and repair equipment, the teacher can devote more time to the children and curriculum. Another advantage can be the special friendships that many times develop between parents and teachers.

A major disadvantage of a parent cooperative is the lack of control on the teacher's part.

Although the teacher acts as an adviser, parents alone are usually responsible for making rules. At times, there may be differences of opinion between teacher and parents. For instance, parents may feel that children do not have to help return toys to the storage place. The teacher may feel differently. This can cause problems for many teachers.

### Sessions

Parent cooperatives usually run for two or three hours, two to five days each week. Sometimes these groups take form based on the children's ages. For example, on Tuesday and Thursday mornings, a group of two-year-old children will be scheduled. On Monday, Wednesday and Friday mornings, three-year-olds may attend. Other centers may prefer to use the "family-type" grouping. In this type of setting, children of mixed ages may all be included in one group.

### Fees

Due to the parent's involvement, fees charged at a parent cooperative are often less than at private programs. Costs are reduced by hiring only a head teacher. Parents serve as the classroom aides. Generally, each parent will assist in the classroom several times each month. In addition, parents volunteer to perform many of the service activities. They may clean and maintain the building, prepare snacks, type newsletters, and/or do some special jobs, such as painting the classroom.

## LABORATORY SCHOOLS

*Laboratory schools,* or campus schools, are located on a post secondary or college campus, 28-6. Although they provide excellent programs for children, their primary purpose is to train future teachers and to serve as a study group for research. Most of these schools have a highly qualified staff, a well-planned curriculum, and excellent equipment.

## SECONDARY SCHOOL PRESCHOOLS

In the last decade, many secondary schools have started running preschools. Usually there are two purposes for these programs. First, many of these schools stress vocational education. Like the laboratory schools, these programs train future child care aides. At the same time, students in the school who are also parents can continue their education and receive guidance.

## SPONSORSHIP

Early childhood centers can be grouped based on sponsorship. Basically, there are three kinds of sponsorship: public, private, and employer sponsored centers.

### Public sponsorship

*Publicly sponsored programs* are funded by the government, school district, and/or division of social services. Operating money comes through federal, state, or local governments.

An example of a publicly sponsored program is Head Start. Its tuition, if any, is very low. Most of the expenses for the program are funded through grants received from the federal government. Funding is usually on a yearly or bi-yearly basis.

State funds may help support programs designed for educational purposes. These programs may be housed in a university, college, secondary school, or vocational school. Ex-

28-6 Laboratory schools generally have highly qualified staffs, well-planned curriculum, and excellent equipment.

amples include day care centers, preschool centers, laboratory schools, and secondary preschool programs.

Publicly funded day care centers, preschools, and laboratory programs may also receive other financial support. For instance, a publicly funded day care center may also receive funds from the United Way, community donations, and tuition. Likewise, a laboratory school on a college campus may receive donations through alumni groups.

### Private sponsorship

In the past, the largest group of privately sponsored programs has been the privately owned center. These centers rely on tuition to cover all operating expenses. As a result, the margin of profit is low.

A *privately sponsored program* may be sponsored by a church, hospital, charitable organization, or an individual. Most programs are sponsored by individuals. Their motivation is more likely to be profit oriented.

### Franchised centers

In the past five years, there has been a rapid growth of privately *franchised centers.* Such centers are associated with a main school. They may be owned by the main school, or a local owner may have purchased the right to be in the school's franchise. These schools often provide their centers with curriculum guides. They may or may not have one design used as a floor plan for all their buildings.

Day-care chains are the largest group of franchised centers. Chains are owned by companies. The number of these centers is growing quickly. They are largely found in cities. To make a profit, the number of children enrolled in one center must be high. As a result, chains tend to house several programs in one building.

### Employer sponsorship

A small number of companies provide their employees with child care. The employer may pay part or all of the costs of the services. These companies provide *employer sponsored programs,* 28-7.

Employers sponsor day care to reduce the conflict between family and work responsibilities. Studies show that there is less employee turnover and absenteeism at companies that provide for child care. At such companies, employees have better work attitudes, new employees are attracted, community relations improve, and good publicity is received. Moreover, there are tax incentives for companies who sponsor child care.

The company owned, on-site child care center is located at or near the work site. With this type of program, the company may hire a director to run the program. Other companies contract with child care franchises or firms specializing in child care.

There are advantages and disadvantages to this model. One advantage is that parents can spend breaks and/or lunch hours with their children. In large cities, however, this model may not work. Employees who commute long distances to work may find it difficult to travel with children on public transportation or in car pools.

The off-site center is another option. This model is often used when several companies form a group. In some cases, each company may not have enough need for their own child care center. The costs and risks are shared by all the companies in the group.

The off-site location may be closer to the parent's home. Therefore, transportation times are shorter. If space is available, this type of

---

**TYPES OF EMPLOYEE SPONSORED CHILD CARE PROGRAMS**

- Company owned, on-site center.
- Off-site center sponsored by one or more companies.
- Company sponsored, vendor provided centers.
- Vouchers provided by company to subsidize care.
- Sick child care.
- Referral services.

28-7 Companies may assist families with child care in many ways.

model may also serve other community children.

The vendor model allows companies to purchase space in a day care center or several centers. This model is ideal for small companies. It is not as costly as opening a center. There are no costs for start-up, investment in a building, or center administration.

Companies respect parental choice when the voucher model is provided. Parents receive a voucher or coupon worth a certain amount of money from the company. Some companies will pay for all day care costs, while others pay only a portion. This model may be preferred by parents who do not live close to the work site. Thus, it is a useful model for companies in large cities.

One disadvantage of the voucher model is that the money the voucher provides must be declared as income on tax returns. However, the employee can deduct the cost of child care from federal taxes (and state taxes where allowed).

Sick child care is a model used by some companies to provide for sick children. This model can take two forms. A center may provide services for children who are ill and cannot attend school. When this is done, the health department as well as the state licensing agency must be notified. This model works best for children who are almost over an illness but not well enough to return to school. The second form allows for a nurse to be sent to a sick child's home to provide care. This allows the parent to go to work.

Finding a good day care program within a reasonable distance of the home is a problem for many parents. To assist parents in this process, some companies provide a referral service that matches the parents' needs with centers. The company may hire their own resource specialist or contract a referral agency.

Generally, parents are given a list of community day care centers. Specific information on each center is collected and given to the parents. Included are the center's location, fees, hours of operation, enrollment capacity, policies, activities, staff qualifications, and special services. Maps showing the location of

the center are often provided to help the parents in the selection process.

## SELECTING A CHILD CARE PROGRAM

Selecting a child care program is important for parents. Studies show that a large percentage of parents choose a program on the advice of a friend. In most cases, the friend has had one or more children attend the program.

Other factors that influence selection of a child care program include location and type of program provided. Parents whose children will attend an all-day program are influenced more by location. These parents have heavy demands on their time. As a result, programs located in the neighborhood or on a route to work are most convenient.

The type of program provided will most likely influence parents with children in half-day programs. Music, art, and other creative experiences interest some of these parents. Other parents are most interested in a program that stresses the development of the whole child—intellectual, physical, social, and emotional, 28-8.

In addition to talking to friends, parents will seek information about the program in several

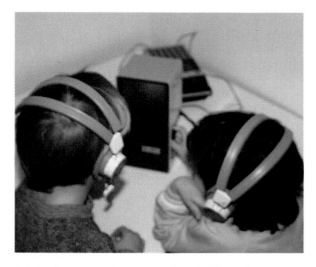

28-8 Parents choose early childhood programs based on what they want most for their children.

other ways. Before visiting a center, many parents will call the director to ask questions about the school policies, program, and fees. After this, if they still are interested, they may visit the center.

Visits to a program may take place before, during, or after program hours. More parents visit during program hours. A larger percentage of parents seeking half-day programs visit centers.

Parents will ask many questions related to the program and staff. They usually are interested in the type of program and related activities provided for the children. Questions related to staff experience and background may also be asked. For example, a parent may ask if the staff is trained in child development.

An example of an information sheet to share with parents is shown in 28-9. This sheet may help them in their selection process.

---

**SELECTING CHILDCARE**

|  | Yes | No |
|---|---|---|
| 1. Are all staff members trained in early childhood education? | | |
| 2. Does staff attend professional meetings and conferences on a regular basis? | | |
| 3. Does staff maintain records on individual children to better understand their development and needs? | | |
| 4. Are staff meetings conducted regularly to plan and evaluate program activities? | | |
| 5. How long has each staff member been employed at the center? | | |
| 6. Is there sufficient indoor and outdoor space? | | |
| 7. Is there sufficient equipment for the number of children attending? | | |
| 8. Is there equipment provided to meet all four areas of development—social, emotional, intellectual, and physical? | | |
| 9. Are safe and sanitary conditions maintained within the building and on the play yard? | | |
| 10. Are there positive teacher-child interactions? | | |
| 11. Are the children's feelings important? | | |
| 12. Do the children appear to be happy, contented, and secure? | | |
| 13. Do teachers make daily and weekly lesson plans? | | |
| 14. Does the program meet your needs in terms of cost and hours of operation? | | |

28-9 In order to help ease the burden of choosing child care for their children, you may wish to supply interested parents with this questionnaire.

## The selection process

Because early childhood programs vary in cost, hours of operation, and program goals, it takes time to select a program that fits individual needs. As a teacher, it is vital that you understand the process parents go through in selecting a program.

The first step many parents take is to talk to other parents. They list all programs that are conveniently located. After this, they may call each center to discuss fees, hours of operation, and whether the center is licensed.

Parents then may visit those centers that meet family's and children's needs. While at the center, they may talk to the director and teachers.

Programs with high staff turnover may cause suspicion. Directors, teachers, and aides often resign due to low wages and/or poor working conditions. In either case, high staff turnover often causes morale problems. Remember, too, in order to feel secure, children need consistent care.

While at the center, parents will observe to see if sufficient space is provided for play and personal belongings. There should be at least 35 square feet of free indoor play space and 100 square feet of outdoor play space for each child. In addition, space should be provided for each child to store personal belongings and a change of clothes.

Parents will also look to see that there is enough equipment for the number of children in attendance. There should also be a wide variety.

To protect their children's health, parents may look for safe, sanitary conditions. The building and grounds should be safe. Electrical outlets should be covered. A smoke alarm and fire extinguisher should be available. An emergency evacuation plan should be posted.

You may be asked whether meals and snacks are provided for the children. If they are, provide a menu. The menu should consist of well-balanced and varied meals. The menu should appear to meet children's nutritional requirements.

Parents may also observe the program to see if the staff is patient and responsive to the children. There should be frequent and supportive staff contact with the children. Also, the staff should work together as they perform their duties.

Quality programs follow a well-planned schedule. To see if such a schedule is followed, some parents may wish to observe. They may also ask to see a daily and weekly schedule. They may look for a balance between active and quiet activities. Weather permitting, there should also be a balance of indoor and outdoor activities.

Parents may also study the way children use materials. In a good center, teachers encourage children to make their own products, 28-10.

Parents will also observe to see if feelings are important. If they are, concern is expressed for the rights of others. Staff should be helping children learn how to take turns, to consider other's feelings, and to stand up for their own when necessary. Angry children should be helped to work through their feelings. All children in the group should be made to feel good about themselves.

Parents will also observe the children. They will be encouraged by children who appear happy, contented, and secure. This is often a sign that the center's program is meeting each child's needs.

Finally, before parents decide whether a center is best for their child, they need to consider whether it met their needs. Did they feel welcome in the program? Did the director and/or teacher welcome them? Did they receive encouragement to observe? Are the children's experiences in the program shared through a newsletter, conference, or group meeting? Parents' answers to these questions will help determine whether or not they have found the right center for them.

## SUMMARY

There are many types of early childhood programs. These include family day care, day care centers, Montessori schools, Head Start, kindergartens, latch-key programs, parent cooperatives, laboratory schools, and secondary school preschools. Each type of program takes a unique approach to meeting children's physical, intellectual, social, and emotional needs.

Programs may be sponsored in a variety of ways. The type of sponsorship may affect goals and philosophies. Programs may be publicly or privately funded. Franchised centers are privately owned centers affiliated with one main program. Employer sponsored programs are designed to lessen some of the burdens of child care for working parents.

With the variety of programs available, parents may use careful evaluation methods to choose programs for their children. Many parents choose programs based on a friend's recommendation. Other factors that parents consider include the type of program, quality of staff, and condition of facilities. As a teacher you need to know what parents look for in a program. Then you can strive to make your center the type that parents choose for their children.

28-10 In a good center, adults encourage children to use materials in their own ways.

## to Know

checking-in services
custodial care
day care centers
employer sponsored
  programs
family day care
franchised centers
Head Start
kindergarten

laboratory schools
latch-key programs
Montessori schools
parent cooperatives
practical life experiences
privately sponsored
  programs
publicly sponsored
  programs

## to Review

1. The most common type of day care in the United States is _____ _____ _____.

2. True or false. Day care centers offer full day programs for young children.

3. Montessori's theory of education stated that children learn best when they are _____.

4. What are practical life experiences?

5. The Montessori teacher's role is:
   a. Passive.
   b. To acknowledge children's accomplishments often.
   c. To encourage experimentation with materials.
   d. All of the above.

6. Describe the purpose of Head Start.

7. True or false. Nutrition is a vital part of the Head Start program.

8. Name the three basic kindergarten schedules.

9. List five objectives for a kindergarten program.

10. _____ _____ are formed and run by parents who wish to take part in their children's preschool experiences.

11. What is the primary purpose of a laboratory school?

12. Publicly sponsored programs are funded by:
    a. The government.
    b. Tuition.
    c. Fund raising.
    d. All of the above.

13. _____ sponsored child care reduces the conflict between family and work responsibilities.

14. A large percentage of parents select a child care center on the advice of _____.

15. How can high staff turnover harm children?

## to Do

1. Visit a family day care home. Ask the provider to outline the schedule followed on the average day.

2. Invite a panel of preschool teachers to speak to your class. Include day care, parent cooperative, kindergarten, and Montessori teachers. Ask them questions on their philosophy, program goals, and curriculum.

3. Visit a Montessori program. Make a list of materials used for practical life experiences, sensory training, and writing and reading.

4. Collect schedules from half-day, full-day, and full-day/alternating day kindergartens. Discuss similarities and differences.

5. Arrange a visit to a latch-key program. Ask to review the curriculum.

6. Discuss the advantages and disadvantages of teaching in a parent cooperative from the viewpoint of a parent.

# Chapter 29

# *Job Hunting*

After studying this chapter, you will be able to:
- ☐ Rank your job preferences.
- ☐ Compile your resume.
- ☐ List various methods for seeking employment.
- ☐ Compute a salary range on which you could live.
- ☐ List questions to ask at an interview.
- ☐ Explain the basic interviewing process.
- ☐ Discuss illegal questions and how to handle them.

Job hunting is an important, challenging task. To be successful, it must be approached in a thoughtful manner. Successful candidates often treat job hunting as a full time job. They commit themselves to the process 100 percent. They approach the hunt with a plan.

Many child care teachers have been successful using several types of job searching techniques. One method has been to apply directly to the employer or center director. This contact may be in the form of a request for an application, a visit to the center, or a telephone call. Usually these contacts are made just before courses are completed.

Answering newspaper ads is one more useful way to seek employment, 29-1. Want ads are checked on a daily basis. If an appealing position is noticed, the center can be contacted at once. If a telephone number is listed, a call can be made. Many times positions need to be filled immediately. Therefore, timing is important.

## RANKING JOB PREFERENCES

There are many types of jobs in child care. Before you begin hunting, make a list of the types of jobs you would enjoy most. This will help you find the right job. While going through this process, consider your skills. If

29-1 Many new child care teachers find their first jobs through newspaper ads.

the interview. After the interview, your resume will help the employer recall your experiences, as well as the interview.

### Preparing a resume

A good resume should instantly create a good impression. It should create, on the part of the employer, a desire to meet you. To do this, it should focus on your educational background and work experiences.

All resumes contain key information about the applicant: name, current address, and telephone number are always included. If you are applying for jobs outside of your hometown, include the area code.

Many applicants place their job objective before listing their educational background. Work experience, professional activities, and other qualifications are also included. Illustration 29-3 is an example of a resume.

### Helpful hints

Directors will quickly look at a resume to find out if you have enough educational back-

you are good with infants and enjoy them, think about working in an infant center or as a home child care specialist who is responsible for an infant.

Chart 29-2 lists a number of child care positions. Rank them in order, number one being your first choice. This process should help you determine your ideal job.

## RESUMES

To prepare for your job search, first prepare a resume. A *resume* is a brief summary of your qualifications, skills, and job experience. The purpose of a resume is to secure an interview and/or inform a potential employer of your qualifications and experience.

Resumes also serve many other purposes. First, a resume may serve as your own self-inventory. Having an objective list of your background and skills can be quite helpful when looking for a job. It can also serve as a starting point in an interview. Your resume will give the employer information on which to base

---

**JOB PREFERENCE LIST**

| | |
|---|---|
| 11 | infant teacher |
| 4 | toddler teacher |
| 1 | preschool teacher |
| 2 | day care teacher |
| 5 | Montessori teacher |
| 6 | parent cooperative teacher |
| 8 | teacher's aid |
| 9 | center director |
| 10 | assistant director |
| 3 | kindergarten teacher |
| 7 | kindergarten aid |

(Number one denotes most desirable)

29-2 How would you rank this list in terms of job preference?

Resume

Sandra Winder
1109 Liberty Street
Valders, Wisconsin 14893
Telephone 414-555-4422

**Objective**

To obtain a teaching position in a preschool or kindergarten setting.

**Education**

- Bachelor of Science Degree in Early Childhood Education, Wisconsin State University-Stout, 1985.
- Two-year certificate from Eau Claire Technical School, Eau Claire, Wisconsin, 1982.
- Graduated from Valders High School, 1980.

**Work Experiences**

- Preschool student teaching, Child and Family Study Center, University of Wisconsin-Stout, Menomonie, Wisconsin, November-December, 1985.
- Kindergarten student teaching at Hillcrest Elementary School, Chippewa Falls, Wisconsin, August to October, 1985.
- Menomonie Day Care, substitute teaching, part-time, September 1984 to December 1984.

**Professional Activities**

- Member of the Wisconsin Early Childhood Association (WECA/AEYC).
- Member of the Menomonie Association for the Education of Young Children (MAEYC). Served as secretary in 1984.
- Attended the University of Wisconsin-Stout early childhood conferences in 1984 and 1985.

**Interests**

Makes friends easily . . . willing to do extra work . . . enthusiastic . . . resourceful . . . dependable . . . always on time . . . committed to teaching.

References available upon request.

29-3 This is one example of a resume. Remember, there is no right or wrong way to prepare a resume.

ground and experience to qualify for the position. If your experience appears to meet the requirements of the job description, the resume is read more closely. During this closer look, employers will look for gaps in your employment dates, the amount of space given to earlier jobs, and the emphasis on education.

Are there gaps in your job history? These gaps may make directors wary of problems in your job history. They may signal that you are unemployed between jobs. You may choose to leave out a job on your resume because it does not apply to the position you seek. Or you may have been unemployed for a legitimate reason, such as returning to school. Be sure to explain such gaps in your cover letter.

When you give the time of your employment, be sure to specify month and year of each job's starting and ending date. Listing only years can be confusing to directors. Such a listing can also give the impression that gaps in employment are being concealed.

A good resume should reflect progress in a career over the years. Also, directors are more interested in an applicant's most recent accomplishments. Therefore, the most recent job experience should be emphasized. Some resume writers devote more space to an earlier teaching position. This usually means one of two things. It may simply be due to poor judgment. Or it could mean the applicant has updated an old resume by simply adding a few lines about the new job. Overall, these errors convey a feeling of laziness and/or poor planning on the part of the applicant. These errors may not always rule out an applicant from an interview. However, they do signal that the applicant needs to be closely reviewed during this process.

The director will also review a resume to see if there is too much stress on education and non-job factors. When an applicant has been out of school for several years, the resume should stress work experience. Applicants who stress post-secondary honors may be focusing too much on the past. If the applicant stresses more non-job factors, this may indicate where his or her real interests lie.

Students who are recent graduates have a special challenge. How can you stress work ex-

perience if you have little or none? Do not overlook any unpaid work experience you may have had. Any lab work or volunteer work in your field of study can be included on your resume. Any involvement in organizations related to your field of study may also be included. You may wish to explain any leadership roles you took on, or any skills you developed that will help you on the job.

Poor typing or writing skills will always reflect badly on the applicant. In fact, some highly qualified applicants have lost out on interviews because of poor writing skills. It is wise to ask a friend who has outstanding writing skills to proofread any cover letters and resumes before sending them to an employer.

## AVENUES FOR SEEKING EMPLOYMENT

Early childhood job seekers may use a number of methods to find employment. These methods include mailing out resumes and placing or answering ads in the newspaper. Successful applicants also do not overlook the hidden job market.

### Newspaper ads

Answering newspaper ads can be helpful when looking for work. As a job seeker, make a habit of reading the ads every day. Newspaper ads are alphabetized from A to Z. Ads for day care center staff may be listed under different areas. Therefore, study the entire section. Examples of titles related to child care include child care teacher, infant teacher, toddler teacher, preschool teacher, day care teacher, early childhood teacher, program coordinator, curriculum specialist, and activities director. If you are looking for an administrative position, look closely for descriptions such as director, administrator, or coordinator.

If an ad appeals to you, respond according to the instructions given in the ad. Some ads contain telephone numbers. In this case, do not wait; call right away, 29-4. Telephone numbers are most often included when a position must be filled as soon as possible.

If a phone number is not given, send your resume to the address or post office box listed.

Attach a cover letter noting the date you are able to begin work and your interest in the position. Successful candidates tailor their letters to fit ads' specifications.

If a newspaper does not ask for your salary requirements, do not mention them in your letter. By including salary, you could be screened out and therefore not even have the chance to interview.

Some ads state the exact salary or range they will pay. For instance, an ad might note the exact dollar figure per hour or a range of several thousand dollars. Many times when a range is provided, the ad might state that salary is open "based on experience" or "based on educational background." See 29-5.

**Placing ads.** Newspaper ads can help you make your availability known. They are quite helpful if you are moving to another area. For example, you may want to work as a child care

> Head Teacher at the Sheboygan Early Childhood Center. Applicant must hold a two-year certificate from an accredited institution of higher learning. Salary range from $1,000-$1,300 per month.
> Call 1-414-555-4598.

29-5 Newspaper ads give a short summary of the open position.

29-4 Quick action is needed if a phone number is included with a newspaper ad.

teacher in New York City after graduation, but you live in Chicago. You could place an ad in the New York Times in the *positions wanted* section of the paper.

Before placing an ad, write and find out the cost. The cost of placing an ad varies depending on the city, circulation of the paper, size of the ad, and the number of days it will run. Many times charges are either on a per word or per line basis. Depending on your budget and the costs of advertising, you may have to limit the length of your ad.

Placing a position wanted ad is a "passive" job search technique. It requires employers to seek you out. However, most employers will actively pursue only the most qualified candidates. Therefore, this method works best for those people who have a great deal of experience. It is best to also use "active" job search techniques.

### College or school placement offices

Most certificate and degree programs provide a placement service. The purpose of this service is to find positions for graduates. To do this, placement offices are usually located on campus. Employers are encouraged to call the office to post job opportunities, 29-6. Likewise, employers are given help finding qualified graduates when they contact the office.

As a student, you will be asked to prepare a file concerning yourself. This file will usually include a standard form prepared by the college or school placement service. The form lists your current address, schools attended, degree earned, and past work experiences. In addition, your file will contain your resume and letters of recommendation from faculty and/or previous employers.

## The hidden job market

Many job candidates are most successful when they focus most of their efforts on the *hidden job market.* These are jobs advertised informally; through word of mouth. Many child care positions are never listed in help wanted ads, in early childhood journals, or with placement offices. Rather, these jobs are filled through word of mouth. To find out about such openings, you as a job seeker should contact center directors directly. This can be done through a letter or a telephone call. Some candidates have met with success by arranging a visit to the center and then asking about job openings. Even if no position is open at the time of the visit, some applicants have been called later when jobs become available.

Get to know early childhood staff workers in the community. One way to do this is to join the local chapter of the National Association

| POSITION: | Head Teacher, Preschool Program<br>Half-Time Position<br>Yearly contract renewal for a maximum of three years. |
|---|---|
| DATE AVAILABLE: | January 3, 19XX |
| JOB RESPONSIBILITIES: | Head Teacher of preschool and/or day care program. Plan and implement a conceptual developmental curriculum with an intergenerational focus. Supervision of student teachers and practicum students. Plan and implement parent meetings and conferences. Participate in committee work in Child and Family Study Center and department. Promote early childhood programs in the community and state. Continuous enrollment in graduate courses is expected if applicant holds only a B.S. degree. |
| QUALIFICATIONS: | • B.S. degree in Early Childhood Education is required, graduate work preferred.<br>• Must be able to be certified to teach preschool in Wisconsin.<br>• Experience in curriculum development, implementation, and program evaluation.<br>• Demonstrated excellence in teaching young children for a minimum of three years.<br>• Demonstrated ability to interact positively with people and work cooperatively with other staff members, parents, students, volunteers, and children.<br>• Must be able to organize and coordinate preschool program and activities with practicum students.<br>• Must be able to motivate children and college students in a creative environment.<br>• Must be able to demonstrate initiative and continuous professional development. |

29-6 Notices posted in school placement offices often give a comprehensive summary of the open position.

for the Education of Young Children. When you attend meetings, try to meet as many people as possible. Always let them know of your job search and when you will be available. In addition, become active in the organization. Volunteer for committees. Show the membership you are willing to work and are professionally motivated.

### Maintaining a filing system

Keep a file of all of the centers or schools you have contacted. Make a photocopy of each cover letter you send out. You may also prepare index cards for each contact and start a card file, 29-7. A card file is convenient because you can keep it by the telephone for quick reference. If you get a call from a director, you can quickly pull the card and refresh your memory on the open position. If you use cards, record the name of the school, address, telephone number, person contacted, and date the contact letter was mailed.

29-7 A card file is one method of keeping your job search information organized.

If you have answered an ad, you may want to attach a copy of the ad to your cover letter or index card. When you receive a response (whether negative or positive), record this on your cover letter or index card. Make notes of interviews, thank you notes, and other contacts on each letter or card as well.

### Salaries

Salaries for early childhood workers vary. Before starting a job search, you need to determine your minimum net income requirements. Your *net income* is the amount of pay you have to spend after taxes and other deductions are taken from your salary. For some people, this is simple. They simply add up essentials such as food, housing, clothing, and car expenses. For others, this process is more complex. If you are one of these people, you will need to prepare a second budget. The second budget could be labeled the "I wish budget." See 29-8. Figures in this budget should reflect an ideal salary.

After you have finished figuring your budget, add all the categories in each column and enter a subtotal. Most people tend to underestimate their needs. Therefore, add 20 percent to the budget. This can also account for miscellaneous expenses. Finally, make an allowance for pay deductions such as federal and state income taxes, health insurance, and social security. You now have a salary range on which you can live in a reasonably comfortable style.

## PREPARING FOR AN INTERVIEW

When preparing for an interview, think positively. Picture yourself walking into the interview confident and relaxed. Get in the habit of being enthusiastic. Remember, enthusiasm is catching. Often, if you are enthusiastic, the interviewer will also share this feeling.

Employers want to hire self-directed people who have a range of skills. They want people who are dependable, enthusiastic, and committed to the child care profession. They also want people who work hard and learn fast. And they want people who manage their time well and

# A MONTHLY BUDGET

|  | "Rock Bottom" $ Spent Per Month | "I Wish" $ Spent Per Month |
|---|---|---|
| **I.  Necessities** | | |
| food | _____ | _____ |
| housing | _____ | _____ |
| transportation | _____ | _____ |
| personal care | _____ | _____ |
| health care | _____ | _____ |
| clothing | _____ | _____ |
| insurance | _____ | _____ |
| other: _____ | _____ | _____ |
| **Subtotal I:** | _____ | _____ |
| **II.  Extras** | | |
| entertainment | _____ | _____ |
| recreation | _____ | _____ |
| gifts and contributions | _____ | _____ |
| savings | _____ | _____ |
| education (optional) | _____ | _____ |
| other: _____ | _____ | _____ |
| **Subtotal II:** | _____ | _____ |
| **III.  Taxes and Social Security** | | |
| Add 30 percent of Subtotal I + Subtotal II **Subtotal III:** | _____ | _____ |
| **IV.  Miscellaneous** | | |
| Add 20 percent of Subtotal I + Subtotal II **Subtotal IV:** | _____ | _____ |
| **V.  Total** | | |
| Subtotal I | _____ | _____ |
| Subtotal II | _____ | _____ |
| Subtotal III | _____ | _____ |
| Subtotal IV | _____ | _____ |
| **TOTAL:** | _____ | _____ |

29-8 It is important to know your salary needs before applying or interviewing for jobs.

look for extra work when their work is done. In order to run a quality center, directors need to hire people who are resourceful.

Chart 29-9 outlines traits for which employers look when hiring people to work in early childhood centers. In preparation for an interview, read the statements and check those that match qualities you would be able to bring to a position. Doing this task will bolster your own self-image. The exercise will help you get a clear picture of your skills. It will also prepare you to make a persuasive presentation that is needed during an interview.

### Preparing your questions

In nearly all interviews, applicants are given the opportunity to ask questions. Thus, smart applicants always prepare questions for an interview. You might form questions by talking to teachers who have taught at the center or asking questions of parents who have children attending the center. You can get general information about the center from the local Chamber of Commerce.

Some questions you may wish to ask during an interview include:

- What is the educational philosophy of your center?
- To what extent may I implement my own ideas?
- Is the staff encouraged to attend conferences? If so, how often may a staff member attend, and who pays the fees?
- What audio-visual materials are provided by the school?
- How often are parent conferences scheduled?
- Does the center send home a weekly parent letter or monthly newsletter? If so, who is responsible for writing and editing them?

Asking questions tells the interviewer that you are serious about a job. You want the job to be right for you.

### THE INTERVIEW

When you go to a job interview, take a copy of your resume, arrive on time, and look pro-

---

| TRAITS OF GOOD EARLY CHILDHOOD WORKERS | |
|---|---|
| • Cooperative | • Willing to do extra work |
| • A fast learner | • Easy to get along with |
| • A good time manager | • Creative |
| • Cheerful | • Resourcesful |
| • Dependable | • A good planner |
| • Committed to teaching | • Open to new ideas |
| • Self-disciplined | • Dedicated to hard work |
| • Motivated | • Thorough |
| • Self-reliant | • Friendly |
| • Self-directed | |
| • Energetic | |
| • Enthusiastic | |

29-9 Deciding which of these traits best fit you will help you focus on your best traits and skills during an interview.

fessional. If you are female, wear an attractive dress or skirt and blouse. If you are male, wear a nice pair of slacks (no blue jeans), and a shirt or shirt and sweater, depending on the weather. Avoid overdressing. Instead, try to wear clothes that an early childhood professional would wear on the job. A simple rule is that you should always dress for the job for which you are applying.

Have a good hair cut, shined shoes, and clean clothing. Do not smoke or chew gum during the interview. This may offend the interviewer(s). Remember, you want to come out a winner.

Greet the employer with a handshake. Many employers begin an interview simply by introducing themselves and welcoming you to the school. This is usually followed by small talk that might include the weather or an activity at school. After this, you will probably be told information about the job. The interviewer may then ask you structured questions concerning your education or experience. After all questions have been answered, the employer will ask you if you have any questions. At this point, you can ask those questions you prepared beforehand. Avoid asking questions about vacation time. The interviewer may think your main concern is with non-work functions.

Follow the lead of the person interviewing. Throughout the interview, listen with an intelligent, intent look on your face. When necessary, ask questions that will help you better understand the job. Other tips for successful interviewing are listed in 29-10.

Be careful not to volunteer negative information about your former employer or yourself. Employers are seeking positive people to work for them. If you were not happy in a previous job or jobs, you may not be happy with this job either. Thus, it is vital not to mention anything negative.

Throughout the interviewing process, you will need to sell yourself. When asked what you did during your practicum, student teaching, or last job, do not recite the daily schedule or curriculum. Instead, state specific things you did to improve the center or classroom. These are your success incidents. You will be sharing your worth. For example, you might tell about how you made protective education part of the curriculum. Or perhaps you revised the format for parent letters and reorganized the children's library, in addition to teaching a group of three-year-olds.

## Interview questions

Prospective employers usually decide before the interview what information they need to share with you about a job. Job expectations, duties, and benefits are often included. Specific questions that you may be asked are also recorded, 29-11. These are often listed in order of importance. The following questions are often included:

- Will you please share your educational background?
- What philosophy of education did that school have?
- What type of course work did you have?
- Do you have previous job experience? If so, describe your positions.
- Why are you looking for a new job?

---

### TIPS FOR A SUCCESSFUL INTERVIEW

- Be on time.
- Present your best appearance.
- Great the interviewer with a handshake.
- Bring a resume with you.
- Remain relaxed and friendly.
- Convey a positive attitude.
- Show your enthusiasm.
- Stress your strengths.
- Personalize your questions.
- Respond to questions carefully.
- Be truthful—if you do not know an answer, say so.
- Provide more than a "yes" or "no" response to questions, but be concise.
- Thank the interviewer for his/her consideration at the end of the interview.

29-10 The interview is your chance to make a good impression. Following these tips will help you.

29-11 Interviewers often prepare questions for the applicant ahead of time. They may record the applicant's answers during the interview.

460

- How would you describe yourself as a teacher?
- Where do you see yourself professionally ten years from today? Describe that job.
- Why are you interested in this job?

In addition, any of the following questions may also be asked:

- What is the value of children's play?
- How would you handle a child that is always hitting others?
- How would you describe the ideal curriculum for a preschool child?
- How do you think your references described you when they were contacted?
- How would you handle transitions?
- How would you relate to parents?
- What is most annoying about children?
- On what basis do you plan curriculum for young children?
- What would you do if a child kicked you and said, "I don't like you"?

Employers who have had training in interviewing techniques may ask the following questions to find out more about your performance in your previous position:

- What disappointments did you face in your last teaching position?
- In what areas did your supervisor criticize you?
- In what areas did your supervisor compliment you?
- For what things did you need guidance or help from your supervisor?

Questions will also be asked to determine your level of motivation:

- Why did you select teaching young children as a career?
- Why did you apply for this job?
- What is your long-term career objective?
- What are you looking for in this position that you have not had in past positions?
- What type of position would you like to hold in three years? Ten years?

It is not unusual for an interviewer to ask, "What are your weaknesses?" If this happens, sit quietly for a moment. It is always a mistake to quickly answer a question off the top of your head. Give each question some thought, then form a response in your mind. Then respond carefully and positively. Do not put yourself down while answering this question. Rather, share your growth by saying something like, "I have really grown a lot in relationship to classroom control," or "My parent interaction skills really grew during the last few weeks of my student teaching." Or express your weaknesses in a positive way: I care too much about the children, I take my work too seriously, I try too many new ideas, etc.

## Legal problems in interviewing

Affirmative action employers are forbidden to discriminate against women, ethnic minorities, and people from poverty areas. At both the state and federal level, it is also illegal to discriminate on the basis of age, sex, national origin, race, or religion.

Most employers do not intend to use information obtained from an interview in order to discriminate. However, such information could affect the hiring decision. Therefore, it is illegal for an employer to ask questions about an applicant's race, national origin, or religion.

During an interview, there is usually little doubt about an applicant's sex. However, interviewers are also limited in the questions that can be asked about a person's sex. For example, a mother of small children cannot be asked how the children will be cared for while she is working. Likewise she cannot be asked about spouses's employment or salary. This question cannot be asked of a male, either.

Women cannot be asked if they are planning to have a family or are currently pregnant. Interviewers are also forbidden to ask applicants their marital status or the number of children they have. Chart 29-12 lists questions that may be asked. During an interview, to prevent discrimination, all applicants for a job should be asked the same questions.

Despite the fact that they are illegal, you may still find yourself being asked some of these questions. Some prospective employers may purposely ask such questions to discriminate. Others, however, may simply ask them in an effort to get to know you better or make you feel at ease. These interviewers may not even know that the question(s) they ask is illegal.

## LEGAL QUESTIONS

| SUBJECT | INTERVIEWER |
|---|---|
| **Age** | Date of birth |
| **Arrests** | Nothing |
| **Marital status** | Nothing |
| **Convictions** | Only on convictions that would affect the job position. |
| **Education** | Only questions related to training and experience related to the position. |
| **Family** | Only questions related to meeting work schedule. |
| **Handicaps** | Only questions about handicaps that would affect job performance. |
| **National origin** | Only questions about ability to read, speak, and write the language the job requires. |
| **Organizations** | Only questions about participation in professional organizations related to the position. |
| **Pregnancy** | Only questions about anticipated absences from the center. |
| **Religion** | Only questions about anticipated absences. |

29-12 Interviewers are not allowed to ask questions that may result in discrimination.

If you are ever asked an illegal question, it is up to you to decide what the intent of the interviewer is. Based on your judgment, use discretion and tact to handle the situation. You may decide to simply answer the question. If you believe the person's intent was to discriminate, and then you are offered the job, you may ask why the question was asked. If the person's answer concerns you, you may decide to decline the job offer.

You may also choose to not answer the question. Do not accuse the person of discrimination. Instead, you may say simply and calmly, "I am sorry, but I am not required to answer that question."

### Ending the interview

An interview can be ended with words and/or through actions. Verbally, the interviewer may thank you for coming to signal the end of the interview. Nonverbally, the interviewer may sit up straight or stand up. This gesture means the interview is over. At this point, the interviewer has gotten all of the information from you that is needed. Respond by thanking the interviewer for his or her time. See 29-13.

Many people feel bad when they learn they were not successful in getting the job. If you feel this way, do not think something is wrong with you. It is not unusual to feel depressed or feel an erosion of your self-esteem. These feelings will pass.

### Thank-you's

Always write a brief note thanking the people who interviewed you. Mention the secretaries, if appropriate. This is a basic courtesy. Also, your letter will serve as a reminder to those you

29-13 Be sure to leave the interviewer with a positive impression of you.

met. Even if you are not hired for that position, these people may remember you for future openings. They may even pass your name on to someone else who is searching for a child care employee.

## ON THE JOB

Positive human relations are key in any position. As a new employee, make every effort to get along with the staff, 29-14. The best way to do this is to observe, listen, and gently question.

Make a list of questions to show you are interested in knowing more about your job and improving your skills. As you think of each question, write it down. When there is time, ask your supervisor. If this person does not know the answer, he or she will likely direct you to someone who knows. Show respect for the knowledge and experience of your fellow employees. This will bring about good working relationships on the job and mutual respect in the future.

## SUMMARY

Searching for a job is a rewarding, but sometimes frustrating, experience. During a job search you can learn a great deal about yourself: likes, dislikes, strengths, weaknesses. A well-organized job search is never boring!

While every person's search is different, there are some generally accepted guidelines for conducting your hunt. Start with a resume. Use your resume when you meet with or talk to potential employers.

When you secure an interview, be prepared. Have questions to ask the interviewer, and be ready to answer his or hers. Conduct yourself in a professional manner and show your enthusiasm for the child care field.

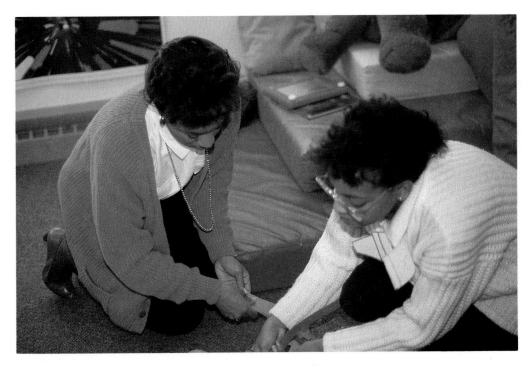

29-14 Getting along with staff members is as important to job success as working well with children.

## to Know

hidden job market
net income
resume

## to Review

1. A _____ should include a list of your qualifications, skills, and job experience.

2. True or false. The job objective must always come before a listing of your educational background.

3. How can the recent graduate stress job experience on his or her resume?

4. The cost of placing an ad in a newspaper varies depending on the:
    a. City.
    b. Circulation.
    c. Number of days printed.
    d. All of the above.

5. What is the major disadvantage of placing a position wanted ad?

6. What is the hidden job market?

7. What steps might you take to learn about job openings through the hidden market?

8. When preparing for an interview:
    a. Think positively.
    b. Put the interview out of your mind until the time it is scheduled.
    c. Prepare answers for all questions you may be asked.
    d. None of the above.

9. Asking questions about a job shows the interviewer you are _____ about the position.

10. True or false. Men and women should always wear suits to an interview.

11. If an interviewer asks you what your weaknesses are, you should:
    a. Answer quickly.
    b. Think for a moment before answering.
    c. Refuse to answer.
    d. None of the above.

12. It is illegal to discriminate on the basis of an applicant's:
    a. Age.
    b. Sex.
    c. Religion.
    d. All of the above.

## to Do

1. Prepare a resume. When you finish, ask your teacher for suggestions on how you might improve it.

2. Clip ads for early childhood care positions from the newspaper. Rank these positions according to your preference.

3. Attend a meeting of a local chapter of the National Association for the Education of Young Children. Talk with a variety of the members to learn about their work.

4. Conduct a survey of the salaries paid to teachers and assistant teachers in your area.

# *Appendix*

## DEVELOPMENTAL TRAITS OF CHILDREN FROM BIRTH TO AGE FIVE*

| BIRTH TO TWO YEARS OF AGE | |
|---|---|
| **MOTOR SKILLS** | |
| **1 Month** | Does not control arm and leg movements since movements are still reflexive.<br>Needs support for head. Without support, head will flop backward and forward.<br>Lifts head briefly from the surface in order to turn head from side to side when lying on tummy.<br>Twitches whole body when crying.<br>Keeps hands fisted or slightly open.<br>May hold object if place in hand, but drops it quickly.<br>Follows moving object briefly if the object is within the line of vision. |
| **2 Months** | Can keep head in midposition of body when lying on tummy.<br>Can hold head up for a few minutes.<br>Can turn head when lying on back.<br>Cycles arms and legs smoothly. Movements are mainly reflexive, but may become voluntary.<br>Grasps objects in reflex movements, but grasps are becoming voluntary.<br>May hold object longer, but drops object after a few minutes.<br>Uses improved vision to look at objects more closely and for a longer time. |
| **3 Months** | Can move arms and legs together.<br>Turns head vigorously.<br>Can lift head for several minutes.<br>Can sit briefly, with support. |
| **4 Months** | On tummy, can lift head and chest from surface, using arms for support.<br>On tummy, may roll from side to side.<br>Can maintain a sitting position for several minutes if given proper support.<br>Uses hands more skillfully.<br>Begins to use mitten grasp for grabbing objects.<br>Looks from object to hands to object.<br>Swipes at objects, gradually improving aim. |
| **5 Months** | On back, can lift head and shoulders off surface.<br>Can roll from tummy to back.<br>When supported under arms, stands and moves body up and down, stamping feet alternately.<br>Helps when being pulled to a sitting position.<br>Can sit supported for 15 to 30 minutes with a firm back.<br>Reaches for objects such as a cradle gym with good coordination and aim.<br>Begins to grasp objects with thumb and fingers.<br>Grabs objects with either hand.<br>Transfers objects from one hand to the other, dropping objects often. |
| **6 Months** | Rolls from back to tummy.<br>On tummy, moves by pushing with legs and reaching with arms.<br>Gets up on hands and knees in a crouching position, but then may fall forward.<br>Is able to stand while supported. |

*The items listed are based on average ages when various traits emerge. Many children may develop certain traits at an earlier or later age.

| | |
|---|---|
| | May be able to sit for short periods of time.<br>Reaches with one arm and grasps object with hand. Then transfers the object to other hand. Then reaches for another object.<br>Holds an object in both hands.<br>Learns to drop an object at will. |
| **7 Months** | Crawls awkwardly, combining movements of tummy and knees.<br>Likes to bounce when in standing position.<br>May be able to pull self up to a standing position.<br>Can lean over and reach while in sitting position.<br>Has mastered grasping by using thumb in opposition to fingers.<br>Holds an object in each hand. Brings objects together with banging noises.<br>Keeps objects in hands most of the time.<br>Fingers, manipulates, and rattles objects repeatedly. |
| **8 Months** | Sits alone, steadily, for longer periods of time.<br>Crawls.<br>Achieves sitting position by pushing up with arms.<br>Learns pincer grip, using just the thumb and forefinger.<br>Is able to pick up small objects and string. |
| **9 Months** | Sits alone.<br>May try to crawl up stairs.<br>May be able to move along furniture, touching it for support.<br>Uses index finger to point, to lead, and to poke.<br>Waves "bye-bye." |
| **10 Months** | Likes to walk holding on to caregiver's hands.<br>Climbs up on chairs and other furniture.<br>Stands with little support.<br>Can release grasped object instead of dropping it. |
| **11 Months** | Stands alone.<br>Is able to stand and pick up objects.<br>Likes to grasp feeding utensils and cup.<br>May carry spoon to mouth in feeding attempt.<br>Takes off shoes and socks. |
| **12 Months** | Climbs up and down stairs.<br>May show preference for one hand.<br>May be able to take off clothes.<br>Walks with one hand held. |
| **13 to 15 Months** | Builds a tower consisting of 2 one-inch cubes.<br>Turns pages in a book 2 or 3 at a time.<br>Walks without assistance.<br>Builds tower of two blocks.<br>While walking, cannot maneuver around corners or stop suddenly. |
| **16 to 18 Months** | Walks up steps.<br>Walks well while carrying a toy or pulling a pull toy.<br>Hurls a ball. |
| **19 to 22 Months** | Draws with spontaneous scribbling.<br>Complets a 3 piece formboard.<br>Places 4 rings on post in random order.<br>Rolls, pounds, squeezes, and pulls clay.<br>Kicks backward and forward. |
| **22 to 24 Months** | Attempts to stand on balance beam.<br>Builds tower of 6 cubes.<br>Runs without falling. |

| | Pedals a tricycle.<br>Kicks a large ball. |
|---|---|
| **INTELLECTUAL SKILLS** | |
| **1 Month** | Prefers to look at human faces and patterned objects.<br>Listens attentively to sounds and voices.<br>Cries deliberately for assistance.<br>Is comforted by the human voice and music. |
| **2 Months** | Coordinates eye movements.<br>Shows obvious preference for faces to objects.<br>Makes some sounds, but most vocalizing is still crying.<br>Shows some interest in sounds and will stop sucking to listen. |
| **3 Months** | Is able to suck and look at the same time, thus doing two controlled<br>actions at once.<br>Discovers hands and feet as an extension of self.<br>Searches with eyes for sounds.<br>Begins cooing one syllable, vowel-like sounds—ooh, ah, aw. |
| **4 Months** | Likes to repeat enjoyable acts like shaking a rattle.<br>Enjoys watching hands and feet.<br>Looks at an object, reaches for it, and makes contact with it.<br>Makes first consonant sounds—p, b, m, l.<br>Smiles and coos when caregiver talks to him or her. |
| **5 Months** | Recognizes and responds to own name.<br>Smiles at self in mirror.<br>Can recognize people by their voices. |
| **6 Months** | Grabs at any and all objects in reach.<br>Studies objects intently, turning them to see all sides.<br>Varies volume, pitch, and rate while babbling. |
| **7 Months** | Enjoys looking through books with familiar pictures.<br>May begin to imitate an act.<br>May say mama or dada but does not connect words with parents. |
| **8 Months** | Likes to empty and fill containers.<br>Begins jargoning by putting together a long series of syllables.<br>May label object in imitation of its sounds, such as choo-choo for train. |
| **9 Months** | Responds appropriately to a few specific words.<br>Likes to look for content in a container. |
| **10 to 12 Months** | Links specific acts or events to other events.<br>Can point to body parts.<br>Likes to look at pictures in a book.<br>Puts nesting toys together correctly.<br>Begins to find familiar objects which are not in view but have permanent<br>locations (looks for cookies after being told he or she can have one). |
| **13 to 15 Months** | Identifies family members in photographs.<br>Gives mechanical toy to caregiver to activate toy.<br>Has an expressive vocabulary of four to ten words; most nouns in<br>vocabulary refer to animals, food, and toys. |
| **16 to 18 Months** | Demonstrates knowledge of absence of familiar person (points to door, says<br>"gone").<br>Enjoys cause-effect relationships (banging on drum, splashing water, turning<br>on the television set).<br>Has expressive vocabulary of 10 to 20 words. |

| 19 to 24 Months | Mimics adult behaviors.<br>Points to and names objects in a book.<br>Plays identification games using body parts (points to ears, nose, eyes, teeth, etc. upon request).<br>Has expressive vocabulary of 20 to 50 words. |
|---|---|
| **SOCIAL-EMOTIONAL SKILLS** | |
| 1 Month | Reacts to discomfort and pain.<br>Recognizes a parent's voice.<br>Is comforted by the human face. |
| 2 Months | Smiles.<br>Is able to show distress, excitement, contentment, and delight.<br>Can quiet self by sucking.<br>Looks at a person alertly and directly.<br>Quiets in response to being held.<br>Shows affection by looking at person while kicking, waving arms, and smiling.<br>May perform to get attention. |
| 3 Months | Shows feelings of security when held or talked to.<br>Senses that the hands and feet are extensions of self.<br>Whimpers when hungry; chortles when content.<br>Communicates with different sounds and facial expressions.<br>Responds with total body to a familiar face.<br>Tries to attract attention of caregiver. |
| 4 Months | Expresses delight and laughs.<br>May form an attachment to one special object.<br>Responds to continued warmth and affection.<br>Shows increased pleasure in social interactions.<br>Enjoys social aspects of feeding time.<br>Becomes unresponsive if left alone most of waking hours. |
| 5 Months | May begin to show fearful behavior as separateness is felt.<br>Distinguishes between familiar and unfamiliar adults.<br>Builds trust when cries are answered; becomes anxious and demanding when cries are unanswered.<br>May be able to play the peek-a-boo game. |
| 6 Months | Enjoys playing with children.<br>Responds to affection and may imitate signs of affection.<br>Likes attention and may cry to get it.<br>May begin clinging to a primary caregiver.<br>Laughs when socializing.<br>Smiles at familiar faces and stares solemnly at strangers.<br>Desires constant attention from caregiver. |
| 7 Months | May show more dependence on caregiver for security.<br>Has increased drive for independence but senses frightening situations.<br>Shows desire for social contacts.<br>Thoroughly enjoys company of siblings.<br>Begins to have a sense of humor. |
| 8 Months | Exhibits fear of strangers.<br>May anticipate being left and, if so, becomes disturbed.<br>Values quick display of love and support from caregiver.<br>Likes to explore new places, but wants to be able to return to caregiver.<br>Enjoys playing with own image in a mirror.<br>Definitely prefers caregiver to strangers.<br>Is more aware of social approval or disapproval. |

| 9 Months | May show fear of heights; may be afraid to crawl down from a chair. |
|----------|---------------------|
|          | May show a fear of new sounds, such as a vacuum cleaner. |
|          | Shows interest in play activities of others. |
|          | Likes to play games like pat-a-cake. |
|          | Recognizes the social nature of mealtimes. |
| 10 Months | Cries less often. |
|          | Expresses delight, happiness, sadness, discomfort, and anger. |
|          | May be able to show symbolic thought by giving love to a stuffed toy. |
|          | Is more aware of and sensitive toward other children. |
|          | Enjoys music and may mimic movements others make to music. |
| 11 Months | May not always want to be cooperative. |
|          | Recognizes the difference between being good and being naughty. |
|          | May say ''no'' while shaking head, but will continue to do the forbidden thing. |
|          | Seeks approval and tries to avoid disapproval. |
|          | Imitates movements of other adults and children. |
|          | Likes to say ''no'' and shake head to get response from a caregiver. |
|          | Tests caregivers to determine limits. |
|          | Objects to having his or her enjoyable play stopped. |
| 12 Months | May reveal an inner determination to walk. |
|          | Begins to develop self-identity and independence. |
|          | Shows increased negativism. |
|          | Enjoys playing with siblings. |
|          | Likes to practice communication with adults. |
|          | Continues to test caregivers limits. |
| 13 to 15 Months | Shows pride in personal accomplishment. |
|          | Likes to exhibit affection to humans and to objects. |
|          | Prefers to keep caregiver in sight while exploring environment. |
|          | Demands personal attention. |
|          | May show fear of strangers. |
|          | Shows increased negativism. |
|          | Enjoys solitary play. |
|          | Shows preference for family members over others. |
|          | Recognizes self in mirror and may communicate with sounds. |
| 16 to 18 Months | Is emotionally unpredictable and may respond differently at different times. |
|          | Is unable to tolerate frustration. |
|          | May reveal negativism and stubbornness. |
|          | May exhibit fear of thunder, lightning, large animals, etc. |
|          | Is very socially responsive to parents and caregivers. |
|          | Responds to simple requests. |
|          | May punch and poke peers as if they were objects. |
|          | Will perform for an audience. |
|          | Is unable to share. |
| 19 to 21 Months | May become possessive about toys, hiding them from others. |
|          | Likes to claim things as ''mine.'' |
|          | Gives up items that belong to others upon request. |
|          | Begins to show sympathy to another child or adult. |
|          | Continues to desire personal attention. |
|          | Indicates awareness of a person's absence by saying ''bye-bye.'' |
|          | May enjoy removing clothing and is not embarrassed about being naked. |
|          | Reveals a sense of trust in adults. |
|          | Plays contentedly alone if near adults. |
|          | Likes to play next to other children, but does not interact with them. |
|          | Is able to play some simple interacting games for short periods of time. |

| 22 to 24 Months | Displays signs of love for parents and other favorite people. |
|---|---|
| | Is easily hurt by criticism. |
| | Becomes frustrated easily. |
| | May show some aggressive tendencies, such as slapping, biting, hitting. |
| | May assume an increasingly self-sufficient attitude. |
| | Wants own way in everything. |
| | May dawdle but desires to please adults. |
| | Is more responsive to and demanding of adults. |
| | Still prefers to play alone, but likes to be near others. |
| | Engages in imaginative play related to parents' actions. |
| | Uses own name in reference to self when talking to others. |
| | Is continually testing limits set by parents and caregivers. |
| | Likes to control others and give them orders. |

## TWO- AND THREE-YEAR-OLDS

### GROSS MOTOR SKILLS

| 24 to 29 Months | Runs without falling. |
|---|---|
| | Pedals a tricycle. |
| | Kicks a large ball. |
| | Jumps in place. |
| | Plays on swings, ladders, and other playground equipment with fair amount of ease. |
| | Throws ball without falling. |
| | Bends at waist to pick up object from floor. |
| | Walks up and down stairs, both feet on step, while holding on to railings. |
| | Stands with both feet on balance beam. |
| 30 to 36 Months | Walks on tip toes. |
| | Performs a standing broad jump 8 1/2 inches. |
| | Attempts to balance on one foot. |
| | Walks to and picks up a large ball. |
| | Balances on one foot for 5 seconds. |
| | Catches a large ball with arms. |
| | Walks up stairs with alternating feet. |
| | Rides a tricycle. |
| | Performs 1 to 3 hops with both feet together. |
| 37 to 48 Months | Walks toe-to-heel for four steps. |
| | Balances on one foot for 8 seconds. |
| | Catches a beanbag while standing. |
| | Performs 1 to 3 hops on one foot. |
| | Catches a bounced ball with hands. |

### FINE MOTOR SKILLS

| 24 to 29 Months | Inserts key into lock. |
|---|---|
| | Turns pages in a book singly. |
| | Strings large beads. |
| | Copies a circle. |
| | Copies a vertical line. |
| | Copies a horizontal line. |
| | Builds a tower consisting of 6 to 7 cubes. |
| | Uses two or more cubes to make a train. |
| | Uses one hand consistently for most activities. |
| | Holds scissors correctly. |
| | Opens and closes scissors. |

470

| | |
|---|---|
| **30 to 36 Months** | Builds a tower consisting of 8 cubes.<br>Copies an "H."<br>Copies a "V."<br>Copies a circle.<br>Imitates building a three-block bridge.<br>Snips paper with scissors. |
| **37 to 48 Months** | Pours liquid from a pitcher.<br>Copies a cross.<br>Builds a tower of 9 to 10 cubes.<br>Completes simple puzzles.<br>Wiggles thumb.<br>Folds paper twice (in imitation).<br>Draws a person with three parts.<br>Cuts a 5-inch piece of paper in two.<br>Traces a diamond.<br>Cuts along a 5-inch line within 1/2 inch of the line. |
| **SELF-HELP SKILLS** | |
| **24 to 29 Months** | Cooperates in dressing.<br>Removes shoes, socks, and pants.<br>Pulls on simple garments.<br>Unzips zipper.<br>Unsnaps snap.<br>Verbalizes toilet needs.<br>Usually remains dry during the day. |
| **30 to 36 Months** | Seldom has bowel accidents.<br>Unbuttons large buttons.<br>Closes snaps.<br>Sits on toilet without assistance.<br>Puts on shoes.<br>Pours well from a pitcher.<br>Uses a knife for spreading. |
| **37 to 48 Months** | Washes and dries face and hands.<br>Unbuckles belt.<br>Usually remains dry at night.<br>Turns faucet on and off. |
| **EXPRESSIVE LANGUAGE SKILLS** | |
| **24 to 29 Months** | Combines two or more words (boy hit).<br>Developing three term relations such as, "I kick ball," "You go home," "See my daddy."<br>Yes/no questions marked only by intonation (Mommy go? You see me?).<br>No and not used to negate entire sentence (No eat; Mommy no; No sit down).<br>Preposition "in" used (Go in house; Ball in box).<br>Plural used (More cookies; cats). |
| **30 to 36 Months** | Negative elements no, can't, and don't used after subject (I can't eat; Mommy, don't go).<br>Use of different modifiers: qualifiers (some, a lot, all one); possessives (mine, his, hers); adjectives (pretty, new, blue).<br>Overgeneralization of regular past with an "ed" (He eated it; I woked up). |
| **37 to 48 Months** | Preposition "on" used (book on table; sit on chair).<br>Possessive ('s) used (mommy's coat; daddy's car). |

| | "When" questions appear. |
|---|---|
| | Negatives cannot and do not appear. |
| | Double negatives appear when using negative pronoun (nobody, nothing) or negative adverb (never, nowhere). Examples include, "I can't do nothing," or, "I don't never get to go." |
| | Sentences with two clauses are joined (then it broke and we didn't have it anymore). |

| LANGUAGE COMPREHENSION SKILLS | |
|---|---|
| 24 to 29 Months | Child answers routine questions (What is that? What is your name? What is [person] doing?). <br> Points to six body parts on doll or self. <br> Provides appropriate answers to yes/no questions that deal with the child's environment (Is mommy sleeping? Is daddy cooking?). <br> Comprehends pronouns: I, my, mine, me. |
| 30 to 36 Months | Follows two-step directions. <br> Provides appropriate answers for "where" (place) questions that deal with familiar information (Where does daddy work? Where do you sleep?). <br> Comprehends pronouns: she, he, his, him, and her. |
| 37 to 48 Months | Provides appropriate answers for "whose" questions (Whose doll is this?). <br> Provides appropriate answers for "why" (cause or reason) questions (Why is the girl crying?). <br> Provides appropriate answers for "who" (person or animal) questions (Who lives at the North pole?). <br> Understands the pronouns you and they. <br> Provides appropriate answers for "how" questions (How will mother bake the pie?). |

| MATH READINESS SKILLS | |
|---|---|
| 30 to 36 Months | Gives "just one" upon request. <br> Comprehends concepts soft and heavy in object manipulation tasks. <br> Comprehends size concepts big and tall in object manipulation tasks. <br> Comprehends spatial concepts on, under, out of, together, and away from in object manipulation tasks. |
| 37 to 48 Months | Gives "just two" upon request. <br> Distinguishes between one and many. <br> Understands the quantity concept "empty" in object manipulation tasks. <br> Understands "smaller;" points to smaller opjects. <br> Eighty percent understand "largest." <br> Counts while correctly pointing to 3 objects. <br> Understands quantity concepts full, more, and less in object manipulation tasks. <br> Comprehends spatial concepts up, top, apart, and toward in object manipulation tasks. <br> Comprehends spatial concepts around, in front of, in back of, high, and next to in object manipulation tasks. |

| SOCIAL SKILLS | |
|---|---|
| 24 to 29 Months | Likes to play near other children, but is unable to play cooperatively. <br> Becomes a grabber, and may grab desired toys away from other children. <br> Does not like to share toys. <br> Has not learned to say please but often desires the toys of other children. <br> Likes to give affection to parents. <br> May pull hair or bite before giving up a desired possession. |

| 30 to 36 Months | Continues to have a strong sense of ownership but may give up a toy if offered a substitute.<br>May learn to say "please" if prompted.<br>Has increased desire to play near and with other children.<br>May begin cooperative play.<br>Distinguishes between boys and girls.<br>Likes to be accepted by others.<br>Enjoys hiding from others.<br>Likes to play with adults on a one-to-one basis.<br>Enjoys tumble play with other children and caregivers. |
|---|---|
| 37 to 48 Months | Is learning to share and take turns.<br>Follows directions and takes pride in doing things for others.<br>May act in a certain way just to please caregivers.<br>Makes friends easily.<br>Seeks status among peers.<br>May attempt to comfort and remove cause of distress of playmates.<br>Seeks friends on own initiative.<br>Begins to be choosy about companions, preferring one over another.<br>Uses language to make friends and to alienate others. |

## EMOTIONAL DEVELOPMENT

| 24 to 29 Months | Continues to be self-centered.<br>May exhibit increasing independence one minute and then run back to security of parents the next.<br>Likes immediate gratification of desires and finds it difficult to wait.<br>May exhibit negativism.<br>Continues to seek caregiver approval for behaviors and accomplishments.<br>Displays jealousy.<br>May develop fear of dark; needs reassurance. |
|---|---|
| 30 to 36 Months | May display negative feelings and occasional bad temper.<br>May exhibit aggressiveness.<br>May dawdle but insists on doing things for self.<br>Likes to dress self and needs praise and encouragement when correct.<br>Feels bad when reprimanded for mistakes.<br>Desires caregiver approval.<br>Wants independence but shows fear of new experiences.<br>May reveal need for clinging to security object.<br>Needs an understanding, orderly environment.<br>May have trouble sleeping if the day's events have been emotional. |
| 37 to 48 Months | Is usually cooperative, happy, and agreeable.<br>Feels less frustrated because motor skills have been improved.<br>May still seek comfort from caregivers when tired or hungry.<br>Learns more socially acceptable ways of displaying feelings.<br>May substitute language for primitive emotional feelings.<br>May show fear of dark, animals, stories, and the bogeyman. |

## FOUR- AND FIVE-YEAR-OLDS

## GROSS MOTOR SKILLS

| 4 Years | Catches beanbag with hands.<br>Skips on one foot.<br>Walks down stairs with alternating feet.<br>Throws ball overhand.<br>Carries a cup of liquid without spilling.<br>Rides bicycle with training wheels. |
|---|---|

| | |
|---|---|
| | Balances on one foot ten seconds.<br>Skips with alternating feet.<br>Walks backward toe-to-heel for four consecutive steps. |
| **5 Years** | Marches to music.<br>Jumps from table height.<br>Climbs fences.<br>Attempts to jump rope.<br>Attempts to roller skate.<br>Walks forward, backward, and sideways on balance beam.<br>Catches ball with hands. |
| **FINE MOTOR SKILLS** | |
| **4 Years** | Builds a three block bridge from a model.<br>Completes a six to eight piece puzzle.<br>Folds paper diagonally (three folds).<br>Copies a square. |
| **5 Years** | Copies a triangle.<br>Prints first name.<br>Prints simple words.<br>Dials telephone numbers correctly.<br>Models objects with clay.<br>Colors within lines. |
| **SELF-HELP SKILLS** | |
| **4 Years** | Laces shoes.<br>Buckles belt.<br>Cuts with knife.<br>Dresses and undresses with supervision.<br>Distinguishes front and back of clothing.<br>Zips separating zipper. |
| **5 Years** | Dresses and undresses without assistance.<br>Washes self.<br>Puts shoes on correct feet.<br>Unbuttons back buttons. |
| **LANGUAGE SKILLS** | |
| **4 Years** | Understands has/doesn't have and is/is not.<br>Identifies penny, nickel, and dime.<br>Follows three commands in proper order (clear the table, wash the table, and get ready to go outdoors).<br>Understands the pronoun we.<br>Uses irregular verb forms (ate, ran, went).<br>Uses regular tense (ed) verbs.<br>Uses third person present tense verbs (runs, shops). |
| **5 Years** | Uses third person irregular verbs. (He has a ball.)<br>Uses compound sentences. (I went to the grocery store and I went to my grandmother's.)<br>Uses descriptions in telling a story.<br>Uses some pronouns correctly.<br>Uses words to describe sizes, distances, weather, time, and location.<br>Asks the meaning of words.<br>Recalls the main details of a story.<br>Recognizes some verbal absurdities.<br>Tells original stories. |

## MATH READINESS SKILLS

| 4 Years | Understands the concepts beside, bottom, backward, and forward in object manipulation tasks. Understands size concepts short, fat, and thin in object manipulation tasks. Counts 1 to 4 chips and correctly answers questions such as "How many altogether?" with cardinal number. Says correct number when shown 2 to 6 objects and asked, "How many?" Can rote count 1 through 9. Understands the concepts of triangle and circle. Understands the concepts tallest and same size. |
|---|---|
| 5 Years | Understands square and rectangle. Understands the concept of same shape. Understands the position concepts first and last in object manipulation tasks. Understands position concept middle. Rote counts 1 through 20. Recognizes the numerals 1 through 10. Writes the numerals 1 through 5. May count 1 to 20 objects correctly. |

## SOCIAL-EMOTIONAL DEVELOPMENT

| 4 Years | May not be as pleasant and cooperative as at age three. May be more moody. Strives for independence; resents being treated like a baby. May be stubborn and quarrelsome. Resents directions; thinks he or she knows it all and can do it all. Learns to ask for things instead of snatching things from others. Is increasingly aware of attitudes and asks for approval. Needs and seeks parental approval often. Has strong sense of family and home. May quote parents and boast about parents to friends. Becomes more interested in friends than in adults. Shares possessions and toys, especially with special friends. Suggests taking turns but may be unable to wait for his or her own turn. Likes to play with friends in cooperative play activities. |
|---|---|
| 5 Years | Shows increased willingness to cooperate. Is more patient, generous, and conscientious. Expresses anger verbally rather than physically. Is more reasonable when in a quarrel. Develops a sense of fairness. Likes supervision, accepts instructions, and asks permission. Has a strong desire to please parents and other adults. Still depends on parents for emotional support and approval. Is proud of mother and father. Delights in helping parents. May act protective of younger siblings. Shapes ideas of sex roles by watching parents' behavior. Is increasingly social and talkative. Is eager to make friends and develop strong friendships. May pick a best friend. Prefers cooperative play in small groups. Prefers friends of same age and most often of same sex. Stays with play groups as long as interests hold. Learns to respect the property of friends. |

**Adapted from Verdene Ryder,** *Parents and Their Children,* Goodheart-Willcox Publishing Company, Inc., 1985.

# Acknowledgements

Through the long months of writing this manuscript, there were many individuals whose encouragement, support, and expertise helped me immeasurably. My sincere thanks to all of them.

First, to my husband, Dr. James Herr, and Mark and John, my sons, who supported me throughout this process.

To Dr. Judy Jax who saw a need for this textbook.

To Robin Muza and Shirley Gebhart, my typists, who so ably transcribed my writing.

To Eileen Zenk, Margaret Brunn, Judy Gifford, Paula Noll, Peg Saienga, Lori Register, Patti Herman, Janet Massa, Mary Ann Spangler, Teresa Mitchell, Rita Devery, Dr. Priscilla Huffman, Candy Jordon, Carla Ahmann, Nancy McCarthy, Diane Carriveau, Linda DeMoe, Dr. Karen Zimmerman, Dr. Joan Herwig, Elaine Staaland, Charlotte Cummins, Sung Jee Chung, Janet Maffet, Cari Parent, Nancy Graese, Nan Olson, Karen Stepens, Angela La Bonne Kaiser, Paulette Fontaine, Paula Iverson, Jeannette Daines, Pat Resinger, Betsy Halden, Sharon Kaminski, Sandra Winder, Sally Olm, Phyllis Barilla, Irene Larson, Florence Burke, Lori Pioske, Elizabeth Kaster, Jill Behnke, and Melba Rolland for their support and encouragement throughout this project.

To Yvonne Libby, a colleague and co-author with me on other publications, who listened to my complaints about writers' block and encouraged me to continue.

To Mary Pugmire who assisted me with all phases of the book.

To May Broines, Kathy Rucker Schaffer, Greg Ross, Kathy Yeager, and Kim Moore for assistance with contributing pictures.

Finally, to all of the early childhood education majors at the University of Wisconsin-Stout and the children enrolled in the Child and Family Study Center who have facilitated my thinking for this book.

**Judy Herr**

# Photo Credits

# Glossary

## A

**abrasion:** a scrape that damages a portion of the skin, such as a skinned knee, scratched arm, or rope burn.

**acceleration:** process in which a gifted child is assigned to a class with older children.

**acoustic material:** material used to deaden or absorb sounds. Carpets, drapes, bulletin boards, pillows, stuffed toys, and sand are examples.

**active listening:** listening to what is said, then repeating what was just said.

**activity patterns:** levels of movements in infants.

**ageism:** stereotyping of the elderly.

**allergy:** a sensitivity to a substance, possibly causing rashes, swelling, sneezing, or other reactions.

**amblyopia:** the result of a muscle imbalance caused by disuse of an eye. Often called lazy eye.

**ambulatory:** being able to move from place to place.

**anecdotal records:** notes kept by the teacher concerning children's play.

**animal stories:** books giving animals some human qualities. Usually, the animal hero has some unusual success or ability.

**anophylactic shock:** extreme allergic reaction to insect stings causing shock symptoms and could possibly death.

**arthritis:** condition brought on by inflammation of joints and surrounding tissues.

**articulation problems:** omissions, distortions, or substitutions of vowels or consonants or both. It is possible for a child to have one or more of these problems.

**articulation:** the ability to speak in clearly pronounced sounds.

**asthma:** a disease characterized by a recurrent shortness of breath. An annoying cough, wheezing, and whistling breathing also often occur with asthma.

**attachment behaviors:** behavior showing that infants care for and respond to certain people who are important to them.

**audible:** making clear, easily heard sounds.

**audio-visual board:** a smooth wall board that serves as a bulletin board, chalkboard, and movie screen. It is usually white, off white, or beige.

**auditory discrimination skills:** the ability to detect different sounds by listening.

**auditory learner:** a child who learns best through hearing. This child is the first to hear a fly in the classroom or a snow plow outdoors.

**auditory signals:** informing children of a change through the use of sound, such as a bell, timer, autoharp, tambourine, or piano.

**autoharp:** a simple chording instrument used to accompany singing.

## B

**Babinski reflex:** reflex that occurs when stroking the sole of the foot, causing the infant to fan the toes upward.

**bacteria:** small living organisms causing foodborne illnesses.

**behavioral expectations:** rules that children are expected to follow.

**behavioral objectives:** outcomes of an activity, used to plan teaching strategies.

**behaviors:** refers to any visible activities done by the child. It tells what the child will be doing.

**bentonite:** a clay product used as a thickening agent for powdered tempera paint.

**block plan:** a written overall view of the curriculum.

**body percussion:** musical movement activities such as stomping feet, clapping hands, patting thighs, and snapping fingers.

**burn:** an injury caused by heat, radiation, or chemical agents, generally classified by degree or depth.

## C

**capillaries:** small veins in the body.

**cautious:** slower to make decisions.

**cephalocaudal principle:** principle of development stating that development tends to proceed from the head downward. According to this principle, the child first gains control of the head, then the arms, then the legs.

**cerebral palsy:** condition resulting from damage to the brain and characterized by lack of control of voluntary movements.

**chalk talk:** storytelling method using drawings made on chalkboard, tagboard, or newsprint. Also called draw and tell.

**chant:** song that has word patterns, rhymes, and nonsense syllables in one to three tones repeated in a sequence.

**checking-in services:** program assigning caregivers to children in self-care. These caregivers call the children to make sure there are no problems.

**chronic health needs:** needs for special care caused by an illness that persists over a period of time.

**chronological age:** age determined by a birth date. Also known as physical age.

**class A fire:** fire involving ordinary combustible materials, such as common plastics, fabrics, paper, and wood.

**class B fire:** fire involving flammable liquids, including gases, grease, paints, and solvents.

**class C fire:** electrical fire.

**classification:** the process of mentally grouping objects or ideas into categories or classes based on some unique feature.

**closed wound:** an injury to the tissue directly under the skin surface, not involving a break in the skin, such as a bruise.

**close-ended questions:** questions requiring few decision-making skills and most often answered with yes or no. Also referred to as single-answer questions.

**closure:** how an activity will end.

**coaching:** teaching skill that provides children with ideas for difficult situations.

**color blindness:** the inability to see a color. This problem, also referred to as color deficiency, is hereditary.

**color deficiency:** the inability to see a color. This problem, also referred to as color blindness, is hereditary.

**communicable diseases:** illnesses that can be passed on to other people.

**conditions of performance:** list of tools a child will use, including puzzles, paper, scissors, beads, or any other materials and/or equipment found in early childhood settings. This list can also include what the child will be denied.

**conflict:** two or more forces that oppose each other.

**congenital defect:** a condition caused before birth but not hereditary.

**consistency:** enforcing rules in a regular, unchanging manner.

**consumable supplies:** supplies that, in most

cases, cannot be used again. Clay, paper, paint, paste, and other art materials are examples.

**contactants:** objects that make contact with the body through touch.

**cool colors:** colors, such as blue and green, that make a room appear larger and create a feeling of openness.

**co-op:** group of people or groups who join together so they have more buying power.

**cooperative play:** type of play in which two or more children interact with one another. At this stage socio-dramatic play begins.

**crawling:** a skill in the motor sequence occurring shortly after the infant learns to roll onto the stomach.

**creeping:** movement in which infants support their weight on their hands and knees, moving their arms and legs to go forward.

**cubbies:** top sections of lockers used to store finished artwork, library books, parent letters, and other valuable items.

**culture:** a group's ideas and ways of doing things—such as traditions, language, beliefs, and customs—which become a learned pattern of social behavior.

**custodial care:** type of family day care where emphasis is a safe and healthy environment, and one in which meals are provided.

**cystic fibrosis:** a chronic hereditary disease that involves persistent and serious lung infections, failure to gain weight, and loose, foul-smelling stools.

## D

**Daily Food Guide:** a guide to planning a well-balanced diet, ensuring good nutrition. This guide contains the five food groups.

**dawdling:** eating slowly or having a lack of interest in food. Sometimes used as an attempt to gain attention.

**day care centers:** full-day child care facilities that focus on the child's basic nutritional, social, emotional, intellectual, and physical needs.

**deferred imitation:** watching another person's behavior, then acting out that behavior. This occurs between eighteen and twenty-four months.

**demonstrating:** showing children how to do a task, such as buttoning, zipping, pulling on boots, tying shoes, and putting fingers in gloves.

**desensitized:** a process in which a doctor injects small amounts of an allergen into the body over a period of time building immunities to an irritant.

**development:** change or growth in a human being. Development is usually measured in terms of physical, intellectual, social, and emotional growth.

**developmental age:** a child's skill and growth level compared to what is thought of as normal for that physical age group.

**developmental scales:** lists of characteristics considered normal for children in certain age groups. Sometimes referred to as normative scales.

**diabetes:** a disease in which the body cannot properly control the level of sugar in the blood.

**direct guidance:** physical and verbal actions, such as facial and body gestures, that influence behavior.

**direct learning experiences:** learning experiences planned with a specific goal in mind.

**dramatic play:** a form of play in which a child imitates others.

**draw and tell:** storytelling method using drawings made on chalkboard, tagboard, or newsprint. Also called chalk talk.

## E

**early childhood:** the period of life from birth up to nine years of age.

**ecology:** study of the chain of life, focusing on water, land, air, grass, trees, birds, and insects.

**egocentric:** people concerned only with themselves.

**elimination:** bowel and bladder release.

**emetic:** a substance used for emergency poisonings. When swallowed, it will induce vomiting.

**emotional abuse:** abuse of a child's self-concept by parents or guardians through such acts as providing insufficient love, guidance, and/or support.

**employer sponsored programs:** child care provided by an employer.

**empty set:** a set without any members, such as a set of tables without legs or a set of children with beards.

**enrichment:** a process to broaden the range of experiences with special curriculum.

**epilepsy:** a convulsive disorder caused by damage to the brain causing a person to have periodic seizures. There are two types of seizures, grand mal and petit mal.

**expansion:** technique that involves taking a child's mispronounced words and correctly expanding them into sentences.

**expressive language:** the ability to produce language forms. Used to express a person's thoughts to others.

**extended preschool centers:** full-day child care facilities that focus on the child's basic nutritional, social, emotional, intellectual, and physical needs.

# F

**fairy tales:** books having a theme of achievement. The characters or heroes of these stories must perform difficult tasks in order to succeed.

**family day care:** child care that is provided in a private home.

**family life stories:** books containing the theme of social understanding.

**farsightedness:** difficulty in seeing things that are close. Also referred to as hyperopia.

**feely box:** a box with a circle cut in it large enough for children to put their hands into and identify different objects and materials placed inside.

**felt board:** a board covered with felt or flannel that is used as a background for placing felt characters and props to tell a story.

**field-independent:** children who are more independent and prefer to work on their own. They enjoy competition as well as individual recognition.

**field-sensitive:** children who are more interactive with others; volunteering, assisting, and helpful, they also try to gain attention.

**fine motor development:** improvement of skills using the small muscles, such as grasping, holding, cutting, and drawing.

**first-degree burns:** burns to the top layer of skin. They are the least severe of all burns. Signs include redness or mild discoloration, pain, and mild swelling.

**flannel board:** a board covered with felt or flannel that is used as a background for placing felt characters and props to tell a story.

**flexible rules:** rules that can be adapted to the needs of an individual or a situation.

**flipcharts:** stories drawn on large tagboard cards used for storytelling.

**food poisoning:** an infection occurring in the gastrointestinal tract from eating food with a high bacterial count. Common symptoms are vomiting and diarrhea.

**franchised centers:** centers associated with a company. They may be owned by the company or a local owner may have purchased the right to be in the company's franchise.

**frustration:** feelings of defeat or discouragement causing tension.

**functional stage:** second stage of material use. During this stage, a child will use a prop as intended while playing with other children.

# G

**gender roles:** behaviors expected of girls or boys. Though not as clearly defined as they once were, they are still an important part of learning.

**gerontology:** study of the aged.

**giftedness:** having exceptional skills in one or more of six areas: creative or productive thinking, general intellectual ability, leadership ability, psychomotor ability, specific academic aptitude, and/or visual or performing arts.

**glaucoma:** condition caused by failure of the eye fluid to circulate in the proper way, resulting in increased pressure on the eye. Over time, this pressure can destroy the optic nerve.

**grand mal seizure:** a reaction, or seizure, caused by epilepsy. During a grand mal seizure a child will lose consciousness, jerk, thrash, or become stiff.

**grasping reflex:** reflex that occurs when touching the infant's palms. This reflex disappears after the first three or four months after birth.

**gross motor development:** improvement of skills using the large muscles, such as running, skipping, and lifting weights.

**guidance:** direct and indirect actions used by an adult to help children develop socially acceptable behavior.

**guidance problems:** difficulty in controlling or teaching a child or children.

## H

**hand-eye coordination:** muscle control that allows the hand to do a task in the way the eye sees it done.

**head lice:** small bugs that make their homes on the hair and scalp. They lay small, round eggs, called nits, that feed on human blood.

**Head Start:** a program developed by the federal government to strengthen the academic skills of children from low-income homes, and designed for the social, emotional, physical, and intellectual needs of four- and five-year-olds.

**hemophilia:** genetic blood disease in which the blood cannot clot normally.

**hidden job market:** jobs advertised informally through word of mouth.

**hitching:** movement that occurs after an infant is able to sit without support. From this position, infants move their arms and legs, sliding their buttocks across the floor.

**hyperopia:** difficulty in seeing things that are close. Also referred to as farsightedness.

## I

**ignoring:** avoiding an acknowledgement to a child's inappropriate behavior if the behavior is not dangerous.

**imaginative stage:** the third and final stage of material use. Children in this stage do not need real props; they are able to think of substitutes.

**impulsive:** quick to make decisions.

**incidental learnings:** learning experiences that happen during the course of a normal day.

**indirect guidance:** outside factors influencing behavior, such as the layout of the center.

**indirect learning experiences:** learning experiences that occur on the spur of the moment.

**individual transition:** quietly informing a particular child of a change, such as cleaning up or going to the snack table.

**Individualized Educational Plan:** a written strategy for learning designed to ensure that each special needs child is educated in the most appropriate manner for him or her.

**induce:** to produce on purpose.

**infant:** term used to refer to a child for the first year after birth.

**ingestants:** foods, drugs, or anything taken through the mouth.

**inhalants:** airborne substances that are inhaled.

**injectables:** chemicals or drugs injected into the body.

**insulin:** a hormone that is needed to keep sugar in the blood at a proper level. As insulin is released, the blood sugar level drops.

**insulin reaction:** occurs in a person with diabetes when the amount of insulin is not properly adjusted.

**intellectual development:** growth in the mental processes used to gain knowledge, such as thought, reasoning, and imagination.

**internal:** under the skin.

**irritability:** tendency to feel distressed.

**isolation area:** special room or space in the center for children who become ill or show signs of a communicable disease.

## K

**kindergarten:** school for children who are at least four years old. Some kindergartens stress pre-academics, while others focus more on social development. Many kindergartens are part of public school systems.

## L

**laboratory schools:** schools located on a post secondary or college campus with a primary purpose of training future teachers and serving as a study group for research.

**language comprehension:** an understanding of language. Sometimes referred to as receptive or inner language.

**latch-key programs:** programs which provide care during after-school hours for children.

**lazy eye:** an eye disorder that is the result of a muscle imbalance caused by disuse of the eye. Also referred to as amblyopia.

**lesson plan:** a written plan outlining specific actions and activities that will be used to meet goals.

**letters:** written communication most often addressing only one subject and sent out on an "as needed" basis.

**leukemia:** a form of cancer that affects the blood-forming organs and the blood. This cancer causes a sharp increase in the number of white blood cells in the bloodstream.

**level of performance:** states the minimum standard of achievement and how well one might want the child to do.

**licensing specialist:** a person employed by a state to ensure that the state's child care rules and regulations are followed.

**limits:** classroom rules that protect the health and safety of the children, helping them feel freer to explore.

**listening:** giving full attention to another person or people.

# M

**mainstreaming:** term used for placing special needs children in a regular classroom, allowing children to learn in a less restrictive environment.

**malnutrition:** lack of nutrients caused by lack of nutrients in the diet or by the inability of the body to use the nutrients in the food. Malnutrition can occur even in children who eat the proper amounts of food.

**manipulative stage:** first stage of material use. Children in the manipulative stage will screw and unscrew a baby bottle cap.

**manuscript writing:** a simple form of calligraphy not requiring the sustained muscle control that cursive writing does. This writing involves unconnected letters made of simple, separate strokes.

**matching:** a form of classification involving putting like objects together.

**maturation:** sequence of biological changes in a child giving children new abilities.

**modeling:** verbal and nonverbal actions by one person, setting an example for others.

**Montessori schools:** schools providing children freedom within limits by a rather structured approach, and a fixed method in which materials are presented.

**Moro reflex:** reflex that occurs when a baby is startled by a noise or a sudden movement. The infant will fling the arms outward and quickly draw the arms into the chest. Lasts from birth to about three months of age.

**motivation:** in a lesson plan, a method of gaining children's attention.

**motor sequence:** order in which a child is able to perform new movements. Motor sequence depends on the development of the brain and nerves.

**multicultural toys:** toys that represent a variety of racial and ethnic groups.

**multipurpose dry chemical extinguishers:** only type of fire extinguisher designed to put out Class A, Class B, and Class C fires.

**myopia:** difficulty in seeing things that are far away. Also referred to as nearsightedness.

# N

**nanny:** a child care worker who provides care for a child in the child's home.

**nearsightedness:** difficulty in seeing things that are far away. Also referred to as myopia.

**negative reinforcement:** rewarding children for unacceptable behavior, such as laughing at a child who is acting silly at group time.

**neglect:** form of child abuse in which the child is not given the basic needs of life. Neglected children may be deprived of proper diet, medical care, shelter, and/or clothing.

**net income:** the amount of pay a person has after taxes and other deductions are taken from his or her salary.

**newsletters:** written communication most often including information concerning a variety of subjects.

**nonaccidental physical injury:** physical abuse

inflicted on the child on purpose. The most visible type of child abuse.

**nontoxic radiopaque plastic:** special plastic added to children's toys making it possible for this plastic to clearly show up on X rays in the event the toy has been swallowed by the child.

**normative scales:** lists of characteristics considered normal for children in certain age groups. Sometimes referred to as developmental scales.

**novelty transitions:** unusual, new actions or devices to move children from one activity to another.

**nutrients:** chemical substances found in foods that are needed for growth and maintenance of health.

**nutrition:** the science of food and how the body uses it.

# O

**obesity:** a major health problem caused by overeating. A condition in which the body weight is 20 percent above the normal weight for a given height.

**object permanence:** an understanding that objects continue to exist even if a person cannot see them. Object permanence occurs between six and nine months.

**observation:** informal viewing of a child during self-selected activities, watching for specific behaviors.

**omission:** implication that some groups have less value than other groups in our society caused by not mentioning or including a group in teaching.

**open wound:** an injury involving a break in the skin, such as a cut or scrape.

**open-ended questions:** questions promoting discussion and requiring decision-making skills.

**overeating:** the intake of more food than is needed by the body to function properly, often causing health and emotional problems.

**overfamiliarity:** lack of interest in a particular toy shown by children who are given the same toy day after day.

**overstimulate:** to cause to become overexcited.

# P

**pantomiming:** telling a story with body movements rather than words.

**parallel play:** a type of play in which children play by themselves but stay close by other children. All the children may be involved in similar activities, but play between and among the children does not exist.

**parent cooperatives:** child care programs that are formed and run by parents who wish to take part in their children's preschool experience.

**parent involvement:** activities parents do related to their roles as parents, including volunteering in the classroom, assisting with fund raising activities, and home teaching.

**parquetry blocks:** geometric pieces that vary in color and shape. They are used to teach shape concepts.

**passivity:** term for describing the level of involvement with a child's surroundings, such as withdrawing from a new person or event.

**perceptions:** ideas formed about a relationship or object as a result of what a child learns through the senses.

**personification:** giving human traits to nonliving objects, such as dolls or puppets.

**persuading:** encouraging children to act or behave in a certain way by appealing to their basic wants and needs.

**petit mal seizure:** an epileptic condition in which the person may have a few muscles twitch briefly or may become confused with the surroundings. These seizures are milder than grand mal seizures.

**phrase method:** method of teaching songs using short sections of a long song, having children repeat these sections. These sections are increased until the children know the entire song.

**phrase/whole combination method:** method of teaching a song stressing key phrases with rhythmic movement or visual props.

**physical age:** age determined by a birth date. Also known as chronological age.

**physical development:** physical body changes in a growing individual, such as changes in bone thickness, size, weight, vision, and coordination.

**pica:** a craving for unnatural foods such as paper, soap, rags, and toys.

**picture books:** books having single words or simple sentences and simple plots.

**policy:** a course of action that controls future decisions, such as a center's health policy.

**practical life experiences:** experiences in the Montessori curriculum that stress independence for children.

**praising:** giving children recognition for their accomplishments.

**preschooler:** term used to refer to children ages three to six.

**principle of proximodistal development:** principle noting that development of the body occurs in an outward direction. The spinal cord develops before outer parts of the body; arms develop before hands; hands develop before fingers.

**privacy law:** a law designed to protect children. It states that a child's records cannot be given to anyone other than parents, without the parents' permission.

**privately sponsored programs:** child care programs sponsored by a church, hospital, charitable organization, or an individual.

**problem-solving file:** file containing helpful information on problems parents may face.

**process-centered approach:** teaching philosophy in which learning is seen as a constant process of exploring and questioning the environment with hands-on curriculum stressed. All four areas of child development are included.

**program goals:** broad statements of purpose that reflect the end result of education. They state what is important.

**projection:** a type of play allowing children to place feelings and emotions he or she feels onto another person or an object, such as a puppet. Through this play, a child may share his or her inner world.

**prompting:** making a verbal or nonverbal suggestion that requires a response. Used either to stop an unacceptable action or start an acceptable one.

**prop box:** box containing materials and equipment needed for certain roles in socio-dramatic play.

**prosthesis:** an artificial limb, such as an arm, a hand, or a leg.

**publicly sponsored programs:** child care programs funded by the government, school district, and/or division of social services.

**puppetry:** using puppets in play.

**puppets:** figures designed in likeness to an animal or a human, used to enact stories, actions, or thoughts.

**purple K dry chemical extinguisher:** extinguisher used to fight Class B and Class C fires. It is slightly more effective against Class B fires.

## R

**rabies:** a disease caused by a viral infection of the nervous system and brain. Rabies is transmitted through the saliva of a rabid animal.

**racism:** stereotyping of people who have different skin coloring, food preferences, and/or languages.

**rational counting:** attaching a number to a series of grouped objects.

**recognizing:** the ability to relate past and present experiences and classify items. Recognizing is made possible by using the senses to learn from repeated experiences.

**redirecting:** diverting, or turning, a child's attention in a different direction.

**referral:** directing a parent to obtain a diagnosis from a professional when a problem exists with a child.

**reflex:** an automatic body response to a stimulus. At birth, an infant's physical abilities are limited to reflexes.

**reinforcement:** the process of using a parent's name in conversation. Through repetition, a teacher will engrave the parent's name in his or her memory.

**resource people:** center guests or field trip hosts.

**resume:** brief summary of a person's qualifications, skills, and job experience. The purpose of a resume is to secure an interview and/or inform a potential employer of a person's qualifications and experience.

**reviews:** lists and descriptions of books. These lists and descriptions can be found in public libraries.

**rheumatoid arthritis:** common form of juvenile arthritis which can also strike adults. General fatigue, loss of appetite, aching joints, and a stiffness of joints are the first signs of the disease.

**role playing:** a type of play allowing children to mimic the actions of others, such as wife, husband, mommy, daddy, doctor, or police officer.

**rote counting:** reciting numbers in their proper order.

**routines:** everyday experiences such as dressing, undressing, eating, napping, toileting, and changing activities.

**rules:** guides to actions and behaviors that reflect the goals of the center.

## S

**science table:** a table used to display items related to the science area.

**science:** the study of natural processes and their products. A way of viewing the universe.

**second-degree burns:** burns causing damage to underlying layers of skin, requiring medical treatment. These burns are marked by pain, blistering, swelling, and discoloration.

**self-concept:** qualities a child believes he or she possesses. A result of beliefs, feelings, and perceptions a child has of himself or herself as part of the world.

**sensory table:** table in the sensory area that gives children practice in social situations. Also known as a water or sand table.

**separation anxiety:** a child's difficulty in separating from parents, often occurring between nine and twelve months of age.

**separation distress:** attachment behavior shown when a child is unhappy because a familiar caregiver is leaving.

**set:** a group of objects that are alike in some way and, therefore, belong together.

**sexism:** any action, attitude, or outlook used to judge a person based only on the sex of that person.

**sexual abuse:** abuse that involves adults using children for their own pleasure, including rape, fondling, incest, and indecent exposure.

**single-answer questions:** questions requiring few decision-making skills and most often answered with yes or no. Also referred to as close-ended questions.

**skywriting:** demonstrating the correct way to make a letter by writing it in the air.

**social-emotional development:** growth in the two related areas of social and emotional skills. Social development involves learning to relate to others. Emotional development involves refining feelings and expressions of feelings.

**socio-dramatic play:** social play in which several children play together as they imitate others.

**solitary play:** independent play.

**sorting:** a form of classification involving the process of physically separating objects based on unique features.

**specific task assessment:** giving children set activities to determine skill and/or needs.

**spectator toys:** toys requiring little action on the child's part, such as battery-powered cars and talking dolls.

**spina bifida:** a condition in which the bones of the spine fail to grow together, resulting in paralysis.

**spiral curriculum:** a curriculum based on the fact that as children grow, their circle of interests becomes larger.

**staff room:** room provided for staff to spend work-related time away from the classroom.

**standard dry chemical extinguishers:** extinguishers used to fight Class B and Class C fires.

**staple supplies:** art supplies, such as paper, scissors, paste, glue, collage materials, crayons, watercolor markers, chalk, tape, and paint, that are used in the center on a frequent, regular basis.

**stationary equipment:** permanently installed equipment in the play yard, such as jungle gyms, slides, and tree houses.

**statute:** formal document drawn up by elected officials outlining a teacher's legal responsibilities in a case of child abuse.

**stepping reflex:** reflex that occurs while holding

the infant so that the feet are flat on a surface. The infant will move the legs in a walking motion.

**stereotypes:** preset ideas about people based on one characteristic such as sex, nationality, or religion.

**stereotyping:** showing people in a rigid, traditional way ignoring individual differences.

**story records:** records telling stories with sound effects and music.

**storybooks:** books that contain pictures but have more words and more complex plots than picture books.

**storytelling:** reciting a story or reading aloud from a book.

**stress:** the body's reaction to physical or emotional factors, often taking the form of tension.

**stuttering:** speech disorder that is often characterized by repetition, hesitation, and prolongation.

**suggesting:** placing thoughts for consideration into children's minds.

**sunshine calls:** telephone calls made by teachers to parents to communicate praise and support for children. The purpose of these calls is to share with parents something outstanding or interesting the children have done recently.

**swimming reflex:** reflex that occurs when holding the infant horizontally, face down. The infant will stretch out the arms and legs in a swimming motion.

## T

**tactile senses:** senses related to touch, which are stimulated by such activities as cutting and drawing.

**temperament:** ways in which children react to their environment, such as passivity, irritability, and activity patterns.

**theme walks:** simple field trips taken in and around the center based on a theme.

**third-degree burns:** burns that destroy the skin layer and nerve endings, requiring prompt medical attention.

**time out:** a form of punishment used when a child's behavior cannot be ignored. The teacher moves the child to a place where the child must sit quietly for a period of not more than three minutes.

**toddler:** term used to refer to a child from the first year until the third birthday. The term is used because of the awkward walking style of children in this age group.

**traffic pattern:** the way in which people move through the classroom area, affecting its arrangement.

**transition:** changing from one activity to another and/or moving from one place to another.

## U

**undernutrition:** lack of proper nutrients in the diet caused by not eating enough food in an otherwise well-balanced diet.

## V

**vegetable printing:** art technique that involves dipping molds made from vegetables into paint and then pressing the molds onto surfaces to make prints.

**visual learner:** a child who depends a great deal on the sense of sight. This child will notice small visual changes in the environment.

**voice flexibility:** good speaking voice during routine conversation using a variety of pitches and loudness levels.

## W

**warm colors:** colors including red, yellow, and orange that make a room appear smaller. Studies show children prefer warm colors until about age six.

**warning:** reminding children to follow classroom rules, stating the misbehavior and the consequences.

**water soluble:** a substance that can be dissolved in water, such as powdered tempera paint.

**water-type extinguishers:** extinguishers designed for use strictly on Class A fires and should not be used on any other type of fire.

**whole song method:** method used to teach short, simple songs by having the children listen and then sing along.

**wound:** damage to the surface of the skin or body tissue. There are two types of wounds, closed and open.

# Index

Molding clay, 218, 219
Mono painting, 217
Montessori schools, 440, 441
Moro reflex, 32
Motivation, 367
Motor sequence, 32, 33
Movement activities, 334-336
Movement experiences, 332-334
Multicultural concept activities, 304, 305
Multicultural concepts, 302-305
Multicultural toys, 152
Multipurpose dry chemical
    extinguishers, 163
Music, 320, 321
    benefits of, 321
    classroom rules, 74, 75
    movement activities, 334-336
    movement experiences, 332-334
    rhythm instruments, 325-329
    scheduling, 329, 330
    teacher's role, 322-325
Music activities, 330-332
Music area, 134
Music center, 322
Myopia, 424

# N

Nannies, 16
Napping, health policies, 190
Napping routines, 100-102
Nearsightedness, 424
Negative reinforcement, 87
Negativism, 113
Neglect, 168
Net income, 457
Newsletters, 376
Noise, guidance problems, 109
Nonaccidental physical injury, 168
Nontoxic radiopaque plastic, 402
Normative scales, 30
Novelty transitions, 104
Nutrients, 174-176
Nutrition, 173
    meal and snack planning, 179-181
    meal serving, 181-184
Nutrition concepts, 312, 313
Nutrition planning, 172-186

# O

Obesity, 174
Object permanence, 35
Observation, 81, 262
Omission, 304
Open wound, 197, 198
Open wound care, 199
Open-ended questions, 80, 278
Outdoor play area, 137-141
Overeating, 174
Overfamiliarity, 405
Overstimulation, 108

# P

Painting activities, 216-218
    chalk, 217, 218
    easel, 216, 217
    finger, 217
    mono, 217
    spice, 218
    string, 217
    vegetable, 218
Pantomiming, 336
Paper, art, 213, 214
Parallel play, 236
Parent bulletin board, 386
Parent cooperatives, 443, 444
Parent involvement, 375-392
    discussion groups, 384, 385
    infant-toddler programs, 410
    objectives, 376
    parent-teacher meetings, 378-384
    volunteering, 387-390
    written communication, 376, 378
Parent volunteers, 387-390
Parent-teacher meetings, 378-384
    follow-up, 384
    planning, 378, 380-382
    the meeting, 382-384
Parquetry blocks, 265, 266
Passivity, 38
Paste, 215
Perceptions, 299
Personal characteristics for careers
    in child care, 20-23
    commitment, 23

Toileting routines, 102
Toy selection planning sheet, 145
Toys,
  infant-toddler programs, 402-405
  safety, 152, 153
Toys and equipment, 143-158
  selecting, 154, 155
  sources, 153, 154
Traffic pattern, 128
Transitions, 103-105, 371
Two-year-olds,
  intellectual development, 44, 45
  physical development, 42-44
  social-emotional development, 45-47
  teaching, 47, 48
Tying shoes, 96

## U

Undernutrition, 174

## V

Vegetable painting, 218
Vendors, 153
Vision disorders, 423-425
Visual learners, 363
Voice disorders, 423
Voice flexibility, 423
Volume concepts, 270
Vomiting, 100
  health policies, 203

## W

Warm colors, 126
Warning, 91
Water concepts, science, 281, 282
Water soluble, 212
Water-type extinguishers, 163
Whole song method, 325
Woodworking area, 133
Wounds, 197-199